Najib George Awad

Orthodoxy in Arabic Terms

Judaism, Christianity, and Islam – Tension, Transmission, Transformation

---

Edited by Patrice Brodeur, Carlos Fraenkel,
Assaad Elias Kattan, and Georges Tamer

Volume 3

Najib George Awad

Orthodoxy in Arabic Terms

A Study of Theodore Abu Qurrah's Theology in Its Islamic Context

DE GRUYTER

ISBN 978-1-61451-677-4
e-ISBN (PDF) 978-1-61451-396-4
e-ISBN (EPUB) 978-1-61451-953-9
ISSN 2196-405X

Library of Congress Cataloging-in-Publication Data
A CIP catalog record for this book has been applied for at the Library of Congress.

Bibliographic information published by the Deutsche Nationalbibliothek
The Deutsche Nationalbibliothek lists this publication in the Deutsche Nationalbibliografie; detailed bibliographic data are available on the Internet at http://dnb.dnb.de.

Printing and binding: CPI books GmbH, Leck
♾ Printed on acid-free paper
Printed in Germany

www.degruyter.com

Contents

Preface — IX

Introduction — 1

I. On Theodore Abū Qurrah, the Melkite Bishop of Ḥarrān — **1**
II. Abū Qurrah in this Study: Going beyond Mere Apologetics — **8**
III. Outline of the Volume and Abū Qurrah's Works — **14**

Part One: **The Historical and Religious Settings**

Chapter One. "If Indeed They Were Known At All": Christians' Attitudes towards Islam — 23

I. The Dawn of the Arabs' 'Invasion' in the Eyes of Christians — **23**
II. Between Social and Cultural Appraisal and Simply Seeking to Survive — **31**
III. From Social Indifference to Apologetic Reaction — **49**
IV. Conclusion — **57**

Chapter Two. Abū Qurrah and the Christian Apologetics of the Melkite Church — 58

I. From Emperor to Caliph: The End of Christian Triumphalism — **58**
II. The Christian Response to Islam and the Beginning of Apologetics — **64**
III. The Melkite Church in the Land of Islam: The Birth of Arabic Theology — **74**
IV. Theodore Abū Qurrah as an Apologetic *Mutakallim:* Remarks on Style — **88**
V. Towards a 'Positive' Orthodox Apologetic: On Being a *Mutakallim* after Abū Qurrah — **103**

Part Two: **The Dogmatic Framework of Abū Qurrah's Orthodoxy**

Chapter Three. From Nicene Trinitarian Trends to Chalcedonian Christological Terminology — 115

I. Introduction — **115**

II. On *Hypostasis* in Greek Trinitarian Terminology — **118**
III. On *Qnoma* in Syriac Trinitarian Terminology — **140**
IV. Using Trinitarian Ontology in Re-reading Christological Terminology — **150**
V. Conclusion — **161**

Chapter Four. Theodore Abū Qurrah's Trinitarian Theology, or Orthodoxy in Dialogue with Muslim Monotheism — 163
I. Introduction — **163**
II. Abū Qurrah's Trinitarian Theology in *al-Mujādalah* — **164**
A. On *Shirk* and the Allegory of 'Intellect' — **165**
B. When Oneness Prevails over Trinitarian Unity — **183**
III. Abū Qurrah's Trinitarian Theology in His *Maymar on the Trinity* — **192**
A. The Theological Argument of the Maymar — **193**
B. Some Remarks on the Trinitarian Terminology — **212**
IV. Abū Qurrah and the Melkites' Trinitarian Legacy — **234**
A. John of Damascus and the Trinity — **235**
B. Maximus the Confessor and the Trinity — **245**
C. Abū Qurrah's Trinitarian Theology: Confession or Innovation? — **259**
V. Conclusion — **266**

Chapter Five. Theodore Abū Qurrah's Christological Discourse and the Muslims' Jesus — 267
I. When 'Jesus the Son of God' and ''Īsā Ibn Maryam' Collided — **267**
II. On Jesus as Kalimat Allāh' and Rūḥ Minhu — **284**
A. On Using the Terms 'God's Word' and 'Spirit' in Christian and Muslim *Kalām* — **284**
B. Abū Qurrah's Use of 'God's Word' and 'Spirit' in *al-Mujādalah* and Other Maymars — **292**
III. Jesus' Divine Sonship and the Muslim God, Who *'Lam Yalid Wa-Lam Yūlad'* — **314**
A. God's Taking a Child unto Himself in the Qur'an and *Kalām* — **314**
B. Abū Qurrah's Defense of Jesus' Divine Sonship before the Muslims — **328**
IV. The Incarnation in Abū Qurrah's Christology — **359**
A. The Incarnation between *Tajassud/Taʾnnus* and *Ḥulūl* — **359**
B. On the Incarnation as *Ḥulūl* in Abū Qurrah's Apologies — **369**

V. Abū Qurrah and Melkite/Chalcedonian Christological Orthodoxy —— **380**
A. Some Christological Views from John of Damascus —— **380**
B. Some Christological Views from Maximus the Confessor —— **389**
C. Abū Qurrah's Christology and the Melkite Tradition: Concurrence or Divergence? —— **398**
VI. Conclusion —— **408**

Concluding Postscript. Theodore Abū Qurrah: A Melkite Orthodox *Mutakallim* in *Dār al-Islām* —— 411

Bibliography —— 430

Name Index —— 460

Subject Index —— 465

Preface

It was Beirut, Lebanon, in the fall of 2007. The Near East School of Theology in Beirut was celebrating its 75th anniversary. The school organized a series of meetings, worship services, public lectures, and panels to celebrate the history and legacy of the oldest Protestant theological school in the Near East. One of the keynote speakers who were invited by NEST to speak on that occasion was the author of *The Cross and the Prodigal* and *Poet & Peasant: Through Peasant Eyes*, Kenneth E. Baily, the long-serving ex-Professor of New Testament at the school. Bailey was invited to give two key public lectures related to his scholarship on Near Eastern interpretation of the Scriptures and its relation to his life in the Middle East and work experience in NEST. The main, unforgettable prelude of Bailey's first lecture was actually a critique conveyed in an invitation-like accent. Bailey stated that during his decades of service in the school he had the great chance of acquainting himself with the theological and biblical heritage of the Arab and Syrian Christian fathers who produced their intellectual discourses in the midst of the Islamic milieu and developed their understanding of Christian faith in vivid, consistent, and multi-faceted dialogue with Islam. Bailey's invitational critique lay in his (rather embarrassingly truthful) realization that among the Protestants of Syria and Lebanon, one can hardly detect any serious interest in studying this aforementioned 'theologically very precious treasure' (thus Bailey described it) or any tangible encouragement of the young generation of Protestant theology students and ministers to produce any education or research on it. Among those Arab-speaking church fathers, whose heritage he said that he had to read for the first time in his scholarly career in the Near East, Bailey named people like Theodore Abū Qurrah, ʿAmmār al-Baṣrī, Abū Rāʾiṭah at-Takrītī and Yaḥyā ibn ʿAdī. Bailey ended his critique-invitation statement by saying: "I was puzzled and saddened to see that the Protestants of the Near East spend all their time studying western theologians, while they hardly know any one of these names which I mentioned or hardly read any of their writings."

In that year, and on that occasion, it happened that I was in the region, residing in Beirut and working at my *Alma Mater* (NEST), and I was one of the audience members who were listening to Kenneth Bailey's lectures with closed mouths and embarrassed, red-cheeked faces. Bailey was absolutely right in his critique of the Protestant theological education that day. For all the time I spent at NEST between 1992 and 1997 to earn my BA in Theology, I do not remember at all any of my professors mentioning one of the above-mentioned names of the Arab-speaking fathers, which Bailey invited us to read and study. Bailey's words have been anchored deeply within my mind since that day, and the names of the Arab church fathers he mentioned never vanished from my memory. Since then I never stopped asking myself: "Who are these figures? How come I know nothing about them? How come no one taught me about them in my entire theological education?" For the first time in my professional academic life, I realized how ignorant I was of my own oriental-Arab culture, its theological and historical background, and how alienated my professional training as a Systematic Theologian (by that time I had earned my first PhD in Systematic Theology from King's College University of London) could actually be since it did not equip me with the necessary knowledge, learnedness, and training to contribute to scholarly education and research on Arab Christianity and on the relation of its theological discourse to Islam. No theologian can teach theology in the Arab world, if not around the globe nowadays, without touching upon these dimensions.

During the following academic year, 2008–2009, I was privileged to be offered a scholarship from the Langham Trust to spend an academic year as a Research Fellow in the Centre for Faith and Culture at Yale University Divinity School. My plan in that year was to work toward finishing writing my second book (my first book was *God Without a Face? On the Personal Individuation of the Holy Spirit*) in Systematic Theology on the Trinity and the notions of 'personhood' and 'relationality' in dialogue with modernist and postmodernist forms of intellectual inquiry (this would become my second book, *Persons in Relation: An Essay on the Trinity and Ontology*). Yet, during that research time in Yale Divinity School's library, I stumbled upon Sidney Griffith's book, *The Church in the Shadow of the Mosque*. It was the very first serious and complete book I read on Arab Christianity and Christian theology in the shadow of Islam. Griffith's book was like a profound, transformative theophany experience for me. It was the first time I realized how rich, sophisticated, and stimulating were the Christian-Muslim encounters during the 7th–10th centuries CE. In that fascinating book, I met again the names of these Arab Christian *mutakallimun*, which Kenneth Bailey had uttered before me a little bit more than a year earlier in his public lecture on NEST's 75th anniversary: the same names and the same figures and their theological heritage, about which I knew almost nothing until the moment of reading Griffith's book.

Reading Sidney Griffith's book was a moment of conversion that inaugurated the start of a pivotal transformation in my scholarly track ever since the summer of 2009. It was at that moment that I decided to seriously pursue a paradigm shift in my academic and scholarly career. I decided to move from being a crude Systematic Theologian (in the classical Western sense), who strictly studies and contributes scholarship on Christian doctrines, philosophical and methodological aspects of western Christian (mostly Protestant) theological heritage

alone, into a historian of theological and religious ideas in their oriental, Arabic-Islamic, and contextual dimensions. I decided to train myself regarding the Oriental Christian theological legacy in its dialogue with, and formation within the context of, Islam. That shift enabled me for the first time in my intellectual career to reconcile my western training and scientific education on one side, and my personal cultural-contextual background and identity on another. For the first time, being 'a Near Eastern, Christian Arab systematic and historical theologian' made profound sense to me. This conversion led me eventually into a four-year adventure, between 2010 and 2014, of learning, researching, and developing my own scholarly contribution to the field of Arabic Christianity and Arabic Christian-Muslim *Kalām*, and it will continue driving me through that adventurous and profoundly enriching and stimulating track in the coming years.

Orthodoxy in Arabic Terms is the child that was birthed by the above-mentioned story. My study of Theodore Abū Qurrah is my very first (yet not the last, as I believe) humble attempt at contributing an addition to the vast and immeasurably precious amount of scholarship many other great scholars, from different generations and backgrounds and nationalities, have already offered to the theological and religious heritage of the Near East. In it, I offer my most sincere discipleship and appreciation to each one of these great scholars, who still admirably dedicate the crown jewel of their professional careers to the study of the Arab Christian-Muslim *kalām* and invite further generations of students to pursue this scholarship. My monograph on Abū Qurrah is my endeavour to become a disciple in this field and to serve it scientifically and academically as best I can.

I produced this monograph on Abū Qurrah's Theological discourse in dialogue with Islam between 2010 and 2014. I did this as a research thesis written for gaining the 'Dr. Theol. Habil' status (*Venia Legendi*) in Oriental/Arabic Christian Historical Theology from Phillips Universität in Marburg, Germany. I first started working on this second PhD degree in collaboration with The Centre for Religious Studies in Westfälische Wilhelms-Universität Münster and finished the work in collaboration with Marburg. Through the past four years, I was supported and helped by a group of wonderful and excellent scholars and friends, without the contributions of whom I would not at all have been able to finish this project and produce the manuscript as I eventually did.

My very first and most sincere gratitude and deep indebtedness goes to my dear friend, Prof. Dr. Assaad Elias Kattan of Münster University. Prof. Kattan was the very first and most influential interlocutor I was privileged to have in this adventure. His vast knowledge of Byzantine theology, Arab-Melkite Christian tradition and patristic studies were the foundational counter-voice which I learned a lot from, and I always had to find meticulous methods to attend to its challenging questions and corrections: there is nothing better than that in the pursuit of serious learning and intellectual growth. I would not have been able to produce such a monograph without his belief in the project, in me, and in the potential of the entire adventure. Assaad was not only a greatly patient friend, but a qualified co-thinker and very stimulating conversationalist. There are paragraphs in the text that would not have been written at all in the way that they are now without his intellectual fingerprints on them.

I am also as deeply and gratefully indebted to my friend Prof. Dr. Karl Pinggera of Marburg University. It was Karl who embraced my project toward the last year of the work and welcomed it warmly and enthusiastically, offering me the possibility of submitting the text in the school there and gaining the hoped-for result. Karl's very perceptive and sharp suggestions and corrections also crystalized my arguments and sharpened my analyses at different parts of the monograph. His advice toward producing the final draft of the text and readying it for review and later for publication were beyond valuable. Without his help and unflinching support, I would have not been able to achieve 'Dr.Theol. Habil' status after all.

I also want to express my consistent and wholehearted indebtedness to Prof. Sidney H. Griffith. Father Griffith has not stopped being a very supporting and inspiring encouragement to me on different levels throughout the past four years. I had the great privilege of receiving his detailed feedback on the very first draft of the project's proposal. Prof. Griffith's words were very encouraging and inviting, and they were the fuel that energized me to pursue the work. Prof. Griffith also generously agreed to review my monograph's final draft and report on it to the review committee at Marburg University. Without the support and appreciation of one of the foremost skilled and prolific authorities in this field, I would not have been able to achieve my final goal for the whole project.

To the three above-mentioned dear friends and colleagues, I remain indebted beyond words, and I therefore gladly dedicate this volume to them. I must also express my thanks and appreciation to so many other people who also helped make possible the finishing of this project. I am thankful for the initial remarks I generously received from Prof. Dr. Theresia Hainthaler, who in 2010 looked at the very first draft of what is now the third chapter in the monograph. Prof. Hainthalr provided me with many very valuable corrections and suggestions for reading on the Nestorian-Cyrilan Christological controversy that substantially improved the sections on this subject. I am also grateful to Prof. Sebastian Brock for his very kind feedback and comments on a first draft of the same chapter. With his valuable remarks and vast knowledge, Prof. Brock sharpened and improved the sections in that chapter that are related to Syriac Christian theology. I must also most sincerely thank Ms. Carol Rowe from England for the highly professional and meticulous copy-editing work she brought to the manuscript. Carol's professional work turned the text into a properly written English manuscript and substantially improved the clarity and form of its content. For her performance I remain deeply grateful. My most sincere appreciation also goes to Dr. Terry Wright for preparing the book's indices. I am also highly appreciative of the faculty of the theological school at Marburg University for allowing me to submit my thesis in their school, for voting unanimously in approval of it, and for eventually granting me the relevant academic status. I also thank the editors of the De Gruyter series Judaism, Christianity and Islam – Tension, Transmission, Transformation (JCIT) for deciding to publish my volume as part of the series. I am also grateful to De Gruyter press for accepting my book and for the professional, high-quality work they dedicated to the process of readying it for publication. I am also truly thankful to all the libraries and study centres that offered their resources to me to enable me to finish writing this book: ITF Hermannsburg; Georg-August-Universität Göttingen; Westfälische Wilhelms-Universität Münster; Central Public Library, Vienna; and Hartford Seminary, CT, USA.

Last but never least, I remain, in my present personal and professional life and in the successful finishing of this project alike, fully indebted to the love, companionship, support, patience, and altruism of my dearly beloved soulmate, friend, and wife, Verena. Despite her full occupation with her own research and daunting work requirements, she never tarried or balked in backing me up, believing in me, and anticipating the great outcome of the entire adventure at those moments when I was trapped in doubts. For her presence in my life, for her belief in me, for her support and tolerance of all the difficulties of living with someone obsessed with research, I am deeply grateful and indeed indebted for this project and far more beyond it.

Hartford, CT 2014 Najib George Awad

Introduction

I. On Theodore Abū Qurrah, the Melkite Bishop of Ḥarrān

Theodore Abū Qurrah is one of the earliest theologians to write in Arabic. He belonged to the Melkite[1]-Chalcedonian community during the Abbasid period in the 9th century. Historians of Arab Christianity like to introduce him as "an itinerant controversialist in the Chalcedonian cause during the early Abbasid caliphate, from the time of al-Mahdī (775–785) to midway in the reign of al-Ma'mūn (813–833)."[2] Though it is believed that Theodore's mother tongue was Syriac, scholars give him credit for his fluency in Arabic,[3] praising him for ultimately being "both one of the first Christians to write in Arabic and one of the first to undertake a sustained theological defence of Christianity against the rival claims of Islam."[4] Furthermore, Abū Qurrah has been considered "extremely in-

1 In this study, I follow Sidney Griffith's historical use of the term 'Melkite' to refer specifically to the Chalcedonian Orthodox church at the time of Theodore Abū Qurrah, excluding the modern "Greek Catholic" churches known in the Middle East today. The adjective 'Melkite' in the present work designates, as Griffith defines it, the "Arabic-speaking Christians in the world of Islam who accepted the doctrinal formulae determined by the first six ecumenical councils of Roman and Byzantine orthodoxy." Sidney H. Griffith, "Apologetics and Historiography in the Annals of Eutychios of Alexandria: Christian Self-Definition in the World of Islam," in *Studies on the Christian Arabic Heritage: In Honour of Father Prof. Dr. Samir Khalil Samir, S.I. at the Occasion of his Sixty-Fifth Birthday*, ed. Rifaat Ebied and Herman Teule (Leuven: Peeters, 2004), 65–90, p. 65.

2 Sidney H. Griffith, "Muslims and Church Councils: The Apology of Theodore Abū Qurrah," *Studia Patristica*, 25, 1993, 270–299, p. 271. See also S.H. Griffith, *The Controversial Theology of Theodore Abū Qurrah (c. A.D. 750–c. 820); A Methodological, Comparative Study in Christian Arabic Literature* (PhD Diss., Washington: Catholic University of America. Ann Arbor, MI: University Microfilms, 1978); John Lamoreaux, "Introduction," in *Theodore Abū Qurrah*, trans. John C. Lamoreaux (Provo, UT: Brigham Young University Press, 2005), xi–xxxv; and Ignace Dick's introduction to Abū Qurrah, *Maymar fī Wujūd al-Khāliq wad-Dīn al-Qawīm* (Maymar on the Existence of the Creator and the Right Religion), ed. Ignace Dick, (Jounieh: Librairie S. Paul/Rome: Papal Oriental Institute, 1982), 37–57.

3 S.H. Griffith, "The Monks of Palestine and the Growth of Christian Literature in Arabic," *The Muslim World*, 78(1) (1988), 1–29, p. 22. In his edition of Abū Qurrah's Arabic *mayāmir*, Constantine Bacha states that Abū Qurrah himself told us that he wrote texts in Syriac, which for Bacha is evidence that, in contrast to the Melkites of Syria, the Melkites of Ḥarrān and some other regions, where Greek culture had not entered, knew Syriac and used it in their writings: Constantine Bacha [Qusṭanṭīn Bāshā] (ed.), *Mayāmir Thāūdūrūs Abī Qurrah 'Usquf Ḥarrā: 'Aqdam Ta'līf 'Arabī Naṣrānī* (Mayāmir Theodore Abū Qurrah, Bishop of Harran, the Oldest Arabic Christian Book), Beirut: Maṭba'at al-Fawā'id, 1904, pp. 3–5, esp. p. 5.

4 Lamoreaux, *Theodore Abū Qurrah* , pp. xi-xii.

novative … [in the] attempt to articulate a new vision of Christian identity using the language and conceptual tools of Muslim theologians."[5]

This has led to the view, expressed by Ignace Dick, the noted editor of Abū Qurrah's works, that Theodore merits being considered a theological and intellectual link between the Greek Church Fathers and the Arab Christian authors of the 8th and 9th centuries CE, and one who proved himself to be both the rightful heir of Greek-speaking theological thinkers (John of Damascus and Maximus the Confessor) and a reliable and innovative Arab Christian theologian, who reflected in his Muslim context during the age of Harūn al-Rashīd and al-Maʾmūn an open-minded Christian stance on Islamic thought and society.[6] Ignace Dick is, therefore, right to praise Theodore's vast knowledge of both Christian theology in its Greek and Syriac versions and Islamic religion and *kalām* to an extent that was not matched by any other Christian theologian of his time. Theodore's authentic intellectual grasp of Islam and masterly fluency in Arabic must have been the ultimate motivator of his systematic attempt to build close connections with Muslim intellectual circles by writing theological and philosophical texts addressed directly and openly to Muslim *mutakallims*, whom he must have met and conversed with on a variety of occasions.[7] Ignace Dick further suggests that this orientation toward Islam and Arabic lies behind the fact that Theodore Abū Qurrah's legacy persisted for many years after his death in the Muslim intellectual context of Abbasid Baghdad. One may note, for instance, many of Theodore's ideas and claims being implicitly struggled with and responded to in the writings of the famous 9th-century Muslim *mutakallim*, Abū ʿĪsā al-Warrāq.[8] Another Muʿtazilite, ʿAbd aj-Jabbār al-Hamadhānī (d. 1025), also reveals knowledge of Abū Qurrah and presents him as the authoritative Melkite voice on Christian doctrine. Theodore was also mentioned in the *Fihrist* of Ibn an-Nadīm around the 10th century CE, where the famous Muslim biographer speaks of Abū Qurrah as the bishop of Ḥarrān.[9] Ibn al-Nadīm actually speaks of a bishop of the Melkites

---

5 J.C. Lamoreaux, "The Biography of Theodore Abū Qurrah Revisited," *Dumbarton Oaks Papers*, 56 (2002), 25–40, p. 25.

6 Ignace Dick in the introduction to Abū Qurrah, *Maymar fī Ikrām al-Aiqūnāt* (Maymar on the Veneration of Icons), ed. Ignace Dick, (Jounieh: Librairie S. Paul/Dhūq Michael: Christian Arabic Heritage/Rome: Papal Oriental Institute, 1986), p. 17.

7 Dick's introduction to Abū Qurrah, *Maymar fī Wujūd al-Khāliq wad-Dīn al-Qawīm* (Maymar on the Existence of the Creator and the Right Religion), p. 50.

8 Ibid. p. 49. Dick relies here on the study by A. Abel, *Le livre de la refutation des trois sectes chrétiennes de Abū ʿĪsā Muḥammad ibn Harūn al-Warrāq. Sa date, son importance, sa place dans la littérature polémique arabe* (Diss., Bruxelles, 1949), p. ix.

9 Lamoreaux, *Theodore Abū Qurrah*, p. xvii. See also Ignace Dick's introduction in Abū Qurrah, *Maymar fī Wujūd al-Khāliq wad-Dīn al-Qawīm* (Maymar on the Existence of the Creator and the

in Ḥarrān by the name of *Abū ʿIzzah*, and not Abū Qurrah.[10] But scholars tend to believe that the person meant here is none other than Theodore Abū Qurrah, and that Ibn al-Nadīm's text contains a scribal error.[11] However that may be, the longevity of Theodore's legacy can also be seen in the fact that some of his Greek works continued to be published until the 17th century by the Jesuits in Ingolstadt.[12]

So, who was Theodore Abū Qurrah? John Lamoreaux answers as follows: "[Abū Qurrah] is one of those too numerous figures about whose theology we know a great deal, while their lives remain shrouded in darkness."[13] That is, only a brief sketch of the life of this Melkite figure can be drawn from a few minor scraps of information scattered here and there in a variety of Islamic-Arabic and Greek, Syriac, and Arabic Christian sources.

Concerning Abū Qurrah's birth-place and native homeland, contemporary scholars tend to generally agree that Theodore was born and grew up in the

---

Right Religion), pp. 36–38; and Sidney Griffith, "Reflections on the Biography of Theodore Abū Qurrah," *Parole de l'Orient*, 18 (1993), 143–170, p. 155.

10 Muḥammad Ibn Isḥaq Ibn an-Nadīm, *Al-Fihrist* (Cairo: Al-Maktaba at-Tijāriyya al-Kubrā, 1929), Vol. I, ch. 2, p. 36:

... وأبو عزة وكان أسقف الملكية بحران وله من الكتب كتاب يطعن فيه على أسطورس الرئيس وقد نقضه عليه جماعة

... and Abū ʿIzzah, and he was the bishop of the Melkites in Ḥarrān and, of the books, he has a book wherein he appeals against the chief Asṭūrus and some people vetoed him [i.e. Abū ʿIzzah] on it.

11 Dick's introduction in Abū Qurrah, *Maymar fī Wujūd al-Khāliq wad-Dīn al-Qawīm* (Maymar on the Existence of the Creator and the Right Religion), p. 36. Dick believes that the figure called "chief Asṭūrs" is Nestorius. On the other hand, Dick also pauses at Ibn al-Nadīm's speech, a few lines earlier, referring to someone called *Theadūros* as a translator (*nāqil*) of philosophy and logic into Arabic. Dick believes that the person meant here is our Melkite bishop of Ḥarrān (ibid. p. 36).

12 Alfred Guillaume, "Theodore Abū Qurra as Apologist," *The Muslim World*, 15 (1925), 42–51, p. 42.

13 Lamoreaux, *Theodore Abū Qurrah*, p. xii. Lamoreaux goes on to say "documentary evidence is absent. There is no ancient narrative of his life, certainly nothing like a traditional *vita*. Furthermore, his own works are almost wholly devoid of autobiographical information." For brief, yet valuable information on Theodore Abū Qurrah the person and the man of the Church, one can also read Aaron. M. Butts, "Theodoros Abū Qurra," in *Gorgias Encyclopedic Dictionary of the Syriac Heritage*, ed. Sebastian P. Brock et al. (Piscataway, NJ: Gorgias Press/Beth Mardutho: Syriac Institute, 2011), pp. 403–405; and John C. Lamoreaux, "Theodore Abū Qurra," *Christian-Muslim Relations: A Bibliographical History*, Vol. 1: *600–900*, ed. David Thomas and Barbara Roggema (Leiden: Brill, 2009), 439–491; and the brief note in Sidney Griffith, "Faith and Reason in Christian *Kalām:* Theodore Abū Qurrah on Discerning the True Religion," in *Christian Arabic Apologetics during the Abbasid Period (750–1258)*, ed. Samir Khalil Samir and Jørgen S. Nielsen (Leiden: Brill, 1994), 1–43, pp. 6–9.

city of Edessa (*Rahā/Urhāy*, or *Urfa* in modern-day Turkey).[14] Sidney Griffith finds evidences of Theodore's Edessan origin first in the Syriac text, *The Chronicle of Michael the Syrian*, which refers to Theodore Abū Qurrah as the "Edessan Chalcedonian," and second in Abū Qurrah's own description of the city as "our own city, Edessa the Blest."[15]

On the other hand, scholars generally agree that Theodore Abū Qurrah was connected with Ḥarrān and that "a vast number, both Christian and Muslim, remember him to have been the bishop of Ḥarrān."[16] Ignace Dick also rejects claims that Theodore was actually the bishop of '*Qārah*', not Ḥarrān, and that is indicated by his nomenclature 'Qurrah.' Dick argues that Ḥarrān used to be called in Greek '*Corrhae*,' and that this accounts for Theodore's being called 'Abū Qurrah.' Dick also conjectures that the name 'Qurrah' is a proper name that used to be generally attributed to the people of Ḥarrān.[17] Sidney Griffith in turn points to existing textual data that refers to Abū Qurrah's removal from his see of Ḥarrān by Patriarch Theodoret at some point between 785 and 799 CE. Griffith and Lamoreaux both refer to the only source that mentions this demotion, namely *The Chronicles of Michael the Syrian*. They acknowledge the difficulty of specifying the reason behind this deposition or its temporal duration, but they nevertheless consider it to be reliable evidence of Abū Qurrah's connection with Ḥarrān.[18] They conclude that Abū Qurrah's consecration to, and demotion from, his bishopric indicate that he was a bishop, most probably of the see of Ḥarrān. Ignace Dick adds that it is sufficient to know that his demotion did not damage Abū Qurrah's reputation or erase his name from the Church's records, for the patriarchate of Jerusalem still reveres Theodore Abū Qurrah

---

14 Lamoreaux, *Theodore Abū Qurrah*, p. xiii; Ignace Dick in Abū Qurrah, *Maymar fī Wujūd al-Khāliq wad-Dīn al-Qawīm* (Maymar on the Existence of the Creator and the Right Religion), pp. 40–42; Griffith, "Monks of Palestine," p. 22.

15 Griffith, "Reflections on the Biography," p. 149. Griffith adds that "the fact that on his own testimony Abū Qurrah also wrote in Syriac supports his Syrian origin, and Edessa of course, was in his day the metropolis *per excellence* for the speakers in Syriac" (ibid., p. 149).

16 Lamoreaux, *Theodore Abū Qurrah*, p. xiii; Griffith, "The Monks of Palestine," p. 22; Bacha, *Mayāmir Thāūdūrūs Abī Qurrah* (Mayāmir Theodore Abū Qurrah), p. 3; and Abū Qurrah, *Maymar fī Wujūd al-Khāliq wad-Dīn al-Qawīm* (Maymar on the Existence of the Creator and the Right Religion), p. 37.

17 Abū Qurrah, *Maymar fī Wujūd al-Khāliq wad-Dīn al-Qawīm* (Maymar on the Existence of the Creator and the Right Religion), p. 37.

18 Griffith, "Reflections on the Biography," pp. 164–167; and Lamoreaux, *Theodore Abū Qurrah*, pp. xv–xvi.

today, and the extant manuscripts speak of him as a 'saint' and as the 'bishop of Ḥarrān.'[19]

When it comes to determining the dates of Abū Qurrah's birth and death, scholars can only conjecture. Sidney Griffith tries to set out a general temporal framework, opining that "whatever else can be learned about Abū Qurrah's life must then take these forty some years between 785 and 829 as his *floruit*."[20] Griffith argues that, within the boundaries of these 40 years, one can put Theodore's deposition from the bishopric of Ḥarrān by Theodoret between 785 and 799, and that his probable birthdate would have been appropriately earlier. Griffith also proposes the conversation with the Caliph al-Maʾmūn as a point for estimating the year of Theodore's death. This would mean, Griffith concludes, that Abū Qurrah was born around 755 and died sometime shortly after 829.[21] On the other hand, John Lamoreaux prefers not to suggest dates for Abū Qurrah's birth and death, pointing out the unreliability of the extant sources, such as the Syriac chronicles, for pursuing such attempts to fix dates.[22] Ignace Dick, for his part, while acknowledging the difficulty of fixing precise dates for Abū Qurrah's birth and death, concludes, principally from Abū Qurrah's extant intellectual heritage, that this father of the Church must have lived between the second half of the 8th century and the first third of the 9th. Dick develops his conjecture in conversation with Georg Graf, who suggests 740 as Abū Qurrah's birth date and 820 as the date of his death. Dick believes that both dates should be pushed forward by at least ten years,[23] seeming, eventually, to concur with the proposal of Samir Khalil Samir and Sidney Griffith, and surmising that Theodore Abū Qurrah was born around 750 and died between 825 and 830.[24]

Finally, when it comes to his link to the monastery of Mar Sabas and the question of whether or not Abū Qurrah was a monk there, there are differences between modern scholars and their proposals diverge conspicuously. One may note a slight difference of opinion, in degree if not in substance, between the two classical editors of Theodore's Arabic texts, Constantine Bacha and Ignace Dick. They both associate Theodore with Mar Sabas. Yet, while Bacha leans on

19 Abū Qurrah, *Maymar fī Wujūd al-Khāliq wad-Dīn al-Qawīm* (Maymar on the Existence of the Creator and the Right Religion), pp. 43–45.

20 Griffith, "Reflections on the Biography," p. 148.

21 Ibid., p.149. Father Samir Khalil Samir agrees with this proposition; see S.K. Samir, "La somme des aspects de la foi, œuvre de Abū Qurrah?" in *Actes II*, Samir Khalil, 1986, 93–121, pp. 119–120.

22 Lamoreaux, *Theodore Abū Qurrah*, pp. xi xviii.

23 Abū Qurrah, *Maymar fī Wujūd al-Khāliq wad-Dīn al-Qawīm* (Maymar on the Existence of the Creator and the Right Religion), p. 52.

24 Ibid., pp. 57–58.

probability and surmises that the bishop of Ḥarrān *may* be the saint of Mar Sabas,[25] Ignace Dick seems to be certain, as he claims that the evidence for Theodore's monastic life in Mar Sabas is beyond doubt.[26]

In his reflection on Abū Qurrah's association with Mar Sabas, Sidney Griffith acknowledges the scholarly opinion that traces a "manifest intellectual debt to St. John of Damascus, the monastery's [i.e., Mar Sabas'] most illustrious theological scholar."[27] Griffith spots evidence of the association of Theodore with John, not only in the wording of the former's own texts (e.g., Theodore's Greek text, *Opusculum 18*), but also in the contents of some Syriac texts (e.g., Bar Hebraeus' texts). Going against the classical claims of Georg Graf and Msgr Joseph Nasrallah, Griffith does not agree that Theodore's affinity with John of Damascus' thought means that Theodore must have been at Mar Sabas during John's time there. He argues, instead, that Theodore could have learned John's thought and theology during his time in Mar Sabas long after the latter's departure or even after his death.[28] Relying positively on the Georgian version of a document that narrates the passion story of a monk of the monastery called Michael, Griffith concludes:

> One may then reasonably suppose that the first period of his monastic life was in all probability prior to his episcopal consecration as the bishop of Ḥarrān, sometime between 775 and 785, his presumed twentieth and thirtieth birthdays ... it is also not unlikely that Abū Qurrah had a second stint as a monk of Mar Sabas.[29]

In 2002, John Lamoreaux published an essay on the biography of Theodore Abū Qurrah, in which he presents his revision of the classical reading (i.e., by scholars such as Ignace Dick, Georg Graf, Sidney Griffith, Joseph Nasrallah and Samir Khalil Samir) of Theodore Abū Qurrah's link to the monastery of Mar Sabas. Lamoreaux's re-examination of Abū Qurrah's Sabaite monastic background leads him to pursue a rigorous historical-critical assessment of both Abū Qurrah's Greek text, *Opusculum 18*, and the story of *The Passion of Michael the Sabaite*. He casts a skeptical eye on the historical reliability of these texts and other possible ancillary sources and data, and argues that all scholars can actually be certain of is that there is no authentic evidence to prove that Abū Qurrah was really

---

25 Bacha, *Mayāmir Thāūdūrūs Abī Qurrah* (Mayāmir of Theodore Abū Qurrah), p. 4.
26 Abū Qurrah, *Maymar fī Wujūd al-Khāliq wad-Dīn al-Qawīm* (Maymar on the Existence of the Creator and the Right Religion), p. 42.
27 Griffith, "Reflections on the Biography," p. 150.
28 Ibid.
29 Ibid. p. 152.

a Sabaite monk. The only truth we can surely claim to know about this church figure is that he was at one point the Melkite bishop of Ḥarrān.[30] Lamoreaux goes on to say that the evidence "that Abū Qurrah was a monk at the monastery of Mar Sabas is slight at best and nonexistent at worst."[31] He then intriguingly concludes that severing Abū Qurrah from the monastery of Mar Sabas would prevent us from taking for granted "that Abū Qurrah was the '*continuateur arabe*' of that monastery's most famous theologian, John of Damascus, ... one should not, in particular, be too quick to extrapolate from Abū Qurrah's notions to those of the monastery of Mar Sabas."[32]

John Lamoreaux's, Sidney Griffith's, and other scholars' discussions on Abū Qurrah's association with the monastery of Mar Sabas fall under the rubric of historical-critical examination of the textual and historical extant resources from the early Abbasid era. This scholarly method is not the primary research track that I intend to follow in the present study, which is fundamentally theological and hermeneutical, not historiographical, in nature and *telos*. I acknowledge the historians' disagreement on Theodore's Sabaite monastic background and do not claim to bring to the discussion any new proposal that is pertinent to this matter *per se*.

That said, and without forgetting the purely introductory nature of these first pages, I allow myself to suggest here that, just as other scholars may be too quick in linking Theodore to Mar Sabas, John Lamoreaux seems to me to be as quick, if not quicker, to conclude that dissociating Abū Qurrah from Mar Sabas automatically divorces him intellectually and theologically from John of Damascus and sets a division between Theodore's theological mind and the Damascene-Sabaite, Melkite theological legacy. I believe that the theological link between Abū Qurrah and John of Damascus stands on intellectual rather than primarily geographical or historiographical evidence. In chapters four and five of the second part of this book, I will demonstrate both textually and theologically the close and far-from-deniable affinity between Theodore and John. This affinity stands on solid theological and intellectual ground, regardless of whether Theodore Abū Qurrah was a Sabaite monk, or whether he was just the bishop of Ḥarrān and never entered Mar Sabas monastery at all. Neither the evidence for, nor the questionability of Theodore Abū Qurrah's Sabaite monastic background should be the basis on which we either affirm or deny that his theological legacy warrants awarding him the title of '*continuateur arabe*' of the legacy of John of

30 Lamoreaux, "Biography of Theodore Abū Qurrah Revisited," p. 37.
31 Ibid., p. 40.
32 Ibid.

Damascus, or even of Maximus the Confessor. Whether there is or is not such an intellectual continuity should rather be tested on the basis of a thorough *ad intra* comparison between Theodore Abū Qurrah's Arabic theological works, on the one hand, and the Greek works of John of Damascus and Maximus the Confessor, on the other.

On the basis of this methodological conviction, it is my goal in the ensuing chapters of this study to show that I accept the view that associates Theodore Abū Qurrah with Mar Sabas and the Jerusalemite Christian Melkite sphere (I find no convincing reason not to do so), and I will build my theological and hermeneutical study on the consensus of the majority of the historians of Arab Christianity, without however engaging in any way with their theories. Rather, on the basis of the methodological conviction outlined above, I aim to demonstrate the theological link between Theodore Abū Qurrah and the Palestinian-Syrian Melkite tradition, including John of Damascus. The evidence for this theological affinity, as I will show in the second part of this book, is altogether too persuasive to be denied.

II. Abū Qurrah in this Study: Going beyond Mere Apologetics

The study presented in this book attempts to make the first comprehensive systematic and hermeneutic analysis of Theodore Abū Qurrah's Arabic theological discourses and doctrinal thinking on the Trinity and Christology, in dialogue with Islam. It introduces a new dimension by approaching the subject from the perspective of considering the extent of Abū Qurrah's allegiance to, or divergence from, the doctrinal orthodoxy of the Chalcedonian-Nicene, Byzantine-Melkite Christian legacy, which he learned from theologians such as John of Damascus and Maximus the Confessor, whose theological perspective, in turn, stems intellectually from the doctrinal stream of the Cappadocian fathers and Cyril of Alexandria. Studying Theodore Abū Qurrah's Arabic apologetics from the perspective of his rootedness in Christian doctrinal orthodoxy takes the scholarship of this Arab Christian *mutakallim* beyond the boundaries of previous studies of his extant works, which have been undertaken thus far by Islamicists and specialists in the history of Arab Christianity in the early Abbasid era.

This introduction began with some quotations from contemporary scholars who attribute to Theodore Abū Qurrah the pioneering role of dialoguing on Christian theology with Muslims and defending it before them in Arabic. The intention was to point to the fact that Abū Qurrah is primarily, if not exclusively, praised for pursing this 'apology in Arabic' mission in relation to its impact on Islam and Muslims. However, in this study I endeavour to argue that this approach to, and praise of, Theodore's legacy reinforces the tendency, on the part of present-day scholars, to study his writings from the angle of the apologetic purpose that they believe appears in Theodore's writing in Arabic "with an eye to the Muslim *Mutakallimūn* of Baṣrah, Kūfa and Baghdād."[33] On this point, Sidney Griffith goes even further in noticing that Abū Qurrah and his Arab compatriot theologians set about explaining Christian doctrines to arabophone Christians in terms and idioms that are derived from, and determined by, Qur'anic language and thinking, leave alone by Islamic theology.[34] It is not far from truth to say that the pressure of the Islamic challenge was a main factor influencing the apologetic style of argument Abū Qurrah uses in order to present the Christian faith to/in his context.[35] At the time of this remarkable Arab theologian, the teachings of the Bible and the councils of the Church on Jesus Christ's identity and his two natures, as well as the incarnation and the Trinity, were still topics of great controversy in the territories under Islamic rule.[36]

I am convinced that the full dimensions and content of Abū Qurrah's theological thinking have not yet been explored in modern scholarship. It is also my belief that, instead of carefully examining Abū Qurrah's intellectual impact on Christian theology, scholars have tended to read and interpret his writings rather one-sidedly, emphasizing his apologetic interaction with Islam and studying him only from an interfaith perspective. Such concern about his writings stems from a prior interest in the interreligious apologetic approach they demonstrate.

In the scholarship on Abū Qurrah's legacy, we find a general emphasis on him mainly because he was 'the first theologian to write in Arabic' and someone who 'undertook a defence against the rival claims of Islam.' The facts that he was an orthodox *Christian* and that he wrote *theological and doctrinal* discourses against the claims of Islam and of other Christian sects are almost taken for granted, while his theological premises and assertions are yet to be comprehensively studied. The interest of current scholarship in the interreligious encounter between Christianity and Islam has led to an eagerness to study the heritage of the Arab fathers as a means of understanding Eastern Christians' experience of living and practicing Christian faith in a predominantly Muslim society, like Theodore's. It is within this context that Abū Qurrah is studied as a historical image related to Christian-Muslim encounter. The preoccupation with this encounter makes scholars pay more attention to the fact that he wrote on Christian faith and theology in Arabic rather than in Greek or Syriac, than to the core content

33 Griffith, "Muslims and Church Councils," p. 272.
34 Ibid., p. 273.
35 Ibid., p. 274.
36 Ibid., p. 285.

and assertions of his theology *per se*. What scholarship has so far presented to us on Abū Qurrah are studies on his writings as reflecting a Christian discourse written in an Islamic culture and presented to Muslim readers in their own language; a discourse, that is, that can be taken as a case study on how the Christian community of the East spoke to Islam in the 8th and 9th centuries through the theology of Christian Arabs like Abū Qurrah. As significant and valuable as this concern may be, the attention to Theodore Abū Qurrah's style of apologetic discourse (the *how* of his discourse) should not overshadow the importance of analysing the content of his theological propositions (the *what* and *whence* of his claims). Theodore's relationship to his Islamic context should also be interpreted taking into account his relationship to the Christian theological heritage of earlier centuries – the heritage that the Church deemed definitive of its orthodox interpretation of faith. Theodore's understanding and interpretation of Niceno-Constantinopolitan and Chalcedonian theologies is a very seminal and essential area of research that invites us to deeper and more careful study.

Sidney Griffith once perceptively noted the following:

> A feature of Christian apologetics in Syriac and Arabic in the early Abbasid period was the appeal writers sometimes made to the Muslims on behalf of the reasonableness of their own christology, by contrast with that of their fellow Christian adversaries. In this respect, the influence of Islam, and the distinctive christology of the Qur'ān, served to sharpen the christological debates among the Christians in the caliphate.[37]

Griffith's claim raises for scholars a plethora of questions about the nature, the content, and the systems of doctrine that are reflected in the writings of Arab theologians such as Theodore Abū Qurrah. Griffith points to this potentially very fruitful field of research without so far himself engaging in it. It is into this as yet insufficiently studied field of Theodore Abū Qurrah's orthodox legacy that I attempt to enter in the present volume. By studying Abū Qurrah's Arabic texts and suggesting another, theologically centred, reading and translation of the Arabic *mayāmir*, I attempt to examine the extent of the influence of Islamic and Qur'anic theology, and Arabic language, in shaping the Christological and Trinitarian argumentation of Christian apologists such as Abū Qurrah. One may describe this study as an attempt to discover whether or not Islamic-Arabic influence on Christian theology during the early Abbasid era amounts to a kind of 'islamization' of the orthodox, Chalcedonian, and Nicene theological heritage. To frame this as a question, if Sidney Griffith is right in his claim that "for Abū Qurrah, the argument with the Jacobites was an essential part of the vindication

37 Ibid., p. 295.

of Christian doctrine in the Arabic-speaking milieu of the Muslims,"[38] would this imply that the goal of gaining the acceptance and support of Islam made Abū Qurrah compromise by any means imaginable some of the claims that are constitutive of Chalcedonian and Nicene Christology and Trinitarian thinking? And if there seems to be evidence of such a compromise, in what sense could one still say with Abū Qurrah's contemporary opponents (i.e., Jacobites and Abū Rā'iṭah, for instance) that his theological masters were Maximus the Confessor and John of Damascus?

Sidney Griffith invites us elsewhere to think about this issue from the perspective of questions as to whether Abū Qurrah is one of those Christian authors who decisively attempted to produce theology in Arabic. Griffith points to the allegation of the Abbasid Muslim author al-Jāḥiẓ that "the Christian doctrinal formulae, at least when expressed in Arabic, simply make no sense," and that the Christians' 'ugly' doctrines demonstrate "their ignorance of the figures of speech and the inflections of languages, and the translation of one language into another, and of what is possible [to say] about God, and what is not possible."[39] I find in the words of this Muslim *mutakallim* a serious, challenging invitation to examine the accuracy of his allegation, specifically in relation to Abū Qurrah's theology. Has Abū Qurrah's presentation of Chalcedonian and Nicene doctrinal discourse in Arabic terms ultimately produced figures of speech and translations that are intellectually inflected, not only from an Islamic religious point of view, but also, more essentially, with regard to Christian dogma? Is there a linguistic distortion that is sufficient to make us doubt that Abū Qurrah's Arabic theology truly represents, rather than revises or re-models, Chalcedonian and Nicene orthodoxy in a new language?

Touching upon these dimensions of Abū Qurrah's writing of theology within an Islamic context, and in controversies with other Christian sects, takes us directly to the core of the research undertaken in this volume. In order for the above questions to be answered, a coherent analysis of Abū Qurrah's legacy must be made: one that takes into account the facts that he was an *orthodox* Christian who wrote about specific lines of theological thought in Arabic, and that he was a Christian theologian *in* the church as much as an apologist *for* it. I have, therefore, attempted to study the theological mindset that motivated the man of the 8th – 9th-century Christian-Muslim exchange, the historical and intellectual context of whom invites us, in fact, to study and understand him and

38 Ibid., p. 296.
39 Sidney Griffith, "Ḥabīb Ibn Ḫidmah Abū Rā'iṭah: A Christian *Mutakallim* of the First Abbasid Century," in *The Beginnings of Christian Theology in Arabic: Muslim-Christian Encounters in the Early Islamic Period* (Aldershot, UK: Ashgate Variorum, 2002), 161–201, p. 165.

his legacy deeply. I consider *what* Theodore's theology in itself consists of, and I attempt to integrate this with the recent preoccupation with *how* his theology counters the rival ideas of Islam on major doctrines such as the Trinity, Christology, and the incarnation. I will do this because I believe that, methodologically, understanding the *how* requires a clear understanding of the foundational *what*.

My study will tackle questions such as: what kind of *orthodox* theologian was Abū Qurrah – not denominationally, but theologically? What kind of theological language and rationale do his apologies reflect? Abū Qurrah is known to be a defender of Chalcedon, and of orthodoxy in general, not only by present-day scholars but also by 12th-century monophysite chroniclers, who call him "the Chalcedonian of Edessa."[40] It is significant for the assessment of Theodore's contribution to the history of Christian thought to study what is *Chalcedonian*, *Nicene*, and ultimately *orthodox* in Abū Qurrah's theology. Is his understanding of Chalcedonian orthodoxy 'orthodox,' or is it not? What are the similarities and differences between his theological hermeneutics of Chalcedonian and Nicene doctrines and the thinking of the main Nicene and Chalcedonian Fathers, such as the Cappadocians, Cyril of Alexandria, John of Damascus, and Maximus the Confessor?

Abū Qurrah's texts show, for example, that one of the key features in his understanding of Chalcedonian, and even Nicene, thinking is the terms he uses to speak about 'personhood' and 'nature' or 'essence.' In his Greek texts, Abū Qurrah uses *hypostasis* and *physis*, while in his Arabic texts he uses the Arabic words *wajh*, *uqnūm* and *jawhar*. Also, in his texts on the incarnation and the divine-human union in Jesus Christ, Abū Qurrah states that "nature is never in any way predicated of a nature." Rather, nature is predicated of a *hypostasis*. It is of immeasurable importance for understanding Abū Qurrah's thinking to see what he means by 'nature' and *hypostasis* in the context of writing about these two notions for an Arabic-speaking readership. Does his understanding of these terms, whatever it may be, represent in content a reiteration of Chalcedonian and Nicene thinking and terminology, or does it in fact take the theological legacy of Christian orthodoxy beyond the original connotations of the terms? And, if the latter, does Abū Qurrah's understanding make him theologically an authentic voice speaking about Christian faith as it is, or rather someone who is bringing the Christian voice into tune with the Muslim mind?

In addition, Abū Qurrah speaks about 'the *hypostasis* of union' in Christ, invoking language prominent in the writings of Cyril of Alexandria and Maximus the Confessor. He concedes that in this '*hypostasis* of union,' the human and the

---

40 Lamoreaux, *Theodore Abū Qurrah*, p. xii.

divine are simultaneously in total equality and total particularity. Yet Abū Qurrah also speaks about the *hypostasis* of each nature, especially the *hypostasis* of the eternal Son, which is predicated on the eternal nature. In this study, I consider what Theodore means theologically by '*hypostasis* of union' and what the connotations are of the Arabic terminology he uses to speak about this notion. I discuss the sense in which speaking about the *hypostases* of two natures as well as 'the *hypostasis* of union' between them is expressive of a line of thinking within theological orthodoxy. I examine whether or not Theodore attempts to reconcile Cyrilan concern about the unity in terms of '*hypostasis* of union' with a Nestorian-like concern about personal individuation in terms of 'the *hypostasis* of the nature,' which in fact implies giving attention to Nicene-Constantinopolitan theology's concern about personal particularity. Moreover, does Abū Qurrah's adoption of an Arabic term like '*wajh*' to translate *hypostasis* in some of his Arabic texts[41] have any implications for the various connotations of *hypostasis*, and does it create any new theological dimension in use of the Greek term in orthodox theology?

Delving into the linguistic, conceptual, and doctrinal components of Abū Qurrah's theology and analysing them as such will show whether his apologies represent a Christian orthodox theology or rather exemplify a Christian thinking that is slavishly assimilated to his Islamic context, which may actually mean that he offers a new form of orthodoxy that is adapted to his context and not properly orthodox in substance. More broadly, this will show us whether, when the Syrian-Palestinian Melkites of the $8^{th}-9^{th}$ centuries began to craft their own distinctive theological tradition because of their subordinate position after the Muslim conquest, they produced a new variation on the creedal theology of Nicaea and Chalcedon, or whether they generated a new doctrinal theological discourse altogether: Did they present a new 'arabized' version of Chalcedonian Christology and Niceno-Constantinopolitan Trinitarian theology or a totally new interpretation of faith in Christ and the triune God?

This study of the theological content of Theodore Abū Qurrah's apologetic discourse and the relation of this theology to its Christian doctrinal heritage is very important for present-day scholarship. It first takes Arabic patristic studies into areas of knowledge not yet fully explored by shedding light on the *ad intra* relationship(s) between Arabic theology in the age of Islam and earlier theological currents within Christianity, especially those of the ecumenical councils. This expansion is necessary, even essential, if we are to develop a comprehen-

41 Bo Holmberg, "'Person' in the Trinitarian Doctrine of Christian Arabic Apologetics and Its Background in the Syriac Church Fathers," in *Studia patristica*, 25 (1993), 300–307, p. 302.

sive understanding of the theology of that period in the Islamic world. Such an Arabic theology is an important link in the chain of the self-development of Christian theology through history. It should not be undermined by any tendency to focus only on one issue that is characteristic of the Christian-Muslim exchange of the 9th century.

Furthermore, by studying the degree of Theodore's success or failure in confining his theological discourse to the orthodox faith of the ecumenical councils despite, or because, of his concern to make Christian faith appealing to, or defensible before, Muslims, we find an inspiring historical case study about the difference between interaction with non-Christians that is an opportunity for enriching and improving Christian thinking[42] and interaction that may cause the conversion of Christian faith into something that is no longer really representative of Christianity's core content and original identity. Though Theodore's historical context and the present-day situation are noticeably dissimilar, discerning this notional difference between these two forms of interfaith interaction is extremely relevant to today's passionate Christian endeavour to launch (at all costs, even if they are eventually paid by Christianity alone) interactions with Islam and, sometimes, to twist the expression and compromise the content of Christian faith in order to make it sound acceptable and appealing to the ears of Muslims.

Exploring the theological content of Theodore Abū Qurrah's texts constitutes a historical and theological case study on such a difference. It is a journey from the apologetic story that Abū Qurrah was involved in toward the theological mind that lies behind his role in this story. It is a journey that will, eventually, uncover the consequences and ramifications of Theodore's apology for the faith that he tried to convey and represent.

III. Outline of the Volume and Abū Qurrah's Works

This study is divided into two parts comprising five chapters overall, with a chapter-like concluding postscript. The first part sets out the general contextual and historical scene in Syria-Palestine during the 7th–9th centuries CE, when the Muslim Arabs of the southern Peninsula invaded the area and established the rule of the caliphate.

42 As Mark Swanson believes dialogue with Muslims can do to the Christian theology of the Trinity. See Mark N. Swanson, "The Trinity in Christian-Muslim Conversation," *Dialog: A Journal of Theology*, 44(3) (2005), 256–263.

The analysis of the historical context is presented in two chapters. The first chapter considers the Syrian-Palestinian Christians' reaction to the Islamic invasion, their cultural and sociological stances towards the newcomers, and their intellectual and societal status. The chapter aims to show that the transfer of power from the Byzantines to the Muslims represents a radical and sweeping transformation that presented the Christian inhabitants of the land with the challenge of reading themselves through new lenses shaped substantially by the new factor called 'Islam.' The Church prelates in particular found themselves faced with the urgent responsibility of finding a plausible and positive explanation for the presence of Islam that would enable their churches' members to survive the radical and irreversible shift from being a 'majority' to being a 'minority' in their homeland.

The second chapter in part one will continue to portray the broader historical and cultural scene of Syria-Palestine during the early Islamic centuries and will also focus on the situation of the Byzantine-Melkite Christian community of Syria-Palestine, which was Chalcedonian in its theological stance and Arabic- and Greek-speaking in its language. This chapter will begin to shed particular light on one figure in this church tradition, the main subject of the book, Theodore Abū Qurrah, and his intellectual legacy during the 8th–9th centuries. It will show that, with the transformation from the age of the Byzantine Emperor into the era of the Muslim Caliph, the Melkite church of Syria and Palestine experienced a parallel transformation from being a follower of the theological orthodoxy of Byzantium-Constantinople to becoming a distinct church in the process of developing its own particular Chacedonian-Melkite, Arabic theological orthodoxy. In this chapter, I will show that this transformation is exemplified in the distinction between John of Damascus' theological reasoning and that of Theodore Abū Qurrah. By developing a particular intellectual methodology characterized by prioritizing reason over the religious text, Abū Qurrah launched a new theological discourse that is different from those of other Byzantine theologians (notably John of Damascus) not only in terms of language (i.e., Arabic), but also, and more crucially, in terms of apologetic method and content. This difference represents a step ahead in Eastern Christian attitudes to the changes that were taking place in their lives with the arrival of Islam in the region.

After setting the historical, sociological, and general intellectual scene of Theodore Abū Qurrah's era, the second part of the book concentrates on how he reflects this intellectual and theological transformation in Byzantine-Melkite theology through his theological apologies and debates with the Muslim *mutakallims* of the 8th–9th centuries. This part consists of three chapters. The first (chapter three) will attempt to show the connection of Theodore Abū Qurrah's theological orthodoxy with the Greek and Syriac legacy of Nicene and Chalcedonian orthodoxy. It aims to tackle the following question: Has Abū Qurrah's presentation of Chalcedonian and Nicene doctrinal discourse in Arabic terms eventually produced figures of speech and translations that are intellectually inflected, not only from an Islamic point of view, but also, more essentially, with regard to Christian dogma? This chapter attempts to answer this question by going back and carefully considering how pre-8th-century Greek- and Syriac-speaking fathers understood the key Christological and Trinitarian notions of the orthodox creedal discourse and how the use of these notions in Syriac and Greek played an indelible role in creating a serious misunderstanding and consequent conflict in the Church.

The ensuing chapters in the second part build upon the theological-linguistic contextual framework that was visited in chapter three. Chapters four and five attempt to answer the question posed above from within the Arabic texts (*mayāmir*) of Theodore Abū Qurrah himself. Chapter four sheds light on Theodore's theology of the Trinity, while chapter five tackles some elements in his Christological thought. These two central chapters in the book aim to show whether expressing Nicene and Chalcedonian orthodoxy in Arabic, especially the technical theological terminologies of the previous Greek and Syriac fathers, did or did not create another misunderstanding of the content of Christian faith, and whether such a misunderstanding, if there was one, drove Abū Qurrah's theological discourse along a track that was satisfactory and feasible to the ears of Muslims and Arabic-speaking community in his context but pushed his wagon, in turn, far from the track of Christian orthodoxy. This endeavour is undertaken by: 1) thorough, meticulous, analytical and critical hermeneutics of Abū Qurrah's theology of the Trinity and Christology in his extant Arabic works; and 2) comparing and contrasting this hermeneutics with the theology of the Trinity and Christology in the writings of John of Damascus and Maximus the Confessor. As will become apparent in chapters four and five, I pursue this comparison after analysing Abū Qurrah's hermeneutics strictly in the extant Arabic works that demonstrate his thought on these two themes. It will also be noted that I pursue this comparison starting with John of Damascus' writings and then moving on to the texts of Maximus the Confessor, rather than considering them chronologically. I deliberately start with the later of the two, John of Damascus, rather than with the earlier, Maximus the Confessor, because I want to trace the roots of Theodore Abū Qurrah's theological thought first in the soil of the Church father who was temporally closer to Theodore (i.e., John of Damascus) and then dig deeper to see whether these roots find a possible location within the soil of the earlier, no less influential Chalcedonian thinker, Maximus the Confessor (whose legacy was by no means dead in the time of Abū Qurrah, let alone in the days of the Damascene). I shall consistently make my comparison and contrast of Abū Qurrah with earlier Chalcedonian orthodoxy starting with John of Damascus and then going back to Maximus the Confessor.

The study ends with a chapter-like concluding postscript, in which I offer my conclusions on Theodore Abū Qurrah's theological and ecclesial character as Melkite, orthodox *mutakallim* in the world of Islam. I do this by proposing answers to questions such as: What kind of 'orthodox' does Abū Qurrah emerge as in his theological career? Is he someone who rejects innovation in the service of confessing the faith of his church, or someone who bravely embarks on innovation because he believes in its value in transmitting faith to others plausibly and understandably? Does Abū Qurrah's theological legacy suggest a new understanding of 'orthodoxy' that indicates an Arabic-Christian innovative meaning that goes beyond the traditional, Byzantine connotations of the term? Last but not least, what might be some of the contextual implications of Abū Qurrah's attempt to do more than merely transmit confessional orthodoxy in traditional terms by taking an innovative, productive approach, and do these implications mean that he stands out as an early Arab Christian contextual theologian in dialogue with Islam?

This study is an intensive analysis of Theodore Abū Qurrah's Arabic works in particular. I rely in my study of his extant Arabic *mayāmir* on the Arabic edition by Constantine Bacha, *Mayāmir Thāūdūrūs Abī Qurrah Usquf Ḥarrān: Aqdam Ta'līf 'Arabī Naṣrānī* (Mayāmir of Theodore Abū Qurrah, the Bishop of Ḥarrān: The Oldest Christian Arabic Composition), which was republished in Beirut in 1904. This edition of Theodore's entire Arabic oeuvre is still very valuable and useful for studying his thought and linguistic conceptuality. In addition to this main text, I also refer to other editions of some of Theodore's extant Arabic *mayāmir* edited by Ignace Dick: *Maymar fī Ikrām al-Aiqūnāt* (Maymar on the Veneration of Icons) and *Maymar fī Wujūd al-Khāliq wad-Dīn al-Qawīm* (Maymar on the Existence of the Creator and the Right Religion), both published by Librairie S. Paul (Jounieh, Lebanon) and the Papal Oriental Institute (Rome), the former in 1986 and the latter in 1982. In addition, I use Samir Khalil Samir's edition of Theodore's *Maymar fī al-Ḥurriyyah* (Maymar on Freedom), published in two issues of *Al-Mashriq* in 2005 and 2006. I also rely heavily on the Arabic text of Abū Qurrah's debate with Muslim *mutakallims* in the court of the caliph, al-Maʾmūn. The critical edition used in this study is that by Wafīq Naṣrī, *Abū Qurrah wal-Maʾmūn: al-Mujādalah* (Abū Qurrah and al-Maʾmūn: al-Mujādalah), published in 2010 by CEDRAC (Beirut) and Librairie S. Paul (Jounieh). Some scholars (e.g., Graf, Griffith, Bertaina) do not believe that the text of the debate in al-Maʾmūn's court is authentically Abū Qurran. While I agree that it is impossible to prove that this text came from Theodore's pen, I side with those scholars who believe that the content of the text is reflective of authentic Abū Qurran theological thought and logic (e.g., Bacha, Guillaume, Dick, Khalīl, Naṣrallah, and lately Naṣrī). I thus treat the text as a reliable part of Abū Qurrah's theological legacy.[43]

Throughout the book, Arabic texts from Abū Qurrah's works, as well as from the Qur'an and Muslim *kalām*, are given in Arabic script and only transliterated whenever this is necessary. I try to include as many texts in their original Arabic format as possible, because this seems to me more appropriate and useful from a scholarly point of view. All of the English translations (and transliterations) of these texts are my own, unless otherwise stated. I opted for making my own English translation of the Arabic texts because I was not fully satisfied with the translations I found of Abū Qurrah's Arabic works. I did consult the English translations of Theodore's *mayāmirs* that are available today: Sidney Griffith's English translation of Theodore's *Maymar fī 'Īkrām al-Aiqūnāt* (Maymar on the Veneration of Icons) published by Peeters (Louvain) in 1997, and John Lamoreaux's English translation of Theodore's Arabic *mayāmir* in *Theodore Abū Qurrah*, published by Brigham Young University Pess (Provo, UT) in 2005. Griffith and Lamoreaux undoubtedly offer admirable and valuable translations. However, I have reservations about Lamoreaux's translation of Abū Qurrah's Arabic terms, especially the technical Greek and Syriac theological vocabulary. In chapter four, I shall consider Lamoreaux's translation of Abū Qurrah's terminology in his *Maymar fī ath-Thālūth* (Maymar on the Trinity), where Abū Qurrah speaks of the *hypostases* in the triune Godhead using the terms *uqnūm* (which is an Arabic transliteration of the Syrian *qnumo*) and *wajh*. In his translation of the *maymar*, Lamoreaux translates both Arabic terms as either *hypostasis* or *uqnum*, without, in my view, paying sufficient attention to the conceptual and philological nuances that distinguish the two Arabic terms Abū Qurrah uses. I therefore decided to present my own English translation of the Arabic texts, not only the Arabic *mayāmir*, but also, and more extensively, Wafīq Naṣrī's Arabic critical edition of the text of Abū Qurrah's debate in al-Ma'mūn's court. Naṣrī offers us the first up-to-date critical version of the Arabic text of the debate. What we still

43 On the authenticity of this text, see, for example, Theodore Abū Qurrah, *Abū Qurrah wal-Ma'mūn: al-Mujādalah* (Abū Qurrah and al-Ma'mūn: The Debate), pp. 43–93; David Bertaina, "The Debate of Theodore Abū Qurra," in *Christian-Muslim Relation, A Bibliographical History*, Vol. 1: *600–900*, ed. David Thomas and Barbara Roggema (Leiden: Brill, 2009), 556–564; S.H. Griffith, *Theodore Abū Qurrah. The Intellectual Profile of an Arab Christian Writer of the first Abbasid Century* (Tel. Aviv: Tel Aviv University, 1992), pp. 23–25; A. Guillaume, 'A Debate between Christian and Moslem Doctors," *Journal of the Royal Asiatic Society of Great Britain and Ireland* Centenary Supplement (1924), 233–244; and G. Graf, *Die arabischen Schriften des Theodor Abū Qurra, Bischofs von Ḥarrān (ca. 740–820)* (Paderborn: Ferdinand Schoningh, 1910), pp. 77–85.

need is an English translation of such an edition, but this is not yet available. Therefore, in this study of Abū Qurrah, I have allowed myself to offer an English translation of various paragraphs cited from the text of the debate, as an initial contribution to scholarship in the field, and hoping that one day I may be able to work on a complete English translation of this text.

Part One: **The Historical and Religious Settings**

Chapter One. “If Indeed They Were Known At All”: Christians’ Attitudes towards Islam

I. The Dawn of the Arabs’ ‘Invasion’ in the Eyes of Christians

At the first half of the 7th century, the history of the Middle East took an irreversible turn that would change the face of that region for the following millennium. In almost no time, Eastern Christians in the area found themselves no longer under allegiance to the rule of the Byzantine Empire and coming within the domain of a new ruling power – a domain that encompassed people who differed not only in their principal language and culture, but also in their religious views. The newcomers’ appraisal of the Christians’ view of God and Jesus Christ was more or less antagonistic towards and intolerant of Christian orthodoxy (Chalcedonian and non-Chalcedonian alike).

The traditional view has been that Muslims from the Arabian Peninsula took control of Syria and Palestine after defeating the Byzantines in a series of major battles, usually called in Muslim and Christian texts from the early-Islamic era *al-futūḥat al-ʿArabiyya* (the Arab conquests). For example, in *Byzantium and the Early Islamic Conquests*,[44] Walter Kaegi defends the historicity of the written sources about the famous battle of Jabiya-Yarmuk, when the Muslims invaded the southern parts of Syria and Palestine in vast numbers and captured these areas from the Byzantines. Kaegi concedes that the Byzantine sources do not contain a coherent account of these conquests and acknowledges that they need to be read with caution as “historical texts.”[45] He also concedes that the Byzantine sources depend on fragmentary and dubious Muslim and Oriental historiographers’ narrations of the same events, which ultimately, he admits, complicate the attempts to interpret and weigh the reliability of what are “not entirely free-standing” Byzantine and Arabic sources.[46] That said, Kaegi still believes that there is enough textual evidence to claim that the Muslim occupation of Palestine and southern Syria from 634 onwards has a plausible *military*, and not only social, economic, religious, and socio-cultural, explanation: the Byzantines were constantly defeated in major battles with the nomads of the Peninsula, who

44 Walter Kaegi, *Byzantium and the Early Islamic Conquests* (Cambridge: Cambridge University Press, 1992).
45 Ibid., p. 6.
46 Ibid., p. 9.

invaded Byzantine territories with vast armies. It is thus possible, Kaegi maintains, to justify on the basis of Byzantine and Arabic textual evidences the use of the military term 'conquest' *fatḥ* (pl. *futūḥ* or *futūḥāt*) to describe the Peninsulan Arabs' takeover of the eastern and southern Syrian territories from the Byzantines.[47]

Admitting, however, that the military explanation is not the only one, Kaegi refers the defeat of the Byzantines to the decision made by King Heraclius, who, after his victory over the Sassanians and his peace treaty with them in 629, decided to decrease the number of Byzantine troops in Syria and Palestine. Heraclius, Kaegi states, did this out of self-confidence, not realizing that the situation in these regions was soon to change rapidly. The Muslim conquests, as Kaegi says, followed on too swiftly from the victory over the Sassanians for the Byzantines to cope with, leaving Heraclius no time to re-stabilize the empire or make adequate military preparations for major battles against the Arabs.[48] Although most of the Byzantine troops were stationed on the northern borders of Syria, far from the battlefields, this did not exempt them from fighting against the Muslims. The Byzantines, Kaegi explains, had a clear "mobile defence-in-depth"[49] strategy, which led them into harsh battles with the Muslim troops and was used by Byzantium in its attempt to reassert its authority in the areas formerly under imperial control. This strategy, Kaegi adds, made the Byzantines keep masses of troops and recruit huge armies in certain areas (e.g., Ma'āb) in order to resist the Muslims' troops and try to defeat them (e.g., at Wādī al-Mūjīb, Fusṭāṭ, and Balqā'). In conclusion, Kaegi defends the traditional view that there was a series of major battles between large Byzantine and Muslim armies, which ended with a massive victory of the latter, followed by the complete transformation of the area from a Byzantine-Christian into an Arab-Muslim region.[50]

---

47 Ibid., p. 18: "there is no sensible reason to avoid such terms ['conquest'] or to seek alternatives," because such an alteration, Kägi continues, "can only result in very inadequate and incomplete historical comprehension."

48 Ibid., p. 33. Heraclius, according to Kegi, found it was of no avail to pay huge amounts of money to recruit armies of Arabs and non-Arabs to help him fight the Arabs of the Peninsula on the southern borders of the Empire (p. 35).

49 Ibid., p. 59.

50 Ibid. p. 87: "Islamic tribesmen['s] ... invasions occurred while Byzantium was still in the process of restoring her authority over the full extent of the former eastern borders of her empire. Heraclius was in that region because he was personally involved in overseeing that restoration and reunification. If he had had more time, he might have succeeded. The Muslim invasions caught him and the empire off balance at a very awkward time, and kept them off balance."

In the past few years, the question of the reliability and historical plausibility of this traditional view has been put on the table for discussion by scholars who rely in their reading of history on archaeological factors, rather than on ancient written sources. In 2003, a book titled, *Crossroads to Islam*,[51] was produced by the archaeologist, Yehuda Nevo in collaboration with Judith Koren, and published after Nevo's death. In this book, Nevo and Koren persuasively question the traditional view of an Arab conquest and major military victory over the Byzantines on the eastern and southern borders of the empire, finding it hard to accept from a scientific point of view the claim made in the written texts that there was a ‘conquest’ or real major battles between the nomads of the Peninsula and the Byzantine armies. Trusting the reliability of the archaeological, material remains for gleaning what really did or did not happen,[52] Nevo and Koren argue that there are no archaeological traces that can be cited as evidence of Byzantine armies and military campaigns on the eastern and southern borders of the empire during the 7th century. Nevo and Koren also argue that one cannot verify archaeologically the occurrence of perpetual raids of large forces of Muslims from the Peninsula or major wars and battles, either with the Byzantine armies or with the local troops of their Arab allies.

Contrary to Kaegi's ‘re-expansion’ theory, Nevo and Koren argue that the Byzantines, for political and strategic reasons, decided as early as the 5th century to withdrew from the eastern and southern parts of Syria and Palestine, gradually ceding to the Arab *foederati* the responsibility of defending the empire's remaining borders, and also the burden of ruling the territories.[53] From then on, the inhabitants of these areas became accustomed to being ruled by Arab tribesmen and protected by their followers and to paying taxes to them alone.[54] By the time the Arabs of the Peninsula started to create skirmishes that could disturb the daily life of these populations, there were no Byzantine rulers or armies left in the region to deal with such matters. The Peninsulan Arabs, Nevo and Koren maintain, did not need to come in large numbers in order to be able to

---

51 Yehuda D. Nevo and Judith Koren, *Crossroads to Islam: The Origins of the Arab Religion and the Arab State* (Amherst, NY: Prometheus Books, 2003). For a critical assessment of Nevo's and other researchers' scholarship on early Islam, see David Grafton, “The Politics of Pre-Islamic Arab Christianity in Contemporary Western Scholarship,” in *Theological Review*, 34(2013), 3–21.
52 Nevo and Koren, *Crossroads to Islam*, p. 8: “an archaeological site represents what people did, not what a more or less contemporary author and/or his later copiers thought they did or wanted others to believe they did.”
53 Ibid., pp. 36 ff. “It is our opinion more likely that repaired and/or manned fortresses in the southern sector of the *limes* reflect the presence of other Arab *foederati* in this sector and right down to ʿAqabah, including the Wādī Sirḥān leading to Phoinikon” (p. 42).
54 Ibid., p. 44.

bully and terrify the inhabitants, because there was no big, organized force to fight them back. They only made small-scale raids every now and then, which were sometimes ignored and even allowed by the Byzantines when such raids could serve their political and strategic agenda.[55] Thus, instead of there having been major battles and large-scale wars between Byzantium and the Muslims of the Peninsula over the eastern and southern borders of the empire, the transfer of power from the former to the latter, Nevo and Koren maintain, was smooth and did not disturb the daily life of the local population.[56] Battles such as the battle of Dāṯin, which the traditional view takes to have happened near Gaza, for example, was just a local, 'minor affair' "caused by a town official's decision to resist paying taxes to tribesmen, [who are] no longer (apparently) backed by imperial authority, or possibly as the result of his decision to resist raiders."[57] The Muslims, Nevo and Koren conclude, never 'conquered' Syria and Palestine and never fought wars on any major military scale with the Byzantines or their *foederati*. If such wars did take place, and if large armies of both sides camped in these areas during the 7th century, their presence, Nevo and Koren say, must have been totally unnoticed and had hardly any impact on the inhabitants' daily life. Otherwise, how can one explain the fact that there is no archaeological evidence for such presence and alleged battles?[58]

Whether the Muslims arrived into the Byzantine territories with major military actions, or the takeover was smooth and peaceful,[59] what concerns me in

---

55 See the interesting discussion at ibid., pp. 51–65, where Nevo and Koren point out how Byzantium prevented or allowed the persecution of the monophysites or the monothelities according to its own political interests and calculations.

56 Ibid., p. 94.

57 Ibid., pp. 99–100.

58 Nevo and Koren conclude from this the following: "the local written sources down to the early 8th century do not provide any evidence that a planned invasion of Arabs from the Peninsula occurred, and that great and dramatic battles ensued which crushed the Byzantine army and vanquished the empire" (ibid., p. 134).

59 For other readings on the Muslim conquest of Palestine and Syria and its nature and extent, see also Robert Schick, *The Christian Communities of Palestine from Byzantium to Islamic Rule: A Historical and Archaeological Study* (Princeton, NJ: Darwin Press, 1995), pp. 68–84; Fred Donner, *The Early Islamic Conquests* (Princeton, NJ: Princeton University Press, 1981); and Muḥammad al-Bakhīt and Iḥsān ʿAbbās (eds.), *Proceedings of the Second Symposium on the History of Bīlad al-Shām during the Early Islamic Period up to 40 A.H/640 A.D.: The Fourth International Conference on the History of Bīlad al-Shām* (Arabic papers) (Amman: University of Jordan, 1987), Vol. 2. On the other hand, between the two above mentioned positions, stand other scholars who find historical value in the Muslim chroniclers' narrations on the Muslim conquests and battles of invasion in Syria-Palestine, although without denying that there is serious historical distortion in the Muslim versions. One of these scholars, for example, is James Howard-Johnston, who opines that

this chapter is the fact that the transfer of power represented a radical, even sweeping, change that put Eastern Christians face-to-face with the inescapable task of reading the new phenomenon called 'Islam', as well as themselves in the light of it, through new lenses, by means of a new language-game and even from a totally unprecedented theological perspective. This new conquest was completely unexpected. Yet, the Christians could not just allow it to happen without attempting to explain it and trying to understand their fate in the light of it.[60] Church leaders found themselves burdened with the difficult duty of presenting a plausible explanation for this conquest to their fellow local Christians. It was impossible for them to ignore the need to interpret the new situation positively, not only to help the people maintain their faith, but also, and more importantly, to enable them in the coming centuries to survive the radical, irreversible shift from being a majority in a Christian empire into becoming a *dhimmī* minority in a Muslim one. In sum, what the Church found itself obliged to do in the face of this challenge was, as John Lamoreaux states, "to find a way to live in the new and sometimes hostile environment ushered in by the Muslim invasion."[61]

"both in terms of substance and the chronology of individual conquest narratives, early Islamic sources can be shown to have performed more than competently." Yet, he also points out "there is but one damaged section in this generally sound Islamic version of events. Something has gone seriously awry with the start of the *futuh*. ... sceptics may quite legitimately argue that this provides strong *prima facie* evidence for their doubts about the validity of early Islamic historical traditions": James Howard-Johnson, *Witnesses to a World Crisis: Historians and Histories of the Middle East in the Seventh Century* (Oxford: Oxford University Press, 2011), p. 379. Howard-Johnston convincingly discloses that Muslim historians such as Ibn Isḥaq, al-Balādhurī, al-Ṭabarī, al-Madā'inī and al-Wāqidī, to mention but a few, actually inserted in their record of the Muslims' battles with the Byzantines and the Persians many heroic and superhuman exploits on part of Muslim warriors and leaders, as well as allowing many noticeable chronological slippages to permeate their narrations. This, Howard-Johnston believes, proves that the accounts of these Muslim historians are not to be considered as historical records, but must rather be treated as mere historiographical re-narration that is corroborated, at least in outline, from non-Muslim [older] sources and as following the method of *isnād* (ibid. pp. 370–379; and see the whole of pp. 354–394). Howard-Johnston, nonetheless, refuses to consider this to be evidence of falsification, or even corruption, of history on the part of the Muslim authors, and thus a reason to consider the Islamic accounts as historically unreliable. It is rather, according to him, an attempt to enlist history in the service of the religious message: "we must remember at all times that Islamic history is religious history, that religion played, as it still plays, an unusually large part in the everyday life and politics of the Muslim community. Historical truth had to compete with religious truth" (ibid., pp. 379–380).

60 John C. Lamoreaux, "Early Eastern Christian Responses to Islam," in *Medieval Christian Perceptions of Islam*, ed. John V. Tolan (New York: Routledge, 2000), 3–21, p. 3.

61 Ibid.

Christian chronicles from the $8^{th}-9^{th}$ centuries onwards tell us that the Christians of the region, responding to the Islamic conquest of the Byzantine world (c. 634), had mixed feelings towards the invaders. On one hand, they found in them their saviours from the tyrannical and oppressive rule of the Roman-Byzantine Empire.[62] One of those who viewed the Saracen conquest as a divine, just salvation from the atrocities of the Byzantines is the Egyptian bishop, John of Nikiu, as he indicates in his late-7th-century *Chronicle.*[63] Another, less positive, example can be found in Jacob of Edessa (ca. 708 AD), who in his *Scolion on I Kings XIV:21*, says, in reaction to the campaign in Syria: "Christ has delivered us up because of [our] many sins and iniquities and subjected us to the hard yoke of the Arabians."[64] Walter Kaegi points out that the reading of the collapse of Byzantium as both salvation from Byzantine tyranny and punishment for the Christians' sins is evident in texts written in the Western, as well as the Eastern, Christian world. Kaegi cites as Western example the French historian Fredegarious, writing in Gaul at the end of the 650 s, who describes those who defeated the Byzantine army in Yarmuk as "the sword of God."[65] A similar view can also be found expressed in apocalyptic texts written by Jewish rabbis in the 8th century.[66]

On the other hand, other chronicles, such as the *Zuqnīn Chronicle* (775), reflect a different appraisal; it states that nothing positive whatsoever resulted from the Arab conquest. Rather, it brought disaster on the Christians because

62 As Michael the Great (d. 1199) states in his chronicle, quoted in an essay by Jan J. van Ginkel, "The Reception and Presentation of the Arab Conquest in Syriac Historiography: How Did the Changing Social Position of the Syrian Orthodox Community Influence the Account of their Historiographers," in *The Encounter of Eastern Christianity with Early Islam*, ed. Emmanouela Grypeou; Mark Swanson & David Thomas (Leiden: Brill, 2006), 171–184, p. 171. On Michael the Great's speech on Islam, see also Jobst Reller, "Christian Views of Muslims in Syria before 1300 AD: Some Remarks on Christian-Muslim-Relations," *Ostkirchliche Studien*, 59(1) (2010), 55–69.

63 John of Nikiu, *Chronicle*, trans. R.H. Charles (London: Oxford University Press, 1916), 120.33; 121.2, 11; 123.5 (pp. 195, 200–202 in the translation).

64 As quoted in F.E. Phillips, *Scholia on Passages of the Old Testament by Mar Jacob, Bishop of Edessa* (London: Williams and Norgate, 1864).

65 Kaegi, *Byzantinum and the Early Islamic Conquest*, p. 213 (and see ibid., pp. 213–218).

66 See, for example, the apocalyptic text called *The Secrets of Rabbi Simon ben Yoḥai,* in which an angel called 'Metatron' explains to the rabbi the invasion of the Ishmaelites/Arabs in the following words: "Do not fear, son of man, for the Almighty only brings the kingdom of Ishmael in order to deliver you from this wicked one (Edom)." See Robert G. Hoyland, *Seeing Islam As Others Saw It: A Survey and Evaluation of Christian, Jewish and Zoroastrian Writings on Early Islam* (Princeton, NJ: Darwin Press, 2007), pp. 308–312.

it "was on the Christian empire," and the empire lost and soon after collapsed.[67] A similar totally negative appraisal of the Arabs' disastrous conquest also exists in the text known as *The Apocalypse of Pseudo-Methodius*, written probably by a miaphysite from northern Mesopotamia and circulated around the end of the 7th century. There, the Arabs are seen as sheer destroyers and bringers of doom and desolate devastation, who are defiled and love defilement.[68]

Other chroniclers evince yet another view. They look at the Arab conquest as a punishment from God for the religious sinfulness of the Chalcedonian Byzantines, and their distorted Christological views in particular. In his study of nascent Islam in the 7th century and the Syriac Christians' stance towards it, Abdul-Massih Saadi points to the Nestorian John of Phenek (d. 690 s), who argues that the invasion by the Arab newcomers – usually called *Mhaggrayê* in Syriac texts, which means 'immigrants' (*muhājirūn*, in Arabic) – is a sign of God's punishment of Christian heresies and the sinful empires of Byzantium and Persia.[69] On the other hand, Jan van Ginkel cites as an example of the same stance the Syriac text known as *The History of Patriarch Dionysius of Tel Maḥrē* (d. 845), or in fact what remains of it, preserved in the 12th-century chronicle of the patriarch Michael the Great. There, Patriarch Michael cites Patriarch Dionysius' argument that the Christological corruption of the Chalcedonians brought God's

---

67 van Ginkel, "Reception and Presentation of the Arab Conquest," p. 176. In his Christmas sermon, which he delivered in Jerusalem, in December 634, the patriarch of Jerusalem, Sophronius (634–638) reflects the Christians' frustration at their inability to go on pilgrimage to Bethlehem, the birthplace of Christ, and the negative feelings the Christians had because the roads to Jerusalem and Bethlehem had fallen into the hands of raiders from the Arabian Peninsula. See on this and on Sophronius' encounter with the Muslim Caliph 'Umar Ibn al-Khaṭṭāb, Daniel Sahas, "The Face to Face Encounter between Patriarch Sophronius of Jerusalem and the Caliph 'Umar Ibn Al-Khattāb: Friends of Foes?" in *The Encounter of Eastern Christianity with Early Islam*, 33–44, p. 34. Commenting on Sophronius' devastation at the fall of Jerusalem, Sahas says "delivering up the Holy City must have been a painful task and a traumatic experience for him. It may not, therefore, be a coincidence that his death occurred only a few months, if not weeks, later" (ibid., p. 39).

68 Sebastian Brock (trans.), *The Apocalypse of Pseudo-Methodius*, in *The Seventh Century in the West-Syrian Chronicles*, ed. Andrew Palmer, Sebastian Brock and Robert Hoyland (Liverpool: Liverpool University Press, 1993), 233–234.

69 Abdul-Massih Saadi, "Nascent Islam in the Seventh Century Syriac Sources," in *The Qur'ān in Its Historical Context*; ed. Gabriel Said Reynolds (London: Routledge, 2008), 217–222, pp. 218–219. Saadi quotes the words of John of Phenek from Alphonse Mingana, *Sources Syriaques* (Leipzig: Harrassowitz, 1908), 146–147. Another author who reflects the same view, according to Saadi, is George of Rish 'Ayna in his Syriac *Life of Maximus*, where he also argues that the invasion of the Arab immigrants is a sign of God's wrath (Saadi, "Nascent Islam," p. 219).

judgment and just punishment upon their heads at the hands of the Islamic conquerors. Dionysius' words are very evocative and worth quoting at length:

> However, the God of vengeance ... when he saw that the measure of the Romans' sin was overflowing and that they were committing every story of cruelty against our people and our churches, bringing our confession to the verge of extinction, He stirred up the sons of Ishmael and enticed them hither from the land of the South. This had been the most despised and disregarded of the peoples of the earth, if indeed they were known at all. By their hands we acquired salvation. In this manner it was no light benefit for us to be delivered from the tyrannical rule of the Romans ...[70]

In the following sections, I shall analyse the language of some Christian authors' readings of the Peninsulan Arab attacks on Byzantium, including Dionysius, and draw from the analysis some of the elements of local Christians' reactions and attitudes toward the newcomers and their religious beliefs. In examining the texts of such readings, I shall address questions like: Were the Christians interested from the beginning in embarking on a dialogue with the Muslim Arabs who became their rulers from the first third of the 7th century, or were they, in fact, uninterested in initiating such a dialogue? How did the Christians regard the newcomers and how did their view of them shape their attitude towards the new Islamic rule, religiously, politically, and socially? When carefully considering the language in Dionysius' text, I shall read it in the light of other texts that also reflect an early interaction between the Christians and their new rulers. I shall look in parallel at the text of the conversation between Patriarch Timothy I (727/8 – 823) and the Caliph al-Mahdī, because it contains a certain dialogue strategy that may help us to acquire a deeper perception of the core of the Christians' attitude towards Islam and their view of themselves in relation to it during the early Islamic period. I shall also look at the 12th-century chronicle of Michael the Great, in which Michael quotes Dionysius. Michael does this only after making some important amendments to the latter's original text. These amendments not only change the wording of Dionysius, but also reflect the particular attitudes of each patriarch's community towards Islam.

70 van Ginkel, "Reception and Presentation of the Arab Conquest," p. 177. See also an analysis of Syriac-speaking Christians' attitude to the Muslim conquests in John Moorhead, "The Monophysite Response to the Arab Invasions," *Byzantion*, 51 (1981), 579 – 591.

II. Between Social and Cultural Appraisal and Simply Seeking to Survive

We may note two points in Dionysius’ appraisal of the Arab conquest that is quoted above. The first is related to the image of the new invaders in Dionysius’ text. It is interesting that he does not call them directly ‘Muslims’ or ‘Muhammadans’ and says nothing about their religious ideas or affiliation, as if these were irrelevant to the crucial change in the fate of the region. Dionysius does not seem to be really interested in these people’s religious identity, because, as we can conclude from his words, the invaders are considered “the most despised and disregarded of the peoples of the earth.” Van Ginkel is also aware of Dionysius’ negative perception of the Arabs when he says that he views the invasion as “too good to be true.”[71]

Dionysius’ words are not unusual or exceptional, in fact. Their accent is, rather, reminiscent of even more bluntly negative tone regarding the Arab invaders that is found in other writings from the early Islamic era. For example, in a text he wrote in the late 7th century, John Bar Penkāyē describes the Arabs as ‘barbarians’[72] and uncivilized savage people, whose comfort “lies in blood that is shed without reason,” and whose food is “hatred and wrath.”[73] In his turn, Maximus the Confessor also describes the Arab invaders as a “barbarous nation of the desert overrunning another land as if it were their own,” and as “wild and untamed beasts who have merely the shape of a human form.”[74] Another Christian author from the Syria-Palestine region, Cyril of Scythopolis, similarly calls

---

71 van Ginkel, “The Reception and Presentation of the Arab Conquest,” p. 182. Van Ginkel adds that such aggressive language can also be traced in Michael the Great’s text, where he does not refrain from calling the Arabs ‘Bano Hagar’ (the children of Hagar), which connoted the Arabs’ origin from a harlot.

72 According to Nevo, the Yemenis are not included among the ‘barbarian’ inhabitants of the Arabian Peninsula, but are traditionally considered “the best warriors: easily regimented into military troops and very easily disciplined, in obvious contrast to the other Arabs, who were considered unruly barbarians”: Nevo and Koren, *Crossroads to Islam*, pp. 100–101. However, Nevo proposes that al-Yaman is not actually in the south-west of the Peninsula, but in the north, that is, in the area known to the Byzantines as Phoinikon, and that its inhabitants were independent pagan nomads (p. 101).

73 On John Bar Penkāyē, see Sebastian P. Brock, “North Mesopotamia in the Late Seventh Century. Book XV of John Bar Penkāyē’s *Rīš Mellē*,” *Jerusalem Studies in Arabic and Islam*, 9 (1987), 51–75, pp. 58, 66. See also Kaegi, *Byzantinum and the Early Islamic Conquest*, pp. 216–217.

74 As translated in John Lamoreaux, “Early Eastern Christian Responses to Islam,” pp. 14–15; and also in John V. Tolan, *Saracens: Islam in the Medieval European Imagination* (New York: Columbia University Press, 2002), p. 43.

the oí Σαρακηνοί (Saracens) "the wolves of Arabia."[75] Also, the Byzantine historiographer Theophylact Simocatta (ca. 630) also shows his scorn and disdain for the Peninsulan Arabs because of their lifestyle and behaviours when he says "the Saracen tribe is known to be most unreliable and fickle, their mind is not steadfast ... ."[76] Last but not least, Sophronius, the Patriarch of Jerusalem, describes the invaders as "barbarians," "cruel and beastly ... irreverent and ungodly daring spirits." [77] And, in a synodal letter probably written as late as the summer of 634, Sophronius ends his theological discussion with a prayer to Christ to save the Church from the Saracens, whom he describes as "barbarians," "impious" and "vile creatures" who are madly insolent.[78] In his Christmas sermon of the same year, Sophronius also uses negative words, describing the Arabs as "filled with every diabolical savagery."[79] Far from spending any time reflecting on the Saracens' religious beliefs and convictions, Sophronius associates the Arab invasion of Jerusalem and Palestine with the unspiritual and sinful state of his church's members. He admonishes his audience and calls them to sincere repentance, in the conviction that this would make God crush the southern invaders to the ground

> therefore, I call on and I command and I beg you for the love of Christ the Lord, in so far as it is in our power, let us correct ourselves, let us shine forth with repentance, let us be purified by conversion and let us curb our performance of acts which are hateful to God. If we constrain ourselves, as friendly and beloved of God, we should laugh at the fall of our Sar-

75 Cyril of Scythopolis, *The Lives of the Monks of Palestine*, trans. R. M. Price, annotated by John Binns (Kalamazoo, MI: Cistercian Publications, 1991), p. 20.

76 Hoyland, *Seeing Islam as Others Saw It*, p. 24; citing Michael and Mary Whitby (trans.), *The History of Theophylact Simocatta: An English Translation with Introduction and Notes* (Oxford: Clarendon Press, 1986), 3.XVII.7 (p. 100).

77 Sahas, "Face to Face Encounter" p. 42. Sahas, nevertheless, concedes that Sophronius' view of ʿUmar is different and more positive, and that his respect for the latter's need to pray in the church was genuine and sincere.

78 Hoyland, *Seeing Islam as Others Saw It*, p. 69; citing Sophronius, *Epistola Synodica*, in *Patrologiae Graecae Cursus Completus*, ed. J. P. Migne, Vol. 87 (Paris, 1857–1866), 3148–3200, 3197D–3200 A. For further texts from Sophronius' writings with descriptions of Muslims, see Daniel J. Sahas, "Why Did Heraclius Not Defend Jerusalem, and Fight the Arabs?" *Parole de l'Orient*, 24 (1999), 79–97. For a short but valuable presentation of Sophronius' life and ministry, see James Howard-Johnston, *Witnesses to a World Crisis*, pp. 171–174.

79 Hoyland, *Seeing Islam as Others Saw It*, p. 70, citing Sophronius, *Christmas Sermon*, H. Usener (ed.), *Weihnachtspredigt des Sophronios*, in *Rheinisches Museum Fuer Philologie*, 41 (1886), 500–516, p. 506.

> acen adversaries and we would view their not distant death, and we would see their final destruction.[80]

Such scorn like the above displayed one indicates that the local Christians of Greater Syria did not give any serious attention to the religious convictions of these new occupiers. One might even go as far as saying that Dionysius' and other Christian authors' words indicate that this lack of interest stemmed not only from the Arabs' perceived intellectual inferiority, but also from assumptions on their social status.[81] Supportive of this proposal is the fact that such attitudes and feelings were not restricted to the Syrians' and the Greeks' appraisal of the Arabs – leave alone how the members of these two groups viewed each other[82] – but were also found among Jews, too.[83]

From what Dionysius' *Chronicle* says about these Arabs, one conjectures that the Christians (at least the non-Chalcedonians) considered these invaders as merely a tool in the hand of God – functional and powerful, but humanly lowly and mean. Though it may not be his independent personal opinion, Dionysius' description of the Arabs as the most despised and inconsequential people does not indicate that the Christians of Byzantium's northern territories had a high opinion of the southerners of the empire. While Dionysius, like other Syrian

---

80 Quoted in Tolan, *Saracens*, p. 42, citing the translation of Sophronius' *Christmas Sermon* in Walter Kägi, "Initial Byzantine Reactions to the Arab Conquest," *Church History*, 38 (1969), 139–149, p. 141.

81 David Cook refers to a conversation between the Prophet Muhammad and a man called ʿAbdullāh b. Ḥawwāla, in which the Prophet states that the people of Syria consider the Arabs "more contemptible than the lice which inhibit the buttocks of camels": David Cook, "Syria and the Arabs," in *A Companion to Late Antiquity*, ed. Philip Rousseau and Jutta Raithel (Chichester: Blackwell, 2009), 467–478, p. 469. See also Sulaymān b. Aḥmad aṭ-Ṭabarānī, *Musnad ash-Shamiyyīn*, ed. Ḥamdī ʿAbd al-Majīd as-Salāfī (Beirut: Muʾassasat ar-Risāla, 1996), Vol. 3, p. 396.

82 There seem to have been similar discriminatory ideas of social status between the Syrians and the Greeks. Robert Hoyland points, for example, to the astronomer and logician Severus Sebokht's (d. 667) pride in his Syrian origin vis-à-vis the Greeks. Hoyland says: "having noted the dependence of Ptolemy on Babylonian science, [Severus] adds 'that the Babylonians were Syrians I think no one will deny, so those who say [i.e. the Greeks] that it is in no way possible for Syrians to know about these matters (astronomy) are much mistaken": Hoyland, *Seeing Islam as Others Saw It*, p. 21.

83 Ibid., p. 22. Hoyland cites the comment of a Jewish taverner called Samuel about the Arabic surname (*kunya*) he was forced to adopt: "no Arab *kunya* can honour me, nor fill me with pride and lend me high rank. Though light and made up of few letters, unlike others, yet it was created as a burden [for me]", quoting from Philip Kennedy, "Abū Nuwās, Samuel and Levi," *Studies in Muslim-Jewish Relations*, 2 (1995), 109–125, pp. 112–113.

historians (each from his own hermeneutic perspective) regarded the Arabs' *conquest* of Byzantium positively, this does not make the polemic and scornful language about the Arab *people* in Dionysius' text less negative. The positive attitude towards the Arab conquest stems from either political enmity towards Byzantium or a theological antagonism against Chalcedonian orthodoxy. Either way, the Arabs as people were not regarded very positively.[84] Moreover, this lack of appreciation of the Arabs did not only colour the Christians' attitude towards the matter of co-existence and social communion with the newcomers, but also underpinned their lack of interest in interacting with these Arabs or discussing with them issues related to religious ideas. It is likely, as Muriel Debié notes, that, while Christians had been accustomed for centuries to discussing theological issues with Jews, during the early Islamic period they were not yet giving any attention to launching similar discussions in response to Muslims' questions, or even to inaugurating a serious religious dialogue with the invaders.[85]

In her study of the Syriac text called *Revelations and Testimonies about Our Lord's Dispensation* (the date and place of composition of which are unknown), Muriel Debié reads in this manuscript an early Christian attempt at constructing arguments against Islam. The example Debié cites is the author's explanation of why Jesus rode a donkey rather than a horse for his entry into Jerusalem. "When the author [of the text]," Debié states, "needs to explain why Christ was riding a donkey when he entered Jerusalem, he says that it is not because he did not have a horse to ride but because 'he wanted to show that he is the Lord of all creatures, quiet and humble' (Test. 37)." Debié concludes that this argument "could be a response to mockery from the Arabs who were fond of horses, especially in the battle field."[86] Debié also points out the claim made by the author of the text that the Syrian Christians are more excellent in their religion than any

---

84 See van Ginkel, "Reception and Presentation of the Arab Conquest," p. 183. Christine Shepardson points out that a similar ethnic prejudice characterized Greek-Western Christians' view of the Syrian-Eastern Christians. The people of Syria, Shepardson maintains, "were commonly described as too inferior, effeminately eastern, hedonistic, and morally suspect to be properly 'Roman'...": Christine Shepardson, "Syria, Syriac, Syrian: Negotiating East and West," in *A Companion to Late Antiquity*, ed. Philip Rousseau and Jutta Raithel (Chichester: Blackwell, 2009), 455–466, p. 456.

85 Muriel Debié, "Muslim-Christian Controversy in An Unedited Syriac Text: *Revelations and Testimonies about our Lord's Dispensations*," in *The Encounter of Eastern Christianity with Early Islam*, ed. E. Grypeou, M. Swanson and D. Thomas (Leiden: Brill, 2006), 225–236, p. 231. Debié describes this time as "a period of transition, when Christian apologists found the weapons of anti-Jewish controversy at hand and used them to create, little by little, a new defence directed to the Muslims."

86 Ibid., pp. 231–232.

other because they pray facing east. Debié concludes from these examples that "we may have here the very beginnings of controversy with Islam about the direction for prayer, something that would become an important topic in 9th-century texts."[87]

Contrary to Debié's suggestion, I do not think we have in the *Testimonies* an early example of Christian-Muslim dialogue on theological issues. Rather, we have in this text clear evidence of the Christians' disengagement and lack of interest in launching any serious dialogue about faith with people they seem to have been deemed inferior and unworthy of attention. It may be that the *Testimonies* offer an explanation for certain Christian practices or practical behaviour with Muslims' questions or mockery in mind. However, these examples do not in themselves sufficiently prove that Christians started this early to take the initiative in, or were preparing themselves for, theological dialogue with Islam by constructing counter arguments and apologies. The issue of Christ riding a donkey does not even reflect religious mockery, leave alone represent any kind of a theological argument, even from the Muslim point of view. The invaders from the Arabian Peninsula used to ride mainly camels, because horses could only with difficulty survive in the harsh environment of the deep desert, and the Arab nomads would measure levels of social status and nobility by means the size of the herd of camels an individual possessed.[88] Reverence for the camel, which the Prophet Muhammad used to ride, was also a sign of respect for the Prophet himself.[89] So, if the question of 'why a donkey rather than a horse' has any apologetic connotation, it must be of a cultural and societal nature, and not theological at all. On the other hand, the matter of facing east to pray also seems to have sociological and ethnic connotations, rather than theological, in that it is used in the context of speaking about the excellence and distinction of the Syrian Christians in comparison with the newcomers: the Syrian Christians were believed to be ethnically and culturally superior to other ethnic tribes in the

---

87 Ibid., p. 232.

88 On the economic and social significance of the camel, see D. T. Potts, "Camel Hybridization and the Role of *Camelus Bactrianus* in the Ancient Near East," *Journal of the Economic and Social History of the Orient*, 47(2) (2004), 143–165. See also on the importance of camels in the history of the Arabian Peninsula, Richard W. Bulliet, *The Camel and the Wheel* (Cambridge, MA: Harvard University Press, 1977).

89 In Arab films about the Prophet, only his camel appears, not the Prophet himself. In a Jewish apocalyptic text from the 8th century AD, known as *The Secrets of Rabbi Simon ben Yoḥai*, the Arabs of the Peninsula are described as the Ishmaelites who ride on 'chariots of camels', in contrast to the promised Messiah, who rides on a chariot drawn by asses when he brings salvation to Israel. See the translation of this text in Hoyland, *Seeing Islam as Others Saw It*, pp. 309–310, and Nevo and Koren, *Crossroads to Islam*, p. 210.

region.[90] This is in line with Dionysius' rather ethnically discriminatory tone when, in his *Chronicle*, he describes the Arabs as the most despised and disregarded among people.

Last but not least, even if, for the sake of argument, we concede that we have here an attempt at developing a theological argument with Muslims, the fact that the answer to the question, 'why a donkey and not a horse?' is given in response to mockery only proves that Christians found themselves constructing an apologetic rather than a descriptive and explanatory discourse on Christian faith. It evinces, that is, that the Christians' arguments were in *response* to a Muslim initiative; one does not usually start with an apology when one is taking the initiative. Apologetic arguments are always responsive and reactive in nature and origin. The polemic language of the Christians about the Arabs' social status and intellectual attainment invite us to realize that their interest in dialoguing with the new conquerors on issues of faith and religious beliefs in the centuries that followed was from the very beginning dressed in various styles of communication. The Christians, for the sake of survival and in response to pressure, sometimes adopted an apologetic stance that was defensive in purpose and nature. They were forced into this for self-protection when those whom they had considered to be insignificant and marginal gained the upper hand and took power. The invaders not only entered Christian religious circles and started to discuss religion openly and directly, but also managed by means of the edge of the sword and the power of the mind, politics or persuasion, to draw Christians out of their churches[91] and bring them to their own faith.[92] Now that they

---

90 Samir Khalil Samir notes in an Arabic essay the fascination and amazement with which the Arab newcomers reacted to the cultural and civilizational developments they witnessed in the Byzantine territories and that they asked the local inhabitants, i.e. the East Syrians, the Byzantine Syrians and the Copts, to transmit it to them: S. Khalil Samir, *Lāhūt ash-Sharq al-Adnā al-Ḥadīth fī aṣ-Ṣilah bayn al-Hawiyyah wal-Ghaiyriyyah* (The theology of the modern Near East in relation to the link between identity and otherness," *Al-Mashriq*, 75(1) (2001), 25–55, p. 37. See also on this intellectual prerogative S. Khalil Samir, "Religion et culture en Proche-Orient: arabe-islam et christianisme comme facteurs d'intégration et d'éclament," *Proche-Orient Chrétien*, 39 (1989), 251–309.

91 In the Umayyad and Abbasid eras, Christian churches were sometimes taken over. However, in contrast there is the story, famous in the history of Christian-Muslim relations, of the Caliph ʿUmar's refusal to pray inside the Church of the Resurrection (in Jerusalem) in order to prevent the Muslims from using the fact that he had prayed in it as an excuse to take possession of it after his death. For an English translation of this narrative, see Sahas, "The Face to Face Encounter," pp. 38–39.

92 The conversion of Christians, Jews and others to Islam was a phenomenon characteristic of the Islamic era, and it was usually the final, and easiest option, for non-Muslims who wanted to ease the restrictions imposed on them by their Muslim rulers and to improve their living condi-

had the upper hand, the Muslim rulers were able easily to intimidate and threaten the Christians and force them to resort to adopt a reconciliatory and diplomatic tone, even when the rulers seemed simply to be enquiring out of curiosity about the Christians' faith and their view of Islam.

A good example of such an intimidation is the famous 8th-century encounter between Patriarch Timothy I and the Caliph al-Mahdī sometime in 781 CE. Patriarch Timothy records the conversation that took place at this meeting in a letter written in Syriac to a friend of his, who was a monk. This text is usually known today as Timothy's apology for Christianity to the Caliph al-Mahdī.[93] Among the subjects the caliph asked the patriarch about at that meeting was Christianity's view of Islam and what Christians thought of the Prophet Muhammad. Perceiving instantly the sensitivity and delicacy of the situation he was put in, Patriarch Timothy emphasized that Christians acknowledged the prophetic identity of Muhammad and stressed that the Prophet was worthy of all praise. Why? Because the Prophet, like other real prophets, walked in the way of the lovers of God, taught the unity of God, called people to good deeds, brought them

tions in the caliphate. Conversion in such cases brought material and social advantages in addition to its redeeming-from-coercion prerogative. See on islamization Milka Rubin, "Arabization versus Islamization in the Palestinian Melkite Community during the Early Muslim Period," *Sharing the Sacred: Religious Contacts and Conflicts in the Holy Land, First-Fifteenth Centuries CE*, ed. Arieh Kofsky and Guy G. Stroumsa (Jerusalem. Yad Izhak Ben Zvi, 1998), 149–162; G.C. Anawati, "Factors and Effects of Arabization and Islamazation in Medieval Egypt and Syria," in *Islam and Cultural Change in the Middle Ages*, ed. Speros Vryonis (Wiesbaden: Harrassowitz, 1975), 17–41; Richard W. Bulliet, "Conversion Stories in Early Islam," in *Conversion and Continuity: Indigenous Christian Communities in Islamic Lands, Eighth to Eighteenth Centuries*, ed. Michael Gervers and Ramzī J. Bikh'āzī, (Toronto: Pontifical Institute of Medieval Studies, 1990), 123–134, and in the same volume Donald P. Little, "Conversion to Islam in Syria and Palestine and the Survival of Christian Communities," 263–288.

93 The English translation of the debate's Syriac text can be found in Alphonse Mingana, *Woodbroke Studies: Christian Documents in Syriac, Arabic and Garshūni; Edited and Translated with a Critical Apparatus*, Vol. 2 (Cambridge: Heffer, 1928), 1–162; and also in A. Mingana, "Woodbrooke Studies: Patriarch Timothy I and the Caliph Mahdi," in *The Early Christian-Muslim Dialogue: A Collection of documents from the First Three Islamic Centuries (632–900 A.D.), Translations wit Commentary*, N.A. Newman (ed.), (Hatfield, Penn: Interdisciplinary Biblical Research Institute, 1993), 169–267. The most recent and reliable critical edition of Timothy I and al-Mahdī's debate, nevertheless, exist today in German translation done by Martin Heimgartner. See: Martin Heimgartner, *Timotheos I., Ostsyrischer Patriarch: Disputation Mit dem Kalifen al-Mahdī*, in *Corpus Scripturum Christianorum Orientalium*, (Leuven: Peeters, 2011). The Anglophone scholarly world needs definitely a new critical edition of that debate that will exceed the mistakes and weaknesses of Mingana's version.

out of polytheism and idolatry and finally taught about God, his Word and Spirit.[94]

Scholars view usually Timothy's conversation with the caliph as an ideal example of the courageousness of Christians in their theological encounters with early Islam, as well as a model of how Christians took the initiative in conveying Christian doctrines to Muslims. In Timothy's response to al-Mahdī, David Thomas, for instance, finds the prudent involvement of a theologian in a doctrinal re-interpretation, or even 'Christianization', of the teaching of Islam, conducted in diplomatic, dialogical language. Thomas does not want to deny that Timothy's diplomacy may in fact simply be hiding a negative and scornful attitude towards Islam, which Timothy shared with his Christian contemporaries. However, Thomas still wants to impute to Timothy's conversation with al-Mahdī, and to what he says about the Prophet Muhammad, a clear and deliberate theological intention and orientation when he says that Timothy's smartly-chosen words about the Prophet's teaching about 'God, his Word and Spirit' shows his endorsement of the doctrines of the Trinity and the divinity of Christ. Beside David Thomas, scholars' appraisals of Timothy's speech on these issue before the caliph fluctuate between seeing this as "a Christianization of the teachings

94 See the words of Patriarch Timothy in David Thomas, "Changing Attitudes of Arab Christians towards Islam," *Transformation*, 22(1) (2005), 10 – 19. Thomas quotes Timothy's words from A. Mingana, "The Apology of Timothy the Patriarch before the Caliph Mahdi," *Bulletin of the John Rylands* Library, 12 (1928), 137 – 292, p. 197. Patriarch Timothy says of the meeting: "And our gracious and wise King said to me: 'What do you say about Muḥammad?' – And I replied to his Majesty: 'Muḥammad is worthy of all praise by all reasonable people, O my Sovereign. He walked in the path of the prophets and trod in the track of the lovers of God. All the prophets taught the doctrine of one God, and since Muḥammad taught the doctrine of the unity of God, he walked, therefore, in the path of the prophets. Further, all the prophets drove men away from bad works and brought them nearer to good works, and since Muḥammad drove his people away from bad works and brought them nearer to good ones, he walked, therefore, in the path of the prophets. Again, all the prophets separated men from idolatry and polytheism, and attached them to God and to His cult, and since Muḥammad separated his people from idolatry and polytheism, and attached them to the cult and knowledge of one God, beside whom there is no other God, it is obvious that he walked in the path of the prophets. Finally Muḥammad taught about God, His Word and His Spirit, and since all the prophets had prophesied about God, His Word and His Spirit, Muḥammad walked, therefore, in the path of all the prophets." A longer English record of this conversation can be found in Samir K. Samir, "The Prophet Muḥammad as Seen by Timothy I and Other Arab Christian Authors," in *Syrian Christians under Islam: The First Thousand Years*, ed. David Thomas (Leiden: Brill, 2001), 75 – 106, pp. 93 – 96, and Mingana's complete text in Newman's *The Early Christian-Muslim Dialogue*, 169 – 267.

of Islam and a consequential implicit diminution of the faith,"[95] or as a Christian attempt to prove to Muslims that the doctrine of the Trinity is implicit in the monotheistic message of the Prophet and the Qur'an.[96]

I concede the prudence and wittiness of Patriarch Timothy's response to the caliph. However, I do not see a clear doctrinal and Christian form of evangelism from within anywhere in the text of the conversation as the patriarch himself recorded it. In his translation of the conversation, Alphonse Mingana says at one point that the conversation between Timothy and the caliph elapses between two days.[97] On a careful reading of Timothy's argument on these two days, one realizes that, while on the first day Timothy bluntly casts doubt on the authenticity of Muḥammad's identity as a prophet, on the second day he states just the opposite with almost the same bluntness and clarity. He even points to a similarity between Muḥmmad and Moses and Abraham, after arguing at length on the first day that Moses and the Arab prophet were not at all the same and that Muḥammad's prophethood could not be proved by means of such a comparison.

In their readings of Timothy's apology, David Thomas, Sidney Griffith and Samir Khalil Samir do not take note of Timothy's recording that he and the caliph had two meetings on two different days. They tend, instead, to read Timothy's rather different, and even sometimes contradictory, discourses in these two meetings as one, continues conversation. I think one should not underestimate the possibility that we have here a narration of two different conversations conducted on two separate days, and that on the second day Timothy felt that he needed to refine and soften his caustic references to the prophethood of Muḥammad before the caliph. One could then say that Timothy the politician prevailed over Timothy the theologian and made him adopt a more diplomatic and conciliatory tone that was probably aimed at lessening the threat of any violent reaction to his polemic in the first discussion with the caliph.

---

95 Thomas, "Changing Attitudes of Arab Christians towards Islam," p. 13. Sidney Griffith seems to back this reading when he says, commenting on the same meeting with the Caliph al-Mahdī, "Patriarch Timothy was also one of the first Christian apologists to bring the defence of Christian beliefs and practices right into the Caliph's court": Sidney Griffith, *The Church in the Shadow of the Mosque: Christians and Muslims in the World of Islam* (Princeton, NJ: Princeton University Press, 2008), p. 47.

96 Barbara Roggema, "Muslims and Crypto-Idolaters: A Theme in the Christian Portrayal of Islam in the Near East," in *Christians at the Heart of Islamic Rule, Church Life and Scholarship in 'Abbasid Iraq*, ed. D. Thomas (Leiden: Brill, 2003), 1–18, p. 16.

97 A. Mingana, "Woodbrooke Studies: Patriarch Timothy I and the Caliph Mahdī," in *The Early Christian-Muslim Dialogue*, p. 170. See also Heimgartner, *Timotheos I., Ostsyrischer Patriarch: Disputation Mit dem Kalifen al-Mahdī*, p. xxxiv.

It is not my goal here to undertake a redaction or literary criticism of the text of Timothy to see whether it contains later redactionist and editorial fingerprints, or multi-layered temporal revisions. Timothy I's debate is not the main focus of my research in this monograph, and I do not claim any expertise on his writs in the first place. I am just referring to some aspects of communication-style in his debate with the Caliph to make a point on the Christians' attitudes toward their new Muslim rulers and environment during the early Muslim era. In what follows, I shall read Timothy's discourse on the second day of his conversation with the caliph in its own terms; that is, without, allowing his argument on the first day to colour my appraisal.

It is my belief that separating for a while Timothy's discourse on the second day from his discourse on the first will help us perceive more clearly what was driving Timothy's responses to the caliph's questions when he was summoned again to the court. I intend to suggest a parallel reading to the recently dominant belief that Timothy's apology coherently demonstrates the thinking of a theologian par excellence at the forefront of explaining Christian faith and addressing challenging doctrines such as the Trinity and Christology to a Muslim leader by showing him that his own scripture and prophet refer to them both explicitly and implicitly. I suggest that the diplomacy we note in the patriarch's words at the second meeting invite us to consider a socio-political context in which the patriarch found himself in the demanding situation of having to explain to the powerful ruler of the Islamic state whether Christians venerated the central character in Islam, and whether, consequently, their religious beliefs constituted a potential source of stability and security or threat and treason.

In his brief presentation of the history of the East Syrian Church under the Arab-Muslim rule, Wilhelm Baum accurately, if indirectly, invites us, when we study any interfaith conversation between church prelates and Muslim caliphs, at least during the 8th and 9th centuries, to keep in mind the historical context to which the interlocutors belonged and its influence on their manner of speech and approach to each other. During the 8th century, and as the centre of Islamic power shifted from Damascus in Syria to the Abbasids' capital, Baghdad in Iraq, the Catholicos of the East Syrian Church became the official representative of the Christians before the Abbasid caliphs. This was not at all an easy time to bear such a responsibility and to represent the Christians positively and sympathetically to the new Muslim rulers, who tended to associate the local Christians with their Byzantine Christian enemies. And we know that, during that last quarter of the 8th century, a severe, mass persecution of *Zanadiqa* (Manichaeans)[98] took

98 Read on the *Zanadiqa*, for example, Mahmood Ibrahim, "Religious Inquisition as a Social

place by order of the Caliph al-Mahdī himself, who started after this to view many groups and movements, the Christian groups probably included (he personally ordered the destruction of so many churches as well[99]), in his territories with considerable suspicion.[100] It is in the light of this historical context that one should consider Timothy's language and manner of speech before the persecuting caliph. Timothy was expected not only to convince the caliph intellectually on matters of faith, but also to give the caliph sufficient reason to spare the lives of the Christians who remained in the Islamic territories by changing his suspicious attitude toward them.[101]

This rather politico-sociological concern appears, for instance, in Timothy's elaboration on the prophetic identity of Muḥammad. Instead of comparing him to Jesus, for example, Timothy deliberately chooses the figures of Abraham and Moses from the Old Testament, not only because he knows the reverence in which the Qur'ān holds Abraham and Moses and their prophetic role, but also because of the similarity of Abraham's and Moses' roles as fighting and war-launching prophets with that of Muḥammad. Instead of comparing their messages and religious ideas with those of Muḥammad, Timothy speaks of them as fighters for God against idolaters and pagans.

> **15.8.** and who would not exalt/praise and commend and honour/dignify the one, who has not only fought for God with words, but also has shown with the sword his zeal for God?
> **15.9.** for he behaved like Moses over against the children of Israel: when he saw that they made a golden calf and honoured it, he raised his sword and killed all the calf's adorers (Ex. 32:27 f). Exactly in the same way, Mohammad also demonstrated his eagerness/zeal for God and [he] loved and honoured God more than his own self, and his group [of followers]/community and his tribe.
> **15.12.** and as Abraham behaved – God's favourite and friend (Js 41:8; Jac 2:23), who turned his face away from idols and [from] his clan and kept an eye on God alone and became for

---

Policy: the Persecution of the Zanadiqa in the Early Abbasid Caliphate," in *Arab Studies Quarterly*, 2(16), 1994, 20 – 53; Faroak Omar, "Some Observation on the Reign of the Abbasid Caliph al-Madhi 185/775 – 196/785," in *Arabica*, 2(21), 1974,139 – 150; and Muḥammad Qāsim Zamān, *Religion & Politics under the Early ʿAbbāsids, the Emergence of the Proto-Sunnī Elite*, (Leiden: Brill, 1997).

99 See Timothy I's speech on this in one of his letters in the critical edition and German translation of Timothy's texts in Martin Heimgartner (ed, trans.), *Die Brief 42 – 58 Des Ostsyrischen Patriarchen Timotheos*, in *Corpus Scriptorum Christianorum Orientalium*, (Leuven: Peeters, 2012), Ep. 50, pp. 32 – 33.

100 Wilhelm Baum and Dietmar W. Winkler, *The Church of the East, A Concise History* (London: Routledge Curzon, 2010), Ch. 2, pp. 42 – 83, p. 59 (pp. 58 – 64).

101 The Christians, Wilhelm Baum explains, "were accused by the caliph of praying day and night for the triumph of the Byzantines," and the Caliph al-Mahdī had many churches destroyed because of this (ibid., p. 60).

> his people the instructor of the one God – so turned Mohammad away his face, as well, from the idols and their adorers – be they people from his clan, [or] be they foreigners – [he] turned [his face] away and only honoured and venerated who adored the only God.[102]

Patriarch Timothy's speech clearly focuses on likening the prophet of the Arabs to two Old Testament prophets whom he knows the Qur'an not only venerates but also portrays as Muḥammad's forebears. On the other hand, Timothy's following words reveal the political import of his discourse. He focuses on the Prophet's defeat of the two empires surrounding the Islamic territories, which were still in existence at the time of al-Mahdī and represented a threat. Timothy puts aside for a while Christ's message of peace, reconciliation, and sacrifice and avoids comparing Muḥammad with Jesus in this respect. He adopts instead witty politicized language that basically gives the war-like tone of the Islamic prophetic message a religious justification and legitimacy. To achieve his ultimate goal, namely gaining the caliph's trust and approval, Timothy even avoids mentioning the Trinity completely and emphasizes his total commitment to monotheism:

> **16.1.** And our king said to me: "Then, you must also adopt the words of the prophet."
> **16.2.** But I said to his majesty: "Which words our king means [that] we must adopt?"
> **16.3.** And our king said to me: "That God is one and there is no other except Him."

---

102 The above is my own English translation of the German translation of the text in the critical edition of M. Heimgartner, *Timotheos I., Ostsyrischer Patriarch: Disputation Mit dem Kalifen al-Mahdī*, p. 70. One can find an English translation of the same lines of the debate's text in S. Kh. Samir, "The Prophet Muḥammad as Seen by Timothy," where Samir translates them into English on pages 94–95 in the following way
19. who will not praise, honour and exalt the one who fought for God,
20. not only in his words, but with the sword showed his zeal for Him?
21. as Moses did with the Children of Israel when he saw that they had fashioned a golden calf which they worshipped,
22. and killed all of those who were worshipping it,
23. so also Muḥammad evinced an ardent zeal towards God and loved Him and honoured Him more than his own soul, his people and his relatives.
...
31. and what Abraham, that friend and beloved of God, did
32. in turning his face from idols and from his kinsmen, and looking only towards the one God, and becoming the preacher of the one God to other peoples, this also Muḥammad did
See also for another English translation of the same lines A. Mingana's translation in "Woodbrooke Studies: Patriarch Timothy I and the Caliph Mahdi," in *The Early Christian-Muslim Dialogue*, pp. 218–219. I personally believe that Heimgartner's German translation of the original Syriac text is more reliable. Thus, I allow myself to develop my own English translation of the German edition. I remain here gratefully indebted to martin Heimgartner for kindly double-checking my translation – here and in the following citation on the next page.

> **16.4.** But I answered: "I learn [and still] this belief in one God, our king, both from the Torah, as well as from the prophets and the Gospel; in [this belief] I believe and on it I die."[103]

I can hardly find in this answer a refusal of the caliph's invitation to Timothy to follow the Prophet's teaching on the oneness of God.[104] Nor can I glean from it any evidence of Timothy's rejection of the prophethood of Muḥammad like that we find in his words on the first day of the meeting with al-Mahdī, which gives the impression that Timothy's personal opinion tended to such a rejection.[105] Nor can I find a clear rejection of Muḥammad's prophetic role in the discussion that follows between Timothy and the caliph on whether or not the biblical text proclaims the coming of the Prophet. Had Timothy wanted to be consistent with his earlier words, he would have denied Muḥammad's prophetic role, as he did on the first day, but it seems that something made Timothy reconsider this option after realizing that it would put at risk the trust and confidence he wanted the caliph eventually to grant him.

The discussion between the two men proceeds to address the question of whether the Gospels refer to another prophet to come after Christ and whether Christians should follow another prophet after Christ's ascension to heaven.[106] Timothy here was honest and wisely adhered to the way he had presented the message of scripture at the first meeting. He could not do otherwise because it would have been difficult to twist his direct and explicit reading of the biblical text to make the scripture say what the Muslims wanted to hear, ultimately compromising his credibility and consistency in the eyes of the caliph. This would have made him lose what his tone and attitude on the second day suggest he was primarily searching for: gaining the caliph's trust and admiration. It is one of the signs of a politician's prudence and intelligence that he knows

---

103 My English translation of the German version of M. Heimgartner, *Timotheos I., Ostsyrischer Patriarch: Disputation Mit dem Kalifen al-Mahdī*, p. 71. The English translation of the same lines in Samir, "The Prophet Muḥammad as Seen by Timothy," p. 96, read as follows

48. and our King said to me: 'You should, therefore, accept the words of the Prophet'

49. and I replied to him: 'About which words does our King speak?'

50. and our King said to me: 'That God is one and that there is no other one besides Him'

51. and I replied: 'This belief in the one God, O Sovereign, I have learned from the Torah, from the prophets and from the Gospel.

52. I stand by it and shall die in it.

See also the English translation of A. Mingana's translation in "Woodbrooke Studies: Patriarch Timothy I and the Caliph Mahdi," in *The Early Christian-Muslim Dialogue*, p. 219.

104 Roggema, "Muslims and Crypto-Idolaters," p. 17.

105 Samir, "The Prophet Muḥammad as Seen by Timothy," p. 105.

106 Ibid., pp. 97–104.

what can and cannot be used to win the audience's heart, lest the misuse of certain claims may have impact adversely on the achievement of the intended goal. Timothy's refusal to follow any prophecy after that of Jesus would be more in line with the caliph's expectations (especially after what he had heard on the first day) than escaping the confrontation and saying that the Bible alluded to Muḥammad or allowed Christians to follow another prophet after Christ. Timothy plays safe by taking the realistic and more convincing option of sticking to what he had said about the scriptural message at the first meeting.

This does not in itself mean that what we have here is a blunt, audacious rejection of the Prophet of Islam. Rather, it is a prudent and perceptive presentation of a religious leader's image that consequently earned the caliph's trust, rather than his disbelief and suspicion. Timothy won the caliph's admiration and, more importantly, his confidence because it seems that he was able to convince him that the Christians were not basically against the prophethood of Muḥammad. Although they could not become his, or any other prophet's, followers because they obey Christ and the teaching of their scriptures instead of the prophet and the book of Islam, the Christians could still be reliable and trustworthy citizens in the caliphate. Achieving this goal becomes commendable when we remember that persecution of Christians during the Islamic era was as real and present a danger as it was under Roman and Byzantine rule.[107]

In his book on the history of Abbasid rule, Hugh Kennedy indicates the discriminatory treatment to which Christians in the Muslim empire were subjected and points to the differences between the treatment of Christians on the individual and the communal levels. Though the caliphs frequently had Christian personnel among their courtiers and staff (who enjoyed a good standing of living and social status among the Abbasid aristocrats), the majority of the Christian population received rather discriminatory treatment by being regarded as *dhimmīs*. For example, in the time of the Caliph al-Mutawwakil, in the 9th century, all *dhimmīs* (both Christians and Jews), "were required to wear yellow on their clothes. Upper-class *dhimmis* had to wear yellow hoods, simple belts and to

107 We have in the history of early Islam stories of Christians who publically challenged Islam and where persecuted and eventually executed. Examples are the monk Michael the Sabaite, Peter of Capitolas and ʿAbd al-Masīḥ al-Najrānī al-Ghassānī and others. On such martyrs, see Sidney H. Griffith, "Christians, Muslims and Neo-Martyrs: Saints' Lives and Holy Land History," in *Sharing the Sacred: Religious Contacts and Conflicts in the Holy Land*, ed. Guy G. Stroumsa and Arieh Kofsky, Jerusalem: Yad Izhak Zvi, 1998, pp. 163–208; also Rubin, "Arabization versus Islamaization," pp. 149–153, and Mark N. Swanson, "The Martyrdom of ʿAbd al-Masīḥ, Superior of Mount Sinai (Qays al-Ghassani)," in *Syrian Christians under Islam: The First Thousand Years*, ed. David Thomas (Leiden: Brill, 2001), 107–130.

ride with wooden stirrups with two pommels on the backs of their saddles." Kennedy also points to al-Mutawwakil's order that all places of worship undergoing renovation are to be confiscated and converted into mosques if they were spacious enough, or demolished if they were not.[108] What Kennedy describes is not restricted to the situation of Christians and Jews in the Islamic empire. Every new prevailing power always tends to subordinate the citizens of its previous enemy in an attempt to ensure their loyalty and compliance with the new order. This policy is followed regardless to these citizens' religious, ideological, or cultural background. However, the treatment of the *dhimmīs* in the Abbasid era, when Patriarch Timothy I lived and served the Church, shows that the position of Christians was not at its best. It is not unlikely, therefore, that there were always serious doubts about their loyalty and respect for the values and doctrines of their new Muslim rulers. That being so, the easiest way to obtain their loyalty was through the conversion of Christians to Islam. This was the option chosen, for instance, by al-Mahdī when, after arriving in Aleppo from Baghdad and meeting there the Arab tribe of Tanūkh, the Abbasid caliph was enraged to discover that there were not Muslims. He demanded, therefore, that almost 5000 men of the tribe should convert to Islam.[109]

Sidney Griffith reminds us that Timothy decided at one point to transfer his patriarchal see from Seleucia/Ctesiphon in the Persian enclaves to the territories of the Islamic Caliphate, specifically Baghdad. Griffith perceptively comments that this noteworthy move to the new centre of power was not made for simply practical reasons related to Timothy's administration of his far-flung dioceses. Griffith refers this decision back to what he describes as the patriarch's willingness to "support the church's missionary enterprises, which in his time, even under Muslim rule, extended eastward far into central Asia along the so-called Silk Road and southward into India."[110] The fostering of missionary work is compatible with Timothy's line of argument on the first day of his conversation with al-Mahdī, which depicts him as a missionary bringing the Good News of Christianity to the supreme leader of the Muslims in an intelligent, courageous, and commendable evangelism strategy. However, it is my belief that the Christi-

---

108 Hugh Kennedy, *When Baghdad Ruled the Muslim World: Tthe Rise and Fall of Islam's Greatest Dynasty* (Cambridge, MA: Da Capo Press, 2005), p. 240. Christians' treatment under the Abbasid's is reminiscent of what they experienced under the Umayyads too; in Egypt, for instance, the Copts, who maintained their Christian faith and remained devoted to Egyptian soil, were, as Kennedy says, "obliged to wear lead seals around their necks and carry written passports if they wished to move from one town to another" (ibid., p. 1).

109 Hoyland, *Seeing Islam as Others Saw It*, p. 1.

110 Griffith, *The Church in the Shadow of the Mosque*, p. 45.

ans' situation in Islamic Abbasid society and the generally scornful view of Christians toward the Arabs made the claim that the Christians reflect a theological prudency in their dialogues with Muslims on Christian faith in the court of the caliph rather unlikely and unconvincing interpretation, especially in the light of the change in Timothy's tone on the second day of his meeting with the caliph. What if Timothy actually moved from Seleucia/Ctesiphon to Baghdad because he found himself, as the patriarch of the Church of the East, responsible for protecting Christians from serious suspicions, nurtured by the Muslim majority in the empire, that they were potential traitors?

In his assessment of the Byzantine rulers' treatment of the Church when they started to experience perpetual raids by the rising Muslim power, Walter Kaegi states

> Constantinople was very suspicious of anyone who made or might make unauthorized contacts with Muslims. The outcome was suspicion of treason against any governor or ecclesiastic who showed hesitation about any aspect whatever of imperial policy, whether civil or religious. Constans II's efforts to censure Pope Martin I for unauthorized contacts with Muslims are consistent with those of his grandfather Heraclius to prevent unapproved negotiations between local leaders and Muslim commanders.[111]

What would lessen the likelihood of such suspicions of treason in the Islamic campaign on the part of Christians who lived in the territories of the Caliphate? Just as the Byzantines were cautious about shift of non-Chalcedonian Christians' loyalty in the struggle with Islam, the Muslim rulers were most probably as suspicious and vigilant about the Christians' commitment to the new regime's best interests and the Muslim nation's peace and stability. And, just as the Byzantine rulers' were intolerant of any disobedience to imperial policy, whether civil or religious, the Muslim caliphs were also probably as strict about the Christians' obedience to their political policies and their acquiescence to their religious beliefs as their Byzantine foes had been. One may even say that proof of such loyalty and allegiance was demanded especially intensively and strictly from the *dhimmīs* of the Caliphate because of their non-Muslim religiosity. Be that as it may, what if Patriarch Timothy moved his patriarchal see from Ctesiphon directly to the Muslim Caliphate's heart (Baghdad) because he thought that he should deal personally with the caliph's suspicions regarding the Christians' loyalty and peaceableness, leaving aside their view of Islam and the Prophet? Seen

---

111 Walter E. Kaegi, "The Early Raids into Anatolia and Byzantine Reactions under Emperor Constans II," in *The Encounter of Eastern Christians with Early Islam*, ed. Emmanouela Grypeou, Mark Swanson and David Thomas (Leiden: Brill, 2006), 73–93, p. 79.

from this angle, Timothy's presence at al-Mahdī's court may have been an acquaintance-building interview between him, as the leader of the Christians, and al-Mahdī as the 'Prince of the Believers.'

Timothy must have realized on the second day that he could not continue in the court to pursue a missionary task that was theological or evangelistic in nature and may thus have decided at the second meeting to stop trying to convey to his Muslim counterpart a critical and challenging Christian view of Muḥammad. Timothy's carefully chosen terminology 'God, his Word and Spirit' shows that he had abandoned introducing the doctrine of the Trinity to the caliph in Christian terms, and preferred using without reservation these very Qur'anic terms. Any orthodox reference to the Trinity would usually use the terms 'Father, Son, and Holy Spirit.' Reference to 'God, his Word and Spirit' is more familiar in Christian Gnostic, Arian, and Nestorian circles, and it probably entered the language of the Qur'an via the interaction of the Arabs of the Peninsula with the Nestorians, Arians, and other Christian Gnostics in the 'Ukāẓ market in the Christian centre of Najrān.[112] Patriarch Timothy's personal allegiance to Nestorian Christology is likely to have meant that he was trying to show al-Mahdī that Nestorians and Muslims were not really divided in their religious language and way of thinking of God after all.[113] So, just as these two parties had found common ground since the time of the Prophet in the birthplace of Islam, the Arabian Peninsula, so they could maintain this affinity under the rule of the Prophet's successors in Baghdad. On the other hand, it is unlikely that the caliph, as someone who had never before heard Christian belief claims, would have invited the patriarch to introduce himself and the faith of the Church (although Timothy's narration of the conversation depicts the caliph as only asking for information, rather than presenting highly sophisticated theological counter-claims). Al-Mahdī must have known in the least the Qur'anic view and what Muslim thinkers taught about what the Christians believed. It is more logical in the light of the wider historical, political, and practical circumstances of the time that al-Mahdī summoned the church's highest prelate to the court to inquire about negative rumours he must have heard about the Christians' arrogance and scorn for

---

112 On the presence of Arians and even Nestorians and their impact on the Arabs of Mecca, see Irfan Shahīd, "Islam and *Oriens Christianus:* Makka 610–622 AD." in *The Encounter of the Eastern Christianity with Early Islam*, ed. Emmanouela Grypeou, Mark Swanson and David Thomas (Leiden: Brill, 2006), 9–32; and idem, *Byzantium and the Arabs in the Sixth Century*, 2 vols (Washington, DC: Dumbarton Oaks/Chichester, UK: John Wiley, 2010).

113 On the Nestorian presence in the Arabian Peninsula, see Christoph Baumer, *The Church of the East: An Illustrated History of Assyrian Christianity* (London: I. B. Tauris, 2006), pp. 137–168, esp. pp. 137–147.

Muslims and Islam. He wanted to examine the extent of the Christians' allegiance and support for the Caliphate's cause, despite the negative views they held about Islam.

Patriarch Timothy, as legally responsible for the good conduct and loyalty of his co-religionists,[114] found himself standing before the caliph trying, as prudently and persuasively as he could, to prove that the Christian *dhimmī*s were not traitors or the enemies of the Prophet and his 'earthly' legacy (though they did not consider it heavenly), whose representative was none other than the caliph himself. Claiming that Christianity venerated the Arabian prophet and recognized that he taught what other prophets had taught before him would not have been an overwhelmingly enchanting theological refrain to the ears of a political ruler like al-Mahdī. In a dynasty whose history was full of conspiracies, assassination plots, and threats of riots and rebellions against the legal right of the descendants of al-ʿAbbās (i.e., not of the descendants of ʿAlī, for example) to rule the Muslim nation, it would rather resonate politically and it tells al-Mahdī that the Christians were obedient and loyal to his rule and leadership. This pragmatic framework would explain why Timothy, in his apology before al-Mahdī, would say that the Arabs "are today held in great honour and esteem by God and men, because they forsook idolatry and polytheism, and worshipped and honoured one God. For this they deserve the love and praise of all."[115]

Knowing that al-Mahdī commissioned Timothy to translate the works of Aristotle from Greek into Arabic, and then listening to him arguing with an Aristotelian philosopher in the royal court itself,[116] may indicate, in the light of the above context, that Timothy succeeded in his defence of the Christians' allegiance to his Caliphate, despite the scornful and arrogant attitude of common Christians towards their Muslim compatriots. History tells us that Patriarch Timothy survived the rule of other five caliphs over a period of four decades, thanks to his remarkable diplomatic abilities in dealing with the fluctuating strategies of the civil authorities.[117] Instead, then, of merely a brave theological speech, we have here a good example of the intelligent and fruitful politically-oriented diplomacy that the Christians needed to gain some secure and peaceful space in the Islamic era.

What we may finally conclude from the language of the Christians on Islam and the Arabs in some early Christian texts is that it is likely that the Christians, who were meant to admit their inferiority to their new Muslim rulers, reacted, on

114 Ibid., p. 148.
115 Hoyland, *Seeing Islam as Others Saw It*, p. 24.
116 Griffith, *The Church in the Shadow of the Mosque*, pp. 46–47.
117 Baumer, *The Church of the East*, pp. 153–155, esp. p. 153.

the contrary, towards the newcomers with lack of interest and a scornful attitude for a considerable period of time, because, as David Thomas says, they simply found it easy to “regard themselves as culturally and intellectually superior to their employers and rulers.”[118]

III. From Social Indifference to Apologetic Reaction

The second observation that catches the attention in Dionysius’ chronicle of the Arab conquest is also related to the Christians’ apologetic-defensive attitude to the Muslim conquerors, but this time, from the perspective of Christian-Christian relations. In this regard, it is helpful to compare Dionysius’ words with the revised record of them in Michael the Great’s citation of the patriarch of Tel Maḥrē. Michael the Great sometimes quotes Dionysius’ words verbatim but at others he makes revisions that introduce a new realm of implications and meaning. One can probably see in this a reductionism similar to that which the Jewish scholar Jacob Neusner perceives in Jewish rabbinic literature, where “one’s authorship goes through the motions of copying the work of a prior author, even while introducing striking innovations.”[119] Let us first note the words of Michael the Great as recorded in Jan van Ginkel’s important essay “The Reception and Presentation of the Arab Conquest in Syriac Historiography”

> Heraclius did not allow the orthodox to present themselves before him, and he refused to hear their complaints about acts of vandalism committed on their churches. This is why the God of vengeance ... seeing the cruelty of the Romans, who, wherever they ruled, cruelly plundered our churches and our monasteries and condemned us mercilessly, brought from the land of the south the children of Ishmael that by their hands we would acquire salvation from the hands of the Romans ...[120]

The synoptic reading of Dionysius’ and Michael’s interpretation of the Islamic conquest reflects editorial activity similar in style and method to what we find when we read synoptically the first three gospels in the New Testament, Matthew, Mark, and Luke: we find texts and stories that are recorded by all three gospels, but each exhibits changes and revisions that demonstrate the point of view and theological purpose of the author of each gospel. A similar synoptic

---

118 D. Thomas, “Changing Attitudes of Arab Christians towards Islam,” p. 11.

119 Jacob Neusner, *From Tradition to Imitation: The Plan and Program of Pesiqta Rabbatic and Pesiqta de Rab Kahana* (Brown Judaic Series 80) (Atlanta, GA:, Scholars Press, 1987), p. 223; and Hoyland, *Seeing Islam as Others Saw It*, pp. 34–40, esp. p. 35.

120 van Ginkel, “The Reception and Presentation of the Arab,” p.171.

revision happens in Michael the Great's borrowing from Dionysius' text. Jan van Ginkel notes this, saying "because Michael used the work of Dionysius extensively, his perspective appears to be comparable to that of Dionysius; yet often he abbreviated Dionysius' account, removing some of the nuances present in it."[121] I would go further and argue that, rather than merely briefly introducing small differences of opinion, Michael employs Dionysius' words in an almost totally new and substantially different hermeneutics. Michael the Great reads the Arab raids in a very different way from Dionysius, and clearly chooses to replace certain key words in Dionysius' text with others more congenial to his own interpretation. Michael's hermeneutics of the Arab conquest is *political*, not theological, in content: God punished by means of the Ishmaelites those Christians who exploited their good relationships with the Byzantine state and their political prerogative in confiscating and looting the places of worship of their Christian compatriots. The Arabs enact God's vengeance for the atrocities committed by the Byzantine rulers and their Christian followers. Though this instrument of God did not fully serve the best interest of orthodox Christians (the non-Chalcedonians, according to this logic), they at least eradicated the enemies of the orthodox and enabled them to regain some power. There is here a depiction of Christian-Christian polemic of a clearly political and ecclesio-materialistic nature.

The case is different in the earlier version of Dionysius' interpretation of the Arab conquest. For Dionysius, the political connotations of the event do not seem to be central and do not take priority in his hermeneutics. There, Dionysius refers to the Arab invasion not as God's vengeance for Byzantium's vandalism and looting, but as a punishment for 'sin,' which he specifies as that action that brings the 'confession' of the Church to the brink of extinction.[122] Dionysius'

---

121 Ibid., p. 181. John Lamoreaux thinks that one reason behind the fact that it was two Syrian Orthodox (and not Nestorians, for example), Michael and Dionysius, who saw in the Islamic invasion a punishment for Byzantium, is that, while the Nestorians flourished in Persia, away from Byzantine authority, the Jacobites' territories were at the heart of the Byzantine enclaves and so they suffered, along with Jews and the Samaritans, from the growing Byzantine intolerance of religious minorities in the century following their defeat by the Arabs: Lamoreaux, "Early Eastern Christian Responses to Islam," p. 4.

122 The same theological reading of historical events as a consequence of human sin and God's justice or mercy also appears in other places of Dionysius' chronicle, where at one time he reads, for example, an epidemic that afflicted horses, donkeys and mules as a sign of God's justice retribution for human sin and evil, and at another time as a sign of God's mercy and of His abundant love and kindness towards humankind, in that He diverted the plague from humans to animals. See on this Witold Witakowski, "The Syriac Chronicle of Pseudo-Dionysius of Tel-Maḥrē:

reading also reflects a Christian-Christian polemic, but one that is of a clear theological – more specifically Christological – nature. The struggle that God found himself forced to resolve between the Christians of the East is, for Dionysius, not primarily political or a matter of ecclesial and societal authority. It is rather deeply theological in its nature and in its consequences: the Chalcedonians are jeopardizing the confessed faith of the Church of Christ with their Christology. This is the greatest sin of the Romans. 'Romans' here has also a theological rather than a political connotation: it stands in contrast to 'Syrian,' which here denotes a theological, not an ethnic, affiliation, since the Chalcedonians included Syriac- and Arabic-speakers, just as the non-Chalcedonians included Greek-speakers. This jeopardizing of the confessional faith of the Church is, according to Dionysius, the great sin. Notably, Dionysius' claim here is that what threatened the confession of the Church was a different Christian theology, and not a different religious discourse, such as Islam. This implies that the Arabs' religious ideas were not at the centre of Christian attention at the beginning of the Islamic era. As far as Dionysius' text is concerned, one can explain this lack of interest by the fact that the 'sons of Ishmael' as a group of people were not even recognized, but rather disregarded.

This lack of concern about the religious thought of the new invaders and the focus, instead, on Christian-Christian controversies was more relevant in the time of Dionysius' (9th century) than in the days of Michael the Great (12th century). In Michael's time, Muslims became the ruling power and Islam the dominant religion throughout the region. Christian communities of all theological traditions, as one might expect, were busy surviving in the new context and maintaining their existence as a numerically decreasing religious community, unique and distinct from its Western sister. By that time, the Christian-Christian controversies and polemics had receded to the second or third level of importance, with Christian-Muslim co-existence taking the first. The theological clash between the Christian groups, which was characteristic of the officially Christian state and society of Byzantium, had now, predictably, given way to another identity-forming orientation that focused first and foremost on maintaining a Christian-based identity in a society that was now structured at all levels in accord with a different religious worldview and agenda.[123] This explains why,

---

A Study in the History of Historiography," PhD diss., (Motala: Uppsala University, 1987), pp. 103–118, esp. pp. 115, 110.

123 David Olster would like to argue that, more than the people's endeavour to form a new communal identity, the Arab invasion also deeply impacted the institutional conditions of the imperial offices in the Byzantine state as early as the seventh century: David Olster, "Ideological Transformation and the Evolution of Imperial Presentation in the Wake of Islam's Victory," in

during the time of Michael the Great, terms such as 'anti-Nestorian' (which is a theological category par excellence) received the least emphasis in the process of group-identity formation,[124] leaving the stage to other more general, inclusive terms life 'Christians' or 'Syrian Christians.'

It seems that this situation did not apply in the time of Dionysius of Tel Maḥrē. During the early centuries of Islam, the clash between Chalcedonian and non-Chalcedonian Christological views was still capable of influencing the fate of Christians on the level of relations between the churches themselves and relations between the churches and the Byzantine rulers, as well as relations with the rules of the newly established Islamic empire. Islam then was only a newcomer to the scene, just about starting to participate in the intellectual and theological game. Dialoguing on religion with the new Arabs from the south was not yet within the range of urgent priorities for the Christians of the area, who were still concerned to discover what kind of state and societal and civil order this new empire would bring. In addition, the Christians' underestimation of these newcomers on the basis of their ethnicity, would even make the initiating of such interreligious dialogue appear to be an idea that was not worthwhile or valuable. One eloquent example of the Christians' lack of interest in developing a serious view of Islam, and thus taking a significant initiative in addressing Christian faith in dialogue with Muslims, is the fact that a major Church Father, John of Damascus, who lived at the centre of the Islamic rule, hardly mentions explicitly in his magnum opus, *The Fount of Knowledge*, any Islamic theological claim or teaches Christian faith with a clearly stated reference to Islam in itself.

In an essay on the encounter between the Christians of the East and early Islam, David Thomas touches upon this. Thomas notes that, despite, on the one hand, the Damascene's upbringing in the Umayyad court and his later employment by the caliph, and on the other, the increasing influence of Islam at the time, "it is difficult to see any but the merest traces of Islamic influence upon the composition of [John's] work."[125] While the book contains many chapters on God's being and on the incarnation, Thomas continues, it hardly contains any apologetic, constructive exposition that aims at responding to inquiries about how, for instance, one can reconcile the triune nature of God, as understood

The Encounter of Eastern Christianity with Early Islam, ed. Emmanouela Grypeou, Mark Swanson and David Thomas (Leiden: Brill, 2006), 45–72, pp. 46–47.

124 van Ginkel, "The Reception and Presentation of the Arab Conquest," p. 183.

125 David Thomas, "Christian Theologians and New Questions," in *The Encounter of Eastern Christianity with Early Islam*, ed. Emmanouela Grypeou, Mark Swanson and David Thomas (Leiden: Brill, 2006), 257–276, pp. 257–258.

in Christian faith, with monotheism in Islam. Thomas concludes from this that what concerns John of Damascus is still Christian-Christian, rather than Chrisian-Muslim, dialogue. Even in chapters 100 – 101 of the second part of the Damascene's *On Heresies*, John does not make a detailed theological comparison or analysis of Christian and Islamic doctrines. These two chapters merely state that Islam is just, as Thomas comments, "a mishmash of beliefs concocted from Christianity and entirely human in origin."[126] When Thomas attempts to explain this attitude, he concedes that for the Christians at that time it seems that Islam was not "a faith to take seriously, and certainly not a force that might dictate new directions for Christian doctrinal explanations and defences."[127] Furthermore, when it comes to his opinion of Muḥammad, John of Damascus' tone is no less negative and pejorative: the Ishmaelites' prophet adopted heretical Christian ideas and spread mere rumour that God gave him a scripture from heaven, which contains laughable claims.[128]

Thomas admits that the Damascene's virulent reaction is definitely not because of his ignorance of Islam. As one who grew up and worked and lived as one of the courtiers in the Islamic palace, leave alone his theological and intellectual calibre and learnedness, he must have had encountered Muslim thinkers and heard about Islam on a regular basis. John of Damascus' attitude, as Thomas also concedes, is "a product of his own sense of superiority both intellectually and spiritually, and also as an attempt to insulate himself and his coreligionists from its cultural and political as well as religious potency, by denying its validity as a God-given revelation."[129] Thomas' argument suggests that this belittling attitude is in harmony with the language of scorn and disregard towards the Arabs that we find in Dionysius' chronicle. It demonstrates a conviction that, with regard to this lowly, marginal group of people, it is not worth spending time initiating any qualitative fruitful conversation about their own religious ideas.

In his tracing of the formation of a renewed Christian identity in the context of the new Arabic empire, Sidney Griffith also touches upon the driving force behind the Christians' attitude towards Islam. In his investigation, Griffith goes back even earlier than the time of Michael the Great to the period between the

126 Ibid., p. 258.

127 Ibid., p. 259; also on John of Damascus' comments on Islam, see Daniel J. Sahas, *John of Damascus on Islam: The 'Heresy of the Ishmaelites'* (Leiden: Brill, 1972), and Andrew Louth, *St John Damascene: Tradition and Originality in Byzantine Theology* (Oxford: Oxford University Press, 2002), pp. 76 – 84.

128 Thomas, "Changing Attitudes of Arab Christians towards Islam," p. 11, citing from John of Damascus, *On Heresies*, Chs. 100 – 101.

129 Thomas, "Changing Attitudes of Arab Christians towards Islam," p. 12.

middle of the 8th century and near the end of the 10th. He maintains that, during that time, the monastic communities and the churches of Jerusalem cut their link with Constantinople and the Byzantine world, and started, instead, deliberately to develop a new identity derived from, and relevant to, their new societal, cultural and religious Arab-Islamic context. Griffith reads this identity-formation process as the genesis of the Melkite Christians, who were, as Griffith says, "Arabic-speaking by necessity, Byzantine Orthodox in their faith, and religiously challenged by the ever more insistent 'call to Islam.'"[130] Out of this attempt, the Melkite community would produce a theologian such as Theodore Abū Qurrah, who would become known in historical and theological studies of Late Antique Eastern Christianity as the pioneer of the attempt to write theology in Arabic terms.[131]

I shall cover in detail the results of Abū Qurrah's mentioned endeavour in the following parts of this study. What I want to draw attention to now in relation to the shift from Byzantine to Arab identity is Griffith's statement that Christians of that time found themselves *in need*, or 'by necessity' in Griffith's words, of shifting into Arabic in their daily life practice and their religious affairs. Why? Because they were challenged, if not threatened, by the Arab newcomers' initiative of calling to Islam the local people, who now inhabited an evidently non-Christian empire. 'Necessity' here designates obligation and urgent reaction to an imminent and direct threat. It is not a freely willed intention to seek full voluntary

130 Sidney H. Griffith, "A 'Melkite' Arabic Text from Sinai and the Doctrines of the Trinity and the Incarnation in 'Arab Orthodox Apologetics'," in *The Encounter of Eastern Christianity and Early Islam*, ed. Emmanouela Grypeou, Mark Swanson and David Thomas (Leiden: Brill, 2006), 277–310, p. 279. For a comprehensive view of Griffith's reading of the shift from Byzantine to Arab identity, see S. H. Griffith, "Byzantium and the Christians in the World of Islam: Constantinople and the Church in the Holy Land in the Ninth Century," in *Medieval Encounters*, 3, 1997, pp. 231–265; idem, "Monks of Palestine,"; idem, "The Church of Jerusalem and the 'Melkites': The Making of an 'Arab Orthodox' Christian Identity in the World of Islam, 750–1050 CE," in *Christians and Christianity in the Holy Land: from the Origin to the Latin Kingdom*, ed. Ora Limor and Guy G. Stroumsa (Turnhout: Brepols, 2006), 173–202.

131 Scholars believe that the role of the Christians of Palestine is central in this. On the situation of Christians in Palestine in Late Antiquity, see, for example, Robert L. Wilken, *The Land Called Holy: Palestine in Christian History and Thought* (New Haven, CT: Yale University Press, 1992); L. Perrone, "'Four Gospels, Four Councils' – One Lord Jesus Christ: The Patristic Development of Christology within the Church of Palestine," in *Liber Annuus Studium Biblicum Franciscanum*, 49 (1999), 357–396; Sidney Griffith, "The View of Islam from the Monasteries of Palestine in the Early Abbasid Period," *Islam and Christian-Muslim Relations*, 7 (1996), 9–28; and on Palestine' importance in early Islam, see Arieh Kofsky and Guy Stroumsa (eds), *Sharing the Sacred: Religious Contacts and Conflicts in the Holy Land, First-Fifteenth Centuries CE* (Jerusalem: Yad Izhak Ben Zvi, 1998), pp. 149 ff.

integration. We have a community trying, on the one hand, to break free from the pressure of the bad situation it experienced under Byzantine rule, , and, on the other, to preserve its existence in the face of the threat of proselytizing activity by the new ruling power.

Furthermore, the concern to develop an Arab identity did not have, as it seems, a clearly identifiable theological nature or intention either. Griffith notes that the Melkites, though conceding the need to Arabize their cultural and religious traditions, leave alone their language, remained, nevertheless, Byzantine orthodox in their faith. This is a significant point that should not be ignored or belittled. It, first, says that the local Christians (the Melkites at least) broke their ties to Hellenism not for theological or intellectual reasons, but rather for purely political, sociological and pragmatic ones. These people maintained their orthodox theology; and Abū Qurrah's writings show, as I shall demonstrate later, that defending this orthodoxy occupied the epicentre of his apologetic discourse. Whether or not Abū Qurrah succeeded in keeping his reading of orthodox theology on the 'Chalcedonian' and 'Nicene' tracks is a question to be attended to later. What matters here is that, in their attempt to develop a new Arab identity, the Christians of the Middle East did not give up their Christian theology, no matter how provocative and wearying its Christological and Trinitarian elements were to the sensibilities of their Muslim rulers and co-citizens. They did not even deem it necessary to take the initiative in sharing this theology with the newcomers. When they did later start to engage in discussion and writing on their Christian thinking, they did so out of a concern similar to that of the Christians in the time of Michael the Great: recreating an identity that would secure their existence and grant them safety and survival among Muslims. In other words, Griffith's attention to the Melkites' move to using Arabic in 8th–10th-century Palestine does not conflict with my suggestion that the Christians of the East did not really initiate a theological dialogue with Islam, and that launching such a theological dialogue with the Arabs was not an initiative they voluntarily undertook. Griffith in fact inspires us to consider the possibility that, when the Christians got involved in such dialogue and started to Arabize their identity, they did this reactively and out of necessity, with the result that they found themselves almost always taking a defensive and apologetic stance, rather than one that was interactive, pro-active and reciprocal.

One may conclude from the above that even before the 12th century, concern about survival as a minority community took precedence over all other interests. And, if any attention was given to theology, it was basically related to Christian-Christian controversies that had already been taking place before Islam, and not primarily to launch a religious conversation with Muslims, except when their criticism of Christian theology threatened to erode Christian numbers and the status of the church. The local Christians soon realized that they were becoming a minority and found themselves involved in the demanding task of re-forming their Christian identity.[132]

Sidney Griffith is right in recognizing the challenge of Islam "as itself having been a factor in the Christian, community-building process," and perceiving that the three determining factors in this process were these Christians' "encounter with the Muslims, their adoption of the Arabic language and their isolation from other Christian communities outside the Islamic world."[133] Griffith perceptively notes in the writings of some of the Christians of the 11th century an awareness of the need for one shared identity that could help the Christians to survive as a minority in the Islamic world, and eloquently expresses this as follows

> There were also some ecumenists among the Christian writers who thought that in the face of the multiple challenges from Islam it would behove the Christians to look beyond their mutual differences for the sake of presenting a united defence of Christianity's claim to be the true religion.[134]

Considered from this angle, Michael the Great is perhaps not different in approach from those ecumenists. In order to shift the focus of his Christian readers away from the antagonism and enmity that existed between the Christian churches, he directed their attention to the reality of their existence in a new historical and contextual setting by means of Dionysius' reading of the Arab defeat of the Christian empire, Byzantium. However, he only referred to that chronicle after substantial editing. Instead of Dionysius' theological, Christian-Christian hermeneutics of the conquest, Michael offers a rather political reading, which focuses on the tyranny and governmental misdemeanours of the Byzantine rulers (rather than on their theological allegiance to Chalcedon), thereby inviting the Christians to see in the new Muslim rule an opportunity to reconsider God's will for their situation as a community.

132 Sidney Griffith does not deny the link between the community-building process and the Christian-Christian controversies in the East. He says: "In these circumstances, the Nestorians, Jacobites/Copts and Melkites, the classical denominations of the Christians in the Islamic world, can be seen emerging in their mature identities, formulating their differences in polemical reactions to one another in tracts most often written in Arabic": Griffith, *The Church in the Shadow of the Mosque*, p. 131.

133 Ibid., pp. 129–130.

134 Ibid., p. 141.

IV. Conclusion

When the Christians declined freely to take the initiative of dialoguing with the new invaders, leaving this for the Muslims to assume at their own time and pace, they backed themselves, by their own choice, into a narrow corner of reactive defensiveness, rather than pro-active interaction. They became consistently challenged to offer plausible apologies to justify their faith, rather than instructively interpreting it and freely explaining its elements and constituents. This narrow, apologetic, defensive margin forced itself upon the Syrian and Arab Christians’ interreligious interaction with Islam from the beginning and throughout the following centuries. Arab and Arabic-speaking Christian theologians, such as Theodore Abū Qurrah, far from being able to interpret faith from a doxological standpoint, found themselves controlled by the necessity either to counter-attack Islam and refute it altogether, or to modify and compromise the fundamental doctrines of Christian faith (e.g., Christology, the incarnation, the Trinity) in order to make Christianity acceptable and Christian faith plausible and appealing to the Muslims.

The crucial questions here are: In their attempt to achieve one of these two goals by theologizing apologetically, did the Arab church fathers – Theodore Abū Qurrah in this study – compromise the theological discourse of Christian orthodoxy? Does the apologetic tendency in Abū Qurrah’s arabization of the theology of Nicea and Chalcedon, and his attempt to make that theology plausible to the Arabic-sensitive ear of Muslims, force him to make his theology less ‘Nicene’ and ‘Chalcedonian’ (whatever those terms may mean) than it should be? Such questions take us from the historical to the theologico-doctrinal level of the study of the relationship between Islam and Arab Christianity, which demands a systematic analysis of Theodore Abū Qurrah’s reading of orthodox Trinitarian theology and Christology and a critical assessment of the ramifications of his attempt to express these doctrines in Arabic.

Chapter Two. Abū Qurrah and the Christian Apologetics of the Melkite Church

I. From Emperor to Caliph: The End of Christian Triumphalism

By the time Theodore Abū Qurrah began to be involved in writing theological texts to address the religious challenges of Islam, Christianity had already lost authority and retained hardly any tangible autonomous influence in the Near East, whether ecclesially, intellectually, politically, or even culturally. The adoption of the Roman rhetoric of triumphalism and the investment of this triumphalist *topos* in establishing the Lord of the church, Jesus Christ, as the greatest god of victory, which the Christians of the once dominantly Byzantine Near East had earlier adopted easily and swiftly,[135] was no longer feasible in the light of the increasing prevalence of Islam, its hegemonic control of the region and its determination of all aspects of life therein. Christ could no longer be seen as "mightiest in battle"[136] after the Byzantine retreat from the southern parts of the Empire (Syria and Palestine), and with it the arch-episcopal sees of Alexandria, Jerusalem and Antioch, starting from the 7th century, and the gradual conquest of the southern parts of the 'Christian-Roman Empire' from the 630s and 640s by the Bedouins from the Arabian Peninsula.

This new situation influenced not only the Christian view of Jesus Christ as *Christus victor*, but also the relationship between church and state that the church had enjoyed in previous centuries. Some scholars have found in the early Islamic rulers' behaviour and leadership style features that indicate a convergence between Christianity and Islam. One such scholar is Daniel Sahas, who suggests that whenever we consider the relationship between Islam and Christianity, we should always keep in mind the "geographical and cultural proximity of Byzantine Christianity to Islam."[137] The majority of Eastern Christians, Sahas continues, viewed Islam as a religious teaching that was loaded with Christian, albeit heretical, ideas and elements. The Christians of Syria, therefore, never

---

135 David Olster, "Ideological Transformation ...," p. 47.
136 Ibid., p. 48.
137 Daniel J. Sahas, "The Art and Non-Art of Byzantine Polemics: Patterns of Refutation in Byzantine Anti-Islamic Literature," in *Conversion and Continuity: Indigenous Christian Communities in Islamic Land*, ed. Michael Gervers and Ramzī J. Bikh'āzī (Ontario: Pontifical Institute of Mediaeval Studies, 1990), 55–73, p. 57.

questioned the existence of Muslims among them and openly intermingled with these Arab southerners socially and culturally, though they simultaneously believed that the religious ideas of these Peninsular Arabs were a superstitious, distorted form of Christianity that was in serious need of correction, if not complete refutation.[138] Sahas goes as far as stating that "Orthodox Christianity and Islam mirror each other in many ways. Not only several significant experiences were the same, but several developments were also contemporary."[139] The similarity between Byzantium and Islamic rule is hardly to be missed, and one may say, as Sahas believes, "that Byzantium was not destroyed by the earliest conquests, but it survived in an Arabized and Islamized form, as a 'neo-Byzantine empire.'"[140] One of the examples Sahas uses to support his conclusion is the system of theocracy that, according to him, both the Byzantine emperors and the Muslims caliphs adopted. The Muslim caliphs' offices were shaped after a theocratic model that thoroughly resembled that of the Byzantine emperors, for, had the caliph's behaviour and style of rule not been so, no Byzantine would have taken him or his authority seriously.[141]

Sahas' general observation of a convergence between the Byzantine and the Islamic traditions to the extent that it may be said that the latter was an adoption of the former, may, broadly speaking, be theoretically possible. However, conjecturing this convergence is not absolutely accurate and seems to be rather unrealistic in practice. The mere fact that the Muslim rulers treated Christians, including the 'Arabs' among them, as *dhimmīs* indicates that the two communities did not in fact intermingle so easily, even though the Christian *dhimmīs* played a significant role in expanding the cultural, artistic, political and economic life of the caliphates.[142] David Cook is probably right in saying that the Arabic-speakers of

138 Ibid., p. 57. Sahas supports this openness towards the Muslims by noting that both the Eastern Christians and the Muslims were, after all, Arabs. For Sahas, the clash between the Syrian locals and the Peninsular Arabs had no real cultural or sociological dimension. It was from the very beginning purely religious.

139 Ibid., p. 58.

140 Ibid., p. 60.

141 Ibid., p. 62. Robert Hoyland would further trace a similar adoption of political and social systems in relations between Christian Arabs' and the Roman imperial order before Islam, in the third-sixth centuries: Robert G. Hoyland, "Arab Kings, Arab Tribes and the Beginning of Arab Historical Memory in Late Roman Epigraphy," in *From Hellenism to Islam: Cultural and Linguistic Change in the Roman Near East*, ed. Hannah M. Cotton et al. (Cambridge: Cambridge University Press, 2009), 374–400.

142 Sahas, "The Art and Non-Art of Byzantine Polemics," pp. 59–60. See also David Cook, "Syria and the Arabs," in *A Companion to Late Antiquity*, ed. P. Rosseau and J. Raithel (Chichester: Blackwell, 2009), 467–478.

Syria, most of whom later became Muslims, were the cultural heirs of Hellenistic civilization, and that the Muslim conquerors of the region did not make an immediate decisive break with that cultural background.[143] However, this does not in itself, in my opinion, prove that the Islamic caliphate treated these non-Muslim citizens as compatriots who belonged with the Muslim population to the same cultural framework (Byzantine) and differed from each other only in religion. On the other hand, David Cook is also correct in pointing out that the Umayyad caliphs, who benefited from Byzantine culture in establishing their rule, "strongly supported Islam and made strenuous efforts not to be assimilated into the cultural sphere of the Christian Mediterranean basin."[144] One may credibly say that there were many elements other than Islam itself that divided the Christians, with their Byzantine cultural and socio-political background, from the Peninsular Muslim invaders. It may be that no complete societal break took place at that time, but a fundamental change definitely occurred in the life of the Christians of Syria that started to create division between them and the Muslim population of the newly founded state – a division caused by an escalating zeal for islamization, which created a gap that would soon grow wider and wider.

One of the dividing elements was related to the 'religion-state' relationship and the way it was understood in the context of the Muslim caliphs' ruling practices. Although the caliphs were as theocratic in their rule as the Byzantines, the separation between the role of the lay ruler and the religious leader, especially in terms of theological teaching and religious matters, was much clearer and wider in the Byzantine case than in the Islamic one. In the centuries that preceded Islam, the Church was substantially able to maintain an ecclesial and theological dividing-line that marked out the area of clerical jurisdiction from the political, royal and lay authorities. The division between the temporal and the spiritual authorities was preserved, at least on the intellectual level – despite occasions of interference, when clerical and political actors were involved in affairs within

---

143 D. Cook, "Syria and the Arabs," p. 475 – 476. "The Greek language," Cook notes, "continued to be employed in the court for some fifty years after that conquest, and even after that time it was still widely used. Byzantine artisans and architects planned and built the major buildings used by the Arabs, such as the Dome of the Rock in Jerusalem, the Umayyad Mosque in Damascus ..., and the desert castles" (p. 475).

144 Ibid., p. 474. Cook gives as an example of this break ʿAbd al-Malik b. Marwān's Arabization of the language of administration, replacing the coinage of Byzantium with a new coinage bearing Islamic slogans and symbols.

the other's realm of responsibility.[145] It was still possible to entertain the conviction, as David Olster eloquently states, that "while Christ presides in the upper register, the emperor, arrayed as military victor crushes Christ's enemies in the lower register, while the enemies of the God-guarded emperor lie prostrate or kneeling in submission in the lowest register."[146]

This was no longer exactly the case under the rule of Islam. During the Islamic era, the Church could no longer maintain this distinction. The Christians found themselves from the 7th century onwards ruled by a new regime that almost totally blurred the religious with the secular and by a religion whose founder (the Prophet Muhammad) was referred to in the earliest Islamic texts as 'the first king of the Arabs' (*malik al-ʿArab*) as often as he was called 'the messenger of God' (*Rasūl Allāh*).[147] The Muslim rulers who succeeded him were considered the protectors and guardians of faith, as were as the Byzantine emperors. However, they were, in addition, not only viewed as the political rulers of the Arabs, but also, and more importantly, as the primary spokesmen and higher arbitrators of Islamic religion, with responsibility for deciding what was the right accepted content of Islam.[148] In their study of the history of Caliphate rule, Patricia Crone and Martin Hinds go even as far as to surmise that authority, in the original notion of 'caliphate,' was both political and religious in nature and was exclusively concentrated in the ruling caliph. The caliphs, Crone and Hinds suggest, "were free to make and unmake Sunna as they wished."[149]

---

145 On such interference, see, for example, Olster, "Ideological Transformation," pp. 50 ff. See also David Olster, "Justinian, Rhetoric and the Church," *Bzyantinoslavica*, 50 (1989), 65–76, and F. Dvornik, *Early Christian and Byzantine Political Philosophy: Origins and Backgrounds*, (Washington, DC: Dumbarton Oaks Studies, 1966), Vol. 2.

146 Olster, "Ideological Transformation," p. 49.

147 On the use of these two titles for Muhammad in Islamic texts, see Y. D. Nevo and J. Koren, *Crossroads to Islam*, pp. 130–131, 247–270.

148 Tilman Nagel conjectures that this role in the history of Islam started with the Abbasid Caliph al-Maʾmūn, who endeavoured, according to Nagel, "to determine from the top what was the right and generally accepted content of Islam, a content that could be explained rationally and was supposedly acceptable to everyone": Tilman Nagel, *Geschichte der Islamischen Theologie* (Munich: Verlag C. H. Beck, 1994). I here use the English translation: Tilman Nagel, *The History of Islamic Theology: From Muhammad to the Present*, trans. Thomas Thornton (Princeton, NJ: Markus Wiener, 2010), p. 24.

149 Patricia Crone and Martin Hinds, *God's Caliph: Religious Authority in the First Centuries of Islam* (Cambridge: Cambridge University Press, 2003), pp. 24, 52. See a discussion of this and of Crone's approach to Islamic historiography in Ibn ar-Rawāndi, "Origins of Islam: A Critical Look at the Sources," in *The Quest of the Historical Muhammad*, ed. and trans. Ibn Warraq (Amherst, NY: Prometheus Books, 2000), 89–124, pp. 97–98.

In the Byzantine world, questions about Christian faith and the orthodox catechism of the Church were to be addressed to and discussed primarily between the Church's theologians and clerics. It is true that church prelates would occasionally use their good relations with the emperor, or the religious disposition of his wife (as in the cases of Empress Theodora and her niece Empress Sophia) to endorse their theological view throughout the empire. It is also true that the Christian communities of the 6th century have witnessed a growing and intensive imperial involvement in religious affairs,[150] as, for example, when the emperors found it easy to bully the prelates of Constantinople into conformity by threatening patriarchs with removal and replacement if they did not follow the imperial line. Some emperors could even enlist the prelates' support by means of persuasion and argument, since some members of the royal family were theologically qualified and competent in their own right.[151] This conceded, the Church usually resisted and rejected the emperor's interference in theological and ecclesial affairs. John Hussey points to this when he invokes the example of John of Damascus' and Theodore the Studite's blunt challenge to the emperor's intervention in theological-ecclesiological matters, citing the Studite's saying to Emperor Constantine VI, "your responsibility, emperor, is with affairs of state and military matters. Give your mind to these and leave the church to its pastors and teachers."[152] Well known also is Maximus the Confessor's argument against the theoretical right of Emperor Constans II to intervene in matters of dogma and decisions regarding the nature of orthodoxy. As we see in the papers from his trial and other correspondences, Maximus strongly rejected the identification of the secular ruler as both emperor and priest and denied his authority to summon Church synods and councils and ratify clerical appointments. In the record of his trial, we find Maximus even stating bluntly that the emperor is "nei-

150 Philip Wood, *‚We Have no King but Christ', Christian Political Thought in Greater Syria on the Even of the Arab Conquest (c. 400–585)*, (Oxford: Oxford University Press, 2010), p. 177 (also pp. 163–208). See also in relation to this Mary Whitby, *The Propaganda of Power: the Role of Panegyric in Late Antiquity*, (Leiden: Brill, 1998). In his monograph, Philip Wood focuses on studying the Syriac ascetic and hagiographical texts that goes back to the sixth century, trying to show therein evidences of a 'miaphysite *Kaiserkritik*', which shows that the criticism of the imperial interference in religious affairs was not just a practice in the chalcedonian, but also the non-Chalcedonian, churchly circles alike.

151 John F. Haldon, *Byzantium in the Seventh Century: The Transformation of a Culture*, rev. ed. (Cambridge,: Cambridge University Press, 1997), p. 285, see also pages 281–323.

152 John M. Hussey, *The Orthodox Church in the Byzantine Empire* (Oxford: Oxford University Press, 2010), p. 56. Hussey borrows this example from Paul J. Alexander, *The Patriarch Nicephorus of Constantinople: Ecclesiastical Policy and Image Worship in the Byzantine Empire*, rev. ed. (Oxford: Oxford University Press, 2001), pp. 130–133.

ther a priest nor a monk, but a pander."[153] Generally speaking, despite the dynamic, and far from statically parallel relationship that linked Church and state in Byzantine history, there was also, as John Haldon states, a "tension between Church and state, emperor and patriarch, which subsisted throughout Byzantine history and was effectively resolved in the East only with the replacement of the Byzantine emperor by an Ottoman sultan."[154]

This complicated and tense relationship between Church and state and secular and religious leaders was not really a problem in Islam, at least not during the first three centuries. The caliph was both the sole ruler of the kingdom, and also, and more centrally, 'the prince of the believers' (*amīr al-Mū'minīn*). He had the duty, and not only the authority, to speak on behalf of the community (*'umma*) in matters of faith and arbitrate in the rightness of its religion. Though Islam does not have a 'priesthood' like Christianity, one can still say that the role of the prelates as protectors of belief and defenders of it before others has similarities in the role of Muslim caliphs. Be that as it may, Christian prelates and thinkers found themselves involved in face-to-face theological debates with Muslim caliphs, and not only with the Muslim *mutakallimūn*. It became one of the inescapable duties of the Christian theologians and patriarchs to stand in the caliph's court and face challenging questions and charges against Christianity, or even to hear an invitation to convert to Islam, from none other than the caliph himself. Far from merely enjoying ruling powers that are directly derived from the heavenly grace of God (like the Byzantine rulers), the Muslim caliph was viewed by Muslims as the supreme guardian of the Prophet Muhammad's religion, and the one who should lead the campaign to 'call' (*ad-da'wah*) Christians to Islam.[155] In other words, the Muslim political leader was almost another *mu-*

153 See "Record of the Trial (CPG 7736)," in Pauline Allen and Bronwen Neil (trans. and ed.), *Maximus the Confessor and his Companions: Documents from Exile* (Oxford: Oxford University Press, 2004), pp. 48–74, §. 10. In explaining why he does not entitle the emperor the rank of 'priest', Maximus says: "no, he isn't, because he neither stands beside the altar, and after the consecration of the bread elevates it with the words: 'Holy things for the holy'; nor does he baptize, nor perform the rite of anointing, nor does he ordain and make bishops and presbyters and deacons; nor does he anoint churches, nor does he wear the symbols of the priesthood, the *pallium* and Gospel book, as [he wears the symbols] of imperial office, the crown and purple" (§. 4, p. 57). See also in relation to Maximus' trial, Haldon, *Byzantium in the Seventh Century*, pp. 304–313.

154 Haldon, *Byzantium in the Seventh Century*, p. 282.

155 Dimitri Gutas says that this formalization of the caliph's religious role did not exist before al-Ma'mūn's time: Dimitri Gutas, *Greek Thought, Arabic Culture: The Graeco-Arabic Translation Movement in Baghdad and Early 'Abbāsid Society (2nd – 4th/8th – 10th Centuries)*, (New York: Routledge, 1999), p. 79. I believe, however, that this view is traceable in Islam before al-Ma'mūn made

takallim and Islamizer among the host of Muslim intellectual and religious *mutakallimūn*. Similarities may likely be traced between the Islamic 'religion-state' and 'caliph-guardian of faith' and the fusion of the heavenly and earthly realms that some Byzantine emperors (such as Heraclius and Constantine IV) followed and imposed during the early Islamic era as an expression of belief in Christ's union with the emperor.[156] But this similarity should not conceal the changes Eastern Christians experienced under the rule of Islam. After all, the discussions some Church prelates had with Byzantine rulers were discussions between two leaders who held the same faith and considered themselves guardians of its orthodox and generally acceptable interpretation.

The new challenges faced by Christians were related to the consequences and ramifications of infusing the earthly with the heavenly in the Islamic view of the caliph's role and duties. Rather than simply exchanging views on various interpretations and teachings of the same faith, the Church fathers found themselves obliged to present to the Muslim caliph convincing apologies that would persuade him to grant security and freedom of belief to Christians in the Islamic territories. The challenge was now to ensure the very survival of the Christian religion community, not just to protect certain Christian groups or followers of certain theological teachings from persecution and punishment.

II. The Christian Response to Islam and the Beginning of Apologetics

How did Christians react to this new, challenging situation, and how did they deal with the threat of Islamic pressure and then survived the numerical decline of the Christian community within the Islamic empire? They did so in various ways and by following diverse strategies that were shaped according to each Christian community's circumstances and the polemical and dialogical stances that were taken by particular Church fathers. Some Christians pragmatically wel-

---

it an official policy and promulgated the view that the caliph was the ultimate arbiter of Islamic dogma. The dialogue between Timothy I and the Caliph al-Mahdī, for example, challenges Gutas' claim and suggests that we should take seriously Muslims' expectations that their caliphs would act as the successors of the Prophet Muhammad in arbitrating in matters of faith and fostering it in the earliest decades, and that they would attempt to prove to their people their worthiness to fulfil this duty.

156 Olster, "Ideological Transformation," pp. 56 ff. According to Olster, there were times when "the emperor … was presented not only as Christ's co-emperor, but also employed a legend that had episcopal connotations" (ibid., p. 69).

comed the Muslim invaders. By resorting to peaceful, welcoming diplomacy, they tried to please the new rulers, to prove themselves useful in the attempt of the latter to build a new state, or to benefit from the caliphs' tolerance by gaining some religious independence and clerical freedom. In contrast, other Christians refused to bend down to the flow of the new religion. They tended to view the new Islamic rule from an almost purely religious perspective and focused on withstanding the newcomers' attempts to convert them. Some courageously counter-attacked Islam and revealed a readiness to pay the high price for choosing to do so, while others opted for an intellectual stance rather than an actual, if diplomatic, confrontation. They either developed intellectual, philosophical and theological counter-discourses to introduce the Christian faith to Muslims and clarify central doctrinal elements and to clarify central components of faith in response to these latters' questions, or they constructed catechetical and pedagogical works directed primarily to members of the Christian churches, not to Muslims, in order to train Christians and prepare them intellectually to deal with Muslim polemics against Christianity.

The first of these approaches was mainly adopted by church prelates, who found themselves responsible for rescuing the Christian community from the grave challenges of decline and discrimination when they fail to substantiate their loyalty to the new regime. These prelates included the Nestorian Patriarch Timothy I, who dialogued with the Abbasid Caliph al-Mahdī on Islam and Christian faith,[157] Patriarch Sophronius of Jerusalem, who negotiated the handing over

157 See Timothy's dialogue with the Caliph al-Mahdī in Mingana, *Woodbroke Studies*, Vol. 2, pp. 1–162. See also N.A. Newman, *the Early Christian-Muslim Dialogue: A Collection of Documents from the First Three Islamic Centuries (632–900 AD). Translations with Commentary* (Hatfield, PA: Interdisciplinary Biblical Research Institute, 1993), pp. 163–267; Samir K. Samir, "The Prophet Muhammad as Seen by Timothy I; S.K. Samir, *The Significance of Early Arab-Christian Thought for Muslim-Christian Understanding* (Washington, DC: Center for Muslim-Christian Understanding, History and International Affairs, 1997); S. Griffith, "Disputes with Muslims in Syriac Christian Texts: from Patriarch John (d. 648) to Bar Hebraeus (d. 1286)," in *The Beginnings of Christian Theology in Arabic*, ed. S.H. Griffith, (Aldershot, UK/Burlington, USA: Ashgate/Variorum, 2002), V, 251–273, pp. 262–265; Griffith, *The Church in the Shadow of the Mosque*, pp. 45–48, 76–91; R.G. Hoyland, *Seeing Islam as Others Saw It*, pp. 472–476; T.R. Hurst, "The Syriac Letters of Timothy I (727–823): A Study in Christian-Muslim Controversy" (PhD Dissertation), (Washington, DC: Catholic University of America, 1986); Sebastian P. Brock, "Two Letters of the Patriarch Timothy from the Late Eighth Century on Translations from Greek," in *Arabic Sciences and Philosophy*, 9 (1999), 233–246; andMartin Heimgartner, *Die Disputation des ostsyrischen Patriarchen Timotheos (780–823) mit dem Kalifen al-Mahdī. Einleitung, Textedition Übersetzung und Anmerkungen* (Halle, 2006).

of Jerusalem[158] to the Caliph ʿUmar ibn al-Khaṭṭāb,[159] and Manṣūr ibn Sarjūn, John of Damascus' grandfather, who was said to have negotiated the terms of surrender of Damascus to Khālid ibn al-Walīd in 635 and opened its Eastern Gate (*Bāb Sharqī*) to his army. In Abū al-ʿAbbās Aḥmad b. Yaḥyā b. Jābir al-Balādūrī's book, *Kitāb Futūḥ al-Buldān* (the Book of the Countries' Conquests) (892), Manṣūr was called 'the bishop of Damascus'.[160]

On the other hand, the second option was followed by those Christians, individuals and groups, who refused to convert to Islam and were audacious enough to confront the Muslims with what they (the Christians) believed to be the irrefutable evidence of the falsity and pitfalls of the Arabs' religion. They were ready to lay down their lives for the sake of maintaining their belief in Jesus Christ and their allegiance to the Church, although many of them were not blindly loyal to the Byzantine emperor, despite his Christian affiliation, but were sometimes harshly critical of Byzantium's treatment of the Church and the emperor's interference in ecclesial affairs. These people became the martyrs of the Church during the early Islamic period. Among them were the sixty martyrs of Gaza (638), the sixty pilgrims in Jerusalem (724), Michael the Sabaite and ʿAbd al-Masīḥ an-Najrānī al-Ghassānī.[161]

---

158 An explanation of why a prelate such as Sophronius, rather than the lay leaders of the city, would negotiate such a political situation with the Muslim invador can be gathered from Jonathan Berkey's claim that "what civil life remained in Roman cities in the late sixth and seventh centuries was overseen by the bishop or patriarch, and so it was with them that the Muslim Arabs would negotiate the terms of the cities surrender": J. P. Berkey, *The Formation of Islam: Religion and Society in the Near East, 600–1800* (Cambridge: Cambridge University Press, 2003), p. 52.

159 Sahas, "The Face to Face Encounter"; Heribert Busse, "'Omar b. al-Khattāb in Jerusalem," *Jerusalem Studies in Arabic and Islam*, 5 (1984), 73–119; H. Busse, "'Omar's Image as the Conqueror of Jerusalem," in *Jerusalem Studies in Arabic and Islam*, 8 (1986), 149–168; Oleg Grabar, *The Shape of the Holy: Early Islamic Jerusalem* (Princeton, NJ: Princeton University Press, 1996), pp. 46–49; Griffith, *The Church in the Shadow of the Mosque*,, pp. 24–27.

160 Saʿīd b. Batrīq Eutychius, *Annals*, in *Corpus Scriptorum Christianorum Orientalium*, ed. Louis Cheikho, B. Carra de Voux and H. Zayyāt (Louvain: Imprimerie Orientaliste, 1954), Vol. 51, Bk. II, p. 15; Aḥmad b. Yaḥyā al-Balādhuri, *Kitāb Futūḥ al-Buldān* (The Book of the Conquest of Countries), trans. Philip Hitti (New York: Columbia University Press, 1916), Vol. 1, pp. 172, 187; Louth, *St. John Damascene*, pp. 3–5; Sahas, *John of Damascus on Islam*, pp. 17–22; and Tolan, *Saracens*, p. 50.

161 Hoyland, *Seeing Islam As Others Saw It*, pp. 336–386; S. Griffith, "Michael the Martyr and Monk of Mar Sabas Monastery at the Court of the Caliph 'Abd al-Malik: Christian Apologetics and Martyrology in the Early Islamic Period," in *Aram*, 6(1994), 115–148; Griffith, "The Arabic Account of ʿAbd al-Masīḥ an-Nağrani al-Ghassānī," *Le Muséon*, 98 (1985), 331–374; Griffith, *The Church in the Shadow of the Mosque*, pp. 147–151; Griffith, "Christians, Muslims and Neo-Martyrs"; Swanson, "The Martyrdom of 'Abd al-Masīh"; Nehemia Levtzion, "Conversion to

Finally, a third option was taken by 7th – 9th-century Christian theologians and intellectuals, known by Muslims as the 'Christian *mutakallimūn*,' who shaped for the first time in history an apologetic, doctrinal catechism and philosophically-based theological discourses in Arabic. These theologians lived in and wrote from Palestine and other parts of Syria. They are referred to by scholars of Arab Christianity as the 'monk-scholars' of Palestine, who lived and produced the first ecclesiastical literature in Arabic at the heart of the context that witnessed the radical shift from Byzantine-Christian to Arab-Islamic rule. Instead of either compromising some Christian principles for the sake of survival and security, or sacrificing their own life and being commemorated as heroes by attacking Islam, these *mutakallimūn* endeavoured in their intellectual projects to establish an 'Arab Orthodox' or 'Arab Christian' identity in the world of Islam by interacting with Islam, and not despite Islam's existence. They included the author of *Disputatio Saraceni et Christiani*, thought by some scholars to be John of Damascus,[162] and Stephen ar-Ramlī, the author of what scholars today call *Summa Theologiae Arabica* (British Library oriental MS 4950; 877 AD),[163] in addition to the three main Christian apologists and catechists, who not only countered Islamic polemics, but also developed the first Arabic theological catechism and Christian doctrinal and philosophical pedagogy at the era of Islam: the Ja-

---

Islam in Syria and Palestine and the Survival of Christian Communities," in *Conversion and Continuity: Indigenous Christian Communities in Islamic Lands Eighth to Eighteenth Centuries*, ed. Michael Gervers and Ramzī Jibrān Bikh'āzī (Toronto: Pontifical Institute of Medieval Studies, 1990), pp. 289 – 311; Michael G. Morony, "The Age of Conversions: A Reassessment," in *Conversion and Continuity*, 135 – 150; Tolan, *Saracens*, pp. 55 – 57.

162 Sahas, *John of Damascus on Islam*, pp. 99 – 130; Sahas, "The Arab Character of the Christian Disputation with Islam: The Case of John of Damascus (ca. 655 – ca. 749)," in *Religionsgespräche im Mittelalter*, ed. Bernard Lewis and Friedrich Niewöhner (Wiesbaden: Otto Harrassowitz, 1992), 185 – 205. Andrew Louth follows an interesting proposal on John of Damascus' authorship of this text when he says that "it has plausibly been suggested that the *Dispute* is based on John's oral teaching, rather than having actually been written down by him": Louth, *St. John Damascene*, p. 77.

163 Griffith, *The Church in the Shadow of the Mosque*, pp. 81– 85; Griffith, "Greek into Arabic: Life and Letters in the Monasteries of Palestine in the 9th Century; the Example of *Summa Theologiae Arabica*," *Orientalia Christiana Analecta*, 226 (1986), 123 – 141; Griffith, "The First Christian *Summa Theologiae* in Arabic: Christian *Kalām* in the Ninth-Century Palestine," in *Conversion and Continuity: Indigenous Christian Communities in Islamic Lands Eighth to Eighteenth Centuries*, ed. Michael Gervers and Ramzī Jibrān Bikh'āzī (Toronto: Pontifical Institute of Medieval Studies, 1990), 15 – 31; Griffith, "Islam and the Summa Theologiae Arabica; Rabīʿ I, 264 A. H," *Jerusalem Studies in Arabic and Islam*, 13 (1990), 225 – 264.

cobite Ḥabīb b. Khidmah Abū Rā'iṭah,[164] the Nestorian ʿAmmār al-Baṣrī,[165] and finally the leading *mutakallim* among them, the Melkite scholar and bishop of Ḥarrān, Theodore Abū Qurrah, who is the subject of the present study.

The three responses to the presence of a new empire with a new religious orientation that have been outlined above put the Christians face-to-face not only with the challenge of survival in the midst of what was now a predominantly Muslim context, but also, and more crucially, with new confrontational questions and fierce intellectual attacks on their religious faith. The previous chapter in this study presented some Christian historiographical texts and ecclesial epistles on the Christians' haughty scorn and lack of appreciation of the Muslims, culturally, socially and ethnically. One may assume that, at the very beginning of the Islamic era, the newcomers from the Arabian Peninsula either ignored or swallowed the native inhabitants' contempt because they were fascinated and deeply impressed by the Byzantines' and Syrians' cultural, civilizational, socio-economic, artistic and civic achievements. Instead of reacting to these negative condescending attitudes towards them, the new arrivals focused on learning from the locals, adopting most of their cultural and urban traditions and using their expertise and knowledge to establish their own kingdom and create their own imperial glory.

The above reaction is probably characteristic of the first decades of Islamic rule. It is not, however, applicable to the following, late Umayyad and early Abbasid eras, despite the Abbasid caliphate's continuous reliance on the Christians for translating Greek scientific and philosophical literature into Arabic.[166] By that

164 See, for example, Griffith, "Ḥabīb ibn Ḫidmah Abū Rā'iṭah"; Sandra Toenies Keating, "Ḥabīb ibn Khidma Abū Rā'iṭa al-Takrītī's 'The Refutation of the Melkites Concerning the Union [of the Divinity and Humanity in Christ] III," in *Christians at the Heart of Islamic Rule*, ed. David Thomas (Leiden: Brill, 2003), 39–54.

165 See, for example, S. Griffith, "ʿAmmār al-Baṣrī's *Kitāb al-Burhān:* Christian *Kalām* in the First Abbasid Century," in *The Beginnings of Christian Theology in Arabic: Muslim-Christian Encounters in the Early Islamic Period*, Aldershot, UK: Ashgate Variorum, 2002, 145–181; Mark Beaumont, "ʿAmmār al-Baṣrī's Apology for the Doctrine of the Trinity," *Orientalia Christiana Analecta*, 218 (1982), 169–191.

166 On the impact and role of Greek-speaking Christians in the Greek-Arabic translation of the Greek scientific and philosophical heritage, see Dimitri Gutas, *Greek Thought, Arabic Culture*; and Cristina D'Ancona, "Greek into Arabic: Neoplatonism in Translation," in *The Cambridge Companion to Arabic Philosophy*, ed. Peter Adamson and Richard Taylor (Cambridge: Cambridge University Press, 2010), 10–31. On the impact of Syriac-speaking Christians on the Greek-to-Arabic cultural transition, see also Sebastian Brock, *Syriac Perspectives in Late Antiquity* (London: Variorum, 1984), and Sebastian Brock, "From Antagonism to Assimilation: Syriac Attitudes to Greek Learning," in *East of Byzantium: Syria and Armenia in the Formative Period*, ed. N. Garsoian, T. Matthews and R. Thompson (Washington, DC: Dumbarton Oaks, 1980), 17–34.

time, and with the improvement of the Muslims' knowledge of ancient sciences and philosophies, Muslim intellectuals and leading religious figures could no longer ignore being regarded as intellectually and culturally inferior. They started instead, as their writings show, to strike back and defend the rational, logical and theological supremacy of Islam over the irrationality and falsehood of Christian faith. Why did they decide to demonstrate their cultural and intellectual superiority via religious polemics? This might be explained by considering the organic link in Islamic thought between the religious and the worldly, between personal spirituality and theological thought and the communal cultural web of meaning and societal behaviour. This essential connection invites the assumption that an individual's social life is founded on, and should mirror, his or her religious convictions and affiliation. The more solid and truthful these religious convictions are, the higher will be the value of this person's cultural background and the more reliable and authentic is his social status. This 'from-faith-to-culture' hypothesis reflects the Islamic firm paradigmatic association and unification of 'faith' with 'culture,' of 'religiosity' with the notion of '*ummah*,' in the Islamic socio-cultural and socio-anthropological mindset. Within this framework, establishing Muslims' cultural and civilizational status would depend on showing the logical reliability and solid rational foundation of the Islamic religion, and in demonstrating to Christians that they were not more cultured and civilized than Muslims by means of demonstrating to the formers the illogical and fragile foundations of Christian religious beliefs, theological convictions and scriptural sources.

In one of his essays on Arab Christianity in the early Islamic era, David Thomas successfully perceives this shift in the Muslims' attitude toward the Christian *dhimmīs*' religious convictions. He states that the radical contextual changes that took place in the 7th and 8th centuries brought Eastern (Syrian) Christians into a confrontation with a new form of monotheistic belief they had not encountered or dealt with before. Rather than just facing another Christian heresy about God or Christ, the Christians faced new thinkers, who, in their attempt to reflect their religious differences and qualifications, challenged their opponents with new and unexpected questions and accusations. Thomas then concludes that in such confrontations "lay the beginnings of what became a tradition of misunderstanding that inevitably led to indifference and condemnation."[167] Muslim intellectuals, Thomas argues, set themselves the goal of demonstrating the wide quality-gap between the authenticity and truthfulness of Islam and the falsehood and absurdity of Christianity.

167 Thomas, "Christian Theologians and New Questions," p. 257.

As an example of these Muslim intellectuals, Thomas pinpoints two 9th-century Muslim *mutakallimūn:* the Zaydī Imām, al-Qāsim b. Ibrāhīm ar-Rassī (d. 860), who wrote a book called *Radd ʿalā an-Naṣārā* (a Response to the Christians); and the Shīʿī theologian Abū ʿĪsā Muḥammad b. Hārūn al-Warrāq (d. 864), who wrote *Radd ʿalā ath-Thalāth Firaq min an-Naṣārā* (Response to the Three Groups of the Christians). In the first text, ar-Rassī attacks Christianity by attempting to prove the refutability and illogicality of its belief in a divine Son of God, before arguing that the overall doctrines of Christianity are logically unacceptable. They, therefore, do not match Islam, which is now considered the *a priori* criterion of logicality and tenability.[168] In his turn, al-Warrāq also develops a much longer refutation of Christian faith that aims to prove its logical inauthenticity and falsehood. The three main sections of his treatise not only support ar-Rassī's refutation of Christ's divinity, but also, on the basis of rationality, argue even more strongly against the incarnation and the Trinity, revealing the extent of their author's knowledge of the three (Melkite, Jacobite and Nestorian) interpretations of these doctrines.[169] After studying these two polemics, Thomas notes the difference between the content of these two treatises, deducing the different goals of their authors. However, Thomas equally concedes many unmissible similarities between ar-Rassī's and al-Warrāq's styles. Both, Thomas maintains, demonstrate a vast, insightful knowledge of Christian belief, and both go on from that to make a rigorous attack on the logicality and rationality of the content of Christian doctrines. For both *mutakallims*, the criterion for judging this rationality is Islam itself, as they both believe that Islam is pure reason incarnate. Thomas deduces from this that the strategic method behind this approach is the conviction that "[the] refutation of the opposing faith is intimately related to the defence of one's own." [170] Refuting Christianity, therefore, serves the purpose of strengthening the position of Islam and proving its superiority.

Persuasive as Thomas' argument is, I would go still further in saying that the goal of this strategy is not only to show the religious superiority of Islam over Christianity, but also, and primarily, to counter Christians' scorn of Muslims by showing that the latter are more intellectually and culturally advanced than the former because Muslims follow a purely rational and authentically logical belief, while Christians are far from doing so. These clashes over socio-cultural status and attempts at counter-discrimination become clear when one realizes that the Muslim refutation of Christianity was conducted on the sole basis of

168 Ibid., pp. 260–267.
169 Ibid., pp. 268–274.
170 Ibid., pp. 274–275.

proving Christians' irrationality and the logical deviance of their beliefs, and not by using Qur'anic or scriptural proof-texting. Even when Christian interlocutors sometimes cited verses from the New Testament, they did not do so to prove a point by referring to the biblical text. Rather, they tried to show, using the best rational arguments they could assemble, that these biblical verses were not contradictory or illogical. Similarly, the refutations of Christianity that were made by Muslims cannot be considered as expressions of a polemic that relied on 'proof-texting,' even when they contained biblical references. This cannot be the case for two reasons. First, the strategy of refuting Christianity by means of *taḥrīf* (*abrogation/falsification*) accusation did not begin to characterize the Muslim discourse before Ibn Ḥazm in the 11th century.[171] Second, references to biblical or Qur'anic verses in early Christian-Muslim encounters were not made in order to explain such verses, but rather to show that the text, which contains these verses, was irrational and illogical.[172] The point Muslims wanted to make is that those who were religiously irrational, and who based their beliefs on unreasonable and unreliable sources, could not lay claim to any cultural superiority or social precedence over others. During the rule of al-Maʾmūn, for instance, a similar conviction would pave the way for a new ideological drive behind the Muslims' war against the Byzantines, who were then to be deemed benighted and culturally inferior to the Muslims because they (the Byzantines) had not preserved the intellectual heritage of their Greek ancestors while the Muslims had done so, by translating the ancient sciences into Arabic.[173]

---

171 Thus Martin Accad, "The Ultimate Proof-Text: The Interpretation of John 20.17 in Muslim-Christian Dialogue (Second/Eighth-Eighth/Fourteenth Centuries)," in *Christians at the Heart of Islamic Rule* ed. David Thomas, (Leiden: Brill, 2003), 199–214, p. 213. I disagree with Accad's calling of the Muslims' use of biblical verses, especially from John's Gospel, a 'proof-text' strategy. I believe that the mere reference to a biblical verse does not in itself mean that the Muslims used the Bible as a reliable text. Proof-texting surely indicates that the text cited is considered authentic and reliable by the user. In this case, however, the Muslims' concern was not to use the Bible to support their critique of Christian doctrines, but to show that these doctrines were based on a source that was rationally and logically unreliable.

172 Thus, Mark Swanson calls for the recognition of a "beyond prooftexting" use of religious texts in Christian-Muslim encounters in the second Islamic century: Mark N. Swanson, "Beyond Prooftexting: Approaches to the Qur'ān in Some Early Arabic Christian Apologies," *The Muslim World*, 88 (3–4) (1998), 297–319.

173 Dimitri Gutas, *Greek Thought, Arabic Culture*, pp. 84–85: "The total war against the Byzantines that [al-Maʾmūn] initiated had an ideological component that was new. The Byzantines were portrayed as deserving of Muslim attacks not only because they were infidels...but because they were also culturally benighted and inferior not only to Muslims but also to their own ancestors, the ancient Greeks. The Muslims, by contradistinction, in addition to being superior because of Islam, were also superior because they appreciated ancient Greek science and wisdom,

This socio-cultural context invites us, then, to reconsider the sequence of Christian-Muslim controversies and realize that it did not start with the Christians taking the initiative and writing explanations to their religious doctrines and then the Muslims replying negatively and polemically.[174] In fact, Christians were not initially concerned to initiate presenting a theological explanation of their faith to the Muslim invaders because they did not take their intellectual abilities seriously, but regarded them as culturally and ethnically inferior. Church prelates of various denominations in Syria and Palestine were occupied with either refuting other Christians' theologies or building diplomatic connections with their new rulers, hoping to save the Church's properties from confiscation and trying to persuade the Muslim caliphs that the Christian inhabitants of the Caliphate were not traitors or secret allies of the Byzantines. Theological knowledge was considered part and parcel of the cultural and educational prerogatives of urban citizens, who were by then mostly Christians and Jews. It was a knowledge restricted to the elites and not to be discussed or exchanged with the lowly common people, who were for the Christians of Syria, as their texts tell us, the newly arriving Peninsular Muslims.

Far from responding to a Christian theological initiative, the Muslims started to strike back against the cultural and ethnic contempt in which they were held by initiating challenging inquiries and critical arguments that demonstrated their rational abilities and cultural qualities and at the same time challenged the intellectual status of their Christian neighbours. As far as theology was concerned, the Christians found themselves on the defensive from the beginning and never on the offensive or the initiative-taking side. This is why they decided to write theological defences in the language used by the Muslims – not because they voluntarily and freely chose to do so, but because, contextually and strategically, they had no other option. Furthermore, it was the Muslims' attempt to prove their cultural and social standard by demonstrating their rationalism in

and had translated their books into Arabic." Gutas goes even further by linking this superiority to religion as well, in that the Byzantines had lost their intellectual heritage because they followed Christianity, whereas the Muslims welcomed this scientific and cultural excellence because they followed Islam (ibid., p. 85).

174 This seems to be David Thomas' view. He says: "Muslims of the early Abbasid era found little to agree with or approve of in attempts by Christians to explain their doctrines or defend them. The records that survive from the Muslim side of the encounter in the first four centuries of Islam show that far from being persuaded or even daunted by the arguments put forward by their Christian counterparts, Muslims were confident both of having truth and logic on their side, and of being able to prove the superiority of their own beliefs with a finality that put Christians very much on the defensive": D. Thomas, "Early Muslim Responses to Christianity," in *Christians at the Heart of Islamic Rule*, ed. David Thomas (Leiden: Brill, 2003), 231–254, p. 231.

religion and the extent of their scientific knowledge, and by undermining the rational basis of the Christians' religiosity, that, in turn, drove the Christian *mutakallimūn* to confront this challenging situation by a parallel reliance and equal emphasis on reason and logic. These Christians found themselves, as Sidney Griffith has said, "called upon also to defend their faith in the very idiom in which [Christianity] was challenged and critiqued."[175]

Given this cultural-social context, Dimitri Gutas' reading of interreligious dynamics during the Abbasid era – which witnessed the birth of the first Arabic apologetic reaction to the Islamic initial attack – is persuasive. Gutas accurately notes the Abbasid caliphs' ambition to establish a "commonwealth of Muslim citizens with equal rights and privileges."[176] It was to be expected that this ambition would make them encourage the non-Muslim inhabitants of Baghdad, who were then in the majority, to enjoy access to powerful positions and high intellectual and prestigious social status in order that Muslims would have the opportunity to learn from Christians and adopt their cultural and administrative skills, and then, later, replace them and continue building the Caliphate's glory. Yet, this would also create, as Gutas correctly notes, a new form of Islam that is different from that of the Umayyad era, namely an Islam with a clear and strong proselytizing orientation and energised by a growing self-confidence among Muslims about their religious faith, and their ability both to defend and prove the plausibility of their religion and to challenge non-Muslims, no matter how intellectual and educated they were, in religious and philosophical debates.[177] From this setting, Gutas draws the following accurate conclusion:

> The encroachment of Arabic Islam into the religions in the Near East was felt on many fronts, and indeed in unexpected ways of which non-Muslims had no experience from Umayyad times. Hence the palpable need to explain themselves and to maintain, enlarge, and at times even re-establish their rights and positions. As a result, the first Abbasid century saw an unprecedented rise in *Arabic* Christian apologetic writings directed against Islam (italics original).[178]

---

175 S. Griffith, "Answers for the Shaykh: A 'Melkite' Arabic Text from Sinai and the Doctrines of the Trinity and the Incarnation in 'Arab Orthodox 'Apologetics'," in *The Encounter of Eastern Christianity with Early Islam*, ed. Emmanouela Grypeou, Mark Swanson and David Thomas (Leiden: Brill, 2006), 277–309, p. 278.

176 Gutas, *Greek Thought, Arabic Culture*, p. 62.

177 Ibid., pp. 63–69. Gutas attributes the increase in the Muslims' confidence in their debating abilities to the massive translation movement, which the Abbasid caliphs strongly supported and fostered. This movement availed the Muslims for the first time of Greek texts, such as Aristotle's *Topics*, from which they learned how to argue logically and dialogue apologetically as effectively and skilfully as the Christians and the Jews.

178 Ibid., p. 66.

It is in this growing intellectual, apologetic context that one witnesses the birth of an orthodox theology, apologetically oriented and rationally founded, but most importantly written for the first time in Arabic and for a non-Christian, Arabic-speaking audience. This theological discourse was specifically and primarily shaped and developed, as Griffith correctly states, by the Melkite Christians of Syria and Palestine before, and even more influentially than, any other Christians "to meet the challenges of the Christian theological adversaries of the Melkites, to address in Arabic the Islamic critique of Christian doctrines and to find a vocabulary in Arabic that is sufficient to express the developing theological profile of Melkite creedal identity."[179]

III. The Melkite Church in the Land of Islam: The Birth of Arabic Theology

During the 8th and 9th centuries, the Melkite Church of Syria and Palestine found itself in the midst of this intellectually polemic atmosphere. The Muslim *mutakallimūn* started openly to promulgate the rational and philosophical arguments that disparaged the Christian faith, essentially maintaining that Christianity was unacceptably illogical and irrational. They tried to show that Christians had strayed in their religious beliefs and thinking from the scientific and philosophical truths that have been arrived at by the ancient Greek philosophers, such as Aristotle, Plato, Hippocrates, Democritus, Euclid and Galen. The Muslim *mutakkalims* made this allegation while they were simultaneously claiming that they themselves had adopted the precious legacy of Antiquity's intellectual sources, translated them into Arabic and taken them into account when structuring the religious thought of Islam. For instance, the refutation of Christianity by one of the prominent propagandists and supporters of al-Ma'mūn's policy, aj-Jāḥiẓ

179 Griffith, "Answers for the Shaykh," p. 280. See also on the birth of this orthodoxy S. H. Griffith, "The View of Islam from the Monasteries of Palestine"; Griffith, "The Monks of Palestine"; Griffith, *The Church in the Shadow of the Mosque*, pp. 45–74; Griffith, "The Church of Jerusalem and the 'Melkites'; Griffith, "The First Christian *Summa Theologiae*"; S. H. Griffith, "Comparative Religion in the Apologetics of the First Christian Arabic Theologians," in *The Beginnings of Christian Theology in Arabic: : Muslim-Christian Encounters in the Early Islamic Period* (Aldershot, UK: Ashgate Variorum, 2002), I, 63–87; Griffith, "From Aramaic to Arabic: the Languages of the Monasteries of Palestine in the Byzantine and Early Islamic Periods," in *The Beginnings of Christian Theology in Arabic: Muslim-Christian Encounters in the Early Islamic Period* (Aldershot, UK: Ashgate Variorum, 2002), X, 11–31; S. K. Samir, "The Earliest Arab Apology for Christianity (c. 750)," in *Christian Arabic Apologetics during the Abbasid Period (750–1258)*, ed. S. K. Samir and J. S. Nielsen (Leiden: Brill, 1994), 57–114.

(full name: Abū ʿUthmān ʿAmr ibn Baḥr al-Kinānī al-Fūqaymī al-Baṣrī), points out that what makes the Byzantine Christians and the Jews inferior in their religion is the latter's rejection of philosophy and the former's simplistic appropriation of Greek philosophical literature without a true and deep understanding of its content.[180] For aj-Jāḥiẓ, The Byzantines, despite their architectural and artistic achievements, cannot claim to have a philosophical and rational mind if they follow a religious belief that claims "there are three gods, two secret and one visible" and that "a creature became creator, a slave became master, a newly created being became an originally uncreated being, but was then crucified and killed with a crown of thorns on the head, and he disappeared only to bring himself back to life after death."[181] The core argument here is not that Christian faith is rationally and philosophically *less in degree* than Islam. It is rather that Christian faith is not rational or philosophical at all, and that, despite its Byzantine followers' usurpation of Greek philosophical literature, the claims of this religion, when judged by this very philosophical heritage, are totally false.

In this kind of polemics, the Christians were facing interreligious attacks and charges that were reminiscent, for example, of those, whom theologians and apologists such as Clement, Origen and Justin Martyr had to deal with during the 2nd and 3rd centuries. In Christian-Christian or Christian-pagan debates in previous centuries, Christian theologians used philosophy as a tool to strengthen their elaborations of faith, and to back up their clarifications and interpretations of certain biblical claims and terminological expressions about God and Jesus Christ. Rationalism and philosophy were just hermeneutical instruments rather than foundational criteria. During the age of Islam, Christians found themselves facing protagonists who not only rejected certain interpretations of Christian faith, but questioned the plausibility and rational truth of the faith itself. This brought into the interreligious arena of the region a new intellectual requirement. The Christians realized that they now had to show the Muslims that they were not only good theologians, but also qualified *philosophers*, or *mutakallimūn* as skilful as the Muslims. The Christians concluded that they could no longer bring the apologetic strategies they had employed in their internal debates to the table of dialogue with Muslims. They needed, instead, to write new apologetic literature capable of addressing a new kind of polemic. They equally perceived

180 aj-Jāḥiẓ, *Radd ʿalā an-Naṣārā* (A Response to the Nazarenes), in *Rasāʾil aj-Jāḥiẓ* (Aj-Jāḥiẓ's Letters), ed. A.M. Hārūn (Cairo: al-Khānjī, 1979), Vol. 3, 314–315; also cited in Gutas, *Greek Thought, Arabic Culture*, pp. 86–87.

181 aj-Jāḥiẓ, *Kitāb al-'Akhbār* (The Book of Chronicles), cited in F. Rosenthal, *The Classical Heritage of Islam* (London: Routledge & Kegan Paul, 1994), pp. 44–45; and also in Gutas, *Greek Thought, Arabic Culture*, p. 85.

that this new literature should not be simply an Arabic translation of the Christian literature of earlier centuries, but that they needed to develop a totally new literature, using new apologetic strategies and styles of argumentation that would demonstrate the philosophical and rational nature of Christian dogma.[182]

In the light of this demand for a new apologetic, the theological role of the fathers of Syria-Palestine's Melkite Church, the most prominent among whom is Theodore Abū Qurrah, stands centre-stage and deserves utmost appreciation. It is in Theodore Abū Qurrah's writings that we have the birth of this new form of Christian apologetic literature. There, we have for the first time a Christian apologetic text written in Arabic, shaped in line with philosophical and logical debate criteria and aims to prove, first and foremost, the philosophical solidity and rational tenability of orthodox Christian belief by means of the very same standards of reasoning that his Muslim opponents acknowledged. One should not undermine the extent of the transformation that was brought about by Theodore by narrowing it into a concern from Abū Qurrah's side to merely make Christian thought available to the Muslims in their own language. Abū Qurrah was not just a translator of texts. He was also a scholar of ideas. One should, thus, also examine carefully whether or not, in his translation of theological, Greek and Syriac, doctrinal and biblical terminology into Arabic, Abū Qurrah took Christian theology itself into new horizons of meaning, gave it new connotations and introduced into it new ideas. It is worth exploring whether Abū Qurrah drove orthodoxy itself into new linguistic and conceptual realms where Christian pedagogy had not ventured before. We should examine whether one can say that, in the attempt of theologians like Theodore Abū Qurrah to produce Christian *kalām* in Arabic, the Church was not only translating its thinking, but actually *re-forming* or even *transforming* it too.

---

182 Sidney Griffith eloquently describes this paradigm shift in the Christian apologetic tradition when he states: "Most of the major Christian writers in the early Abbasid period ... wrote general apologetic pamphlets, including both the principal and the secondary topic. Their methods of argumentation were parallel, *mutatis mutandis*, to the style of the discourse one may find in contemporary Muslim *kalām* texts." Griffith concludes from this, that the Christian *mutakallims* "actually adopted a way of presenting the traditional teachings of the church in an Arabic idiom conditioned by the Islamic frame of reference in the midst of which they lived. In other words, Christian *kalām* was an exercise in what modern day commentators might call enculturation, a process in which the doctrinal development consisted in the exploration of new dimensions of Christian truth, when that truth was considered from a hitherto unavailable or unexploited frame of reference": Sidney Griffith, "Faith and Reason in Christian *Kalām:* Theodore Abū Qurrah on Discerning the True Religion," in *Christian Arabic Apologetics during the Abbasid Period (750–1258)*, ed. Samir Khalil Samir and Jørgen S. Nielsen, Leiden: Brill, 1994), 1–43, pp. 4–5.

The features of this possible transformation of the theological mindset in the process of translating orthodoxy into Arabic will be traced, discussed and studied in detail in the chapters of the next part. Nevertheless, in the following paragraphs, I would like to set Theodore Abū Qurrah's theological discourse, and his attempt to defend before Muslims the rational and philosophical tenability of Christian faith, within the context of his ecclesial and theological tradition. I shall briefly consider this in the light of the orthodox, apologetic tradition that is found in other Melkite texts, with specific attention to the writings of John of Damascus, who lived and served in the context of the Christian community of Syria and Palestine, and to whom Theodore personally acknowledges his apprenticeship and intellectual allegiance. I will not do a compare-and-contrast analysis of the theological teachings of these two great Eastern theological minds, but will restrict my exposition in this chapter to how they touched upon Islam and how they thought one should interact with Muslims in theological-intellectual debate. Whenever necessary, I shall also refer to other Melkite apologetic texts to shed further light on the new apologetic style and argumentation strategy the Melkites developed in the age of Islam.

In his studies of the first Christian apologetic texts written in Arabic during the 9th and 10th centuries, Sidney Griffith pays careful attention to the theological texts composed by theologians and monks from the Melkite Church of Syria and Palestine, deeming them the first and pioneering Christian Arabic texts in history. Griffith divides this Christian Arabic literature into two main categories. The first he calls the 'church-books,' written for Christian education and to serve the internal purposes of Church life (i.e., expositions of the scriptures, patristic classics, inspirational homilies, lives of saints, creeds and canons). These books were written in Arabic in order to meet the growing needs of the members of the Melkite churches in Syria and Palestine, whose vernacular was dominantly Arabic, especially after those Melkites who lived in the Caliphate started to focus on their new eastern context and to cut their contacts with Byzantium during the first two centuries of the Abbasid rule.[183]

The second genre is the 'apologetic texts,' which mainly addressed the external inquiries and challenges that were raised by the surrounding Islamic atmosphere. Griffith maintains that the Melkites developed this literary genre "to bring the traditional theological considerations of their own Christian party to bear on the intellectual challenges of the day, in the very idiom of the current socio-political scene."[184] This contextualization of Christian theological tradition served

183 Griffith, "The Monks of Palestine," pp. 10 – 11.
184 Ibid., p. 4.

the following twofold purpose: responding directly to Muslims' criticisms of Christianity, and equipping the Christians themselves with, first, the persuasive reasoning needed to maintain their faith, and, second, the methods of persuasion necessary to counter increasing Islamization with a successful Christianization strategy. In this attempt to produce apologetic literature in fluent Arabic, Griffith spots the beginning of the historical attempt of Arabic-speaking Christians (the Melkites) to address issues beyond the boundaries of the life of their own communities – issues that must certainly have been raised in Arabic and which called for a fluent and persuasive response in the same language.[185]

In his *The Church in the Shadow of the Mosque*, Griffith elaborates further on some of the apologetic texts produced by the Melkites during the early Islamic era. Among the oldest Christian Arabic texts he points to is one preserved in a manuscript from Sinai (Sinai Arabic MS 154), and known in English as "On the triunity of the one God" (*fī Tathlīth Allah al-Wāḥid*).[186] The text is believed to have been written around 755. It presents an explanation of the doctrines of the Trinity and the incarnation, the messianic history of salvation and the Church's proclamation of the messianic identity of Jesus of Nazareth. It builds its argument upon a rigorous reliance on the scriptural attestation, and marrying this with an implicit invocation of ideas and claims from the Qur'an, though without precise citations.[187] Another text Griffith points to is one known as "Summary of the ways of faith." The text's unknown author explains in twenty-five chapters the cultural and religious circumstances that led Christians to develop literature about their faith, and then argues that, while the creedal, Nicene-Constantinopolitan, faith had been known to all the members of the Church because it was taught in the common language they all spoke in earlier centuries (i.e., Greek), the new generations of church members are not as well-versed in Christianity because the creed is not recited and taught in the current dominant spoken language: Arabic. The "Summary" therefore implicitly alludes to the historical need to develop a Christian theological apology not only to de-

185 Ibid., p. 10.

186 Griffith, *The Church in the Shadow of the Mosque*, pp. 53ff. See the English translation of this text in Margaret Dunlop Gibson (ed. and trans.), *An Arabic Version of the Acts of the Apostles and the Seven Catholic Epistles, with a Treatise on the Triune Nature of God*, Studia Sinaitica 7 (London: C.J. Clay and Sons, 1899), 74–107 (Arabic), 2–36 (English); see also M. Swanson, "Some Considerations for the Dating of *Fī tathlīth Allāh al-wāḥid* (Sinai Ar. 154) and *Aj-Jāmiʿ Wujūh al-Īmān* (London British Library, Or. 4950), in *Actes du quatrième congrès international d'études arabes chrétiennes*, ed. Samir Khali Samir (ed), in *Parole de l'Orient*, 18 (1993), 117–141; Samir, "The Earliest Arabic Apology for Christianity"; and Hoyland, *Seeing Islam as Others Saw It*, pp. 502–504.

187 Griffith, *The Church in Shadow of the Mosque*, pp. 54–55.

fend the faith against Muslim claims, but also to persuade Christians of the tenability and validity of the faith they inherited from their ancestors. These Christians need to be aided in understanding their religion in their present vernacular and in terms accessible to their present mindset, developed within the Islamic cultural setting.[188]

Other apologetic Arabic texts Griffith refers to and considers exemplary of Melkite theological literature during the Islamic era are those that follow a writing style found in earlier Syriac apologetic writs composed by Nestorians and Jacobites, that is, the 'question-and-answer' style.[189] Griffith finds an imitation of this apologetic style in an Arabic Melkite text, Oriental manuscript number 4950 in the British Library collection, written by the Melkite Stephen al-Ramlī in 877 at the monastery of Mar Chariton, which is usually given the title "Summary of the ways of faith in the Trinity of the unity of God, and in the incarnation of God the Word from the pure Virgin Mary." Griffith personally prefers to call this text *Summa Theologiae Arabica.*[190] Griffith adds to this text others, mostly still unpublished, that also follow the 'question-and-answer' style, such as the dialogue between the Christian monk and a Muslim *shaykh* on the Trinity and the incarnation, known as "Questions and answers, rational and divine" (*Masā'il wa-'Ajwibah, 'Aqliyya wa-Ilahiyya*).[191]

Griffith draws our attention to other Melkite texts that are reflective of different, though no less solidly and carefully composed, apologetic strategies and dialogical styles (e.g., 'epistolary exchange' and reports on conversations in the caliph's court[192]). These apologetic forms of writing are somewhat typical of the apologetic style that seems to have been dominant and central in the Melkite theological tradition, and which can be seen in the works of two major theologians in the history of that church: John of Damascus and Theodore Abū Qurrah. In the writings of these two theologians, though the first wrote in Greek and the second in Arabic, we find similar attempts to respond directly to the Muslim criticisms of the orthodox Christian faith and offering the members of the church some sources to prepare them intellectually for dealing with any threat to Christianity. Craig Hanson is persuasive in his suggestion that, for John of Damascus

188 Ibid., pp. 57 ff.
189 Ibid., pp. 81–86.
190 Ibid., p. 82.
191 Ibid., p. 83. see also Griffith, "Answers to the Shaykh". Outside the Melkite circle, Griffith points to the Nestorian, Arabic-speaking theologian 'Ammār al-Baṣrī's text "Book of Questions and Answers" (مسائل وأجوبة). On 'Ammār al-Baṣrī's apology, see Griffith, "Ammār al-Baṣrī's *Kitāb al-Burhān*"; Hoyland, *Seeing Islam as Others Saw It*, pp. 504–505.
192 Griffith, *The Church in Shadow of the Mosque*, pp. 77–81, 85–88.

and Theodore Abū Qurrah, the new threat did not come from the Arabs as people, for these two orthodox fathers and their church communities in Syria/Palestine already shared the same culture as the Arabs. Rather, the foe was a new religion called Islam. This explains the emphasis that was placed on facing Christianity's detractors as well as on fortifying the believers in their orthodox allegiance.[193] In the works of the Damascene and Abū Qurrah, we find a similar reliance on the 'question-and-answer' (*Erotupochriseis*) strategy as well as a defence of the same doctrines – of the Trinity, Christology and the incarnation – that dominated the defensive discourse of other apologetic texts written in Greek and Syriac.

Among the works of John of Damascus (Yūḥannā ibn Manṣūr ibn Ṣarjūn) are two texts that address Islam: chapter 100/101 of his book *De Haeresibus* (On heresies) – which comprises the second part of his major work *Pēgē Gnoseōs* (The fount of knowledge) – and a separate text called *Disputatio Saraceni et Christiani* (A dispute between a Muslim and a Christian). Scholars debate the authenticity of these two texts and doubt John's authorship,[194] but considering the historical

193 Craig L. Hanson, "Manuel I Comnenus and the 'God of Muhammad': A Study in Byzantine Ecclesiastical Politics," in *Medieval Christian Perceptions of Islam* (ed. John V. Tolan, New York: Routledge, 2000), 55–82, p. 58. Hanson further believes that "for such Christians the Byzantine emperor was still the legitimate ruler of their lands," and that there were Christian, Byzantine loyalists in the Muslim-dominated territory (ibid., p. 58). Andrew Louth also seems to concur with this view: Louth, *St. John of Damascus*, pp. 15ff. It is worth arguing, nevertheless, that John's official role in the Umayyad caliphs' courts and his family's long history of service to the Muslim caliphate, though historically and scholarly debated, and Theodore's cultural and geographical origin, indicate that the theological allegiance of these two fathers, which affiliates them to Byzantine orthodoxy, does not necessarily prove their political allegiance to Byzantine rule and the Byzantine state. One should not here identify ecclesial and theological adherence with political affiliation. On this, Sidney Griffith and Daniel Sahas are more convincing in reminding us that John used to be called 'Saracen-minded' by the iconoclast Christians of Constantinople: D.J. Sahas, *Icon and Logos: Sources in Eighth-Century Iconoclasm* (Toronto: University of Toronto Press, 1986), p. 168. Griffith is right in critiquing the allegation of allegiance to Byzantium as an attempt to read "John of Damascus's works entirely from the point of view of Byzantium, where John never lived and where his writings on subjects other than the veneration of the holy icons made no notable impression until some centuries after his lifetime": Griffith, *The Church in Shadow of the Mosque*, p. 40, referring also to Basil Studer, *Die theologische Arbeitsweise des Johannes von Damaskus* (Ettal, Germany: Buch-Kunstverlag, 1956), p. 131.

194 On the authenticity of these two texts, see Louth, *St. John Damascene*, pp. 76–83; Hoyland, *Seeing Islam as Others Saw It*, pp. 485, 489; Sahas, *John of Damascus on Islam*, pp. 99–122; Hanson, "Manuel I Comnenus," p. 63; John Meyendorff, "Byzantine Views of Islam," *Dumbarton Oaks Papers*, 18 (1964), 115–132, pp. 116–118; Speros Vryonis, *The Decline of Medieval Hellenism in Asia Minor and the Process of Islamization from the Eleventh through the Fifteenth Century* (Aldershot: Ashgate Variorum, 2001), p. 422. See also on the authenticity of the *Disputatio*, Daniel

authenticity of these texts, leave alone verifying the historical data about John of Damascus himself, is beyond the scope of this study.[195] In the following paragraphs, I shall comment on these texts on the basis that they were *at least* written by a Melkite theologian and point to some elements characteristic of this author's apologetic style. I shall investigate how this Melkite theologian – say John of Damascus – uses the 'question-and-answer' apologetic method and what is the nature of his response to Islam. I shall then do the same with respect to some of Theodore Abū Qurrah's texts, looking for the similarities and differences between John's and Abū Qurrah's use of the 'question-and-answer' strategy and what it is in the latter's apologetic use of this strategy that makes his dialogical approach to Islam unique and special in his church tradition.

Let me start, then, with John of Damascus' two texts. What is striking in chapter 100/101 of John's *De Haeresibus* is the tone and method of argument John uses to appraise the Ishmaelites' religion. Robert Hoyland describes John's words in the first part of the chapter about Islam's origin and emergence as "a succinct introduction" to Islam and "a concise exposition" of its views about God, Christ and Muhammad.[196] I agree with Hoyland about the conciseness of the Damascene's description of Islam. However, I would not call his exposition an attempt to introduce what is Islam and what its followers believe. John's language indicates that, rather than introducing Islam to his readers, he is actually trying to alarm them about this new heresy and to lure them away from any association with its followers. And in order to achieve this purpose, the Damascene uses the most polemic and offensive language one can imagine: the Ishmaelites are superstitious deceivers and the "for-runners of the Antichrist;"[197] they are idolaters and worshipers of the moon, and have lately become followers of a false prophet and believers in a scripture that is full of

Sahas, *John of Damascus on Islam*, pp. 99–102; and Peter Schadler, "The Dialogue between a Saracen and a Christian," in *Christian-Muslim Relations, A Bibliographical History (600–900)*, David Thomas and Barbara Roggema, et. al., (Leiden: Brill, 2009), Vol. 1, pp. 367–370.

195 One good presentation and discussion of some aspects of the data on John of Damascus' life is Rocio Daga Portillo, "The Arabic Life of St. John of Damascus," *Parole de l'Orient*, 21 (1996), 157–188.

196 Hoyland, *Seeing Islam as Others Saw It*, pp. 485–486.

197 In reading chapter 100/101 and also the text of *Disputatio Saraceni et Christiani*, I follow the English translation of these Greek texts in Sahas, *John of Damascus on Islam*, Appendix I, pp. 133–141. On John of Damascus' disputative tone in his polemics against Islam, see also Radko Popov, "Speaking His Mind in a Multi-Cultural and Multi-Religious Society: John of Damascus and His Knowledge of Islam in Chapter 101 ("The Heresy of the Ishmaelites") of His Work Concerning Heresy," in *Two Traditions One Space: Orthodox Christians and Muslims in Dialogue*, ed. George C. Papademetriou (Boston, MA: Somerset Hall Press, 2011), 109–143.

pronouncements worthy of laughter. In this polemic tone, one can see the same scorn and arrogance as in other texts (see the previous chapter) in which Christian authors belittled the social and cultural background of the newcomers from the southern Peninsular desert.

One wonders here how a man who lived most of his adult, religious and civil life in the Arab cultural context of the dominantly Muslim Syria/Palestine, who was even called by an Arab name (Yūḥannā ibn Manṣūr ibn Ṣarjūn) and who was despised by the Byzantine orthodoxy of Constantinople because of his "Saracen mind",[198] could use such aggressive, scornful language to describe the religion of the people he lived among and served for almost a lifetime. Was this chapter written in this inimical tone to 'let off steam,' now that John was a monk in Mar Sabas and no longer a civil servant in the caliphal palace, where he had to excel not only in carrying out his administrative duties but also in diplomatic eloquence and pliability and in showing submission to, and respect and support for his leaders' dogmas? Did John write in this blunt aggressive language in an attempt to be regarded as Christian-minded rather than 'Saracen-minded' by his Byzantine fellow Christians, now that he had dedicated his life to the service of the Church and their wellbeing and was seriously concerned to affirm his descent from Syro-Palestinian, Arab Christianity and his allegiance to its causes[199] – an allegiance that may have fuelled along other things the posthumous

---

198 Sidney Griffith points to John's tangential relation with the Christian atmosphere and his marginal interest in the theological debates that characterized the Byzantine Christianity of Constantinople and maintains that John's reputation for being "Saracen-minded" deprived his writings and theology of a positive reception in Byzantium, until the 12th – 13th centuries: Griffith, "The Church of Jerusalem and the 'Melkites'," pp. 191 – 192. Griffith disagrees here with Andrew Louth, who believes that John is to be seen as a "Byzantine churchman," whose heart always felt that it belonged there: Louth, *St. John Damascene*, p. 27. Also, in his comment on the conviction of some scholars that John of Damascus was appreciated and respected in Constantinople during his lifetime, Sidney Griffith conspicuously rejects this view and affirms that, on the contrary, the Damascene was rather "despised" during his life-time by Constantinopolitan Byzantium and his works were only appreciated there long after his death. Griffith describes the opinion of these scholars as a "thoroughly anachronistic view, based on a reading of John's work through lenses crafted after his time in Byzantium and long after the final triumph of 'orthodoxy' in Constantinople in the ninth century. This approach co-opts John of Damascus out of his own milieu and into a Byzantine frame of reference which was never his own, often discounting the issues which were in fact most important to him and highlighting others which reflect more the concerns of latter day scholars of Byzantine theology": S. Griffith, "John of Damascus and the Church in Syria in the Umayyad Era: The Intellectual and Cultural Milieu of Orthodox Christians in the World of Islam," *Hugoye: A Journal of Syriac Studies*, 11 (2) (2008), 1 – 34, p. 23.

199 On the Damascene's allegiance to the Arab Christianity of Syria/Palestine, rather than to the Byzantine, Daniel Sahas says "notwithstanding the fact that the general iconoclastic climate

negative image the Greek-speaking Byzantine Christians imposed on the Damascene in its 754 synodal anathema?[200] Or, could John's humiliating polemic severity really have expressed the Damascene's personal conviction, arrived at through his first-hand, human-level experience of Islam, that these so-called 'Ishmaelites' had gone totally astray and were to be completely condemned for following a false religion?

These options are equally possible but cannot all be true. They remain questions that are open to historical scholarship. Whatever the case may be, the point here is that in his apologetic interaction with Islam in *De Haeresibus*, John of Damascus does not adopt an objective, neutral approach towards Islam. The text does not depict an interlocutor who comes to the dialogue with an open interest in knowing the other. Rather, John starts with a clear judgment that Islam is a false, superstitious religion, whose followers are the antichrist. His language indicates that, for John, Muslims are not really "in the same world of discourse with the Christians when it comes to religious matters."[201] They are actually outside the sphere of discourse on right religion altogether. Islam for John is not another religion, or a mistaken interpretation of Christianity. Rather, Islam is not a 'religion' at all; it is a false religion, whose followers are "mutilators (*coptas*) of God."[202] The fact that John includes Islam within the list of Christian heresies does not in itself militate against the possibility that he considered it a 'non-religion,' because one cannot deny the clear offensiveness and negativity in John's words. On the contrary, John's evident negativity against Islam may actually shed doubt on whether chapter 100/101 was originally part of *De Haeresibus* or whether it was added by a later editor, who, by including John's pages on Islam within

---

and the official hostility of the Greek speaking Byzantium toward the cult of saints might have been the cause of composing the life of an ardent iconophile in Arabic rather than in Greek, one can also read in this action the Arab Christian desire to affirm John of Damascus as the product of Syro-Palestinian Arab Christianity, and a saintly man of *Arab* Christian descent and spirituality": Sahas, "The Arab Character of the Christian Disputation with Islam," p. 188, see also Sahas' discussion on pp. 186–190, and note especially footnote 26 on p. 190.

200 The 754 Synod in Hiereia, which was called by Emperor Constantine V, anathematized John in the following terms: "to Mansur, the one with a vile-sounding name and of Saracen opinion, anathema
to the worshiper of icons and writer of falsehoods, Mansur, anathema
to the insulter of Christ and conspirator against the empire, Mansur, anathema
to the teacher of impiety and miss-interpreter of the Holy Scripture, Mansur, anathema.": Louth, *St John Damascene*, p. 197. See also Sahas, *Icon and Logos*, pp. 168–169.

201 Thus Griffith, *The Church in the Shadow of the Mosque*, p. 42. Griffith does not understate the substantial difference between these two religions.

202 Sahas, *John of Damascus on Islam*, p. 137.

his book on heresies wanted, in fact, to emphasise the Damascene's enmity to the Byzantine Church by making readers conclude that John considered Islam as much a religion as Christianity, albeit full of mistaken ideas. Be that as it may, I believe that the author of this last chapter on Islam is totally denying the religious nature of this purported 'religion.' Regarding Sahas' description of this text as a "brief but systematic summary and refutation" of Islam,[203] I agree with calling it a systematic and brief *refutation*, but not a summary.

After pouring scorn on Islam as a religion, John of Damascus addresses certain Muslim criticisms of the Christian faith. The prophet of Islam, John first notes, acknowledges Jesus' prophetic status and miraculous birth from a virgin. He calls Jesus "the word of God, and his spirit." Yet, John affirms, the Muslim prophet also maintains that Jesus is merely "created and a servant", and rejects his crucifixion and death, stressing instead that God took him up to himself because he loved him and allowed the Jews to crucify the shadow of the real person.[204] From Muhammad's view, John moves to the Arab prophet's followers' contradictory ideas about Christ. He points to their allegation that Jesus himself denied before God that he ever attributed a divine nature to himself or boasted about his service to God, blaming for these sayings men among his followers who went astray and fell into error.[205] In addition to the question of the identity of Jesus, John goes on to address in the following paragraphs the Muslims' challenge about the nature of God (the issue of Association) and the veneration of the cross.[206]

The worthwhile question here is how does John of Damascus deal with these challenging inquiries? Does he offer a full-fledged, rationally structured theological response? John's discussion style shows that, rather than presenting a sophisticated and skilfully designed 'question-and-answer' apology, he opts for responding to the Muslims' questions with a counter-inquiry, a 'question-question' strategy. To the Muslims' questions about Jesus' divinity and the evidence for it, John responds with questions on the evidence for the authenticity and reliability of the Qur'anic text, and on the authentication of Muhammad's prophethood:

> "We ask: and which is the one who gives witness that God has given to [Muhammad] the Scriptures? And which of the prophets foretold that such a prophet would arise? … How did the scripture come down to your prophet, this is what we are asking?"[207]

203 Sahas, "The Arab Character of the Christian Disputation with Islam," pp. 195–196.
204 Ibid., p. 133.
205 Ibid., p. 134.
206 Ibid., pp. 135–141.
207 Ibid., p .135.

To the Muslims' accusation that Christians associated other deities with God, one might expect John, with his sharp and powerful theological mind, to offer a theological explanation of the doctrine of the Trinity, or at least to refer inquirers to the doctrinal and philosophical discourse on the Trinity and Christology that he had developed in other parts of his three-volume work, *The Fountain of Knowledge*. But we find none of these in the text. Instead of a truly theological or philosophical answer, the Damascene again presents counter-questions: "Since you say that Christ is word and spirit of God, how do you scold us as Associators?"[208] And similarly, to the Muslims' criticism of Christian veneration of the cross, John neither develops a soteriological discourse, nor explains the ecclesiological and practical-religious dimensions of such veneration. He turns instead to the Islamic religious texts and practices and raises questions about their validity, morality and logical plausibility. On venerating the cross, John reacts by asking: "How is it that you rub yourselves against a stone by your *Habathan*, and you express your adoration to the stone by kissing it?" And, then, on the Qur'anic stories about the camel and paradise, he asks in almost ironic mockery: "How, then, did your prophet not think of all these, that they might happen to you in the paradise of delight?"[209]

In this apologetic style, we find an absence of any attempt to begin by introducing the main elements of the Islamic faith, proceed to an explanation of Christian faith that would be accessible and understandable (even if not eventually adoptable or acceptable) to Muslims, and finally present adequate theological answers to the Muslims' questions. What chapter 100/101 of *De Haeresibus* presents is an orthodox author resorting to a disparaging description of Islam and changing the 'question-and-answer' strategy to a 'question-question' approach; as if the main goal is to show that what counts is not whose answers are more persuasive and unbeatable, but whose questions are more intellectually subtle and rationally solid. The text on the heresy of the Ishmaelites in *De Haeresibus* does not reflect a Christian-Muslim dialogical interaction in the real sense of the word. It rather evinces the same cultural and intellectual haughtiness and scorn with which the urban inhabitants of Byzantine Greater Syria in general, and Greek-speaking Christians in particular, regarded the Muslim, bedouin invaders from the Arabian Peninsula in the early Islamic era (as shown in Chapter One).[210]

---

208 Ibid., p. 137.

209 Ibid., pp. 140 – 141.

210 Perceiving John's strong polemic and even inaccurate distortion of Islam, Sidney Griffith gives the following convincing explanation: "No doubt an important part of his polemical purpose in this enterprise would have been to provide a debater's arsenal of arguments for deploy-

The other text attributed to John of Damascus (or at least to a Melkite theologian), *Disputatio Saraceni et Christiani*, is notably different, however. If we do not follow the line of assuming that the author of this text was a Melkite John other than the Damascene, then we are left with the proposition that we have here the same John of Damascus, albeit writing on a different day, in a different mode and with other intentions in mind.[211] This time, John is less crude and polemic, far more responsive and thoughtful and more clearly systematic and dialogical in his approach. The differences in tone, argumentation strategy and orientation between chapter 100/101 of *De Haeresibus* and *Disputatio Saraceni et Christiani* are too obvious to pass unnoticed. This is the most probable explanation for why readers of these texts have come to the conclusion that they originated from the pens of different authors, and may even reflect Christian-Muslim interactions from totally different historical eras. This conceded, the remaining, no less noticeable common feature between the two texts is their orthodox content and Greek language, which conspicuously paves the way for deeming them to be the intellectual and literary production of a Melkite apologist.

What the *Disputatio Saraceni et Christiani* has in common with chapter 100/101 on the heresy of the Ishmaelites is the argument about the description of Jesus in the Qur'an as 'word and spirit of God' and whether this allows the Muslims to say that he was created like other creatures.[212] In addition, the *Disputatio* records Christian responses to a Saracen on two other subjects: 1) the origin of Good and Evil in relation to human free will, human conduct and God's redemption,[213] and 2) the two natures of Jesus Christ.[214] In discussing these two subjects, the author follows a clear 'question-and-answer' strategy and avoids challenging the Saracen with a counter-question that endeavours to prove the logical untenability or intellectual poverty of Islam. On the contrary, the Christian interlocutor appreciates the sophistication and wit of the Muslim's questions, which may be read as the author's implicit acknowledgment of the Muslim's intellectual abilities. Furthermore, the author's appreciation of the profoundness of the Saracen's questions appears in the Christian's full engagement in presenting Christian answers that are sufficiently detailed and solidly structured.

---

ment against Christians tempted to convert to Islam": Griffith, "The Church of Jerusalem and the 'Melkites'," p. 195.

211 Andrew Louth offers a reasonable justification for studying this text as one of John's writing when he says "it is appropriate to discuss it here, for it concerns issues that were live in the Damascene's time, issues to which he certainly devoted attention": Louth, *St John Damascene*, p. 81.

212 Sahas, *John of Damascus on Islam*, Appendix. II, pp. 143–155, 149–153.

213 Ibid., pp. 143–149.

214 Ibid., pp. 153–155.

What we read in the *Disputatio*, in obvious contrast with *De Haeresibus*, is not even as argumentative as a dispute or a debate. It is more likely a friendly conversation with a Saracen who is almost *learning* about Christianity, rather than someone eager to show its intellectual unreliability. Moreover, the text reflects a positive attitude towards the Saracen's religious text that is worth pondering. Except for the final paragraph of the chapter on the Ishmailites in *De Haeresibus*, the Qur'anic stories cited there are referred to in a sarcastic and derogatory manner and the Qur'an's authenticity is explicitly questioned in order to denigrate the religious identity of Islam. Things are different in the *Disputatio*, where the Christian speaker refers to the Muslim's religious scripture and uses it comparatively to clarify to the Saracen what the Bible states about Christ, aiming ultimately at persuading him of the commonality between the Bible and the Qur'an.[215] Sidney Griffith notes that, in their concern to develop a theological, apologetic discourse in Arabic, the Melkites realized the necessity of adopting "an Islam-inspired approach" different from the traditional Christian way of defending Christian doctrines.[216] One may then propose that in a text such as the *Disputatio* we have perhaps one of the earliest versions of a revision of Christian apologetic methods. What matters more here is to note that, instead of defensive contempt and haughty indifference, we have in the *Disputatio* an author opting for positive engagement and tolerant discussion. Instead of ignoring the Muslim's questions by throwing in his face defensive and ironic counter-questions, we have a Christian thinking seriously about the issues and trying to formulate plausible answers using the best techniques of logic and persuasion that he knows.[217]

One may, then, propose that from chapter 100/101 to the *Disputatio* there is a development in Melkite orthodox apologetic strategy towards Islam from a polemic attitude motivated by scorn and underestimation to an intellectual interac-

215 Ibid., p. 151. "And if [the Saracen] tells you, 'How did God descend into the womb of a woman', say to him, 'let us make use of your scripture and of my Scripture; your scripture says that God cleansed the Virgin Mary above all other women and the Spirit of God and the Word descended into her; and my Gospel says, 'The Holy Spirit will come upon you, and the power of the Most High will overshadow you.' Here is one voice in both statements and one meaning."

216 Griffith, "The Church of Jerusalem and the 'Melkites'," p.197.

217 This seriousness supports Sidney Griffith's belief that John of Damascus was familiar with the writings and questions of the famous Muslim thinkers and authors who were known in Umayyad Damascus, such as Maʿbad al-Juhānī, al-Ḥasan al-Baṣrī, Ghaylān ad-Dimashqī, Jahm ibn Ṣafwān, Wāṣil ibn ʿAṭāʾ and ʿAmr ibn ʿUbayd. This knowledge may be reflected in the questions he addresses in his controversy with Islamic polemicists. See: Griffith, "John of Damascus and the Church in Syria," p. 19.

tion driven by a concern for explanation, persuasion and relationality. In the Melkite literary tradition, this process reaches its peak in the writings of Theodore Abū Qurrah.

IV. Theodore Abū Qurrah as an Apologetic *Mutakallim*: Remarks on Style

Abū Qurrah's works indicate that his main concern was to give a specific response to the Muslim *mutakallimūn*'s attack on the logical and rational plausibility of the Christian faith. Perennially speaking, his writings may suggest that he occasionally resorted in his discourse to strong, crude and even harshly offensive and aggressive apologetic language, similar to that used by John of Damascus. We find examples in his debate with Muslims in the court of the Caliph al-Maʿmūn (*al-Mujādalah*) and *Maymar fī al-Ḥuriyyah* (Maymar on freedom). There, Abū Qurrah sometimes calls his interlocutors – whether Muslims or Christians from other churches – ignorant, mentally blind, stupid, led astray, and ungrateful. He also rejects many Islamic religious claims bluntly and assertively without using any irenic diplomatic expressions.[218] One can see in this a sign of Abū Qurrah's allegiance to the polemic legacy of his theological mentor, John of Damascus. Having said that, one should go beyond the offensive, harsh terms that Abū Qurrah uses in some of his texts and pay more attention to his argumentation strategy and apologetic purposes.[219]Abū Qurrah's overall

---

218 Theodore Abū Qurrah, *Abū Qurrah wa-al-Maʾmūn: al-Mujādalah* (Abū Qurrah and al-Maʾmūn: The Debate), ed. Wafīq Naṣrī, SJ (Beirut: CEDRAC (USJ), 2010); and Abū Qurrah, *Maymar fī al-Ḥurriyah* (Maymar on freedom), ed. Samir Khalil Samir, SJ, *Al-Mashriq*, 79 (2) (2005), 437–468, and 80 (1) (2006), 191–222. Some of Abū Qurrah's Greek apologetic texts even contain insulting references to the Prophet Muhammad. For instance, in his *Opusculum 20* (written in Greek; PG 97: 1545C), Abū Qurrah describes Muhammad as the "deranged pseudoprophet of the Hagarenes," who is "under the influence of the devil": cited in Daniel Sahas, "'Holosphyros'? A Byzantine Perception of 'The God of Muhammad'," in *Christian-Muslim Encounters*, ed. Yvonne Yazbeck Ḥaddād and Wadīʿ Zaidān Ḥaddād (Gainesville: University Press of Florida, 1995), 109–125, p. 111. We do not find similar offensive language used about the Prophet in Abū Qurrah's Arabic works. A plausible reason for this is that the Arabic texts would be read by the Muslims, so the language had to be as unoffensive as possible, lest the Muslims refuse to follow the argument openly and tolerantly, while the Greek texts were mostly addressed to Christians, so there Abū Qurrah could be less diplomatic and more explicitly expressive of his personal convictions.

219 Abū Qurrah's vigorous criticism of the Qur'an and offensive disparagement of his Muslim interlocutors in the *Mujādalah* has led scholars seriously to doubt that this text was the production of Abū Qurrah's own quill. See on this Wafīq Naṣrī's introduction to Abū Qurrah's *Mujāda-*

debate methodology, as I shall show in this section, goes beyond the earlier 'question-question' apologetic style of his Melkite predecessors and reflects a concern to present clearly philosophical explications and persuasive theological answers to questions put by non-Melkite Christians and non-Christians.

One of Abū Qurrah's works that reflects this methodology is his *Maymar fī Wūjūd al-Khaliq wad-Dīn al-Qawīm* (Maymar on the existence of the Creator and the right religion). Instead of starting with ready-made assumptions, our theologian starts his discourse there by listening to the followers of other religious ways. He gives these interlocutors space to introduce their beliefs without interacting personally with what they say or debating its content. Instead of a polemic appraisal or negative prejudices, the Melkite interlocutor reveals openness and readiness to let the others speak their mind and express their convictions freely and fairly.[220] Underlying this beginning is the following main question: how do we come to know which of all the religions is the true religion? Abū Qurrah's *maymar* states that, first, we start knowing each religion from those who follow it, not by means of any prior knowledge we may have about what these religions claim. Second, we set these religions' claims alongside each other within a comparative, analytical framework. From this comparative analysis, Abū Qurrah eventually concludes that all religions more or less speak about deity, good and evil and reward and punishment. These three elements demonstrate a commonality between religions. However, religions differ from each other in how each understands these three elements and how each expresses that understanding.

From the stages of exposition and comparison, Abū Qurrah moves to the third stage of solving the religious dilemma and deciding which religion is the true one. The basic guiding principle here is that only one of the religions must represent the belief that people should follow, and the thinker should find out which one is it.[221] According to Abu Qurrah, one of the common ways

---

lah, pp. 53–65; and Georg Graf, *Die Arabischen Schriften des Theodore Abū Qurrah*, pp. 78–83. And, for a scholarly response to this scepticism and an affirmation that this text is authentically Abū Qurran, see also Wafīq Naṣrī in Abū Qurrah, *al-Mujādalah*, pp. 67–93; and Alfred Guillaume, "Theodore Abū Qurrah as Apologist," pp. 42–45.

220 Abū Qurrah, *Maymar fī Wujūd al-Khāliq wad-Din al-Qawīm* (Maymar on the existence of the Creator and the right religion), ed. Ignace Dick (Jounieh: Librairie St Paul/Rome: The Papal Oriental Institute, 1982). For a valuable analysis of Theodore Abū Qurrah's argument in this maymar, see also Griffith, "Faith and Reason in Christian *Kalām*," pp. 9ff; and Orsolya Varsanyi, "The Role of the Intellect in Theodore Abū Qurrah's *On the True Religion* in Comparison with His Contemporaries' Use of the Term," *Parole de l'Orient*, 34 (2009), 51–60, pp. 52–54.

221 Abū Qurrah, *Maymar fī Wujūd al-Khāliq wad-Din al-Qawīm* (Maymar in the existence of the Creator and the right religion), prt. 2, ch. 8, pt. 6–8.

people follow to decide which is the true religion is to consider as reliable the religion that claims that God sent to his followers a 'messenger' (*rasūl*) and provided them with a 'book' (*kitāb*) to guide them to the truth and lead them away from the fate of condemnation. But Abū Qurrah then comments that, although these are occasionally reliable criteria, it is easy to see that all the religions without exception, speak of a 'messenger' from God and argue that the 'book' this messenger brought to them as the message from God is the only true 'book.' That being so, the question "Which religion is the true one?" then becomes "Which religious 'messenger' among the messengers and which religious 'book' among the books are the true ones? Can we know this with the help of religions?" Abū Qurrah affirms that this is not possible, for the religions' messengers speak against each other and each one presents an argument to prove the falsehood and fraudulence of the others' messages.[222]

One concludes from this argument that Abū Qurrah has serious reservations about the religions' habit of refuting each other, though not necessarily about every element in the content of such refutations. This is why he argues that instead of offensiveness and enmity, one needs to assess the validity and plausibility of the claims of all religions – about themselves as well as against each other – by means of an external, reliable criterion of investigation that makes it possible to see: 1) which religion's claims about God's characteristics are in harmony with God's reality and which are not, and 2) whose prescription for healing from sin concurs with what is known about 'healing' and whose does not.[223] Now, when we track down the investigation criterion Abū Qurrah refers to, we realize that it is the power of reason that God has bestowed upon humankind and commanded us to use in order to know the divine, to know and do what is good and to know and avoid evil.[224]

What makes us able to know the true religion from the false? Abū Qurrah says it is not the scriptures of these religions, but rather human reason. The scriptures and their messengers' claims should both be judged by reason

---

"6. وأمرهم على أحد وجهين: إما ألا يكون فيهم ولا واحد جاء من عند الله، وإما إن كان فيهم أحد فهو واحد.7. ويجدر أن يكون فيهم واحد مما يعرف من فضل الله وعنايته بأمر خلقه. 8. ولكن كيف الحيلة إلى معرفة هذا الواحد؟"

"6. the situation [of these religions] is one of two cases: either none of them is from God, or if any is from God, it is only one. 7. there must be among them one [religion] expressive of the known providence and grace of God towards His creatures. 8. but how can one get to know [which religion it is]?"

222 Ibid., 2.8.20 – 21.

223 Ibid., 2.8.26.

224 Ibid., 2.8.30.

والآن ينبغي لنا أن ندع الكتب ناحية ونسأل العقل كيف عرفت صفات الله التي لا تبصرها الحواس ولا تدركها العقول من شبه طبيعة الإنسان. وإذا أخبرنا بذلك وعرفناه قسنا هذه الكتب التي عندنا...فالكتاب الذي نجد فيه ذلك، عرفناه أنه من الله

> Now, we should ... put the scriptures aside and ask reason: how did you know the attributes of God, which the senses cannot perceive or minds apprehend, from its image in human nature? ... if [reason] answered us and we knew how, we could then examine the books we have, and the book that contains the same knowledge, we would know that it is from God, we will [then] accept and confirm it, throwing others away.[225]

When in the following chapters of his maymar Abū Qurrah applies the criterion of reason to the scriptures of the religions, he discovers that only the Christian Gospel contains the rational understanding of God, good and evil and salvation and condemnation, to which the criterion of reason naturally leads. The Gospel speaks about God, he says, exactly as our reason tells us about God from his image in our human nature.[226] The Gospel alone calls us to follow the way of righteousness and love as we learned about them by virtue of their image in our human nature.[227] It is also the Gospel alone that offers the promise of being truly with God that concurs fully with what our human nature seeks rationally and aspires to from the relationship with God.[228] From studying the Christian texts and judging their content by the rules of reason and logic, Abū Qurrah concludes:

لذلك نؤمن بهذا الدين ونتخذه ونتمسك به ونصبر على البلايا في الدنيا من أجله، للرجاء الذي وعد، ونموت على ذلك ونؤمل أن نلقى وجه الذي الله عليه، ونرمح ما سواه ونبعده ونقصيه ولا نعده شيئاً

> Therefore, we believe in this religion, we adopt it and we adhere to it, tolerating for its sake the world's tribulations, for the sake of the hope it promises, and we die with it hoping to meet the face of God on it, and we cast away anything else and reject it and do away with it and consider it nothing.[229]

In the rest of the maymar, Abū Qurrah moves from justifying the use of reason as a criterion for deciding which is the true religion, into pursuing an apologetic elaboration on the correctness and reliability of the religion that he now deems

---

225 Ibid., 2.8.37–38.

226 Ibid., 2.12.4–5, 16.

"[الإنجيل] وصف الله على ما علمنا ثلاثة وجوه: آب وابن وروح قدس...هذا ما علمتنا طبيعتنا من شبهها بالله سواء"

"[The Gospel] describes God, as it teaches us, as three faces: Father, Son and Holy Spirit ... this is what our [human] nature taught us from its likeness to God."

227 Ibid., 2.13.1 ff.

228 Ibid., 2.14.1–24.

229 Ibid., 2.14.30–31.

to be the only true faith according to reason. Thus, he responds to the Marcionites' rejection of the Old Testament by citing the Gospel, and then he argues for the reliability of Christianity on the basis of miracles. One might wonder here whether Abū Qurrah is contradicting his previous claim that the validity of any message should not be proved by proof-texting or by referring to the textual content of the message itself. What Abū Qurrah is doing here, however, is relying on the Gospel's textual testimony *after*, and not before, verifying by the use of reason that this scripture alone meets the criterion of rationality and represents true logic. His rationale here is as follows: texts do not prove the truth of anything. However, it is ascertained that if the content of a certain text meets the demands of human reason, that text can then reliably be used to validate any other claim. If the text meets the criterion of reason, it can be used as a criterion of truth, but one should first prove that the text can be logically verified.

The same process of starting with argument *from* reason and then ending with interpretation of scriptural and traditional texts is characteristic of Abū Qurrah's apologetic discourse in his *Maymar fī Ikrām al-Aiqūnāt* (Maymar on the veneration of icons). Before identifying some of the main elements in Abū Qurrah's argumentation strategy in this text, let me first point to an important aspect of his apologetic that can be gleaned from discerning the identity of the other involved parties in this debate: Abū Qurrah's friend, who asked him to write this maymar, and Abū Qurrah's interlocutors. In his discussion on the identity of Abū Qurrah's friend, Ignace Dick claims that he is a person residing in ar-Rahā and that he is John, the Melkite bishop of that city, who is said in other manuscripts to have taken part in a debate on Christian faith at the court of Hārūn ar-Rashīd. Dick also avers that this John was a friend and compatriot of Abū Qurrah, who addressed him as a church prelate of a similar rank to his own, since Abū Qurrah calls him 'our brother' (*akhāna*). Dick supports his proposal by citing the sentence with which Abū Qurrah begins his maymar:

إنك أخبرتنا يا أخانا أنبا ينة المقدس وأنت عندنا بالرها أنَّ كثيراً من النصارى يتركون السجود لصورة المسيح إلهنا، الذي أمكن أن يكون له صورة لتجسده من روح القدس ومن مريم العذراء برحمته من أجل خلاصنا.

You have informed us, our holy brother John, *while you were with us* in ar-Rahā that many Christians are quitting prostration to the icon of our Lord, of whom an image, by [God's] mercy, has become possible because of his incarnation from the Holy Spirit and Virgin Mary for the sake of our salvation.[230]

230 Abū Qurrah, *Maymar fī Ikrām al-Aiqūnāt* (Maymar on the veneration of icons), ed. Ignace Dick (Jounieh: Librairie St. Paul/Dhūq Mikhāyil: Christian Arabic Heritage/Rome: Papal Oriental Institute, 1986), intro., section I, pt. 1.

In my view, the Arabic text here does not prove conclusively that this friend is John, the bishop of ar-Rahā, or that he is resident in the city. The relevant words form a circumstantial clause and point to a past event. Dick[231] seems to be reading it to mean: "You told us ... *as* you are with us in Rahā," but the Arabic should be construed as: "You told us ... *while you were* with us in ar-Rahā," or even more precisely: "You told us ... *while you were at our place* in ar-Rahā." This reading implies that we have here a Christian friend, who might or might not be a church prelate. He is not necessarily an inhabitant of ar-Rahā, but he had visited it sometime in the past and had a conversation there with Abū Qurrah. I would suggest that this John was an inhabitant of Palestine or one of the eastern regions of Byzantium's Syrian districts. He either visited Abū Qurrah in ar-Rahā, or happened to be there during one of the latter's pastoral visits to the city. At that meeting, John shared with the bishop of Ḥarrān some disturbing news about the situation of the Christians in his (John's) homeland.

On the other hand, one may also argue that calling this John 'our brother' does not necessarily indicate that Abū Qurrah is addressing a clerical equal. Terms such as 'brother' and 'sister' are still used today among Eastern Christians, both clergy and lay, as a common form of address that signifies fellowship.

Furthermore, in his discussion of John's identity, Dick claims that the Syriac-speaking Christians of Syria and the eastern parts of Byzantium were, along with the Jews, the creators of the iconoclastic controversy in the Church. Dick maintains that the mentioned John was telling Abū Qurrah about the spread of iconoclastic tendencies in ar-Rahā itself, which was at the heart of the Syriac-speaking church. In making this claim, Dick is responding specifically to Mor Gregorios Yūḥannā Ibrāhīm, the Syrian Orthodox bishop of Aleppo, who argues in his book, *As-Suryān wa-Ḥarb al-Aiqūnāt* (The Syriac Christians and the war of icons), against the Syrians' having of any part to play in creating this conflict. Yūḥannā Ibrāhīm justifies his claim by affirming that the Syrian Church of Antioch remained remote from the Byzantine scene and detached from the Greek parts of the empire from the middle of the 5th century.[232] I do not concur with Bishop Yūḥannā Ibrāhīm about the absence of links between the Syrians and the Greek-speaking churches and regions of the Byzantine Empire. I believe that Greek philosophy's and culture's impact on Syrian theology is more evident

231 Griffith also makes the same inaccurate translation of the Arabic text: Sidney Griffith, "Crosses, Icons and the Image of Christ in Edessa: The Place of Iconophobia in the Christian-Muslim Controversies of Early Islamic Times," in *Transformations of Late Antiquity: Essays for Peter Brown*, ed. Philip Rousseau (Farnham, UK: Ashgate, 2009), 63–84, p. 77.
232 Gregorios Yūḥannā Ibrāhīm, *As-Suriyān wa Ḥarb al-'Iyqūnāt* (The Syriac Christians and the war over icons) (Aleppo,1980), p. 11.

and stronger than scholars have admitted until recently. In fact, I believe that there were groups within the Syriac- and Arabic-speaking churches of Syria and Palestine at the time of Abū Qurrah who hesitated to support the iconodule view and held, instead, a somewhat negative attitude that reflected a certain tendency to avoid the public veneration of icons, which can be seen during the time of both John of Damascus and Theodore Abū Qurrah.

Discussing John of Damascus' refutation of iconoclasm, Andrew Louth claims that the Damascene's attacks on the Imperial Byzantine support for iconoclasm needs not negate the fact that this Melkite father also intended to address a variety of iconoclastic movements that were spreading in Palestine, especially in the neighbourhood of Jerusalem. The archaeological evidence, Louth postulates, shows that this area witnessed the defacement of images of animals and humans. This defacement was carried out carefully, Louth maintains, in order to pre-empt a more extensive destruction of images that might take place either by order of the Muslims or be inspired by Islamic religious convictions.[233] Louth then moves on many decades from John Damascene's era to the time of Theodore Abū Qurrah, and detects that there were Islamic pressures on the Christian use of icons in general at that time too. Perceiving the similarity of the two church fathers' contexts, Louth suggests Abū Qurrah's inheritance of almost all John's iconophile arguments. When at once he concedes a potential difference between the two Melkite fathers' positions, Louth attributes it to a mere difference in terms of the addressed settings, opining that Abū Qurrah, in particular, was addressing Christians who lived among Muslims and were not able to venerate icons in public.[234] One may say, in other words, that Abū Qurrah was trying to address a sort of esoteric or crypto-iconophile group, who, driven initially by their fear of social pressure and trapped later by Islamic and Jewish iconoclastic critiques and challenges, had begun to question the iconophile stance and gradually to underplay in their daily practice the value of their faith in icons veneration.

---

233 Louth, *St. John Damascene*, pp. 193–222, esp. 197. Griffith also points to this defacement: Griffith, *The Church in the Shadow of the Mosque*, p. 144. For a good presentation of the Eastern Orthodox theology of icons, see Jaroslav Pelikan, *The Christians Tradition: The Spirit of Eastern Christendom (600–1700)* (Chicago, IL: University of Chicago Press, 1977), Vol. 2, pp. 117–133; and Leonid Ouspensky, *Theology of the Icon*, trans. Anthony Gythiel and Elizabeth Meyendorff, 2 vols., (Crestwood, NY: St Vladimir's Seminary Press, 1992). On the history of iconoclasm, see Hussey, *The Orthodox Church in the Byzantine Empire*; and Leslie Brubaker and John Haldon, *Byzantium in the Iconoclast Era, c. 680–850: A History* (Cambridge: Cambridge University Press, 2011).

234 Louth, *St. John Damascene*, pp. 220–221.

In his description of the religious scene in Syria/Palestine during the rule of Islam in the 8th and 9th centuries, Sidney Griffith, in turn, points to the Melkite theological tradition of John of Damascus and Theodore Abū Qurrah, finding there a reaction to challenges from the Syriac-speaking Jacobites and Nestorians, as well as from the Muslims and the Manicheans. Among these challenges, Griffith underlines "an enthusiasm for iconophobia which arose among some Christians living under Muslim rule in the 8th century."[235] Because of the Muslim discouragement of representational art, these Syriac- and Arabic-speaking iconophobes were, for example, antagonistic to the portrayal of Jesus' crucifixion and death in a style similar to the graphic presentation, which the Melkite Anastasius of Sinai makes in his Greek Christological apology, *Hodegos.*[236] Their compromise over the veneration of images, as Griffith elsewhere demonstrates, extended to damaging the mosaics in their own churches in order to protect the security and integrity of their premises.[237] This group of accommodators and peace-seekers experienced growth among the Syriac- and Arabic-speaking Christians of Syria/Palestine, who, as Griffith states, "in the face of Jewish and Islamic polemic, were becoming iconophobic and abandoning the practice of publically venerating the cross and the icons."[238] Daniel Sahas backs up this attention to the Islamic influence on the Christians of Syria/Palestine, claiming that John of Damascus' treatises on the veneration of icons were actually written to address Islamic iconoclastic pressure and, more specifically, to respond "to Beser's influence upon the iconoclastic policies of Yazīd II (720–4), rather than in response to Leo III's edict (726) against the icons."[239] Sidney Griffith, in turn, presents a plausible argument when he says that "it seems inconceivable that John of Damascus would be primarily concerned with imperial policies in far-off Con-

235 Griffith, "John of Damascus and the Church," p. 12.

236 Ibid., p. 14.

237 Griffith, "Crosses, Icons and the Image of Christ," p. 70.

238 Griffith, "John of Damascus and the Church in Syria," p. 30. See also Robert Schick, *The Christian Communities of Palestine*, pp. 180–224.

239 Sahas, "The Arab Character of the Christian Disputation," p. 186. On Yazīd's edict, see also A. A. Vasiliev, "The Iconoclastic Edict of the Caliph Yazīd II, A. D. 721," *Dumbarton Oaks Papers*, 9–10 (1955–1956), 25–47. In his essay on the Islamic attitude towards the Byzantine Christians, Ahmad Shboul suggests that Yazid's edict was actually issued not for the purpose of dictating the way in which Christians should worship, but to ban "the display of the remaining symbols of the old imperial ecclesiastical influence in his domains". In other words, the Umayyad caliph's wish was to reduce the manifestations of the fading Byzantine era from the territories of the newly established Islamic empire: Ahmad M. H. Shboul, "Arab Islamic Perceptions of Byzantine Religion and Culture," in *Muslim Perceptions of Other Religions: A Historical Survey*, ed. Jacques Waardenburg (New York: Oxford University Press, 1999), 122–135, p. 127.

stantinople and inattentive to the very real pressures exerted on the Christian community in his own milieu."[240] Moreover, Griffith does not stop in the time of the Damascene or find an iconophobic position only earlier than that era. He further argues that the same problem became more vigorous later, in Theodore Abū Qurrah's generation, when the latter called on the Christians of Syria/Palestine to maintain the obligation of prostrating before the cross and the holy icons, notwithstanding the opposition and obloquy of their non-Christian surroundings.[241] The continuation of the compromising policy of defacing figurative images in the mosaic floors of the churches to please the Muslims proves to Griffith that the iconophobic position had persisted into a second generation among the Christians during the early 9th century.[242]

One should note here that prominent scholars of Syriac, such as Sebastian Brock, are not supportive of the view that there was any group among the Syriac-speaking Christians, especially the Monophysites, that was antagonistic or clearly doctrinally opposed to images and icons.[243] That said, such scholars do not deny that we may find evidence from the 5th to 8th centuries of division of views on icons between the Monophysites and the Melkites. In support of this opinion, Marlia Mundell, after admitting that some Monophysites definitely used images, maintains that the non-figurative and plain walls in many Monophysite churches in Syria indicate "a [dominant] preference for abstract church decoration."[244] Though there is no comprehensive proof that the abuse of icons in Syria was as extensive as in other corners of the Byzantine Empire, one may

240 Griffith, "Crosses, Icons and the Image of Christ," p. 73.

241 Griffith, "John of Damascus and the Church in Syria," p. 31. See also Griffith's English translation of Theodore Abū Qurrah, *A Treatise on the Veneration of the Holy Icons*, trans. S. Griffith (Louvain: Peeters, 1997), p. 29; and Griffith, *The Church in the Shadow of the Mosque*, p. 145.

242 Griffith, "Crosses, Icons and the Image of Christ," p. 81.

243 In his study of iconoclasm among the Monophysites of Syria/Palestine, Sebastian Brock rejects completely the suggestion that iconoclasm was present in this Christian community. Brock acknowledges that references to icons and other figurative mosaics and paintings were not common in Monophysite literature in the iconoclastic age, but he does not see this as evidence of a hostile attitude towards icons. On the contrary, he maintains that there is enough evidence to state that venerating icons was the norm for the Monophysites: Sebastian Brock, "Iconoclasm and the Monophysites," in *Iconoclasm*, ed. Anthony Bryer and Judith Herrin (Birmingham: University of Birmingham/Centre of Byzantine Studies, 1977), 53–57. Others agree with Brock; see, for example, Hussey, *The Orthodox Church in the Byzantine Empire*, p. 33; and Henry Chadwick, "John Moschus and His Friend Sophronius the Sophist," *Journal of Theological Studies*, 25 (1974), 41–74, p. 67, n.. 3.

244 Thus Marlia Mundell, "Monophysite Church Decoration," *Iconoclasm*, ed. Anthony Bryer and Judith Herrin (Birmingham: University of Birmingham/Centre of Byzantine Studies, 1977), 59–74, p. 74.

note, Mundell affirms, that ritual options other than figurative art were preferred in Syria during that period,[245] and she proposes that this may be viewed within a historical context of radical cultural and religious change in Syria that was brought about by the rapid increase of the power of Islam during the 8th century, when there was a growing tendency towards iconoclasm similar to that in Byzantium.[246] The Islamic and Jewish factors probably made an indirect contribution to creating an atmosphere that could potentially pave the way for avoiding the veneration of icons in Syria/Palestine.[247] While there may not be solid grounds for calling this position 'iconoclasm,' one can still describe it with Sidney Griffith as 'iconophobia.' And, if one accepts Hélène Ahrweiler's extension of the understanding of people's veneration or destruction of images to an expression of their political attachment or opposition to the authority of Constantinople,[248] one may conclude that an iconophobic attitude may simply have been the last resort of

245 Ibid.
246 Hussey, *The Orthodox Church in the Byzantine Empire*, p. 34. Hussey goes as far as suggesting "contacts, and debts if any, between Byzantium and Islam in initiating the policy of banning the use of icons."
247 Patricia Crone, "Islam, Judeo-Christianity and Byzantine Iconoclasm," *Jerusalem Studies in Arabic and Islam*, 2 (1980), 59–95. In his chronicles, Theophanes points to the influence of the Jews on the Muslim ban on icons when he narrates that on 31 August, 723, "a Jewish wizard who made his headquarters in Phoenician Laodikeia came to Yazid. He told him that he would rule the Arab state for forty years if he would condemn the honoured and revered icons in the Christian churches throughout his entire empire. The senseless Yazid believed him and promulgated an all-embracing edict against the holy icons": Theophanes, *Anni Mundi 6095–6305 (A.D. 602–813)*, ed. and trans. Harry Turtledove (Philadelphia: University of Pennsylvania Press, 1982), AM 6215, 7.4.9.18, p. 93. See also a longer version of the same story in Cyril Mango, *The Art of the Byzantine Empire, 312–1453: Sources and Documents* (New York: Prentice-Hall, 1972), p. 182. For further reading on the Islamic influence, see D. Stein, *Der Beginn des byzantinischen Bilderstreites und seine Entwicklung bis in die 40er Jahre des 8. Jahrhunderts*, Miscellanea Byzantina Monacensia XXV (Munich: Institut für Byzantinistik und Neugriechische Philologie der Universität München, 1980), pp. 139–141; and G. Von Grunebaum, "Byzantine Iconoclasm and the Influence of the Islamic Environment," *History of Religions*, 2 (1962), 1–10. On the Jewish influence, see Andrew Sharf, *Byzantine Jewry, from Justinian to the Fourth Crusade* (New York: Oxford University Press, 1984). Scholars do share a consensus about the lack of any historical or textual evidence for the existence of such an edict, but one should, nevertheless, not reject out of hand the possibility that Yazid, like his father, had negative attitude towards figurative images.
248 Hélène Ahrweiler, "The Geography of Iconoclasm," in *Iconoclasm*, , ed. Anthony Bryer and Judith Herrin (Birmingham: University of Birmingham/Centre of Byzantine Studies, 1977), 21–27, pp. 21–22. "The controversy over icons was therefore only a pretext, a convenient touch-stone, by which the people could express their agreement or disagreement with imperial policy."

Syriac- and Arabic-speaking Christians to prove their allegiance to Muslim[249] rule and society and their break with the trends of thought in the Greek-speaking Christian world.

Looking to the issue from this broad perspective, as Ahrweiler realizes, would make mapping the geographical spread of iconoclasm over against the territory held by the iconodules a highly complex and almost unachievable task. Consequently, just as it is plausible to propose that there were people in Constantinople and its surroundings, who, out of fear of punishment by the Byzantine emperor, would outwardly reject the veneration of icons but secretly sympathise with it,[250] so it is valid to propose that there were among the Syriac- and Arabic-speaking Christians of Syria/Palestine those who would avoid venerating icons, even profess scepticism about image veneration in itself, out of fear of the reaction of the Muslim and Jewish[251] communities. It is, in my opinion, quite likely that these iconcophobes were mainly Syriac- and Arabic-speakers with a Monophysite and Nestorian background, who made up the majority of Christians, at least in Syria.

In the light of this discussion, I believe it is plausible to propose here that Abū Qurrah's text on the veneration of icons was not just a pedagogical, apologetic tool that the iconophiles of Syria/Palestine could use against the Muslim

---

249 Some scholars tend to argue that the rejection of figurative images was not initially a characteristic of Islamic thought, but that it developed over time. On the development of the Muslim view from indifference to the prohibition of images in art (iconoclam), see the argument in Oleg Grabar, "Islam and Iconoclasm," in *Iconoclasm*, ed. Anthony Bryer and Judith Herrin (Birmingham: University of Birmingham/Centre of Byzantine Studies, 1977), 45–52.

250 Ahrweiler, "The Geography of Iconoclasm," p. 25. This realization supports Ahrweiler's conclusion, which is worth pondering: "The fact is that iconoclasts and iconodules lived side by side throughout the empire; the difference in their attitudes was founded on social and economic factors rather than geographical, and on their fidelity to traditions rooted in differing cultures. All in all, individual attitudes, rather than geography, dictated who was iconoclast and who was orthodox."

251 In discussing the validity of accusing Judaism of iconoclasm, Andrew Louth draws attention to the archaeological clarification that even in the Jewish community there was an acceptance of figurative images in art. As an example of this, Louth points to the synagogue of Dora Europos: "Dura Europos, with its richly decorated synagogue and church, dating from no later than 256, when Dura Europos felt to the Persians, is but one example among many": Louth, *St John Damascene*, p. 195. See also Lee I. Levine, *The Ancient Synagogue: The First Thousand Years* (New Haven, CT: Yale University Press, 1999). Later in his book (p. 211), Louth concedes, nevertheless, the occurrence of Jewish-Christian polemic in the seventh century specifically against the veneration of icons. Louth says that the systematic *florelegium* of the third treatise against iconoclasm among John of Damascus' texts on the divine images is an example of a debate shaped after the 7th-century polemic (ibid., p. 212).

and Jewish iconoclasts, and that it was mainly an admonition and corrective to those Christians who had started, out of fear, to lose their iconodule beliefs. And to come back to the text itself, Abū Qurrah's use of Syriac words in Arabic transliteration form (*Mortriam* for the Virgin Mary, *uqnum* for 'person' and *Sellyḥyyn* for apostles, for example) throughout his maymar indicates that some of his readers were *Suryān*, or Arabs who had incorporated some Syriac terms into their religious terminology. On the other hand, I disagree with Dick's reliance, in his response to Bishop Yūḥannā Ibrāhīm, on Abū Qurrah's introductory sentence in this maymar. As I have argued above, the Arabic syntax here more probably implies that someone called John from Syria or Palestine happened to be in ar-Rahā at the same time as Abū Qurrah, and that, when they met, reported on the spread of iconoclasm among the Syriac- and Arabic-speaking Christian majority, and asked the renowned bishop and theologian of Ḥarrān to write a theological response to them on the matter. Abū Qurrah would not actually need a local inhabitant of ar-Rahā to tell him what was happening in a city close to his ecclesial seat in Ḥarrān. He would already have had first-hand knowledge of the spread of iconoclasm in his diocese, if it were taking place. Abū Qurrah, nevertheless, would have needed someone living in the regions under Islamic rule to convey to him first-hand news about the state of the Church there, and this role was fulfilled by this friend called John.

Be that as it may, one may agree with Sidney Griffith's claim that Abū Qurrah's presumed addressees in this maymar were not only or primarily the iconoclast Jews (notwithstanding his reliance on the Old Testament in his discussion and his reference to the Jews at some points), but also, and more significantly, the Muslims.[252] However, I would also argue that Abū Qurrah, even though he had in mind Islamic and Jewish polemics against icons, hoped that the main community that would read his text were the iconophobic Christians, who had started to lose their orthodox faith under the influence of their Muslim and Jewish compatriots. In the introduction to his maymar, Abū Qurrah hints at these two groups of opponents. He speaks about 'those who stand against Christianity' (*mukhālifū an-Nuṣrāniyya)*, who specifically "claim to have a book descended from God in their hands."[253] Those who claim to have 'a book descended from God' are usually the Muslims, and this is how Abū Qurrah commonly refers to

---

252 Griffith, Griffith, "Crosses, Icons and the Image of Christ in Edessa: the Place of Iconophobia in the Christian-Muslim Controversies of Early Islamic Times," pp. 77–78.

253 Abū Qurrah, *Maymar fī Ikrām al-Aiqūnāt* (Maymar on the Veneration of Icons), intro.I.3. "ذلك أنه لا يزال مخالفوا النصرانية، لا سيما من يدَّعي أنَّ بيده كتاباً منزلاً من الله ..."

them in his writings.[254] In addition, Abū Qurrah also calls his opponents 'the outsiders' (*al-barrāniyyn*) [255] and 'strangers' (*al-ghurabā'*)[256] more than once in the maymar on icons and says that these 'outsiders' are those who, because of the doctrines of the Trinity, incarnation and redemption deem Christians mad and deluded.[257] But even though Abū Qurrah's main concern is the Muslim view of the veneration of images, his main addressees, or the main readers of his text, were expected to be those Christians who were influenced by the Muslims' mockery and criticism, and who, more specifically, followed the Old Testament literally and preferred it to the Greek thinking of the earlier Church fathers – namely the iconophobes among the Syriac- and Arabic-speaking Christians of the Nestorian and Jacobite traditions.

On the basis of this analysis of Abū Qurrah's addressees, I would point out the following: as in his apology for the right religion and God's existence, Abū Qurrah's defence of the veneration of icons similarly targets various audiences and different religious views at the same time. If this reflects anything about Abū Qurrah's thinking, it demonstrates that he does not intend to attack one religion in particular or to defend Christianity against a single enemy. Rather, he is an apologist for religious belief that accords with reason and can establish that the fabric of its beliefs is logical. This is why Abū Qurrah is as critical of what he considers contrary to reason and logic in some Christian theological trends (the Syriac Christians' rejection of the veneration of icons) as he is critical of Islamic religiosity. The maymar on the veneration of icons shows that Abū Qurrah's apologetic principle is to defend venerating religious images not just because it is a Christian practice but because those who argue against such veneration, whether Muslims or Christians, are irrational and hardly persuasive in either their allegations or their understanding of the core content of the orthodox Christian theology of icons.

This apologetic strategy leads Abū Qurrah to associate true Christianity and accurate theology with the notions of 'wisdom' and 'truth,'[258] maintaining in parallel that Muslims' rejection of the Christian theology of icons stems from sheer

254 See, for example, Abū Qurrah's saying to his Muslim interlocutors in the debate in al-Ma'mūn's court: "and you also say that the Qur'an is the descended word]of God[, uncreated, originating from God, and returning to him."

"كما أنك تقول إنَّ القرآن كلام الله منزل، غير مخلوق، منه بدأ وإليه يعود"

Abū Qurrah, *Abū Qurrah wa-al Ma'mūn*, Ch.V, Section E, pt. 3.390.

255 Abū Qurrah, *Maymar fī Ikrām al-Aiqūnāt* (Maymar on the Veneration of Icons), intro. I.7; Ch. 1.II.1.

256 Ibid., 1.II.2.

257 Ibid., 1.II.4–17.

258 Ibid., 1.II.3.4–9.

ignorance and from following inappropriate earthly wisdom. We may conclude that the 'outsiders' here are not only the Muslims, but also all those (non-orthodox Christians, Jews, or any other sceptics) who do not have the rational ability or intelligence to perceive the deep heavenly wisdom that underpins Christian orthodoxy. Here too, as in other texts, the Christian Gospel alone is taken as the reliable source of this heavenly wisdom because it alone of all religious books can be proven to accord with natural reason.[259] Those from other religions, who fail to realize this fact by using their rational judgment, are not necessarily to be charged with following false religions and then called to follow Christianity; proving the falsehood of other religions and converting them to Christianity is not the key purpose of Abū Qurrah's argument, which simply just reveals that they are ignorant about their own religions and have no logical, persuasive justification for following it.[260]

It is significant here to realize that Abū Qurrah does not consider reason an alternative to faith or as its enemy. He rather believes that reason is faith's caretaker, which reviews faith and preserves it.[261] Reason is what enables one to investigate what she believes in and to discover its truth or falsehood. It is what guides one to the true faith, even if the content of that belief is not according to what our feelings like and our desires seek.[262] It is this standard of rational examination, according to Abū Qurrah, that makes Christianity the most reason-

259 Ibid., 1.VI.3.5.

"وقد وضعنا نحن أهل الجسارة ميامر مما استفدنا من دقائق تعليم آبائنا القديسين حققنا بها أنه لا كتاب يثبت من العقل الحق بتّة اليوم إلا الإنجيل"

"We, the people of daring, have composed maymars from the precise teaching we have acquired from our holy fathers, proving thereby that no book can be rationally proved to be completely true today except the Gospel."

260 Ibid., 1.VI.3.9.

فأما إن جعل يقبل من ذلك بعضاً ويرد بعضاً وكان ما قبل وما ردَّ واحداً في إنكار العقل الجسداني إياه فقد حقق على نفسه أنه لا بصيرة له بدينه وأنه لا يدري لأي سببٍ هو مقيم عليه

and since he simultaneously accepted and rejected what is actually the same thing according to the mentioned corporal reason's denial, he then proved that he has no perception of his own religion and he is ignorant about the reason of abiding with it.

261 Abū Qurrah, *Maymar fī Taḥqīq annahu la Yalzam an-Naṣārā an Yaqūlū Thalāthat Āliha idh Yaqūlūn al-Āb Īlāh wal-Ibn Īlāh wa-Rūḥ Qudus. Wa-anna al-Āb wal-Ibn wa-Rūḥ Qudus Īlāh wa-law Kāna Kull Wāḥid Minhum Tāmm ʿalā Ḥidatih* (Maymar affirming that the Nazarenes do not necessarily mean to speak of three gods when they say the Father is God, the Son is God and Holy Spirit. And that the Father, Son and Holy Spirit are God even if each one of them is perfect in itself), in *Mayāmir Thaoudorus abū Qurrah, Usquf Ḥarrān, Aqdam Ta'līf 'Arabī Naṣrānī* (*Mayāmir* ofTheodore Abū Qurrah, Bishop of Ḥarrān, the oldest Arabic Christian work), ed. Qusṭanṭīn Bāshā (Beirut: Al-Faw'id Press, 1904), 23–47, p. 23.

262 Ibid., p. 26.

able religion, because "there is nothing in Christianity (*Naṣrāniyyah*) that can be used to claim that its first followers accepted it by means of other than the best consultation and the most rigorous attention."[263] That being so, Abū Qurrah concludes that those who freely choose not to join Christianity base their refusal on personal free choice alone, not on any rational verification. Reason, Abū Qurrah affirms, offers many logical explanations and foundations that support the tenability and rational authenticity of Christianity above all other religions.[264] In other words, the main goal of Christian apologetics is not to proselytise, but to use logic and reason, not proof-texting, as the main referential criteria for proving the truth of Christianity. Abū Qurrah explicitly affirms his foundational reliance on reason first and foremost in his maymar

3. إنَّ قصدنا في كتابنا هذا أن نثبت ديننا من العقل، وليس من الكتب

...

5. فلسنا نقبل من وجه العقل دينا من عند الله إلا الإنجيل وحده، لما ذكرنا من التمام والصواب الذي أتى به

> 3. our purpose in this book is to prove our religion from reason, and not from the books
>
> ...
>
> 5. for we do not accept, from the perspective of reason, a religion 'from God' except the Gospel alone, due to what we have pointed out about the perfection and accuracy which it [the Gospel] brought.[265]

---

263 Ibid.
"وذلك أنَّ النصرانية ليس فيها شيء يوقع التهمة على قابليها الأولين أنهم قبلوها إلا بأفضل المناصحة وأشد الاحتياط. لأن ليس فيها شيء يغتر إليه ولا يدعو إليه الهوى أن يقبله قابلوه ممن يدعوهم إليه."

264 Ibid., p. 47.

265 Abū Qurrah, *Maymar fī Wujūd Al-Khāliq wad-Dīn al-Qawīm* (Maymar on the existence of the Creator and the right religion), 2.15.3,5. Abū Qurrah also refers to his argument in this maymar in his other treatises on the veneration of icons. There, Abū Qurrah states that his concern in the former maymar and other earlier ones was primarily to prove from the evidence of reason alone that only the Gospel contains the truth: Abū Qurrah, *Maymar fī Ikrām al-Aiqūnāt(*Maymer on the veneration of icons), 1.6.3.5

5. وقد وضعنا نحن، أهل الجسارة، ميامر مما استفدنا من دقائق تعليم آباءنا القديسين، حققنا بها أنه لا كتاب يَثبُتُ من العقل الحق بتة اليوم، إلا الإنجيل وكل ما يحققه الإنجيل لتحقيق الإنجيل إياه

5. and we, the people of daring, have composed maymars from what have we benefited from the preciseness of our holy fathers' teaching, wherein we verified that no book at all today can be verified by true reason except the Gospel [*al-Injīl*] and whatever the Gospel verifies, because of its verification by the Gospel

V. Towards a 'Positive' Orthodox Apologetic: On Being a *Mutakallim* after Abū Qurrah

Studying the apologetic style of Theodore Abū Qurrah and his mentor and co-religionist, John of Damascus, shows that the difference between their discourses lies not only in the identity of their presumed opponents – the former's are the Muslim *mutakallimūn* of Baṣra, Kūfa and Baghdad, while the latter's are the intellectuals of Constantinople[266] – but also, and more importantly, in their writing style and their understanding of the nature of interreligious interaction. More importantly still, this study shows clearly the unique value that Abū Qurrah grants to logic and reason in verifying the truth of any religion; reason rather than scripture is the foundation of any authentic and reliable religiosity. The way Abū Qurrah argues this, and the content with which he fills this belief, distinguish him not only from his Melkite predecessors, but also from his non-Melkite Christian contemporaries, as well as Muslim *mutakallimūn.*[267]

In his response to the accusation that he resorts to an apologetic approach in writing about the Christian faith, the philosopher of religion, Dewi Z. Phillips, states that he sees himself as a scholar endeavouring to acquire a clear perception of a cluster of beliefs that many men and women consider essential to life. Phillips affirms that his aim in this endeavour is not to persuade others into belief, nor is it to convince them of the plausibility of conceding God's existence. He is simply attempting to give people an opportunity to understand the nature and character of what they believe and to enable them personally to discover the consequences of accepting God's existence.[268] Rather than developing a kind of a 'negative apologetic' and turning belief into a polemic, reactive epistemological theory, Phillips stresses that his ambition is restricted to the following

> If I can get a philosopher to see that his objections to religious belief are confused, he may or may not become a believer as a result. Nevertheless, he must appreciate something about the character of religious belief which he did not appreciate before ... this in itself takes us, in certain respects, beyond the limits of negative apologetics.[269]

266 Thus Griffith, "Muslims and Church Councils," pp. 271–272.

267 This is, for instance, what Varsanyi shows when she points to difference between Abū Qurrah and the emphasis commonly placed on reason by Abū Rā'iṭah and other Muslim *mutakallimūn* for finding the right religion: Varsanyi, "The Role of the Intellect," pp. 54 ff.

268 D. Z. Phillips, *Faith after Foundationalism: Plantinga – Rorty – Lindbeck – Berger – Critiques and Alternatives* (Boulder, CO: Westview Press, 1995), p. 95.

269 Ibid., p. 96.

It is not my intention here to make an anachronistic link between Abū Qurrah's legacy and philosophical thinking that belongs to a different historical context and intellectual framework. I just want to borrow Phillips' words about the role of apologetics and how the theologian can offer a discourse that is not negative and polemic in approach and purpose. A careful reading of the tradition of apologetics in Christian history demonstrates that there were many times in Christianity's history when Church fathers and theologians wrote discourses that attempted to prove Christianity's superiority and truthfulness in comparison with either paganism (as in Augustine's *The City of God*), or Judaism and Islam (as in Thomas Aquinas' *Summa Contra Gentiles*). Nevertheless, one can also see set out in parallel to this negative approach a more positive apologetic that aims to make Christianity look reasonable and credible to the sceptics (as in Pascal's *Apology*, and Schleiermacher's *Speeches on Religion to its Cultured Despisers*). If one wants to place Abū Qurrah's and John of Damascus' apologetics within one of these two traditions, one could say that the Damascene's texts reveal a negative apologetic, while Abū Qurrah's evince a uniquely positive approach. His is a discourse that does not aim primarily at proving Christianity's hierarchical status above other religions or ultimately converting his audience to that faith. Abū Qurrah's apologetic approach, like Phillips', attempts to clarify to his interlocutors the character of Christian faith and enable them eventually to appreciate its rational and logical credentials, even if they do not finally become Christians. One may conclude from Abū Qurrah's writings that his positive apologetic is characterized by the following four elements:

1. In this apologetic, Christianity is seen as one religion among many others. It does not stand alone against or above them, and it is not the standard judging reference by means of which the truth and validity of other religions is to be decided. Christianity's truth and validity, like the truth and validity of other religions, is to be verified and proven by a criterion *from without* its content's boundaries.

2. In this apologetic, the content of the religions' source texts and the words of their prophets are not in themselves sufficient to prove which one of them is the true belief. The content of religions is more or less similar in its purpose, its constitutive elements and its ultimate goal: they all speak about God's self-introduction, his description of our weakness and sin, and how we can be healed from it. One needs to judge this content by another criterion: reason and logic. In this, Abū Qurrah's apologetic thinking differs in method from that of other Christian and Muslim apologetics, which resort to scriptural evidence to affirm their own

faith against the other.[270] For Abū Qurrah, the scriptures must also be judged and measured by the rules of rational thinking. Rather than resorting to the proposition that faith transcends and even contradicts reason and relies on God's grace, Abū Qurrah clearly argues that Christian faith is the true belief because it resonates fully with the rules of rational thinking.

In his discussion of the Eastern fathers' reliance on patristic tradition and the scripture in their apologies, Jaroslav Pelikan states that the orthodox fathers did not only rely on scriptural authority and did not cite only biblical verses in their arguments because the heretics, with whom they were in dispute, also acknowledged the authority of the Bible. So, Pelikan concludes, "It did not suffice simply to declare that one stood with the orthodox tradition of the fathers in their interpretation of the faith on the basis of Scripture when both the orthodox and the heretic were claiming this authority as well."[271] When it came to Theodore Abū Qurrah's controversies with Muslims, he did not face this situation since the Muslims used another religious text (the Qur'an) and did not attribute any authority to the Christian scriptures. This may have discouraged Theodore from citing the Scripture alone and relying on its authority far less than other Church fathers in their writings, since the authority of the Bible was not a belief shared by him and his interlocutors. This is why Theodore relies on the judgement of reason primarily and more extensively than on scriptural authority. He invites his Muslim interlocutors to resort to rational verification rather than to proof-texting, subjecting all religious texts to the ultimate appraisal and assessment of rationality. While other Melkite fathers relied on how the scriptures were interpreted in the patristic legacy, Abū Qurrah based his use of the Bible and the patristic tradition alike on how the content of these texts could be judged as true or not by means of the criterion of reason.

---

270 Abū Qurrah's method does not prove Jacques Waardenburg's over-generalized belief that both Muslims and Christians resorted to scriptural evidence as their primary defence strategy, and it also defies Waardenburg's belief that Christians differed from Muslims in their belief that religion contradicts reason and lies in God's grace: Jacques Waardenburg, *Muslims and Others: Relations in Context* (Berlin: Walter de Gruyter, 2003), pp. 155–156.

271 Pelikan, *The Christian Tradition*, p. 21. Though expressing himself slightly differently, Khaled Anatolios has recently put forward the same idea in relation to the Trinitarian controversies of the fourth century, stating that "there was general agreement on the contents of the scriptural canon; its normativity as the prime source of divine revelation, and the attribution of its ultimate authorship to the Holy Spirit. Thus all parties in the trinitarian conflicts constructed their arguments in scriptural terms, without any disagreements on canonicity": Khaled Anatolios, *Retrieving Nicaea: The Development and Meaning of Trinitarian Doctrine* (Grand Rapids, MI: Baker Academic, 2011), p. 36.

3. It follows from the previous point that, in this apologetic, the purpose of the argument is not to defend the validity of the scriptures' attestation to religious faith and its truthfulness over against attestation in other religious texts. It is rather to defend the validity of reason and logic as standards to measure and examine validity and truth in principle. It is also to try to see whether, according to this criterion and nothing else, Christian faith is justifiable and then using rationality as the foundation for Christians' reliance on the Christian scriptures' witness to that faith, and their belief in its authenticity and reliability.

This prioritization of reason and rating it more highly as a criterion than religious texts is unique in Theodore Abū Qurrah's apologetic discourses, even though it is true that in other contemporary Melkite apologetic texts, one can see a similar principal attention to reason and attempts to respond to Muslim criticism of Christian faith on the basis of reason. One good example of this is pointed out by Sidney Griffith. In his study of the early 9th-century apologetic text from Sinai Arabic MS 434, which he calls *Answers for the Shaykh*, Griffith recognizes the Sabaite monks' reliance on reason to respond to the Muslim interlocutor's questions on the Trinity and the incarnation. Yet, Griffith states that each of the monks' responses offers arguments that are derived from reason, as well as from the revealed texts of the Bible. In the light of this, and after conceding that this derivation is "a standard feature of most apologetic discourses in the early Islamic period, both Christian and Muslim," Griffith concludes that the rational argument is actually used here to prove none other than the validity and authenticity of the biblical attestation on the Trinity and the incarnation, so much so that "the presentation of proof-texts from the Scriptures was [after all] to have pride of place."[272] This tendency to invest reason in verifying the validity of relying on the Bible for defending (or refuting) Christian (or Muslim) faith is common in almost all Christian and Muslim apologetic texts from the early Abbasid era onwards. Nevertheless, my previous study of Abū Qurrah's rational discussion of Christianity in his *Maymar on the Existence of God and the Right Religion* shows that, for Abū Qurrah, the most ostentatiously important place in his apologetic discourses is kept primarily for reason and rational logic.[273]

---

272 Griffith, "*Answers for the Shaykh*," p. 288.

273 Elsewhere, Griffith points to a Greek text in Abū Qurrah's works, where Abū Qurrah more or less explains to his readers the reason behind his prioritization of the evidence of reason over proof-texting, or even over proving the validity of the scriptural verification. In that text, Abū Qurrah recalls that his Muslim interlocutors are the reason for this option, as one of them once challenged him saying "persuade me not from your Isaiah or Matthew, for who I have no slightest regard, but from compelling, acknowledged, common conceptions": Griffith, *The Church in the Shadow of the Mosque*, p. 94; quoting from Abū Qurrah's Greek *Opusculum 24*,

4. In this apologetic, the apologist's argument must reflect a positive correspondence to the historical context and intellectual culture of society. Abū Qurrah is an Arabic-speaking *mutakallim* from the Abbasid era. This is an important factor for understanding why in his theological writings he opts for a rational, philosophical method that is indelibly distinguished from the conventional apologetic language and style of his orthodox predecessors. It actually shows the pioneering status of Abū Qurrah's dialogical style for debate with Muslims, which makes him one of the earliest Christian Arab *mutakallimūn* to believe that rational verification rather than any other criterion is the standard measure of truth in every religion. In his edition of Abū Rā'iṭah's letter on the Trinity, Father Salīm Dakkāsh claims that Abū Rā'iṭah is the first of the Christian *mutakallimūn* to offer a complete system of rules and pre-conditions for dialogue. Dakkāsh justifies this claim by noting that none of the Christian *mutakallimūn* who came after Abū Rā'iṭah, such as Yaḥya ibn ʿAdī, Elias of Nesseben and Patriarch Timothy I, mentions anything about rules of dialoguing with others.[274] Father Dakkāsh's observation grants Abū Rā'iṭah pioneering status in relation to his successors, but excludes those who preceded or were contemporaneous with him, such as Theodore Abū Qurrah. Before Abū Rā'iṭah, Abū Qurrah's understanding of the criterion of truth in interreligious dialogue makes it plausible to consider him the first Arab Christian *mutakallim* to consider the judgment of reason as having the foundational role in comparing and contrasting between religions and to pioneer in construing logic and rational verification as the criteria for the validity of any religious belief.[275]

PG, Vol. 97, col. 1556B. For further discussion of the Muslim view of the Christian Bible and its valid use in debates, see S. Griffith, "Arguing from Scripture: The Bible in the Christian/Muslim Encounter in the Middle Ages," in *Scripture and Pluralism: Reading the Bible in the Religiously Plural Worlds of the Middle Ages and Renaissance*, ed. Thomas Hefferman and Thomas Burman (Leiden: Brill, 2006), 29–58.

274 Salīm Dakkāsh, *Abū Rā'iṭa at-Takrītī wa-Risālatuh fī ath-Thālūth al-Muqaddas: Dirāsah wa-Naṣṣ* (Abū Rā'iṭah at-Takrītī and his epistle on the holy Trinity: Study and text), (Beirut: Dār al-Mashriq, 1996), p. 34.

275 There are indications that some other Melkite texts earlier than Abū Rā'iṭah's mentioned similar ideas about dialogue. For example, Abū Rā'iṭah warns that Christians and Muslims sometimes use similar terms, but with different meanings. He then emphasizes that one of the preconditions of proper dialogue is to keep this factor clearly in mind: Ibid., pp. 35–36. Sidney Griffith points to a similar claim in the earlier Melkite texts known as *Summa Theologiae Arabica:* "By 'there is no god but God' they mean a god other than the Father, Son and Holy Spirit. According to what they say, 'God neither generates nor is generated [Q. 112:3]'. Nor according to what they say, is the Holy Spirit anything other than a creature among creatures. So, their saying 'there is no god but God' is the same as what we say in words, but it is different in meaning": Griffith, "The First Christian *Summa Theologiae*," p. 20.

In their attempt to present theology in the Abbasid era, Christian thinkers such as Abū Qurrah realized that they had to demonstrate convincingly the philosophical and rational calibre of their religious knowledge, not only about Christianity, but also about other contemporary religions and trends of thought. Why did they have to appeal passionately to reason and philosophy? Because the age of the Abbasids was one, wherein Muslim intellectuals, as Franz Rosenthal reminds us, "based themselves ideologically on the Muʿtazilah ... to whom can be ascribed the chief merit of introducing into the realm of Islamic culture the philosophical treatment of theological problems based on ideas and methods originally found in Greek philosophy."[276] Abū Qurrah produced a major cluster of his theological literature during the reign of the Caliph al-Maʾmūn; that is, when the Muʿtazilah, as well as the Greek-Arabic translation movement, flourished and the formers' influence on the Caliphate emerges in orienting Muslim rule towards an official adoption of the heritage of classical Antiquity and a rigorous appreciation of reason and scientific argument.[277] Abū Qurrah's sensitivity to this intellectual and cultural context appears in the fact that, rather than busying himself with the condemnation and polemic humiliation of other religions, he addresses the religious convictions of the members of Syrian/Palestinian society, Christians, Jews, Muslims and pagans alike, from within their cultural and intellectual setting. He occupies himself not with attacking non-Christian religions, especially Islam, but with proving the foundational role of knowledge (*ʿīlm*) and reason (*ʿaql*) in Christianity and showing that Christian thought meets the intellectual standards of the time. In this positive apologetic approach lies the particularity of Abū Qurrah's legacy in interreligious dialogue. One can undoubtedly see in his writings a development in Christian orthodox apology and a step forward for the Eastern Christian attitude towards, and in interaction with, the radical historical changes that occurred in their lifetime with the arrival of Islam to the area.

What we need to investigate now is: If Abū Qurrah's apologetic discourse on Christianity had a positive impact and represented a fruitful relation with the Arabs and Muslims, can we ascertain whether his writing of theology in Arabic, and his concern about defending orthodoxy before Muslims, had any negative consequences for the content of orthodox theology? Did it take the Melkite Church away from the older, Greek and Syriac, Nicene-Constantinopolitan, and Chalcedonian creedal tradition? In other words, is it possible that Abū Qurrah's openness to Arab culture and Islamic thought cost the Melkite Church no less a

---

276 I cite the translation in Rosenthal, *The Classical Heritage of Islam*, p. 4.
277 Ibid., p. 5.

price than the abandonment of the theological elements that were constitutive of its theological pedagogy? Having examined the form of Abū Qurrah's apologetic methodology, it will be my goal in the next part to examine the content of his orthodox theology. I shall try to find out whether, in his attempt to present theology in Arabic, Abū Qurrah had to change the conceptual connotations and theological meanings of some central Trinitarian and Christological terms to make them more understandable and acceptable to the Muslim mind.

Part Two: The Dogmatic Framework of Abū Qurrah's Orthodoxy

In this part, I will study in depth Theodore Abū Qurrah's theological discourse in relation to the trends in orthodox theological thinking that are expressive of the Trinitarian thought of Nicaea-Constantinople and the Christological thought of Chalcedon. The main questions I aim to answer are: Did Abū Qurrah's presentation of Chalcedonian and Nicene doctrinal discourse in Arabic eventually produce figures of speech and translations that are intellectually out of kilter, not only with Islamic religious thinking, but, and more importantly, from the point of view of Christian dogma as well? Is the linguistic adaptation extensive enough to make us doubt that Abū Qurrah's Arabic theology truly represents, rather than revises or remodels, Chalcedonian and Nicene orthodoxy in a new language? Does Abū Qurrah's articulation of his understanding of Trinitarian and Christological terms, whatever that understanding may have been, represent a reiteration of Chalcedonian and Nicene thinking and terminology, or does it rather take the theological legacy of Christian orthodoxy beyond its original connotations? And, if the latter was the case, is Abū Qurrah's an authentic Christian theological voice, or is he tuning the Christian voice to please the Muslim ear?

In order to develop answers to the above questions that are as comprehensive and thorough as possible, one needs to trace how doctrinal terminology developed and how its use progressed from the Trinitarian discourses of the 4th-century Nicaea-Constantinople context to the Christological debates and discourses of the 5th and 6th centuries in the context of Ephesus and Chalcedon. Within the framework of this process and its aftermath in the following centuries up to the early Islamic era, we find an attempt to introduce the Greek technical terms that are used to articulate the doctrine of the Trinity (e.g., *hypostasis*, *ousia*, *prosopon*, *physis*, etc.), first, into Syriac (*qnoma*, *kiana*, *etuta*, etc.) and, second, into Arabic (*uqnūm*, *jawhar*, *wajh*, etc.). The attempt to translate doctrinal terms into Arabic is Abū Qurrah's pioneering contribution to the history of Christian thought, along with ʿAmmār al-Baṣrī and Ḥabīb ibn Khidmah Abū Rāʾiṭah. But to see whether or not Abū Qurrah's Arabization of the terminology keeps his feet on the orthodox path of the theologians who preceded him, we need to go back and view carefully, though here only briefly, how pre-8th-century Greek- and Syriac-speaking fathers understood the key Trinitarian and Christological notions of orthodox creedal discourse and how the expression of those notions in Syriac and Greek played an indelible role in creating two trends of thought in 4th-century Trinitarian theology (the Athanasian and the Cappadocian) and also had an impact on the Christological misunderstanding that led to the dispute between Cyril of Alexandria and Nestorius in the 5th century. A consideration of this Greek-Syriac terminological and linguistic context will help in our main aim of finding out whether, in his endeavor to articulate these elements in Arabic, Abū Qurrah found himself forced to compromise on some orthodox connotations and interpretations for the sake of making Christian faith accessible to the Arabic-speaking audience and the Muslim mind, or whether was he not forced to follow that demanding and costly path.

The three chapters of the second part of this study will tackle this issue. The first chapter in this part will be dedicated to a study of Greek and Syriac Trinitarian and Christological language and its influence on the Christological dispute between Cyril and Nestorius. We shall see that using the same terms within different languages created serious misunderstanding and ongoing conflict between the churches of Antioch and Alexandria over the content of faith. From this setting, we shall move in the following two chapters to Abū Qurrah's theological discourse on the Trinity and then Christology in order to see whether transferring the same doctrinal terminology into yet another language, namely Arabic, may have created another misunderstanding of the content of Christian faith, and whether such misunderstanding, if it existed, made Abū Qurrah's theological hermeneutics a discourse that was accessible to Muslims and Arabic-speakers, while derailing it from the track of Christian orthodoxy.

Chapter Three. From Nicene Trinitarian Trends to Chalcedonian Christological Terminology

I. Introduction

In his analysis of the various positions within the Christological spectrum of the Chalcedonian and post-Chalcedonian controversies of the 5th and 6th centuries, Sebastian Brock divides the various Christologies that were the subject of the famous historical debate into the following seven models:

1. True 'Nestorians' (two *prosopa*)
2. Strict dyophysites outside the Roman Empire: Church of the East
3. Strict dyophysites within the Roman Empire
4. Silence over Chalcedon
5. Neo-Chalcedonians
6. Henophysites
7. Eutychians (true monophysites)

Of these seven models, Brock deems the first to be representative of its followers' allegiance to a rejected Christological scheme. At the Council of Chalcedon, this model was declared heretical for reasons that relied heavily in the 'two *prosopa*' wording (derived from Nestorius' theology), which was considered expressive of a belief in two *separate* persons and two *separate* natures in Christ. Brock construes the Chalcedonian decision as unfortunate, and he convincingly argues that it does not reveal a serious willingness "to penetrate behind the wording of [the Nestorian expressions] in order to discover how they were arrived at and (above all) the way in which they were understood by those who put [them] forward"[278]

In the following sections, I would like to build upon Brock's claim and argue that the Chalcedonian reaction also evaded the following very important inquiries: Could the followers of the Antiochene tradition (who supported the Trinitarian theology of Nicaea-Constantinople) allow themselves in principle to speak of two separate natures by using the phrase 'two *prosopa*'? What if the real connotation of 'two *prosopa*' in the writings of Nestorius and his followers is only un-

---

278 S. Brock, "The Christology of the Church of the East in the Synods of the Fifth to Early Seventh Centuries: Preliminary Considerations and Materials," in *Studies in Syriac Christianity: History, Literature and Theology* (Hampshire: Variorum, 1992), XII,. 125–142, p. 132.

derstandable if one starts studying the Nestorian terminology in the light of the wording of the Trinitarian theology of Nicaea and Constantinople, rather than restricting the reading of that terminology narrowly to the context of its use in the Christological controversies of 431 and 451 alone? What if the intention behind the use of the phrase 'two *prosopa*' was to emphasize the notion of 'particularity' (spelled out at Nicaea in the term *hypostasis*) rather than separation or duality? What if the main problem in the 'Nestorian/Antiochene' tradition, as Brock suggests, was completely bound up to Nestorius' inappropriate choice of terms in his endeavor to explain Nicene Trinitarian ontology? What if Nestorius' '*parsope/prosopa*' was intended to express the same meaning as '*qnome/hypostases*' in the theology of the Trinity; meant, that is, to say that the Trinitarian dimensions of particularity and distinction are as foundational as the notions of unity and oneness?

Given these questions, I want to propose in this chapter that a new more perceptive reading of 'Nestorian/Antiochene' Christological expressions calls for serious attention to be given to the link between the 5th-century fathers' terminological choices and the Trinitarian terminology of the 4th-century's supporters of Nicene-Constantinopolitan theology. In what follows, I shall attempt to argue that '*parsopa/prosopon*' was not used at the expense of the important truth of 'the distinction of nature' that is implied in Trinitarian words such as *qnoma* and *hypostasis*. I shall also show that, once we realize that the main concern of Nestorian thinking is to stress the dimension of particularity, it is clear that Nestorius' position would have been clarified had he used the Trinitarian term *qnoma* rather than *parsopa* to refer to 'the personal appearance of the united, yet distinguished, natures' of Christ. In other words, Nestorius paid the price for his linguist-terminological choices, rather than for the implications of his theology.

In recent times, some theologians from the Ancient Oriental Church have begun to concede the importance of re-understanding Nestorian Christology with the help of looking at the Syriac-speaking fathers' traditional allegiance to the Nicene-Constantinopolitan understanding of 'particularity' in their use of the term *hypostasis* (*qnoma*), especially in the context of the relation between 'nature' and 'person' in the Trinity. This can be seen, for instance, in the documented conversations that took place two decades ago in a consultation on dialogue between the 'Oriental/Assyrian' and 'Syriac/Jacobite' churches. In an essay presented at the consultation, a theologian from the Oriental Assyrian Church, Mar Bawai Soro, acknowledges the importance of clarifying the various meanings of the Syriac theological terminology, regarding not only Christology but also the doctrine of the Trinity, and eventually concludes that discerning the connotations of the technical terms (such as *qnoma*) that are used can solve any misunderstanding between the churches with regard to the identity of Jesus Christ.[279]

In addition to following Sebastian Brock's proposal, the present chapter also attempts to take up Bawai Soro's suggestion by: 1) comparing the Greek and Syriac Trinitarian terms that reflect the teaching of Nicaea-Constantinople; 2) showing that the similarity in the Trinitarian terminology used by the Syriac- and Greek-speaking fathers implies that the Christological disagreement between the Chalcedonian and the non-Chalcedonian churches during and after the events of 431 and 451 could have been avoided had Nestorius and his followers used the Greek and the Syriac Trinitarian terms, *hypostasis* and *qnoma* instead of *prosopon* or *parsopa*. I suggest that attention be given to what the impact has been on Christology of the common understanding of the terms '*person*' and '*nature*' in each of these Trinitarian theologies. By highlighting the importance of clarifying the Christological differences vis-à-vis exploring the potential clarity the Trinitarian terminology could have brought to the issue had it been used in Christology, I attempt to encourage theologians to view the Christological schism as an unfortunate result of the reading of the Syriac terms for 'person' and 'nature' in isolation from their original Trinitarian connotations and roots.

In order to show that the extent of the terminological similarity between the Greek- and Syriac-speaking followers of Nicaea is much greater and more evident than some may think,[280] this chapter is divided into three parts. The first is a brief presentation of the understanding of the Greek terms *hypostasis* and *ousia*. The second part is an exposition of the Syriac Trinitarian term *qnoma* and other related terms, in which I shall show that the Greek and the Syriac terms are conceptually synonymous, and thus prove that the two groups of fathers share a common Trinitarian understanding of God. The third part will then argue that this terminological similarity in the doctrine of the Trinity explains in a new way how the fathers on both sides read the Christological differences between them, and it equally shows that this mutual reading not only reveals the centrality of *qnoma* in Syriac Trinitarian theology, but also its foundational importance for interpreting the logic of any Nestorian-like Christology.

---

279 Mar Bawai Soro, "Does the Council of Ephesus Unite or Divide: Re-evaluation of the Council of Ephesus – The Point of View of the Assyrian Oriental Church", in *Syriac Dialogue: Second Non-Official Consultation on Dialogue within the Syriac Tradition*, ed. A. Stirnemann and G. Wilflinger, (Vienna: Pro Oriente, 1996), 179–204, p. 193.

280 Sebastian Brock says, for example: "The connotations of Syriac *kyana* and *qnoma* are by no means precisely the same of those of [*ousia*] and [*hypostasis*], which they regularly represent": Brock, "The Christology of the Church of the East in the Synods of the Fifth to Early Seventh Centuries," XII, p. 130.

II. On *Hypostasis* in Greek Trinitarian Terminology

Up until the end of the 2nd century, the Greek fathers used the term *prosopon* to refer to the three divine persons of the Trinity.[281] The original meaning of this word is "'face' or 'expression' or one's 'individual outward being,'" but it also connotes 'surface' and 'form,' as well as "the mask worn by an actor and then extended to one's 'role' in a drama or to one's 'position' within his or her community."[282] One notes in patristic literature, at least of the first five centuries, that the fathers frequently used the term *prosopon* because it exists in the Septuagint and the New Testament, where it generally refers to the 'whole person' or the person's whole presence. It is even used in relation to the term *ousia* to express the concrete revelation of the latter. In other words, *prosopon* plays the same role that *hypostasis* plays later in Trinitarian and Christological literature, albeit the former is free from the metaphysical connotations of the latter.[283] Some fathers (e.g., Theophilus of Antioch and Origen) would even speak about the Son or the divine *Logos* as the *prosopon* of the Father. 'The *Logos* assumes the *prosopon* of the Father' means here that the divine Son plays the 'role' of the Father and evinces his character, as if the Father stands 'disguised' in the *Logos*.[284]

That is noted, there then came a time when *prosopon* became problematic to the 3rd- and 4th-century fathers, who not only wanted to avoid reducing the Son to a mere disguise or role-player of the Father (for Christological reasons), but also refused (for Trinitarian reasons) to say that God was 'three *prosopa*' because it suggested that God was one person with three masks or roles rather than three divine, fully subsistent persons. An expressive statement of the fathers' reservations about using *prosopon* is Basil of Caesarea's comment: "It is not enough to

---

281 In this brief presentation of the use of *prosopon* and *hypostasis* in Christian theology and also for the use of this terminology by the Cappadocians and Athanasius, I rely heavily on the main points of my exposition of the notion of personhood in patristic ontology in: Najīb G. Awad, *God without a Face? On the Personal Individuation of the Holy Spirit* (Tübingen: Mohr Siebeck, GmbH & Co, 2011).

282 Frederick G. McLeod, SJ. *The Image of God in the Antiochene Tradition* (Washington: Catholic University of America Press, 1999), pp. 91–92. See also the article on *prosopon* in *Theological Dictionary of the New Testament*, Gerhard Kittle and Gerhard Friedrich (eds.), Geoffrey Bromiley (trans.), (Grand Rapids, MI: W. B. Eerdmans, 1968), pp. 768–769.

283 McLeod, *The Image of God*, p. 92. See also G.W.H. Lampe, *Patristic Greek Lexicon* (Oxford: Clarendon Press, 1961), pp. 1186–1189; on the fathers' borrowing of Greek terminology in theology, see Edwin Hatch, *The Influence of Greek Ideas and Usages upon the Christian Church*, ed. A. M. Fairbairn, 5th ed. (Peabody, MA: Hendrickson, 1995).

284 On the use of *prosopon* in this sense, see John J. Lynch, "*Prosopon* in Gregory of Nyssa: A Theological Word in Transition," *Theological Studies*, 4 (40) (1979), 728–738, pp. 729–732.

enumerate distinctions of *prosopa*; rather it is necessary to profess faith in a genuine *hypostasis*."[285] Even when *propsopon* is used in a qualified manner (as sometimes in Gregory of Nyssa and Gregory Nazianzen), the fathers were always aware that this term's meaning of 'face' might create all kinds of theological confusions and misinterpretations unless whoever used the term clearly stated what he meant by it. This eventually made the fathers look for an alternative that is capable 'securely and properly' of speaking about the divine persons *per se* as a subject with a particular nature, as well as each having a unique and real existence. *Hypostasis* seemed to be the most appropriate alternative.[286] It was the theological keyword that these fathers used to define the particular personhood of the three divine persons of God as both 'what lies underneath' *as well as* "what forms the thing without being obscured by empty appearance."[287]

In its Greek etymological form, *hypostasis*, as Frederick McLeod shows, can be derived from two different Greek verbs, *ὑφίστημι* or *ὑφίσταμαι*. While the first connotes "origination, sustenance, actualization and plan," the second holds a wide range of meanings: "source, original existence, being, state of being, reality, nature, substance, substantive entity, concrete entity, individual, setting, property, statement, and finally a person."[288] McLeod adds that the term in its second form was used in medical and scientific Greek texts before the Stoics introduced it to the field of philosophy, understanding by it both 'the being before its becoming into specific existence' *and* 'the being's actual coming into existence,' stressing the second comparatively more than the first.[289]

When the term was transferred from philosophical literature to the theological field, the Church fathers adopted the Stoics' twofold usage: *Hypostasis* pointed to the nature of the subject's existence (i.e., how it is what it is) as well as to the subject's inner substance (i.e., what is its essence). It was considered an appropriate expression of divine personhood in the Trinity because it showed that every divine person in the Godhead was essentially constituted by a substance

285 Basil of Caesarea, *Letters*, in *Nicene and Post-Nicene Fathers*, ed. P. Schaff and H. Wace (Peabody, MA: Hendrickson, 1995), Vol. 8, Lt. 210.5.

286 Uti Possekel shows that scholarly opinion varies as to whether it was the Stoics are the first to introduce the term '*hypostasis*' into the philosophical discussion or the Epicureans before them: Uti Possekel, *Evidences of Greek Philosophical Concepts in the Writings of Ephrem the Syrian* (Leuven: Peeters, 1999), pp. 71ff (n.122). In any case, whoever introduced the term to philosophical and theological debates, it seems that '*hypostasis*' meant both the inner nature of the thing as well as its real existence.

287 C. Webb, *God and Personality* (New York: Macmillan, 1918), p. 34, and: G.L. Prestige, *God in Patristic Thought* (London: SPCK, 1981), p. 163.

288 McLeod, *The Image of God*, p. 90.

289 Ibid., p. 91.

that connotes both particularity and communion.[290] This meant for the fathers that the three particular divine persons of the Trinity were united by virtue of one substance (*ousia*) and that this divine *ousia* was open and relational in characteristics; so much so that the three persons are related to each other by virtue of the common essence they share and communally constitute as a single Godhead. In principle, then, differentiating *hypostasis* from *ousia* was meant to mark a distinction in the Greek fathers' Trinitarian terminology between God's nature and the divine actions that are indicative of God's particular personhood, without this implying any division between who God is as one *ousia* and what God personally and relationally does as three *hypostases*.

One should here point out, however, that some Greek patristic writings during the 4th century demonstrate a kind of identification between 'nature,' 'action,' 'being' and 'existence' by either using *hypostasis* alone and dispensing with the word *ousia*, or treating both terms as totally synonymous and using them interchangeably. Christopher Stead sheds light on this interchangeability in the works of St Athanasius. He shows that this father uses *hypostasis* in place of *ousia* on the basis that the latter is not found in scripture while the former occurs in the Wisdom literature, in Hebrews.1:3; 3:14; 11:1 and in the Pauline epistles (e. g., 2 Cor.9:2ff; 11:17).[291] Athanasius, Stead further argues, equates existence with being when he says that *hypostasis is* 'being,' and *ousia* means that which simply exists.[292] Accordingly, God's essence or substance is God's existence as a divine being and God's being as an ontological existence.

Against, on one hand, the Arians' claim that the Son is alien to and separate from the essence and eternity of the Father and, on the other, the Sabellians' conviction that the divine essence (Godhead) only appears as Son-Father and is not three divine persons *a se*, Athanasius argues in his various writings that the divine essence and its particular, specific form of existence are one and the same thing. The essence does not lie behind its existing mode and actions, for the existence and actions *are* the subsisting essence. In the identification between 'substance' and 'subsistence,' according to Athanasius, lies the core of the mystery of the incarnation: not only did the Son of God, the eternal *Logos*, perform the incarnation and redemption by means of human flesh, but also, in this body and these actions, Athanasius states, the *Logos* was not simply human, but

290 Art. "Person, divine" in *New Catholic Encyclopaedia*, ed. Catholic University of America (New York: McGraw-Hill, 1967), Vol.11, p. 171.

291 C. Stead, *Divine Substance* (Oxford: Clarendon Press, 1977), p. 161.

292 Webb, *God and Personality*, p. 166. G. Prestige further claims that the historical Athanasius never applied '*hypostasis*' to the three persons of the Godhead: G. L. Prestige, *God in Patristic Thought*, p. 181.

God the Word as well.[293] The divine *ousia*, then, was not absent from the human personhood or what Jesus the human person did. Rather, it was in that very personhood as much as "in everything while [still] external to the universe."[294] Had the works of the existing incarnate Word not reflected the divine essence, it would have been plausible to disbelieve the resurrection, Athanasius continues, since the human body is the temple of death and mortality. But, because the divine essence *is* in the human personhood of the incarnate *Logos*, the resurrection of Christ is to be believed, for the body of the incarnate *Logos*, being the abode of the *ousia*, is the temple of life and of life-giving alike.[295] What the incarnate *Logos* did was not only achieved by means of his mere personhood, then, but also, and more substantially, actually in His own substantial belonging to the Godhead.[296]

Contrary to the Arians, Athanasius wants to show that the *hypostasis* of the Son is not alien to the *ousia* of the Father, nor his knowledge of his own *ousia* marred because of his incarnation in human form.[297] The identity of the essence (*ousia*) and its concrete existence (*hypostasis*) must found the oneness-in-substance between the Father and the Son (*homoousion*), lest the scriptural attestation of the hypostatic threeness of the divine Godhead pave the way for partition and division in the Deity, as Athanasius warns in *De Decretis*.[298] Against, on one hand, the Sabellian claim that the Son is the Father in human form and the Fa-

293 Athanasius, *On the Incarnation of the Word*, in *Nicene and Post-Nicene Fathers*. Ed. P. Schaff, and H. Wace (Peabody, MA: Hendrickson, 1995), Vol. 4, Ch. 16, 4–5.

294 Ibid., Ch. 17, 7–5. "And this was the wonderful thing that He was at once walking as man, as the Word was quickening all things, and as the Son was dwelling with His Father. So that not even when the virgin bore Him did He suffer any change, nor by being in the body was [Hid glory] dulled, but, on the contrary, He sanctified the body also."

295 Ibid., Ch. 31, 4.

296 Ibid., Ch. 48, 8–9.

297 Athanasius, *Deposition of Arius*, in *Nicene and Post-Nicene Fathers*, Pt. 4. In his reading of Arius' Christology, Aloys Grillmeier points out that, although Arius also speaks of both the Father and the Son as *hypostases*, what he means by this term is not what Athanasius and Origen meant. Arius simply uses this term to avoid employing Sabellian and Gnostic term *prosopon* for the Father and the Son: "[Arius'] talk of '*three hypostases*' ... does not mean what Origen understood by this phrase ... For Origen understood the only-begotten to be subordinate, but nevertheless the Son of God in essence ... Arius differs: for him only the first *hypostasis*, the monad, is God in the real and unqualified sense. The *hypostases* of the Son and the Spirit are gradated and belong in the creaturely sphere. If they are called '*hypostases*' this is to express their reality in the face of Sabellius or the Gnostics": Aloys Grillmeier, SJ, *Christ in Christian Tradition*, Vol. 1: *From the Apostolic Age to Chalcedon (451)*, trans. John Bowden, (Atlanta, GA: John Knox Press, 1975), Vol. 1, p. 227.

298 Athanasius, *Defense of the Nicene Definition*, in *Nicene and Post-Nicene Fathers*, Ch. 5, 2–4.

ther is the Son in a different form and, on the other, the Marcionite division of the Godhead into three subsistences that are foreign to each other in essence and utterly separate (even contradictory, i.e., the God of the Old Testament and the God the Son in the New Testament), Athanasius emphasizes in this writing the unity of the *hypostases* of the Son and the Father by stressing the oneness of their *ousia* and the almost total identification of that *ousia* with its hypostatic paternal and filial subsistences.[299] The Son is not just one of the functions of the divine *ousia*, but is a hypostatic particularity of that *ousia*.[300] Athanasius believes that there is no other way to maintain the unity and oneness of the triune Godhead than by using the terms 'substance' and 'subsistence' interchangeably and stressing that the essence *is* its existing particularities. Only such emphasis, he argues, prevents speaking of three subsistences (*hypostases*) as the triune Godhead from implying three substances (*ousiai*) or a divided Monad.[301] Against a divided Monad, Athanasius protects the oneness of the substance and the threeness of the subsistences by means of construing as reflective of the Nicene faith the conviction that the word *hypostasis* (subsistence) is the same as the word *ousia* (substance/essence), provided this, on the other hand, does not mean that the Godhead is *one hypostasis*, but rather one *ousia*, as Athanasius states.[302]

It is necessary to understand the Athanasian equation of essence and subsistence in its own terms and avoid thinking that *all* the 4th-century Greek-speaking fathers followed Athanasius in believing that the nature of each divine person in the Trinity was exclusively defined in terms of 'how' that nature existed as what it was.[303] In its own terms, Athanasius' reading of the Nicene Trinitarian terminology serves brilliantly as a plausible explanation of the basic *homoousian* relationship between the Father and the Son, as well as defending the divine na-

299 Ibid., Ch. 6, 26–27.

300 Ibid., Ch. 7, 26. "Neither then may we say divide into three Godheads the wonderful and divine Monad; nor disparage with the name of 'work' the dignity and exceeding majesty of the Lord; but we must believe in God the Father almighty, and in Christ Jesus His Son and in the Holy Ghost and hold that to the God of the universe the Word is united."

301 Athanasius, *Synodal Letter to the People of Antioch*, in *Nicene and Post-Nicene Fathers*, Ch. 5.

302 Ibid., Ch. 6.

303 Robert Jenson makes this mistake: Robert Jenson, *The Triune Identity: God according to the Gospel* (Philadelphia, PA: Fortress Press, 1982), p. 149 (n. 18). Francis Young even states that Athanasius personally maintained "a non-committal attitude towards use of the word *hypostasis* ... and that he did appeal to those united in spirit to sink verbal differences for the sake of peace": Frances M Young, *From Nicaea to Chalcedon: A Guide to the Literature and its Background* (London: SCM Press, 1983), p. 79.

ture of the *Logos*, before but also, and more crucially, after the incarnation. In this, Athanasius is just reflecting the dominant theological logic that shaped the theological decisions of the fathers at Nicaea. The Nicene conveners (influenced by Athanasius, and not the other way round, most probably), as Grillmeier correctly notes, considered *hypostasis* and *ousia* as totally synonymous and had not yet reached that stage in 4th-century theology that would witness a recognition of a distinction in the understanding of the triune God between the term that designates the unity and that which designates the particularity.[304]

Reading *ousia* and *hypostasis* as interchangeable synonyms and reducing the extent of their significations to one narrow connotation or meaning still does not help the endeavor to unpack fully or clearly the depth and the conceptual spectrum of the use of *hypostasis* and *ousia* in 4th-century orthodox theology. Neither can one really develop a clear view of who said exactly what about the oneness of the Godhead and the triune particularity of the divine persons if we sweepingly assume that all 4th-century orthodox theologians concurred without reservation with Athanasius' assertion that "subsistence and essence is [mere] existence; for it is, or in other words exists."[305] Later, I shall argue that Cyril of Alexandria sticks to Athanasius' equating of the terms and uses that criterion when he reads into Nestorius' Christology the reduction of substance to subsistence. In fact, Nestorius, in using his own terms (which are not always well chosen, as exemplified by his use of *prosopon* and *hypostasis* interchangeably, as I shall argue later), stands in line with the Antiochene (and, more specifically, Cappadocian) theological distinction between *ousia* and *hypostasis.*[306] Without discerning this departure from such a Trinitarian, terminological distinction, one misses, as I shall show, the main discrepancies between Cyril's and Nestorius' Christological arguments. But, let us for now remain within the exposition circle of 4th-century Greek Trinitarian terminology. To justify an existence of three *hypostases* as one *ousia* without suggesting the existence of three *ousiai* in God, other 4th-century Greek fathers, especially the Cappadocian fathers, found it necessary to maintain the conceptual distinction between *hypostasis* and *ousia*. For them, speaking about three *hypostases* does not imply many *ousiai* because, rather than being totally identified, *hypostasis* points to one *ousia*

---

304 Grillmeier, *Christ in Christian Tradition*, Vol. 1, p. 272.

305 Athanasius, *To the Bishops of Africa*, in *Nicene and Post-Nicene Fathers*, Ch. 4.

306 In the light of this terminological point of departure, one can actually stand with those who argue for the sake of proving the genuine orthodoxy of Nestorius' theology, even his interpretation of *theotokos*. For an example of such an attempt, see: Milton V. Anastos, "Nestorius was Orthodox," in *Studies in Byzantine Intellectual History*, ed. M.V. Anastos (London: Variorum Reprints, 1979), VI. pp. 119–140.

without exhausting its infinity. The essence and its subsistence(s) (*hypostasis*) are not totally synonymous in the Cappadocians' Trinitarian writings, although they are, as Grillmeier notes, strongly linked to each other: each one's meaning elaborates that the need of each for the other is clear.[307]

This line of thought is clearly seen, for instance, in the theology of Gregory of Nyssa. According to Clement Webb, Gregory of Nyssa does not completely identify 'being' with 'personal subsistence' in his understanding of God or divinity, but maintains, instead, an ontological distinction between *hypostasis* and *ousia*, averring that *hypostasis* refers to the objective presentation of a certain nature, while *ousia* refers to the abstract substance of that *hypostasis*.[308] Occupied, like Athanasius, with refuting the Arian ontology, Gregory of Nyssa argues in his first treatise against the Arian theologian, Eunomius, that one should not ascribe the supreme being of the Godhead to the Father alone and deny it to the Son and the Spirit. For Eunomius, in the first place, denying any existing entity its being means that that entity does not really exist or 'be.' So, denying the Son and the Spirit their divine being would mean that only the person of the Father enjoys divine power, divine goodness and the rest of the divine attributes, since only the Father's personhood has 'being' or 'is.'[309] Against this ontological hierarchy, Gregory of Nyssa stresses that "the personality of the only-begotten and the Holy Ghost has nothing lacking in the way of perfect goodness, perfect power and every quality like that."[310] To assume that the Son and the Spirit are less than perfect in divine attributes would not only deny them their being, but also their real substance and its divinity. This view would further entail that the Father has personal subsistence (*hypostasis*), while the Son and the Spirit have none. And, if they have no hypostatic presence, they then exist only in name.[311] "Everything that is regarded as subsisting [*ἐν ὑποστάσει θεωρούμενον*]," the Nyssan postulates later in the same treatise, "is said by the common custom of all who use language, to 'be': and from the word

307 Grillmeier, *Christ in Christian Tradition*, Vol. 1, p. 481. Grillmeier believes that Nestorius follows the Cappadocians in distinguishing nature from *hypostasis* in Trinitarian theology (p. 460). While this may be true, it is not evident from Nestorius' expression of the distinction between nature and *hypostasis* by using the term *prosopon*. This latter term designates a formal rather than *personal* particularity that is not mere appearance but a substantial being-ness. The Cappadocians would not use *prosopon* to express the distinction they want to retain in the Trinity between nature and *hypostasis*.

308 Webb, *God and Personality*, pp. 17 ff., esp. p. 18.

309 Gregory of Nyssa, *Against Eunomius*, In *Nicene and Post-Nicene Fathers*, ed. Philip Schaff and H. Wace (Peabody, MA: Hendrickson Publishers, 1995), Vol. 5, Bk. 1, 14–15.

310 Ibid., Bk. 1, 15.

311 Ibid.

'be' has been formed the term 'being.'"[312] If this is the case, Gregory concludes, the thing whose 'be' is only nominal does not truly subsist because it does not have real being.

From postulating that the Son and the Spirit have both real substance or being and true subsistence or personhood that is as divine and supreme as the Father's, Gregory of Nyssa moves on to affirm that one should equally refute Eunomius' usage of 'being' and 'person' interchangeably to speak, for instance, of 'three beings' when he means 'three persons.' Things that are common in being, Nyssa argues, are not all identical in terms of personal identities. Peter, James and John, for example, are one and the same in their substance as human beings. However, they are distinguished from each other with respect to each one's particular subsisting properties.[313] What makes them different from each other – what sets each of them apart from the others, is their 'identifying properties' (*gnoristikai Idiotetes*).[314] One cannot therefore replace 'personhood' with 'being' and speak of 'three beings' as if that meant 'three personal-

312 Ibid., Bk. 10, 4.

313 In an essay on the Aristotelian differentiation made by the Cappadocians, especially Gregory of Nyssa, between nature and properties, Lucian Turcescu refutes John Zizioulas' reading of the Cappadocians' understanding of personhood (J. D. Zizioulas, *Being as Communion: Studies in Personhood and the Church*, (Crestwood, NY: St. Vladimir Seminary Press, 1997)) by claiming, contrary to Zizioulas, that the Cappadocians did recognize the notion of individuality as definitive of personhood. Turcescu refers to Gregory of Nyssa and Basil's reference to differences in properties that set each human person apart (e.g., Peter, John and James) from others despite their common humanity: Lucian Turcescu, "'Person' Versus 'Individual', and Other Modern Misreadings of Gregory of Nyssa," *Modern Theology*, 18 (4) (2002), 527–539. I do agree with Turcescu's principal critique of Zizioulas' reading of the Cappadocians: see Najīb Awad, "Between Subordination and Koinonia: Toward a New Reading of the Cappadocian Theology," *Modern Theology*, 23 (2) (2007), 181–204. I also read Zizioulas' concept of person in the light of the influence of modern authors on him: see N.G. Awad, "Personhood as Particularity: John Zizioulas, Colin Gunton and the Trinitarian Theology of Personhood," *Journal of Reformed Theology*, 4 (1) (2010), 1–22. For a counter-argument for Turcescu's critique of Zizioulas, see the response of Aristotle Papanikolaou, "Is John Zizioulas an Existentialist in Discourse? Response to Lucian Turcesco," *Modern Theology*, 20 (4), 2004, 601–607. I believe that, while the Nyssan pays attention to individuality in his understanding of *hypostasis*, he understands it in the sense of particularity and individuation. Gregory is not actually supporting a notion of individualism that is similar to the notion of 'individualism' that Zizioulas is refuting. This last notion reflects a strong sense of individualism in the sense of 'singularism' and 'self-enclosure', which I believe the three Cappadocians would reject, choosing instead to opt for relationality, as Zizioulas notes.

314 Following the translation in J.N.D. Kelly, *Early Christian Doctrines* (London: SCM Press, 1993), p. 263. Elsewhere, as John Lynch points out, Gregory uses other Greek synonyms to refer to the same 'identifying peculiarities': "*idiazon, idioma, idion gnorisma, charakter*, and *morphe*": Lynch, "*Prosopon* in Gregory of Nyssa," pp. 732ff.

ities.'[315] Instead, we should maintain a conceptual and philological distinction wherein we speak about the one essence of God and the three persons of the Trinity. 'Being' and 'particular existence' are not to be totally identified or used interchangeably, lest the one God become three gods.[316] We should rather refer to God's simple and single nature by speaking of one substance, and refer to the particularity and individuation of the Father, Son and Spirit by speaking of three persons.[317] Moreover, speaking of 'essence' *and* 'persons' in or as the Godhead safeguards the incomprehensibility of the divine essence and never reduces the divine essence to one of the three persons alone. This includes the person of the Father, according to the Nyssan, because even the Father "does not present to us the essence, but only indicates the relation to the Son."[318]

---

315 Gregory of Nyssa, *Against Eunomius*, Bk. 1, 19. According to Gregory, this is exactly the mistake Eunomius makes, for he defends the existence of *three persons* in the Trinity "not because he divides the persons only from each other by their recognized characteristics, but because he makes the actual substantial being of each [one] different from that of the others, or rather from itself: and so he speaks of a plurality of beings with distinctive difference which alienates them from each other."

316 Some scholars believe that Gregory of Nyssa is here founding this distinction upon a philosophical attempt at marrying Platonic forms with Aristotelian metaphysics of the universal and the particular. Thus Lucian Turcescu, *Gregory of Nyssa and the Concept of Divine Persons* (Oxford: Oxford University Press, 2005), pp. 63, 97; Christopher A. Beeley, *Gregory of Nazianzus on the Trinity and the Knowledge of God: In Your Light We Shall See Light* (Oxford: Oxford University Press, 2008), p. 306; Lewis Ayres, "On Not Three People: The Fundamental Themes of Gregory of Nyssa's Trinitarian Theology as Seen in *To Ablabius: On Not Three Gods*," *Modern Theology*, 18 (4) (2002), 445–474; Nathan Jacobs, "On 'Not Three Gods' – Again: Can a Primary-Secondary Substance Reading of *Ousia* and *Hypostasis* Avoid Tritheism?" *Modern Theology*, 24 (3) (2008), 332–358; and earlier Anthony Meredith, SJ, "Gregory of Nyssa and Plotinus," *Studia Patristica*, 17 (3) (1982), 1120–1126. On the other hand, some scholars argue that both Basil's and Gregory of Nyssa's works demonstrate a Stoic, rather than Platonist, Neo-Platonist or even Aristotelian, influence on their theological thinking. For this opinion, see, for example, on Gregory of Nyssa: R.G. Tanner, "Stoic Influence on the Logic of St. Gregory of Nyssa," *Studia Patristica*, 18 (3) (1989), 557–584; and on Basil, see David G. Robertson, "Stoic and Aristotelian Notions of Substance in Basil of Caesarea," *Vigiliae Christianae*, 521998), 393–417. Yet other scholars still like to see a Cappadocian borrowing of some apophatic ideas about God's incomprehensibility and transcendence from Jewish apocalyptic, mystical and visionary traditions. Thus, for example, Dragoş Giulea, "The Divine Essence, That Inaccessible *Kabod* Enthroned in Heaven: Nazianzen's *Oratio* 28.3 and the Tradition of Apophatic Theology from Symbols to Philosophical Concepts," *Numen*, 57, 2010, 1–29.

317 Gregory of Nyssa, *Against Eunomius*, Bk. 1, 22.

318 Ibid., Bk. 2, 3.

On the basis of the distinction between 'nature' (*physis*) and 'personhood' (*hypostasis*), Gregory of Nyssa constructs his significant answer to the following question from Ablabius

> How is it that in the case of our statements of the mysteries of the Faith, though confessing the three persons, and acknowledging no difference of nature between them, we are in some sense at variance without confession when we say that the Godhead of the Father and of the Son and of the Holy Ghost is one, and yet forbid men to say 'there are three Gods'?[319]

Gregory starts his response by showing that, just as in the case of human beings, the phrases 'many men' and 'many human natures' do not have the same meaning, in the case of the Godhead, the phrases 'three divine persons' and 'three divine natures' do not mean the same thing, leave aside the fact that the second phrase is incorrect. What signifies the particular distinction between Peter, James and John is not that they are 'human.' It is rather the things that characterize each one's particular personhood in his concrete existence as a human being. It is the personhood, not the nature, which is common to all three, that distinguishes James or John as particular individuals. The enumeration of the individuals is restrictively relevant to the dimensions of particularity and distinction in Gregory's logic. For Gregory, the very notion of *hypostasis* allows this quantity and numeration perspectives and enable us to refer to particularity in terms of numbers.[320] In other words, Gregory proceeds, "Luke is a man, or Stephen is a man; but it does not follow that if any one is a man he is therefore Luke or Stephen."[321] So, when it comes to discerning what makes Luke 'Luke' and not Stephen, it is Luke's personhood; this particular subsistence as a human being is what counts. Whereas, pointing to Luke's human nature *per se* would just point to the commonality between him and Stephen, despite their distinction as two persons. When it comes to nature, numeration is not acceptable; using the analogy of the oneness of the human nature, we cannot speak of God's nature in terms of numbers. In other words, Gregory sees the possibility of the 'enumeration of individuals' as the basic distinction between nature and person, as he states elsewhere

319 Gregory of Nyssa, *On 'Not Three Gods' to Ablabius*, in *Nicene and Post-Nicene Fathers*, Philip Schaff (ed.), (Grand Rapids, Mich: W.B. Eerdmans Publishing Company, 2007), Vol. V, pp. 331–336. In the footnotes that follow, I shall give the page numbers in this edition.

320 See also Turcescu's interpretation in "'Person' Versus 'Individual'," pp. 532ff.

321 Gregory of Nyssa, *On 'Not Three Gods' to Ablabius* p. 332.

> Numerical order does not bring about diversity of the natures, but the numbered items, whatever their nature is, remain what they are, whether they are numbered or not. Number is a sign to make it known how many things are.[322]

From arguing within the boundaries of human ontology, Gregory of Nyssa moves in his logic up to the framework of divine ontology. He argues that, since mixing what 'nature' signifies with what 'personhood' connotes is not applicable to the human (it is rather a 'bad habit' in reasoning and speaking, as Gregory says), it is even more inappropriate to use it when we speak about the divine. We should not, that is, speak of the divine nature using a variety of terms that actually have different, and far from interchangeable, connotations. We should confess 'one God,' that is one *ousia* or *physis*, even though, Gregory says, "the name of the Godhead extends through the holy Trinity."[323] Is this possible? Yes, because the holy Trinity is named as three *hypostases* – i. e., three personal existences – and not as three *ousiai*. The name of the divine essence should not be extended by any mark of plurality, whereas the names of the persons are by nature plural. They point to distinction, not division, to particularity, not separation.[324]

It is within this framework that one should read Gregory's claim that 'Godhead' is the name of the three *hypostases* and not the divine essence. He is not trying here to follow a mystical, apophatic train of thought, according to which God is seen as hidden and unknown. Despite the fact that his understanding of God's being and of God's knowability would indicate that his theology is more apophatic than that of Basil and the Nazianzen, Gregory of Nyssa,[325] like his Cappadocian colleagues, is above all a theologian of revelation and divine-human relationality. His point is not epistemological in nature (i. e., about the knowabil-

---

322 Gregory of Nyssa, *Against Eunomius*, Bk. 1, 201–202. Also quoted in Turcescu, "'Person' Versus 'Individual'," p. 532.

323 Gregory of Nyssa, *On 'Not Three Gods' to Ablabius*, p. 332.

324 One can concur with Daniel Stramara in his conclusion from Gregory of Nyssa's understanding of the particularity of the three persons that, for the Nyssan, the perichoretic, interpenetrative relationship between the three divine persons "does not vitiate the respective individuality and incommunicability of each person": Daniel F. Stramara, Jr, "Gregory of Nyssa's Terminology for Trinitarian Perichoresis," *Vigiliae Christianae*, 52 (1998), 257–263, p. 259.

325 Thus Christopher Beeley states, accurately, I believe: "... Gregory of Nyssa is more apophatic than Basil, and this even more so than Gregory Nazianzen's positive doctrine of divine illumination and revelation": Beeley, *Gregory of Nazianzus on the Trinity and the Knowledge of God*, pp. 306–309, esp. p. 308. I, nevertheless, also agree with the opinion that, though the Nyssan believes that the *ousia* of God is incomprehensible to the human intellect, he also stresses that God is *known* by virtue of faith. On this qualified understanding of the extent of Nyssa's apophaticism, see Martin Laird, "Apophasis and Logophasis in Gregory of Nyssa's *Commentarius in Canticum Canticorum*," *Studia Patristica*, 37 (1999), 126–132.

ity of God and human knowledge). It is rather terminologico-ontological in extent and intention. It aims to show that the use of inappropriate terminology can produce an inaccurate ontological interpretation of the divine mystery of the triune God. Speaking of three *hypostases* in/as the Godhead does not automatically lead to speaking of three *ousiai*, because *ousia* and *hypostasis* are not conceptually interchangeable in relation to the triune being of God. Gregory's claim, therefore, that 'Godhead' is the name of the divine operations does not imply that the substance is hidden behind its activities, but simply means to say that the incomprehensibility and infinity of the divine essence are not exhaustively contained by any action or form of subsistence that is attributable to that essence. If the essence *were* totally its existence, one could claim that there was a different being or *ousia* behind every different action that is performed by one of the divine persons. But, on the contrary, Gregory states:

> The name derived from the operations is not divided with regard to the number of those who fulfill it, because the action of each concerning anything is not separate and peculiar, but whatever comes to pass, in reference either to the acts of his providence for us, or to the government and constitution of the universe, comes to pass by the action of the three, yet what does come to pass is not three things. [326]

Thus, having three *hypostases* that are designative of the operations of the Godhead does not mean that we have a diversity of essences. On the other hand, neither does having one, undivided *ousia* mean that the *hypostases* are just nominal variations or that they are mixed and confused with each other. The distinction between the three persons is to be maintained and their particularities should be stressed *because* of their unity, not despite it. Maintaining the particularity and distinction of the three *hypostases* is essential, and it is not possible without maintaining the difference in meaning between 'substance' and 'subsistence.' But, would not this distinction make the existence or the subsistence of the substance redundant and eventually threaten the substance's being? No, Gregory would answer, because "the question of existence is one, and that of the mode of existence is another."[327]

Moving to the writings of Basil of Caesarea, we find there a similar concern to define Trinitarian ontological terms and differentiate their meanings. Basil also endeavors to show that distinguishing between *hypostasis* and *ousia* is the foundation of a right understanding of the triune Godhead, as conflating them is the source of many heretic claims.

---

326 Gregory of Nyssa, *On 'Not Three Gods' to Ablabius*, p. 334.
327 Ibid., p. 336.

In a letter to his brother Gregory of Nyssa, for example, Basil touches directly upon the problem that arises from the total identification of *ousia* with *hypostasis* and from using them interchangeably. He argues that this conflation makes people think mistakenly that there are three essences or substances because they are spoken of as three *hypostases.*[328] In contrast, Basil states that the difference between *ousia* and *hypostasis* is a difference between generality and particularity. The former stands for the common essence that is shared by many entities, while the latter stands for the particular "limitation of anything, having, so far as the peculiarity extends, nothing in common with what is of the same kind."[329] *Ousia*, then, names a general description of the nature or the substance that combines, let us say, three human persons together. So, while subsistence (*hypostasis*) indicates the particular standing of a concrete present thing, substance (*ousia*) is that general thing that lies 'under' what stands (under-standing/sub-sistence); that 'sub-sists' under a particular subsistence and combines it, despite its distinction, with other concrete forms of standing.[330] That said, we have to confess in the case of the Godhead "one essence or substance so as not to give a variant definition of existence." We confess, that is, one *ousia* in the Godhead, not one *hypostasis*, while we use *hypostasis* to designate the particularity of the three persons of the Trinity, so that "our conception of Father, Son and Holy Spirit may be without confusion and clear."[331] The general or common needs the particular and specific in order to avoid the mistake of Sabellian Modalism. For if we use *ousia* and *hypostastis* interchangeably and at the same time retain the images or figurative roles (*prosopa*) in the biblical reference to God as Father Son and Spirit, we would inevitably speak of God as three *ousiai* and fall into the trap of Sabellianism.[332]

---

328 Basil of Caesarea, *Letters*, Lt. 38.1. This letter is also included among Gregory of Nyssa's letters to their third brother, Peter of Sebaste.

329 Ibid. ,Lt. 38.2.

330 Ibid., Lt. 38.3. On Basil's distinction between *ousia* and *hypostasis*, see John Behr, *The Nicene Faith: Formation of Christian Theology*, Vol. 2 (Crestwood, NY: St Vladimir's Seminary Press, 2004), pp. 293–299; and Stephen M. Hildebrand, *The Trinitarian Theology of Basil of Caesarea: A Synthesis of Greek Thought and Biblical Truth* (Washington, DC: Catholic University of America Press, 2007), pp. 91–92. Stephen Hildebrand's essay on the development of Basil's Trinitarian thinking is also helpful here: Stephen M. Hildebrand, "A Reconstruction of the Development of Basil's Trinitarian Theology: The Dating of Ep. 9 and *Contra Eunomium*," *Vigilae Christiannae*, 58 (2004), 393–406.

331 Basil of Caesarea, *Letters*, Lt. 236.6.

332 Ibid. In his letter to Count Terentius, Basil repeats the same argument in relation to Sabellianism, pointing out again that *ousia* stands for the general and *hypostasis* for the particular: Ibid., Lt. 194.3–4. For a good study of Basil of Caesarea's use of *hypostasis* and *prosopon* in

Without noting the above mentioned terminological and conceptual distinction between *ousia* and *hypostasis*, as well as the emphasis on maintaining a proportionate recognition of oneness and particularity in the Trinity, one can easily misjudge Basil's reservation about saying that the Father and the Son are totally similar in everything. In his letter to Maximus the Philosopher, Basil expresses this reservation while commenting on a statement made by Dionysius, that the Father and the Son are 'alike in essence, without any difference.' Basil clearly states his reservation despite his equal affirmation in the same letter of his support for the *homoousios* phrase.[333] But, how can Basil simultaneously support *homoousios* and have reservations about Dionysius' saying? Does not *homoousios* mean that the Father and the Son are alike in essence?

Basil responds to these questions by saying that he stands against the second part of the sentence, 'without any difference,' not the first. Where does the problem lie here? The answer to this question is only possible by taking account of the terminological and conceptual difference Basil conceives between *hypostasis* and *ousia*. 'Alike in essence' is a basic given presumption without which one cannot defend any oneness or unity between the Father and the Son (i.e., any *homoousian* relation between them). To be *homoousios* with the Father means that there is a general, common essence shared by the Father and the Son *together*. However, to say 'without any difference' is totally different. 'Difference' here is connotative of particularity. It points to what peculiarly distinguishes one entity from another, not in terms of 'what' or 'who' each entity is in nature, but in terms of *how* each entity concretely subsists as what or who it is in existence. So, to say that the Father and the Son are 'without any difference' entails either denying their hypostatic distinction, or defending their common essence at the expense of the distinction between their persons.[334] The di-

---

his literature, see also Lucian Turcescu, "*Prosopon* and *Hypostasis* in Basil of Caesarea's *Against Eunomius* and the Epistles," *Vigiliae Christianae*, 51 (1997), 374–395. From studying Basil's terminology in *Against Eunomius*, Turcescu concludes "In *CEun* [i.e. *Contra Eunomium*] [*hypostasis*] could mean 'substance' ... 'subsistence', 'substratum' or even 'person'. Later, Basil began to distinguish it from 'substance' so much so as to force the interpretation in this direction of the Nicene anathema that condemned those who would discriminate between *hypostasis* and *ousia*" (p. 394).

333 Basil of Caesarea, *Letters*, Lt. 9.3.

334 This reservation on 'no difference' also corresponds, as Basil states, with his concern about rejecting Aetius' and the Neo-Arians' total identification of the Father and the Son to the extent that, as Basil says, the glory of the only-begotten is diminished: Ibid., Lt. 9.3. On Basil's letter number 9, its probable date and its implication for Basil's theology, see Hildebrand, "A Reconstruction of the Development of Basil's Trinitarian Theology.

mension of oneness is over-stressed, in other words, against the dimension of particularity, and Sabellianism here is inevitable.

Maintaining the distinction between *ousia* and *hypostasis*, therefore, not only saves the equation of oneness-particularity in the triune Godhead from a one-sided emphasis, but also protects the concept of *homoousios* from misinterpretation. The only case where one can say that the Father and the Son are both 'alike in essence' *and* 'without any difference' is when instead of *hypostases* one speaks, like Sabellius, of three *prosopa*, or different modes or roles. Then, one needs to assimilate these images by all means in order to maintain the oneness of the divine essence. In other words, one could thus still say that the Son is *homoousios* with the Father, but one would then no longer be speaking about the *hypostases* of the Father and the Son of the triune Godhead.[335] In this Sabellian option, maintaining the oneness of the Godhead requires the rejection of differentiation and particularization. However, without these latter dimensions, the three *hypostases* are torn away from the things that make them who they are as three *distinct* persons, and their personhood is marred by their unity. For Basil, the correct solution to this dilemma is to acknowledge a triune Godhead, wherein oneness and particularity are equally maintained, and the essence and its subsistences are conceptually distinguished.[336]

I would like now to move to third theologian in the Cappadocians' group, Gregory Nazianzen. I have argued elsewhere[337] that Gregory Nazianzen develops a perichoretic hermeneutics of the triune Godhead that undeniably invites us to distinguish his Trinitarian discourse from those of his compatriots, Basil of Caesarea and Gregory of Nyssa. Instead of emphasizing that the Godhead lies in the *hypostasis* of the Father alone and is reflected through the Son and the Spirit by virtue of their causal origination from the Father, the Nazianzen argues that the divine *monarchia* is the perichoretic life of the three *hypostases* together. The Father is the centre of unity in the Trinity, rather than being the only source of divinity.[338] One should not overlook the terminological difference in Gregory's ref-

335 Basil of Caesarea, *Letters*, Lt. 52.3.

336 In Letter 75.1, Basil expresses the same rejection of Sabellianism: "Some, moreover, of the impious following of the Libyan Sabellius...derive ground for the establishment of their blasphemy from the same source, because of its having been written in the creed 'if any one says that the Son is a different substance or *hypostasis*, the Catholic and Apostolic church anathematizes him'. But they did not there state *hypostasis* and substance to be identical." Then Basil retorts with this rhetorical question: "Had the words expressed one and same meaning, what need of both?"

337 Awad, "Between Subordination and Koinonia."

338 John Egan's reading of Gregory Nazianzen's understanding of the Triune Godhead and his use of Trinitarian terminology remains very valuable: John P. Egan, "Primal Cause and Trinitar-

erence to the Father as the *Arche* (originator/cause) of the Son and the Spirit and the Father as the *Aitia* (principle/source) of Creation, but not of the Godhead itself, lest one mistakenly claim, as some scholars have, that there is a contradiction, inconsistency, or even arbitrariness in Gregory's Trinitarian ontology.[339] Noting this crucial difference in understanding the Godhead, as I concluded in my other essay, makes us realize that "we should scrutinize, compare and contrast each of the three Cappadocians' theological discourses, rather than lump them together on the assumption that they are fundamentally the same."[340] We should consider seriously the fact that the Cappadocians' theology is by no means a monologue or a monolithic voice.

That said, when it comes to the question of the accurate use of Trinitarian terminology and, specifically, the precise connotations of *ousia* and *hypostasis*, the Nazianzen stands unreservedly on the side of Basil of Caesarea and Gregory of Nyssa, concurring fully with their refusal to use *ousia* and *hypostasis* inter-

---

ian Perichoresis in Gregory Nazianzen's Oration 31.14", *Studia Patristica*, 27 (1993), 21–28; and J. Egan "Aitios/'Author', Aitia/'Cause' and Arche/'Origin': Synonyms in Selected Texts of Gregory Nazianzen", *Studia Patristica*, 32 (1995), 102–107.

339 I argue against this ontology and explain the implications of this terminological difference for the Nazianzen's understanding of the Trinitarian *Monarchia*; see Awad, "Between Subordination and Koinonia," pp. 193–195. Overlooking this terminological distinction has led scholars to misjudge the Nazianzen's Trinitarian ontology and underestimate its depth and brilliant balance between 'unity' and 'particularity.' See, for example, E. P. Meijering, 'The Doctrine of the Will and the Trinity in the Orations of Gregory of Nazianzen," in *God Being History: Studies in Patristic Philosophy*, ed. E. P. Meijering (Amsterdam: North Holland Publishing Company, 1975), 224–234; and Frederick Norris, *Faith Gives Fullness to Reasoning: Five Theological Orations of Gregory Nazianzen* (Leiden: Brill, 1990), pp. 45–46. The lack of precision in reading the Nazianzen's use of '*arche*' and '*aitia*' and the sweeping belief that he uses them interchangeably continues, it seems, in recent writings on Gregory's works and the warning that this mistake is inappropriate still seems to fall on deaf ears. See, for example, Ben Fulford, "'One Commixture of Light': Rethinking Some Modern Uses and Critiques of Gregory of Nazianzus on the Unity and Equality of the Divine Persons," *International Journal of Systematic Theology*, 11 (2) (2009), 172–189. See especially page 178, where Fulford states "basic to and implicit in this view is the idea that the Father is cause, source, or origin (Gregory uses these terms *interchangeably*) of the divinity of the other two persons, an idea well attested elsewhere in Gregory's corpus" (my italics).

340 Awad, "Between Subordination and Koinonia," p. 199. In my reading of the Nazianzen's Trinitarian theology, I hold the opposite view to Christopher Beeley's conviction that the Nazianzen's understanding of the Trinitarian Godhead echoes literally Basil of Caesarea's patrocentric view that the person of the Father is the source of the divine Godhead of God. See: Beeley, *Gregory of Nazianzus on the Trinity and the Knowledge of God*, pp. 187–234, esp. pp. 201–216, and his earlier essay, Beeley, "Divine Causality and the Monarchy of God the Father in Gregory of Nazianzus," *Harvard Theological Review*, 100 (2007), 199–214. For a critical response to Beeley's reading of Gregory's Trinitarian ontology, see also my N. Awad, *God without a Face?* Pp. 111–130.

changeably. He similarly states that the orthodox faith (i.e., Nicene faith, in the language of the Cappadocians) uses *ousia* to refer to the one essence of the Godhead and *hypostasis* to refer to the properties of the three persons. And when he is asked about the confusion these terms cause in the churches, he traces the roots of this challenge to the inability of the Latin-speaking fathers to find in the 'poor' store of their language's vocabulary appropriate words to express the difference in meaning between the Greek *ousia* and *hypostasis*. Instead of treating them as two different notions, the Latin-speaking fathers read *hypostasis* as another term for essence or substance. Consequentially, they found themselves in need of another word to refer to the three persons (*persona*) in the Trinity and ended up introducing to the theological scene a third term, borrowed from Greek literature: *prosopon*, which means 'mask or role,' and not the 'real, personal and particular existence' that *hypostasis* connotes. What was the result? According to the Nazianzen, this led either to reducing the triune Godhead to three *prosopa* (Sabellianism), or to claiming that there are in the Godhead three *hypostases* (which meant in this case, 'essence'), which are hierarchically ordered (Arianism).[341]

When it comes to his own position vis-à-vis this terminological confusion, Gregory states that he does not follow the line of thought that limits the *monarchia* either to one *hypostasis* or to one *persona*. The Nazianzen principally concedes that one should not recognize a Trinity in the deity without emphasizing the fundamental unity that alone makes the three "made of one equality of nature and a union of mind and an identity of motion and a convergence of its elements to unity ... so that though numerically distinct there is no severance of essence."[342] On the basis of this principal, Gregory says that, when speaking of God, we mean by 'three' the particular individuations (*hypostases*), while by 'one' we mean the substance of the Godhead (*ousia*). These are "divided without division," in the sense that their individuation does not separate them, but rather reveals hypostatically the oneness of their common nature. On the other hand, they are also "united in division," in the sense that the common, general essence of the Godhead does not eliminate or deny each *hypostasis* its own individuation as a particular, concrete personal existence. The Godhead, the Nazianzen states, "is one in three, and the three are one in whom the Godhead is, or to speak more accurately, who are the Godhead."[343]

341 Gregory Nazianzen, *Orations*, in *Nicene and Post-Nicene Fathers*, Philip Schaff and Henry Wace (eds.,), (Grand Rapids, Mich: W. B. Eerdmans Publishing Company, 1974), Vol. 7, Orat. 21.35.

342 Ibid., Orat. 29.2.

343 Ibid, Orat. 39.10. "Excess and defects," he proceeds, "we will omit, neither making the unity a confusion, nor the division a separation. We would keep equally far from the confusion

That said, the *ousia* is revealed in the *hypostases*. It is the common essence that lies behind them, as *who* they are *a se*. It is not an essence that lies behind them as if *standing with* them. It is not an essence that is '*unum in numero*.' It hypostatically exists, instead, as '*ens unum in multis*.' The Godhead is not three *hypostases and* one *ousia*. It is rather one *ousia in* three *hypostases*.[344] From this distinction, the Nazianzen concludes that what is ultimately important is to maintain that there is only one essence in the Godhead, not three, and that the proper way to do this is by not using *ousia* and *hypostasis* synonymously or interchangeably. If that is established, it does not matter whether we speak of the three persons in God as *hypostases* or *prosopa*. It also makes little difference, in Gregory's opinion, whether we speak of the three as 'particular, real forms of existence' (*hypostasis*) or as 'particular representations of a single being' (*prosopon*).[345] For Gregory, this is no longer a source of controversy, and it does not threaten the divine essence, insofar as *hypostasis* and *prosopon* are used to express the fact that the three in God are distinct not in nature but in their properties and particular personhood.[346] What matters is maintaining that the nature of the Trinity is absolutely beyond any degree of *quantity*.[347]

---

of Sabellius and from the division of Arius...for what need is there heretically to fuse God together, or to cut him up into inequality?"

344 As the editors and translators of Gregory Nazianzen's works correctly state in Ibid., p. 280, n. γ

345 Rather than using the term in the Sabellian modalistic sense of a 'mere mask', Gregory Nazianzen is most probably echoing here Gregory of Nyssa's understanding of *prosopon*, that it connotes the individual's separation from others who share the same *ousia* but not the same differentiating qualities: Lynch, "*Prosopon* in Gregory of Nyssa," p. 737. The Nazianzen certainly reiterates Basil of Caesarea's warning of the danger of the unqualified use of *prosopon* and the open charge of Sabellianism this may leave the person with (Ibid., p. 378).

346 Gregory Nazianzen, *Orations*, Orat. 42.16. In his reading of the use of *physis*, *hypostasis* and *prosopon* in late 4th-century Christological literature, A. Grillmeier says: "a being has a *prosopon* in so far as it is a *physis* and a *hypostasis*": Grillmeier, *Christ in Christian Tradition*, Vol. 1, p. 439. The Nazianzen would probably agree that every being that is *physis* and *hypostasis* also has an image in which it exists or a specific role that it plays (*prosopon*).

347 Gregory Nazianzen, *Orations*, Orats. 37.2; 38.7. Christoph Beeley has recently argued that this understanding of the divine nature also lies at the foundation of Gregory Nazianzen's Christology, especially when he uses 'single-nature expressions' to speak of Christ's full divinity even in his human state: C. A. Beeley, "Cyril of Alexandria and Gregory Nazianzen: Tradition and Complexity in Patristic Christology," *Journal of Early Christian Studies*, 17 (3) (2009), 381–419, pp. 398–399. Beeley mainly argues that the idea of 'one nature and one *hypostasis*' that we find in Cyril's works was drawn into his Christology from nowhere but the Nazianzen's understanding of the divine nature and his 'single-nature expression.' Beeley then concludes that Cyril's Christology is mainly shaped after the Nazianzen's and that the influence of the latter on the former may actually be greater than the traditionally accepted influence of Athanasius and the

This exposition of the difference between Athanasius' and the Cappadocians' treatment of the Trinitarian terms, *hypostasis* and *ousia*,[348] shows that the confusion in the Christological controversies since the 5th-century clash between Cyril and Nestorius may have arisen simply from the identification between 'being' and 'personal existence' in 'the Athanasian branch' of 4th-century Trinitarian hermeneutics.

It is important here to point briefly to the fact that the emphasis on maintaining a substantial link between God's *ousia* and the triune *hypostases* in the theology of the 4th-century fathers, especially the Cappadocians, stems from a concern to defend the authenticity of the revelation of God's being in the incarnation of the eternal *Logos*. It wants to show that the divine Godhead did not hide himself from us and did not remain totally unknowable. He rather revealed himself truly and fully in our existence and history through the eternal divine Son. It is precisely by distinguishing God's *ousia* from his three *hypostases* that the Cappadocians wanted to speak of this revealed-ness and its authenticity in the persons of the Son and the Spirit. By virtue of the hypostatic distinction of each divine person, the Cappadocians maintain that the *ousia* itself is authentically and non-exhaustively revealed. Whatever emanates from the *hypostasis* is also from the very *ousia*.

To a certain extent, this attention to the *revealed-ness* of the divine *ousia* is also indicated in Athanasius' identification of 'being' and 'personal existence' in his Christology, showing that his identification of *ousia* and *hypostasis* does not represent an ontological conviction about the triune Godhead, but is primarily as a way of pursuing a Christological defense of the substantial equality of the eter-

---

Alexandrian school (Ibid., pp. 406 ff., esp. p. 417). Though Athanasius, like Gregory, also prefers the language of single-nature, Beeley comments that, "he does so in a way that is less formal and robust then Gregory" (p. 402).

348 This difference between Atahanasius and the Cappadocians tells us that R. P. Hanson was not wrong when he tried to show that these two terms were not treated as synonymous in 4th-century theology, or even earlier: R. P. Hanson, *The Search for the Christian Doctrine of God: The Arian Controversy 318–381*, (Edinburgh: T&T Clark, 1988), pp. 167–168. Hanson, nevertheless, prefers to interpret *hypostasis* as "three distinct realities or entities" and refrains from using the term 'person': R. P.C. Hanson, "The Doctrine of the Trinity Achieved in 381," *Scottish Journal of Theology*, 36 (1) (1983), 41–57, p. 51. On Athanasius' identification of these terms, see also J.T. Lienhard, *Contra Marcellum: Marcellus of Ancyra and Fourth Century Theology* (Washington, DC: Catholic University of America Press, 1999); or the concise essay-length version of this study J. Lienhard, "The 'Arian' Controversy: Some Categories Reconsidered," *Theological Studies*, 48 (1987), 415–437. For a counter-opinion to Hanson and Lienhard, see Jon M. Robertson, *Christ as Mediator: A Study of the Theologies of Eusebius of Caesarea, Marcellus of Ancyra and Athanasius of Alexandria* (Oxford: Oxford University Press, 2007). Robertson states his disagreement with Hanson and Lienhard on pp. 222–223.

nal Father and the incarnate Son. Athanasius is responding basically to the Arians' Christological claims, and he wants to refute their subordinationism by showing that, even *after* the incarnation, the Son is *homoousios* with his Father. In view of this Athanasian Christological concern, the Church fathers conceded at the Council of Nicaea in 325 that what substantially defines the *hypostasis* of the Son and the *hypostasis* of the Father is their divine, unfathomable *ousia* and not only their relational existence: both are God in essence and not only in actions. It is, therefore, very crucial to be aware of the Christological apologetic intention behind Athanasius' claim that *hypostasis* and *ousia* are totally synonymous.

Missing this Christological dimension not only leads to a narrow reading of the full scope of Athanasius' overall theology, and to an underestimation of the wider motif that characterizes the usage of *hypostasis* and *ousia* in the other 4th-century Greek fathers' doctrine of the Trinity. It also misunderstands the basic philological connotations of these two terms in Greek philosophy in general. In Greek philosophy, *ousia* means the being of the *hypostasis* or the essence of a certain subsisting being with a particular character. The *hypostasis* is his *ousia*, yet the *ousia* is more than the *hypostasis*' particular subsistence in an active mode of existence. This is what Prestige shows when he points out that Aristotle, for example, argues that *ousia* exists on its own account and does not belong to any attribute or anything else, but rather every attributive subsistence belong to it.[349] *Ousia*, then, designates the essence of a being that exists on account of itself. The Greek Church fathers take the distinction of *hypostasis* from *ousia* into consideration and claim in the creeds of Nicaea and Constantinople the existence of 'one *ousia*, three *hypostases*,' rather than 'three *ousia*(s), one *hypostasis*.' For them, this terminological specification protects the doctrine of the Trinity from either Tritheism or Modalistic Monism. More importantly, it shows that the being of every divine person (i.e., every *hypostasis*) does not lie in a particular existence that distinguishes him from other *hypostases*. Rather, the being of every *hypostasis* lies ultimately in each person's divine nature, which is common to all three, who *are* single Godhead. Every *hypostasis* is God insofar as he is constitutive of the Godhead, and every *hypostasis* is a particular person insofar as his particular personhood is by virtue of communion with the other two divine persons.[350]

---

349 Prestige, *God in Patristic Thought*, pp. 40 – 42.

350 Within this framework, one can understand why Gregory of Nyssa, for example, as Francis Young points out, has no problem in saying that there are 'three subjects' in the divine Godhead, provided we remember that their infinity means "that they are indistinguishable alongside one another" in terms of their essence and nature as an in-composite, homogeneous and unchange-

Discerning this difference between Athanasius' and the Cappadocians' understanding of the relation between *ousia* and *hypostasis* is crucial for discovering whether the Syriac Nicene fathers follow the Athanasian equation of the two terms, or the Cappadocians' distinction between them. Sebastian Brock seems to be one of the supporters of the Syrian fathers' faithfulness to the Athanasian option, for, as he correctly states, the phrase *mia hypostasis* was a stumbling block to both the Ancient Oriental Church and the Syrian Jacobite Church. Brock explains this rejection by claiming that *both* Syriac traditions (the Jacobite and the Nestorian) share the view that *physis* implies *hypostasis* and vice versa.[351] Some recent theologians of the Ancient Oriental Church, such as Mar Bawai Soro, would even like to qualify this common implication by saying that, for the Nestorians, the Syriac word for 'person,' *qnoma*, expresses the concrete particular representative of the nature – the designation of its substantial particularity – without alluding to any possible exhaustive identification of this nature by its personal presence. '*Qnoma*' (*hypostasis*) means the particular personhood that *designates* this nature among other natures.[352]

Mia hypostasis, accordingly, is understood by the Nestorians as indicating that Cyril and the Alexandrians adopt the total ontological identification of *ousia* and *hypostasis*, thus being close to Athanasius in their use of *ousia* and *hypostasis* to mean one and the same thing. Only such an identification could make it possible for them to speak of *mia physis* on the basis of the following logic: since *hypostasis* is *ousia*, 'one person' entails 'one nature'; *mia hypostasis* thus means *mia physis*. In speaking of the Logos/Son of God who became human, who was born of a virgin, was crucified and died, Cyril of Alexandria is the one who actually follows the Athanasian total equation of *hypostasis* with *ousia* and he cites Athanasius' logocentric process of the divine nature of the Son coming into real human existence. His claim that there is a complete unity of natures, and his emphasis on 'one *hypostasis* in one *physis* of the Logos,'[353] as I shall show in the third part of this chapter, is clearly based on an Athanasian identification of 'being' and 'existence.' The Syrian fathers who follow Nicene-Constantinopolitan Trinitarian thinking, which takes into account

---

able God. "There is existence and non-existence," Young continues, echoing the Nyssan. "There cannot be [i.e. in the Godhead] degrees of Being or priorities of Being; one cannot be more or less existent than another": Young, *From Nicaea to Chalcedon*, p. 111.

351 Brock, "The Christology of the Church of the East," XII, p. 130.

352 Soro, "Does the Council of Ephesus Unite or Divide," p. 189.

353 Thus: Elias Khalife-Hashem, "Does the Council of Ephesus Unite or Divide?", *Syrian Dialogue Second Non-Official Consultation on Dialogue within the Syriac Tradition*, ed. A. Stirnemann and G. Wilflinger, Arabic trans. M. Taraqji (Vienna: Pro Oriente, 1996), 164–178, pp. 170–171.

the Cappadocians' distinction of *ousia* from *hypostasis*, would inevitably reject Cyril's terminology.[354]

However, what if the Nestorian understanding of *hypostasis* and *ousia*, and the Syriac terms that Nestorius uses as their synonyms, do not actually reflect a total allegiance to Athanasius' equation of these terms? Could one then explore the tenability of another possibility, namely that the Trinitarian and Christological logic of Syriac-speaking Nestorians in fact supports the Cappadocian distinction between *ousia* and *hypostasis* and makes a similar distinction between the Syriac Trinitarian and Christological terms, *qnoma* and *kyana/ituta?*[355] If this possibility is tenable, it would allow for the belief that Nestorian theology speaks of the distinction between the two natures of Christ on the basis of a 'distinction' concept that is actually derived from the Cappadocians' reliance on the same notion of distinction in their reference to 'one *ousia* and three *hypostases*' in the Trinity.[356] It might be the case that the philosophical logic that underpins this emphasis on distinction is similar to the logic that characterizes the Cappadocian differentiation of *ousia* from *hypostasis:* the Aristotelian process of cognizing from subsistence in the particular up to the being of the substance by means of analogy. Following this logic, the distinction between the divine and human categories, Christologically speaking, is inescapable. The Alexandrian wording 'the divine Logos who was born, suffered and dies' sounds to the ears of the Syriac-speaking adopters of this philosophical logic like the expression of a categorical conflation that denies the particular qnomic existence of the two distinguished *kyane*.

In the ensuing section, I shall show that the Syriac-speaking Nestorians' adoption of the Nicene attention to particularity in Trinitarian theology vis-à-vis differentiating *ousia* from *hypostasis* is evidently derived from their Syriac-speaking predecessors, namely the Nicene Syrian fathers' writings of the 3rd and 4th centuries. I shall do this by showing that the 4th-century fathers, such as St Ephraim, reflect the distinction between 'nature' and 'person' in the distinction they make between *qnoma* and *kyana*. I shall show that *qnoma* for

---

354 Affirmed by Louis Sako, "Does the Council of Ephesus Unite or Divide?" in *Syriac Dialogue: Second Non-Official Consultation on Dialogue within the Syriac Tradition*, ed. A. Stirnemann and G. Wilflinger, Arabic trans. M. Taraqji (Vienna: Pro Oriente, 1996), 158–163, p. 160.

355 The opposite view is held by other scholars. See, for example: Young, *From Nicaea to Chalcedon*, pp. 236ff; A.R. Vine, *An Approach to Christology* (London, 1948), pp. 113ff; Grillmeier, *Christ in Christian Tradition*, Vol. 1, pp. 501–519; McLeod, *The Image of God in the Antiochene Tradition*, pp. 94 ff.

356 This concern with the terminological distinction between 'person' and 'nature' does underlie, as I shall argue in the third section, Nestorius' reference to the union of two *distinct* natures, rather than to two *separate* persons.

Ephraim never designates 'oneness,' but always points (like *hypostasis*) to particularity. This Trinitarian terminological factor would explain the Nestorian skepticism about Cyril's 'one *hypostasis* of unity.' It mirrors the belief that Cyril's wordings launch a departure away from the Trinitarian understanding of *hypostasis* and pave the way for asserting one nature and one personhood rather than two natures in Christ.

III. On *Qnoma* in Syriac Trinitarian Terminology

If we want to study the Syrian fathers' Trinitarian terminology before (and even after) the Christological debates that led to the councils of Ephesus and Chalcedon, we need to look at the Trinitarian theology of one of the greatest fathers and saints of the East, Ephraim the Syrian.

St Ephraim (ca. 306 – 373) lived and wrote in the great schools of Nisibis and Edessa, two Near Eastern cities that were influenced by Hellenism as much as by Semitic and Persian philosophies. His theological writings show that he strongly supported Nicene orthodoxy and opposed Arianism.[357] Generally speaking, it is difficult to know what language(s) Ephraim was able to speak besides Syriac and what books were available to him to study. Some major scholars of the older generation in the field of Syriac Studies, such as E. Beck and S. Brock, tend mostly to understate the influence of Greek thinking on Ephraim's thought,[358] leave alone the thought of the Syrian fathers before the 5th century.[359] Other scholars of the

357 Possekel, *Evidence of Greek Philosophical Concepts*, p. 18.

358 Despite his emphasis on the tremendous work of translation that was carried out by the Syrians of Greek texts into Syriac, which later played a major mediating role in the transmission of Greek thought into the Arabic Islamic world, Sebastian Brock considers the two major Syrian fathers of the 4th century, Ephraim and Afrahat, as representative of "Christianity in a relatively pure Semitic, and as yet un-Hellenized form": S. Brock, "Greek into Syriac and Syriac into Greek", in *Syriac Perspectives on Late Antiquity*, ed. S. Brock (London: Variorum Reprints, 1984), Art. II (p. 1).

359 One example of such a Harnachian-like division of the 'Greek' from the 'Semitic-Aramaic' background is the saying of Bishop Hilarion of the Russian Orthodox Church of Vienna and Austria that "comparing the theological thinking and language of Ephrem the Syrian and Gregory of Nyssa, two representatives of the same faith, sharing the same spirituality, and near contemporaries yet living in totally different cultural and linguistic contexts, we cannot but notice the enormous difference between them. Gregory's language and manner of thinking turn towards Greek culture; Ephrem, on the other hand, lives in the world of Semitic Christianity; Gregory expresses the richness and diversity of Christian Tradition in the figurative categories of Greek mythology, whilst Ephrem appeals to the characteristic imagery of the Palestinian-Aramaic tradition. As befits a Greek, Gregory is more rational and disposed to definitions, while Ephrem is

younger generation, however, would like to acknowledge the possibility of Ephraim's acquaintance with Greek culture at a late stage of his life.[360] Others still, such as Princeton scholar Uti Possekel, persuasively argue that Ephraim's writings reveal an understanding of the nature of learning and the meaning of knowledge that are undeniably similar to the Hellenistic and Greek views of *episteme* and *paidaea*.[361] Even if some of his writings allude to a perennial hostility to Greek culture, as one gleans, for instance, from Ephraim's saying in his *hymn on Faith* "happy is the man who has not tasted of the venom of the Greeks,"[362] such hostility is not directed against Greek thought in general, but rather toward the reliance of certain theological trends on Greek philosophy to define the begetting of the Son of God in a way that denies the Son's infinity (i.e., Arianism).[363] Paul Russel departs from this apologetic concern per se in his argument

---

more emotional and expressive": Bishop Hilarion Alfeyev, "Theological *Popevki:* of the Fathers, Liturgy and Music," in *Shaping a Global Theological Mind*, ed. Darren C. Marks (Aldershot: Ashgate, 2008), 15–26, p. 19. One cannot but wonder whether the bishop reflects here a division similar in view to the classical 'East-emotional-irrational-Semitic' and 'West-rational-Greek' division of Ernst Renan, which was attacked by Edward Said more than anyone else in the past century, and which actually makes a value-judgment division that is today widely considered implausible and false. See Edward W. Said, *Orientalism*, (New York: random House, 1994), pp. 123–148.

360 Robert Murray, "The Characteristics of the Earliest Syriac Christianity," in *East of Byzantium: Syria and Armenian in the Formative Period*, ed. N. Garsoïan; T. Mathews and R. Thompson (Washington, DC: Dumbarton Oaks, 1982), 3–16, p. 9; and earlier R. Murray, "The Theory of Symbolism in St Ephrem's Theology," in *Parole de l'Orient*, 6–7 (1975–1976), 1–20, p. 13.

361 Possekel, *Evidences of Greek Philosophical Concepts*, pp. 33 ff. Possekel claims that "Ephrem understands learning as a hypostasis that takes intermediate position between human kind and God" (p. 34). S.H. Griffith principally believes that Ephraim's theological defence of Nicene orthodoxy does not show traces of Greek doctrinal influence, but he notes that the content of Ephraim's writings shows a remarkable concurrence with the theology of Basil of Caesarea and Gregory Nazianzen. Griffith even adds that "by Ephrem's day, one could find in Nisibis and Edessa the full range of theological interests that characterized the full intellectual agenda of the wider Roman world in the proto-Byzantine period": Griffith, "The Thorn Among the Tares: Mani and Manichaeism in the Works of St Ephrem the Syrian", *Studia Patristica*, 35 (2001), 395–427, p. 401.

362 Sebastian Brock points to this saying and find in it an indication of the minimal impact that Greek language and culture left on Ephraim's mind as well as of the second-hand rate of knowledge, which Ephraim had of the Greek intellectual world. Brock also likes to interpret Ephraim's words against the Greeks as expressive of his antagonism towards 'pagan wisdom' in particular: Sebastian Brock, "From Antagonism to Assimilation," pp. 17, 19.

363 Possekel, *Evidences of Greek Philosophical Concepts*, p. 47. See also: Kathleen McVey, *The Fathers of the Church*, Vol. 91: *St Ephrem the Syrian* (Washington, DC: Catholic University of America Press, 1994). McVey argues that the existence of contact between the Syriac and the Greek theological and cultural traditions is most likely in a geographical place like Syria, which "stood at the crossroads of the ancient world where Semitic, Hellenistic and Mesopotamian cultures freely intermingled" (p. 969).

that Ephraim's concern to refute Arianism must undoubtedly have involved him in a first-hand contact with Church theological debates and the cultural foundations underpinning them in the greater Roman Empire, both of which were deeply immersed in Greek thought and language.[364]

Possekel's and Russel's similar opinions are convincing because, even if the Greek texts of the Byzantine fathers were not officially translated into Syriac before the beginning of the 5th century,[365] this does not necessarily mean that the Syrian fathers of the earlier centuries were unable to read Greek texts effectively. If the schools of Nisibis and Edessa were as famous as many scholars, including Brock, believe, it is possible that the Syrian fathers who studied and taught there knew Greek literature, and read primary Greek texts, even at this early point in history. Brock himself does not totally deny this possibility when he admits that a number of Greek technical and philosophical terms were known to Afrahat, Ephraim's contemporary.[366] Han Drijvers also argues that Edessa demonstrated the strong link between Greek and Syriac cultures:

> The East Syrian and Northern Mesopotamian area, where Edessa was the centre of early Syriac-speaking Christianity, was not so isolated and untouched by Greco-Roman civilization as is often assumed ... [Edessa] had all the characteristics of a Greco-Roman city in an area in which a Semitic culture was indigenous ... Greek philosophy was taught there in Syriac disguise, but local religious traditions were expressed in Greek artistic and literary forms. Like Palmyra, Edessa was an exponent of Near Eastern Hellenism, where cultural traditions of Semitic origin were transmitted in Greek disguise and vice versa.[367]

---

364 Paul S. Russel, *St Ephraem the Syrian and St Gregory the Theologian Confront the Arians* (Kerala: St Ephraem Ecumenical Research Institute, 1994), pp. 13–14. Sidney Griffith follows the same logic and argues similarly that Ephraim's concern to defeat Arianism must have driven him to acquire substantial and deep knowledge, beyond his linguistic sphere, of the theological discussions that were taking place in the Greek-speaking Christian world: Sidney H. Griffith, "Faith Seeking Understanding in the Thought of St Ephraem the Syrian," in *Faith Seeking Understanding: Learning and the Catholic Tradition*, ed. G. Berthold (Manchester, NH: St Anselm College Press, 1991), 35–55.

365 See Brock, "Towards a History of Syriac Translation Technique," in *Orientalia Christiana Analecta*, 221 (1980), 1–14, where he traces the first serious translation from Greek to Syriac with a clear attribution back to the 5th century and not earlier than that.

366 Brock, "Some Aspects of Greek Words in Syriac", in *Syriac Perspectives on Late Antiquity*, ed. S. Brock (London: Variorum, 1984), p. 81.

367 Han J.W. Drijvers, "East Antioch: Forces and Structures in the Development of Early Syriac Theology," in *East of Antioch: Studies in Early Syriac Christianity* (London: Variorum Reprints, 1984), 1–27, p. 3.

The above mentioned claim, if right, supports the suggestion that the main theological Greek terms were known to the Syrian fathers as early as the 3rd and 4th centuries, especially those who supported the theology of the Nicene Creed. There are even indications that Ephraim knew the Cappadocians in person, as well as their works, and that they admired him as a person as well as his writings. This is evident from the fact that Ephraim's language reflects a similarity with that of Gregory of Nyssa and it is also supported by an assertion by the church historian Sozomen that Basil of Caesarea held a "great admiration to St. Ephraim and had marveled at the width of his education."[368]

Two Syriac terms in Ephraim's writings are of immeasurable importance when considering the similarities between the Greek and Syriac Trinitarian terminologies: *qnoma* and *itya/ituta*. The first, as I shall show below, connotes 'personhood,' and the second 'nature.' Scholars believe that *ituta* is synonymous with the Greek *to hon* (the being),[369] and that it is used for generally existing things. Ephraim (and Afrahat), however, uses this term only with reference to God. For Ephraim, *itya/ituta*, generally designates God's 'being' as well as God's 'existence.' But, more specifically, *itya* means in his doctrine of God the 'uncreated substance' or the 'eternal principle.'[370] It indicates that this eternal principle (God) is not a mere expression of existence, but rather a designation of an independent principle that *has* a real existence. *Itya/ituta* means an infinite, eternal Being who has a unique existence of his own nature. Besides applying *ituta/itya* exclusively to God, the word 'God' itself is for Ephraim the name that expresses the existing mode of this *ituta*; it is not exhaustively the *ituta* as such. God alone is *itya* because there are no other gods (i.e., no other *itye*)

---

368 Possekel, *Evidences of Greek Philosophical Concepts*, p. 49. Some scholars believe that the story of Ephraim's visit to Basil in Cappadocia is almost certainly a fabrication: Stanley M. Burgess, *The Holy Spirit: Eastern Christian Traditions* (Peabody, MA: Hendrickson, 1997), pp. 167–177. Others, however, such as Kathleen McVey, believe that, despite the difficulty of finding enough textual evidences to establish the influence of Ephraim and the Cappadocians on each other, there are noticeable similarities that cannot be ignored and merit further systematic exploration: K.E. McVey, "Ephrem the Syrian's Theology of Divine Indwelling and *Aleia Pulcharia Augusta*", *Studia Patristica*, 35 (2001), 458–465, p. 463. Geoffrey Ashe also narrates a story of Ephraim's visit to Caesarea in Cappadocia in 371 and his meeting with the three Cappadocian fathers there. Describing the deep impression Ephraim made on them, Ashe says: "to judge from remarks by the younger brother, Gregory of Nyssa, Ephraim impressed them deeply. The tiny, venerable man was a strange being from a strange country, speaking an unfamiliar tongue, giving the mysteries of faith an exotic colour and freshness": Geoffrey Ashe, *The Virgin* (London: Routledge & Kegan Paul, 1976), pp. 174–175.

369 Possekel, *Evidences of Greek Philosophical Concepts*, p. 56.

370 Ibid., pp. 56–57.

who have the same nature as God. There is only one real deity, so there is only one *ituta*, which is comprehended in the name 'God,' yet not exhausted by it.

In Ephraim's doctrine of the Trinity, *ituta*, and not *qnoma*, refers to the oneness of the divine being, which the divine Son and the divine Spirit share by virtue of sonship and spirit-hood.[371] The idea of the Son's participation in God's *ituta* indicates that *ituta* is the Godhead of God. One may say that, in this understanding, Ephraim follows the same Trinitarian logic as Gregory Nazianzen, who argues that the Godhead is constituted by the reciprocal *koinonia* of the three divine persons, who both participate in God's essence and are co-constitutive of that essence. Even if Ephraim does not elaborate on the Trinity in a way that shows his complete adoption of the Nazianzen's view, one can still say that *ituta/itya* is not for him the name of God the Father alone, but rather the name of the divine Being of the triune God; the *ousia* of the Godhead.

Another even more important key term in Syriac Trinitarian terminology is *qnoma*. The Syrian fathers of the 4th century supported the use of the Greek word *hypostasis* rather than *prosopon* for the three divine persons in the Trinity. Their writings clearly show that they use *qnoma* as a synonym for *hypostasis*, and not as a synonym for *prosopon*. In a short but important article, Bo Holmberg shows that the Syriac word for 'person' is *qnoma* (which is still used in Arabic theology today: *Uqnūm*/أقنوم). This Syriac word means, according to Holmberg, "an essence or *ousia* existing in its particular being."[372] When the Greeks, for instance, theologically translate the saying in Hebrews 1:3 "the Son is ... the exact representation of [God's] being" as "the Son is the *hypostasis* of God's *ousia*", the Syrians translate it "the Son is the *qnoma* (*uqnūm*) of God's essence (*ituta/jawhar*)." This means that the essence of God exists in a "concrete manner in a given individual."[373] The crucial point here is that the Syrian fathers did not understand *hypostasis* to mean merely a 'mask' or 'role' (i.e., *prosopon*). Instead of *qnoma*, the Syrian fathers used the word *parsopa*, which means 'face,' as a synonym for *prosopon*. They did not, however, use *parsopa* to refer to the persons of the Trinity, because they believed, according to Holmberg, that using this term

371 Ibid., p. 59. Possekel further says that, for Ephraim, '*itya*' is primarily said of God the Father and only in a derivative sense of the Son. This if correct, which I doubt if Ephraim is Nicene in conviction, it makes Ephraim's Trinitarian ontology similar to Basil's, in which the Godhead is restricted in terms of origin to the Father alone.

372 Holmberg, "'Person' in the Trinitarian Doctrine of Christian Apologetics," p. 302.

373 Ibid.

would imply Trinitarian Modalism.[374] They preferred to speak of three *qnome* with one * itya/ituta*.

The conceptual difference between *ituta* and *qnoma* reflects the reason behind the Nestorians' unease with speaking about 'one *hypostasis*' in Christ. Yaroslav Pelikan correctly reveals that understanding the reason behind their rejection of the use of *hypostasis* in this regard starts not from the doctrine of Christ's personhood, but from the doctrine of the Trinity.[375] *Hypostasis* designates the special properties that the nature possesses in its personal identity. The personal appearance of the hypostatic particularity of the nature is expressive of that which keeps this nature from being other than itself. And, because the *hypostasis* exists in its being, it cannot be assumed or added to this being by another *hypostasis* or to become one *hypostasis* with it. In contrast, this does apply to the appearance (*prosopon/parsopa*) of the nature's hypostatic particularity, which, Pelikan maintains, "can be assumed and yet remains in its own *hypostasis*."[376] Having the Syriac (Nicene-based) Trinitarian terminology in mind, we can say that the qnomic particularity of the nature cannot be assumed by another qnomic particularity. In other words, the two *qnome* cannot become 'one *qnoma*.' And the unity of the *parsope* does not nullify the qnomic distinction of their natures. This shows that the particular hypostatic existence of the nature (*qnoma*) can never be treated as just an appearance or a role that is assumable or conflated with another. In Christology, this does not demonstrate a belief in a duality or a separation of the qnomic particularities of the two natures, as it does not, according to the Nicene-Constantinopolitan doctrine of the Trinity, imply a tritheistic division in the Godhead. It rather points to the centrality of the notion of 'particularity' and of the unity-in-distinction paradigm.

In addition, *qnoma* in Ephraim's writings does not connote individualism, as it does not mean merely a mask or role. Rather, it means both the essence of something and its substantial, particular existence or personhood. Ephraim believes that that which has substantial existence, or *qnoma*, is ontologically superior to that which has no *qnoma*. Accordingly, the three persons of the Trinity must have a substantial, concrete existence. In other words, they must have real existence in themselves because they are ontologically superior and divine

---

374 Ibid., p. 303. Holmberg rightly notes that another Arabic word for *hypostasis* that was used by the Syrian fathers was *shakhṣ*", which is equivalent in meaning to the English 'person.' In Arabic, this word means a body seen in a silhouette from a distance. But, contrary to Holmberg's claim that the Arabs use this word for the Trinity today (p. 304), contemporary Christian Arabs of all denominations prefer *uqnūm* to *shakhṣ*.

375 Pelikan, *The Christian Tradition*, Vol. 2, pp. 44 ff.

376 Ibid., p. 45.

as *qnome*. Their personal existence as *qnome* is a reflection of their real nature, which means that they are not mere metaphors symbolizing a hidden reality, but that they are three eternal realities that have real existence by virtue of their single, divine essence. In *Memra on Faith*, Ephraim says: "If you confess [the triune] names, but you do not confess their *qnome*, you are a worshipper in name, but an unbeliever in deed."[377]

Ephraim considers 'Father, Son and Spirit' a designation of three personal identities, or three *qnome*, and not merely a designation of three names. He would not say, for instance, like Augustine, Anselm and Aquinas, that 'Father, Son and Spirit' are merely three names of the relational modes of subsistence of one, simple, divine substance.[378] Stanley Burgess makes an important observation when he says that Ephraim does not consider the Spirit to be the bond of love between the Father and the Son, as Augustine, Anselm and Aquinas do. Rather, he speaks of love as a common characteristic that is shared by the *three* divine persons alike.[379] Moreover, even when Ephraim occasionally describes 'Father, Son and Spirit' as 'names,' he is referring to the ontological gap between the human mind and the reality of God that cannot be perceived by human reason or cognitive investigation. He wants, that is, to state that, although we may speak analogically of three divine persons (*qnome*) of the Trinity 'Father, Son and Spirit,' this does not mean that the essence of these *qnome* is thereby cognitively captured. Even when he reveals himself in the Trinity, God remains the incomprehensible reality, the one beyond reach (*mstyk'al*). This emphasis just means that God's nature cannot be rationally captured, but only humanly praised and glorified in and as 'the Father, the Son and the Spirit.'[380] More importantly still, Ephraim always affirms that these three are actually designations of three infinite, unfathomable *qnome* and not mere names of one, single Being. The purpose of this affirmation is to stress that the essence of these three persons is not directly captured by human reason, and that their *qnoma*, or their personhood, is comprehended through their names, but not reduced to these names per se.

---

377 Ibid., p. 67.

378 See, for instance: Augustine, *De Trinitate*, trans. Edmund Hill, in *The Works of St Augustine*, ed. John E. Rotelle, Brooklyn, NY: New City Press, 1996), Bk. 7, Ch. 3.7–8; Bk. 8, Ch. 4.11; Anselm of Canterbury, *Monologion*, trans. and ed. J. Hopkins and H. Richardson (London: SCM Press, 1974), Ch. 51, 79; Thomas Aquinas, *The Summa Theologia*, 2nd ed. (London: Burns, Oates & Washbourne Ltd, 1920), QQ. 28.2, 29.4, 30.1–4.

379 Burgess, *The Holy Spirit*, p. 180.

380 Possekel, *Evidences of Greek Philosophical Concepts*, p. 44.

In addition, for Ephraim the names of the three divine persons are designations of the uniqueness of their eternal personhood and its substantial difference from human personhood. Thomas Koonammakkal eloquently articulates this Ephraimite view: "If God is put on our terms, types, symbols and metaphors, it does not mean that the '*qnoma*' of these 'names' belongs to God's nature but [that] the *qnoma* of divine proper names is not ours by nature."[381] Here, the claim that the divine *qnoma* that is reflected through human words and metaphors does not belong to God's nature does not mean that the persons of the divine Trinity merely symbolize a historical imagery of the Godhead rather than revealing substantially the Godhead per se. What is meant here is that: 1) each divine person is revealed in a substantial way that shows his particularity and declares his substantial difference from any human personhood, and 2) the personal nature of each divine person is itself inexhaustible, exactly as the Godhead is. This is a particular way of saying that the three divine persons are each 'God from God.'

The emphasis on the inexhaustibility of the personhood of the Father, the Son and the Spirit is similar to the Greek fathers' emphasis on the infiniteness of God's triune hypostatic nature. Paul Russell persuasively points out that Ephraim's emphasis on God's incomprehensibility is similar in perspective and intention to Gregory Nazianzen's. The Nazianzen shows this incomprehensibility by speaking of God as 'the primary cause,' 'the primary nature,' 'the primary light,' 'the primary good,' and as the one with 'unchangeable nature,' indissoluble nature,' 'incomprehensible and ungraspable nature,' and 'un-nameable divine.'[382] Ephraim also speaks of the incomprehensibility of God by referring to God as 'the primary nature' (*itaya qdema*) and 'the incomprehensible one' (*mstyk'al*), as well as when he speaks of God as 'maker, former and creator.'[383] That said, *qnoma* does not designate a non-personal substance but rather a personal nature that is not exhausted by human reason or human analogy because it re-

---

381 Thomas Koonammakkal, "Divine Names and Theological Language in Ephrem," *Studia Patristica*, 25, (1993), 318–324, p. 321.

382 Gregory Nazianzen, *Orations*, Orat. 28.5,7,13, 31; Orat. 29.2; Orat. 30.13, 16–17.

383 See Russel, *St Ephraim the Syrian and St Gregory the Theologian*, pp. 76–98. Russel quotes extensively from Ephraim's Hymn 29.3.7–8. He cites at length Ephraim's saying: "mixed with him [the Father] and divided from Him, He [the Son] is in his bosom and on his right hand. If he were not mingled with Him, His beloved would not be in His bosom. If He were not separated from Him He would not sit at His right hand … . Fatherhood is the name of the Father and it is His name which safeguards His glory. Begottenness is the name of the Son and it is His name of which safeguards His generation. This distinguishing characteristic of the Father is in His name and the Explanation of the Son is His name. In the order of their names is guarded the order of their genealogies" (ibid., p. 88).

flects the incomprehensibility of the essence it represents. This is what Ephraim means when he says in *Memra on Faith:*

> Father and Son and Holy Spirit are comprehended in their names. Do not
> Study their substances (*qnome*), contemplate their names.
> If you investigate the substance, you will perish, but if you believe in
> The name, you will live.
> Let the name of the Father be the limit of you, do not transgress, do not
> Investigate his nature.
> Let the name of the Son be a wall for you, do not transgress, do not
> Investigate his begetting.
> Let the name of the Spirit be a fence for you, do not enter into its investigation.
> Let the names be limits for you, with the names restrain the questions.[384]

The goal here is to show the limitation and inadequacy of human investigation before the infinite personhood of the three divine persons and the infinity and unfathomability of their eternal being. This is similar in intention to the Greek fathers' use of *hypostasis*, which was meant to show that each divine person is neither a mere relationship nor a static modal of divine communicability, but rather a being in a communion that does not absorb his infiniteness.

Qnoma clearly means that God's existence in his Trinity is ontologically different from a human's existence. God and humans are not only different in name; they are ontologically different in terms of being and in terms of existence. For Ephraim, the names 'Father, Son and Spirit' are empty and void unless they point to the real three divine *qnome* or persons, who are unique and self-existing. The names of 'Father, Son and Spirit' exist by virtue of the unique ontological existence of their *qnoma*, which is different from human personhood. Moreover, each one of these names designates the difference and the particularity of its *qnoma* in comparison with, and in relation to, other *qnome*. One cannot deny that at some points Ephraim speaks about the Father's and the Son's close relationship in terms that indicate that they intermingle to the extent of mixing (*mzyge*): the Son is mixed fully with all that the Father is.[385] Ephraim's concern here is to show that the Son's divinity is equal to the Father's to such an extent that the divinity of the Son exempts him from depending on the divinity of the Father, as other created things do: the Son is peer to the Father. But it is not to say they do not each have a particular, concrete form of personhood. On the contrary, like his Greek orthodox colleagues, Ephraim also desires to show the relatedness, as well as the distinction, of the three divine persons of the Trinity. He

384 Koonammakkal, "Divine Names and Theological Language," p. 46.
385 Russel, *St. Ephraem the Syrian and St. Gregory the Theologian*, p. 87.

also believes that 'Father' designates a certain substantially existent reality that is distinct from the other two substantially existent realities called 'Son' and 'Spirit.' Again, in *Memra on Faith* Ephraim uses metaphorical language to convey the idea of the particularity of each *qnoma:*

> The name 'fruit' belongs only to the fruit, and the name 'tree' to the planet; two names and two *qnome* ... But as the tree exists in name as well as in *qnoma*, likewise the fruit, which also exists in name and in truth.[386]

Qnoma is not, then, merely an expression of a mode of being, but is also a designation of the *unique* existence of an essence. The *qnome* of the Father, the Son and the Spirit do not, further, only represent particular, real modes of existence. Their *qnome* also point to an inner divine Godhead of Father, Son and Spirit. This is not only a demonstration of 'how' they truly exist, but also a disclosure of the inner nature of those persons who are truly existent. In other words, *qnoma* does not only describe the essence's (*itya*/*ituta*) mode of existence. It also points to the divine essence (*ituta*) itself in a profound and a mysterious way. What we have here is a conceptual distinction between 'personhood' and 'nature' that is noticeably similar to the distinction the Cappdocians make when they speak of *hypostasis* as distinguished from *ousia*. Nothing better articulates the existence of a similar concern in Syriac theology to maintain the particularity and the unity of the three persons equally and proportionately than Ephraim's words in Sermon 4.197:

> You must not think that there is confusion [between the divine persons] because they are mingled. Even though they are distinguished you must not think that there is separation. They are mingled but not confused and they are distinct but not divided. Their mingling is not confused and their distinction is not divided.[387]

One can agree with Paul Russel's conviction that in these words one can see a Syriac passage that Gregory Nazianzen, if not all three Cappadocians, "would have been happy to call his own."[388] The Cappadocians would also have been happy to claim for themselves Ephraim's distinction between the commonality that is designated by means of speaking of the nature, on one hand, and particularity that is expressed by means of the names of the persons, on the other, when Ephraim says in Sermon 4.45:

---

386 Koonammakkal, "Divine Names and Theological Language in Ephraem," p. 68.
387 As translated in Russel, *St. Ephraem the Syrian and St. Gregory the Theologian*, p. 89.
388 Ibid.

> You have heard 'Father', 'Son' and 'Spirit': grasp the individuals by means of the names (*shma*). It was not the names that were mingled; the Three are mingled in reality. If you confess faith in their names but not their realities, you will be a worshiper in name, but a denier of fact.[389]

In this differentiation between *qnoma* and *itya/ituta* lies one of the main reservations of the Syriac-speaking theologians regarding Chalcedonian and post-Chalcedonian Christological terminology. As we saw in Ephraim's texts, *qnoma* and *itya/ituta* are not to be confused or used interchangeably as if they connoted one and the same thing. One should not therefore speak of 'one *qnoma*' in Christ as if it meant 'one nature,' lest one thereby corrupts the 'two natures' confession. According to the scriptural testimony, as the 7th-century Syriac Catholicos, Ish-oʿyahb, says criticizing Chalcedon, "many *qnome* can be found in a single 'nature,' but it has never been the case, and it has never been heard of, that there should be various 'natures' in a single *qnoma*."[390] In this terminological distinction lies a major difference between Nestorius and Cyril of Alexandria, which ultimately reflects a difference in Trinitarian terminology between two central Nicene branches of thought, Athanasian and Cappadocian.

IV. Using Trinitarian Ontology in Re-reading Christological Terminology

Using this understanding of *qnoma* as the true and particular existence of a unique real nature, we may rethink the meaning of the Nestorian fathers' Christological assertion of two distinct realities in Jesus Christ. The concern to stress the particularity of the natures with the help of the notion of 'the triune qnomic distinction in the Trinity' is reflected in Nestorian Christology through its prioritizing of the particularity of the two natures when it refers to two hypostatic appearances in Christ. The Nestorians allude to a Christological understanding derived from the notion of 'qnomic particularity in the Trinity' because they believe that this demonstrates their faithfulness to the teaching of Nicaea. They aver that the Nicene doctrine calls for the interpretation of Christ's identity to start from the inquiry: "'What, then, is to be done with the duality [of] the divinity and humanity' in Christ?"[391] For them, this question is much more relevant to the di-

---

389 Ibid., p. 92.

390 As quoted in Sebastian Brock, "The Christology of the Church of the East," in *Fire from Heaven: Studies in Syriac Theology and Liturgy* (Aldershot: Ashgate, 2006), III, 159–177, p. 162.

391 Pelikan, *The Christian Tradition*, Vol. 2, pp. 37–75, here p. 39.

mension of particularity than the emphasis on the notion of 'unity' that is inherent, for example, in the claim that Christ is 'one *hypostasis*.' '*Mia hypostasis*' is untenable because it is, first and foremost, contrary to the teaching of the 318 holy fathers of Nicaea. This faithfulness to the Nicene faith shows that what underpins the Nestorian reference to 'two *prosopa*' is actually an attempt to preserve the emphasis of Nicaea's and Constantinople's Trinitarian teaching on particularity and hypostatic (qnomic) distinction. One can argue, therefore, that what was at issue in the disputes between Nestorius and Cyril was the continuity of Nicaea and Constantinople in the Christological proposals and counter-proposals they exchanged.[392] Being concerned to distinguish 'one of the *hypostases* of the Trinity' from 'one of the *hypostases* of humanity'[393] while remaining faithful to the Trinitarian theology of Nicaea indicates that the Nestorian understanding of *hypostasis* that is applied here follows the Cappadocian differentiation of *hypostasis* from *ousia* and aims, by means of stressing particularity, at avoiding any confusion or subordination between the two natures of Jesus Christ.

In order to capture the dimensions and ramifications of Nestorius' unsuccessful terminological reliance on *parsopa* rather than *qnoma* in his and his followers' Christology, let us look at the terms that scholars believe Nestorius uses to refer to the two natures of the incarnate *Logos*. It is generally believed[394] that, when Nestorius refers to the incarnate *Logos* and the human Christ, he speaks of two natures with two distinct *prosopa* (*parsope*) and never of two *qnome*/*hypostases*. There are, nevertheless, some indications that Nestorius was willing to accept the use of the Greek equivalent of the Syriac *qnoma*, namely *hypostasis*, in certain circumstances. This is what A. Grillmeier believes, as he maintains that *hypostasis* is the term Nestorius uses to refer to the three persons in the Trinity.[395] Grillmeier further argues that Nestorius even uses *hypostasis* in his early Chris-

---

392 Pelikan believes that the same concern also underlies the intentions of the Nestorian Orientals in their later debates with the Chalcedonians: ibid., p. 40.

393 Ibid., p. 41.

394 In email correspondence with Prof. Sebastian Brock (to whom I am greatly indebted for his perceptive corrections, suggestions and comments), he alerted me to the general conviction among scholars that what Nestorius really taught about the two natures of Christ is, historically speaking, disputed and that opinions on the real content of Nestorius' doctrine, and even the extent to which it was heretical, are deeply divided. I take on board Prof. Brock's warning and refer to Nestorius' own ideas with great caution. However, I also assume, like the majority of scholars, that what Nestorius' opponents claim he said is at least true as regards the content, if not always as regards the implications. After all, this chapter is not on Nestorius per se but rather on the influence of Syriac Trinitarian terminology on the Christological assertions that led to the famous debate.

395 Grillmeier, *Christ in Christian Tradition*, p. 458.

tological writings, of which only fragments have survived (i.e., the fragments from his *Hypomnemata*, or the 'First Apology of Nestorius,' which have only been handed down by Severus), when he elaborates on the concrete particularity of each of Christ's two natures.[396]

Frederick McLeod also points to Nestorius' interest in *hypostasis*. He maintains that, for Nestorius, *hypostasis* designates the determinative properties of the essence or the nature of something, when something has 'such and such' as its personal characteristics. It is what makes a nature or an *ousia* what it particularly is in terms of existence, and it connotes this nature's distinct activity as 'the subject of its own actions.'[397] *Prosopon*, on the other hand, is considered by Nestorius to be the correct term to use for the hypostatic presence of the *ousia* in a manner that point to the particularity of that *hypostasis* in a tangible, visible form. He uses this term, McLeod explains, as the expression of *how* this *ousia* "reveals or can reveal itself to others."[398] In this sense, *prosopon* does not designate a mere figurative appearance or a temporary, circumstantial image. It is rather a real element in a permanent appearance of the *ousia*'s hypostatic particularity. It is this *ousia*'s very real visible particularity alone. By having a prosopic visibility, the hypostatic particular existence of the *ousia* enjoys an actual presence and role in the visible world that goes beyond the *hypostasis*' general essence and specific nature.[399]

Although in his later, and the most complete extant, work *The Acts of Heraclides*, Nestorius started to rely on *prosopon* rather than *hypostasis*, it is my conviction that his terminological shift to *prosopon/parsopa* does not indicate that he was starting to abandon Nicene thinking. On the contrary, he uses *prosopon* in order to convey the same idea of particularity that is central to Nicaean-Constantinopolitan Trinitarian theology. *Prosopon* becomes Nestorius' key term for explaining how the two particular natures function as one person. They do this, he says, as two natures that *appear* in particular forms that are characteristic of particular actions (*prosopon*).[400]

One of the reasons behind Nestorius' opting for *prosopon* rather than *hypostasis* may be his willingness to use a term that is usually employed in theology to designate the reality of the presence of a self-existing nature, especially in relation to human beings. He may think that the reality of the particular appearance of Christ's human nature is not given adequate attention or taken seriously

---

396 Ibid., pp. 458 ff.
397 McLeod, *The Image of God*, pp. 144 ff.
398 Ibid., p. 145.
399 Ibid., pp. 146–147.
400 Ibid., pp. 160–161 ff.

enough, so he uses *prosopon* to defend the reality of the personhood and characteristics of the human in whom the *Logos* dwelt, even after the incarnation or the union. The humanity of the incarnate *Logos* is not a mere appearance or a mask. It is rather a 'prosopic' appearance that is designative of a real human essence with its own hypostatic (i.e., personal) particularity. This human *prosopon* is joined with the divine *Logos*. Their hypostatic concrete characteristics interpenetrate each other without confusion, yet in a complete unity. They reflect the unity of the divine and human natures, which are joined together without conflation or subordination. This may be the background to Nestorius' belief that "a prosopic union ... allows that each of Christ's two wills can function independently according to their own hypostatic natures and yet be combined so that they both appear as one."[401] Here, the understanding of 'union' may be similar to that expressed in Cyril's '*hypostasis* of union' with a slight terminological difference, in that Nestorius refers to a '*prosopon* of union' rather than a '*hypostasis* of union.' Thus, as McLeod suggests, Nestorius seems to be treating *prosopon* as "a metaphysical term, rather than declaring it to be a descriptive word that seeks to affirm how Christ has functioned .... .in divine and human ways."[402]

John McGuckin also believes that the problem between Nestorius and Cyril of Alexandria lies heavily in the former's failure to convince the latter that by emphasizing the distinction of the two natures he (Nestorius) is not denying the single subjectivity of the incarnate Lord.[403] I agree with McGuckin's conviction, and would add that Nestorius failed because of the technical terms he opts to use, and not because of what he wants his terminology to convey. Nestorius loads *prosopon* with the metaphysical connotations that are usually inherent in the Greek term *hypostasis*. One may say, therefore, that, rather than his use of words being evidence of misunderstanding and faulty hermeneutics, it was rather a case of the imprecision of his choice of language and its failing clearly and accurately to convey his meaning. His discourse's weakness is ultimately more linguistic than doctrinal, because what he wants to convey does not in principle depart from what other earlier Syriac-speaking, pro-Nicene fathers want to express when they refer to oneness and distinction in the doctrine of the Triune God. Nestorius is trying to apply to Christology a logic that is usually accepted in the doctrine of the Trinity, but he tangles his statements in a linguistic maze when he refers to 'distinction' in terms that are not acceptable to either

401 Ibid., p. 147.
402 Ibid., p. 148.
403 John A. McGuckin, *St Cyril of Alexandria: The Christological Controversy – Its History, Theology and Texts* (Leiden: Brill, 1994), p. 132.

the Greek-speaking or to the Syriac-speaking fathers who support Nicene-Constantinopolitan theology.

Like Nestorius, Cyril is as keen to maintain the distinction between Christ's two natures in order to protect the incarnate *Logos* from any substantial Appollinarian-type confusion. In addition, and also like Nestorius, Cyril is equally concerned to distinguish the existence of two evenly substantial natures, but in his case it is to negate the Arian skepticism regarding the full divinity of Christ.[404] However, it is difficult for Cyril to glean the same concern from Nestorius' insistence on the distinction between the natures, because Nestorius does not use the term *qnoma*, the Syriac word that expresses 'unity-in-distinction,' to convey this intention. Cyril would have accepted Nestorius' view had Nestorius' terminology helped Cyril to grasp Nestorius' concern to maintain the unity of the two natures on the basis of their concrete distinction. Cyril accepts in principle the possibility of speaking of 'two natures,' which Nestorius likes to do often, because he knows that it refers to the distinction, not the division, of the two natures.[405] The concern to convey that distinction is, nevertheless, obscured by Nestorius' use of *prosopon*/*parsopa*.

Nestorius wants to say that there is a real human personal particularity *alongside* the personal particularity of the *Logos* in the individual Lord. He is not talking about another separate individual being that exists alongside the divine being of the *Logos*. He knows very well that none of the fathers who support the Nicene-Constantinopolitan creedal terminology would stand with him in that. The problem is that Nestorius' use of *parsop* does not help him to show that he does not mean an individual personal subject, but rather a distinct personal particularity. Had he used *hypostasis* or *qnoma* as they are used in explaining the doctrine of the Trinity (i. e., to express a personal particularity of a certain nature), he would have conveyed the idea of distinction and proved his rejection of separation more plausibly. Nestorius wants to say that the human nature in Christ is real and not just a theoretically existing genus. He should, however, have spoken of the *hypostatized natures*, for then his intention to maintain the equality and the equal con-substantiality of the two natures of Christ by virtue of their distinction, not despite it, would be clearly perceived. The same concern for consubstantiality in distinction characterizes the wording of the Nicene-Con-

404 Ibid., p. 134.

405 Grillmeier, *Christ in Christian Tradition*, pp. 478–480. Grillmeier is convinced that some of Cyril's Christological texts are close in perspective and language to those of the Antiochene fathers: "The event of the union of 433 and the correspondence with the Antiochenes at all events show that Cyril knew an account of his own Christology in terms which could match Antiochene language" (p. 480).

stantinopolitan doctrine of the Trinity, which refers to three *hypostases* (*qnome*) rather than three *prosopa* (*parsope*). *Hypostasis* and *qnoma* designate the particular personal appearance of the nature *in*, and not against, its union with another. They designate particularity and equality without confusion.

One may validly challenge this proposal and point out here that, had Nestorius used *hypostasis* instead of *prosopon*, Cyril could have rejected Nestorius' approach even more strongly and that it would have been much more difficult for Cyril to grasp Nestorius' concern to make clear the personal particularity of each of the two united natures. I respond to this challenge by saying that the possibility of this misconception is due to Cyril's adoption of an Athanasian-like total identification of *ousia* and *hypostasis*. Contrary to the way the Cappadocian fathers understand *hypostasis* in the doctrine of the Trinity, Cyril echoes Athanasius' understanding of *hypostasis* (as he would probably understand *qnoma*) as designative of a concrete subject or nature.[406] While Cyril (like Athanasius) uses *hypostasis* to point to the factor of unity, the Trinitarian discourse of the Greek- and Syriac-speaking fathers, at least before the 5th century, includes *qnoma* and *hypostasis* as pointers to distinction and particularity that are non-indicative of division in God's being. The difference in the understanding of *qnoma* is one of the causes of Nestorius' critical reservation regarding Cyril's, and Chalcedon's, formula '*one qnoma*/*hypostasis* of the two united natures.' In the view of Nestorius' followers, the assertion that there was *one hypostasis* undermines the doctrine of the existence of two natures.[407]

What most concerns me here, however, is that, while Cyril's misunderstanding of Nestorius' use of *hypostasis* was possible, Nestorius' argument could have been clearer had he, in his Syriac text, used *qnoma* to express the distinction of the natures, for it is the synonym of the Greek Trinitarian term *hypostasis*, which designates a concrete personal particularity rather than an individual, separate subject. The later oriental fathers who sympathized with Nestorius could have salvaged the latter's intention and shown that Christ's humanity is real and not notional had they used *qnoma* rather than *parsopa* to emphasize the particularity and the concrete distinction of the two substantially united natures. Had they used *qnoma* to refer to the particularity of the two natures of the incarnate

---

406 I would like to believe that even if he attempted to, Nestorius could not prove to Cyril his faithfulness to the Nicene-Constantinopolitan usage of *hypostasis* because, instead of using *hypostasis* in its Cappadocian and Ephraimic meaning, he uses *physis* and *prosopon*, which also convey what Cyril understands by 'concrete separate subject.'

407 According to Sebastian Brock, Ishóyahb II, the Syrian Catholicos from 628 to 646, for example, articulates this criticism of the Chalcedonian confession: Brock, "The Christology of the Church of the East in the Synods of the Fifth to Early Seventh Centuries", p. 129.

Logos, it would have been possible to perceive that the Syriac-speaking supporters of Nicene-Constantinopolitan orthodoxy were not speaking about two separate natures of two separate beings in Jesus of Nazareth, but were pointing to two ontologically distinct natures, one divine and one human, each with its own unique, substantial and real presence and impact.

What increases the confusion in Nestorian Christological terminology is that, after the 5th century some Syriac texts started to refer to the divine personhood of the incarnate Son as *qnoma* (*hypostasis*), while calling the personhood of the child who was born from the Virgin Mary as *parsopa* (*prosopon*). This wording is equally found in some of the texts of the Syrian Monophysite fathers, the fathers of the Ancient Oriental Church, the fathers who support the 'single nature' theory, especially the Copts, and the crudely Diaphysite texts that hold a 'two-separate-natures' view of the person of Christ.[408] However, one should keep in mind that an earlier Syriac-speaking father, St Ephraim, does not even literally refer to two 'natures' or two 'beings' in his writings on the Son of God. Instead, he often speaks about two things: 1) one incarnate person, who is the first-born without whom no human can approach the essence of God; and 2) a *distinction* in that person between the earthly body that was born and the heavenly invisible divine *power*. In *Hymns on the Nativity of the Son*, Ephraim says:

> While [the Son's] body was forming within the womb, His power was fashioning all members ... Not as His body was weak in the womb, was His power weak in the womb. So too not as His body was feeble by the cross, was His might also feeble by the cross.[409]

One may think that Ephraim is undermining the divine Son's humanity when he says in the same hymn, "the Son's own person shaped an *image* in the womb," or when he says: "Who is able to speak of the Son of the hidden one who came down and *clothed Himself with a body* in the womb?"[410] In fact, Ephraim's language here is not evidence of an ontological interpretation of Christ's nature, but rather of a conviction that the real body of the incarnate and born child (the reality of which is evident by virtue of his finiteness and feebleness) does not prevent the infinite influence of the Son's particular divine power. This is clear in the

---

408 Holmberg, "'Person' in the Trinitarian Doctrine of Christian Arabic Apologetics," pp. 303–304. On Monophysite Christology, see Roberta C. Chesnut, *Three Monophysite Christologies: Severus of Antioch, Philoxenus of Mabbug and Jacob of Sarug* (Oxford: Oxford University Press, 1976).
409 Ephraim the Syrian, *Hymns on the Nativity*, in *Nicene and Post-Nicene Fathers*, ed. Philip Schaff and Henry Wace, Vol. 13 (Peabody, MA: Hendrickson, 1995), Hymn 3.
410 Ibid., Hymn 3. My italics.

following hymn: "Let every human chase away his weariness, since that majesty was not wearied with being in the womb nine months for us."[411] The intent here is not to deny the real humanity of the divine Son, but to show that the humanity does not hinder the appearance of the divinity's particularity. In the same hymn, Ephraim depicts the Virgin Mary as praising God in words that reveal Ephraim's acknowledgement of the existence of two natures in the Son:

> The day that Gabriel came unto my low-estate, he made me free instead of a handmaid, of a sudden: for I was the handmaid of the divine nature, and am also the mother of thy human nature, O Lord and Son.[412]

Even if Ephraim here means that the Virgin's motherhood is restricted to the human in nature, and even if he is speaking here about the personhood as *par-sopa* and not as *qnoma*, a supporter of Nicaea like Ephraim would not promote belief in the division of the incarnate Son's two natures. Ephraim's language here is most probably an expression of Mary's humility and submission to God's will. If there is a substantial Christological message in Ephraim's words, beyond praising the greatness and proclaiming the mystery of the incarnation, it is about the *soteriological* mission of the divine Son. The mystery of the incarnation shows, for Ephraim, that the Son of God became low beyond measure so that he might make us great beyond measure. In *Homily on Christ*, Ephraim says: "Glory to the one who took from us in order to give to us, so that we should all the more abundantly receive what is His by means of what is ours."[413] This same soterio-logical view of the incarnation clearly marks the theology of major 3rd- and 4th-century Greek-speaking fathers, such as Irenaeus, Athanasius and the Cappado-cians.

One of the metaphors Ephraim uses is 'the tree and the fruit.' In the perspective of the understanding of his attention to the particularity of the natures, as presented above, we conclude that a Christological claim that there were in Christ two distinct natures with two kinds of true, particular modes of existence does not suggest a division in the person of Christ, as the distinction of the tree from the fruit does not suggest a total division and non-commonality between them. 'Fruit' and 'tree' name two distinct modes of 'real existence,' but they still both belong to the same reality called 'plant.' Similarly, 'Son of Man,' 'Em-

---

411 Ibid., Hymn 4.

412 Ibid.

413 Ephraim the Syrian, *The Homily on Our Lord*, in *The Fathers of the Church*, ed. K. McVey, trans. Roy J. Deferrari, Vol. 91 (Washington, DC: Catholic University of America Press, 1977), Sect.10.1.

manuel,' and 'Messiah,' on one hand, and 'Son of God' and 'logos,' on another, designate two distinct modes of a substantial existence that truly belong to the same being called Jesus of Nazareth. In other words, while the Syrian fathers speak of the personhood of Christ using terms other than *qnoma*, the meaning they have in mind is similar to what they intend when they speak of three *qnome* in God. The reference to the existence of two *prosopa* rather than two *qnome* in Christ is just an inappropriate choice of words that cannot maintain the distinction between the being of God and the human being without at the same time implying absolute division or subordination.

Despite the terminological ineptness, this theology is similar in content to the Chalcedonean affirmation that the two natures of Christ are equal and united without confusion or subordination. It similarly shows that the distinction in nature points to a distinction in terms of *how* each nature reflects its unique real existence. The distinction aspect that is expressed in the term *qnoma* is proof of the existence of two natures, divine and human, side by side in and as Christ.

If I am right in positing a similarity between the Syriac *qnoma* and the Greek *hypostasis*, in that they designate concreteness and personal particularity, the Syriac-speaking fathers, and in order to be faithful to their Trinitarian beliefs, should focus on the issue of particularity and not claim that nature is totally and exhaustively implied in its concrete existence. Sebastian Brock concedes that a distinction between nature and its concrete existence is noticeable in the writing of the dyophysite Syrians, who refer to two *kyane* with two *qnome*.[414] If this is the case, the Nestorian fathers' language is more in harmony with the Trinitarian language of earlier Syrian theologians (e.g., St. Ephraim), where *qnoma* designates three persons in God without turning the Godhead into three separate natures. On the other hand, if Brock is right in stating that, in the Syriac-speaking orthodox tradition, *physis* is almost identical with *prosopon*,[415] then the ambiguity of the understanding of the relation between 'nature' and 'personhood' lies in the Christological terminology of this Syriac-speaking tradition, for in the equation of 'nature' with 'appearance' there is an evident departure from the Trinitarian framework that makes the particular, concrete mode of existence expressive but not exhaustive of the nature. One has to say, however, that despite this terminological misuse, the Syriac-speaking orthodox tradition is no less concerned than that of the Syriac-speaking Nestorians to emphasize the manifestationality of *kyana* – whether in a form of appearance (*prosopon*) or in a

414 Brock, "The Christology of the Church of the East in the Synods of the Fifth to Early seventh Centuries", p. 130.
415 Ibid., pp. 130–133, esp. p. 131.

form of a concrete particular existence (*hypostasis*) – in order to stress the key importance of the notion of 'particularity' for Christology. Content-wise, this emphasis reflects what the Syriac-speaking theologians of both groups mean by *qnoma* in their doctrine of the Trinity, for *qnoma* does not mean 'unique true existence' alone, but also, and more essentially, that this unique existence is of a certain unique essence. In this sense, and even when the term designative of it is not used, one can say that the use of *prosopon* is meant to indicate that particularity and not oneness is the key basis of the equality and the unity of Christ's two natures.

In speaking of the incarnate Son's two distinct natures even *after* the union or the incarnation, the Nestorians are not necessarily proposing that there were two sons linked together by a purely moral union, even if the word they use to convey this idea is not as clearly expressive of this as it should be. They are just avoiding the Alexandrian habit of speaking about *God's* birth and about *God's* death on the cross, rather than about the birth and the death of the second person of the Trinity.[416] J.N.D. Kelly argues that this was even the logic behind Nestorius' own Christology. Contrary to Cyril of Alexandria's belief in 'hypostatic union,' Nestorius believed that we cannot acknowledge two distinct and non-confused natures unless each one of them has its own distinct *hypostasis* and concrete subsistence. Kelly believes that Nestorius "meant to convey, not that each nature was an actually subsisted entity, but that it was objectively real."[417] In the mind of Nestorius, the word *hypostasis*, as it is used by Cyril, is synonymous in concept with *qnoma*, not *prosopon*.

The point of the above is to show that despite Nestorius' use of *prosopon* to refer to both the divine *Logos* and the human flesh, it is possible that he wants to say what the Syriac-speaking fathers mean when they use *qnoma* – at least with regard to the divine Son – which is synonymous, as I have shown, with the Greek *hypostasis*. Even if the Syriac-speaking fathers do not use *qnoma* conspicuously in their Christological texts, they do clearly read the person of the union or the incarnation, who originated from the union between the divine personhood of the *Logos* and the human personhood of the born child, on the basis of their understanding of the personal particularity of the Son in the Trinitarian doctrine of God. Instead of the dyophysite-like claim that "a divine *prosopon* and a human

---

416 Kelly, *Early Christian Doctrines*, pp. 311–312.

417 Ibid., p. 313. Nestorius' Christology may then recognize the particularity of the divine and the human in Jesus Christ in a way that avoids confusion. However, there is still, I believe, a terminological problem in this theory, which lies in the use of *prosopon* to refer to the human personhood, which could after all imply that the incarnate Son's human personhood is just an image or a garment and not a real, substantial personhood.

prosopon united as the *prosopon* of Jesus Christ," the Syriac-speaking fathers try to speak of a divine *qnoma* and a human *qnoma* united as Jesus Christ.[418] If this is not read within the context of their Trinitarian theology, the Syriac-speaking fathers' discourses fall into terminological ambiguity.

This Syriac terminology is not far, theologically, from Cyril's use of *hypostasis* to refer to both the divine Son before the incarnation and the two-natured person of Jesus Christ after the incarnation.[419] This explains why, as Kelly says, at the Council of Ephesus in 431, the Syriac-speaking fathers passed over the name of Nestorius "in discrete silence" despite their refusal to agree to his personal condemnation.[420] This may also explain the 6th-century Syrian fathers' willingness to accept, with certain reservations, Cyril's Christology and criticize Nestorius' assertions, as some Syriac extant writs narrate.[421] Important Syriac manuscripts from the late 5th and 6th centuries refer to a conversation that took place in 532 between five Syrian bishops, known as the Severan bishops (i.e., followers of Severus of Antioch who wrote on Christology after Chalcedon to show that the disagreement at that council was only one of words[422]) and five Chalcedonian bishops, retained by order of the Emperor Justinian to resolve the debate on the issue of Christ's two natures.[423] In one of the sections of the manu-

---

418 One could probably argue that, had Nestorius used *hypostasis* instead of *prosopon* for Christ's manhood, his intention to show that this manhood is "objectively *real*" may have been more successfully achieved.

419 Kelly, *Early Christian Doctrines*, p. 320. For Cyril, *hypostasis* is used in its original meanings as: 1) a 'concrete being' in relation to the divine Son, and 2) as a 'concrete existing reality' in relation to the person of union, Jesus Christ.

420 Ibid., pp. 327–328.

421 Brock argues that the Oriental fathers' reliance on Antiochene christological notions derived from the writing of some ones who write in this tradition, like Nestorius, is due to sheer political factors that made the churches that exist under the Sasanian rule segregated from the ones under the Roman rule. Brock concludes from the previous that the reliance of the Orientals on Nestorius' writings does not deem him of a referential authority in that church and does not support any claim of a 'nestorianization of the Persian Church". Such claims are, in Brock's opinion, "rhetorical hyperbole of the theological opponents of the church of the East": Brock, "The Christology of the Church of the East in the Synods of the Fifth to Early seventh Centuries", p. 130.

422 For subtle analysis of Severus' christology, see Iain R. Torrance, *Christology after Chalcedon: Severus of Antioch and Sergius the Monophysite*, (Eugene; OR: Wipf & Stock Publishers, 1998), pp. 75–145. See also for further views on Severus and on monophysite christology Roberta C. Chesnut and Roberta C. Bondi, *Three Monophysite Christologies: Severus of Antioch, Philoxenus of Mabbug and Jacob of Sarug*, (Oxford: Oxford University Press, 1985); and Pauline Allen and C.T. Hayward, *Severus of Antioch*, (New York; Routledge/Taylor & Francis Group, 2005).

423 Brock, "The Orthodox-Oriental Orthodox Conversations of 532", in, *Syriac Perspectives on Late Antiquity*, Art. 11 (pp. 219–227).

script that records the moments of that conversation (which was unfortunately unsuccessful for all kind of circumstantial and political, though not theological, reasons), the Severan bishops reveal their agreement with Cyril's Christological view that is expressed in his, *Letter to Eulogius.* The bishops said: "We are of a like opinion [with Cyril] ... and we do not *divide up* the single Christ after the union into a duality of natures, even though we recognize their difference."[424]

V. Conclusion

Mar Bawai Soro succinctly unveils the fact that, although the Ancient Oriental Church continues today to speak of the incarnate Christ as one human of two hypostatic or qnomic natures – or of two natures with two particular modes of presence – it still avoids using the word *qnoma* to express this teaching in its official creeds.[425] I have tried in this chapter to argue that the avoidance of using *qnoma* obscures: 1) the Nestorians' faithfulness to the Nicene-Constantinopolitan understanding of *hypostasis* and its Trinitarian teaching; as well as 2) their concern to emphasize particularity and unity on the basis of personal distinction. The use of *prosopon/parsopa* instead of *qnoma* is the 'Achilles Heel' in the Nestorians' rather correct attention to the personal, particular distinction of the two natures. The comparison between the Syriac and the Greek Trinitarian terminology shows that understanding the Syriac-speaking fathers' Christological views by taking into consideration the meaning of *qnoma* would shed light on the real theological conception that are brought to this Christology. The commonality between the Greek- and Syriac-speaking fathers becomes much more apparent when the theological meaning of this term is seen from the angle of their Trinitarian conceptions.

This chapter's main purpose has been to show that the choices a theologian makes with regard to language and terminology play a crucial, and sometimes fatal, role in deciding the destiny of that theologians' legacy in the Church. Nestorius' main theological contention is not substantially wrong, and his concern regarding the particularity factor is rather valid. However, the Syriac terms he used to convey that concern fatally undermined his theological sincerity and faithfulness. In the light of this, the question this study will address in the fol-

424 Ibid. Art. 11 (p. 22). The Syriac manuscript, according to Brock, even says that the Severan bishops anathematized Eutyches' christology and that the Chalcedonian fathers in response considered Eutyches "neglectful of important points" rather than a heretic who totally rejects orthodox faith (Art.11, pp. 221–222).

425 Souro, "Does the Council of Ephesus Unite of Divides ...", p. 190.

lowing chapters is whether one can see in Theodore Abū Qurrah's attempt to translate orthodox Trinitarian and Christological theology a similarly inappropriate choice of terms that doomed to failure his effort to explain to Muslims the meaning of key words such as *qnoma*, *hypostasis*, *kiana*, *ousia*, *itya*, *ituta* etc. in relation to Christians' belief about God and Christ. Did Abū Qurrah unwittingly take his theological legacy outside orthodoxy when he tried to express and convey specific Nicene, Constantinopolitan and Chalcedonian theological assertions by using inappropriate Arabic terms, leading eventually to an understanding that is not exactly consistent with the content of the creedal faith? Did Abū Qurrah make a crucial mistake in relation to Arabic that is comparable to Nestorius' mistake in relation to Greek and Syriac? This is what the two ensuing chapters are going to offer answers to.

Chapter Four. Theodore Abū Qurrah's Trinitarian Theology, or Orthodoxy in Dialogue with Muslim Monotheism

I. Introduction

In a manifesto-like defence of Orientalism in his book, *For Lust of Knowing*, Robert Irwin endeavours to overturn the widespread accusations of colonialism, imperialism and history-distortion that have been made against Western Orientalists and their writings. He argues that, in their preoccupation with the Orient and with introducing it to their own societies, these Westerners were essentially driven by pure passion for learning new languages and studying new cultural and literary heritages, rather than being eager to make themselves instruments in the service of Western colonialist ambitions or Orientalist hierarchism.[426] One of the interesting aspects of the Orientalists' relation to Islam that Irwin points to is their contact with Muslims and Islamic culture in the Near East during the era of the crusades. Among the individuals Irwin names is a 13th-century Dominican missionary called Ricoldo de Monte Croce. Monte Croce was based in Baghdad, Iraq, during his missionary work in the region and was there when the crusader city of Acre fell into the hands of the Muslims in 1291.[427] Deeply immersed in studying Islam and seriously convinced of the value and validity of missionary interaction with Muslims, Monte Croce recorded in 1310 his experience in Iraq, and made an intriguing observation: "It was very difficult to convey a correct idea of the Trinity to a Muslim audience and ... it was easier to attack Islam than to defend Christianity."[428]

Many Christians at that time, as now, would not have disagreed with Ricoldo's frustration, and would probably sympathize with his preference for polemically refuting Islam rather than trying in vain to make the doctrine of the Trinity understandable, let alone acceptable, to Muslims. This standpoint, however, is not the position Theodore Abū Qurrah took as his writings clearly show. Rather than pessimism about the possibility of dialoguing with the Muslims on the Trinity, Abū Qurrah expresses a conspicuous belief in the validity of such dialogue

426 Robert Irwin, *For Lust of Knowing: The Orientalists and their Enemies* (London: Penguin Books, 2007).
427 Ibid., p. 38.
428 Ibid., p. 39.

and its potential for success. Moreover, he not only believed that it was possible to explain the doctrine of the Trinity and make sense of it to the Muslim mind, but was also convinced that this task could, and should, be carried out in Arabic. Whether or not his attempt to put his conviction into practice bore fruit, and whether or not what he eventually presented was a truly orthodox doctrine of the Trinity, are the two questions this chapter is about to try to answer.

In the sections that follow, I shall start with an exposition of Theodore Abū Qurrah's Trinitarian logic as it is recorded in the text of *mujādalah* in al-Māʾ-mūn's court. There, Abū Qurrah discusses the Trinity and defends the validity of Christian belief in it in an interreligious, face-to-face dialogical setting. Second, I will touch upon the Trinitarian discourse in Abū Qurrah's other works, especially the text known as *Maymar on the Trinity.* In my reading of these two texts, I shall study Abū Qurrah's Trinitarian logic in the light of the Trinitarian theologies of other orthodox fathers, such as the Cappadocian fathers, John of Damascus and Maximus the Confessor. This, I believe, will enable us to see whether, in his attempt to defend the Trinity and prove its rational tenability to Muslims, Abū Qurrah managed to give a presentation of genuinely orthodox Trinitarian lines of thought, or whether he found himself forced to compromise over some elements of that orthodoxy and to resort to non-orthodox alternatives that resonated more positively with Muslim monotheistic belief.

II. Abū Qurrah's Trinitarian Theology in *al-Mujādalah*

In studying Abū Qurrah's explanation of the Trinitarian nature of God in his debate with Muslim interlocutors in al-Māʾmūn's court, I first point to Abū Qurrah's reliance on allegorical language that seems to be reminiscent of Augustinian language and metaphors, when he speaks of God as 'Mind, Word and Spirit' strictly in relation to a *filioque*-like explanation of the Trinity, and then suggests the source from which Abū Qurrah may have derived such an Augustinian association of the 'mind, word, spirit' metaphor with a *filioque* logic. I must state that it is not my intention to offer here a theological comparison and contrast between Abū Qurrah's and Augustine's Trinitarian theologies. Such an attempt, let alone the question of Augustine language's possible influence on Eastern theology, merits a detailed study by itself, which is not possible to pursue here. I am not here suggesting that Theodore has studied Augustine's writings and shaped his theology after them. I am just drawing the readers' attention to a rather interesting similarity between the theological allegories these two church fathers use in their Trinitarian discourses. In addition to this, I shall point out the attention Abū Qurrah paid to proving the oneness of the Christian God despite his Trinitarian nature and shall show that, in doing so, Abū Qurrah was opting for a Trinitarian orthodoxy that prefer to prioritize the defence of God's oneness over explaining the divine unity of the three *hypostases*. I shall seek an explanation for this approach by tracing Abū Qurrah's option back to the influence exerted on him of the theologies of Maximus the Confessor and John of Damascus. All these analyses will help us see whether or not Abū Qurrah ultimately remained within the mainstream of orthodox Trinitarian theology or whether he was carving out a new path.

A. On *Shirk* and the Allegory of 'Intellect'

Generally speaking, the text of Abū Qurrah's *mujādalah* indicates that most of the questions he had to face in the debate were predominantly Christological in nature. One can plausibly call this debate in the caliph's court a Christological dialogue par excellence. However, the Muslim interlocutors' arguments and charges against Christology made it inevitable that Abū Qurrah would find himself, while offering a rational defence of the Christian belief in Christ's two natures and divinity, developing in parallel another logical explanation for belief in the Trinity.

The text of the debate demonstrates that the Muslim participants started their Christological inquiries by accusing the Christians of polytheism and replacing God with other deities (*shirk*). This charge connected with Christology when it touched on the Christian claim that Jesus of Nazareth not only was a prophet and a human person guided by 'God's' spirit, but also had a divine nature and was called by his followers 'the Son of God'; that is, he represented, to the Muslims, another divine entity beside God. At the same time, starting the discussion on the identity of the Messiah and his divinity with an accusation of *shirk* inevitably takes the debate beyond the boundaries of Christology alone. If the charge of *shirk* meant accusing Christians of calling a human being 'God' beside the real God, and if for Muslims there is strictly one and only God – *la-'ilāh 'illa hū, al-wāḥid al-aḥad*[429] – then any Christian confronting the charge of *shirk* would inevitably find himself defending the doctrine of the Trinity as well as explaining Christology. This is what Abū Qurrah too found himself doing as he started his debate with the Muslims precisely on the accusation of *shirk*.

429 e.g., Q 2:163; 4:171; 29:46; 9:31; 21:92; 37:4; 112:1.

It is very valuable here to note how Abū Qurrah responds to the charge of association and how he debates with the Muslims on it and eventually refutes their claims and arguments, as his interlocutors and the caliph themselves admit. We can discern Abū Qurrah's refutation strategy in responses like the one we find in chapters three and four of the text of the debate. There, Abū Qurrah responds to the accusation of *shirk* as follows:

152. وقال: "لتجدن النصارى محكمين بما أنزل عليهم من ربهم"
153. وأنت لبغيك علينا وحسدك لنا تسمينا مشركين
154. كأنك تكذب نبيك وتجحد قرآنك وتبطله مما قد نَسَبَنا الله إليه
155. وقد قال في كتابك: "إنَّ من أشركَ بالله فقد ضل ضلالاً مبيناً"
156. وقال أيضاً: "لتجدن النصارى محكمين بما أنزل عليهم من ربهم"
157. فكيف تقول أنت إنّا مشركون وقد قبلنا ما أنزل علينا من الزبور والإنجيل؟
158. ونحن أقدم منكم ونبيكم يشهد لنا بالحق والحكمة.

152. And it [the Qur'an] said: "You will find the Nazarenes firm in what was sent down to them from their God."
153. And you, because of your hostility against us and your envy of us, call us *mushrikūn* [replacers].
154. As if you belie your prophet and deny your Qur'an and discount what God attributed to us therein
155. and in your book, [He] said: "He who replaces God [with others] (*yuskrik*) is in a clear and grave error."
156. And [He] also said: "You will find the Nazarenes firm in what was sent down to them from their God."
157. So how do you say that we are *mushrikūn* (replacers) if we accepted what was sent down to us in the Psalms and the Gospel?
158. And we are your predecessors and your prophet testifies in support of us with truth and wisdom.[430]

As these lines show, the first apologetic strategy Abū Qurrah followed to defend Christian belief about Christ and also the Trinity, was to weaken the Muslims' accusation of *shirk* by quoting their own religious book and their prophet's words. Before launching into a critical analysis and deconstruction of the Muslims' in-

430 Theodore Abū Qurrah, *Abū Qurrah wal-Ma'mūn: al-Mujādalah* (Abū Qurrah and al-Ma'mūn: The Debate), ed. Wafīq Naṣrī, SJ (Beirut: CEDRAC (USJ)/Jounieh: Librairie St Paul, 2010), III.B.4.152–158 (p. 133); and V.D.1.603–605 (p. 207). Unless otherwise stated, all the English translations of Abū Qurrah's Arabic texts in this chapter are my own. One interesting factor in Theodore Abū Qurrah's apologies in the *mujādalah* is that one does not find in the Qur'an a verse which states what Theodore recites as a Qur'anic claim in points 152 and 156. On the other hand, Theodore's quotation from the Qur'an in point 155 seems to be his recalling of verse 116 in *sura* 4 (*surat an-Nisā'*). In general, Theodore never quotes *verbatim* his citations from the Qur'an or names the *suras* he refers to. He mainly relies on recalling these claims and verses sheerly from memory.

terpretation of the Trinity as a form of *shirk*, Abū Qurrah demonstrates that this accusation is in itself invalid according to Islam: it implicitly rejects the authenticity of the testimony of the Qur'an and the Prophet's insistence on the genuineness and truthfulness of the Christians' Gospels and belief. Before the rational plausibility of the Christian belief in the Trinity is set out, the validity of the Muslims' attack on the Trinity is here cleverly nullified by a demonstration that, before anything else, it goes against these Muslims' own beliefs.

In the next sections of the text of the debate, we see Abū Qurrah resuming the same apologetic method, as he gets deeper into discussion with his interlocutor; he does not explain the Christian scriptures, but rather sheds strong light on statements made in the Qur'an. In response to the *shirk* accusation of a Muslim interlocutor from Mosul called Ṣaʿṣaʿa ibn Khālid, Abū Qurrah refers again to the Qur'an, saying:

253. ونبيك وكتابك يسميائنا صالحين مهتدين.
254. وأنت بمخالفتك وبغضتك تنسبنا إلى الكفر وتجعلنا مشركين
255. فاعلم أن نبيك أراد ألا يتركك في شكّ
256. بل إنه عرّفك بأنا نحن غير مشركين ولا كافرين.
...
258. وأعلمك أيضاً أنَّ المشركين هم الأعراب، ليس النصارى.
259. بقوله لهم: "إنَّ الأعراب أشدُّ كفراً ونفاقاً"
260. لا يريد بذلك الذين كانوا يعبدون الأصنام بل من أسلم من الأعراب. فإنَّ الإسلام غير الإيمان.
...
263. فقد أبعد كتابك جميع النصارى من الشِرك وأبرأهم من الكفر بذكره إياهم بالشرف والفضل.

253. And your Prophet and book call us righteous and guided,
254. and you in your disagreement and hatred attribute unbelief to us and make us replacers (*mushrikīn*).
255. Know that your Prophet did not want to leave you in doubt.
256. He even made it known to you that we are neither replacers [*mushrikīn*] nor unbelievers.
...
258. And he informed you also that the *mushrikīn* [replacers] are the Bedouins [*aʿrāb*], not the Nazarenes.
259. By his saying to them [i.e., to the believers]: "The Bedouins are more blasphemous and hypocritical,"
260. he did not mean those who used to worship idols, but those among the Bedouins who entered Islam. For entering Islam is different from faith.
...
263. So your book distanced the Nazarenes from *shirk* [replacing God with others] and exculpated them from unbelief when it attributed to them honour and merit.

For Abū Qurrah, then, the replacers (*al-mushrikūn*), according to the Qur'an (i.e., Q 9:77, 101) and the Prophet, were not the Christians but those who had worshiped idols instead of God and later turned to Islam untruthfully and became 'Muslims' only in name, instead of becoming true 'believers.' The true believers, Abū Qurrah shows, are those Nazarenes, who proclaim, as the Qur'an states, God's mercy and grace. According to genuine Islam, these Christians are to be rewarded on the day of the resurrection. So, despite their belief in the Trinity, Abū Qurrah concludes, the Christians are not replacers (*mushrikīn*) because the Qur'an itself declares them innocent of replacing God with other deities and of unbelief, and it grants them honour and merit.[431]

One of the interesting elements in Abū Qurrah's argument in *al-Mujādalah* is what he says about Jesus Christ as *both* God's Word and Spirit. Instead of speaking of 'God's Son and Word' and 'God's Holy Spirit,' Abū Qurrah says that 'God's Word and Spirit' are both God's *walad* (child). He refers to the Spirit and Word using the grammatical dual, but tends to refer to each of them in the singular when he speaks of God's *walad*. Instead of clear Trinitarian language, we have here a seemingly binitarian one (see *al-Mujādalah* V. A.437; V. A.2.445; VII. A.1.705). Speaking of both the Spirit and the Word as God's *walad* goes side by side with Abū Qurrah's attention to Trinitarian particularity when he sometimes points to the particular tasks of the Spirit and the Word, as when he ascribes the growth of Adam to the Spirit and his creation to the Word.[432]

The first explanation for Abū Qurrah's calling both the Spirit and the Word 'God's Messiah' (e.g., *al-Mujādalah* V. A.437; V. A.2.445; VII. A.1.705), instead of maintaining the Trinitarian rule of distinction and individuation (i.e., speaking about the Word alone as the Son and about the Spirit as an 'other' alongside him), is that Abū Qurrah argues his Muslim interlocutors from Qur'anic thought and not primarily from the Gospels. In the Qur'an, 'Īsa ibn Maryam is called God's Word and Spirit (as in Q 3:45,[433] but most clearly in Q 4:171[434]), that is,

---

431 Ibid., IV. A.5.263 (p. 150), as I jotted it down above.

432 Ibid., IV. B.2.320 (p. 156):

302. الذي اتخذ من مريم ابنه آدم، وآدم بكلمة الله خلق وبروحه نشأ.

302. who has from Mary his son Adam, and Adam was created by the Word of God and grew by His Spirit.

433 Q 3:45:

"إذ قالت الملائكة يا مريم إنَّ الله يبشركِ بكلمة منه اسمه المسيح عيسى ابن مريم وجيهاً في الدنيا والآخرة ومن المقربين" (آل عمران 3: 45)

for the angels said: O Mary, lo God giveth thee glad tidings of a word from him whose name is the Messiah, Jesus, son of Mary, illustrious in the world and the hereafter, and one of those brought near (unto God)" Translations of Qur'anic verses are from www.holyquran.net

using an expression that could be described in Christian theological terminology as binitarian rather than Trinitarian. Abū Qurrah here uses Qur'anic language, regardless of its compatibility with Christian Trinitarian logic, in order to begin by showing the Muslims that the Qur'an itself speaks of God in plural terms when it calls ʿĪsa ibn Maryam both God's Word and his Spirit. By pointing to this plurality in the Qur'anic text, Abū Qurrah hopes that the Muslims' conceding that this language is found in the Qur'an will pave the way for them to admit the logical tenability of the pluralism in the Christian reference to God as a Trinity of Father, Son and Holy Spirit. He hopes, that is, to invite the Muslims to go below the surface of the Qur'anic words and discover implications in their own scripture that would make it possible for them rationally to embrace the logical tenability of the Christian belief in the Trinity. This strategy harmonizes with Abū Qurrah's apologetic method, explained above in Chapter two.

In using this method, as I have argued above, Abū Qurrah bases the tenability and truth of Christian faith on the rational validity of its general religious language, which is similar to, though more accurate than, the religious languages of other faiths, especially Islam. Within the framework of this logic, Abū Qurrah's method reflects the following rationale: if I can show Muslims that their religious texts speak of God in dualist terms (God and his Word-Spirit), this may offer a path toward making them realize the rational validity of what the Gospels say about God in plural-Trinitarian terms (Father, Son and Holy Spirit). If, in order to achieve this, it is necessary to adopt, for the sake of argument, the Qur'an's view of the Word and Spirit as *both* being God's *walad*, even if this duality (binity!) is problematic from a Christian Trinitarian perspective, so be it. On the other hand, if taking this line does not lead the Muslims to perceive the rational tenability of what the Gospels say about Father, Son and Holy Spirit, the authentic rationality and truth of the Gospels would not be invalidated. Rather, it would call into question the validity of the Qur'an and the authenticity of the Prophet, who both, Abū Qurrah stresses, command Muslims to accept the Christians'

---

434 Q 4: 171:
"يا أهل الكتاب لا تغلوا في دينكم ولا تقولوا على الله إلا الحق إنما المسيح عيسى ابن مريم رسول الله وكلمته ألقاها إلى مريم وروح منه فآمنوا بالله ورسله ولا تقولوا ثلاثة انتهوا خير لكم إنما الله إله واحد سبحانه أن يكون له ولد وله ما في السموات ومافي الأرض وكفى بالله وكيلا" (النساء 4: 171)

O People of the Scripture do not exaggerate in your religion nor utter aught concerning God save the truth. The Messiah, Jesus Son of Mary, is the messenger of God and His word which He conveyed unto Mary, and a spirit from Him. So believe in God and His messengers, and say not 'three' – cease (it is) better for you – God is only One God. Far is it removed from his transcendent majesty that He should have a son. His is all that is in the heavens and all that is in the earth. And God is sufficient as defender"

theological discourse.[435] One of the interlocutors in the debate in the caliph's court eloquently summarizes this strategy of Abū Qurrah when he asks the caliph to excuse him from resuming discussion with Abū Qurrah, confessing that the latter "shoots me with arrows from my own quiver. My weapon is perishable, his weapon is enduring."[436]

Theodore Abū Qurrah's explication of the Christian belief in the Trinity follows on from his attempt to show his interlocutors the existence of a dualist-pluralist tone and terminology in their Qur'an. In the debate, Abū Qurrah faces challenging questions from a nobleman of Quraysh, one of which is on the oneness of God and its congruence with Christian belief in the Trinity. Abū Qurrah responds to the challenge by using a metaphorical description that is, as I shall argue below, reminiscent of Augustinian Trinitarian logic and terminology.

Abū Qurrah begins by affirming God's incomprehensibility, which transcends human reason, thus preparing the ground for his reliance on the metaphorical use of the terms 'soul' (*nafs*), 'spirit' (*rūḥ*), 'word' (*kalima*) and 'reason' (*ʿaql*). These four, Abū Qurrah argues, exist in the body and the body lives by virtue of them, yet 1) they cannot be seen or captured by the human eye, and 2) they are all constituent parts of one human being. Abū Qurrah then applies these terms metaphorically to God, in an Augustinian fashion:

465. قال أبو قرة: وكذلك الله (سبحانه) المسمى أباً والكلمة المسمى ابناً والروح القدس، إله واحدٌ هم أيضاً.
466. فالآب هو العقل، والابن هو الكلمة المتولد في العقل، والروح هو المنبثق من العقل والكلمة.
467. فالآب المبدي، والابن المنشي، والروح القدس المحيي.
468. وهو المعبود، بثلاثة أقانيم، الجوهر الواحد، الأزلي.

465. Abū Qurrah said: Thus also God (praise be to Him), who is named Father, the Word, who is named Son, and the Holy Spirit, they are also one God.
466. So the Father is the mind and the Son is the Word who is begotten in the mind and the Spirit is the one who proceeds from the mind and the Word.
467. So the Father is the Originator, the Son is the Creator and the Holy Spirit is the Life-giver.
468. And He is the [one who is] worshiped in three *hypostases* [*qnome*], the one essence (*ousia*) [*ituta/kyana*], the eternal.

---

435 Abū Qurrah, *al-Mujādalah*, IV.C.3.358–359 (p. 166).

358. قال أبو قرة: إن صدقت أنا فكتابك يصدق.
359. فإن كنت أنت تجحد كلامي هذا، فلنبيك تجحد ومن دينك تخرج.

358. Abū Qurrah said: If I said the truth, your book says also the truth
359. so if you flout these words of mine, then you are flouting your prophet and you give up your religion.

436 Ibid., IV.C.4.363–364 (p. 167).

363. لأنَّ أبا قرة يرميني بسهامٍ من جعبتي.
364. فسلاحي فانٍ وسلاحه باقٍ.

Al-Mujādalah is not the only text in which Abū Qurrah uses this Augustinian allegory and assimilation of the divine to the human. In his *Maymar on the Trinity*, which I shall consider in further detail later, Abū Qurrah uses this allegory when he states that "God and His Word and Spirit are one God, as the human and his word and spirit are one human ... so now the position of the Son to God is the position of the word to the human, and the Spirit's position to God is the human spirit's position to the human ... thus, one only says God, His Word and Spirit are but one God, as one only says the human and his word and spirit are but one human."[437] Also, in his *Maymar on the Existence of God and the Right Religion*, Abū Qurrah similarly tries to make sense of the Trinity by means of allegorically assimilating it to human nature. He argues that God's begetting-proceeding (Son-Spirit) and headship (Father) are actually imaged in the human qualities of generating and leadership. He says that, if one denies

30. أنَّ آدم شبه الله والله شبه آدم في الولادة والرئاسة كمثلما هو شبهه في سائر فواضله، فإننا نجيبه أنه ما ينبغي له أن ينكر ذلك، لأنه ليس في آدم فضل أكرم ولا أرفع من الولادة والرئاسة.

...

41. إذا مما استخرج العقل من شبه طبيعة آدم، فالله ثلاثة وجوه: والد ومولود ومنبثق.

30. that Adam is similar to God and God is similar to Adam in begetting and headship, as He is similar to him in all his virtues, we then respond that one should not deny this, for there is no virtue in Adam that is more noble and higher than begetting and headship.

...

41. Thus, from what the mind concluded from the similarity to Adam's nature, God is three faces [*wujūh*]: begetter and begotten and proceeding.[438]

What is unique in Abū Qurrah's *Mujādalah*, however, is, first, Abū Qurrah's allegorical comparison between God and human nature not only in terms of characteristics and actions, but more particularly in relation to mind/intellect; and, second and more importantly, his association of this mind allegory with a Trini-

---

437 Abū Qurrah, *Maymar Yuḥaqqiq 'annahu lā Yalzam an-Naṣārā an Yaqūlu Thalāthat 'Āliha Idh Yaqūlūn al-Āb 'Ilāh wal-'Ibn 'Ilāh war-Rūḥ al-Qudus. Wa-'anna al-Āb wal-'Ibn war-Rūḥ al-Qudus 'Ilāh wa-law Kāna Kull Wāḥid Minhum Tāmm ʿalā Ḥidatih* (Maymar affirming that the Christians do not necessarily speak of three gods when they say the Father is God, the Son is God and the Holy Spirit. And that the Father, Son and Holy Spirit are God even if each of them is perfect in Himself), in *Mayāmir Thāūdūrūs Abī Qurrah 'Usquf Ḥarrā* (*Mayāmir* Theodore Abū Qurrah, Bishop of Harran, the oldest Arabic Christian text), ed. Constantine Bacha (Beirut: Maṭbaʿat al-Fawā'id, 1904), 23–47, pp. 44–45. For an English translation of this maymar, see Abū Qurrah, *On the Trinity*, in *Theodore Abū Qurrah*, trans. John C. Lamoreaux (Provo, UT: Birgham Young University Press, 2005), ch. 15, 175–194.

438 Abū Qurrah, *Maymar fī Wujūd al-Khāliq wad-Dīn al-Qawīm* (Maymar on the existence of the Creator and the right religion), ch. 9, pts 30, 41.

tarian logic that is reminiscent to the *filioque* idea. Speaking of God the Trinity in this neo-Platonic language of 'mind and word' is well established in the Christian patristic legacy. It goes back to the time of Origen and it is present in patristic literature up to the time of Theodore Abū Qurrah's teacher, John of Damascus.[439] One can also find the same use of the metaphor of 'the mind, its word and spirit' in an earlier Christian apologetic text on the Trinity, known as *fī Tathlīth Allah al-Wāḥid* (On the Triunity of the One God). This text was probably written by a Melkite author well-versed in John of Damascus' works and teaching. Thus, one of the metaphorical expressions this author uses to speak of the oneness of the three divine *aqānīm* is reminiscent of John's language in the seventh chapter of *De Fide Orthodoxa*. The author of "On the Triunity" says:

> الإنسان وعقله والكلمة التي تولد من عقله بعضها من بعضها، والروح في العقل والكلمة من العقل وبعضه من بعض: لا نفرق بينهم وكل واحد من الآخر يبدو ويُعرَف.... كذلك قولنا في الآب و والابن و روح القدس روح القدس ...
>
> The human and his mind and the word that is generated from his mind each from the other; and the spirit in the mind and the word from the mind and each from the other: we do not differentiate between them, and each one of them appears [distinct] and is known from the other ... . In the same way we speak of the Father and the Son and Holy Spirit ... .[440]

Despite the familiarity of this metaphorical language in Melkite texts that were written before his *mayāmir*, Abū Qurrah's use of the metaphor of 'mind, word and spirit' is still noticeably unique and unprecedented. This is one of the rare occasions on which we see an Eastern father, not a Western follower of Augustine, associating this language with none other than the *filioque*, as we see in Abū Qurrah's saying:

> 466. فالآب هو العقل، والابن هو الكلمة المتولد في العقل، والروح هو المنبثق من العقل والكلمة.
>
> 466. So the Father is the mind and the Son is the Word who is begotten in the mind and the Spirit is the one who proceeds from the mind and the Word.

It is within this framework of speaking about God using the neo-Platonic language of 'that mind and its word' as related to, and expressive of, the double procession of the Spirit from the Father *and* the Son together that one should study Abū Qurrah's terminology and phrases in this text. In what follows, I shall limit my analysis to this particular allegory and its reflection – in Abū

---

439 John of Damascus, *Exposition of the Orthodox Faith*, in *Nicene and Post-Nicene Fathers*, Vol. IX, ed. Philip Schaff and Henry Wace, (New York: Cosimo, 2007), Bk. I, Ch. 6.
440 *Fī Tathlīth Allah al-Wāḥid* (On the Triunity of the One God), in Gibson, *An Arabic Version of the Acts of the Apostles*, f. 104a, p. 76.

Qurrah's mind as it seems – of a *filioque* Trinitarian logic. I shall explore a possible comparison between Abū Qurrah's reference to God as 'mind' and his understanding of God's triunity in the light of human nature with Augustine's Trinitarian allegorical reference to the Trinity as 'mind speaking with itself and loving its knowledge to itself' and as a reality engraved in the human self. What leads me to investigate such a possible similarity is that both Abū Qurrah and Augustine seem to be reading this allegory within the framework of the *filioque*-based expressions of God's unity as a Trinity.

Let me again stress here that using allegory, anthropomorphic or natural, to speak of the Trinity is not an Augustinian innovation, but was inherent in Christian theological discourse from its very beginnings. In contrast, during the early Islamic era, relying on allegorical language to speak of God was totally rejected by the Muʿtazlites, who considered it an anthropomorphic degradation of the divine transcendence and incomprehensibility, and Arab-speaking church fathers of all denominations stood and argued against this negative appraisal of allegorical and analogical language. Theodore Abū Qurrah's *Maymar fī Sabīl Maʿrifat Allah wa-Taḥqīq al-Ibn al-Azalī* (Maymar on the way of knowing God and the verification of the eternal Son) and Ḥabīb ibn Khidmah Abū Rāʾiṭah's *ar-Risālah al-Ulā fī ath-Thālūth al-Aqdas* (First Letter on the Holy Trinity) are two prime examples of a Christian response to the Muʿtazlites with regard to this issue.[441] To go back to Augustine, his allegorical reference to the Trinity in *De Trinitate* as 'lover (Father), beloved (Son) and love (Holy Spirit)' is well known and intensively studied in modern scholarship, as is his allegorical elaboration on the Trinity in terms of the mind's remembering (*memoria*), understanding (*intelligentia*) and will (*voluntas*), which is usually called Augustine's psychological understanding of the Trinity.[442] As an expression of the mind's self-contemplation, the allegori-

---

441 Theodore Abū Qurrah, *Maymar fī Sabīl Maʿrifat Allāh wa-Taḥqīq al-Ibn al-Azalī* (Maymar on the way of knowing God and the verification of the eternal Son) in *Mayāmir Theodore Abū Qurrah, usquf Ḥarrān, aqdam taʾlīf ʿArabī Naṣrānī* (*Mayāmir* Theodore Abū Qurrah, Bishop of Harran, the oldest Arabic Christian text), ed. Constantine Bacha, Beirut: Maṭbaʿat al-Fawāʾid, 1904, 75–91, pp. 75–82; and Abū Rāʾiṭah at-Takrītī, *ar-Risālah al-Ulā fī ath-Thālūth al-Aqdas* (First letter on the Holy Trinity), pts 83–98. Mark Swanson also reminds us of a similar way of speaking of the Trinity using the allegories of thinking and mind in Yaḥyā ibn ʿAdī, who refers to the three as *ʿal-ʿaql, al-ʿāqil, al-maʿqūl*': Mark N. Swanson, "Are Hypostases Attributes? An Investigation into the Modern Egyptian Christian Appropriation of the Medieval Arabic Apologetic Heritage," *Parole de l'Orient*, 16 (1990–1991), 239–250, p. 240.

442 For various interpretations and appraisals of Augustine's Trinitarian thinking and allegories, see, for example: Colin E Gunton, *The Promise of Trinitarian Theology*, 2nd ed. (Edinburgh: T&T Clark, 1999), pp. 42–48; Michel René Barnes, "Rereading Augustine's Theology of the Trinity," in *The Trinity: An Interdisciplinary Symposium on the Trinity*, ed. Stephen T. Davis, Daniel

cal triad of 'memory, understanding and will' is even considered the primary determinative element in Augustine's conception of the Trinity.[443]

In his *De Trinitate*, Augustine uses the allegory of a 'mind remembering, understanding and willing' to explain the divine oneness above anything else. As early as Chapter 5 of Book IV, he invokes this triadic metaphor to speak about the oneness of the three divine persons. He argues that the way we express this triad in words forces us to refer to them (the divine three) separately: "Each name refers to a single thing, yet each of these single names is the product of all three; there is not one of these three names which my memory and understanding and will have not produced together."[444] For Augustine, the oneness of these three elements of mental activity is an appropriate explication of the oneness of the Trinity; therefore, in the following books of his volume, Augustine would assimilate God to a mind conducting threefold self-knowing activity or self-relationship.

In Book IX, Chapter 2, Augustine elaborates on the function of the mind when it knows itself and loves itself. He states that such actions of knowing and loving are not practiced merely voluntarily, but are primarily and previously uttered as a 'word' *inside* the mind.[445] So, if God is mind then God knows and loves his self mainly by thinking and articulating that love within himself (*Logos*). The word of knowledge and the love that the mind expresses to itself are not separate from the uttering mind per se; they are one with it in substance. For Augustine, proper loving knowledge does not only start with wording. It is also in itself a word. Thus, there is no mind that is knowing and loving itself willingly without a word that is inherent in that self-relatedness.[446] In the same analogical manner, God must have a Word (and also, for Augustine, love, thus Spirit) within and alongside him, and God and his Word are one. Speaking of mind, its word to itself and its love of itself does not entail three minds or three entities in a plural division. It rather explains that "these three are shown to be equal to each other and of one being."[447] In the same way, Augustine suggests, speaking

Kendall, and Gerald O'Collins (Oxford: Oxford University Press, 2001), 145–176; Lewis Ayres, *Nicea and Its Legacy: An Approach to Fourth-Century Trinitarian Theology* (Oxford: Oxford University Press, 2006), pp. 364–383; L. Ayres, *Augustine and the Trinity*, (Cambridge: Cambruidge University Press, 2010), pp. 175–271; Najib Awad, "'Another puzzle is ... the Holy Spirit': *De Trinitate* as Augustine's Pneumatology," in *Scottish Journal of Theology*, 65(1), 2011, pp. 1–16; and N. G. Awad, *God Without a Face?*, pp. 61–69.

443 Gunton, *The Promise of Trinitarian Theology*, p. 45.
444 Augustine, *De Trinitate*, Bk. IV, Ch. 5, pt. 30.
445 Ibid., IX.2.12.
446 Ibid., IX.2.15.
447 Ibid., XV.1.5.

of God and his Word and Spirit means that one is referring not to three deities, but to divine being relating to itself. In other words, God's oneness is guaranteed and maintained. God as Trinity is one, single deity; and God's Word, along with the love (charity) that is common to God and his Word, and which proceeds from them both, are also one and the same.[448]

Significant in this context is that Augustine calls the Spirit the love that relates the mind to its word's utterance, and that he relates the word to the mind that knows itself by means of this word. This specifically is how Augustine views the Spirit in the Trinity from the angle of defending and prioritizing God's oneness. If the mind's love is what relates it to its word and what, in turn, relates the word to the mind that utters it, that love must then emanate from both of them equally and commonly in order to be truly something that is reciprocated between them and as them, rather than a third, additional entity. Along the same line, one may refer allegorically to the Holy Spirit who mutually relates God and his Word to each other in the Trinity – who proceeds from both of them and who they both *are* in essence – rather than considering him a third additional deity.[449] The stress on oneness first, and the reliance on the allegory of the mind that knows itself and loves itself by uttering it as a word, , second, are the backbone of Augustine's support for the Spirit's double procession (*filioque*): the Spirit is the Spirit of God and his Word, or God is not one.

Lest I deviate from my study of Abū Qurrah's Trinitarian language, I will leave Augustine's Trinitarian allegory there and return to Abū Qurrah's *Mujādalah* and his reference there to God as 'mind and word and spirit' in order to deal with the following: In the light of my suggestion that there is some similarity between Abū Qurrah's and Augustine's Trinitarian ideas, one cannot but wonder whether it was possible that Abū Qurrah had come across some of Augustine's views. Had Abū Qurrah heard of Augustine's teaching on the *filioque?* Were any excerpts of Augustine's literature, or some ideas from his writings, known to the church fathers of the 8th- and 9th-century Syria-Palestine? If this is feasible, in what language were Augustine's views available in that context? Did Abū Qurrah, for example, know Latin, or were excerpts of Augustine's originally Latin texts known in that region in Greek, Arabic, or Syriac so that these texts or their ideas would have been accessible to Abū Qurrah?

The question of Augustine's presence in, and impact on, the Christian East (not to mention the 'saddening' neglect of his influence on Byzantine authors

448 Ibid., XV.2.10.
449 Ibid., XV.6.41–49.

that some scholars allege[450]), is still an open and complicated area of discussion. In his valuable essay on Augustine's influence on Byzantine theology, Josef Lössl offers the best detailed exposition in English of Augustine theology's presence and status that I could find. Lössl shows that Augustine's personal interest in Greek changed through his lifetime from a lack of interest and appreciation of the Greek language classes he attended in his youth, to a keen interest in and considerable knowledge of Greek in his later years.[451] Although Augustine's own theological texts do not give any strong evidence of any deep indebtedness to the theology of the Eastern fathers, he nevertheless, as Lössl affirms, had ambitions to introduce himself to the Greek world. This became a necessity, in Augustine's view, as the Pelagian controversy rapidly permeated the Eastern and Western churches alike, which led Augustine to try to send Greek translations of his works to the East. Though these translations, Lössl maintains, were "hasty, catering only for immediate needs and carrying the risk of creating further misunderstandings,"[452] and despite the difficulty of determining whether all Augustine's works were translated into Greek by that time, one can at least assert that early Greek translations of Augustine's works were, at his own instigation, in circulation in the East.[453]

In their introductory essay to The Orthodox Readings of Augustine Conference (June 14–16, 2007, Fordham University), George E. Demacopoulos and Aristotle Papanikolaou maintain that, despite his influence on theological traditions through various periods, Augustine remained largely unread in the East and his *corpus* was little known in that region before the 13th century.[454] Being rarely, if ever, read in the East, the two authors continue, does not, how-

---

450 Josef Lössl, "Augustine in Byzantium," *Journal of Ecclesiastical History*, 51 (2) (2000), 267–273, p. 267.

451 Ibid., pp. 267–268. For another earlier study of the development of Augustine's interest in Greek language and theology, see Pierre Courcelle, *Late Latin Writers and Their Greek Sources* (Cambridge, MA: Harvard University Press, 1969), pp. 149–165.

452 Lössl, "Augustine in Byzantium," p. 272.

453 This translation attempt notwithstanding, in German scholarship, the tendency seems to be to give comparatively more emphasis to the view that Augustine ultimately remained hardly recognized in the East. See, for example Berthold Altaner, "Augustinus in der griechischen Kirche bis auf Photius," in *Kleine patristische Schriften* (Berlin: Akademie-Verlag, 1967), 75–98; B. Altaner, "Augustinus und die grieschiche Patristik," *Revue Bénédictine*, 62 (1952), 201–213; Alfons Fürst, "Augustinus im Orient," *Zeitschrift für Kirchengeschichte*, 110 (1999), 294–303.

454 George E. Demacopoulos and Aristotle Papanikolaou, "Augustine and the Orthodox: 'The West' in the East," in *Orthodox Readings of Augustine*, ed. George E. Demacopoulos and Aristotle Papanikolaou (Crestwood, NY: St Vladimir's Seminary Press, 2008), 11–40, p. 11. This is the case, note the authors, notwithstanding Augustine's personal effort to gain attention in the East and his commissioning of translations of his works into Greek.

ever, mean that Augustine was not known, or did not enjoy a good reputation, among Eastern theologians much earlier than that date. On the contrary, Augustine's name is listed with the "holy fathers and doctors of the church" in the *acta* of the fifth ecumenical council of Constantinople (553), where his name is even inserted between those of Gregory Nazianzen and John Damascene.[455] More importantly, Augustine is mentioned in the 9th century by the famous Byzantine anti-*filioque* father, Photius, who around 860, in his *Mystagogia*, argues against the Franks' reference to Augustine's authority to support their belief in the *filioque*. Photius states that a Church father of the quality and stature of Augustine would never stand behind a mistaken teaching such as the double-procession of the Holy Spirit.[456] If Henry Chadwick's assertion that Photius was "ignorant of Latin, His culture was entirely Greek" is correct, Photius must, in order to support his refutation of the *filioque* (proposed by the Franks), have had access to some of Augustine's texts that were already available in Greek for Greek-speaking readers.[457] In any case, the fact that Photius defended Augustine's reputation as an orthodox authority suggests that the latter "remained well respected if rarely read, in 9th-century Byzantium."[458]

It is widely conceded among historical theologians that, despite the acknowledgment of and respect for his orthodox legacy, Augustine's *De Trinitate* would not be translated into Greek until over eight hundred years after his

455 Johannes Straub (ed.), *Acta Conciliorum Oecumenicorum* (Berlin: Walter de Gruyter, 1971), Vol. 1, tome. 4, p. 37; and Demacopoulos and Papanikolaou, "Augustine and the Orthodox," p. 13.

456 Demacopoulos and Papanikolaou, "Augustine and the Orthodox," p. 14. On the *filioque* in both Augustine and Photius, see also Henry Chadwick, *East and West: The Making of a Rift in the Church. From Apostolic Times until the Council of Florence* (Oxford: Oxford University Press, 2005), pp. 27–33, 124–133, 153–157; and A. Edward Siecienski, *The Filioque: History of a Doctrinal Controversy* (Oxford: Oxford University Press, 2010), pp. 51–70, 87–110. As Chadwick concedes Augustine's leaning on a *filioque* argument to refute the Arians, thereby proving Photius' misreading of Augustine, he also reminds us that *filioque* language found a space in the soil of Greek theology earlier than Augustine. "In the 330 s," Chadwick states, "Marcellus bishop of Ankyra (quoted by Eusebius, *Eccl. Theol.* 3.4) had argued that Father and Son are one God because the Spirit comes from the Word as well as proceeding from the Father." The *filioque* theme therefore, Chadwick concludes, expressed during that time, and even within Greek theological circles, "the unity of the Trinity": Chadwick, *East and West*, pp. 27–28. Chadwick adds that this language can also be detected among the Greeks in the writings of Cyril of Alexandria and Epiphanius of Salamis, if not also in one place in Gregory Nazianzen's Orat. 39.12 (ibid., p. 28).

457 Chadwick, *East and West*, p. 125. See also on the *Filioque* in Augustine and Photius, Peter Gemeinhardt, *Die Filioque-Kontroverse zwischen Ost- und Westkirche in Frühmittelalter*, (Berlin & New York: Walter De Gruyter, 2002), pp. 56–65, 166–174.

458 Demacopoulos and Papanikolaou, "Augustine and the Orthodox," p. 15.

death, when Maximus Planoudes made such a translation by order of Emperor Michael VIII Palaiologos.[459] In his historiographical *opus* on the history of Christian tradition, Jaroslav Pelikan in turn concedes that the translation of Augustine's *De Trinitate* into Greek was much delayed. Pelikan perennially conjectures that Greek and Latin theologians in Antiquity were generally alienated from each other and that there was a mutual lack acquaintance with, and sometimes respect for, each other's church fathers.[460] Nevertheless, Pelikan maintains that some of Augustine's works were translated into Greek during his lifetime, and that his *De Trinitate* was occasionally quoted, especially passages that explained the significance of supporting the double procession of the Holy Spirit, in the patristic *Florilegia* that were compiled as a proof for Latin theology.[461]

The fact that Greek translations of some excerpts from Augustine's writings may have been available earlier than the 13th-century Greek version of *De Trinitate* is not in itself evidence that Abū Qurrah read these translations. Nevertheless, it means that the possibility cannot be entirely discounted, and it means that Theodore Abū Qurrah may have heard about some of Augustine's views and ideas via his intensive exposure to the theologies of his Melkite predecessors (such as Maximus the Confessor). More broadly still, this possibility places Abū Qurrah's texts within the theological tradition of his monastic background in Palestine and Mar Sabas, where we also find theological texts that refer to God as 'mind' (*ʿaql*) and a creating Word – a strategy Augustine uses to explain the Trinity.

In his study of the earliest Christian attempts to develop a theology in Arabic, Sidney Griffith sheds light on an anonymous Christian Arabic text from the early Islamic period, known as *Summary of the Ways of Faith*. We have this text today in a copy made by Stephen of Ramla in 877, in the monastery of Mar Char-

---

459 Ibid., p. 15. On this translation, see Elizabeth Fisher, "Planoudes' *De Trinitate*, the Art of Translation, and the Beholder's Share," in *Orthodox Readings of Augustine*, ed. George E. Demacopoulos and Aristotle Papanikolaou (Crestwood, NY: St Vladimir's Seminary Press, 2008), 41–61; Lössl, "Augustine in Byzantium," pp. 273–277. For some recent studies of Augustine's *De Trinitate*, see for example Roland Kany, *Augustine Trinitätsdenken: Bilanz, Kritik und weiterführung der modernen Forschung zu 'De Trinitate'*, (Tübingen: Mohr Siebeck, 2007), Basil Studer, *Augustine De Trinitate, Eine Einführung*, (Paderborn: Ferdinand Schöningh, 2005); Maarten Wisse, *Trinitarian Theology beyond Participation: Augustine's De Trinitate and Contemporary Theology*, (London & New York: T&T Clark, 2011).

460 Pelikan, *The Spirit of Eastern Christendom*, pp. 180–181. Henry Chadwick considers 'alienation' too strong a term to describe relations between the Eastern and Western fathers and opts instead for "mutual irritation": Chadwick, *East and West*, p. 29.

461 Pelikan, *The Spirit of Eastern Christendom (600–1700)*, p. 189.

iton in Palestine.[462] In this text, the author shows that Christians and Muslims use similar Arabic words to speak of their religious beliefs. The author claims that, despite sometimes using the same terms, Christians and Muslims would employ them to mean quite different things. The author gives as an example the saying "لا إله إلا الله" (*lā ilaha illa Allah*/there is no god but God):

> [the Muslims'] saying *lā ilāha illa Allah* and what we say is one in words but very different in meaning. That is because ... we mean by it a living God, endowed with a living spirit (*rūḥ*) which enlivens and lets die, and intellect (*ʿaql*) which gives determination to whatever it wills, and a word by means of which all being comes to be.[463]

As in Abū Qurrah's *Mujādalah*, the text of the summary also speaks of God as intellect and creating word. Accepting the belief that Theodore was a monk in the neighbouring monastery of Mar Sabas, or at least was one of the visitors of the monastery due to his close links to the church in Jerusalem, Abū Qurrah must could have used the library at Mar Chariton, studied the works it held and possibly read the *Summary* and borrowed from its content,[464] But we cannot conclude that Abū Qurrah necessarity knew that the *Summary's* allegory of 'intellect, word and spirit' was Augustinian. On the other hand, Abū Qurrah may actually have been more directly exposed to Augustine-type ideas via his reading of the theological writings of Maximus the Confessor, whose knowledge of Augustine's thought, and familiarity with some of his works, can be more successfully argued for and more probably verified.

In a paper read at the International Conference on Patristics in 2011, Johannes Börjesson supported the idea that Augustine's works were known to Maximus the Confessor. He suggests that this familiarity with Augustine's writings appears in the Confessor's knowledge of the *acta* of the Lateran Synod of 649, where two texts from Book V of Augustine's *Contra Julianum Opus Imperfectum* are cited to show that the attendents of the synod reject Monothelitism. Börjesson even goes as far as claiming that Maximus actually relies on Augustinian

---

462 Griffith, *The Church in the Shadow of the Mosque*, pp. 57–60, esp. p. 57.

463 Ibid., p. 58; citing British Library Oriental MS4950, f.5v.

464 Referring to the Father as 'reason/mind' and the Son as the word that stems from that reason seems to have continued as a legacy in the theological literature that came out of the Mar Chariton monastery. For example, we find the same Trinitarian allegory in the Arabic theological text *Kitāb al-Burhān*, which used to be attributed to Saʿīd ibn Batrīq (also known by his ecclesial name, Eutychius of Alexandria), but is now considered by scholars to be written by a Melkite monk from Mar Chariton sometime during the 10th century: Eutychius of Alexandria, *The Book of the Demonstration (Kitāb al-Burhān)*, ed. Pierre Cachia (Louvain: Secrétariat du Corpus SCO, 1961), Vol. I, pts 44–48, pp. 32–34; and Vol. II, pts 464–467, pp. 42–43.

argumentation structures elsewhere too.[465] Good support for Börjesson's proposal can be detected in Maximus' reference to the Trinity as the 'archetype' of mind, reason and spirit, or the human soul's triadic dimensions, in *Ambigua* 7 and 10.

From a similar perspective, and in his analysis of Abū Qurrah's view of the authority of the Roman See in certifying the orthodoxy of church councils,[466] Sidney Griffith points to Maximus the Confessor's intimate link to the *acta* and the Lateran Synod. Griffith draws our attention to the fact that at the Synod of 649 there were present, and actively supportive of its decisions, monks from Mar Sabas, who, as Griffith points out, even had a "sister house in Rome," and were accompanied to the Synod by "other Melkite prelates and churchmen from Palestine and Arabia."[467] If this was the case, it was not only Maximus

---

465 Johannes Börjesson, "Maximus the Confessor's Knowledge of Augustine: An Exploration of Evidence Derived from the Acta of the Lateran Council of 649," posted on the Patristic Society's blog by Prof. Markus Vinzent: www.patristics.org.uk (accessed July 24, 2011).

466 Abū Qurrah declares this role for example in his *Maymar fī Taḥqīq Nāmūs Mūsā wal-Anbiyā' alladhīna Tanabba'ū 'alā al-Masīḥ wal-Injīl aṭ-Ṭāhir alladhī Naqalahu ilā al-Umam Talamīdh al-Masīḥ al-Mawlūd min Maryam al-'Adhrā' wa-Taḥqīq al-Urthūdhuksiyya allatī Yansibuhā an-Nās' ilā al-Khalkīdūniyya wa-Ibṭāl kull Milla Tantaḥil an-Naṣrāniyya Siwā hādhihi al-Milla Waḍa'ahu al-Mu'allim al-'Āmil wal-Faylasūf al-Kāmil wal-'Ab al-Fāḍil Kīr Thā'ūdūrus Usquf Ḥarrān* (Maymar in confirmation of the law of Moses and of the prophets who foretold Christ and the pure Gospel, which was conveyed to the nations by the disciples of Christ who was born of the Virgin Mary, and a confirmation of the orthodoxy that people attribute to Chalcedonianism and refuting every group that claims to be Christian other than this group, written by the active teacher, and the perfect philosopher and the righteous father Kir Theodore, Bishop of Ḥarrān), in *Mayāmir Thā'ūdūrus Abī Qurrah, Usquf Ḥarrān, Aqdam ta'līf 'Arabī Naṣrānī* (*Mayāmir* of Theodore Abū Qurrah, Bishop of Harran, the oldest Arabic Christian text), ed. Constantine Bacha (Beirut: Maṭba'at al-Fawā'id, 1904), 140 – 179. Bassam Nassif believes that Abū Qurrah here simply echoes the teaching of his theological masters, John of Damascus and Maximus the Confessor: Bassam A. Nassif, "Religious Dialogue in the Eighth Century: Example from Theodore Abū Qurrah Treatise," *Parole de l'Orient*, 30 (2005), 333 – 340, pp. 337 – 339. Nassif correctly questions Abū Qurrah's attribution of a leading role to Rome with regard to the councils, stating, "One naturally wonders if Abū Qurrah was really unaware that none of the Ecumenical Councils gathered at the bidding of the bishop of Rome?" Nassif personally believes that Abū Qurrah certainly knew this, "but he used these claims in order to clear some accusations by his Christian and non-Christian antagonists" (ibid., p. 338).

467 Griffith, "Muslims and Church Councils," p. 297. In an interesting study, the German scholar Rudolf Riedinger argues that the theological statements of the Synod of 649 were actually composed first by the Greek-speaking attendees at the Synod, under the leadership and theological inspiration of Maximus the Confessor, and later, when the Synod convened, were adopted by the Western fathers and translated into Latin: Rudolf Riedinger, "Die Lateransynode von 649 und Maximos de Bekenner," in *Maximus Confessor: Actes du Symposium sur Maxime le Confesseur,*

who was aware of some aspects of Augustine's thought and even able to read excerpts from his texts at the Synod. Other Melkites from Abū Qurrah's monastic and church circles were able to do this too.[468] One can even assume that some of these Melkites could have read the texts in their Latin version. This is not an unlikely suggestion in the light of the reports of some Eastern fathers on local Palestinian monks who had mastered Latin and other languages. Cyril of Scythopolis, for example, refers to a Palestinian monk called Gabrielius who was versed in Latin culture. Cyril says, "Being highly intelligent and also studious, he had learnt to speak and write accurately in Latin, Greek and Syriac."[469]

Relevant to the tracing of the roots of the intellect allegory in Abū Qurrah's writings is the realization that Maximus also speaks about the Trinity, as A. E. Siecienski notes, "as the archetype of mind (νοῦς), reason (λόγος) and spirit (ψυχή), as well as in the triadic structure of the human soul."[470] Along the same lines, Andrew Louth notes Maximus the Confessor's reference to the Trinity as imaged in the human and as pertinent to the intellect. Louth notes an affinity between this discourse and Augustine's. However, Louth thinks that this notion reached Maximus via Gregory of Nazianzus and passed from him to John of Damascus.[471] Revealing his awareness that the Confessor never cites Augustine, Louth nevertheless argues that Maximus' residence in the West for twenty to twenty five years must have put him in direct touch with Augustine's theology, which dominated Western theology at that time.[472] Finally, despite the lack of

Fribourg 2–5 September 1980, ed. Felix Heinzer and Christoph Schönborn (Fribourg: Editions Universitaires, 1982), 111–121.

468 In the Sinai Arabic MS 434, known as a monk's responses to a Muslim shaykh's questions on the Trinity and the incarnation, the monk, who is believed to be a member in the monastery of Mar Sabas in the ninth century, uses allegorical language reminiscent of Augustine's when he says: "[the three *aqānīm* of God] are three names for a single king; selves (*dhawāt*); identities (*ma'ārif*) of the one essence/self (*dhāt*); like the spirit, mind and the word [in a human being]": S. Griffith, "Answers for the Shaykh," p. 289.

469 Cyril of Scythopolis, *The Lives of the Palestinian Monks*, p. 53; Griffith, "From Aramaic to Arabic," p. 15.

470 A. E. Siecienski, "The Authenticity of Maximus the Confessor's *Letter to Marinus:* The Argument from Theological Consistency," *Vigilae Christianae*, 61 (2007), 189–227, p. 196. Maximus' use of this allegorical language is found in his *Ambigua 7*, which is available in English in Paul Blowers and Robert Wilkens (trans.), *On the Cosmic Mystery of Jesus Christ: Selected Writings from St Maximus the Confessor* (Crestwood, NY: St Vladimir's Seminary Press, 2003), pp. 45–78; and in his *Ambigua 10*, available in English in Andrew Louth, *Maximus the Confessor* (Abingdon: Routledge, 1996), pp. 94–154.

471 Louth, *Maximus the Confessor*, p. 211, n. 120.

472 Ibid., p. 202, n. 11. See also George C. Berthold, "Did Maximus the Confessor Know Augustine?" *Studia Patristica*, 17 (1982), 14–17. In this article, Berthold states, "It seems, then, that for a conclusive evidence of a clear connection between Augustine's thought and the theology of the Eastern fathers, including Maximus,' it is my belief that one can still concur with Siecienski's suggestion that "[Augustine's] influence had, by the 7th century, become so widespread that such a connection cannot be excluded."[473] The fact that Augustine lived two centuries earlier in the same area to which Maximus was exiled, and that "the African church in which Maximus was residing as a Byzantine exile was an Augustinian church," invites us to wonder with George Berthold

> would it not have been natural for those Latins with whom Maximus was engaging in discussion at Carthage and elsewhere to produce texts of the Master [i.e., Augustine] and to translate them or at least to explain them to the satisfaction of their Greek-speaking guest? Would it not have been natural for this thoroughly Eastern doctor in his 23–25 years' residence in the West to have read and studied the greatest of the Latin doctors?[474]

Further support for the belief that Theodore Abū Qurrah derived his allegorical language from Maximus lies in the fact that the latter believed that allegories and symbols were naturally fitted to our human mind in its endeavour to acquire the knowledge of God.[475] In his *Ambiguum 10*, Maximus states that there are two universal modes of theology: a pre-eminent and simple one that apophatically affirms the divine (i.e., by means of denial) and exalts God's transcendence via speechlessness, and another that is composite and cataphatic in nature (i.e., by means of affirmation). What leads us, Maximus then affirms, to the realization of these two forms of theology are "symbols naturally fitted to us," which teach us that every symbol that transcends the senses belongs to apophatic theology, while those that relate to the sensible level belong to the cataphatic conjectural knowledge of the divine.[476] Our human mind needs this symbolic language to proceed causally from creation and the sensible level of reality up to transcendent knowledge, which not only reveals to us that God is the cause of everything he has made, but also that he is the transcendent who made himself known in the divine transfiguration of the Lord.[477]

---

period of some fifteen to seventeen years, with the possibility of at least one interruption, the greatest theologian of the Greek-speaking East is resident in the chief city of Roman Africa, and for another eight years or so ... he is resident in Sicily and then in Rome itself" (ibid., p. 14).

473 Siecienski, "The Authenticity of Maximus the Confessor's *Letter to Marinus*," p. 205, n. 47.

474 Berthold, "Did Maximus the Confessor Know Augustine?" p. 15.

475 See my discussion in the third part of this chapter, where I demonstrate why this source is Maximus the Confessor's teaching, not John of Damascus'.

476 Maximus the Confessor, *Difficulty 10*, in Louth, *Maximus the Confessor*, 31b.1165B-c (pp. 131–132).

477 Ibid., 31c.1167D (p. 132).

I shall consider further Maximus the Confessor's influence on Theodore Abū Qurrah later in this section on al-*Mujādalah*, and also in relation to Abū Qurrah's Trinitarian theology in other texts, in an ensuing section. I simply note here that finding some elements of thought in Abū Qurrah's discourse that are reminiscent of Augustine's *filioque* framework, and are supportive of his allegorical and symbolic language of 'mind, word, and their relation,' is not improbable since a similar Augustinian and linguistic influence is traceable in the theological writings of one of Abū Qurrah's Melkite predecessors, i.e., Maximus the Confessor, with whose theology Abū Qurrah's texts indicate that the latter was familiar.

Finally, it is worth mentioning that this allegory and its *filioque* framework proved its usefulness in debate with Muslims on the Trinity on other occasions and in interreligious dialogues conducted with Muslims by other Christians before Abū Qurrah made his case in al-Ma'mūn's court. Speaking of the Trinity by allegorical comparison with the human being was a strategy also known to other non-Melkite theologians who lived at the time of Abū Qurrah. A good example would be the Nestorian Archbishop Timothy I. In his debate with the Caliph al-Mahdī, Timothy I uses the same allegory to prove the oneness of 'God, his Word and Spirit.' Timothy argues that, just as the caliph and his word and spirit are not distinguishable or separated, so are God and his Word and Spirit. Timothy, like Abū Qurrah, also uses this anthropomorphic allegory to prove the Trinity's substantial oneness and to show that the Christians believe in one God, not three.[478] There is nothing to rule out the possibility that Abū Qurrah may have known that this allegory-based argument was successfully used by Timothy I in his debate with al-Mahdī, and decided to use it himself. If this was the case, it suggests that Augustinian ideas were known to many Greek- and Syriac-speaking fathers in 8th- and 9th-century Syria-Palestine, even if Austine's works were not fully translated or intensively read in that region at that time.

B. When Oneness Prevails over Trinitarian Unity

Noteworthy in the discourse on the Trinity in *al-Mujādalah* is Abū Qurrah's invocation of an Augustinian double procession or *filioque* theology, rather than

---

478 A. Mingana's translation in "Woodbrooke Studies: Patriarch Timothy I and the Caliph Mahdi," in *The Early Christian-Muslim Dialogue*, pp. 180–181, 219–221; M. Heimgartner, *Timotheos I., Ostsyrischer Patriarch: Disputation Mit dem Kalifen al-Mahdī*, pp. 14–16, 71–72; and James W. Sweetman, *Islam and Christian Theology: A Study of the Interpretation of Theological Ideas in the Two Religions* (Cambridge: James Clark & Co., 2002), pt 1, Vol. 1, p. 75.

a more dominantly Eastern, mainly Cappadocian, one. The reason most probably lies again in some apologetic necessities. The Muslim interlocutors do not in fact inquire about the rational validity of what Christians say about the three divine persons' particular roles and status in the Godhead. They are not, in other words, concerned (and it probably did not occur to them) to find a theological answer to a traditional doctrinal question, such as: Why speak of Father, Son and Holy Spirit and not of threefold fatherhood, threefold sonship, or threefold spiritual identity? Such inquiry is not the Muslim interlocutors' initial problem with Christianity's belief in the Trinity. First, they are not probably well versed in the complicated details of Christian belief in the Trinity and the internal, Christian-Christian debates on the various aspects and interpretations of that belief. These interlocutors are followers of another religion. They stand with both feet firmly on the track of a strictly monotheistic belief, where there is supposedly no room for plurality or many-ness in the divine Being.

More significantly, and specifically in *al-Mujādalah*, this inquiry about the Trinity is not the Muslims' main focus. Here, they actually ask Abū Qurrah about the Christians' belief in God's *oneness*, not about their understanding of the Triune *unity*. The emphasis on oneness, rather than on unity, is crucial, and one should keep it in mind in order to grasp coherently the kernel of Abū Qurrah's argument. The focus on oneness rather than unity appears in the Muslim interlocutors' inquiry: How can the Christians say that their God is *one* (*wāḥid*), though they believe equally in God and in Christ, who is simultaneously God's Word and Spirit? That is, they are not asking: How are God, the Word and the Spirit *united* (*muttaḥidūn*) in God? It is a question on oneness and not on unity, because it is a *who* and not a *how* inquiry.

Within the framework of defending oneness rather than proving unity-despite-distinction, St Augustine's *filioque* logic serves the purpose of dealing with the Muslims' problem with the Christians' equalization and even divinization of God, the Word and the Spirit. God is one, Abū Qurrath states, because he is mind, and the mind, even in the human case, is one and single. The Word, on the other hand, is not another mind, but the offspring of the single mind (God), and the Spirit, in turn is not another unique mind alongside them. It is rather an emanation from the mind and its word. In style and view, Abū Qurrah's point here is reminiscent of Augustine's *De Trinitate:*

> These three then, memory, understanding and will, are not three lives but one life, nor three minds but one mind. So, it follows of course that they are not three substances but one substance ... for this reason these three are one in that they are one life, one mind, one being;

> and whatever else they are called together with reference to self, they are called it in the singular, not in the plural.[479]

There is no chance in Abū Qurrah's setting to assume three *hypostases*, united in their distinction and intimately reciprocal in their relationships. This latter Cappadocian logic would not sound congenial, let alone meaningful, to the ear of the Muslim monotheists, no matter how strongly Abū Qurrah emphasized the three divine persons' unity at the expense of their relational distinction. In order to make the Trinitarian unity at least understandable, and at most rationally verifiable, to the Muslim interlocutors, as Abū Qurrah perceptively realizes, the Christian apologist needs to present this notion of unity from within Islam, by using the Muslim Qur'anic notion of oneness. Abū Qurrah therefore puts aside the orthodox 'perichoretic relationality' argument and opts for an Augustinian-like one-sided emphasis on 'causal relations of origin' logic. In the context of this logic, it is plausible that Abū Qurrah should use an Augustinian analogy of 'intellect, word and spirit' and follow a double-procession *filioque* view, despite knowing that this will, to say the least, distance him from the mainline Byzantine, and Syrian, (if not also orthodox) Nicene-Constantinopolitan and Cappadocian attention to the relations of reciprocity alongside the relations of origin.

One has here to read Abū Qurrah's theological choices strictly within the context of the *mujādalah.* What matters to Abū Qurrah in the debate is to assure the Muslims that the Christian God is as much one as the Muslim 'Allah,' for God alone is intellect, while the word and the spirit are *from* the intellect, the former as begotten from the intellect, the latter as proceeding from both the intellect and its word. Every scholar of Trinitarian theology knows that narrowing the triune nature of God down into mere relations of origin for the sake of emphasizing the divine oneness threatens not only the particularity of each of the three persons (by making the Son participate in the Father's particularity as *arche*), but also their equality-in-distinction, because it implies a hierarchical subordination between God, the Word and the Spirit and denies real substantial unity. That said, the particularity of the three persons is not at all relevant to the Muslim understanding of oneness, and a substantial hierarchy between God and his Word and Spirit does not, in the Islamic view, jeopardize God's oneness. Rather, it affirms that oneness and centralizes it. Hearing a Christian theologian arguing for such oneness, with the help of binitarian and *filioque* logics, would reassure the Muslims of the authentic truth and rationality of the Christian doctrine of God

479 Augustine, *De Trinitate*, X.4.18.

and, even more significantly, would suggest its affinity with the Muslim monotheistic understanding of the Deity.

The Muslim interlocutors, Abū Qurrah believes, should no longer be disturbed by his calling 'God' both the Word and the Spirit, or the Christ which they both are, or by his worshiping them both as such. Abū Qurrah argues in a neo-Platonic fashion that this should no longer cause a problem, since calling the Word and Spirit 'God' means only that Christ (as Word and Spirit) originated from God (as word and spirit originate from the mind) and end in God,[480] and not that he is equal particular being in unity with God. For Abū Qurrah, this oneness is shown to the Muslims in the affirmation that God's Word and Spirit are his self (*dhātih*),[481] rather than 'God from God' *with* God (as the Trinitarian creed states. For more on this, see Chapter three).

Instead of referring to 'Father, Son, and Holy Spirit,' Abū Qurrah speaks from this point onwards of 'God, his Word, and Spirit,' using these terms to affirm God's oneness and avoiding any elaboration of God's triune unity. He sees the difficulty of interpreting the triunity to his Muslim interlocutors.[482] So, he concentrates in the rest of the debate on postulating that the existence of God's Word and Spirit – understood in the Islamic view as merely God's creation – does not necessarily deny that God is one, and does not, consequently, require the hierarchical subordination of the Word and Spirit to their originating source for the sake of maintaining the oneness of that source. Abū Qurrah suggests that the Qur'an supports this when it affirms that, despite being God's mere Word, the Messiah is God because he is God's Word and Spirit, and must also be God, since one cannot divide God's Spirit-Word from God, exactly as it is impossible to differentiate between the water of different fountains because water is always one and the same.[483] How can it be possible, Abū Qurrah concludes, "to isolate God's Spirit and His Word, which are limitless, without form, unknowable, and intan-

480 Abū Qurrah, *Abū Qurrah wal-Ma'mūn: al-Mujādalah* (Abū Qurrah and al-Maʾmūn: the Debate), V. B.1.477–478 (p. 188).

477. يا لهذا العجب! فما الذي يمكن أن تُسمَّى كلمة الله وروحه إلا إلهاً، إذ هما منه وإليه.

What a wonder! what else can the Word of God and His Spirit be called but a god, for they come from Him and end in Him.

481 Ibid.V. B.1.478 (p. 188).

478. وكلمته وروحه هي ذاته، كما أنَّ ما كان منك لا تنكره

And His Word and Spirit are His self, as what is of you is not denied by you.

482 The thing that Abū Qurrah gathers from his interlocutors' reactions. See for example *al-Mujādalah*, V. B.2–3.

483 Ibid., V. B.6.516–530.

gible?"[484] Such dissociation is impossible, for God begot his Word "as the sun begets the ray and as the fire begets heat and as the mind begets thought."[485]

Abū Qurrah takes the argument for God's oneness, which we have analysed above, to its ultimate monistic extreme when he argues that Christians do not distinguish between God and his Word and Spirit, nor do they make anything that emanates eternally from God stand apart from him as a distinct deity. Again, instead of the triune distinction and unity-in-particularity, Abū Qurrah presents a maximalist version of divine oneness in order to appeal to the Muslims: God "one is He, one Lord, one Creator."[486] This strict emphasis on oneness instead of unity carries Abū Qurrah's ensuing discussion into speaking of God as one who is "known in the oneness of His essence, worshiped in the threeness of His characteristics."[487] In this phrase there is no reference to three *hypostases* or *qnome*. Theodore speaks instead of 'characteristics' (*khawāṣṣ*) and 'attributes' (*ṣifāt*), because saying that God has threefold attributes is compatible with the Muslim view of 'oneness' and sets aside the complication of explaining a 'tripersonal God in substantial unity.' On the other hand, defending ontological oneness demands equating God, or God's *ousia*, with the Father and speaking of the Son and the Spirit as the Father's properties: one his word (the Son) and the other the perfector of creation;[488] implying that a patrocentric hierarchy is inherent in the Christian doctrine of the Trinity.

Now, the question here is: Does what Abū Qurrah says about the Father as God, the Son as the creating Word and the Spirit as the perfector of creation echo Trinitarian orthodoxy, or does he move away from it for the sake of creating common ground with Islamic monotheism? Answering this crucial question takes us directly to the heart of the Trinitarian theology of the Cappadocian fathers, and more specifically to an essential distinction between the Trinitarian ontology of Basil of Caesarea and Gregory Nazianzus.

---

484 Ibid., V. B.6.525.

525. فكيف يتهيأ لأحد أن يفرد روح الله وكلمته التي لا تحدّ ولا تُكيَّف ولا تُعرَف ولا تُحَسّ

485 Ibid.V. B.6.529.

529. واعلم أيها المسلم أنَّ الله (سبحانه وجل جلاله) ولد كلمته، كما تلد الشمس الشعاع وكما تلد النار السخونة وكما يلد العقل الفكر.

486 Ibid., V. B.7.532.

532. قال له أبو قرة: "واحد هوَ! ربٌّ واحدٌ! خالقٌ واحدٌ."

487 Ibid., V.C.1.550 (and VII. D.814)

550. المعروف بوحدانية جوهره، المعبود بثالوثية خواصه.

488 Ibid., V.C.3.580 – 581.

580. وأما الآب فهو الله والابن هو الكلمة.

581. والروح هي روح القدس الذي كَمُلَت بها الخليقة كلها.

I have written elsewhere about Cappadocian Trinitarian theology and proposed that there is a pivotal difference between Basil's patrocentric ontology and Gregory of Nazianzus' perichoretic one.[489] I basically argue that one cannot develop a coherent and inclusive understanding of the Cappadocians' Trinitarian theology without discerning "the internal dynamics of the relations between the diverse Trinitarian approaches of every one of the Cappadocian fathers."[490] Although Basil and Gregory are considered leading fathers of Trinitarian orthodoxy, their theological differences are often concealed under a tendency to lump their contributions together on the assumption that they are fundamentally the same. The difference between Basil's and Gregory's Trinitarian ontology must not be distorted or underestimated, for it is through this difference that we can perceive the richness and versatility that is to be found within orthodox Trinitarian theology.[491] More significantly, by detecting this difference one can understand the theological approach in orthodoxy that succeeding church fathers, such as Theodore Abū Qurrah, opted for and why they did so. In the ensuing paragraphs, I will rely on my previous discussion of Cappadocian Trinitarian ontology in presenting a brief exposition of Basil's patrocentric and Gregory's perichoretic approach. My exposition will be limited to the extent that serves my interest in this section in examining whether or not Abū Qurrah's Trinitarian logic in *al-Mujādalah* echoes Trinitarian, Nicene-Constantinopolitan orthodoxy.

In Basil of Caesarea's theological thought, his belief that the cause of the Godhead is the Father *alone* occupies a central place. Basil, like other orthodox theologians, primarily refuses to recognize a substantial levelling between the Father, Son and Holy Spirit in terms of divinity. He also emphasizes that the three divine persons are equally God from God and none of them is semi-divine or creaturely. This admitted, Basil still wants to make sure that the oneness of the divine Godhead is maintained and he does so mainly by resorting to an almost one-sided prioritization of the causal relations of origin in the Trinity. On the basis of this origination causality, Basil argues that the Father alone can be constitutive of the divine essence and representative of the Godhead's oneness, because the Father alone is 'not caused' (unbegotten and not proceeding), whereas the Son and the Holy Spirit are both caused by him (the first begotten, the second proceeding).[492]

In his, *De Spirito Sancto*, Basil uses this emphasis on the Godhead as the Father alone as a foundation for his belief in a linear, successive connection be-

489 N.G. Awad, "Between Subordination and Koinonia;" *God without a Face?*, pp. 105–129.
490 Awad, "Between Subordination and Koinonia," p. 199.
491 Ibid., p. 199.
492 Awad, *God without a Face?* pp. 105–107.

tween the Father, Son and Holy Spirit, and he prioritizes it over the completely reciprocal communion between them.[493] He believes that rejecting the Spirit's divinity – which in Basil's time was the main tendency of the *pneumatomachoi* – does not directly influence the Father. The linear, successive relation between the Father and the Holy Spirit via the Son protects the Father's divinity from any direct misconception of the Godhead that may stem from rejecting the Holy Spirit's divinity. It is actually the Son who is directly influenced by such a rejection, since the Son's connection, in this linear ranking form, with the Father places the former between the Father and the Spirit.[494] Being at the top of the linearly structured connection between the divine persons, by virtue of being the non-caused Originator, makes the Father alone, for Basil, the representative of God's oneness. The Father *alone* is the representative of the one Originator of all things. Though the Father "creates through the Son and perfects through the Spirit," he does not do so out of need. The Father does not need the Son and the Spirit, Basil maintains. The Father, rather, chooses freely and gracefully to work through the Son, who in a similar hierarchical manner chooses freely, not out of any need, to use the Spirit.[495] Elsewhere, Basil would repeat the same patrocentric linearity, as when in his discussion of the human language's ability to express the Trinity he says that one can speak of three persons in God without falling into tritheism by saying that "the Father is the emperor, and the Son and the Spirit are the emperor's images. Every reaction to the images passes back to the image's owner."[496]

---

493 This linearism shapes Basil's reading of the impact that the denial of the Spirit has on the Trinity. See, for example, Basil of Caesarea, *On the Holy Spirit* (Crestwood, NY: St Vladimir's Seminary Press, 2001), Ch. 16, pt. 37.

494 Ibid.; and Awad, *God without a Face?* p. 106. Basil's patrological hierarchy is expressed in the following allegory: "Notice that [the apostle Paul] speaking the same way we do when we receive gifts: first we thanks the messenger who brought the gift; next we remember him who sent it, and finally we raise our thoughts to the fountain and source of all gifts" (Basil of Caesarea, *On the Holy Spirit*,.Ch. 16, pt 37).

495 Basil of Caesarea, *On the Holy Spirit*, Ch. 16, pt 38; and Awad, *God without a Face?* p. 107.

496 Basil of Caesarea, *Letters*, Let. 52; and Awad, *God without a Face?* p. 108. For an elaboration and appraisal of Basil's patrocentric understanding of the triune Godhead, see various works of Bishop John Zizioulas: John Zizioulas, "On Being a Person: Towards an Ontology of Personhood," in *Persons, Divine and Human*, ed. Christoph Schwöbel and Colin Gunton (Edinburgh: T&T Clark, 1991), 33–46; J. Zizioulas, "The Teaching of the Second Ecumenical Council on the Holy Spirit in Historical and Ecumenical Perspective," in *Credo in Spiritum Sanctum*, ed. J. S. Martins, *Teologia e filosofia* 6 (Rome: Libraria Editrice Vaticano, 1983), 29–54; and J. Zizioulas, *Being as Communion: Studies in Personhood and the Church* (Crestwood, NY: St Vladimir's Seminary Press, 1993). For a critique of Zizioulas' Basilian-like understanding of personhood, and God-

In contrast, Gregory of Nazianzus parts company in his Trinitarian ontology with Basil's patrocentric understanding of the Godhead. He emphasizes that, rather than being the person of the Father alone, the Godhead is the three divine persons *together*. Rather than a linear successive hierarchy, Gregory views the three persons as connected to each other in complete reciprocity and mutual influence.[497] In the Nazianzen's Trinitarian discourse, one finds for the first time in the history of doctrine a comprehensive and thorough consideration of the reciprocity of the three *hypostases*, not only in terms of operations, but more radically in terms of being.[498] The crucial difference in Gregory's argument lies in his claim that the primary Cause and the representative of the *monarchia* in the Trinity is not the person of the Father, but rather the Godhead itself.[499] By this, Gregory goes beyond the boundaries of the causal relations of origin and integrates them with an even attention to the mutual inter-relationality and mutual penetration of the three persons in the Godhead. Unlike Basil, he thereby focuses on explicating the triune *unity*, rather than on proving the divine oneness.

When it comes to God's relation with creation, the Nazianzen sides with Basil in granting the Father causal priority and in construing him as the one who sends the Son and, then, commissions the Holy Spirit. He concedes the logic of the idea that the originating cause is prior to the originated effects within that God-creation framework.[500] Nevertheless, when the Nazianzen endeavours to interpret the *opera ad intra trinitatis* relations within the eternal Godhead (i.e., God's self-relation), he tends to see the causal relations in the form of 'Godhead → Father, Son, Spirit' instead of 'Father → Son and Spirit.' He states that it is not the Father alone who is the source (*aitia*) of the Godhead alone, because, Gregory maintains, one should neither presuppose that in the Godhead "we have a hierarchy of three persons with three different degrees of divinity, but only a hierarchy in terms of origination," nor should one assume mistakenly that the divine *monarchia* is a "sovereignty of one single *hypostasis* with two subordinate *hypostases*."[501] When we say 'God,' therefore, we are not implying a fatherly *mo-*

head as the person of the Father alone, see Awad, "Personhood as Particularity; and Awad, *God without a Face?* pp. 172–183.

497 In the following, I rely on my analysis of Gregory's theology of the Trinity in Awad, 'Between Subordination and Koinonia," pp. 190–198; and Awad, *God without a Face?* pp. 111–130.

498 Awad, *God without a Face?* p. 111. For two recent historical theologians' attention to the Nazianzen's difference from the other two Cappadocians' Trinitarian ontology, see John Behr, *The Nicene Faith: On the Holy Trinity*, Vol. 2, pp. 325–408; and Lewis Ayers, *Nicaea and Its Legacy*, pp. 244–250.

499 Gregory Nazianzen, *Orations*, Orat. 31.4, 14.

500 Ibid., Orat. 31.33.

501 Ibid., Orat. 40.43, 29.2; and Awad, *God without a Face?* p. 113.

narchia of 'Creator, his Word, and Spirit.' What we say in fact is 'Father, Son, Holy Spirit' as one Godhead together in their interpenetrative unity.[502] The Nazianzen is, then, acknowledging with Basil the three persons' distinction in terms of the relations of origin *ad intra trinitatis*. However, and because he wants to argue for the unity, and not primarily to prove the monistic oneness, Gregory grounds the causal relations that are constitutive of the persons' distinction in a triunion of complete equality and reciprocity. He does this "by means of presenting the *ousia* in such a way that does not allow for any possible suggestion of hierarchical subordination of the Spirit [and the Son] by virtue of origination."[503]

This is not the appropriate place to elaborate further on this immensely significant difference between the Trinitarian ontologies of two of the most important contributors to the orthodox legacy. What I want to glean from this brief presentation of the variation in orthodox Trinitarian ontology is a possible answer to the question: Is Abū Qurrah's discourse on the Trinity in his debate with the Muslims in the caliph's court expressive of an orthodox Trinitarian approach, or is it rather evidence that the Melkite father is compromising that orthodoxy and departing from it? It is my certain conviction that Abū Qurrah's explanation of the Trinity in *al-Mujādalah* does not diverge from orthodoxy. What he does, however, is to select one approach to the Trinity from the orthodox thinking package, deliberately not referring to others. He picks up from this orthodox variation the arguments and ideas that serve his eagerness to prove the strict oneness of the Christian God, despite his Trinitarian identity. He dispenses, that is, with comprehensively showing the rational validity of the Trinitarian arguments within the circle of orthodoxy that attempt to explain the Godhead's substantial unity by virtue of, and not despite, the Godhead's Trinitarian nature. One may thus say that, in *al-Mujādalah*, Abū Qurrah was *eclectically* orthodox in his Trinitarian discourse, which, in turn, makes him far from a pragmatist, who is ready to compromise his orthodoxy to win the support and the favour of his interlocutors in the debate, or to save himself from the wrath of the caliph.

But, the question here remains, why would Abū Qurrah opt eclectically for an orthodoxy that stresses oneness in terms of causal hierarchy and leave aside one that stresses unity in terms of Trinitarian consubstantial interpenetration? Is it because the first option resonates with his Muslim interlocutors' con-

502 Gregory Nazianzen, *Orations*, Orat. 45.4.

503 Awad, *God without a Face?* p. 115. See also Gregory Nazianzen, *Orations*, Orat. 31.9: "Neither is the Son Father, for the Father is one, but He is what the Father *is*; nor the Spirit Son because He is of God, for the only begotten is one, but He is what the Son *is*" (my italics).

ception of God and succeeds more than the second in setting common ground between the Christian and Muslim scriptures?

There is no doubt that creating common ground between Christianity and Islam, even with regard to Christian convictions that are highly problematic for Muslims, is one of the main ambitions of Abū Qurrah, or any other Christian apologist, and it is a major goal in any Christian-Muslim debate. This can be clearly verified by Abū Qurrah's insistence on explaining the Trinity from within the Qur'anic attestation and not primarily from the Gospels. Abū Qurrah evidently knows well that the Muslims care as strongly as, if not even more than, the Jews about defending God's oneness. He is well enough versed in Qur'anic monotheism to anticipate his Muslim interlocutors' attack on the Trinity from the common accusation of *shirk* (replacement/displacement), and the text of *al-Mujādalah* reveals that this is what they did. Consequently, Abū Qurrah had to rely on a Christian Trinitarian discourse that aims to defend oneness and monotheism, despite the substantial place triunity occupies in the Christian doctrine of God, because he has in mind the purpose of finding common ground. This is why he speaks of *both* God's Word and Spirit as imaged and represented in the Messiah (ʿĪsa ibn Maryam), instead of using the conventional orthodox Trinitarian terms of 'Father, Son, and Holy Spirit.' In other words, he borrows the Qur'anic terminology in order to show that there are within it the same elements as can be extracted from Christian Trinitarian terminology: they both want to declare God's oneness and they both ultimately aim at reflecting monotheistic faith. Both the Qur'an and the Gospels try to claim this without denying the equal Muslim and Christian confession that God has a divine Word and Spirit, who convey his divine will and incarnate his presence (as Christians see it) or convey his will and message (as Muslims see it) in Creation. In sum, Abū Qurrah is here consciously and deliberately using a Trinitarian argument to persuade his Muslim counterparts that Christians and Muslims believe in the same 'one,' *monos* deity, and that their holy books similarly state that this deity has a Word and Spirit.

III. Abū Qurrah's Trinitarian Theology in His *Maymar on the Trinity*

The most complete Arabic discourse by Abū Qurrah on the Trinity that we have is the maymar entitled, *Maymar lil-Abb al-Fāḍil Kīr Thāūdūrūs Abū Qurrah, Usquf Ḥarrān, Yuḥaqqiq annahu lā Yalzam an-Naṣārā an Yaqūlū Thalātat Āliha īz Yaqūlūn al-Āb Īlah wal-Īn Īlah wr-Rūḥ Qudus, wa-anna al-Āb wal-Ībn wr-Rūḥ al-Qudus Īlah wa-lū kana Kullu Wāḥid minhum Tāmm ʿalā Ḥidatih* (Maymar by the Blessed

Theodore, Bishop of Harran, attesting that the Nazarenes do not necessarily speak of three gods when they say the Father is God, the Son is God and the Holy Spirit. And that the Father, Son and Holy Spirit are God even if each one of them is perfect in himself). In this section, I shall look carefully at this text and make a thorough study of its theology of the Trinity. For an Arabic version of the text, I rely on Constantine Bacha's edition. I occasionally look at the English translation of John Lamoreaux, but I offer my own translation of the Arabic text in general. It is my view that, despite its overall good quality, Lamoreaux mistranslates some key terms, obscuring, if not changing the conceptual connotations of these terms in the original Arabic. I shall point out these mistranslations in due time and suggest a better translation to their original Arabic version.

My reading of Abū Qurrah's *Maymar on the Trinity* (as Lamoreaux names it, and as I shall too from now on out of sheer practicality) will be divided into two parts. The first will analyse the maymar's theological argument and the second will look at the Trinitarian terminology the author uses. As in the study of *al-Mujādalah* in the previous section, I shall read Abū Qurrah's Trinitarian theology in this maymar within the framework of my main inquiry as to whether or not this Melkite father adheres to Trinitarian orthodoxy in his apology, and, if he does remain within the circle of orthodox thinking, which orthodox approach does he select, and which does he set aside, in order to achieve his apologetic purpose?

A. The Theological Argument of the Maymar

In his consideration of John of Damascus' exposition of Christian doctrine in *De fide orthodoxa*, David Thomas perceptively notes that the Damascene is fully occupied with defending his Christology and does not make any substantial space in his text for explaining God's oneness despite his Trinity or how the three, God, his Word and Spirit, are undivided. The Damascene's work, as Thomas concludes, "substantially reflects past traditions of Christian doctrinal teaching and inter-denominational rivalries, and there is no obvious gesture towards Muslim questions about the possibility of God being a Trinity or of His uniting with a human."[504]

An overall look at this father's text supports Thomas' reading of *De Fide Orthodoxa*, which provides evidence that the Damascene felt no urgent need to address with any detectable seriousness the Muslims' questioning of the doctrine of

---

504 Thomas, "Christian Theologians and New Questions," p. 258.

the Trinity. He rather believed that both Christians and Muslims know the differences between them very well and that neither were ready to compromise or revise their rejection of the validity of the others' faith. The Muslims, John says, "called the Christians 'associators' (εταιριστάς), because they placed other beings alongside God in divinity, and [the Christians and the Damascene] in turn accuse the Muslims of being 'mutilators' (κόπτας), because they sheared off all God's attributes, leaving an impoverished divinity devoid of character."[505]

What John Damascene leaves unattended to, his Melkite compatriot Theodore Abū Qurrah deals with directly and intensively and places centre stage. Abū Qurrah's *Maymar on the Trinity* is an impressive intellectual and theological apologetic response to the question posed by the Muslims: How can God, his Word, and Spirit, which the Christians claim to be fully and equally divine, be one single deity? As in *al-Mujādalah*, Abū Qurrah deals here with the issue of oneness and attempts to prove the logical tenability of the Christian (for him, evident) monotheistic doctrine. He does this primarily by means of, and not despite, the equal Christian belief in, and reliance on, a biblical Trinitarian attestation to God. In Abū Qurrah's maymar, one witnesses, then, a transition in the Melkite theological legacy from John of Damascus' *ad intra* interdenominational apologetic focus to Abū Qurrah's *ad extra* interreligious dialogical discourse, at least in relation to the doctrine of the Trinity.

In his English version of *Maymar on the Trinity*, John Lamoreaux translates as follows: "We shall establish briefly that all the scriptures confess for you multiple persons and that they speak of each of these persons as fully God." Lamoreaux goes on, in brackets "(both we and you already recognize that all revealed books forbid us to speak of anything other than one God),"[506] before finally adding in a footnote his personal interpretation of these words: "And thus, this is a subject that we do not need to treat."[507] Lamoreaux thus makes Abū Qurrah state that the subject of his maymar is not going to be the oneness of the Trinity, but rather another issue, and this because Abū Qurrah reveals that he has already touched upon the issue of oneness elsewhere and finds no reason to do so again here.

In Constantine Bacha's Arabic text of this maymar, Abū Qurrah does states once that he has already tackled some of the issues he deals with in this maymar and that there is no need to repeat his elaborate discussion on them here. However, as Bacha's Arabic text stands, there is a subtle difference between it and

---

505 Ibid., p. 259, citing Sahas, *John of Damascus on Islam*, pp. 136–137.
506 Lamoreaux, *Theodore Abū Qurrah*, p. 179.
507 Ibid., n. 29.

Lamoreaux's translation, which should not pass unrecognized. The Arabic text in Bacha says:

> ونحقق من هذه الكتب بإيجاز أنها تقرر عندكم وجوهاً غير واحد ونقول في كل واحد من هذه الوجوه أنه إله تام. ونحن وأنتم قد علمنا أنَّ الكتب المنزلة تنهي أن يقال إلا إله واحد.
>
> we affirm briefly from these books [Abū Qurrah's other texts] that they confess that you have 'faces' (*wujūh*) more than one. And we say of every one of these faces (*al-wujūh*) that it is a complete god. And we and you know that the revealed books forbid speaking of any but one god.[508]

There is nothing in these lines that supports Lamoreaux's conclusion that Abū Qurrah is going to leave aside discussion of God's oneness. The closest wording to Lamoreaux's translation and interpretation in Bacha's Arabic version is when, a few lines earlier, Abū Qurrah states:

> وتحقيق ما ذكرنا بيانه وتلخيصه قد وضعنا فيه ميمراً يقدر من أراد الشفاء لنفسه أن يقرأه فيقنع منه بما قد قلناه. وليس يحسن تكرار ما قد وضعناه هناك وبثه في ميمرنا هذا.
>
> And we have written the affirmation of what we have already declared and summarised in a *maymar*, which everyone [who] wants healing for himself can read and be persuaded by it about what we said. And it is not appropriate to *repeat* [*tikrār*] what we have stated there and spread it in this *maymar.*[509]

Even so, Abū Qurrah here does not say that he will avoid treating the topic of oneness, but only that he will avoid *repeating* what he has said in detail in another maymar on the same topic. There is a significant difference in meaning here that can only be grasped when we note the Arabic word that Abū Qurrah uses. He does not use a word that could be rendered 'treating/dealing with' (such as, for example, *taʿāmul*), as Lamoreaux's translation implies, but rather *tikrār*, which should be translated in 'repeating.' Abū Qurrah means only to avoid 'repeating' his previous elaboration on a certain issue in earlier texts, and not to avoid 'treating' the issue altogether. The Arabic text does not allow the latter translation or interpretation.

On the other hand, what exactly is the subject about which Abū Qurrah says here that he does not want to repeat his earlier arguments? Is it the issue of God's oneness? Reading Abū Qurrah's words here in the light of their location in the maymar makes it clear that neither the Trinity nor oneness-in-triunity is

---

508 Bacha, *Mayāmir*, p. 28. As in the previous part, the English translation is my own, unless I cite from Lamoreaux's and indicate that I am doing so.
509 Ibid., p. 27.

a theme for discussion at this introductory stage. The maymar's purpose, which Abū Qurrah departs from in this Trinitarian apology, is to argue for the rational validity of Christian faith and to propose that only this faith discourse, along with the Christian scriptural attestations of it, is authentically reliable for obtaining the truth; this faith and its scriptural attestation alone are according to reason, though they also stand above mere rationalization. This is the point Abū Qurrah is referring to here and about which he has decided not to repeat the details of his opinion. Why not? Because he has already written a whole maymar on this subject – probably the text known as *fī Wujūd al-Khāliq wad-Dīn al-Qawīm* (On the existence of the Creator and the right religion).

In the light of the above, Lamoreaux's understanding that Abū Qurrah intends to set aside the issue of oneness is not supported by the text. When we read these lines in the light of what comes before and after in the Arabic text, they suggest, in addition to the above mentioned point, that Abū Qurrah is not going to show the Muslims that their Qur'an contains implications of plurality in God, since he has already done this elsewhere (as we have a potential recording of what could have been what he said on this in his presentation of the pluralism in language of the Qur'ān in *al-Mujādalah*). Had Abū Qurrah decided not to give scriptural evidence of Trinitarian language because he had already done so, he would not have referred in the maymar's ensuing pericopes to Old and New Testament verses to prove the oneness of the Trinity. If this task had been already accomplished elsewhere, and if he really thought there was no need to treat this subject again, he would not have spent any time pointing to biblical attestations (or Qur'anic, which he does not cite clearly). Whatever it is that Abū Qurrah does not want to treat here, it is certainly not the subject of the oneness of the Trinity, which is actually, as I shall show, the key topic, the epicentre of his Trinitarian discussion. What he does want to avoid is the repetition of an argument he had developed earlier before other Muslims about the possibility of defending Christian Trinitarian language by pointing to pluralist implications in the Qur'anic reference to 'God, his Word and Spirit.'[510] What

510 In his polemic response to Christian belief, the 9th-century Mu'tazilite *mutakallim*, Abū 'Uthmān 'Amr ibn Baḥr aj-Jāḥiẓ notes the Christians' reliance on the Qur'an's reference to 'Īsā ibn Maryam as 'God's Word and Spirit' to show that the Muslims' religion defends the divine sonship of the Miessiah. Against this, aj-Jāḥiẓ argues that in the Qur'an the angel Gabriel and Adam are also associated with God's spirit and seen as holding it from Him: aj-Jāḥiẓ, *al-Mukhtār fī ar-Radd 'alā an-Naṣārā* (The Selected in Responding to the Christians), ed. Muḥammad 'Abdullāh al-Sharqāwī (Beirut: Dār aj-Jīl, 1991), pp. 81–82; 87–88. The same awareness of the Christian use of the formula 'God, His Word and Spirit' is also tackled by another 11th-century Mu'tazilite judge 'Ābd a-Jabbār ibn Aḥmad al-Hamadhānī, who also argues that what Christians and Muslims say, though their actual words are similar, connote starkly different understandings of

he wants to concentrate on here is affirming and 'briefly demonstrating' (*nuḥaqiq bi-'ijāz*) that all the holy books, especially the Christian scriptures, affirm that one should speak only of one God, regardless the plural-sounding descriptions of this monistic deity in these texts. In the following paragraphs, I shall systematically analyse how Abū Qurrah pursues this goal and argues for God's substantial oneness despite his Trinitarian nature.

Abū Qurrah starts his explanation of the scriptures' attestation to God with the Old Testament. His main goal is to discuss whether the Old Testament presents a polytheistic, associationist view when it gives the title 'Lord' to more than one entity. Abū Qurrah affirms that it does not, but how, then, can the text call various entities 'Lord' and still be considered a monotheistic text? How can the scripture's pluralist language be deemed expressive of something other than polytheism and association?[511] Tackling this question is the driving force of Abū Qurrah's departure from a scriptural attestation, or from second-order evidence (reason and rationality being the first-order evidence according to his *Maymar on the Existence of God and the Right Religion*. See my discussion in chapter 2). He wants to show that scriptural monotheism can be confirmed from within the internal logic of Christian religious texts. That said, Abū Qurrah begins by addressing certain Old Testament texts that might be taken to indicate the existence of more than one God. His selection of these verses rather than others suggests that they were cited by Muslims as an evidence of Christian *shirk*. He therefore tries to explain logically and theologically how the language of these attestations resonates with, rather than militates against, monotheism and divine oneness.

The first Old Testament text Abū Qurrah deals with is Ps. 109:1: "The Lord said to my Lord, sit at my right side so I make your enemies beneath your feet." Abū Qurrah concedes that the author refers here to both the addresser and the addressee as 'Lord,' but this does not in itself, Abū Qurrah opines, indi-

---

God, and it is certainly the Muslim understanding, he insists, that is accurate: ʿĀbd aj-Jabbār al-Hamadhānī, *Tathbī Dalā'il an-Nubuwa* (Confirming the evidences of prophecy), in *ʿĀbd aj-Jabbār: Critique of Christian Origins*, ed. and trans. Gabriel Said Reynolds and Samir Khalil Samir (Provo, UT: Brigham Young University Press, 2010), II.2B.89 (pp.38 – 39).

511 In tackling this inquiry about calling both the one who is worshiped and the one who worships 'lord', Abū Qurrah may be indirectly responding to a criticism one can find in the polemic of the 9th-century Muslim *mutakallim*, al-Qāsim ibn Ibrāhīm ibn Ismāʿil ar-Rassī, who accuses the Christians of making the worshiped lord (*Allah*) and the worshiping servant (ʿĪsā ibn Maryam) one and the same: *fa-ṣayyarū Ar-Rabb al-Maʿbūd fī dhalik kullah kal-Marbūb al-ʿAbid.* See: ar-Rassī, *ar-Radd ʿalā an-Naṣārā* (Response to the Christians), ed. Imām Ḥanafī ʿAbdullāh (Cairo: Dār al-Āfāq al-ʿArabiyya, 2000), p. 29. Many points in ar-Rassī's text find an echo in Theodore's response and defence of the Christian belief in God's oneness, which merits a whole study by itself.

cate numerically the existence of two lords. 'Lord' here has a *status* connotation, not a numerical signification. God (the addressing Lord) is here calling the Messiah (the addressee) 'Lord' in order to unveil the Messiah's eternal sonship, as he was begotten before light (*qabl an-nūr waladtuk*). So, the Psalm is calling the Messiah 'Lord,' as it calls God 'Lord,' not to suggest that there are two gods, but rather to show the divine monarchical position of the incarnate God and to affirm, as Hosiah 1:7 also states, that both God and his saving Messiah are lords in identity. The same logic, Abū Qurrah proceeds, applies to other places in the Old Testament, as when Abraham in Genesis 13:14 and Jacob in Genesis 31:3 speak with the angel of God and hear him as if hearing God himself, and both God and his angel are called 'Lord'; or when in Genesis 9:1–6 God speaks about himself and his creation, telling Noah that the speaker to the Creator and the Creator of Noah are both 'Lord.'[512] The same applies too to the story of the destruction of Sodom, when the one who rains down fire is Lord and the one who hands the fire in to him is also Lord (Genesis 19:24); or in Exodus 3:2, where the angel of God, who appeared to Moses in the burning bush, is called 'the angel of the Lord' and also simply 'Lord'; or again in Genesis 16:7,10, when the angel who appeared to Hagar in the wilderness is also called 'Lord' and 'the angel of the Lord.'[513] All these Old Testament incidents are not meant to be understood as enumerating several deities. They are simply indicating the non-creaturely, lordly status of God and every entity inherent to God's realm of being, whether angels or the Messiah. The plurality in the language here is not numerical, but rather categorical and descriptive in nature. The Old Testament does not attest to various lords but to the lordly, divine identity of God and his eternally existing Son.

From there, Abū Qurrah moves to the New Testament to show that the same status connotation, rather than numerical connotation, is also intended there. He refers first to John 1:1: 'In the beginning was still the Word. And the Word was still with God. And a [God] the Word still is ...'[514] He shows that the New Testament similarly points to the eternal sonship and divinity of God's Word by ascribing it to a lordly status, without this making God and his Word numerically two lords, but rather indicating that they are equally lordly in status. The same applies, Abū Qurrah maintains, to what St Paul writes, referring to the God whom Christ praises and worships, as well as to Christ himself, as 'Lord'; and it also applies to Christ's saying in Mt. 28:19, when he commissioned the disci-

512 Abū Qurrah, *Maymar on the Trinity*, pp. 29–30.
513 Ibid., pp. 30–31.
514 Ibid., p. 32.
"وفي البدء لم تزل الكلمة والكلمة لم تزل عند الله وإلهاً لم تزل الكلمة."

ples to baptize all in the name of 'Father, Son and Holy Spirit,' proving thereby that the Son and Spirit are both 'Lord' in identity, like the Father:

> وقال مار بولس في شأن اليهود أنَّ المسيح ظهر منهم بالجسد الذي هو إله على كل، له التسبيحات والبركات إلى الدهر. فالمسيح الإله والذي يسبحه المسيح إله....وقال المسيح إلهنا لتلاميذه: اذهبوا علموا جميع الأمم وعمدوهم باسم الآب والابن والروح القدس (متى 28: 19). هذا يحقق أنَّ الابن والروح كل واحد منهما إله مثل الآب ولم تجدد الخليقة بالمعمودية باسمهما مع الآب إلا وكل واحد منهما مثل الآب
>
> And St Paul said concerning the Jews that Christ appeared from them in the flesh, He who is the God over all, praise and blessings be to Him forever. So, Christ is the God, and the one Christ praises is God ... and Christ our God said to his disciples: Go and teach all nations and baptize them in the name of the Father, the Son, and the Holy Spirit (Matthew 28:19). This confirms that the Son and the Spirit are each God like the Father, and creation was renewed by baptism in their name along with the Father, only because each one of them is like the Father.[515]

Abū Qurrah ends his biblical explication of the oneness of God in Christianity by affirming:

> ولا نريد من شهادات الكتب المقدسة ما يحقق به أنَّ الابن إله والروح القدس إله أكثر من هذا لأنه ليس هذه إرادتنا في هذا الميمر.
>
> And we do not want to affirm from the holy books' testimonies that the Son is God and the Holy Spirit is God more than this, for this is not our will in this *maymar.*[516]

Again, this is not to say that the topic of the maymar is not to prove the oneness of the Father, Son and Holy Spirit, but simply that the theme of the maymar is not to prove the divinity of the Son and the Spirit but rather to show that the deity is one, though triune, and that the evidence of this is the fact that God, his Word/Messiah and Spirit all have equal divine or lordly status; their oneness is evident by virtue of who they are as 'Lord.'[517] Where can this be found? Abū Qurrah stresses that it can easily be extracted from the Bible by those whose faith is shaped according to true reasoning. Those who resort to reason and listen to its voice, rather than surrendering to the sentiments of the heart, can undoubtedly perceive that the Bible calls the Father, Son and Spirit 'God' in the sin-

---

515 Ibid.

516 Ibid.

517 Ibid., p. 33.

فمن كان سديداً في إيمانه يدبره بعقل فقد وجب عليه الإيمان بما شهدت به الكتب التي قد استبان لكل ذي لبّ أنها من الله. ولزمه أن يقول أنَّ الآب إله وأنَّ الابن إله وأنَّ الروح القدس إله.

So he who is just in his faith ponders it rationally and he must believe in what the scriptures, whose origination from God has become clear to every rational person, attest. And he is bound to say that the Father is God and the Son is God and the Holy Spirit is God.

gular and never 'gods' in the plural, and that all the scriptural texts without exception affirm this singleness. For people of reason, the Christians' reference to Father, Son and Holy Spirit is not a numerical counting of three deities, and those who cannot apprehend this are weak in their mind and emotionally arrogant in their hearts.[518]

From where did Abū Qurrah obtain the argument for oneness by employing a categorical, not numerical, notion of lordship? The elements of his discussion suggest that he borrows it from Gregory Nazianzen's Trinitarian theology via its invocation in the writings of John of Damascus.

In principle, Gregory of Nazianzus is keen to show that the three divine *hypostases* are single Godhead, not only in terms of divinity, but first in terms of *monarchia*. Rather than restricting the Godhead's *monarchia* to the Father alone, the Nazianzen states, for instance in Oration 38, that the Holy of Holies "is hidden even from the seraphim, and is glorified with the thrice repeated Holy, meeting in one ascription of the title Lord and God ..."[519] 'Lord' here is not designative of the particularity of one of the *hypostases* – the Father, say – but is a signification of the Godhead and the three persons alike. It is a title of their oneness.

Some scholars have already argued that Gregory's Oration 25 demonstrates the opposite view, and that he is arguing here for the patrocentric nature of the *monarchia*, ultimately calling the Father 'God,' while naming the Son 'Lord' and restricting the Godhead to the Father alone.[520] I have addressed this idea and presented a different reading of Gregory's Oration 25 elsewhere.[521] Suffice it to say here briefly that there is no doubt that Gregory is concerned in Oration 25 to highlight the particularities of the three divine persons because he specifically wants to avoid what he describes as "a Judaic narrow version of oneness."[522] This acknowledged, the Nazianzen is equally avoiding the trap of 'Greek polytheism,' so that his escape from extreme monotheism would not throw him into extreme tritheism. It is in the light of this concern that one should read Gregory's specifically calling the Son 'Lord' in this oration, which is meant to serve the elaboration of the various titles that point to the Son's lordship from different relational situations. However, nothing in this oration goes against

518 Ibid.
519 Gregory Nazianzen, *St Gregory of Nazianzus: Select Orations*, trans. Martha Vinson, Fathers of the Church 107 (Washington, DC: Catholic University of America Press, 2003), Orat. 38.8.
520 Thus Christopher Beeley, *Gregory of Nazianzus*, p. 204. For Gregory's Oration 25, see Gregory Nazianzen, *St Gregory of Nazianzus: Select Orations*
521 Awad, *God without a Face?* pp. 122ff.
522 Gregory Nazianzen, *St Gregory of Nazianzus: Select Orations*, 25.15.

what the Nazianzen says in Oration 38 – that lordship is designative of the Godhead or the *monarchia* of the three divine persons together. It is here a matter of emphasis not of content. Lordship is the status of the entire triune Godhead and the oneness of the three divine *hypostases* lies in their equal lordship as *monarchia*, as much as it lies in their equal divinity as God.

In his *De Fide Orthodoxa*, John of Damascus follows in the Nazianzen's footsteps when he similarly speaks about the Holy Trinity in the singular, not the plural, calling the three divine persons "master and lord and king over all,"[523] rather than 'masters, lords and kings over all.' The Trinity, the Damascene maintains, is not only one essence, divinity, will, energy and beginning. The Trinity is also "one sovereignty."[524] John also calls the Son 'Lord' without calling the Father so, but he insists that the Son perfectly images the unseen substance of God in his very lordship. On the other hand, the Damascene also ascribes this title to the Holy Spirit, emphasizing the third *hypostasis* as an object of equal adoration and glorification with the Father and the Son and affirming that the Spirit's lordship is co-essential and co-eternal with theirs.[525] In his emphasis on the Spirit's co-essential lordship, John here echoes none other than the Nazianzen in his exhortation to the Christians "being perfected by the Spirit, do not make the Spirit your own equal."[526] This Spirit is as authoritative as the Father and the Son and should not be treated as creaturely. Following the Nazinzen, John affirms that his all-ruling status makes the Spirit, like the Father and the Son, "Lord of all creation and not under any Lord."[527]

In his explication of the biblical language of lordship and his arguement that it expresses oneness rather than polytheism, as shown above, Theodore Abū Qurrah stands firmly within the theological line of Gregory of Nazianzus and John of Damascus. In his insistence that the Bible speaks of one Lord as 'God, his Word and Spirit,' and not numerically of many lords, Abū Qurrah echoes the Damascene's affirmation that the deity is undivided and that the three are identical in essence, power and energy, but also lordship.[528] By this, Theodore equally invokes Gregory of Nazianzus' saying that what we conceive in the *monarchia* is actually one deity.[529] This is why Abū Qurrah stresses that the scrip-

523 John of Damascus, *Exposition of the Orthodox Faith*, Bk I, ch. 8.
524 Ibid.
525 Ibid.
526 Gregory Nazianzen, *Orations*, 37.17.
527 John of Damascus, *Exposition of the Orthodox Faith*, Bk I, ch. 8; and Gregory Nazianzen, *Orations*, 49.
528 John of Damascus, *Exposition of the Orthodox Faith*, Bk I, ch. 8.
529 Gregory Nazianzen, *Orations*, 31.14.

tures speak of *one* Lord rather than many lords. For him, as for his two predecessors, this is the starting place for demonstrating the oneness of the Christian God – not only by proving the equal divinity of the Creator, his Word/Messiah and Spirit, but also by showing the singular lordship status that the three equally share and co-constitute.

From explicating the scriptural language, Abū Qurrah moves on to unpack the inner logic of Trinitarian doctrinal terminology. In his translation of the *Maymar on the Trinity*, John Lamoreaux divides Abū Qurrah's argument into four parts, titling the discussion that follows the biblical analysis, 'The Testimony of Reason.' I would prefer to describe this section as 'argument from doctrinal terminology.' The overall inquiry that Abū Qurrah addresses here pertains to the accusation of association and Tritheism that was made against Christians on the basis of their referring to three divine entitites, Father, Son and Holy Spirit, rather than one. The accusation states that, if the Christians recognize three divine realities, and that each is God from God and each is 'Lord' in status as the Bible says, and if each entity is representative of a self-existing, independent essence, then 'Father, Son and Spirit' are representative of nothing but three beings, and thus they are designative of three deities. The Christians, therefore, are polytheists and not monotheists.

Responding to this allegation, Abū Qurrah explains that the Christians distinguish between names that designate 'faces' (*wujūh*), such as 'Peter,' 'Paul,' and 'John,'[530] and names that refer to 'natures' (*ṭabāʾiʿ*), such as *ʾīnsān* 'human,' *faras* 'horse' and *thaūr* 'ox.' When one wants to count many faces that have one, common nature, one must not predicate number to names that refer to a nature, lest it imply many natures. So, if one wants to count Peter, James and John, one must predicate number to these three names because they designate the differences between their three holders in terms of faces and characters, but one must avoid numbering the name 'human,' for the three are all equally human in nature. Thus, one should not speak here of three humanities, but of one human nature in three distinct faces or characters called Peter, James and John. It is in the same way, Abū Qurrah postulates, that Christians speak of a triune God:

كذلك الآب والابن والروح القدس ثلاثة وجوه لها طبيعة واحدة وطبيعتهم هي إله. فإذا عددتهم
فليس ينبغي أن توقع العدد على اسم الإله الذي هو اسم الطبيعة وإلا فقد جعلت طبيعتهم الواحدة
التي هي اسم الإله دليل عليها طبائع مختلفة وأخطأت خطأً بيّناً.

530 Lamoreaux translates this word as 'persons' throughout his English version of the maymar, which I shall seriously question and critique in the following section.

> Likewise, the Father, Son, and Holy Spirit are three faces [*wujūh*] with one nature and their nature is God. So, if you count them, you should not predicate number to the name God, which is the name of the nature; otherwise you would make their one nature, the signification of which is the name God, various natures, and commit a manifest error.[531]

From distinguishing 'names of nature' from 'names of faces,' Abū Qurrah takes the discussion to a deeper level by presenting a distinction between 'the name of a nature' and the use of that name in an attributive, predicative manner to apply to one of the nature's characteristics. He starts with an allegorical example that is derived from human existence – in an orthodox comparative fashion that we see in the writings of the Cappadocians and Augustine – before moving up to the realm of God. First, Abū Qurrah points out that the term 'human' is (like 'God') the name of a nature and should remain non-countable, even if we sometimes use it as an adjective referring to an attribute of the entity that has the nature called 'human.' So, for example, one can say that Peter is human, but one cannot say that 'human' as a nature is exclusively imaged in Peter alone. The same applies to James and to John as well: we can predicate their characters by using the adjective 'human,' but we should not allow ourselves, because of this possibility, to make the term 'human' a countable name, when it is used as a the name of a nature. If we predicate a number to the term 'human' when it is used as the name of a nature, we shall be "predicating number to what is unnumbered."[532]

From the previous discussion on the level of the human, Abū Qurrah moves up to the realm of the divine, making the following interesting statement:

> كذلك أعلم أنَّ الآب إله ولكن ليس الإله هو الآب. والابن إله ولكن الإله في وجه (إذ اسم الإله دليل على الطبيعة) ليس هو الابن. والروح إله ولكن الإله ليس هو الروح. فإذا عددت الآب والابن والروح القدس فليس ينبغي لك أن توقع العدد على اسم الإله فتقول ثلاثة آلهة. وإلا فقد أوقعت العدد على غير المعدود.

> Likewise, know that the Father is God [or divine], but God is not the Father [alone]. And the Son is God [or divine], but God in a face [*fī wajh*] (since the name God designates nature) is not the Son [alone]. And the Spirit is God [or divine], but God is not the Spirit [alone]. So, if you count the Father, the Son, and the Holy Spirit, you should not predicate number to the name God, saying three gods, lest you predicate number to what is not to be numbered.[533]

This is a very thought-provoking statement. It is crucial here to realize that Abū Qurrah does not reduce the Godhead to one of the three divine *hypostases* alone, whether to the Son or to the Spirit, or, more crucially still, to the Father. I have

---

531 Abū Qurrah, *Maymar on the Trinity*, pp. 33–34.

532 Ibid., p. 34.

"وإلا فقد أوقعت العدد على غير المعدود."

533 Ibid.

already pointed out in this chapter as in chapter three that the patrocentric understanding of the Godhead (i.e., as belonging to the Father alone) was a central trend in Trinitarian, Greek-Byzantine orthodoxy from the 4th century onwards. It seems, nonetheless, that Abū Qurrah stands here aside from this patrocentric stream, emphasizing instead – according to what we can deduce from his overall logic in this maymar – a Trinitarian ontology such as we find in Gregory of Nazianzus: neither the Son nor the Spirit, and nor even the Father, alone is the hypostatic representation of the Godhead.[534] 'God' is the name of the common nature, which the three are, not only in terms of character or face (*wajh*), but primarily in terms of being, of who they are in nature. So, the fact that we can use the term 'God' as an adjective to characterize the Father, the Son and the Holy Spirit as divine and godly in character does not permit us to make the term 'Godhead,' when it is used as the name of the nature and not simply as an adjective, a designation of one of the three (the Father, the Son, or the Spirit) alone. This logic clearly takes Abū Qurrah away from any theology that sees the Godhead in the Father alone, and places him instead within the circle of a Nazianzen-like orthodoxy that views the Godhead as the three *hypostases* together.

Another noteworthy element in Abū Qurrah's statement lies in his saying "and the Son is God, but God *in a face* (*fī wajh*) (since the name 'God' designates nature) is not the Son." This is how the sentence appears in Constantine Bacha's Arabic text of the maymar. In his translation of this sentence, John Lamoreaux omits from the sentence the words "*fī wajh (īz ism al-īlah dalīl 'alā al-ṭabā'ī)*" (in a face [since the name God designates nature]) on the basis of his allegation (Lamoreaux's) that they are "likely to be a scribal interpolation."[535]

Which of these two versions, "the Son is God, but God in a face ... is not the Son" (Bacha) or "the Son is God, but God ... is not the Son" (Lamoreaux) is more authentically expressive of Abū Qurrah's mind? Lamoreaux considers both the phrase "in a face" and the phrase in brackets to be a scribal editorial addition. I totally disagree with this and suggest that we may consider the bracketed explanation "(for the name God designates nature)" as a later scribal insertion,

---

534 Abū Qurrah elsewhere opts for different, more clearly, patrocentric language. See Abū Qurrah, *Maymar fī Wujūd al-Khāliq wad-Dīn al-Qawīm* (Maymar on the existence of the Creator and the right religion), pt 3, ch. 9, pt. 29. There, Abū Aurrah, explicitly attributes the divine headship or Godhead to the Father among the three:

29. ليس بينهم خلاف شيءٍ البتة إلا أنَّ هذا والد وذاك مولود والآخر منبثق، والوالد منهم رئيس

29. There is no differentiation whatsoever between them, except that this is progenitor, that is engendered and the other is emanated, and the progenitor among them is head/chief.

This is a good example of Abū Qurrah's eclectic reliance on, and invocation of, various patristic orthodox modes of expressions to fit his argument and dialogical setting.

535 Lamoreaux, *Theodore Abū Qurrah*, p. 183, n. 71.

but not the phrase "in a face." This latter phrase, I believe, is part of the original text and expresses Abū Qurrah's thought. What Abū Qurrah wants to say is "and the Son is God, but God in a face is not the Son [alone]." Adding "alone" here is useful for interpreting the meaning of the sentence accurately. It is important here to study carefully Abū Qurrah's use of the Arabic term '*wajh*' in reference to the Trinity and whether translating it as 'person' in English is appropriate, but I shall postpone this to the next section and concentrate here on the presence of the term in the above mentioned sentence in the text in specific, suggesting that an appropriate English translation here should be 'face' or 'character.' Thus, I read the sentence as follows: "but God in a face/character is not the Son [alone]."

Which character or face is Abū Qurrah referring to here, the one of the Son in eternity (as the begotten, eternal *Logos*), or the one that represents the Son in history (as the incarnate Messiah-*Logos*, who became flesh)? It is my conviction that Abū Qurrah is here referring to the second personal presence of the Son as the incarnate *Logos*. Why? Because this is the face that Muslims would be concerned to discuss and rationally grasp. They do not care primarily about the Son's personhood in the divine eternity, because, first, they reject the possibility that humans have the ability to speak of God's transcendent being, and, second, they are not versed in Christian traditional doctrinal debates and the hermeneutics of the triune ontology of God. Rather, they are more familiar with the Christians' claim that ʿĪsā ibn Maryam is their Messiah and the incarnate Word of God, who was born miraculously from a virgin. Muslims also have a Qur'anic attestation to *Allāh*, his Word and Spirit, and they concede that God's Word and Spirit are also expressive of the divine supremacy of their source. What the Muslims cannot accept, however, is the Christians' claim that in the person of the Messiah God himself is present and that the Messiah-*Logos* is not just a property of God, but a personal divine face (*wajh*) of the divine being; the *Logos* is the Son of God, is God from God.

Abū Qurrah is dealing here with Muslim audiences and he endeavours to explain to them the triune oneness, taking seriously into consideration their view of God, his Word and the nature of the Word. He knows that if he speaks of the Son as 'God,' he will not break into the Muslim way of thinking and will not be able to draw them into the circle of Trinitarian logic. In order not to lose his audience's attention and interest, Abū Qurrah cleverly adds "in a face" (*fī wajh*) and stresses that God's incarnate Son is just one of the personified images of God and does not exhaust the infinity of the divine being in a single historical manifestation. In this way, Abū Qurrah does not deny the Christian belief that the Messiah is divine and godly in nature, since the incarnate is "*God* in a face" and not just a creaturely image of a divine reality. Theodore equally avoids provoking any negative, offensive reaction from his Muslim audience by maintaining that, even if Christians describe the Messiah-*Logos* as 'God the Son,' they do not thereby limit the divine infinity or deny God's transcendence, for Christians also state that "God *in a face* [God's characteristics and attributes, in Muslim terms] is not the Son [alone]." Christians do not reduce the divine infinite being to the face/character of the Son alone, because they also see this divine infinite nature imaged in the Father and the Spirit.[536]

Reading this mentioned sentence within the context of what Abū Qurrah says about the Trinity in the paragraph as a whole makes his intention clearer and validates his choice of words, especially with regard to his applying "in a face" to the Son alone. Abū Qurrah needed here to add "in a face" to his statement about the Son and not to the points he makes about the Father and the Spirit because he was trying to pre-empt the question: If you say that the Son, whom you Christians claim to be also human, is 'God,' then you are denying God's infinity and incomprehensibility and making God imprisoned in a human, historical – even if prophetic – person. How can you then still say that God is eternal and transcendent? To this anticipated challenge, Abū Qurrah says: Yes, the Son, who is the human Messiah, is 'God.' But, this does not mean that this incarnate face (*wajh*) exhausts the divine being, for God's personal face or character (God in a face) is not the Son alone.

From differentiating the 'name of nature' from its use as an adjective that is descriptive of one of the particular characteristics of those who, while distinct, share one nature, Abū Qurrah returns to the distinction he started with between naming the nature and naming the faces. This time he describes the name of the face as a 'logical name' (*'ism manṭiqī*), meaning by 'logical' that the name of the face (*wajh*) is not restricted to one face per se, but can be used for more than one character. It can rather "fall on the Father, the Son and the Holy Spirit and on every one of the angels and humans and animals and other non-separate enti-

---

536 In the polemical writings of some of the later Muslim *mutakallims*, one can see that Muslims understood *uqnūm* in the writings of the Christian *mutakallims* as referring to an individual (*shakhṣ*) with specific characteristics (*khawāṣṣ*). While what they say about 'specific characteristics' is an accurate perception of the Christian *mutakallims*' explanation of the aspect of particularity in the triune hypostatic nature of God, the Muslim *mutakallims*' association of particularity with the notion of 'individuality' is an inaccurate reading of the Christian terminology, though it serves the Muslims' purpose of nullifying the Trinity. For some examples of such an association of particularity and individuality in Muslim polemical *kalām* on the Trinity, see David Thomas, *Anti-Christian Polemic in Early Islam: Abū ʿĪsā al-Warrāq's "Against the Trinity"* (Cambridge: Cambridge University Press, 1992); and D. Thomas, "The Doctrine of the Trinity in the Early Abbasid Era," in *Islamic Interpretations of Christianity*, ed. Lloyd Ridgeon (Richmond: Curzon Press, 2001), 78–98, pp. 83–88.

ties."[537] The logical name of face can be numbered, while one cannot number the general name of the nature so as not to turn what is common into various different natures. But neither should one apply number to the particular name that one uses for each particular face in its uniqueness, for that would make one particular name, and ultimately its face/character, inclusively representative of all others, thereby overriding their particularities. This means that we cannot generalize Peter's, James', or John's particular name and speak of three 'Peters,' 'James,' or 'Johns.' This is another way for Abū Qurrah to make his previous point that Peter is 'human' in nature, while the nature called 'human' is not Peter alone. In the same way, saying that the Father is 'God' without making God the Father alone means that one cannot speak of the three divine persons as three Fathers (or three Sons or Holy Spirits), for 'Father' names only one particular person and designates his individuation. Naming the nature is different, however, for 'nature' signifies what makes the particulars one and con-substantial. The names 'God' and 'human' are names designative of oneness: "they neither multiply nor diffuse."[538] This, Abū Qurrah affirms, is even more the case with the Father, Son and Holy Spirit, who, unlike humans such as Peter, James and John, are neither separate in location, nor different in terms of image, likeness, or condition.[539] And, when many agree in terms of what is common between them and stands as their nature, we call these many 'one' by virtue of this commonality. In the case of the Father, Son and Spirit, this is even more evident. For, while humans may sometimes not have images, wills, conditions, etc. in common (although they share these things at other times), in the case of the Father, Son and Spirit there is nothing they do not share, and at all times, among each other.

> فأما الآب والابن والروح القدس فليس هذا منهم في موضع ليس فيه للآخر ولا لأحدهم صورة ليست لغيره ولا مشيئة ولا مال ليس لغيره. فإذا كان الواحد من هذه الخصال قد تجعل المتفقين فيها واحداً وإذا كانوا كثيراً فكم ينبغي للآب والابن والروح القدس أن يكونوا واحداً إذ لا يفترقون في موضع وهم متفقون في كل هذه الأشياء والوجوه وما شاكلها.
>
> As for the Father, Son, and Holy Spirit, there is not one of them in a position the other is not in, nor has one of them an image the other has not or a will or a condition [reading the word here with Lamoreaux as *ḥāl* instead of *ma'āl*] which the other has not. So, if one of these characteristics may make those who commonly hold it one, even if they are

537 Abū Qurrah, *Maymar on the Trinity*, p. 35.
"بل يقع اسم الوجه على الآب وعلى الابن وعلى الروح القدس وعلى كل واحد من الملائكة والناس والحيوان وغير ذلك من الغير المنفصلات."

538 Ibid.

539 Ibid.
"مع أنَّ الآب والابن والروح القدس ليسوا كأناس ثلاثة يفترقون في الموضع أو يختلفون في الصورة أو في الشبه أو في الحال."

> many, this oneness is more applicable to the Father, Son, and Holy Spirit, who never part ways and who agree in everything and every respect and other things alike.[540]

But, would not the emphasis on 'oneness' stand against the threeness of the Father, Son and Holy Spirit? Would it not, that is, reveal the meaninglessness of the Christian acknowledgment of Father, Son and Spirit as one God, and invite them, instead, to speak of one God who is Father of all creation, who utters his Word and breathes his Spirit via his prophets' mouth? In other words, if Christians ultimately emphasize the oneness of God's nature and being, why do they still need to give to God, his Word and Spirit three particular 'names of faces,' and why do they need to point to distinctions between these faces, to the extent that it makes their view of God's oneness contradictory, illogical and hardly plausible?

Here, Abū Qurrah reaches the stage of justifying the orthodox Trinitarian core belief in 'God's oneness-in-particularity, not oneness despite distinction.' His strategy in tackling this challenge is basically to differentiate between 'distinction' and 'difference' and show that the individuation and particularity of the three in the Trinity signifies distinction without implying difference. This is the core meaning of his words:

> فأما الآب والابن والروح القدس فإنه لا اختلاف بينهم بتة له أثر في أقنوم أحدهم أكثر من أنَّ كل واحد منهم غير صاحبه. فهم لعمري أولى أن يكونوا إلهاً واحداً وإن كان كل واحدٍ منهم إلهاً تاماً

> Concerning the Father, Son and Holy Spirit, there is between them no difference whatsoever which can be traced in the personhood [*uqnūm*] of one of them more than the fact that each one of them is other than his companion [i.e., the Father is not a Son, the Son is not the Father, and the Spirit is neither]. They are, I swear, more appropriatly to be one God even if each one of them is a complete deity.[541]

What then drives the Christian to believe that the Trinity is one God, though each one of the three persons is fully divine in his particular *hypostasis* (*uqnūm*), is the possible allegorical similarity between this divine situation and human, creaturely cases. For example, one may hear three men reciting one and the same poem. Despite the distinctions between their voices, one can still hear them reciting one and the same poem and cannot say that what one hears are three poems. The same applies to the person who looks at three pieces of gold. She can see that each piece is a complete piece of gold in itself, yet she still speaks

540 Ibid., p. 36.
541 Ibid.

about 'gold,' which these pieces are made of, rather than of three different 'golds.' Such allegorical cases and similarities, Abū Qurrah concludes, are not only attested to in the revealed scriptures (*al-kutub al-munzala*), but more importantly by correct reason (*al-ʿaql al-sadīd*).[542]

By this logic, Abū Qurrah continues, it becomes easy to answer those irrational people who ask Christians: Was creation created by one or by three? The Creator of creation, Abū Qurrah affirms, is one, but, he adds, this does not mean that only one *hypostasis* (*uqnūm)* is divine in status and, thus, the only one able to create, while the other two *hypostases* are not divine enough to enjoy this prerogative. Thus, saying that the Creator is one does not suggest a hierarchy within the Godhead, nor does it negate the completely equal divinity of the three *hypostases*. When Christians speak of the One God as the Creator of the universe, they mean that the three persons act indivisibly in relation to creation (*opera ad extra trinitatis indivisa sunt*). Ascribing the act of creating to the person of the Father does not mean that the Son and the Spirit are not involved in this action. Each one of the three is involved in accordance with the particularity of his hypostatic identity. Again, Abū Qurrah here resorts to allegory: when we look at the sun and observe how its rays enlighten people, we do not say the sun *and* its rays co-enlighten people. We rather say, 'The sun enlightens people by means of its rays.'[543] Similarly, when the carpenter makes a door, we do not say, 'The carpenter *and* his hands made the door,' but 'The carpenter made the door with his hands.' By the same logic, Abū Qurrah opines:

كذلك يقال أنَّ الآب خلق الخلق. ويقال أنَّ الابن خلق الخلق. ولا يقال أنَّ الآب والابن خلقا الخلق لأنَّ الآب إنما خلق الخلق كله بابنه

> Likewise, it is said that the Father created the creation. And it is said that the Son created the creation. And, it is not said that the Father and the Son both created the creation, for the Father created the whole creation by his Son.[544]

Abū Qurrah, then, states his point in the clearest terms possible, saying:

---

542 Ibid., p. 37.

543 Almost the exact apology for the Trinity by the help of the metaphor of 'sun-rays' relaion also exists in the response of Leo III to ʿUmar b. ʿAbdul-ʿAzīz's letter: Arthur Jeffery, "Ghevond's Text of the Correspondence between ʿUmar II and Leo III," in *The Early Christian-Muslim Dialogue: A Collection of Documents from the First Three Islamic Centuries (632–900 A.D.): Translations with Commentary*, N. A. Newman (ed.), (Hatfield, Penn: Interdiscplinary Biblical Research Institute, 1993), pp. 47–132, pt. W, p. 76.

544 Abū Qurrah, *Maymar on the Trinity*, p. 38.

ولا نرى أنَّ الحرارة أولى بأن تكون للنار من الابن أن يكون للآب ولا أنَّ الحرارة أشد اتصالاً بالنار من الابن بالآب [حتى] وإن كان كل واحد منهما أقنوماً، لأنَّ الطبيعة الإلهية لا تقبل تركيباً كما تقبله الأجساد. ولا يكون فيها الهيولى والصورة ولا توجد بتة الغيرية في ذات أقنوم واحد منها، بل موقع الابن من الآب هو كموقع حرارة النار من النار وكموقع الشعاع من الشمس والكلمة من العقل، [حتى] وإن كان الابن أقنوماً تاماً عندنا لأنَّ الطبيعة الإلهية تلطّف أن توجد الغيرية في ذات أقنوم واحد منها كما قلت.

> And we do not think that the heat belongs to the fire more than the Son belongs to the Father, nor that the heat is more attached to the fire than the Son to the Father, [even] if each one of them is person [*uqnūm*], because the divine nature cannot be constructed [of several parts] as [physical] bodies can. Nor can it contain matter or form and there is never any otherness [*ghayriyyah*][545] in the single person among them, but the position of the Son to the Father is like the position of the fire's heat to the fire and of the ray to the sun and the word to the mind, [even] if for us the Son is a complete person [*uqnūm tāmm*], for the divine nature is too refined to accept the existence of otherness within one of its persons, as I said.[546]

It is important here to realize that Abū Qurrah uses the word *ghayriyyah* (otherness), and not *taghyīr/taghayyur* (change), in reference to the core meaning of the Christian recognition of three particular *hypostases* (*aqānīm*) in God. Lamoreaux inappropriately translates this word as 'change,' but Abū Qurrah is not here speaking of 'change,' but rather of 'otherness,' which is more in line with Abū Qurrah's purpose of showing that Christians' recognition of hypostatic particularity and individuation in the Godhead does not mean that they claim that there is a difference between the *hypostases*, or that the divine nature is an eternal Father with a created *Logos* that contains traces of its creator's divinity (against Arianism).[547] Within this framework, it is plausible to emphasize the absence of any 'otherness' (*ghayriyyah*) between the *hypostases* or in any one of them, for such otherness, if it existed, would entail leveling in terms of status, but also difference in terms of being. This would deconstruct the oneness of the Christian God and confirm the Muslim accusations of associationism and polytheism. Rather than making the Father an 'other God' by calling him Creator, explains Abū Qurrah, Christians make the Father 'a particular, completely divine, *hypostasis*,' whose individuation lies in creating the world by the Son. Abū Qur-

---

545 Lamoreaux translates the Arabic *ghayriyyah* as 'change.' I believe that 'otherness' is a more appropriate translation here: Lamoreaux, *Theodore Abū Qurrah*, p. 186.

546 Abū Qurrah, *Maymar on the Trinity*, p. 39.

547 Later in the text, Abū Qurrah alludes to this Arian idea when he states:
"واعلم أنَّ الطبيعة الإلهية لا تقبل التركيب بتة كما قلنا أو غيرية يوجد لها أثر في أقنوم واحد منها [لوحده] بل هي مبسوطة على صرف الانبساط وحقيقته وليس يقبل أقنوم إلهي أن يضاف إليه شيء له أثر فيه."
And know that the divine nature cannot be constructed [of several parts], as we said, nor can there be any trace of otherness in one *hypostasis* (*uqnūm*) [alone]. It [the divine nature] is rather fully and truly simple and no *hypostasis* accepts anything to be added to it that leaves a trace in it": ibid., p. 44.

rah denies *ghayriyyah* here because he wants 1) to affirm oneness by rejecting otherness in *nature* (the name of nature is common and unnumbered) and 2) to defend equality by means of stressing complete hypostatic particularity (the name of the face [e.g., Peter] is also unnumbered for it designates distinction). That said:

> لأنَّ الكنيسة تعلم أنَّ الآب والابن والروح القدس إله واحد على الوجوه التي ذكرنا من قبل...فإنها تقول أنَّ الآب والابن والروح القدس خلق الخلق. ولا تقول خلقوا. وتقول يا آب ويا ابن ويا روح القدس ارحمني. ولا تقول ارحموني وما كان مثل ذلك.
>
> Because the Church teaches that the Father, Son, and Spirit are one God in the faces that we referred to before ... [I]t, therefore, states that the Father, Son, and Holy Spirit created [in the singular] the creation. It does not say they [in the plural] created. And it says "O Father, O Son and O Spirit" have mercy on me [in the singular]. It does not say have mercy [in the plural] on me, or anything like that.[548]

The final question Abū Qurrah deals with is related to his statement that each of the *hypostases* is complete God or completely divine, like the other two. For such a claim, the non-Christian 'irrational person' (*man lā ʿaqla lah*) asks the Christian: "Do you disbelieve (*takfur*) in every God other (*ghayr*) than the Father? Do you disbelieve in every God other than the Son? Do you disbelieve in every God other than the Holy Spirit?"[549] The irrational person thinks that if the Christian answers 'yes' to these questions, either the Father, the Son, or the Spirit would be deemed God while the other two would not (which traps the Christian in the Arian or Eunomian heresy). On the other hand, if the Christian answers 'no' to the questions, he will prove that Christians are polytheists, since they consider more than one to be completely divine.

In the face of this challenge, Abū Qurrah refers his interlocutors to a conceptual distinction he has made earlier between the 'name of nature' and the 'name of face.' By taking account of this distinction, Abū Qurrah argues, one can realize that speaking of the Messiah as complete God does not refer to the Son's hypostatic identity (the name of his face), but rather to the Son's being (the name of his nature). Since the name of 'God,' which is the name of a nature, is a non-logical name; that is, it is not restricted to the Son alone but is applicable to the Father and the Spirit, one can tenably say, 'I disbelieve in every God other than the Son' without denying the divinity of the Father and the Spirit. This would be like saying, Abū Qurrah maintains, that one disbelieves in every divine nature other than the Messiah's nature. This is correct, and does not deny the divine nature of the Father and the Spirit, for their divine nature is not *another* divine nature. It is,

548 Ibid., pp. 40 – 41.
549 Ibid., p. 42.

rather, the same nature, which is common to the Son too.[550] When we speak of the Messiah we are generally referring to his hypostatic identity that is particularly his alone. However, the Messiah's divine status is not related to his *uqnūm*, but more substantially to the divine nature, which he shares with the Father and the Spirit as one, complete God. When one asks about the nature, the inquiry inherently implies the Father, Son and Spirit alike, even if the inquirer names only one of them, since there is no complete divine nature except the one that consists of the three divine persons together. In other words, oneness is not challenged by believing in three completely divine *hypostases*. Oneness is rather the foundation of these three's divinity and equality; because they are one in nature (all are named with the same name of nature, 'God'), the Father, Son and Holy Spirit are each completely God and fully divine in their hypostatic particularity. God's oneness, Abū Qurrah concludes, is not only defended and maintained in Christian faith. It is also deemed the cornerstone of Christians' belief in the Trinity and their rational point of departure in reading the scriptural attestations and in understanding the Church's doctrinal hermeneutics on the divinity of the Father, the Son and the Holy Spirit.

B. Some Remarks on the Trinitarian Terminology

A point of interest in Abū Qurrah's *Maymar on the Trinity* is his use of two different Arabic terms to refer to the three divine persons; *wajh* (face) and *uqnūm* (*hypostasis*). On the basis of the use of these two terms, the text can be divided into two almost equal halves. In the first half of the maymar, Abū Qurrah refers to the divine persons using the term *wajh* (pl. *wujūh*) and in the second he uses *uqnūm*

---

550 Ibid., pp. 42–43.

"كذلك حيث تُسأل عن المسيح فيقال لك 'أتكفر بكل إلهٍ غيره [؟]' ليس عن أقنومه تُسأل، وإن كانت المسألة تشير إليه، بل إنما تسأل عن طبيعة المسيح لأنَّ اسم الإله ليس بخاص للمسيح دون الآب والروح. وإنما اسم الإله اسم طبيعة لا اسم أقنوم كما بيّنا بدءاً. فلذلك يحسن أن تقول إني كافر بكل إله غير المسيح ولا يسقط الآب والروح من أن يكون كل واحد منهما إلهاً. لأنَّ هذه المسألة إنما تشبه أن يقال لك 'أتكفر بكل طبيعة إلهية غير طبيعة المسيح" فتقول 'نعم' وقولك حق لأنَّ طبيعة الابن الإلهية هي طبيعة الآب والروح."

Likewise, when you are asked about Christ, 'Do you disbelieve in every God other than him[?]', you are not being asked about his *hypostasis* (*uqnūmihi*), even though the question may indicate that, but you are being asked about the nature of Christ, since the name of God is not restricted to Christ without the Father and the Spirit. The name of God is the name of nature, not the name of a *hypostasis*, as we initially explained. Therefore, it is appropriate to say, 'I disbelieve in every God other than Christ' and this does not deny the divinity of the Father and the Spirit. For this issue is similar to when it is said to you, 'Do you disbelieve in every divine nature other than the nature of Christ[?]' and you say, 'Yes'. Your saying is true, for the Son's divine nature is the nature of the Father and the Spirit."

(pl. *aqānīm*), which Arab Christians took directly from the Syriac *qnomo/qnoma* (pl. *qnome*). In his English version of the maymar, John Lamoreaux translates *wajh* as 'person' and *uqnūm* as *hypostasis*. However, Constantine Bacha in his Arabic edition of the maymar also suggests that by *wajh* Abū Qurrah means *uqnūm*, although Bacha does not literally apply this suggestion to his edition of the Arabic text.[551] Lamoreaux most probably follows Bacha's suggestion in his English translation of *wajh* as 'person,' since the Syriac *qnomo* is a synonym of the Greek *hypostasis*, as I have already argued in chapter three, and since both designate personhood, or connote a concrete and particular personal subsistence of the *ousia* (Greek) or the *ituta/kyana* (Syriac).

It is my conviction that treating *wajh* as *uqnūm* (Bacha) and translating it as 'person' (Lamoreaux) are both questionable suggestions that need to be carefully examined. Is taking *wajh* as a synonym for 'person' and *uqnūm*, and thus for *hypostasis* too, consistent with its Arabic meaning? What if a more appropriate translation can be suggested that would link the meaning of *wajh* to other Greek and Syriac terms? In the rest of this section, I will touch upon Abū Qurrah's Trinitarian terminology in *Maymar on the Trinity*, starting with a brief reminder of some remarks on *uqnūm* and proceeding to a more detailed discussion of *wajh*.

In Chapter three, I demonstrated that the Greek fathers adopted the term *hypostasis* from the Stoics because they considered it the most appropriate word to use in reference to divine personhood in the Trinity. They used *hypostasis* and the Greek term *ousia* in Trinitarian hermeneutics to distinguish between God's nature (*ousia*) and the divine subsistances that are expressive of God's particular personhood (*hypostasis*), without allowing this to lead to any assumption of a division between who God is as one *ousia* and what God personally and relationally does as three *hypostases*. I also explained in Chapter three that the terms *qnomo* and *ituta/kyana* have the same role in Syrian orthodox Trinitarian theology as *hypostasis* and *ousia* have in Greek orthodoxy, giving the following example: when the Greek fathers understood the biblical verse "the Son is ... the exact presentation of [God's] being" (Hebrews 1:3) as meaning 'the Son is the *hypostasis* of God's *ousia*,' the Syrian fathers interpreted the same verse as meaning 'the Son is the *qnomo* of God's *ituta/kyana*.'

In the light of this terminological affinity, translating *uqnūm* in Abū Qurrah's text as 'person' and '*hypostasis*' – since *uqnūm* is just the Arabic equivalent of the Syriac *qnomo* – is appropriate. It conveys accurately Abū Qurrah's Trinitarian thinking, as shown in the analysis above. That notwithstanding, it is still crucial

551 Bacha, *Myāmir*, p. 28, n. 1.

to ask here whether 'person' is an accurate translation of the Arabic *wajh* and, indeed, whether *wajh* can be treated as synonym of *uqnūm*, thus also of *hypostasis*, in the first place. In the paragraphs that follow, I shall argue that the Arabic word *wajh* carries neither the connotation of *uqnūm/qnomo*, nor the meaning of 'person' in any of the senses implied in the term *hypostasis*. In fact, when we realize the meaning of *wajh* in Arabic, its use by an acclaimed orthodox Melkite theologian like Abū Qurrah becomes quite puzzling.

According to the encyclopedic dictionary of Arabic with its philological roots and usages, *Lisān al-ʿArab*, the word *wajh* (pl. *wujūh*) means something recognized by virtue of facial features, geographical direction, social status, or spatial presence. It also means the future fate of something or its condition. In an extension of the meaning of 'face,' *wajh* indicates a person who is known by certain facial features, and this is even applied in a Ḥadith saying on God: *kullu shay'in hālikun īllā wajhuh* (everything is perishable except his face [i.e., him]).[552] Other variations of meaning can be found in Qur'anic texts (Q 2:144, 272; 13:22; 28:88; 30:38–39; 55:27; 76:9; 92:20) and in a Ḥadith reported by Abū al-Dardā's *"lā tafqah ḥattā tarā ll-Qur'an wjūh"* (you will not apprehend until you see that the Qur'an has many meanings). On the other hand, Muslim mutakallims, such as the Muʿtazilī judge, ʿAbd al-Jabbār, use *wajh* in the sense of a 'facet' or 'aspect' of convictions or knowledge.[553]

In his explanation of the use of *wajh* with reference to God in the Qur'an, especially Q 55:27: "*wa-yabqā wajhu rabbika zū aj-jalāl wal-īkrām*" (there remaineth but the 'face' of thy Lord of might and glory), the 9th–10th-century Sunni scholar from Nishapur, Abū Bakr Muḥammad ibn Isḥaq Ibn Khuzayma (d. 923), supports the use of *wajh* to speak of God on the basis of its occurance in the Qur'an. He justifies this anthropomorphism, which the Muʿtazilites at that time accused non-Muʿtazilite Muslim authors of, by affirming that it is acceptable as long as we remember that God's face (*wajh*) is not to be confused with the faces of mortal human creatures.[554] The impossibility of this assimilation, Ibn

---

552 On God's face in Islamic thought and *kalām*, see, for example, Richard M. Frank, *Beings and Their Attributes: The Teachings of the Basrian School of the Muʿtazila in the Classical Period* (Albany, NY: State University of New York Press, 1978); Johannes R.T.M. Peters, *God's Created Speech: A Study in the Speculative Theology of the Muʿtazilî Qâḍî l-Quḍât Abû l-Ḥasan ʿAbd aj-Jabbār bin Aḥmad al-Hamadhānī* (Leiden: Brill, 1976); and Feras Ḥamza, Sajjad Rizvi and Farḥana Mayer (eds), *An Anthology of Qur'anic Commentaries*, Vol. 1: *On the Nature of the Divine* (Oxford: Oxford University Press, 2008), pp. 67–125. I am grateful to Dr. Jon Hoover, Professor of Islamic Studies at Nottingham University for drawing my attention to these sources.

553 See on this J. Peters, *God's Created Speech*, pp. 47–53, 269–271.

554 On the Muʿtazilites and the influence of their thought on early Islamic theological thinking, see Josepf van Ess, *Theologie und Gesellschaft im 2 und 3. Jahrhundert Hidschra: Eine Geschichte*

Khuzayma argues, stems from the fact that, contrary to human faces, which are creaturely, perishable and lacking in any glory or radiance, God's *wajh*, as Q 55: 27 says, "radiates so much bright light, so much splendor ... and we say that our Lord's face has no beginning and no end, it was always part of the one who remains and never perishes."[555] In other words, it is theologically acceptable in Islam to speak of God's face, according to Ibn Khuzayma, and there is no need to replace this word with another, as long as we remember that God's face is substantially different from the human face and one should not refer to the divine, unseen face out of any attempt to liken it to the human reality.

On the other hand, *wajh* also designates social status, and it means one who plays the role of, or acts like, a chief or noble, who represents or speaks on behalf of his community. '*Rajul wajh*' is a 'notable man,' someone with the rank of representative or leader.[556] *Wajh* is still commonly used in colloquial Arabic in the sense of that part of the head that includes the eyes, the mouth and the nose, and in the sense of one who is a representative, spokesman, or noble chief of a people or community (*wajh al-qawm*).[557]

As we see, none of the various meanings of *wajh*, either ancient or modern, conveys 'person' or 'personhood.' It would, therefore, be rather inappropriate to translate it in Abū Qurrah's text as 'person,' or to consider it a synonym of *uqnūm* and link it to *hypostasis*. The words the Muslim *mutakallims* use to express *hypostasis* are the Arabic terms *maʿnā* (meaning),[558] *shayʾ* (thing), *khawāṣṣ* (properties) and *ṣifāt* (attributes).

Harry Wolfson perceptively points this out in his seminal study of Muslim *kalām*. Wolfson argues that in Christian theology the Greek term for 'things' (*pragmata*; sing. *Pragma*) is used like *hypostases* to describe the three divine persons in the Trinity.[559] Wolfson further shows that the term *pragma* has even been

---

des religiösen Denkens im frühen Islam, Berlin & New York: Walter De Gruyter, 1991, Vol. II, pp. 233–242, 327–342; and Richard C. Martin; Mark R. Woodward and Dwi S. Atmaja, *Defenders of Reason in Islam: Muʿtazalism from Medieval School to Modern Symbol*, (Oxford: Oneworld Publishing, 2003), pp. 25–45.

555 M.I.I. Ibn Khuzayma, *Kitāb at-Tawḥīd wa 'Īthbāt Ṣifāt ar-Rab* (The book of monotheism and the verification of the Lord's attributes), ed. M.K. Harras (Beirut: Dār aj-Jīl, 1983), pp. 10–11, 22–23; also in Nagel, *The History of Islamic Theology*, pp. 131–132.

556 See *Lisān al-ʿArab* at www.alwaraq.net/lisanSearchutf8.htm (accessed 10 August. 2011).

557 See the meaning of *wajh* in www.almaany.com (accessed 10 August. 2011).

558 On the use of the word *maʿnā*, see R.M. Frank, "Al-Maʿnā: Some Reflections on the Technical Meanings of the Term in the Kalâm," *Journal of the American Oriental Society*, 87 (1967), 248–259.

559 Harry Austryn Wolfson, *The Philosophy of the Kalām* (Cambridge, MA: Harvard University Press, 1976), p. 115. Wolfson attributes this usage to Origen in *Contra Celsum*, trans. Henry Chad-

used on some occasions (as in the *Formula Prolixa* of the Council of Antioch, 343) as equivalent not only to *hypostasis*, but also to *prosopon*. Wolfson, then, intriguingly points to a Greek text written by Abū Qurrah on the Trinity, which speaks of the three persons of the Trinity as *pragmata*,[560] which in Arabic would be translated as either *shay'* (pl. *ashyā'*) or *ma'nā* (pl. *ma'ānī*).[561] What catches the attention here is that, though Theodore Abū Qurrah in his Greek *opusculum* uses *pragmata* to speak of the three persons in the Trinity, in his Arabic texts he does not translate *hypostases* (or even *pragmata*) as *ma'nā* (meaning) or *shay'* (thing),[562] but uses instead the Arabic *wajh/wujūh*. Why choose this term and not *ma'nā*, *shay'*, *ṣifah* (attribute), *khāṣṣah* (characteristic), or *īsm* (name) that were commonly used by, and were familiar to, both Christian and Muslim *mutakallims*? More challengingly still, why would Abū Qurrah use the term *wajh*, despite his almost certain knowledge that *wajh* can be synonymous with another word, in Greek and Syriac, that was briefly used to refer to the three divine persons in early Trinitarian literature, before the Church fathers, starting from the 4th century, replaced it with *hypostasis* in Greek, and *qnomo* in Syriac? I refer here to the Greek term *prosopon* and the Syriac term *parsop*.

We have already seen in chapter three that the word *prosopon* was used until the end of the 2nd century in relation to the Trinity's presence and role in creation. In its original meaning, *prosopon* connotes 'face,' 'expression,' 'outer image,' or 'mask,' but also 'role' or 'position.' The Church fathers initially adopted this term because it is found in the Septuagint and the New Testament.[563]

---

wick (Cambridge: Cambridge University Press, 1953), VIII.12 (PG 11, 1533 C); and Tertullian in *Against Praxias*, in *The Ante-Nicene Fathers*, Vol. III, ed. Robert Alexander and James Donaldson (Grand Rapids: W. B. Eerdmans, 1968), pt. 7 (PL 2. 162 A B).

560 Wolfson, *The Philosophy of the Kalām*, p. 116. Wolfson refers here to Theodore Abū Qurrah's *Opuscula* (PG 97, 1480B) and to the discussion on this text's terminology in Georg Graf, "Die arabischen Schriften des Abū Qurra," in *Forschungen zur Christlichen Literature – und Dogmengeshichte*, ed. G. Graf, Vol. 10 (Paderborn: Ferdinand Schöningh, 1910), 67–78.

561 *Ashyā'* and *ma'ānī* appear, for example, in the Arabic apologetic Trinitarian texts of Yahyā Ibn 'Adī, as well as in the texts of Muslim and Jewish *mutakallims*, such as al-Ash'arī, Ibn Hazm, Saadia Gaon and 'Abdullāh Ibn Kullāb: Wolfson, *The Philosophy of Kalām*, p. 117. Wolfson concludes from this that "during the early part of the ninth century, at about the time of the rise of Mu'tazilism, Christians under Muslim rule used the term *pragmata* instead of, or by the side of, the terms *hypostaseis* and *prosopa* as a description of the members of the Trinity and that the term *pragmata* was translated by them into Arabic by *ashyā'* and *ma'ānī*" (ibid., p. 116).

562 Wolfson concedes this and admits the absence of any such translation in Theodore's Arabic works. He, nevertheless, goes along with Constantine Bach's interpretation of Abū Qurrah's Arabic *wujūh* as meaning simply *hypostases* or *aqānīm*, which I do not agree with: ibid., p. 116, n. 20.

563 As I have shown elsewhere, because the term is used about 850 times in the LXX alone, many Church fathers, such as Clement, Ignatius, Tertullian and others, used it in their biblical

There, in particular, the term referred to the person in his wholeness or in his whole presence (in a similar sense to that found in the Islamic Ḥadith mentioned above, which speaks of God in terms of his face). Later, especially in the 4th century, as already argued in chapter three, *prosopon* was deemed problematic because the fathers suspected that calling the Son *prosopon* would undermine the Son's substantial divinity and might reduce him to a mere disguise or role of the Father. The Church fathers also avoided speaking of three *prosopa* in the Godhead, because they also did not want to give the impression that they were speaking of God as one person with three masks or roles and that they, therefore, supported Modalism. Eventually, the Greek fathers discarded *prosopon* and consistently used *hypostasis*. This was at least the clear and affirmative choice of the Cappadocian fathers.

On the Syrian side, the Cappadocians' choice, as shown in chapter three, seems to have found favour among many fathers. Ephraim the Syrian and Afrahat, for instance, avoided using the Syriac synonym for *prosopon*, namely *parsopa*, and used instead *qnomo/qnoma* to refer to the three *hypostases* in the Godhead. The Syrian fathers knew that speaking of three *parsope* in the Godhead would give a problematic modalist impression of the divine persons and the Son's divine substance, just as the term *prosopon* would in Greek-speaking circles. Such a problematic misunderstanding took place for example, as argued in chapter three, when Nestorius used *parsope* instead of *qnome* to speak of the personal, concrete particularity of each of the two natures in Jesus Christ, leading Cyril of Alexandria and the members of the Council of Ephesus in 431 to accuse Nestorius of saying something that he did not mean.

To return to Abū Qurrah's Trinitarian terminology in the subject of this section, if the *Maymar on the Trinity* conveys to us a genuine 'Abū Qurrahan' use of the word *wajh* to refer to the three divine persons in his interreligious debate, it means that Abū Qurrah is using an Arabic term, whose Greek and Syriac synonyms have clearly been avoided in the Trinitarian literature of his Melkite predecessors. For the three divine persons in the Trinity, Greek orthodoxy would use *hypostases*, and never *prosopa*. Abū Qurrah must undoubtedly have known this and been too well versed in the Trinitarian literature of his earlier church compatriots to ignore it or underestimate its constitutive status. He must have known that using *wajh* to speak about the Father, Son and Spirit in the Trinity would make him sound as if he was following Modalism and reducing the three

citations and theological discussions: N. Awad, *God without a Face?*, pp. 143 ff. On *prosopon*, see also Friedrich, *Theological Dictionary of the New Testament*, Vol. 6, p. 769; and Prestige, *God in Patristic Thought* pp. 157–159.

aqānīm to mere facial images or roles of God. Why, then, does Abū Qurrah use *wajh?* And more crucially still, why would he use *wajh* in the first half of the *Maymar on the Trinity* but use *uqnūm* (*qnomo/hypostasis*) in the second?

In their study of Abū Qurrah's Arabic maymars, both Constantine Bacha and Ignace Dick confirm Abū Qurrah's authorship. However, they both also concede that parts of these texts were not written by Abū Qurrah himself, but were the work of other – perhaps his students or disciples who came after him – whose aim was to preserve his theological legacy and pass it on to future generations. For example, we know that this was certainly the case with Abū Qurrah's debate with Muslims in al-Maʾmūn's *majlis*, which was not written down by Abū Qurrah himself but by another scribe.[564] There is nothing to prevent us from assuming that the same applied to the *Maymar on the Trinity*. Even if this text was originally written by Abū Qurrah, the extant manuscripts of the maymar all belong to a later historical period and were produced by later scribes, who must have left their editorial mark on the original.

In the light of this, is it possible that what we have in the manuscript of *Maymar on the Trinity* is just a later, terminologically revised edition of Abū Qurrah's original text? And, if this is the case, can we conclude that the use of *wajh* in the first half of the text, and *uqnūm* in the second suggests that we have here two different revised texts from two different later editor-scribes, who each recorded Abū Qurrah's argument using the words he thought his Melkite master would have used? If this is likely, what we have in our hands is two separate records of some of Abū Qurrah's defence of the Trinity against Muslim challenges, which were later annexed to each other and included in the papers of a third ed-

---

564 W. Nasry believes that Abū Qurrah did not personally dictate the development of the debate to this scribe: Nasry, *Abū Qurrah wa-al Ma'mūn: al-Mujādalah* (Beirut: CEDRAC/Jounieh: Librairie St Paul, 2010), p. 72. Nasry does not think that the text of the debate was written down by Abū Qurrah himself, either, but that he narrated the story of the event and that one or a group of his students recorded what he said later, shaping its development with the help of the ideas and theological thought that is recorded in the texts Abū Qurrah wrote himself (ibid., pp. 90–92). Sidney Griffith points to the anonymous Syriac chronicle *ad annum 1234*, where Abū Qurrah's debate in al-Ma'mūn's *majlis* is reported. There, the author of the chronicle states that "the debate is written in a special book for anyone who wants to read it," without naming the one who recorded the debate and preserved it in a written form: Griffith, "Reflections on the Biography of Theodore Abū Qurrah," p. 147. Griffith here cites Jean-Baptiste Chabot, *Anonymi Auctoris Chronicon ad A.C. 1234 pertinens*, coll. *CSCO*, vols 81, 82, 109, 354, (Louvain: 1916, 1920, 1937 & 1974), Vol. 109, pp. 22–23. Elsewhere, Griffith affirms that the author of the text is not Abū Qurrah himself, but somebody giving an account of the debate: S. Griffith, "The Qurʾān in Arab Christian Texts: The Development of an Apologetic Argument: Abū Qurrah in the *Majlis* of al-Ma'mūn," *Parole de l'Orient*, 24 (1999), 203–233, p. 224.

itor as one, single text in the belief that these two records pertained to the same subject and so would fit harmoniously together in terms of style and ideas.

If we do have here two separate records of some of Abū Qurrah's Trinitarian ideas, the question remains: Which term would be more authentically expressive of Abū Qurrah's own wording – *wajh* as in the first half, or *uqnūm* as in the second? One might plausibly propose that, by using *uqnūm*, the hypothetical second scribe is more true to Abū Qurrah's original choice of words than the first with his use of *wajh*. This would be supported by the fact that, in his other maymars, Abū Qurrah does not always, or only, use *wajh* to refer to the three persons in the Trinity, but sticks more often to the common word *uqnūm*. One sees this clearly, for instance, in what he says about the Trinity in *al-Mujādalah* and the rest of Abū Qurrah's Arabic maymars. Thus it seems that Abū Qurrah's first choice when it came to Trinitarian terminology would have been *uqnūm* and not *wajh*, and so the second part of the *Maymar on the Trinity*, and its scribe – if the two-scribe hypothesis is plausible – would be conveying to us a genuine Abū Qurrahan terminological preference.

But does this mean that Abū Qurrah never used *wajh* to refer to the three divine persons in the Trinity? Not necessarily. There are two other places where Abū Qurrah did use this word. The first is in his *Maymar fī Wujūd al-Khāliq wad-Dīn al-Qawīm* (Maymar on the existence of the Creator and the right religion), where, Abū Qurrah states in chapter six:

1. فلما عرفت ذلك منها، أحببت أن نعلم أيضاً، وجهاً واحداً [هو] أم أكثر من واحد

...

12. إذاً ليست تدل الخلائق على الخالق أنه وجه واحد فرد، من هذا الوجه.

> 1. So, when I knew this from it, I wanted us to know also, [is] He [i.e., God] one *wajh* [face] or more than one[?].
>
> ...
>
> 12. Therefore, the creatures do not signify the Creator as one single *wajh* [face], from this perspective [*wajh*].[565]

In chapter seven, Abū Qurrah uses the term *wajh* to speak directly of the Trinity, and not only of the one God, when he says:

36. ولكن عليك بدين المسيح وتعليمه. وذلك أنَّ الله آب وابن وروح قدس، إله واحد ثلاثة وجوه. وفي هذا الجوهر إله واحد.

---

565 Abū Qurrah, *Maymar fī Wujūd al-Khaliq wad-Dīn al-Qawīm* (Maymar on the existence of the Creator and the right religion), ch. 6, pts 1, 12. Notice here Abū Qurrah's use of the same Arabic term *wajh* in the sense of face and in its frequent use in Arabic in the sense of 'meaning/perspective/direction of thought.'

> 36. But rely on Christ's religion and teaching. For [it states that] God is Father, Son, and Holy Spirit, one God three *wūjūh* [faces]. And, in this essence [*jawhar*] one God.[566]

The same use of *wajh* (face) in reference to both the Trinity and God's oneness is also found in chapter twelve:

4. وذلك أنه وصف الله على ما علّمنا ثلاثة وجوه: آب، ابن وروح قدس...
...
9. وآخرون قالوا أنه وجه واحد فرد

> 4. For it [i.e., the Gospel] describes God, as we taught, as three *wūjūh* [faces]: Father, Son and Holy Spirit ...
> ...
> 9. And others said he [i.e., God] is one single *wajh* [face].[567]

The second place where Abū Qurrah uses this term to refer to the Trinity is in his *Maymar fī Maūt al-Massīḥ* (Maymar on the death of Chirst). There, Abū Qurrah uses the word *wajh* twice. First, in the following sentence:

قد تقول الأرثوذكسية في الإله أنه واحد في الطبيعة وثلاثة في الوجوه

> Orthodoxy may say about God that He is one in nature and three in faces [*wujūh*].

Abū Qurrah then uses the same term a few lines down in the following sentence:

وأنت تتبين في كل واحد منهما ما ذكرنا من جماح عقول أهل الباطل. أحدهما قول آريوس إنَّ الله ثلاثة في الوجوه وثلاثة في الطبائع.

> And you recognize in each one of them what we have mentioned of the unrestrained mind of the people of falsehood. One of which is the saying of Arius that God is three in faces [*wujūh*] and three in natures [*ṭabāʾiʿ*].

In the second sentence, Abū Qurrah refers to Arius, claiming that he used the term *wujūh* to speak of the Trinity. This is not unlikely, since *prosopon* was still used by the church fathers during the first quarter of the 4th century, especially in Alexandria, to refer to the three persons in the Godhead. In any case, Abū Qurrah is here quoting another theologian's choice of words and is not necessarily reflecting his own. However, the first sentence in this maymar and the other sentences cited from his maymar *On the Existence of the Creator and the Right Religion* are more indicative of Abū Qurrah's own wording, and they mirror,

566 Ibid., ch. 7, pt. 36.
567 Ibid., ch. 12, pts 4, 9.

so these texts would suggest, his own understanding of orthodox Trinitarian theology. Though in the rest of these maymars, Abū Qurrah would also use *uqnūm* again, the occurrence of *wajh* here, as his terminology, is noteworthy and may be an indication that the scribe of these texts and the two presumed scribes of the *Maymar on the Trinity* could be one and the same. But it may also suggest that Abū Qurrah occasionally considered alternating between *uqnūm* and *wajh* in his teaching and discourses on the Trinity before his students, friends, scribes and audiences. This would be the most probable assumption if he personally truly believed, as *Maymar on the death of the Messiah* and *Maymar on the existence of the Creator and the right religion* suggest, that this wording was virtually orthodox.

But do we have evidence that *wajh* was used in any orthodox Trinitarian theology, whether during or before the time of Abū Qurrah? In my search, I have found one place where the word *wajh* is used in an Arabic theological text on the Trinity that is earlier than Abū Qurrah's writings. If the author of the earlier apologetic text on the Trinity known as *fī Tathlīth Allah al-Wāḥid* (on the Triunity of the One God) is Melkite, as all contemporary scholars believe, it may be possible to conclude that Abū Qurrah is following the practice of his anonymous predecessor.

In *On the Triunity of the One God,* the Melkite author uses the word *wajh* once to speak about the idea of unity:

وكمثل النفس والجسد والروح لا نفرق بعضهم من بعض ولا نقول ثلثة أناس ولاكن إنسان واحد أسما ثلثة بوجه واحد

> And like the soul and the body and the spirit, we do not differentiate one from the other, and we do not say three persons but one person and three names with one *wajh* [face].[568]

This is no doubt an attractive invitation to assume that Abū Qurrah is just imitating his Melkite predecessor in his choice of words, but a careful reading of the above sentence shows that this is far from being the case. One cannot but pause at the following two important points: First, the author uses *wajh* in reference to the human, not the divine. We do not actually find any use of this word in the sense of 'face' to refer in any direct way to God or the Trinity in this text. Second, *wajh* in this sentence seems to denote the one, single nature or essence, since the one and single entity that combines and unifies the three names is called *wajh*. In either case, the author of this early text is clearly saying something substantially different from Abū Qurrah. For, with regard to the first point, Abū Qurrah uses the term *wajh* to refer plainly and exclusively to the Trinity in God, and not

568 Gibson, *An Arabic Version of the Acts*, f.103b, p. 76.

to the human; not even metaphorically. With regard to the second, *wajh* in the texts by Abū Qurrah that we have referred to above does not designate the 'one essence,' but specifies the 'particular three': God is one in essence and *three* in *wujūh*, according to Abū Qurrah. The case is different in *Fī Tathlīth*, where the sentence means that there are three names for *one* single *wajh*.

Is there another Christian Trinitarian line of thought contemporary with Abū Qurrah, from which he could have derived the idea of speaking of the three in the Trinity as *wujūh?* In his work on the philosophy of *kalām*, Harry Wolfson invites us to consider this as a possibility and points to a specific 'splinter group of Nestorians' of whom the Muslim author al-Shahristānī writes in his *Kitāb al-Millal wan-Niḥal* (The Book of Religious Sects and Groups).[569] Wolfson argues that the group Shahristānī refers to cannot be "the Nestorians as known to us from the history of Christianity and as also known to the Muslims."[570] It is, rather, a special group of Christians, Wolfson argues, that is named after their Nestorian church prelate 'Naṣṭūr al-Ḥakīm' (Nestorius the wise/sage), about whom very little information is available to us today. We only know that this Christian prelate, "appeared in the time of Ma'mūn [that is, between 813–833. AD],"[571] that he and his followers were affiliates of the Nestorian church and formed "an indistinguishable group within the Nestorians."[572] Wolfson further proposes that this 'Nestorius the sage' is probably the same Nestorian bishop, called Naṣṭūr in Arabic, who lived and served in Adiabene on the Tigris river around 800, and was also known to the Muslim caliph al- Maʾmūn.[573] Wolfson maintains that, even if it is not possible to verify that 'Nestorius the sage' is historically this Naṣṭūr of Adiabene, it is extremely unlikely historically that 'Nestorius the sage' was the historical Nestorius of Constantinople, who died in 451.

What is far more important than the historical identity of 'Nestorius the sage' and his followers, according to Wolfson's introduction of this Nestorian figure and his 'splinter group of Nestorians' (as Wolfson calls them), is the Trinitarian theological ideas that this group of Nestorians developed during the first quarter or so of the 9th century. According to Wolfson, this Nestorian group wit-

---

569 al-Shahristānī, *Kitāb al-Millal wan-Niḥal* (The book of religious sects and groups), ed. W. Cureton (London1846). On this Nestorian group, see also Wolfson, *The Philosophy of the Kalām*, pp. 337–349; and his shorter and earlier article, "An Unknown Splinter Group of Nestorians," *Revue des Études Augustiniennes*, 6 (1960), 249–253

570 Wolfson, *The Philosophy of the Kalām*, p. 340. Among the Muslim authors who refer to the Nestorians and their theological thought in their writings, Wolfson mentions al-Masʿūdī and Ibn Ḥazm.

571 Ibid., p. 341. citing from *Kitāb al-Millal wan-Niḥal*, p. 175, l.9.

572 Wolfson, *The Philosophy of the Kalām*, p. 341.

573 Ibid.p. 341.

nessed, within the Islamic *kalām* circle, the debate between the various Muʿtazilite branches of *kalām* and the Muʿtazilites and other Muslim currents of thought on the attributes of God and whether it is permissible to speak of God's attributes as merely figurative (nominalistic approach) or as real substantial and essential properties that are as eternal as God himself (realistic approach).[574] In contrast with these two, the realistic and the nominalistic, extremes in 8th- and 9th-century Islamic *kalām*, some Muslim scholars, such as Sulaymān b, Jarīr (d. 785), and later Abū Hāshim (d. 933),[575] developed a middle proposition that called the attributes of God 'modes' (*wujūh*), rather than either 'names' (*asmāʾ*) or 'properties' (*khawāṣṣ*) and stated, according to Wolfson, that "the attributes of God are neither existent nor nonexistent; they are neither identical with God nor other than God, they are '*Wujūh*/aspects.'"[576]

Notable in Wolfson's discussion is his disclosure that the mid-way Muslim theory of attributes uses the term *wujūh* to refer to God's attributes. What is more intriguing still is Wolfson's claim that Sulaymān b. Jarīr and Abū Hāshim were inspired to use this terminology by the Trinitarian language of the followers of the so-called Nestorius the Sage. These Nestorians, Wolfson argues, also tried in their own way to find, within the Christian circle of debate on the Trinity, a midway between orthodox Trinitarianism and Sabellianism by "attenuating to the reality of the *hypostases*."[577] So, they started to speak of the three persons in the Trinity as three 'modes' or aspects (*wujūh*) that designate the essential properties of the divine essence, without either totally identifying these three modes with the divine *jawhar* (essence), or separating them organically from it. Wolfson goes even further in his proposal when he opines that these Nestorians derived their reference to the three divine *hypostases* in terms of 'modes' (*wujūh*) from another contemporary Islamic, specifically Muʿtazilite, discourse, namely that of the *mutakallim* Abū al-Ḥuḍayl Ibn al-ʿAllāf. In his explanation of the divine attributes, Ibn al-ʿAllāf not only argues for the existence of attrib-

574 Wolfson, "An Unknown Splinter Group," pp. 249–250. In his reading of this Islamic debate on the nature of God's attributes, Sidney Griffith suggests that this Muslim-Muslim quarrel was actually "part of a larger controversy in Islam over the nature of the Qurʾān as the speech of God, over whether all of its statements must be interpreted literally, or if some of them may be understood metaphorically": S. Griffith, "The Concept of *al-Uqnūm* in ʿAmmār al-Baṣrī's Apology for the Doctrine of the Trinity," in *Actes du premier congrès international d'études arabes chrétiennes (Goslar, septembre 1980)*, ed. Samir Khalil Samir, Orientalia Christiana Analecta, 218, (Rome: Pontificium Institutum Studiorum Orientalium, 1982), 169–191, p. 174.

575 Wolfson, *The Philosophy of the Kalām*, p. 343.

576 Wolfson, "An Unknown Splinter Group," p. 249; citing from Abū Manṣūr b. Ṭāhir al-Baghdādī, *al-Farq bayn al-Firaq* (The difference between the sects) (Cairo1910), p. 182, l. 5.

577 Wolfson, "An Unknown Splinter Group," p. 251.

utes in God, but also considers these attributes to be *wujūh* of the divine essence.[578] In other words, this group of Nestorians chose to refer to the three divine hypostases in the divine Godhead as three essential 'aspects,' that is *wujūh*, because they knew that using this term would bring them onto common ground with contemporary Muslim *mutakallims*, since the same term was familiar within Muslim circles that were discussing the question of God's attributes.

From Wolfson's discussion, one can reasonably assume that Theodore Abū Qurrah, who also lived during the rule of al-Ma'mūn and must have been versed in the Muslims' texts and discussions, must also have been exposed to the Trinitarian discourse of this Nestorian group. There is nothing unlikely in the surmise that Abū Qurrah could have found in these Nestorians' adoption of the midway (neither nominalist nor realist) construal of the attributes as 'modes' or 'aspects' in God a prudent and positively fruitful dialogical strategy for discussion with Muslims about the Trinity. Therefore, in some of his maymars on this topic, Abū Qurrah would use the Arabic terms *wajh* and *wujūh* to refer to the three persons in the Trinity. He may have thought that, when they heard him using this term to speak of the three in the divine Godhead, Muslims would receive his Trinitarian discourse as acceptably within the bounds of the valid and familiar discussion that was taking place among Muslim *mutakallims* on the attributes of God.

We do know, if only from his debate in al-Ma'mūn's court, that Abū Qurrah was in touch with the intellectual atmosphere of Baghdad and the eastern territories (e.g., Iraq and Iran) of the Muslim caliphate. Wolfson claims that the Trinitarian hermeneutics of the Nestorian group referred to above were known in Iran and Iraq at the time of al-Ma'mūn, and that some Muslim *mutakallims* developed their theories on God's attributes in intellectual and conceptual exchange with such Trinitarian hermeneutical activities. If this was true, Abū Qurrah must have also been exposed to these Trinitarian discourses and their choices of vocabulary, not only through his debate with Muslim interlocutors in the caliph's court, but also from his own interaction with, and study of, other contemporary Christian, non-Melkite, authors and thinkers.

One may still ask here: But why would Abū Qurrah choose to adopt a term (that is using the Arabic term *wajh* to speak about the *hypostases*) from the Trinitarian discourse of a non-Melkite theological discourse? Was not Nestorian theology considered by Melkite orthodoxy as a non-orthodox, let alone heretical, school of theological thought? Why would Abū Qurrah use the Trinitarian termi-

---

578 Ibid., p. 252, citing from ash-Shahristānī, *Kitā al-Milall wan-Niḥal*, p. 34, ll. 19–20.

nology of non-orthodox Christians and what justified that decision in his own mind?

Opting for a Nestorian theological interpretation would cause Abū Qurrah trouble with his Melkite fellows only if this interpretation were related to Christology, but not if it was used in connection with the Trinity. It is over Christology (Chalcedonian or non-Chalcedonian) that the Melkites and the Nestorians, as well as the Jacobites, fell into serious schisms and enmity from the 5th century onwards. This was not the case, however, with regard to their teaching on the triune nature of God. During the early Abbasid era, at least, even Muslim intellectuals acknowledged that on the level of their belief in the Trinity, the Melkites, Jacobites and Nestorians all adhered to the Nicene-Constantinopolitan orthodox doctrine.[579] That being the case, borrowing a Trinitarian term such as 'modes/aspects' (*wujūh*) from these Nestorians would not bring Theodore Abū Qurrah into condemnation for relying on non-orthodox thinking. He would still be within the circle of orthodox Trinitarian thought even when he relied on Nestorian ways of expression and interpretation, and although doing the same in a discourse on Christology would have been another story altogether.

This demonstration of possible influences on Abū Qurrah's use of the term *wajh* from another Melkite (the author of *On the Triunity of the One God*) and Nestorians (the group of the so-called Nestorius the sage) invites us to delve deeper into understanding the historical and theological context of the early Arab Christian *mutakallims*' attempt to convey the orthodox faith to Muslims without departing from orthodoxy and falling into the pit of Sabellianism, Arianism, or Tritheism. This connection between Abū Qurrah and earlier and contemporary Christian *mutakallimun* demonstrates Theodore's deep indebtedness to, and vast learnedness about, the intellectual and cultural context of his era. He was by no means a hermetically sealed scholar who isolated himself in his rational ivory tower and opted for a 'one-man-show' style of contribution. He rather seems to be an open-minded and bridge-building learner, who seeks to educate himself about every available teaching, and is willing to incorporate any idea or explanation he finds reliable and useful into his own projects.

Nevertheless, Abū Qurrah's reliance on every intellectual source available does not in itself indicate whether or not, by using all these sources, he presented accurately and successfully the core content of orthodox Christian teaching. One of the challenges such an attempt at representation placed before the Chris-

---

579 Wolfson, "An Unknown Splinter Group," p. 250; and Wolfson, *The Philosophy of the Kalām*, pp. 337–338. The non-orthodox schools who differed from these three, as the Muslims noted, were the Macedonians, the Sabellians and the Arians. Thus al-Shahristānī, *Kitā al-Millal wan-Niḥal*, p. 178, l. 13; p. 179, l. 1.

tian *mutakallims* in general, and Abū Qurrah in particular, is whether using terms that were familiar to, and used by, the Muslim *mutakallims* (such as *wajh*, in this case) succeeded in conveying the exact teaching of orthodoxy on the doctrine of the Trinity, or was simply a clever ploy that presented Muslims alone, but not Christians, with what they wanted to hear and could accept.

By looking at the text of *On the Triunity of the One God*, and with the help of Wolfson's attention to the followers of Nestorius the sage, I have argued that Abū Qurrah could have been aware of the use of the term *wajh* in other contemporary (and deemed orthodox) Trinitarian discourses by other Christian authors, whose used words that were known to and accepted by Muslims. I have suggested that Abū Qurrah also decided to use the term *wajh* when he realized that it was acceptable to, and even used by, his Muslim interlocutors. He could do this without fearing any rejection or criticism from his Melkite fellows, since the Trinitarian theology of the anonymous Melkite author of *fī Tathlīth Allah al-Wāḥid*, as well as that of the Nestorians, were acknowledged by the Melkites as orthodox.[580] But, is this enough to prove that what Abū Qurrah conveyed in his use of *wajh* is *per se* authentically orthodox in content and meaning? It is yet to be shown whether it can be solidly proved that, in his use of this word, Abū Qurrah was trying to show that the meaning of *wajh* in Arabic can be revised enough to make this term appropriate for conveying the doctrine of the Trinity to the Arabs, without changing the core meaning of the orthodox understanding of the three in the divine Godhead. In the ensuing paragraphs of this section, I attempt to answer this question.

In his analysis of Christian responses to the Islamic criticism of Christian doctrines in the early Islamic era, Sidney Griffith touches upon such possible attempts at revision by Christian apologists. Griffith states that such efforts were made in order to find appropriate Arabic vocabulary to translate standard Greek and Syriac doctrinal technical terms, and that this enterprise involved "the further effort to define certain Arabic terms in a technical way for purpose of theological discussion, even when the ordinary connotations of the terms in common Arabic-speaking usage militated against the senses intended in doctrinal contexts."[581] As an example of such an attempt, Griffith invokes the use of the Arabic term *jawhar* to translate the Greek term *ousia* and comments that

580 This may explain why the term *wajh/wujūh* is used in the Trinitarian discourse of the followers of Nestorius the sage and also in the anonymous Melkite author's text *On the Triunity of the One God*.

581 Griffith, *The Church in the Shadow of the Mosque*, p. 94.

its initial inappropriateness appears in the Arabic term's inevitable suggestion of "a concrete nugget like a jewel or an atom."[582]

Griffith's perception is very relevant to the point I am making here. It might be that Abū Qurrah found himself in need of making a similar attempt at using the Arabic term *wajh* – the original meaning of which does not fit the scope of the theological connotations of *hypostasis* and *qnoma* – in order to conduct a successful theological discussion with Muslims. Abū Qurrah, in this case would have certainly known that the Arabic term he uses here does not at all serve the purpose of conveying the meaning of the Greek and Syriac terms for personhood. But he may have found himself obliged to resort to such a choice, even if it militated against the sense intended in orthodoxy, and even if it made his discourse comparable to a Modalist way of reasoning. One can assume that Abū Qurrah thought that the Arabic word *wajh* would sound more positive to Muslim ears than other Arabic words, such as *shakhṣ*, for example, which, though it literally means 'person,' would suggest that the Trinity is three separate, individual persons, thus ultimately militating not only against the Trinity, but, more problematically for Muslims, against God's oneness.

Griffith's characterization of this Christian struggle to find appropriate Arabic terms to convey theological discourses to Muslims accurately and coherently (a concern that also characterizes other Melkite apologetic texts from that era, such as *Summa Theologiae Arabica* and *fī Tathlīth Allāh al-Wāḥid*[583]) succeeds in explaining Abū Qurrah's use of *wajh*, despite its problematic connotations, if and only if he used it in clear awareness that, in its original meaning, *wajh* is not in line with orthodox views. But the *Maymar on the Death of Christ* suggests otherwise, as shown above. It tells us that Abū Qurrah believed that *wajh* genuinely conveys orthodox thinking.[584] In other words, his use of it was not an attempt to suggest a new Arabic word to translate a doctrinal term, despite the fact that its normal meaning had connotations inappropriate to this context. The maymar indicates that, for Abū Qurrah, the Arabic term *wajh* does successfully convey an orthodox understanding of what is meant by a 'per-

---

582 Ibid., p. 95. See also S. Griffith, "Theology and the Arab Christian: The Case of the 'Melkite' Creed," in *A Faithful Presence: Essays for Kenneth Cragg*, .ed David Thomas (London: Melisende, 2003), 184–200.

583 This concern led the Christian mutakallims to borrow Qur'anic words, phrases and verses and insert them in their explanation and interpretation of Christian theology in a way that is clearly far more creative than mere proof-texting. On this practice in relation to *Fi Tathlīth Allāh al-Wāḥid*, see Swanson, "Beyond Prooftexting"; and on this practice in *Summa Theologiae Arabica*, see Griffith, "The First Christian *Summa Theologiae*."

584 Abū Qurrah, *Maymar fī Mawt al-Masīḥ* (Maymar on the death of the Messiah), ch. 12, pt 4,9.

son' in the Trinity. It is orthodox, Theodore claims, to say that God is 'one in nature and three in faces (*wujūh*),' and if Arius' Trinitarian doctrine was wrong, its error lay not in his use of a Greek term (*prosopon*) that meant 'face' (*wajh*), but rather in his statement that the existence of three 'faces' (*wujūh*) meant the existence of three natures.

The next question is then: From where did Abū Qurrah get the idea that *wajh* genuinely expresses an orthodox concept? The initial answer to this might be that the Arabic *wajh* is synonymous with the Greek *prosopon*, which is found in the Septuagint and the New Testament, so it has biblical credentials for being used to convey theological ideas. More significantly for Abū Qurrah, the term *wajh* is also used in the Muslim holy book, the Qur'an, where it refers to God's being. For example the phrase *wajh Allah* (the face/countenance of God) occurs in Q 2:115, 272;[585] 6:52;[586] 13:22;[587] 28:88;[588] 30:38–39;[589] 55:27;[590] and 92:20.[591] Abū Qurrah's knowledge not only of the Bible, but also of the Qur'an, must have led him to choose this word, probably in the conviction that what the Bible refers to as *prosopon* is called in the Qur'an *wajh*. I suggest that the scriptural references are enough to make an apologist like Abū Qurrah use *prosopon* as an acceptable term to express the Church's doctrine, and invite

---

585 ولله المشرق والمغرب فأينما تولوا فثمة وجه الله، إنَّ الله واسعٌ عليم"؛ "وما تنفقون إلا ابتغاء وجه الله و ما تنفقوا من خيرٍ يو فى إليكم وأنتم لا تظلمون.
Unto God belong the east and west, and withersoever ye turn, there is God's face [*wajh*]. Lo, God is all-embracing, all-knowing) (2:115); and (When ye spend not save in search of God's face [*wajh*], and whatsoever good thing ye spend, it will be repaid to you in full, and ye will not be wronged.
English translation of all Qur'anic verses from www.holyquran.net.

586 ولا تطرد الذين يدعون ربهم بالغداة والعشى يريدون وجهه
Repel not those who call upon their Lord at morning and evening, seeking his face [*wajhahu*].) The same is repeated almost verbatim in Q 18:28.

587 والذين صبروا ابتغاءِ وجه ربهم وأقاموا الصلاة
Such as persevere in seeking their Lord's face [*wajh*] and are regular in prayer ...

588 كل شيءٍ هالكن إلا وجهه لهُ الحكم وإليه ترجعون
Everything will perish save his face [*wajhih*]. His is the command, and unto Him ye will be brought back.

589 38. فأتي ذا القربى حقه والمسكين وابن السبيل ذلك خيرٌ للذين يريدون وجه الله. 39. وأما ما أتيتم من ذكاة تريدون وجه الله فأولئك هم المضعفون
38. So give to the kinsman his due, and to the needy and to the wayfarer. That is best for those who seek God's face [*wajh*] ... 39. But that which ye give in charity, seeking God's face [*wajh*], hath increase manifold.

590 ويبقى وجه ربّكَ ذو الجلال والإكرام
There remaineth but the face [*wajh*] of thy Lord of might and glory.

591 إلا ابتغاء وجه ربّهِ الأعلى (Except seeking the face [*wajh*] of his Lord most high.)

Muslims to consider the Qur'anic term *wajh* as an accessible Arabic translation of *prosopon*.

But was Abū Qurrah not concerned that this choice of vocabulary would give his fellow Christians the impression that he was a Modalist in his Trinitarian thinking? The question of Modalism is not really relevant to the context of discussing the Trinity with Muslims, for Muslims are called by their religious book to stand firm against Tritheism rather than Modalism (Q 4:171; 5:73).[592] It has recently been argued that the charge of Tritheism was made against the Philoponian (named after John Philoponus) Tritheism of the Monophysites who used to live in the late 6th century in the southern Arabian city of Najran.[593] Modalist implications would not therefore have deterred Abū Qurrah from using an argument that relied on vocabulary used in common by the Bible and the Qur'an, since speaking of God's *wajh* would not have any Modalist connotations in the

592 يا أهل الكتاب لا تغالوا في دينكم ولا تقولوا على الله...ثلاثة... (O people of the Scripture, do not exaggerate in your religion not utter aught concerning God..and say not 'three'); لقد كفر الذين قالوا إنَّ الله ثالث ثلاثة (They surely disbelieve who say: Lo, God is the third of three ...)

593 See on this proposal C. Jonn Block, "Philoponian Monophysitism in South Arabia at the Advent of Islam with Implications for the English Translation of '*Thalātha*' in Qur'ān 4.171 and 5.73," *Journal of Islamic Studies*, 23 (1) (2012), 50–75. On Christianity in Arabia before Islam, see also J. Spencer Trimingham, *Christianity among the Arabs in Pre-Islamic Times* (London: Longman, 1979); Irfan Shahid, *Byzantium and the Arabs in the Sixth Century*, Vol. 1, pts 1–2; ibid., *Byzantinum and the Arabs in the Sixth Century* (Washington, DC: Dumbarton Oaks, 1995), Vol. 2, pt 1; and ibid., *Byzantium and the Arabs in the Sixth Century: Economic, Social and Cultural History* (Washington, DC: Dumbarton Oaks, 1995), Vol. 2, pt 2. In his interesting and intriguing essay, Jonn Block builds his thesis upon his claim that Monophysite Philoponian Tritheism was conveyed to the prophet Muḥammad when the leaders of the Najran Christians, including their bishop Abū Ḥāritha, visited him in 631 (according to Ibn Isḥaq's *Sīra*). Block concludes that "it was his [Abū Ḥāritha's] theology that the Qur'ānic revelations *respond to* in the later sūras" (Block, pp. 66–67, my italics). Despite the general reasonableness and subtlety of Block's historiographical exposition in his "Philoponian Monophysitism", I do not find his rather circular argument (which assumes the Christians of Najran were Monophysites and builds the analysis on that assumption) completely convincing. What if Abū Ḥāritha was in fact against Philoponist Tritheism, and the Qur'an exegete, Ibn ʿAbbās, was not mistaken in calling the Christians of Najran Nestorians; and what if the Qur'an is therefore *echoing*, rather than responding to, Abū Ḥāritha's refutation of this Monophysite version of Tritheism? On the other hand, the 8th-century Khurasānī exegete, Muqātil b. Sulaymān (d. 767), states in his five-volume *Tafsīr* that, of the three groups of the Christians, it is the Melkites (*al-Malkāniyyūn*) who say "God the third of three," and not the Jacobites or the Monophysites, be they Philoponians or not: Claude Gilliot, "Christians and Christianity in Islamic Exegesis," in *Christian-Muslim Relations: A Bibliographical History*, Vol. 1: *600–900*, ed. David Thomas and Barbara Roggema (Leiden: Brill, 2009), 31–56, p. 44. Which claim is historically accurate here, Block's or Muqātil's? The question merits a separate study.

Muslims' minds, and Abū Qurrah does not seem to believe that it implied an understanding of God that would be considered problematic from a Qur'anic point of view. Modalism would have mattered to Abū Qurrah had he been explaining the Melkites' theology of the Trinity to non-Melkite Christians, such as Nestorians or Jacobites, or even to a Melkite audience. Referring to the Father, Son and Holy Spirit as three faces (*wujūh*) might have led some Christians to protest that his theological discourse contained modalist elements. But, for his Muslim interlocutors, it would not have made any significant difference whether the reference was to three *wujūh*, *hypostases* or even *aqānīm*. Any of these in its plural form is equally problematic and likely to be rejected, because it suggests plurality rather than oneness as definitive of God's nature, and conflicts with the Christians' insistence that the God they call Father, Son and Spirit is one, single deity. These contextual and intellectual differences, I believe, provide equally some insight into the reason for the Christians' willingness in the ensuing decades to adopt Muslim terminology and speak of the three persons in the Trinity only rarely as *wujūh*, *hypostases* and *aqānīm* and often as *ṣifāt* (attributes or predicates) or even *'asmā'* (names).

There is another reason why Abū Qurrah may have decided that *wajh* was an appropriate translation of an orthodox Trinitarian term, despite its philological affinity with *prosopon:* it had been used by Gregory of Nyssa in the 4th century.

Patristic scholars differ in their appraisal of Gregory of Nyssa's use of *prosopon*. Lewis Ayres, for example, acknowledges Gregory's readiness to use various terms to speak of the relation between the divine unity and the three divine persons in the Godhead, according to what is deemed useful, and he points that the Nyssan used *ousia*, *physis*, *hypostasis*, and also, and frequently, *prosopon.*[594] For Gregory, Ayres states, the effectiveness of these terms in articulating the possibility of the existence of three eternally distinct entities within the one divine power is more important than examining the specific meaning of each of them in turn.

Much earlier than Ayres, John Lynch wrote an essay in 1979 in which he studied the occurrence of *prosopon* in patristic literature and argued that the term had various uses, depending on the approach of each patristic text, and that it expressed many associated and derivative meanings in accordance with each author's purpose.[595] Among the meanings Lynch pauses at, and draws the attention to, is one that has 'personal' connotations, spotting this use in a text as early as *1 Clement* and in the works of Ignatius and Athanasius.[596]

594 Ayres, "On 'Not Three People'," p. 467.

595 Lynch, "*Prosopon* in Gregory of Nyssa," pp. 729–730. Some of the meanings Lynch invokes are 'expression' (Origen), 'sight' and 'presence' (Ignatius) or 'guise' (Athanasius).

596 Ibid., p. 730.

When Lynch's survey reaches the second half of the 4th century, he locates in particular Gregory of Nyssa's saying in Epistle 38: "The *hypostasis* of the Son becomes, so to speak, form and *prosopon* of the knowledge of the Father, and the *hypostasis* of the Father becomes known in the form of the Son."[597] What is particularly noteworthy here is Gregory's use of both *hypostasis* and *prosopon* interconnectedly, considering them as complementary rather than contradictory. Lynch argues that Gregory justifies this juxtaposition logically by using *prosopon* as a synonym for *morphē*, to designate that which particularizes the *ousia* in its hypostatic manifestation.[598] In other words, the *prosopon* is one of the *morphai* of the *hypostasis*; the *prosopon* of the Father, for example, is one of the particulars (*morphai*) that makes the Father hypostatically unique and not another Son or Spirit. For Gregory, speaking of particular *prosopa* for the *hypostases* of the Father, Son and Holy Spirit does not threaten the unity of God but rather points to one of the common characteristics that reciprocally reveal their co-inherence and common nature in the depth of their distinction.[599]

Lynch concludes that *prosopon*, for Gregory, is definitely not an alternative to *hypostasis*, but rather a "predicate of the *hypostasis*."[600] Lynch also concedes that Gregory also warns against an easy, careless use of *prosopon* in a way that makes it mean mere 'manners of appearance,' especially in the problematic sense of Sabellian Modalism. Yet, Lynch continues, the Nyssan does not hesitate elsewhere to use the term even as a synonym for *hypostasis*, especially in his *Ad Graecos ex Communibus Nationibus*, where he finds *prosopon* helpful to explain to the followers of Athanasian theology the Cappadocians' preference for *mia ousia, treis hypostases*, and how this phrase is far from suggesting three *ousiai*.[601] Gregory initially uses *prosopa* because it is used by his interlocutors, who, after Athanasius, equate *hypostasis* with *ousia* almost indistinguishably. Yet, in his explanation of the particularities of the three persons, Gregory conveys by *prosopa* everything the Cappadocians refer to in their teachings as *hypostases*. Lynch affirms that Gregory's ultimate concern in this terminological choice is to show that those of the Nicene fathers who use *prosopa* to speak of the three do not mean to echo Modalist views, but that they mean by *prosopa* what the Cappadocians mean by *hypostases*, and they endeavour, like the latter, to combat Sabellian Modalism and Tritheism: "We similarly apply to *hypostases* those things [that are related] to the division from each other of *prosopa*, which have the

597 Ibid., p. 731; citing from Epistle 38, 3.
598 Ibid., p. 733.
599 Ibid.
600 Ibid., p. 734.
601 Ibid., p. 735.

same name i.e., *hypostasis*, in common and differ among themselves not in the matters which pertain to *ousia*, but in those which are called accidents (*sumbebekota*)."[602] Lynch's analysis of *prosopon* in Gregory of Nyssa invites us to realize that, despite the prevalence of *hypostasis* in reference to the divine persons in the writings of the main pioneering theologians of the Trinity in the 4th century, *prosopon* maintained a notable philological status in the writings of no less central orthodox Trinitarian theologians than the Cappadocian fathers[603] and other orthodox fathers in the centuries that followed.[604]

Some scholars may be less enthusiastic about stressing the use of *prosopon* in the Cappadocians' orthodox thinking. Michel René Barnes, for example, believes that one should not overstate the importance of *prosopon* in Gregory of Nyssa's theology, claiming that it only appears in the Nyssan's early works, such as *Ad Graecus* and *Epistle 38* (traditionally preserved among the works of Basil, but assumed by almost all scholars to be Gregory's and called *Ad Petrum*),

---

602 Ibid., p. 737; citing from *Ad Graecum*, 185.

603 Even Gregory Nazianzen on one occasion used *prosopon* interchangeably with *hypostasis* to speak of the particular three in the Godhead: "God is three in regard to distinctive properties, or *hypostases*, or, if you like, persons (*πρόσωπα*); for we shall not quarrel about the names, as long as the terms lead to the same conception": Gregory Nazianzen, *Orations*, 39.11.

604 For example, Melchisedec Törönen points to the 8th-century patristic treatise, *Institutio elementaris*, which scholars attribute to John of Damascus. He states that the terms "*hypostasis*, person [i.e. *propson*] and individual are the same thing": Melchisedec Törönen, *Union and Distinction in the Thought of St Maximus the Confessor* (Oxford: Oxford University Press, 2007), p. 51. In turn, Karl-Heinz Öhlig points to the use of *prosopon* in the Syriac tradition to speak of the unity of the two natures in Jesus Christ. Öhlig refers specifically to the 4th-century Syriac father, Diodore of Tarsus (d. before 394), who would use the Greek word *prosopon* in the sense of 'face' or 'outer expression' to speak of the union of the two natures in Christ: K.-H. Öhlig, "Syrian and Arabian Christianity and the Qur'ān," in *The Hidden Origins of Islam: New Research into Its Early History*, ed. Karl-Heinz Öhlig and Gerd-R. Puin (Amherst, NY: Prometheus Books, 2010), 361–401, pp. 378–379. It would be worth studying whether this Syriac tradition is what Theodore Abū Qurrah had in mind as he was conversing with Muslims on the Trinity, and whether he resorted to a Syriac, though still orthodox, tradition of using the word *prosopon* in the sense of 'face' because he thought that this tradition must be familiar to the ears of Muslims in the Abbasid period, who had been in contact with Syriac, Nestorian and Jacobite, Christian theological vocabulary, and borrowed from it some terms that Muslims had found useful for their own Islamic *kalām*. Space does not permit the consideration of this question here. One may simply say that, Abū Qurrah, who was born in a Syriac-speaking context, and was versed in the Greek and Syrian Church traditions, must have known of the existence of this tradition in Syriac theological literature, and might also have thought of borrowing his use of *prosopon* from it, in the conviction that people like Diodore of Tarsus and Gregory of Nyssa alike were offering vocabulary that spoke correctly of Christian faith. This still keeps Theodore within the mainstream of doctrinal orthodoxy.

whereas the term fades out in Gregory's mature theology in *Ad Trinitate*, *On Not Three Gods* or *Great Catechism*.[605] On the other hand, other scholars, such as Lucian Turcescu, argue that one must admit that Gregory was not exceptional in his early reliance on *prosopon* and his later replacement of it with *hypostasis* to avoid Sabellian Modalism. He was just following in the footsteps of his brother Basil of Caesarea, who was also in his early theology prone to use *prosopon*, before later opting for the more appropriate *hypostasis*, which Basil, Turcescu convincingly suggests, picked up from Aristotle's *Metaphysics*.[606]

That noted, my main concern in tracking the use of *prosopon* by Gregory of Nyssa is to link it to Abū Qurrah's thinking and explore the latter's adherence to orthodox Trinitarian theology. In his *Maymar on the Trinity*, the debate in the caliph's *majlis* and *Maymar on the Death of the Messiah*, Theodore Abū Qurrah seems to be following Gregory of Nyssa's choice of words exactly. Like his predecessor's exchange of *prosopon* with *hypostasis*, Abū Qurrah reveals a willingness to use *wajh* interchangeably with *uqnūm*. As already shown in my analysis of Abū Qurrah's Trinitarian logic in the previous sections, for Theodore, too, *wajh* expresses the particular appearance that makes the *uqnūm* of the Father (or the Son or the Holy Spirit) a particular, non-repeatable expression of the divine nature. It is not used here to reduce the three *aqānīm* to three mere faces or guises in a Modalist way. In fact, Abū Qurrah was in a more fortunate situation than Gregory of Nyssa. Unlike the latter, he did not have to worry that Muslims might mistake his discourse for Modalism, since this last was not an issue for them in the first place. It is also reasonable to argue that the Christian *mutakallims* in later centuries were even less concerned about Modalism, and were relaxed in the terminology they used to explain the Trinity in their apologetic conversations with Muslims – so much so that they began to refer to the three divine *aqānīm* as mere attributes, properties, or aspects of God. This is a subject that merits a whole study of its own. As regards our discussion here, Abū Qurrah uses *wajh* as comfortably as Gregory uses *prosopon*, because the former is a term familiar to his Muslim, Arabic-speaking audiences, and is prominent in the discourse about God in both the Qur'an and Ḥadith. He also uses it to en-

---

605 Michel R. Barnes, "Divine Unity and the Divided Self: Gregory of Nyssa's Trinitarian Theology in its Psychological Context," *Modern Theology*, 18 (4) (2002), 475–496, p. 493, n. 34. Barnes thinks that Gregory used this term in his early writings as an inheritance from his brother Basil. On the rare presence of this term in Gregory's *On Not Three Gods*, see Christopher Stead, "Why Not Three Gods? The Logic of Gregory of Nyssa's Trinitarian Doctrine," in *Studien zu Gregor von Nyssa und der christlichen Spätanke*, ed. Hubertus Drobner and Christoph Kock (Leiden: Brill, 1990), 149–162.

606 See Turcescu, "*Prosopon* and *Hypostasis*," pp. 389–394.

deavour to explain to Muslims the uniqueness of the person of the Father (as well as that of the Son and the Spirit) that makes him alone Father (as it makes the Son alone 'Son' and the Spirit alone 'Holy Spirit') in the Trinity, without this *wajh* conveying the sense of a separate nature or an additional deity.

One may say in conclusion that in his (or their) use of *wajh*, the hypothetical scribe(s) of Abū Qurrah's defence of God's oneness-in-Trinity, especially in the first half of the *Maymar on the Trinity*, was insistently using an Arabic term that his teacher or master-theologian may himself have commonly used in his public orations, and which he may have considered an appropriate Arabic translation of a mainstream orthodox term.

IV. Abū Qurrah and the Melkites' Trinitarian Legacy

Are Abū Qurrah's terminological choices for defending the oneness of the divine Trinity determined exclusively by the necessities of his debate with Muslims, or is there another internal factor in his eclecticism that is related to his personal, theological convictions and education? Could Abū Qurrah's preference for Basilian rather than Nazianzen Trinitarian logic in his *mujādalah* in the caliph's *majlis*, for instance, indicate the theological orthodoxy he personally followed and was trained after during his own ecclesial and intellectual formation, regardless of whether it served the purpose of creating a meeting point with Islam? On the other hand, does Abū Qurrah's opting in his *Maymar on the Trinity* for Gregory of Nazianzus' Trinitarian understanding of the reciprocal divine *monarchia* demonstrate his personal choice of orthodoxy, or is it just the continuation of an approach received from his predecessors?

In this section, I shall try to detect possible influences on Abū Qurrah's theological Trinitarian eclecticism in the theological writings of some earlier 6th- and 7th-century Byzantine fathers. I shall try to see whether his total focus on a Basilian-like defence of hierarchical oneness in the *mujādalah*, and his different attention to a Nazianzen-like prioritization of a reciprocal Trinitarian unity in *Maymar on the Trinity*, reached Abū Qurrah via his Melkite predecessors, such as Maximus the Confessor and John of Damascus, or whether his use of this patristic literature reflects a personal reading and interpretation of orthodoxy that is different from the way the Cappadocians were read in the mainstream Melkite church circles of the Damascene and the Confessor.

A. John of Damascus and the Trinity

In his trilogy, *The Fountain of Faith*, John of Damascus states the elements of the Christian faith and its main doctrinal components in a catechetical and simply introductory fashion. He does this almost without getting into any serious argumentation or analytical presentation of any elements of doctrine. One may say that he seems to be setting out the ABC of Christian orthodoxy either for Christian beginners, or for an audience that wants to be taught the basics of Christianity. The fact that the Damascene wrote his exposition in Greek and that we have no evidence to suggest that he wrote another version in Arabic (though it is highly probably that later scribes produced such a version) suggests that he was offering a Martin Luther-type 'big catechism' on Christian orthodoxy. It was probably prepared for the novice monks of Mar Sabas (or other Melkite monasteries in Palestine),[607] But it is also likely that it was addressed to the laiety of Syria-Palestine's Melkite community, in general or of the Jerusalem patriarchate in particular.[608] With regard to John's methodology, it is interesting here that he listed short entries on every old and contemporary heresy in the second book of his trilogy, *On Heresies*, just before presenting the constituents of the orthodox faith. This suggests that John's purpose was to prepare his readers for understanding how the Church had challenged the internal, Christian religious heresies, such as Modalism, Nestorianism, Apolinarianism, Adoptionism, Sabellianism, etc. in previous centuries, and how it should now confront the current external heresy of Islam, which was rapidly growing in influence and clearly oriented towards proselytization. This explains the clear cut, simple and concise expressions and statements that John uses in his discourse, and his avoidance of any detailed "studied explanation of precisely how it might be possible for the three divine persons to be one single and undivided God, [and] of ... any demonstration of exactly how the infinite, unbounded God could become united with the finite, constricted human Jesus."[609] Instead of arguing rationally about

---

607 Some scholars have been sceptical of the Damascene's monastic affiliation to Mar Sabas, as Sidney Griffith points out in *The Church in the Shadow of the Mosque*, p. 40, n. 50. Whether or not he was himself a monk there, one can still assume that John could have written his text for the monks of that monastery or other nearby monasteries in Palestine.

608 Louth, *St John Damascene*, p. 37.

609 Thomas, "Christian Theologians and New Questions," p. 258. The same opinion is shared by S. Griffith: "'Melkites', 'Jacobites' and the Christological Controversies in Arabic in Third/Ninth-Century Syria," in *Syrian Christians under Islam, the First Thousand Years*, ed. David Thomas, Leiden: Brill, 2001, 9–55, pp. 19–22. Griffith differs from Thomas slightly in his appraisal of John's context, however; see Griffith, *The Church in the Shadow of the Mosque*, pp. 40–42. In another essay, David Thomas points to the Damscene's avoidance of any explanatory or justifi-

how the Trinity can be one, John of Damascus is content to state simply *that* the Trinity is one divine being. His text is thus far from clearly apologetic or extensively analytical. It is rather an intelligent and eloquent accumulation and systematic recitation of various orthodox voices from previous centuries, brought together despite their various nuances of meaning, into one theological, descriptive and introductory melting-pot. David Thomas convincingly reads this as a demonstration of the Damascene's "unshakable confidence in the teachings of [his] own faith."[610]

One can, consequently, conjecture that John of Damascus presents here an 8th-century 'textbook' for junior theology students and trainees for the priesthood, which he may quite naturally have been asked to prepare for monks and novices in the monasteries and the patriarchate of Jerusalem. The influence of the Damascene's catechetical contribution continued long after his death and reached the theological circles of the West. There is no reliable evidence of this propagation other than the fact that it was used as the "reference node" for Thomas Aquinas' *Summa Theologiae*,[611] and that it left its mark on the writings of

catory language in his presentation of the Christian belief in the Trinity: "[John's discourse] is evidently intended for an audience who share [John's] presuppositions and technical vocabulary, and who seem to require no more than a brief description of the doctrine [of the Trinity] .... [John] writes for fellow Christians in familiar forms and terminology, and is not aware of having to defend the doctrine at any length for anyone else": Thomas, "The Doctrine of the Trinity in the Early Abbasid Era," p. 81.

610 Thomas, "Christian Theologians and New Questions," p. 275. However, I do not agree with Thomas that this is also a sign of John's indifference to the faith of others, namely Islam. The fact that he was by that time an inhabitant of the Islamic territory of Syria-Palestine, and had been for a long time an official in the caliph's court makes the possibility that he was indifferent to Islam most unlikely. In this regard, Sidney Griffith seems more accurate in his sensitivity to John of Damascus' rootedness in the intellectual concerns of Christians in the Palestinian and Syrian world of Islam rather than in the immediate concerns of the theologians of Constantinople: Griffith, *The Church in the Shadow of the Mosque*, pp. 40–41; and idem, "John of Damascus and the Church in Syria," p. 23. If this is the case, one of John's main concerns would then be to train and educate the monks and the church members of the Melkite communities in the main elements of the orthodox faith. John's larger purpose, Griffith eloquently states, "would have been to provide the Christian teachers of the burgeoning Melkite community with a compendium of orthodox doctrine useful for their response to the whole range of challenges facing them, the attacks of their Christian rivals, the Jacobites, the Nestorians and the Manicheans as well as the Muslims, whose rule allowed the Christian rivals of the Melkites also to flourish": ibid., p. 42.

611 John A. McGuckin, "The Trinity in the Greek Fathers," in *The Cambridge Companion to the Trinity*, ed. Peter C. Phan (Cambridge: Cambridge University Press, 2011), 49–69, p. 66.

Bonaventure, who cites John of Damascus over 200 times, despite the fact that he rarely refers to any other Eastern fathers.[612]

Let me now briefly go through the Trinitarian teaching contained in the Damascene's textbook. As an experienced teacher, and lest students slip into the trap of assuming they can capture God by means of their intellectual contemplation in the classrooms, John starts his exposition by affirming God's incomprehensibility and transcendence above human reason. He stresses that the only knowledge of God available to us is in the testimonies of the prophets, apostles and evangelists.[613] These scriptural testimonies are our evidence of God's existence, and they alone show us that, despite his incomprehensibility and transcendence, God has implanted in us the reality of his being. So, the evidence of God's existence is first and foremost scriptural in the witness that God's people, led by the grace and power of the Holy Spirit, lay open before us.[614] Asserting that reason has no real role in proving God's existence does not mean for the Damascene that the scriptural texts do not stimulate the mind to deduce God's existence from creation. On the contrary, John affirms that the scriptures awaken the natural human capacity to know God that is innate in us and which invites us to deduce the existence of a Creator from the things created (causal proof of God's existence).[615]

The attention to causality and to the 'Creator-creation' relation is not to be construed as the Damascene's proof of God's existence *from* reason or on the basis of rational logic. Far from that being the case, the Damascene is showing that this causal logic reflects the witness of the scriptures. It is to be accepted and relied on because the scriptural testimony uses it. The strategy here is to base rational logic on textual authenticity, and not the other way round. Beyond the boundaries of the scriptural testimony, logic does not help us to comprehend the incomprehensible. Apart from the logical arguments that the texts use and certify, one cannot speak of God's essence and nature in terms of what he is, but only in terms of what he is *not*.[616] In an apophatic tone reminiscent of Dionysius the Areopagite's, John stresses God's transcendence not only above rea-

612 Kenan B. Osborn, "The Trinity in Bonaventure," in *The Cambridge Companion to the Trinity*, ed. Peter C. Phan (Cambridge: Cambridge University Press, 2011), 108–127, p. 113.

613 John of Damascus, *Exposition of the Orthodox Faith*, Bk 1, ch. I–II.

614 Ibid., ch. III.

615 Ibid. "But things that are created must be the work of some maker, and the maker cannot have been created. For if he had been created, he also must surely have been created by someone, and so on until we arrive at something uncreated. The Creator, then, being uncreated, is also wholly immutable. And what could this be other than Deity?"

616 Ibid., ch. IV.

son and human knowledge, but also above essence.[617] Later in Book I of *De fide orthodoxa*, the Damascene even takes this apophatic approach to its pseudo-Dionysian extreme:

> The Deity being incomprehensible is also assuredly nameless. Therefore, since we know not His essence, let us not seek for a name for His essence. For names are explanations of actual things. But God ... not only did not impart to us His essence, but did not even grant us the knowledge of His essence. For it is impossible for nature to understand fully the supernatural.[618]

If God is above knowledge and is separate from our realm of existence, how can we claim that God is Father, Son and Holy Spirit, or that he is one? For the Damascene, the knowledge of God is not totally made impossible by the limitations of human reason, since God's knowability does not primarily lie in rational verification. Also, since we derive any logical awareness of God's existence from the scriptural attestation and not from reason, we have to search for the knowledge of God in the Bible and nowhere else. For those who believe in the scriptures, the Damascene points out, "that God is one and not many is no matter of doubt."[619] In the Bible, God is perfect, without blemish, good, wise, powerful, without beginning and without end, everlasting, uncircumscribed and totally perfect. These attributes do not allow the possibility of a multiplicity of deities, because plurality would mean that these attributes would be subject to difference, circumscription and degree, which are not to be ascribed to God. God's oneness, then, cannot be doubted rationally, for it is affirmed by biblical reasoning, which is, for believers, beyond doubt.

After beginning with an apophatic affirmation of God's incomprehensible existence and then moving to a scriptural attestation of God's oneness, what can one glean from this oneness about the Son and the Holy Spirit? John dedicates the ensuing two chapters to answering this question. In the first chapter, he argues that being above reason does not mean that God is without reason (*alogon*), or, thus, wordless. On the contrary, God has his Word eternally and substantially: "There never was a time when God was not Word: but He ever possesses

617 Ibid. Further, John states: "When we use the term darkness in reference to God, we do not mean darkness itself, but that He is not light but above light; and when we speak of Him as light, we mean that He is not darkness." On John's reliance on Pseudo-Dionysius apophatic approach to the knowledge of God, see the brief but perceptive comments in Wolfhart Pannenberg, *Systematic Theology*, trans. Geoffrey W. Bromiley, Vol. 1 (Grand Rapids, MI: W.B. Eerdmans, 2001), pp. 343–346.

618 John of Damascus, *Exposition of the Orthodox Faith*, Bk 1, ch. XII.

619 Ibid., ch. .V.

His own Word ... having a subsistence in him and life and perfection, not proceeding out of Himself but ever existing within Himself."[620] John here uses the allegory of the human mind that utters a Word, showing by this analogy that, as the human word is not utterly diverse from the mind that spells it out, so the Word of God is also attached to the divinity who utters it. Although in the case of the divine Being the Word gains a distinct subsistence that lies in its emanation from God (causal relations of origin, probably validated by the Damascene's previous extraction of Creator-creation causality from scripture), this Word still has all the attributes that are found in God: "It is of the same nature as God."[621]

In the ensuing chapter, John of Damascus touches upon the Holy Spirit's status and conjectures that, as God must own a Word since God is not reason-less, the Word, in turn, needs to possess Spirit. Resorting again to allegorical analogy, the Damascene opines that, just as the human word "is not destitute of spirit," and since the divine Word "is not more imperfect than our own word," the divine Word also owns a Spirit that is neither from-without God, nor without its own subsistence. The Holy Spirit is "the companion of the Word and the revealer of His energy, and not as mere breath without subsistence."[622] In addition, as God has never been without a Word, so also the Word has never been without a Spirit, for "never was the Father at any time lacking in the Word, nor the Word in the Spirit."[623]

Interesting here is John of Damascus' implementation of a linear form of relationality, rather than a reciprocal or circular one, to explain the existence of God, the Word and the Spirit: the Word's existence is related to God alone, apart from the Spirit, as the existence of the Spirit is linked restrictively to the Word without directly referring the Spirit back to the Father. This theological opting for linearity does not only mirror the Damascene's allegiance to an orthodox logic that is prominent in the discourse of Basil of Caesarea and Gregory of Nyssa. It also reflects a specific, far from inclusive, biblical trend, which John follows in harmony with his overall scripture-based disposition.[624]

John echoes a Basilian linear Trinitarian discourse and uses it exactly as Basil does in his *De Spirito Sancto*, that is, to show that the Spirit and the Word are not different from God and are not creaturely (i.e., from-without

620 Ibid., ch. VI.
621 Ibid.
622 Ibid., ch. VII.
623 Ibid.
624 For other biblical trends such as the alongsided-ness between the Father and the Spirit without the direct mediation of the Son, see Awad, *God without a Face?* pp. 212–222.

God). Basil's defence of the unity and non-differentiation of the three in a linear fashion underpins, for example, his statement that "He who rejects the Spirit rejects the Son, and he who rejects the Son rejects the Father."[625] Basil's structuring of the reciprocity between the three *hypostases* is dominantly linear and mediatorial in order because he departs from an emphasis that the Father alone remains the source or the centre of the Godhead.[626] This Basilian trend of linearity, as Dorothea Wendebourg convincingly argues, was taken up by other Eastern orthodox fathers in the following centuries, but at the expense of other Cappadocian, more reciprocal approaches (such as that of Gregory of Nazianzus).[627]

The same preference for Basilian linearism also appears to be favoured by John of Damascus in his explanation of the necessity for the existence of a Word and a Spirit with God. This reliance on a linear approach does not necessarily express the Damascene's siding with Basil more than other orthodox voices, but only reflects John's preference for what resonates with his departure from a specifically scriptural criterion, which John uses to explicate the oneness of God. Whether the linear understanding of the Trinity is the only option in the Bible, or whether the Damascene acknowledges other understandings in scripture, is not the main issue here (though it merits serious attention). What matters here is to realize how John of Damascus relates to earlier orthodox tradition and how he uses it. This would later contribute to the understanding of how his successor Abū Qurrah relates to and invests in the same tradition.

To return to the Damascene's exposition of orthodox Trinitarian theology, chapter eight is an extensive presentation of the Church's understanding of the Trinity and occupies the major part of the first book of *De Fide Orthodoxa*. In this chapter, John starts his discourse with God's oneness, rather than with the three divine persons' particularities. Christians, he states, "believe, then, in one God, one beginning."[628] If in the previous chapters of Book One John follows in the footsteps of Basil's causal linearity when he speaks of the existence of the Word and the Spirit, in this chapter he initially follows a parallel Cappadocian (Nazianzen) logic of unity by understanding the oneness in a reciprocal manner;[629] he deems God to be the *arche* of himself, rather than attributing that

625 Basil of Caesarea, *On the Holy Spirit*, II. 27; and Awad, *God without a Face?* pp. 89–91.
626 Awad, *God without a Face?* p. 91.
627 Dorothea Wendebourg, "From the Cappadocian Fathers to Gregory Palamas: The Defeat of Trinitarian Theology," *Studia Patristica*, 17 (1982), 194–197. See also Awad, *God without a Face?* pp. 97–98.
628 John of Damascus, *Exposition of Orthodox Faith*, Bk. 1, ch. VIII.
629 John relies on the Nazianzen's logic in *Oration* 35 about the reciprocal ontological necessity of the Father and the Son to each other to conclude that the Father "could not have received the

status to the person of the Father alone.[630] John's main concern here, nevertheless, is different from that of Gregory of Nazianzus. While the latter speaks of the Godhead of the three *hypostases* together as the *arche* in order to show the equal consubstantiality and divinity of the three, John of Damascus uses the same idea (deriving it, most probably, from the Nazianzen) to defend the oneness of God.

It is my conviction that, although what John says in Book One is about the Trinity and how the three reciprocally relate to each other, his methodological point of departure here is still the oneness of God: "one essence, one divinity, one power, one will, one energy, one beginning, one authority, one dominion, one sovereignty."[631] When John is asked: Who are the three, then? his initial answer is that they are the perfect subsistences (*hypostases*) or hypostatic concrete personal forms of existence that make God manifest to us. They are the revealing means of God's knowledge, which is bestowed upon us as a gift from God, rather than as an outcome of the human attempt to capture the divine rationally.[632] These three are neither mixed nor separated; neither indistinguishable in terms of individuation, nor plural in terms of essence. They are, rather, the revelatory particulars of the divine one God.

One may be ostensibly misguided by John's reference to the reciprocity and interpenetration of the Father, Son and Holy Spirit at the very end of Book 1, chapter XIV:

> The subsistences dwell and are established firmly in one another. For they are inseparable and cannot part from one another, but keep their separate courses within one another, without coalescing or mingling, but cleaving to each other. For the Son is in the Father and the Spirit: and the Spirit in the Father and the Son: and the Father in the Son and the Spirit, but there is no coalescence or commingling or confusion. And there is one and the same motion: for there is one impulse and one motion of the three subsistences, which is not to be observed in any created nature.[633]

---

name Father apart from the Son: for if He were without the Son, He could not be the Father: and if He thereafter had the Son, thereafter He became the Father, not having been the Father prior to this, and He was changed from that which was not the Father and bcame the Father": ibid.

630 On *arche* in Gregory of Nazianzus' Trinitarian ontology, see Awad, *God without a Face?* pp. 112ff; and Awad, "Between Subordination and Koinonia," pp. 181–204.

631 John of Damascus, *Exposition of Orthodox Faith*, Bk 1, ch. VIII.

632 On God's knowledge as a divine gift and on the philosophical and theological dimensions of knowing in relation to Church tradition in the Damascene's thought, see George Metallidis, "Theology and Gnoseology and the Formation of Doctrine in St John Damascene," *Studia Patristica*, 42 (2006), 341–346, pp. 341–343.

633 John of Damascus, *Exposition of Orthodox Faith*, Bk 1, ch. XIV.

It is clear that John of Damascus is here using expressions of interpenetration and reciprocity that are similar to those found in Gregory of Nazianzus' Trinitarian writings, but, while the Nazianzen uses this notion of 'reciprocity' to emphasize the total equality and consubstantiality of the three divine persons in terms of divine nature and monarchical status,[634] the Damascene uses this language to affirm the strict, ontological oneness of God.

This is what the theme-context of the whole of chapter XIV suggests. John starts there by conceding that there are many properties in the divine being. This is reminiscent of the way Islam speaks about God's attributes, for John indirectly draws attention to what Christians commonly say about various attributes of God. Yet John endeavours carefully to save what he says from any accusation of polythieism that may arise from his association of the various attributes with what Christians also say about the existence of three subsistences in God. In order to avoid the suspicion that he is falling into the trap of Tritheism or associationism, the Damascene uses the notions of 'interpenetration' and 'reciprocity' to prove that, although there are three subsistences in God, they are not three 'Gods' (as the various properties do not necessarily, not even for Muslims, suggest various deities). These three are inseparable and firmly one. This is why, style-wise, John sandwiches what he says on interpenetration and reciprocity between clear and emphatic statements on oneness and inseparability. The central concern about oneness also explains why in the ensuing paragraph he speaks of the divine nature as totally simple, indivisible and existing in one motion of the three subsistences.[635]

The other question that John tackles in chapter 8 is related to the individuation of each of the three *hypostases*; the particularities, that is, that prevent the subsistances from conflating into each other. Here, the Damascene resorts to the notion of 'causal operations,' thereby distinguishing the three persons in terms of their roles: what they do (i.e., the Father creates, the Son redeems and the Spirit perfects), rather than who they are. Within the framework of the causal operations, John retrieves his earlier Cappadocian linear choice, invoking again reference to the Father as the *arche* of both creation ("Creator of all") and of the other two persons' nature and being ("causer or generator"): the Father is the unbegotten, begetting Cause of the Son, who is, in turn, the only begotten Lord, and finally (to complete the linear equation) the Son is the 'producer' (*probolea*) of

---

634 Reminiscent of the Nazianzen's saying in *Oration 31.41* "When then we look at the Godhead or the first cause, or the *monarchia*, that which we conceive is one, but when we look at the persons in whom the Godhead dwells, and at those who timelessly and with equal glory have theirs from the first cause – there are three whom we worship."

635 John of Damascus, *Exposition of Orthodox Faith*, Bk 1, ch. XIV.

the Holy Spirit.[636] Using this Greek term (which the 3rd- and 4th-century fathers consciously avoided, except Gregory of Nazianzus, who uses it in *Oration* 13.35 and 29.15[637]) to refer to the Son's activity, instead of *arche* (which is used here for the Father alone) has the intention of distinguishing the Father from the Son and demonstrating the difference in their roles. If the Father is the begetter of the Son, the Son is the producer of the Spirit. Linearity is again transported here from its conventional use in the works of the Cappadocians into the circle of showing that the oneness of the divine God is not threatened by the particular, functional status of each of the three persons.

Does this distinction in terms of activity conflict with God's oneness and suggests otherness in the deity? John stresses that this is far from being the case. Though the Father begot the Son, this does not make the Son other in divinity, for he is consubstantial with the Father and is begotten from the Father's very own nature.[638] Nor does the action of begetting indicate a change in God from the state of no-fatherhood before the begetting to a state of fatherhood after it, for there was no time when the Son was not: the Son, unlike creation, "co-existed from the beginning with the Father," and he is an offspring of the Father's essence, and thus identical to the begetter in nature.[639]

How can the three *hypostases* be one, single deity if they are distinct in terms of subsistance and perform different actions? They can be one God, John explains, because their individuation lies not in their substance or divine status, but merely in each one's role and each one's position in relation to the unique roles of the other two *hypostases*. The Son is everything God the Father is in essence, except in playing the Father's role of begetting; he is the begotten, while the Father is the begetter. On the other hand, the Holy Spirit is everything the Father and the Son are in nature, yet She proceeds from the Father, and is not begotten like the Son.[640] This is how the Damascene rephrases Basil of Caesar-

---

636 Prof. Dr. Assaad Elias Kattan of Münster University has drawn my attention to the fact that the Greek text is slightly ambiguous here, since *probolea* may also refer in this sentence to the Father and not indisputably to the Son. This also seems to be behind Andrew Louth's translation: Louth, *St John Damascene*, p. 105. That said, John's overall theological rationale in this chapter, which seems to follow a linear understanding of the causal relations between the three divine persons' operations, actually supports a translation that attributes to the Son the direct production of the Spirit, while making the Father's causation of the Spirit mediated through the Son's action.

637 So states John's translator, S.D.F. Salmond: John of Damascus, *Exposition of Orthodox Faith*, p. 6, n. 9.

638 John of Damascus, *Exposition of the Orthodox Faith*, Bk 1, ch. VIII.

639 Ibid.

640 Ibid.

ea's logic in *Contra Eunomium*, Bks II and VI, and Gregory of Nazianzus' in *Orations* 35–37.

One of the interesting elements in John of Damascus' exposition of the Trinitarian faith of orthodoxy is what he says about the twofold generation of the Holy Spirit: first, the Spirit is the production of the Son in particular by virtue of the causal will of the Father, but second, the Holy Spirit "proceedeth from the Father and resteth in the Son," and is "derived from the Father, yet not after the manner of generation, but after that of procession."[641] It is not quite clear why John attributes the Holy Spirit's generation first to the Son's producing activity before echoing the conventional patristic attribution of the Spirit's generation to the Father alone. It is nevertheless clear in the text that the Damascene is not willing to speak of the Holy Spirit as the outcome of any common, equally generating role performed together by the Father and the Son. He is evidently and firmly standing with both feet within the stream of the Eastern fathers' dislike of an Augustinian 'Filioquism.' This is likely the case, despite John's emphasis on the complete equality and strict oneness of the divine Godhead and his methodological starting point with the substantial single nature, instead of the substantial Trinitarian particularities.

One of the explicators of John's shift to an emphasis on the proceeding of the Spirit from the Father alone, and his dispensing with the earlier assertion of the generating role of the Son, lies, as it seems, in the Damascene's decision to pay a clear Basilian attention to the particularity of the *hypostasis* of the Father. John opts for this because it serves the ultimate goal of proving the oneness of the divine triune God. Following Basil of Caesarea's founding of oneness on the person of the Father alone (thus stressing oneness more than unity), John states:

> [A]ll then that the Son and the Spirit have is from the Father, even their very being: and unless the Father is, neither the Son nor the Spirit is. And unless the Father possesses a certain attribute, neither the Son nor the Spirit possesses it: and through the Father, that is, because of the Father's existence, the Son and the Spirit exist ...[642]

---

641 Ibid.

642 Ibid. This goes against Richard Cross' claim that in John of Damascus "the *monarchia* of the Father cannot be appealed to...as a necessary condition for the *homoousion*. The *Homoousion* is simply the fact that the three divine persons share one and the same (universal) essence": Richard Cross, "Two Models of the Trinity?" *Heythrop Journal*, 43 (2002), 275–294, p. 295. If all what the Son and the Spirit are is from the Father and not from the shared universal essence, then even *homoousion* for John of Damascus depends on the Father's originating status in relation to the Son, and not on any common-sharing attestation of the divine essence.

From this framework of reliance on a patrocentric approach to defend the divine being, one can extract a plausible explanation for why the Damascene stopped involving the Son in any particular generating role pertaining to the Spirit (other than the traditional Eastern 'receiving the Spirit from the Father'). His defending almost exclusively the unique hypostatic role of the Father is intended to singularize the causing-generating source in the Godhead, thus showing that, despite the existence of the three subsistances, the divine substance is strictly and ontologically one. Far from an Augustinian defence of oneness by showing the strict inseparability of the three in terms of action (thus the *filioque*), John of Damascus defends oneness by resorting to a Basilian attribution of all God's roles to one causing *hypostasis* among the three, namely the Father.

B. Maximus the Confessor and the Trinity

It is not unfair to Maximus the Confessor to say that Trinitarian theology per se was not really an 'issue' in his writings.[643] One reason for this is that he lived at a time when controversies over Christology with the Monothelites/Monoenergists dominated totally the scene.[644] A second reason may be Maximus' taking for granted the sufficiency of his Christian audiences' deep embrace of the Trinitarian theology of the Church councils, and his primary interest in showing how the Christian participates in the inner life of the triune Godhead via unity with Jesus Christ, rather than in probing the inner nature of the Godhead.[645] Yet another reason is suggested in Georges Florovsky's description of Maximus' theological discourse as a "grand symphony of experience" that is far from any "perfectly contoured and self-enclosed doctrinal system."[646] The absence of systematic

643 I amm again, grateful to Assaad Elias Kattan of Münster University for initially bringing this important fact into my attention and inspiring me to examine it further.

644 Andrew Louth believes that the hotly disputed subject at the time of John of Damascus was, as at the time of Maximus, Christology and not the doctrine of the Trinity and that one cannot, therefore, find the doctrine of the Trinity dealt with directly as a central topic in any of the Damascene's works: Louth, *St John Damascene*, p. 96.

645 Siecienski, "The Authenticity of Maximus the Confessor's *Letter to Marinus*," p. 194.

646 Georges Florovsky, *The Byzantine Fathers of the Sixth to Eight Century*, trans. Raymond Miller et al. (Vaduz: Büchervertriebsanstalt, 1987), p. 213; as also cited in Blowers and Wilken, *On the Cosmic Mystery of Jesus Christ*, p. 16. Contrary to Florovsky, Lars Thunberg believes that Maximus "developed a very consistent *system* of theology" (my italics), and that, far from following the Western medieval scholastic tradition, Maximus avoided fragmentation and presented rather a holistic vision of the cosmos, within which "the Trinitarian dimension is fundamental": Lars Thunberg, *Man and the Cosmos in the Vision of St Maximus the Confessor* (Crestwood, NY: St.

structuring makes finding the Trinitarian *loci* of the Confessor's theological thinking a more difficult task. This by no means implies that Maximus the Confessor was not a Trinitarian theologian like other orthodox (Byzantine/Melkite) fathers before or after him. In fact, all Maximus' thought is shaped after, and framed within, the Trinitarian discourse of the 4th-century Church fathers. This rather suggests that it is very difficult to locate Maximus' views on the Trinity in one or two texts in his writings, for his Trinitarian logic and allegories are scattered through almost all his *Gesamterke*.[647] That being the case, in this section I shall not endeavour to piece together the 'jigsaw puzzle' of Maximus' understanding of the Trinity, but only to shed light on some of his Trinitarian ideas on the basis of a few selected texts, with the primary aim of detecting any affinity that may exist between them and the analysis of Theodore Abū Qurrrah's Trinitarian theology, which was set out above. I shall follow a method similar to that used to trace the possible influence of John of Damascus on Abū Qurrah's Trinitarian thinking.

Like John of Damascus, Maximus the Confessor also follows the patristic emphasis on the incomprehensibility of God and that the knowledge of God is beyond human reason. In his second letter on love to Cubicularius, for instance, Maximus states that "creation cannot know God from Himself, as he is in Himself."[648] From this apophatic approach, some scholars[649] conclude that Maximus, again like John of Damascus, was clearly indebted to the mystical theology of Denys the Areopagite (maybe even to Gregory of Nyssa[650]).

Vladimir's Seminary Press, 1985), p. 31. While Thunberg finds in Maximus' theology a crude systematic presentation, he nevertheless concurs with the principal observation of the absence of a fully-fledged, comprehensive exposition of a doctrine of the Trinity in the Confessor's *opus:* "It is also quite obvious that for Maximus the doctrine of the Holy Trinity is never an isolated theme within the context of his theology. It is precisely a *dimension* in it, with repercussions and consequences all over the field" (ibid., p. 31).

647 Andrew Louth eloquently expresses the same conjecture when he says: "The doctrine of the Trinity in the thought of Maximus is a kind of overarching presence, lying behind and above everything, but to which he only occasionally directs his attention. It would be quite mistaken to suggest that it is unimportant for him or taken for granted, but it is, nonetheless, quite difficult to bring into focus": Andrew Louth, "Late Patristic Development on the Trinity in the East," in *The Oxford Handbook of the Trinity*, ed. Gilles Emery, OP, and Matthew Levering (Oxford: Oxford University press, 2011), 138–151, p. 144.

648 Maximus the Confessor, *Letter 2: On Love*, in Louth, *Maximus the Confessor*, 400D (p. 89). Unless otherwise stated, texts from Maximus and the page numbers given are from Louth's English translation.

649 Louth, *Maximus the Confessor*, pp. 28–32.

650 Blowes and Wilken believe that Maximus' incorporation of Gregory of Nyssa's ideas, especially the reponse of the latter to Origenism, appears most clearly in Maximus' *Ad Thalas-*

Against this conclusion, one can point to examples of difference between Maximus' apophaticism and the Damascene's. One should first concede that both John and Maximus, while preconceiving God's ontological transcendence, initially stress that God makes himself known to creation (out of love, for Maximus, and out of graceful goodness, for John) by means of revelation. That said, while revelation for the Damascene is Trinitarian in nature (as shown in the previous section), for Maximus it is strictly Christocentric. In his second letter on love, after declaring God's incomprehensibility, Maximus goes on:

> This is the way of truth, as the word of God calls himself, that leads those who walk in it, pure of all passions, to God the Father. This is the door, through which the one who enters finds himself in the Holy of Holies, and is made worthy to behold the unapproachable beauty of the holy and royal Trinity.[651]

For Maximus, the ultimate revelatory moment of God's transcendence in the incarnate *Logos'* life is the moment of the transfiguration. In this event, the cataphatic and the apophatic levels of *theo-logia* unite, with the first leading up to the second, raising our mind up to the ineffable truth of the divine Godhead.

This Christocentric attestation of God's knowability, however, should not make us assume that the Confessor's understanding of revelation was, contrary to the Damascene's, anti-Trinitarian. While, for the Confessor, the process of knowing God does not start with the Trinity, as it does for the Damascene, it certainly, along with John's view, ends with the triune reality of the divine God. The Christocentric revelatory passage of knowing is, for the Confessor, not only our window onto Jesus Christ's divine reality, but also our access to the depth of the other two divine *hypostases* in the eternal Trinity. For, "in becoming incarnate, the *Logos* of God instructs us in *theologia*, since he shows in himself the Father and the Holy Spirit."[652] While for John of Damascus the knowledge of God proceeds from the causal and providential actions of the Trinity in creation up to the Trinity in eternity, for Maximus it moves from the incarnate Christ's actions and transfiguration up to the triune Godhead.

The second difference I perceive between the Confessor's and the Damascene's apophaticism is that while in John's *De fide orthodoxa* we have an assertion that God is above knowledge and even beyond essence and naming, we do

---

sium, especially *Ad Thalassium 1:* Blowers and Wilken, *On the Cosmic Mystery of Jesus Christ*, pp. 29–32.

651 Maximus the Confessor, *Letter 2: On Love*, 404 A (p. 90).

652 As Maximus states in his *Commentary on the Lord's Prayer* (CCSG 23:31, pp. 87–89): Blowers and Wilken, *On the Cosmic Mystery of Jesus* Christ, p. 20, n. 26.

not find this extreme apophatic transcendentalization in Maximus. Even when the latter sometimes states that the divine Godhead is above all infinity, he does not conclude from this that God is beyond knowledge and expressibility, or above all forms of knowing and language, but rather that he is "beyond ineffability and unknowability."[653] On the other hand, even when Maximus states in his *Mystagogia* that God is to be called 'non-being,' he equally affirms that God can also be named 'being' in a specific sense (i.e., as the Cause of being), acknowledging both names as equally valid as applicable to the deity.[654] In his longest *ambigua*, nonetheless, where Maximus discusses one of Gregory of Nazianzus' statements on God's knowability (Gregory's *Sermon 21*), the Confessor concedes a role in theology for reason and philosophical contemplation. Instead of denying any role for reason and philosophy in knowing God, he proclaims the existence of a 'divine philosophy' and allows a space for reasoning and contemplation in perceiving the Trinity, despite the fact that he maintains in parallel that no reason can fully explain how God can simultaneously be triad and monad.[655]

In this, Maximus follows the apophatic approach of the Cappadocians in general and Gregory of Nazianzus in particular,[656] more than that of Pseudo-Dionysius (which seems to be John's preference). I have shown elsewhere that the Cappadocians' theology may be apophatic in tone, but it is not so in intention.[657] While Pseudo-Dionysius' understanding of God's mysteriousness is an epistemological affirmation of the absolute limitation of created human reason, the Cappadocians,' especially the Nazianzen's, is an ontological proclamation of God's infinite nature, which does not at all deny any role for human reason (as the Areopagite seems to be doing), but rather stresses that God's mystery cannot be perceived by reason *alone*.[658] In his understanding of God's mysteriousness in rela-

---

653 Maximus the Confessor, *Difficulty 10*, 31d.1168 A (p. 132).

654 Maximus the Confessor, *Mystagogia*, Intro (PG 91:664B) cited in Torstein Theodor Tollefsen, *The Christocentric Cosmology of St Maximus the Confessor*, (Oxford: Oxford University Press, 2008), p. 168.

655 Maximus the Confessor, *Difficulty 10*, 31d.1168B (p. 133).

656 Gregory of Nazianzus believed that the Godhead reveals to us its *nature* and not only its operations, so that the three persons not only disclose God's actions, but provide us with knowledge about God's nature. On how the Nazianzen takes an important step beyond the apophaticism of the other two Cappadocians, see Awad, *God without a Face?* pp. 95–98.

657 Awad, *God without a Face?* p. 104.

658 Ibid., pp. 125–126. On the Cappadocians' apopheticism, see also Alasdair I.C. Heron, *The Holy Spirit: The Holy Spirit in the Bible, in Historical Thought and in Recent Theology*, (London: Marshall, Morgan & Scott, 1983), p. 82. There, Heron shows that the Nazianzen's emphasis on God's unknowability was aimed specifically at defying the Anomoeans' belief that God's essence

tion to knowledge, Maximus follows almost completely in the footsteps of Gregory Nazianzen, ultimately disagreeing with him, not with regard to the role of rationality and philosophizing in understanding God's reality, but only as to whether that philosophizing is *ascetic* in nature.[659]

Maximus believes that ascetic struggle is not alternative to, but rather part and parcel of the philosophical contemplation of the divine triune reality of God.[660] For him, the equation is not 'reasoning versus asceticism' in any monastic or pietistic sense, or apophaticism versus cataphaticism from any conceptual perspective. It is rather an ascetic reasoning versus non-ascetic reasoning, which means that the Confessor aims theologically to reconcile the apophatic and the cataphatic approaches. His ensuing argument in *Ambiguum* 10 indicates that he aims to achieve this not only by proposing a Christocentric notion of revelation, but also by an innovative presentation of a new form of philosophizing, namely an ascetic, supra-sensible reasoning; a reasoning, that is, whose logical justification is the conviction that "nobody is able to seek out God without scrutiny."[661] In the light of this, the understanding of God's Trinitarian reality relates, in Maximus' view, to a proper ascetic philosophical contemplation of God's revelatory triune activity that is no less cataphatic than apophatic in extent and process. This is why Maximus would speak about philosophy, and philosophical argu-

---

can be rationally defined in terms of unbegottenness. The Nazianzen was not standing against any possible knowledge of the divine reality in principle, but rather against the reduction of that reality to the mere relation of begetting alone.

659 Maximus the Confessor, *Difficulty 10*, 1.1108 A (p. 97). "I do not think that I posses defectively the word of the teacher [i.e. the Nazianzen] handed down about the virtue of the Saints, and if, as you wrote, there are some who think this, saying that the divine philosophy belongs to those who pass over by reason and contemplation alone without ascetic struggle, I on the contrary dare to define as solely the truly fully satisfactory philosophy that true judgment concerning reality and activity, supported by ascetic struggle, or rather I undertake to introduce reason, manifested as correcting [philosophy] by reason and contemplation, as ascetic struggle is certainly connected to reason, and the judgment it involves embraced by contemplation."

660 In *Ambiguum 60* (PG 91: 1385), Maximus speaks of this cataphatic, ascetic knowledge as 'practical philosophy' of life, while, in *Ambiguum 47* (PG 91: 1360), he argues that this form of philosophical contemplation enables some believers to rise from the flesh of Christ to his soul, some others to proceed from his soul to his 'mind', yet some very few others still to rise from Christ's mind to his very divine Godhead. See also on this: Pelikan, *The Spirit of Eastern Christendom*, pp. 11–13.

661 As the Confessor states in *Disputatio Inter Maximum et Theodosium, Episcopium Caesareae Bithyniae*. The English translation for this text that I use is Maximus the Confessor, *Dispute at Bizya*, in Allen and Neil, *Maximus the Confessor and His Companions*, pp. 75–119 (CPG 7735), §.4, p. 93. There, Maximus bases his reliance on scrutiny in understanding God's truth on scriptural attestations, invoking verses from Psalms, Proverbs, the Gospels and the Epistles.

mentation, not as challenging the incomprehensibility of God, but as 'virtue,' 'divine power' and 'grace.'[662] It is by such a divine virtuous philosophy that lies in ascetic reasoning and contemplation, Maximus concludes, that "the saints ... worthily draw near to God through natural reflections of the divine indwelling in them, holding apart body and the world in ascetic struggle ..."[663] This positive appraisal of reasoning in relation to God's being and the knowledge of him drives Maximus even to dedicate sections 38 to 41 of his *Ambiguum 10* to a logical verification (rather than just mere spiritual contemplation) of facts related to the divine nature.

In the introduction to their translation of some of Maximus' works, Paul Blowers and Robert Wilken express eloquently the Confessor's positive appraisal of reasoning in relation to God when they say

> *Theologia* – as the aspiration to intimate knowledge of the Holy Trinity that must always remain grounded in, and integrated with, the contemplative and ascetic life of the Christian – entails for this Byzantine sage an intensive, ongoing, multifaceted 'intellectual quest' (εξέτασις) into the foundations and future of the world created by God, recreated through the work of Jesus Christ, sanctified by the Holy Spirit, and summoned to an unprecedented and glorious deification.[664]

By means of a logical philosophizing, of which we also find faint traces in John's *De fide orthodoxa*, Maximus argues that philosophical reasoning in ascetic struggle leads the believing mind via causal process from the sensual level of discerning the harmonious composition of every created thing up to the spiritual cosmological level of reasoning, where we relate "the parts to the whole" and "direct the mind in a single glance ... to the Cause." This causal retroaction from the caused parts on the sensual level back to the causing whole on the spiritual one ("on the level of mind in the Spirit," to use Maximus' words) enables us, he adds, to be "clearly persuaded by an accurate attention to the things that are that there is truly only One God."[665]

---

662 Maximus the Confessor, *Difficulty 10*, 1.1108B (p. 97). I disagree with Lars Thunberg's belief that in his understanding of God's knowability, Maximus is "a follower of Pseudo-Dionysius, Evagrius and Origen": Thunberg, *Man and the Cosmos*, pp. 33–35, 3 sOp. p. 35.

663 Maximus the Confessor, *Difficulty 10*, 3.1113C (p. 101).

664 Blowers and Wilken, *On the Cosmic Mystery of Jesus Christ*, pp. 16–17. The authors refer to what Maximus says about the knowledge of God in terms of 'questing after' the great mystery in Maximus' *Ad Thalassium 59*, in the light of 1. Peter 1: 10–11.

665 Maximus the Confessor, *Difficulty 10*, 19.1137 A-B (pp. 114–115). See also his argument in 35.1176B-C (pp. 136–137), where Maximus says: "So therefore when the Saints behold the creation ... they are taught from the things [God] has made that there is One who fashioned them ...

Moreover, Maximus refers to the same causal process when he speaks of the equality between the Father and the Word by means of an analogical contemplation on Melchisedec's ascetic union with God, which enabled that human creature to bear the divine likeness (his cause/begetter). The Confessor explains this likeness and equality in a causal way, surmising that "in the process of begetting what is begotten is naturally the same as the begetter, for it is said: what is begotten from flesh is flesh, and what is begotten from the Spirit is Spirit: John 3:6."[666] One might ask Maximus: If Melchisedec bears a likeness to God that makes him begotten from God the begetter, why not saying then that Melchisedec is God from God or God's divine Son? Maximus would answer that Milchisedec was God's begotten indirectly or midiatorially; that is *after* the likeness of the *Logos* and by virtue of the grace of the Son's incarnation, which allows him and other God-bearers to unite spiritually with God. Melchisedec bears God's likeness, Maximus states, "on account of divine and uncreated grace, which eternally exists beyond every nature and at all time." This grace, he then adds, is the grace of the divine *Logos*, who is "the eternal and alone acknowledged as wholly begotten from the whole [God]."[667] The causal relation between the begetting Father and God-bearing creatures is linearily mediated through the *Logos*. The creatures' likeness to God happens by virtue of their resembling the Son of God.[668] Though this argument is not really a clear analysis of the Trinitarian nature of God, it at least suggests that in his understanding of God's spiritual, ascetically shaped relation to creation, Maximus depicts a Trinitarian linear-causal interpretation that is similar to a certain extent to the patristic linear-causal Trinitarian logic of which one can find traces of in many Church fathers (such as Basil of Caesarea before Maximus, and John of Damascus after him).

In *Ambiguum 1*, we find some traces of direct Trinitarian thinking and hermeneutics of God's Trinitarian nature. There, Maximus discusses the logical plausibility of Gregory Nazianzen's saying in *Oration 29* (or his first sermon on the Son): "Therefore, the monad is eternally moved towards the dyad until it reaches the triad."[669] The Confessor's interpretation of this saying not only reflects his allegiance to the Nazianzen's particular Trinitarian discourse as distinct from that of the other two Cappadocian fathers, but, more importantly, it demon-

---

[and] they understand that behind everything there is providence, and this they acknowledge as God, the fashioner of all."

666 Maximus the Confessor, *Difficulty 10*, 20a.1140D (p. 117).

667 Ibid., 1141 A-B (p. 117).

668 Ibid., 1141B (p. 117).

669 Gregory of Nazianzus, *Orations*, 29.2.

strates Maximus' profound grasp of the core-interpenetrative character of Gregory's Trinitarian thought.

People ask: How can the 'teacher' (Gregory) speak of God, who is one, as becoming first two and then three? Does change take place within God's being? Does this mean that we actually have three Gods, first separated and isolated, but then joined together in some kind of union? Maximus responds to these questions by demonstrating that none of these options is implied in the Nazianzen's Trinitarian statement. We have to differentiate, explains Maximus, between what the word 'monad' and what the term 'triad' mean in Gregory's thought. For the Nazianzen, 'monad,' as the Confessor clarifies, does not stand for the hypostatic subsistence, the modes of existence (*tropos tês hyparxeôs*) or the 'how' of the Godhead's being. It rather stands strictly for the Godhead's *ousia*, its essence or nature or the 'who/what' this Godhead *is* in being. When we say God is 'monad' we mean that the one *ousia* (monad, in Maximus' terms) is truly monad; that is truly one and only, with no expansion or numerical connotations. By speaking of a monad who becomes triad, the intention is not to say that the one deity has "poured out naturally and led to multitude." It is rather to show that the one *ousia* (monad) exists in its 'how-ness' as a reality of consubstantial three hypostatic modes of existence.[670]

The above explanation means, according to Maximus, that by 'monad' the orthodox fathers mean "that which is common to certain beings [as] their essence or nature, or [their] essential property."[671] But, what about the particular that is not common or universal? This, Maximus proceeds, is what Gregory Nazianzen refers to as 'triad.' 'Triad' in the Nazianzen's thought, the Confessor explains, does not designate three self-existing essences (*ousiae*) or three 'monads,' so to speak. It rather names the three personal modes of concrete personal existence, or how the monad subsists in a Trinitarian manner. Because the triad is "the substantial existence of the three-personed monad [i.e., *ousia*/Godhead]" and not the name of three monadic deities, one should not assume that the procession from monad to triad implies a "synthesis of monads that might suffer division."[672]

The above interpretation is a clever and profound probing of the Nazianzen's association of oneness with the 'what' or 'who' of the Godhead or the divine *monarchia*, on the one hand, and of the triunity of the Godhead with the hypostatic

670 Maximus the Confessor, *Difficulty 1*, 1036B (p. 170).

671 Törönen, *Union and Distinction*, p. 52. That being so, Maximus concludes that the notions of "common, universal and essential go together." See, for example, Maximus the Confessor, *Difficulty 2*, 38–39 (CCSG 48, 9).

672 Maximus the Confessor, *Difficulty 1*, 1036B-C (p. 170).

'how' of the *monarchia*'s existence as three divine and equally consubstantial persons, on the nother.[673] This allegiance to the Cappadocians' understanding of oneness and particularity in the Godhead underpins Maximus' important statement in *Letter 15:*

> If we, too, are to express briefly what we think, we shall say that what the universal is in relation to the particular, the essence is in relation to the *hypostasis*. For each one of us both participates in being by virtue of the common principle (*logos*) of essence, and is so-and-so by virtue of the particularities which are around the principle (*logos*) of essence. In the same way there too the principle of essence is common, like goodness, godhead, or any other concept, but the *hypostasis* is considered in the property of fatherhood, sonship or sanctifying power.[674]

Maximus travels even farther along Gregory of Nazianzus' Trinitarian route when he points out that Gregory's Trinitarian logic does not take shape after any causal-linear imagining of a relationship between the Father, Son and Holy Spirit (constructed, for instance, according to causal relations of origination and a patrocentric foundation). It rather follows a more consubstantial-reciprocal understanding of the oneness-in-threeness that concedes that the *monarchia* means "Father and Son and Holy Spirit, by nature equal in honour, 'whose wealth is continuity of substance [i.e., the three are equally God from God, and equally constitutive of the Godhead, in Gregory's understanding] and the one outburst of radiance ..."[675]

---

673 The Confessor echoes a Trinitarian distinction reflective of the same association of oneness with 'essence' and threeness with 'existence' in his interpretation of the Lord's Prayer, when he states, for instance, "We say and know that the same God is truly Unity and Trinity: Unity according to the principle of essence and Trinity according to the mode of existence. The same reality is wholly Unity without being divided by the Persons, and wholly Trinity without being confused in unity": Maximus the Confessor, *Commentary on the Our Father*, in George C. Berthold (ed. & trans.), *Maximus the Confessor, Selected Writings* (Mahwah, NJ: Paulist Press, 1985), p. 4, p. 111.

674 Cited in Törönen, *Union and Distinction*, p. 53; from Maximus the Confessor, *Letter 15*, 545 A (PG 91). Törönen maintains that the association of *hypostasis* with particularity and distinction continues to be found in the writings of many fathers from the 6th and 7th centuries, such as Pamphilus, Anastasius of Antioch, Anastasius the Sinaite and Theodore of Raithu (ibid., p. 54, n. 29).

675 Maximus the Confessor, *Difficulty 1*, 1036 A-B (p. 170). Maximus here cites from Gregory Nazianzen's *Oration* 40.5, according to Louth, *Maximus the Confessor*, p. 214, n. 4 in the endnotes on *Difficulty 1*. The same logic of unity underpins Maximus' assertion in *Ambiguum 5* that the nature is not an additional entity besides the three *hypostases* as a fourth thing in the Godhead. It is rather the three *hypostases* per se, for "the Son is the same as the Father and the Spirit through their single nature...": Maximus the Confessor, *Difficulty 5*, 1057C (p. 178).

Maximus suggests that we should read what Gregory says on the one monad that subsists personally in three equally consubstantial hypostatic modes of existence on the basis of this perichoretic understanding of the *monarchia*. The triad is then the 'how' of the monad, and the monad is none other than the one and single 'what-ness' or 'is' of the three-personed Godhead. Realizing that 'monad' connotes the one Godhead and 'triad' the Godhead's hypostatic subsistence leads to the conclusion that "the triad is truly monad, because thus it *is*, and the monad truly triad because thus it *subsists*. Thus, there is one Godhead that is as monad, and subsists as triad."[676] If anyone senses in this 'monad-triad' language a process of becoming, he must be aware that this process takes place in us and not in the Godhead.[677] Rather than expressing an ontological process of becoming within the divine being, there is in the Nazianzen's language an eloquent articulation of an epistemological progressive knowing that our mind follows in order to acquire, first, knowledge about the revealed fact *that* the Godhead *is* one (monad) in substance, and in order to apprehend, second, *how* this Godhead subsists as a triad. This gradual epistemic relation to God's reality stems from the gradual, progressive nature of God's disclosure of his triune being in history.[678] Why did God will to reveal himself gradually to humans? Because, Maximus answers, God wanted "to lead those who are being taught to worship the perfect triad in perfect monad, that is, to worship one essence, divinity, power and operation in three *hypostases*."[679]

One can detect traces of linearity in relation to the Trinity in some of Maximus' other writings. For example, in his *Ad Thallasium 2*, Maximus tries to explain Jesus' saying in John 5:17: "My Father is working even now, just as I am working" in a Trinitarian fashion that is reminiscent of what Basil of Caesarea says on the Father as the Creator, the Son as creation's redeemer and sustainer and the Holy Spirit as its perfector

> It is on the basis of this grace that the divine *Logos*, when he became man, said, *my Father is working even now, and I am working.* The Father approves this work, the Son properly carries it out, and the Holy Spirit essentially completes both the Father's approval of it all and

676 Maxumus the Confessor, *Difficulty 10*, 1036C (p. 170) (my italics).

677 Ibid.

678 On the epistemological elements and implications of Maximus' interpretation of Gregory Nazianzen's 'gradual revelation' idea, see Melchisedec Törönen, *Union and Distinction*, pp. 69–71.

679 Maximus the Confessor, *Ambiguum 23*, (PG 91. 1261 A), as quoted in Törönen, *Union and Distinction*, p. 71.

> the Son's execution of it, in order that God the Trinity might be *through all and in all things* (Eph 4:6) ...[680]

Let us note that here Maximus is talking about the Trinity in its historical work in creation, and not the Trinity in its eternal existence or ontological monarchia. In other words, this is an interpretation of the historical subsistence, not of the eternal substance. In relation to the monadic substance, Maximus remains, it seems, Trinitarian after the Nazianzen rather than the Caesarean model, and the consubstantial and reciprocal unity in terms of will and action between the Father and the Son – rather than their causal differences (i.e., in terms of origination: begetter, begotten and proceeded) – plays a significant role in Maximus' Christological defence of the existence of two, divine and human, equally substantial and influential, wills and powers in Jesus Christ. As the Father and the Son commonly will the same purpose despite their hypostatic distinction, the divine and human natures of Christ also concur in willing one common goal (our salvation) despite their distinction.[681] And when it comes to carrying out the task of salvation, it is the three divine persons together, not the second hypostasis alone, who wills and approves the action as their action together.[682] The monarchia, then, is not one of the hypostases alone (the Father, for example), but the three divine persons together. For, as Maximus says in his commentary on the Lord's Prayer, the Son and the Holy Spirit "always coexist in essence with the Father. They are by nature from him and in him beyond cause and understanding, but they are not after him as if they had come about subsequently as being caused by him. For relation has the capacity of joint indications, without at the same time allowing the terms of the relationship to be thought of as coming one after the other."[683]

This opting for a perichoretic-circular, rather than a patrocentric-linear, understanding of the Trinity invites us to note a final characteristic of the Confessor's Trinitarian thinking. Maximus' writings affirm that demonstrating the unity of all the divine activities, and these activities' verification of the triune God's

---

680 Maximus the Confessor, *Ad Thalassium 2*, in Blowers and Wilkens, *On the Cosmic Mystery of Jesus Christ*, pp. 100 – 101 (CCSG 7: 51).

681 See, for example, how Maximus links up the relation of the Father and the Son in the Trinity and the relation of the divine and the human natures in Christ with regard to willing: *Opusculum 6*, in Blowers and Wilkens, *On the Cosmic Mystery of Jesus Christ*, 68 A-C, pp. 174 – 175 (PG 91:65 A – 68D).

682 Maximus the Confessor, *Opusculum 6*, 68D (p. 176).

683 Maximus the Confessor, *Commentary on the Our Father*, in Berthold, *Maximus the Confessor*, pt. 4. p. 106. In the same place, Maximus goes as far as considering the Trinity, not the Father, as the "creative cause of our coming into existence" (ibid.).

whole presence in an undivided manner in his revelatory, historical action, occupies a central place in the Confessor's theological thought. One can, for example, glean this from *Oposculum 6* and also from his discussion in *Ambiguum 22.*[684] There, one can see that, for Maximus, as A. Siecienski surmises, "[the] revelation of God in Christ is not simply an 'economic accommodation of the Godhead to the world's condition, It *is* the only God himself,' revealed as Father Son and Spirit."[685]

The same emphasis on God's undivided action and presence in his inclusive Trinitarian hypostatic particularities appears clearly in Maximus' interpretation of 'our Father' in the Lord's Prayer. There, he states that "in becoming incarnate, the Word of God teaches us the mystical knowledge of God (*Θεολογία*) because he shows us in himself the Father and the Holy Spirit. For the full Father and the full Holy Spirit are essentially and completely in the full Son, even the incarnate Son, without being themselves incarnate. Rather, the Father gives approval and the Spirit cooperates in the incarnation of the Son who effects it.[686] For Maximus, even when in the Lord's Prayer we address only the Father by name, this does not exclude the other two divine *hypostases*, for in every revelatory presence or work that each of the three conducts, the substantial unity of the divine Godhead is affirmed and clearly declared.[687]

> the words of the prayer point out the Father, the Father's name and the Father's kingdom to help us learn from the source himself to honour, to invoke, and to adore the one Trinity. For the name of God and the Father who subsists essentially is the only-begotten Son, and the kingdom of God the Father who subsists essentially is the Holy Spirit.[688]

Perhaps the clearest expression of the unity of the divine *hypostases* in every activity that is historically conducted by the Trinity is found in *Ad Thalassium 60.* There, Maximus argues that even in the incarnation, which is a unique revelatory

---

684 Maximus the Confessor, *Ambiguum 22* (PG 91: 1257B – C). On Maximus' understanding of the triune God's activity, see Tollefsen, *The Christocentric Cosmology*, pp. 167–169.

685 Siecienski, "The Authenticity of Maximus the Confessor's *Letter to Marinus*," p. 196.

686 Maximus the Confessor, *Commentary on the Our Father*, in Berthold, *Maximus the Confessor*, pt. 2, p. 103.

687 Maximus believes that this emphasis on the unity of the three persons in terms of action not only protects the divine oneness from pluralism, but also safeguards the hypostatic particularity of the divine persons from any mistaken assumption of a fourfold deity: Maximus the Confessor, *Dispute at Bizya*, in Allen and Neil, *Maximus the Confessor and His Companions*, §. 4, p. 95.

688 Maximus the Confessor, *Commentary on the Our Father*, in Berthold, *Maximus the Confessor*, pt. 4, p. 106.

declaration that is related to the hypostatic particularity of the Son, the three divine persons make themselves and each other manifested as single Godhead. This is worth citing at length:

> The Father and the Holy Spirit did not ignore the incarnation of the Son. For the fullness of the Father is found essentially in the fullness of the Son, who accomplishes, through His incarnation, the mystery of our salvation. He is there present, not in incarnating Himself [i.e., the Father], but in giving His consent to the incarnation of the Son. Likewise, the fullness of the Holy Spirit is found essentially in the fullness of the Son, not in that He becomes incarnate, but by cooperating at the ineffable incarnation of the Son.[689]

It would, then, not be untenable to say that, for Maximus, the *perichoresis* between the two, divine and human, natures of Jesus Christ is a revelation of another theological *perichoresis* between the three divine persons in the triune Godhead. This perichoretic process invites us to realize that, just as the divine and the human in Christ are equal in terms of existence, though distinguished in terms of nature, so also in the triune Godhead – and though the Father begets the Son and breathes the Spirit – the unbegotten *hypostasis* (Father) is not greater than, but one in nature with the Son and the Holy Spirit, since the nature of the three is one and the same.[690] In addition, this logic not only shows Maximus' concern to follow the Nazianzen's perichoretic understanding of divine unity, but also traces the logical Trinitarian roots of his ideas about the procession of the Spirit from the Father in the presence of the Son, which are indicative of his tendency to find validity in some elements of the Western *filioque* theology.

One can point to Maximus' allusion to this organic relationship between the Son and the Spirit in his *Ad Thallassium 63*, where he states: "For the Holy Spirit, just as He belongs to the nature of God the Father according to his essence, so He also belongs to the nature of the Son according to his essence, since He proceeds

---

689 Maximus the Confessor, *Ad Thalassium 60* (PG 90: 624C). Also cited in Thunberg, *Man and the Cosmos*, p. 41. Thunberg refers us too to a reference to the same idea in Maximus' *Interpretation of the Lords Prayer* (PG 90: 876C-D), where the he states: "Since the entire Father and the entire Holy Spirit were essentially and perfectly with the entire Son, even in His incarnation, without being themselves incarnated, but the Father imagined in His benevolence, and the Spirit cooperated, the incarnation with the Son, who Himself operated it, since the Word remained in possession of His own mind and His own life, comprehensible in its essence by the Father and the Spirit alone, while at the same time He effected, out of love for man (*philanthropia*) the hypostatic union with the flesh": Thunberg, *Man and the Cosmos*, p. 42; and also in Berthold, *Maximus the Confessor*, pt. 2, p. 103.

690 Maximus the Confessor, *Ambiguum 24*, cited in Siecienski, "The Authenticity of Maximus the Confessor's *Letter to Marinus*," p. 199.

inexpressibly from the Father through his begotten Son ..."[691] In *Quaestiones et Dubia 34*, Maximus explains the Son's role in the Spirit's procession in words that echo an Augustinian intention, when he says that "just as the mind [i.e., the Father] is the cause of the Word, so is He also [the cause] of the Spirit through the Word. And, just as one cannot say that the Word is of the voice, so too one cannot say that the Son is of the Spirit."[692] In Maximus, one can see an example of an Eastern father who straddles the Eastern and the Western Trinitarian views and their distinct emphases in speculating about the triune being of God. Maximus remains undoubtedly an Eastern theologian and his allegiance to that tradition is unflinching. Yet, in his theological *opus* there is a noticeable intellectual intermediary flexibility, which shows itself not only in his recognition that there is an acceptable interpretation of the *filioque*, but also in the overall Trinitarian framework of his theological thinking.[693]

The above brief exposition of some aspects of Maximus' Trinitarian logic aims simply at pointing to some elements in it that must have caught the attention not only of John of Damascus (who in his Trinitarian exposition similarly emphasizes the one, undivided activity of the Trinity in history [*opera ad extra trinitatis indivisa sunt*]), but also, and more importantly, of Theodore Abū Qurrah. As shown earlier, in what he says on the Trinity, Abū Qurrah also alludes on some occasions to the *filioque* and speaks of the Spirit as doubly originating from the Father and/with the Son. Since this is not an idea one can find in John of Damascus, it is possible that Theodore picked it up from Maximus, from

---

691 Maximus the Confessor, *Ad Thalassium 63*, in Carl Laga and Carlos Steel (eds), *Maximi Confessionis Quaestiones ad Thalassium*, CCG 22, (Turnhout: Brepols, 1990), p. 155. In his study of this text, Siecienski points to an affinity between Maximus' view and Gregory of Nyssa's argument in *Contra Eunomium:* Siecienski, "The Authenticity of Maximus the Confessor's *Letter to Marinus*," pp. 202ff. Assaad Elias Kattan drew my attention to the fact that in the Greek text of Maximus, the exact wording should be translated in English as "belongs to the Son naturally (*physei*) according to His essence."

692 Maximus the Confessor, *Quaestiones et Dubia 34*, in José Declerk (ed.), *Quaestiones et Dubia* (Turnhout: Brepols, 1982), p. 151. One can also find clearer elements of Maximus' views on the *filioque* in his *Letter to Marinus*, where he elaborates further on why we should state that the Son is involved in the procession of the Spirit and how such a belief is also inherent to the Greek patristic tradition of Tertullian, Gregory of Nyssa and Cyril of Alexandria. See a valuable analysis in Siecieski, "The Authenticity of Maximus the Confessor's *Letter to Marinus*," pp. 203–217. On the authenticity of *the Letter to Marinus*, see ibid., pp. 217–220; and on Maximus' Ttrinitarian logic in this letter, see also Jean-Claude Larchet, *Maxime le Confessor, médiateur entre l'Orient et l'Occident* (Paris: Les Editions du Cerf, 1998); and John Meyendorff, *Imperial Unity and Christian Divisions: The Church 450–680 AD* (Crestwood, NY: St Vladimir's Seminary Press, 1989).

693 Thunberg, *Man and the Cosmos*, p. 33.

whom he probably also borrowed other Trinitarian elements that he found permeating the Confessor's writings that I alluded to above.

Theodore seems also to be relying on the Trinitarian logic of 'undivided actions as a proof of undivided essence' and using it, like the Damascene and the Confessor, to argue for the oneness of the divine essence. As shown in the earlier sections of this chapter, Abū Qurrah argues that, just as in the Qur'anic faith God and his Word and Spirit are always inseparable and in ontological oneness, so God and his Word and Holy Spirit in Christian faith are equally undivided and essentially one too. In the next section, I turn to a further elaboration of Abū Qurrah's reliance on the orthodoxy of his Melkite predecessors.

C. Abū Qurrah's Trinitarian Theology: Confession or Innovation?

Let us now come full-circle and return to the question of the Confessor's and the Damascene's impact on Theodore Abū Qurrah's Trinitarian discourse. In the light of the analyses above, an evident affinity can be detected between the discourses on orthodox Trinitarian theology of the two Melkites and that of Abū Qurrah. It is plausible that Abū Qurrah could have been, or could have visited, at Mar Sabas at a certain time in his life, particularly at the beginning of his spiritual vocation, as one of the novices who studied John's catechetical textbook.[694] It is also likely that, while visiting the Melkite community in Jerusalem, if not later too, Abū Qurrah read the texts of Maximus the Confessor, whose close relation to the Patriarch of Jerusalem, Sophronius, makes the popularity and fame of his writings in Palestine a very plausible conjecture.[695]

That said, it is my conviction that Abū Qurrah's Trinitarian discourse (as the Arabic texts we have on it reveal) also exhibits noticeable, and far from minor, discrepancies with his Damascene intellectual master. One of the preliminary distinctions between John and Theodore lies in their view of the role of reasoning in perceiving the existence of God. For the Damascene, God is totally uncognizable and above reason, even beyond essence and existence. For John, this

---

694 It is plausible that Abū Qurrah studied John of Damascus' systematic catechism on orthodox faith, even if one were to accept Lamoreaux' argument that a historical, personal link between John and Theodore at Mar Sabas is highly questionable. See Lamoreaux, "The Biography of Theodore Abū Qurrah Revisited," pp. 33–35.

695 In support of this conjecture, Sebastian Brock refers us back to the Syriac biography of Maximus the Confessor, which states that Maximus was actually born in the Golan Heights and was baptized by his priest there before being sent to serve in Palestine: Sebastian Brock, "An Early Syriac Life of Maximus the Confessor," *Analecta Bollandiana*, 1 (1973), 302–319.

total transcendence is the natural consequence of God's nature as simple and non-compound.[696] Abū Qurrah, for his part, similarly rejects in his *Maymar on the Trinity* and his arguments in the text of *al-Mujādalah* any combination, otherness (*ghayriyyah*), or dissolution (*tabʿīḍ*) in God, emphasizing at the same time that God is simple (*laṭīf*) and non-compound (*tāmm*). However, Abū Qurrah does not use this latter emphasis to argue for God's total apophatic incomprehension and transcendence beyond knowledge, essence and existence, as the Damascene does.

I have shown in the second chapter of this study that Abū Qurrah differs from John of Damascus in the role he ascribes to reasoning in religion and in interreligious debates. The Damascene, as we deduce from his exposition, only acknowledges the form of reasoning that is attested by the scriptures (i.e., causal argument), deeming scriptural attestation to be the criterion for what is allowable or unallowable in relation to the knowledge of God, and ultimately resorting to an apophatic Pseudo-Dionysian approach to God. Abū Qurrah, on the other hand, assesses the tenability of the scriptural attestation and examines it on the basis of reason. He opts for a less apophatic approach to God, using in his maymars various paradoxical, causal, analogical, teleological and apophatic arguments for both the existence and knowledge of God.[697] For Abū Qurrah, God remains transcendent, infinite and inexhaustible by human reason, but reasoning also plays for him a more influential and reliable role in knowing and understanding God's triune-oneness than it is allowed to do for John of Damascus. Why is this so? Because for John, the scriptures and the arguing strategies they contain decide the acceptable rational standards for the hermeneutics of God, whereas, for Abū Qurrah, reason and rational scrutiny decide the best means of proving the authenticity of any religious textual attestation.

In his support of a role for cataphatic reasoning to acquire knowledge of God, Abū Qurrah seems to favour Maximus the Confessor's belief that unity with the divine lies also in intellectual, ascetic striving. Though the Confessor does not speak of reason as a criterion for judging the correctness of any theological understanding of God, he acknowledges that reasoning and philosophizing (though in a strictly qualified, spiritual form) have a more positive and substantial role to play than John of Damascus seems to say in his writings. In this,

696 John of Damascus, *Exposition of Orthodox Faith*, Bk 1, ch. VIII. There, John surmises, "combination is the beginning of conflict, and conflict of separation, and separation of dissolution and dissolution is altogether foreign to God."

697 See for example Abū Qurrah, *Maymar fī Mawt al-Masīḥ* (Maymar on the death of Christ), pp. 48–49; and Abū Qurrah, *Maymar fī Sabīl Maʿrifat Allāh wa-Taḥqīq al-Ibn al-Azalī* (Maymar on the way of knowing God and verifying the eternal Son), pp. 76–82.

Maximus is more Cappadocian than Dionysian in his apophaticism, and Theodore Abū Qurrah seems to be treading the same path and siding more clearly with the orthodox approach of the Cappadocians, than of Pseudo-Dionysius.

Another distinction between Abū Qurrah's and the Damascene's expositions of the Trinity lies in their explanation of the oneness of the three persons. In his *De fide orthodoxa*, John of Damascus, as I have shown, relies on a linear, patrocentric attestation of the relations of origin in the Trinity: the Father alone is the *arche* of the divine existence and essence. Abū Qurrah, as shown in the previous sections, allows himself to take a more flexible and context-driven position by resorting to a linear logic in the debate at the caliph's court, speaking of the Word and the Spirit as the properties of God, rather than as 'with him,' and calling only the Father 'God,'[698] although he focuses predominantly on the reciprocity and mutual relations in the Trinity in his *Maymar on the Trinity.* Abū Qurrah's strategy corresponds with the nature of the questions his Muslim interlocutors challenge him with, as well as expressing his appraisal of what in the orthodoxy tradition would be useful and relevant in his attempt to make the doctrine of the Trinity verifiable to Muslims.

This apologetic context makes Abū Qurrah's task more demanding and complicated than that of John of Damascus. The latter is just conveying his understanding of orthodox Trinitarian theology to educate and pastorally train his fellow Christians, who already believe in that orthodoxy and follow its content regardless of whether they find it rational or not. In contrast, Abū Qurrah is doing his best to unpack the core meanings of Trinitarian orthodoxy for the purpose of apologetically, and sometimes polemically, convincing non-Christian sceptics about the Trinity, or at least making them confess their failure to refute its rational plausibility. In order to fulfil this daunting task, Abū Qurrah needed to be as flexible and pragmatic as possible in drawing on various orthodox arguments in different dialogical settings, even if in the eyes of his Christian readers this gave the impression that he was inconsistent, paradoxical and opportunist, seemingly following the Machiavellian principle of 'the end justifies the means.'

This pragmatic flexibility and readiness to invest in various theological approaches also explain another distinction between John of Damascus and Abū Qurrah, which lies in the former's exclusion of any traces of the *filioque* principle in his exposition and his insistence on a patrocentric causality, compared with the latter's use of a *filioque* assertion, as when he says in the text of *al-Mujādalah* that "the Spirit proceeds from the mind and its Word" (*war-Rūḥ munbathiq min*

698 Abū Qurrah, *al- Mujādalah*, where he calls fatherhood the origin (*arche*) (*aṣliyyah*) (V.C.1.564) and the Father God (*amma al-Abb fahūa Allah*) (V.C.3.580).

al-ʿaql wal-kalimah).[699] The explanation for this also lies in the particular demands of Abū Qurrah's apologetic setting, which leads him to depend on 'the goal justifies the means' strategy, more than would be the case for a theologian, like John of Damascus, discussing with fellow-believers ideas about what they acknowledge as reliable or unreliable in faith.

In *al-Mujādalah*, Abū Qurrah appeals to any theological idea that is capable of serving his defence of the oneness of the Christian deity. This is why he frequently refers there to 'God, his Word, and Spirit,' rather than 'Father, Son, and Holy Spirit.' That is, he borrows from the official Muslim store of vocabulary in his endeavour to bring them onto a common ground with what Christians say about monotheism. John of Damascus did not need to do this (or at least he did not reveal in his writings any concern with this challenge), and could thus always safely restrict himself to the traditional Trinitarian language of 'Father, Son and Holy Spirit.' Had he in fact used the phrase 'God, his Word and Spirit,' his students would have mistaken his ideas for Arianism and Pneumatomachianism, or even Modalism. This reaction was not a threat for Abū Qurrah, since 'God, his Word and Spirit' is the crucial Qur'anic and Islamic vocabulary, and the Christian heresies were of no interest or concern to his Muslim interlocutors.[700] Using 'Father, Son and Holy Spirit,' on the other hand, would have been quite problematic and would have been misunderstoood by Abū Qurrah's Muslim counterparts, for it would invite them immediately to see in it evidence of Tritheism and *shirk*. So, in order to pre-empt this misperception, Abū Qurrah speaks of 'God, his Word and Spirit' in a deliberate *filioque*-like tone in order to stress the divine oneness. He must have been aware that this language would not have been accepted by his intellectual mentor or other theologians from the Melkite tradition (except Maximus the Confessor, as Theodore was certainly aware from his works), but he nevertheless follows this Augustinian-like

699 Ibid., V.4.A.466.

700 Andrew Louth believes that in his exposition of the Trinity John of Damascus had the Muslims firmly in view and aimed at emphasizing God's oneness in an imaginary response to them: Louth, *St John Damascene*, pp. 101, 103. However, I do not think that the Damascene takes Islam's claims and beliefs seriously into consideration, as the dismissive tone of what he says about Islam in his *On Heresies* clearly shows. Stressing God's oneness would serve a possible concern about the Jewish monotheistic criticism of Christian Trinitarianism. Prof. Assaad Kattan also explains the Damascene's repetitive statements on the oneness of God by pointing out that in Chapter 8, he is following the statements of the orthodox creed, almost verbatim, and composing a commentary-like exposition of them. This, according to Kattan, explains why John seems to be consistent in what he says about God the One, and goes against Louth's claim that the Damascene was developing a specific way of speaking about monotheism to respond to Muslims. John's concern is more monological, than dialogical, in nature.

approach, believing that it serves well the purpose of defending orthodox Trinitarian thought. Abū Qurrah relies extensively on John of Damascus' Trinitarian catechism, and he must have been familiar with the orthodox Trinitarian legacy, especially that of the Cappadocians, via the writings of his Melkite predecessor from Damascus. This strong affinity notwithstanding, Abū Qurrah begs in his apologies to differ even from his mentor and to part company with the latter's theological choices when he found it necessary to do so. He differs not only in his hermeneutics of some orthodox statements, but also in his eclectic theological selection of some theological ideas for which his Damascene predecessor revealed no support.

The question now, however, is: Is it possible that what Abū Qurrah did not derive from John of Damascus he actually borrowed from Maximus the Confessor? Or, is it the case that where Abū Qurrah differs from John of Damascus he also differs from the Confessor? From my brief study of Maximus the Confessor's Trinitarian ideas in the previous section, I suggest that the perspectives and approaches in which Abū Qurrah differs from John of Damascus were actually offered to him in the earlier, 4th- and 5th-century patristic legacy via the writings of Maximus the Confessor. There, one can also trace elements of 'the goal justifies the means' strategy when, despite his consistent allegiance to the Trinitarian thinking of Gregory Nazianzen, Maximus sometimes borrows a different Trinitarian logic from Basil of Caesarea or Gregory of Nyssa, such as his use of linear logic to speak of the work of the Trinity in *Ambiguum 10* and *Ad Thalassium 2*. In this, Maximus stands with John of Damascus, who also uses, at the beginning of his *De Fide Orthodoxa*, a Basilian patrocentric-linear Trinitarian line of though. Elsewhere, however, Maximus leaves this Damascene usage and more often follows Gregory Nazianzen's reciprocal or perichoretic Trinitarian ontology, stressing that the monad's *monarchia* is the three together. In this preference for the Nazianzen's approach, with occasional readiness to appeal to a Basilian approach when it suited his purpose, Theodore Abū Qurrah seems to be clearly indebted to Maximus and follows the strategy and eclecticism of his argumentation.

One can conclude from the above comparison between Theodore Abū Qurrah, John of Damascus and Maximus the Confessor that Abū Qurrah is indebted to both his predecessors for his knowledge of patristic orthodoxy and that many of the Cappadocian, Nicene, or Constantinopolitan ideas that his writings are seeded with had arrived on his desk via the seminal, hermeneutical mind of one or other of them. This is not to say, however, that Abū Qurrah was just a sincere imitator of old theology and not innovative or original in his thinking. Abū Qurrah learns orthodoxy from his Melkite predecessors, but re-uses and re-interprets it in his own very unique way with an able and perceptive awareness of the nature of his dialogue setting, the background of his interlocutors and contemporary rules of plausible reasoning.

Moreover, Abū Qurrah reflects a readiness to use vocabulary and allegorical expressions that went beyond the philological boundaries of the Greek Trinitarian terms used by Maximus or John in order to translate orthodoxy into Arabic, without allowing that linguistic innovation to change the main connotations of orthodox Trinitarian terms. We have seen Abū Qurrah doing this, for example, when he speaks of the three *hypostases* by using the Arabic term *wajh* in his *Maymar on the Trinity* and other texts. The content of his argument there is a reiteration of what one finds in the Cappadocians' Trinitarian theologies, but the Arabic terms Theodore uses goes beyond the traditional philological framework of the Greek (or Syriac) Trinitarian terminology and takes orthodox Trinitarian vocabulary to the heart of his Muslim interlocutors' cultural world.

Theodore Abū Qurrah does not compromise orthodox doctrine in his apologetic discourse on the Trinity. He, rather, maintains Nicene-Constantinopolitan orthodoxy, which he learned primarily from the legacy of John of Damascus and Maximus the Confessor. Theodore does not, however, copy mechanically his predecessors' interpretations and mimic their expression of patristic orthodoxy. Rather, he reproduces that orthodoxy by interpreting eclectically and innovatively, adding variations whenever necessary.

The Church historian Jaroslav Pelikan once shed light on the particular understanding of the theologian's role in the Byzantine tradition: "In any theological argument … it is necessary to produce the voices of the fathers as evidence for the faith of the church, so that the theologian, in the Byzantine tradition, can clearly record at the beginning of his texts that he has inserted nothing of his own, but has collected everything from the Holy Scriptures and from the fathers."[701] In other words, it was the tendency in Byzantine Christianity to expect theologians to merely testify to and faithfully pass on the faith and teaching of the patristic authorities from generation to another, rather than playing any creative or original role.[702] They should not, that is, be "independent, original and

701 Pelikan, *The Spirit of Eastern Christendom*, pp. 8–9. Such a statement, according to Pelikan, is found, for instance, as part of the title of Simeon of Thessalonica's *Against Heresies* (15th century).

702 The same view is also characteristic of how the fathers of the Church in the 5th and 6th centuries, such as Severus of Antioch, viewed their role as theologians. See L. R. Wickham, "Severus of Antioch on the Trinity," *Studia Patristica*, 24 (1993), 360–372, p. 361: "[Severus] was not valued for originality, partly for the good reason that it is absurd to value theologians for originality: ours is a hermeneutical not a creative skill whereby we play the tunes devised by others more important than ourselves."

productive" with regard to the Christian heritage, but should rather "preserve, protect and defend the doctrine that had been handed down by the fathers."[703] This understanding of the theologians' role applies on the whole to what John of Damascus and, more importantly, Maximus the Confessor said about the Trinity in the 7th century.

With regard to Abū Qurrah's Trinitarian theology, one may say that he does not deviate from the patristic Trinitarian tradition, which Maximus and John not only preserved and passed on intact, but also protected and strongly defended decades before his birth. Like them, Theodore also produced apologetic testimonies to patristic orthodoxy and set out to protect and defend its authenticity and truthfulness, not just against heresies within Christianity, but also, and primarily against the challenge of Islamic monotheism. That being the case, Theodore can be described as a protector and defender of patristic orthodoxy, but not as a mere testifier and witness to it. Thus, one may speak of 'Maximus the Confessor' – or even of 'John the Confessor' – but not of 'Theodore the Confessor,' at least not in regard with the doctrine of the Trinity. While Maximus hardly develops his own interpretation of the Trinity, and John hardly goes farther than repeating, and almost literally passing on, earlier patristic teaching on the Trinity, Theodore's Trinitarian discourse reflects an independent mind that is ready to deliberately produce original and innovative arguments to defend the triune faith of the Church whenever this was needed. Theodore needed to be original in his language and representation of the biblical and patristic faith because, unlike Maximus and the Damascene, he was impelled to take orthodoxy on a journey beyond the territories of its Christian homeland into the land of Islamic monotheism, and from the sphere of Greek-Byzantine culture into the sphere of the Arabic-Abbasid context. Theodore uses Maximus' Byzantine theological heritage and the Damascene's Greek catechetical legacy to fulfil this task, but he does not merely reiterate mechanically and totally neutrally these two fathers' attestations of the Tradition. He rather re-decorates, re-structures and re-verbalizes their confession of the Tradition, and the Tradition they confessed along with, in an eclectic and innovative way that stands the doctrine of the Trinity before the Muslims on a solid rational and theological ground.

703 Pelikan, *The Spirit of Eastern Christendom*, p. 8.

V. Conclusion

In his attempt to defend the doctrine of the Trinity and present it to Muslims in rationally plausible and valid Arabic terms, Abū Qurrah not only revealed originality and creative eclecticism in his use of the earlier, Greek, Syriac and Byzantine patristic orthodoxy that he learned from his Melkite masters, John of Damascus and Maximus the Confessor. He also introduced to the Christian orthodox theological scene a new term from the Arabic language-package in order to speak creatively of the three divine persons in the triune Godhead (i.e., *wajh/wujūh*), a term, that is, which none of either contemporary or later Christian *mutakallims* use as clearly and noticeably as he in their texts. It would not be far from the truth to say that, in his apologetic discourse on the Trinity in response to Muslim polemics, Theodore Abū Qurrah was willingly and ably taking the risk of being an innovative and creative voice, rather than a mere imitator.

In the 13th century, Ricoldo de Monte Croce was convinced of the impossibility of giving any clear, let alone persuasive, explanation of the Trinity to Muslims. In contrast, the innovative interpretation and defence of patristic theology in the Trinitarian apologies of Theodore Abū Qurrah reveal unmistakably that for this 8th–9th-century Church father it was far from impossible.

Chapter Five. Theodore Abū Qurrah's Christological Discourse and the Muslims' Jesus

I. When 'Jesus the Son of God' and "'Īsā Ibn Maryam' Collided

There is no doubt that "Muslims have been in dialogue with Christians from the very beginnings of Islam,"[704] and there seems to be a general tendency among modern scholars to see the apologetic Christian and Muslim texts from the early Islamic era as an early effort at inter-confessional theology; an enterprise that attempts to do theology in the idiom of another religious community, for the sake of achieving a measure of rapprochement between religions in an inter-religious discourse that respects the parameters of the faith of the other, while at the same time commending the verisimilitude of the doctrines of the writer's own confession in as positive and accurate way as possible.[705] However, the attempt to pinpoint stances of 'positivity' in the early Christian-Muslim debates – in the sense, that is, of "respecting the parameters of the faith of the other" and eagerly "achieving a measure of rapprochement between religions" – demonstrates these scholars' personal inclinations, rather than revealing the actual stance or intentions that can be exegetically extracted from the debates of these apologetic texts.

Inescapably explicit in the writings of the Christian *mutakallims* of the 8th and 9th centuries, especially Theodore Abū Qurrah, is their concern to defend the Christian faith, and not merely explain it in the theological idioms of Islam. What is clear is their passionate and relentless intellectual striving to prove the rational tenability and textual plausibility of Christian theological claims and biblical foundations. This defensive and combattive stance is far clearer in the texts than any presumably charitable attempt to give priority to achieving a 'rapprochement' with Islamic thought. One may initially concede, of course, that a positive, reconciliatory reading, like Sidney Griffith's cited above, is detectable in the Christian and Muslim *mutakallims*' dialogues over issues such as the meaning of prophethood, the notion of inspiration, the understanding of the last days and the final judgment, and the unknowability and infinite transcendence of the divine being of God. That said, one cannot but

---

704 Griffith, "Answers for the *Shaykh* ...," p. 278.
705 Ibid., pp. 308–309.

equally conclude from the same controversies (which contains these reconciliatory elements) that there is no evidence of a similar positive and reconciliatory approach when the Christian and Muslim *mutakallims* start delving into discussions on their frankly conflicting understandings of issues such as the nature of God (one or three), the nature of Jesus Christ (God's servant and messenger, or God's Son and the second *uqnūm* of the Trinity) and the destiny of ʿĪsā b. Maryam (raised up to heaven, or crucified, dead, and raised from the dead).

Of these last three highly controversial subjects, the questions of the identity and fate of Jesus Christ are evidently the most significant in the deep difference between Christians and Muslims, as the 8th- and 9th-century Christian *mutakallims*' texts invite us to realize. I would even go as far as to say that Christological issues were more problematic, and far more causative of a religious rift, than issues related to questions of God's oneness and triunity. In their inquiry as to how Christians interpret and explain their belief that God is one and three at the same time, the attitude of the Muslim *mutakallims* is that of people who seek understanding and further knowledge of how Christians elaborate on this belief. The new inhabitants of Syria-Palestine, who invaded the region from the Arabian Peninsula in the first third of the 7th century, must have already heard the Christian inhabitants of Arabia entertaining claims and ideas on God's triune being, and must have known before they arrived in the dominantly Christian region of Syria-Palestine, Egypt and Iraq that belief in the Trinity was central and basic to Christianity. However, they had probably not acquired a full knowledge, and so did not have a real sense, of the whole Christian doctrinal discourse on the Trinity before their arrival in the territories of Syria and Palestine. There, they started to hear about this doctrine at length and in detail from the prelates and theologians of the diverse churches, and started to interact with the full-fledged hermeneutics of the Trinity in a way that later inspired them to launch a Muslim-Muslim debate on God's attributes and to interpret these attributes by importing some ideas and notions from the Christian intellectual circle.

I believe the situation is noticeably different with regard to Christology. The new Muslim invaders brought with them not only their religious discourse on 'God' the one and only, and his prophet Muḥammad ibn ʿAbdallāh ibn ʿAbd al-Muṭṭalib, but also their own, particular narrative of ʿĪsā b. Maryam. They had, one might say, their own full-fledged and complete version of 'christology.' For them, interacting with Christians on religious matters related to Jesus was not just a chance to learn openly and understand as neutrally as possible the Christian discourse on the messianic founder of their faith. It was rather an encounter in which they intended to judge the accuracy and authenticity of Christian Christology by means of, and with reference to, the Qur'ānic teaching on ʿĪsā b. Maryam. The Qur'an rejects the Trinity altogether and never tries to offer any new understanding of the idea of 'triune' as such. On the other hand, the Qur'an does not reject the theology of Jesus Christ altogether, but develops its own, particular 'Christology,' so to speak, and sets it over against the Christian one. If, with regard to the Trinity, Muslims were looking for Christian explanations of what they (the Muslims) did not fully grasp, with regard to the theology about Jesus Christ Muslims reacted against Christians, adopting the attitude of those who *alone* understood and upheld *the* accurate and true theology about the prophet of the Christians. Far from an attempt at real rapprochement and inter-confessional meeting, the Christian and Muslim *mutakallims*' encounters on the questions of Christology demonstrate a dismal collision between the Christians' 'Jesus the Son of God' and the Muslims' 'Īsā b. Maryam.'

The Qur'anic view of Jesus the Christ states that God's messenger to *al-Naṣārā* is called 'Īsā b. Maryam (Q 2: 136; 3: 52, 55, 59, 84; 4:163; 6:85, 42:13, 43:63). Being conceived by a breath from the mouth of God, 'Īsā b. Maryam is fatherless and is named after his mother, the daughter of 'Imrān (Q 2:87, 253; 3:45; 4:157,171; 5:46, 78, 110, 112, 114, 116; 19:34; 33:7; 57:27; 61:6, 14). Like Abraham and Moses before him, and like Muḥammad after him, 'Īsā b. Maryam is God's messenger to his people (Q 2:87; 4:157, 171; 5:75; 61:6), and he is God's servant among them (Q 4:172; 19:30).[706] Yet, the Qur'ān also calls 'Īsā by his Christian title *al-Masīḥ* (messiah) as well (Q 3:45; 4:157, 171–172; 5:17, 72, 75; 9:30–31). This messianic title does not, however, mean that any divine or supra-human prerogatives can be strictly ascribed to this servant-messenger. Like the remaining list of God's messengers and followers, 'Īsā is God's creature and he was made, like Adam, from the clay of the earth (Q 3:59). The only distinction from other messengers and prophets that 'Īsā b. Maryam enjoys is his description in the Qur'an as God's Word (*kalimatah/kalimah minhu*) (Q 3:45; 4:171) and as either a spirit from God (*rūḥ minhu*) (Q 4:171) or a messenger supported and empowered by a spirit from God (*bi-rūḥin minhu*) (Q 2:87, 253; 5:110; 21:91). This 'Word and Spirit' of God, in addition, is going to be raised from the dead and lifted up to God's glory (Q 19:15, 33), which means, according to the Qur'an, that this messenger is vulnerable to death like any other human creature, although the Qur'an rejects associating his death with any human evil or atrocity. More essentially still, it dissociates his death from any crucifixion

706 The tradition of calling the Messiah 'God's servant' may be traced back to the Eastern, Syrian traditions of the Christianity of Grand Syria, which one can find, for example, in the *Didache* and the *Martyrdom of Polycarp*, according to Öhlig, "Syrian and Arabian Christianity, p. 373. Öhlig refers here to *Didache* 10:2, and *Martyrdom of Polycarp*, 41:1, both in *Die apostolischen Väter* [Greek-German parallel edition], ed. Andreas Lindemann and Henning Paulsen (Tübingen: Mohr Siebeck, 1992), p. 15 and p. 275, respectively.

event, such as Christians believe in (Q 4:157). The fact of ʿĪsā b. Maryam's death does not warrant belief in his crucifixion, but rather proves, in the Qur'anic discourse, that Jesus cannot be considered a god or as having any sort of godly nature (Q 5:17, 72, 116; 9:31), nor can he be called the 'Son, (*walad/ibn*) of God,' for God has no offspring or spouse (Q 9:30; 2:11; 4:171; 6:101; 10:68; 17:111; 18:4; 19:35, 88, 91–92; 21:26; 23:62, 91; 25:2; 37:152; 39:4; 43:81; 72:3; 112:3).[707]

The Christian orthodox understanding of Jesus Christ, on the other hand, is stated in the creedal confessions of the Church. The creed of faith that was formulated at the Council of Nicaea in 325 CE states:

> We believe ... in one Lord Jesus Christ, the Son of God, begotten from the Father; only-begotten, that is, from the substance of the Father, God from God, light from light, true God from true God, begotten not made, of one substance with the Father, through whom all things came into being, things in heaven and things on earth; who because of us men and because of our salvation came down and became incarnate, becoming man, suffered and rose again on the third day, ascended to the heavens, and will come to judge the living and the dead.[708]

At the Council of Ephesus, in 431 CE, and due to the strenuous reaction of Cyril of Alexandria against the Christological teaching of Nestorius, the patriarch of Constantinople, the orthodox Christological teaching of Nicaea was expanded and elaborated theologically, as follows:

> We confess, therefore, our Lord Jesus Christ, the only-begotten Son of God, perfect God and perfect Man, consisting of a rational soul and a body, begotten of the Father before the Ages as touching his Godhead, the same, in the last days, for us and for our salvation; born of the Virgin Mary, as touching his Manhood; the same of one substance with the Father as touching his Godhead, and of one substance with us as touching his Manhood. For of

---

707 For a short but precise collection of Qur'anic references to the person and history of Jesus, see the appendix list in George Patronos, "Jesus as a Prophet of Islam," trans. George C. Papademetriou, in *Two Traditions, One Space: Orthodox Christians and Muslims in Dialogue*, ed. George C. Papademetriou (Boston, MA: Somerset Hall Press, 2011),15–36, pp. 33–35. See also Geoffrey Parrinder, *Jesus in the Qur'ān* (Oxford, UK: Oneworld, 1995); Oddbjørn Leirvik, *Images of Jesus Christ in Islam* (London: Continuum, 2010), pp. 19–35; J. Dudley Woodberry, "The Muslim Understanding of Jesus," *Word & World*, 16 (2) (1996), 173–178, and Mark Beaumont, *Christology in Dialogue with Muslims: A Critical Analysis of Christian Presentations of Christ for Muslims in the Ninth and Twentieth Centuries* (Eugene, OR: Wipf & Stocks, 2005), pp. 1–11.

708 Kelly, *Early Christian Doctrines*, p. 232. On the canons and documents of the Council of Nicaea, see Henry R. Percival, *The Seven Ecumenical Councils of the Undivided Church, their Canons and Dogmatic Decrees*, in *Nicene and Post-Nicene Fathers*, ed. P. Schaff and H. Wace. 2nd ser. (Oxford: Benediction Classics, 2011), pp. 37–117.

two natures a union has been made. For this cause we confess one Christ, one Son, one Lord.[709]

In the two decades that followed, orthodox Christological hermeneutics experienced another expansion and attempts at elaboration. These endeavours took place at the Council of Chalcedon, in 451CE, where the orthodox Christological doctrine was stated in the following words:

> Wherefore, following the holy fathers, we all with one voice confess our Lord Jesus Christ one and the same Son, the same perfect in Godhead, the same perfect in Manhood, truly God and truly man, the same consisting of a reasonable soul and a body, of one substance with the Father as touching the Godhead; the same of one substance with us as touching the Manhood, like us in all things apart from sin; begotten of the Father before the ages as touching the Godhead; the same in the last days, for us and our salvation, born from the Virgin Mary, the *Theotokos*, as touching the Manhood, one and the same Christ, Son, Lord, only-begotten, to be acknowledged in two natures, without confusion, without change, without division, without separation; the distinction of natures being in no way abolished because of the union, but rather the characteristic property of each nature being preserved, and concurring into one Person and one subsistence, not as if Christ were parted or divided into two persons, but one and the same Son and only-begotten God, Word, Lord, Jesus Christ; even as the prophets from the beginning spoke concerning him, and our Lord Jesus Christ instructed us, and the Creed of the fathers has handed down to us.[710]

When the Muslims established their first kingdom in Syria-Palestine, with Damascus as its capital, the Christians of that newly formed state were still deeply occupied, if not torn apart, with Christological controversies. It did not take the newcomerss more than few decades to start hearing their Christian neighbours presenting new Christological ideas and claims that were this time derived from a newly written chapter in the Church's theology of Jesus Christ, developed at the sixth ecumenical council, held in Constantinople in 680–681 CE Building upon the previous five councils' chapters in the story of Christ, the theologian-clergy there added to the ecclesial Christological discourse some further exegetical elaborations inspired by the *Tome* of Leo the Great:

> We glorify two natural operations invisibly, immutably, inconfusedly, inseparably in the same our Lord Jesus Christ our true God, that is to say a divine operation and a human op-

709 Leo Donald Davis, *The First Seven Ecumenical Councils (325–787), their History and Theology*, (Collegeville, MN: Liturgical Press, 1990), pp. 161–162. See also Percival, *The Seven Ecumenical Councils*, pp. 295–363.

710 Davis, *The First Seven Ecumenical Councils*, p. 186, see also Percival, *The Seven Ecumenical Councils*, pp. 364–435.

> eration, according to the divine preacher Leo, who most distinctly asserts as follows: 'for each form does in communion with the other what pertains properly to it, the Word, namely, doing that which pertains to the Word, and the flesh that which pertains to the flesh.' For we will not admit one natural operation in God and in the Creature, as we will not exalt into the divine essence what is created, nor will we bring down the glory of the divine nature to the place suited to the Creature.[711]

The prelates also added to the story further Christological explanations and details inspired by the teaching of Cyril of Alexandria:

> We recognize the miracles and the sufferings as of one and the same [Person], but of one or of the other nature of which He is and in which He exists, as Cyril admirably says. Preserving therefore, the inconfusedness and indivisibility, we make briefly this whole confession, believing our Lord Jesus Christ to be one of the Trinity and after the incarnation our true God, we say that his two natures shone forth in his one subsistence in which he both performed the miracles and endured the sufferings through the whole of his economic conversation and that not in appearance only but in every deed, and this by reason of the difference in nature which must be recognized in the same person, for although joined together, yet each nature wills and does the things proper to it and that indivisibly and inconfusedly.[712]

Nowhere else, and at no other time before, in their intermingling and co-existence with Christians in the Arabian Peninsula had Muslims heard so intensively, or been exposed so directly and closely, to the daunting and puzzling details of Christological discours as they did when they settled in Syria-Palestine. Nothing in the Christian faith was as confusing, challenging and provocative to the Muslims' intellect and irritating to their religiosity as the unsettling labyrinth of Christian Christological teachings and the seemingly irreconcilable schisms between the Christian churches caused by these Christological interpretations.[713] One can validly surmise that in their writings on the divisions between the Christians over the sophistications of Christological doctrine, the Muslim *mutakallims* were not only presenting their polemical disapproval of these Christological differences and challenging their rationality, but also disclosing their profound puzzlement and weariness at these disputes and their total failure to grasp

711 Davis, *The First Seven Ecumenical Councils*, p. 283.

712 Ibid., pp. 283–284. See also on the sixth ecumenical council, Percival, *The Seven Ecumenical Councils*, pp. 470–502.

713 One of the puzzling schisms for Muslims considering the Christological maze must have been the 'monothelite-dyothelite' schism that eventually generated the two denominations of the "largely Syriac patristic and liturgical heritage" of the Maronites, and that of the Melkites, "with a major investment in Christian Hellenism": Griffith, "'Melkites', 'Jacobites', and the Christological Controversies," p. 35.

their arguments. The issue was not, that is, that Christology made no religious sense in Arabic, but that the Muslim mind could not make any sense *at all* of what the Christians wanted to express in their orthodox christological statements, be they articulated in Syriac or Greek or even Arabic.

In their co-existence with the Christians of the south-western territories of Arabia (specially Najrān), and in their interaction with the Christians of Nabataea and southern Syria during their trading journeys, the first followers of Islam must have heard Christians, especially Monophysites and Nestorians, voicing some of these Christological assertions and ideas. One may also add the factor of the pre-Islamic Christian background of many of the new converts to Islam in the Peninsulan Najrān and the territories of the Ḥimyarites in Yemen.[714] These two elements constitute the source of the early Peninsulan Muslims' awareness that Christians speak of Jesus the Christ as a divine Lord and Son of the Lord, who was crucified for our sake,[715] and that beliefs are very different from both the teaching of the prophet Muḥammad, and the teaching of his successors, or even from the earliest fragments of the *Ur-Qur'ān*.[716]

---

714 On these Christians in the pre-Islamic Najrān and Yemen, see Suhayl Qāchā, *Ṣafaḥāt min Tārīkh al-Masīḥiyyīn al-ʿArab qabl al-Īslām* (Pages from the History of the Christian Arabs before Islam) (Junieh: Paulist Press, 2005), pp. 25–46, 243–284; and Irfan Shahid, *Byzantium and the Arabs in the Sixth Century.*

715 Suhayl Qāchā gives two examples of some of the statements made by the Christians of pre-Islamic Arabia to the inhabitants of Yemen and Najrān. The first is the saying of the martyr Rumī bint Āzmaʻ before her Jewish persecutor: حاشا لي أن أكفر بالمسيح الإله الذي آمنت به، واعتمدت وبناتي باسم الثالوث الأقدس، وأنا ساجدة لصليبه، ومن أجله أموت مسرورة أنا وبناتي مثلما تألم هو بالجسد من أجلنا ، (I forbid myself from disbelieving in Christ the Lord, whom I believed in and was baptized with my daughters in the name of the Holy Trinity, and to whose cross I bow down and for His sake I and my daughters are glad to die, as He suffered in the flesh for our sake). The second example is the saying of the martyr al-Ḥārith an-Nabīl إننا نكفر بكل من لا يعترف بأنَّ المسيح هو الإله وابن الإله...ها إنني أسمُ نفسي ورفاقي كعادتنا بسمة الصليب الحية، باسم الآب والابن والروح الروح القدس (We reject everyone who does not confess that Christ is God and the Son of God ... here I am marking myself and my fellows, as is our custom, with the living sign of the cross, in the name of the Father, the Son and the Holy Spirit): Qāchā, *Ṣafaḥāt min Tārīkh al-Masīḥiyyīn al-ʿArab Qabl al-ʾIslām* (Pages from the History of the Christian Arabs before Islam), pp. 184–185 (and see pp. 195–208 on the Chalcedonian Himyarite martyrs in the 6th century).

716 On the historical origin of the Islamic religious text and its earliest oral and fragmentary versions, see Gabriel Said Reynolds (ed.), *The Qur'ān in Its Historical Context* (London: Routledge, 2008); C. Luxenburg, *Die syro-aramäesche Lesart des Koran*, 2nd ed. (Berlin: Schiller, 2002); translated into English as *The Syro-Aramaeic Reading of the Koran: A Contribution to the Decoding of the Koran* (Berlin: Schiller, 2007); R.G. Hoyland, "Language and Identity: The Twin Histories of Arabic and Aramaic," *Scripta Classica Israelica*, 23 (2004),. 183–199; B. Gruendler, *The Development of the Arabic Scripts from the Nabataean Era to the First Islamic Century* (Atlanta, GA: Scholars Press, 1993).

When these early Muslims invaded the dominantly Christian territories of Syria-Palestine,[717] they found themselves at the heart of Christian theological cultural and religious thinking and inevitably in contact with sophisticated and puzzling Christological debates. They started to acquire first-hand experience not only of Christian teaching on Jesus Christ, but also, more challengingly, of the relentless clashes between the Melkites, Nestorians and Jacobites over which Christological understanding most accurately and verifiably represented the official orthodox faith of the Christian Church.[718] In Mecca, Medina, Najrān and Yemen, Muslims had had closer and more frequent contact with some so-called 'Arians' (one of whom we know was the legendary East Syrian monk Sargīs Baḥīrā, who was based in Buṣra[719]) and Ebionite Jewish-Christians.[720] They also had opportunities to converse about religious beliefs with Nestorian and Jacobite merchants, slaves, monks and priests, apart from their exposure to the oral indigenous heritage (narratives and poetry), which spread news about the Christians and their religious and life rituals in the Arab Peninsula before the

717 Sidney Griffith alludes to this dominant population factor when he says: "Conversely, during these same first four centuries of the Muslim government of these large territories, ... the Muslims themselves still did not make up the absolute majority of the population everywhere in the caliphate, not even in Mesopotamia, Syria, Palestine and Egypt, where by the end of the ninth century the largest populations of the speakers of Arabic lived": Griffith, *The Church in the Shadow of the Mosque*, p. 11. On the demographic and religious changes in Syria-Palestine in the 8th-9th centuries, see also Richard W. Bulliet, *Conversion to Islam in the Medieval Period: An Essay in Quantitative History* (Cambridge, MA: Harvard University Press, 1979); Bulliet, "Conversion Stories in Early Islam"; Levtzion, "Conversion to Islam in Syria and Palestine"; and Youssef Courbage and Philippe Fargues, *Christians and Jews under Islam*, trans. Judy Mabro (London: I. B. Tauris, 1997), pp. 1–28.
718 Griffith, *The Church in the Shadow of the Mosque*, p. 13.
719 On this monk and his relation to the prophet Muḥammad, see Sidney Griffith, "Muhammad and the Monk Bahira: Reflections on a Syriac and Arabic Text from Early Abbasid Times," *Oriens Christianus*, 79 (1995), 146–174 (repr. In idem., *The Beginnings of Christian Theology in Arabic*, ch. 7; and Barbara Roggema, "AChristian Reading of the Qur'ān: The Legend of Sergius-Baḥīrā and Its Use in Qur'ān and Sīra," in *Syrian Christians under Islam, the First Thousand Years*, ed. David Thomas (Leiden: Brill, 2001), pp. 57–74.
720 On the Christian presence in the Arabian Peninsula before and during the very early years of Islam, see Ghada Osman, "Pre-Islamic Arab Converts to Christianity in Mecca and Medina: An Investigation into the Arabic Sources," *The Muslim World*, 95 (2005), 67–80; Shahid, *Byzantium and the Arabs in the Sixth Century*; and Najib G. Awad, "Is Christianity from Arabia? Examining Two Contemporary Arabic Proposals on Christianity in the Pre-Islamic Period," in *Orientalische Christen und Europa: Kulturbegegnung zwischen Interferenz, Partizipation und Antizipation*, ed. Martin Tamcke (Wiesbaden: Harrassowitz, 2011), 33–58.

birth of Islam.[721] But their first real first-hand encounter with the complicated theological and philological controversies over the nature and work of Jesus Christ, in which these three denominations were fully engaged, must have taken place outside Islam's original homeland.[722]

In Syria-Palestine, and also in Egypt and Iraq, Muslims were exposed in an intensive and direct way that they had not experienced before to discourses on Jesus Christ composed in Greek and Syriac and, more problematically, highly philosophical in content and definitely far from easy to understand by recourse to any Islamic terms that are familiar to Muslims or present in the Qur'ān and the Hadiths of the prophet (both of which spoke negatively of many Christian statements about Christ). Muslims realized that the 'Nazarenes' actually had a variety of interpretations of Christ's identity,[723] and that these hermeneutical variations

---

721 Wilhelm Baum states that the 10th-century Muslim author, Abū al-Faraj al-Aṣfahānī narrates that the prophet Muhammad himself had learned many Christian theological ideas from such encounters. He reports, for example, that the prophet developed his apocalyptic view of the resurrection from "the eschatological preaching of the East Syriac bishop (?) Quss b. Sa'ida while in 'Ukaẓ": Baum and Winkler, *The Church of the East*, p. 42.

722 On the knowledge of the Christians of Arabia of the teachings of Christianity, Suhayl Qacha states that theys were not at all well versed in the Christian faith and had a noticeably shallow knowledge of its teachings. It was a superficial and fragmented Christianity, to the extent that ʿAlī ibn Abī Ṭālib once said of these Christians that all they knew about Christianity was that it allowed them to drink alcohol: Qāchā, *Ṣafaḥāt min Tārīkh al-Masīḥiyyīn al-'Arab Qabl al-'Islām* (Pages from the History of the Christian Arabs before Islam), p. 44.

723 On these Christological variations and complications in the non-Peninsulan territories, Sidney Griffith gives the following, explication, which is worth citing in full: "Most Syriac-speaking Christians at the time of the Islamic conquest accepted christological formulas in Greek by Severus of Antioch (ca. 465–538) and in Syriac by Philoxenus of Mabbug (ca. 440–523), echoing the earlier theology of St. Cyril of Alexandria (d. 444) (the so-called Jacobites or monophysites), or they accepted formulas articulated in Syriac by Narsai (d. 503) and Babai the Great (551/2–628), composed originally in Greek a hundred years earlier (the so-called Nestorians). In other words, already at the time of the Islamic conquest and throughout the early Islamic period, most Aramaean Christians, along with the Copts in Egypt and the Armenians of the Caucasus, did not accept the 'Byzantine' imperial orthodoxy of the first six ecumenical councils. The resulting schisms had already estranged the majority of Christians in the Oriental Patriarchates from both Rome and Constantinople by Muḥammad's day. Nevertheless, there remained among them, in Alexandria, Antioch and Jerusalem, communities who did accept the orthodoxy of the 'six councils', enforced by the Byzantine emperors. In consequence of this loyalty, those who accepted Byzantine orthodoxy, who lived in the newly conquered Islamic world, came soon after the sixth council (III Constantinople, 681) to be called 'Melkites' ('imperialists', 'royalists') by their 'Jacobite' and 'Nestorian' adversaries": Griffith, *The Church in the Shadow of the Mosque*, pp. 11–12. See also on these churches' theological differences in the early Islamic period, Griffith, "'Melkites', 'Jacobites' and the Christological Controversies," pp. 9–55; and D.S.

were as confusingly flexible as the differences between the Christian denominations that taught them.[724] Although in their gradually Islamizing environment the Christians spoke with almost one voice with regard to the Trinity, in Christology the un-concealable discrepancies, and far from simple or lucid differences, in Christian teachings represented a daunting and confusing challenge to the followers of Islam. One may find it totally plausible that, in response to this disunity and schism that the Christologies of the Melkites, Jacobites and Nestorians created, the Muslims would hold fast, and more conservatively, to the Qur'anic discourse on ʿĪsā b. Maryam, deeming it the only authentic source for teaching on the prophet of the Christians, and using it both as a corrector of the Christians' 'blasphemies' and as a protective, unifying means of consolidating the Caliphate's stability and unity against any internal threat of division and instability that might arise from the Christians' theological schisms. At that early stage in its history, the Caliphate could not allow the Christians' theological divisions to drive them into developing various threatening political alliances with Christian Byzantium. There was a fear that the Christians' theological arguments would eventually lead them to develop political orientations that would make them a destabilizing influence in the newly established Muslim realm.

I suggest that two factors lay behind the deep confusion and puzzlement in the minds of Muslims over the Chalcedonian and non-Chalcedonian Christologies. The first is their realization of the stark contradiction between these Christologies and the Qur'anic understanding of ʿĪsā b. Maryam. Of the many elements that made this apparent, one can point to three specifically: 1) the Christians' calling of Jesus 'the Son of God' and its contradiction with the Qur'anic and Is-

---

Wallace-Hadrill, *Christian Antioch: A Study of Early Christian Thought in the East* (Cambridge: Cambridge University Press, 2008), pp. 117–150.

724 Sidney Griffith believes that the Muslims of Arabia knew very well the three main Christian sects of that era, the Nestorians, the Jacobites and the Melkites, even before the invasion of Syria-Palestine and Egypt started in the early 8th century: Griffith, *The Church in Shadow of the Mosque*, pp. 6–11, esp. p. 8. It is quite plausible that the Muslims of Arabia interacted with Christian merchants, monks, priests and travellers, who came to Arabia on a regular basis from the surrounding dominantly Christian territories, and who belonged, in the nature of things, to the three main churches at that time. But this is not to say that the Muslims of Arabia already had a clear and sufficiently comprehensive knowledge of the sophisticated, highly speculative differences between these three churches' Christological discourses. The mere fact that the Qur'an refers to all Christians as 'Nazarenes' and never mentions Nestorians, Jacobites or Melkites indicates that, when it comes to knowledge of the theology of the various churches, the Muslims of Arabia viewed the Christians as 'one-block' and one religious voice. This situation changed, it seems, when they started to live among the members of these three churches in Syria-Palestine. Then, they began to appreciate that, when it came to their belief in Jesus Christ, the Nestorians, Jacobites and Melkites, or the *Nazarenes*, were far from monolithic.

lamic conviction that God can never have offspring, for God *lam yalid wa-lam yūlad* (has neither begotten, nor been begotten); 2) the Christians' belief in the divinity of Christ and their association of this divinity with his virginal birth, which is different from the Qur'anic understanding of ʿĪsā's birth from the Virgin Maryam; 3) the Christians' centralization of Jesus' death on the cross and their belief that it was a sacrificial death, the belief that is bluntly rejected by the Qur'an.

The second factor behind the Muslims' total puzzlement and consequent rejection of the Christians' schismatic Christologies is the occasional failure of the Christians to present their churches' teachings on Christ accurately and clearly. Some of the highly sophisticated, speculative and far from lucid theological and philosophical expressions in Christological hermeneutics were sometimes totally misunderstood by church members, let alone anyone else, so that they might be misrepresented in such a way as to drastically broaden the gap between 'Jesus the Son of God' and 'ʿĪsā b. Maryam,' rather than narrowing it.

In his book, *Jesus and the Muslim*, Kenneth Cragg gives an example that is relevant to such a misrepresentation of Jesus Christ that originates from a Christian misunderstanding of Christology. Hi cites a medieval episode from *Kitāb al-'Ī tibār* (The Book of Construal), the memoirs of the 12th-century author Ūsāmah ibn Munqidh. The story says that Ibn Munqidh witnessed in Jerusalem a meeting between a Christian and a Muslim

> I saw one of the Franks come to Amīr Muʿīn al-Dīn when he was in the Dome of the Rock and say to him: 'Do you want to see God as a child?' Muʿīn al-Dīn said: 'Yes!'. The Frank walked ahead of us until he showed us the picture of Mary with Christ (peace be upon him) as an infant in her lap. He then said: 'This is God as a child'.[725]

Clearly appalled and annoyed by the Frank's statement, Ibn Munqidh ends the story by saying "but God is far exalted above what infidels say about Him," and Kenneth Cragg personally follows Ibn Munqidh's remark with this comment "Indeed, He is, if that is what they, or 'Franks,' say or said."[726] Regardless of this episode's relevance to the question of whether or not Muslims were willing to perceive that Christology must be read within the framework of the Christians' undertadning of God (theology) – which is Cragg's concern in his citation of

725 Kenneth Cragg, *Jesus and the Muslim: An Exploration* (Oxford: Oneworld, 2003), pp. 67–77; citing the story from Usāma ibn al-Munqidh, *Kitāb al-Iʿtibār* (The Book of Construal), trans. Philip Hitti, (Beirut, Gorgias, 1964), p. 164.
726 Cragg, *Jesus and the Muslim*, p. 68.

the story[727] – one can find in the Frank's presentation of Christ as 'God the child' an apt example of how, in their misunderstanding of the core meaning of Christology, Christians sometimes unintentionally bore prime responsibility for increasing Muslims' confusion and misconception of the Christian belief in Christ and, eventually, mobilizing their *mutakallims* against it.

During the 6th and early 7th centuries, these controversies not only jeopardized the stability of the Christian churches in the region, but also threatened the very foundations of the unity and political dominance of both the Byzantine and the Sassanid empires. The question for Byzantine and Sassanid rulers was always about the loyalty of the local Christians who lived in each empire's territories in the Fertile Crescent, and whether they might at some point give their allegiance to hostile powers for religious or doctrinal reasons, thus jeopardizing the security of the state.[728] Both the *basileus* of Constantinople and the *shah* of Persia were therefore deeply concerned about this internal threat to their rule and to social and political stability from the impact of the Christians' ferocious clashes over their belief in Jesus Christ. Both rulers therefore became personally involved in attempts to reconcile the Monophysites with the Dyophysites by any means possible.[729] These attempts included the Persian-sponsored meeting of Monophysite leaders at Ctesiphon in 614 CE, the Heraclius-sponsored synod of the Monophysite Armenians in 633 CE (who eventually accepted Chalcedon as a result of the synod's discussion) or Heraclius' meeting in 629 CE in Mabbough with Athanasius Gammala, the Monophysite patriarch of Antioch, when Heraclius eventually won the Syrians over to the Monoenergist side.[730]

---

727 Ibid., pp. 66–69.

728 Karl-Heinz Öhlig points out that such a threat was felt by the Sassnaid emperor even earlier than the 7th century, as there has been serious suspicion that the Syrian Christians of the Sassanian Empire would transfer their loyalty to the Roman Empire: "It was only after the edict of Milan in 313, and only fully after the elevation of Christianity to the state religion in 380–381, that doubts arose in the Sassanian Empire concerning the loyalty of local Christians, as they could be maintaining relationships with the Roman Empire. This doubt was strengthened through the expectation of the Roman emperor that he had to take care of Christians wherever they might be, even beyond his own borders." Öhligh, "Syrian and Arabian Christianity and the Qur'ān," p. 368.

729 Davis, *The First Six Ecumenical Councils (325–787)*, pp. 258–268. The clergy who orchestrated, or influenced, these reconciliation attempts by lay leaders included Sergius of Constantinople, George Arsas of Egypt, Severus of Antioch, Theodore of Pharan, Paul the Blind of Cyprus and Cyrus of Phasis.

730 Ibid., pp. 261–262. On the historical context, see also Hussey, *The Orthodox Church in the Byzantine Empire*, pp. 13–20.

If Heraclius' unification policy was successful in achieving relative unity among the conflicting Christian schools under the rubric of his imperial support of Monoenergism, his policy was hardly fruitful in finding common ground between Monoenergism and the Chalcedonian Christology of the Melkites. The imperial Monoenergism was fiercely resisted by very influential Chalcedonian theologians, such as Sophronius of Jerusalem, Maximus the Confessor and, two centuries later, Theodore Abū Qurrah.[731] Although Heraclius' favourite ecclesial allies in Constantinople sometimes succeeded in imposing their Monoenergist-Monothelite Christology on the Chalcedonian 'two activities because of two natures' Christology of Sophronius and Maximus, this did not prevent the failure of Heraclius' unification attempts and the tearing apart of his empire, even before the victorious Muslim raids from the south.[732] The Christological complexity of the various theological schools was far too sophisticated and polarized to be dealt with by any policy of reconciliation that involved linguistic or philosophical revision or refinement, and the churches' stark disagreements over how they understood Jesus Christ and how they read the Chalcedonian rationale were too deeper for building bridges.[733]

My argument has so far been that, from the 630s, the troops of the prophet Muḥammad and the first righteous caliphs approached from the Arabian Peninsula and conquered the territories of Syria-Palestine, where Christians were in conflict over Christological questions. Their meeting with the Christian inhabitants of this new land was by no means their first encounter with Christianity. Yet, their domination of the region, and their settlement and establishment of a great Islamic domain there, gave the Muslims, probably for the first time in their history, an intensive first-hand experience of, and an intrusion into, the seemingly insoluble, totally puzzling Christological affairs of the Chalcedonians,

731 Davis, *The First Six Ecumenical Councils (325–787)*, pp. 264–268.

732 Ibid., p. 268.

733 On the ecclesiastical clashes and theological controvesies and their impact on the 7th century, see also Hussey, *The Orthodox Church in the Byzantine Empire*, pp. 9–29; Haldon, *Byzantium in the Seventh Century*, pp. 56–78, 324–375; and Chadwick, *East and West*, pp. 59–70. It may be that the realization of the possible danger of the consequences of such Christological schisms led the later Muslim caliphs to interfere in the internal affairs of the churches and in the appointment of clergy and patriarchs, who were considered loyal and had good connections with the caliphal court. Wilhem Baum alludes to such influence: "... the Islamic rulers gained ever greater influence over the naming of the new catholicos, who was elected only by those metropolitans and bishops designated as delegates. East Syriac secretaries or physicians often had their candidates named by the caliph or his deputies. Between 650 and 1050 twelve of the total thirty catholicoi of the Church of the East were imposed by the Islamic rulers": Baum and Winkler, *The Church of the East*, p. 43.

Nestorians, Monophysites, Monoenergists, Monothelites, etc. Muḥammad and his followers must have heard before about such disagreements, and must have imagined from their contacts with Monophysites and Nestorians in Arabia what these Christological differences might mean. In Syria-Palestine, however, Muslims, I have suggested, found themselves standing firmly within the wrestling arena of Christology. In the regional context of this theological clash, the Muslims stood not as temporary visitors and spectators, but as permanent co-inhabitants of a newly founded, still immature caliphate. They realized that the longevity and survival of this newly founded state could be endangered by these Christian theological battles, as easily as were the earlier Byzantine and Sassanid polities. Like their predecessors, the Muslim rulers were also partial in their stance on the Christian schisms. Political and social calculations and circumstances led the caliphs to support one ecclesial body over against the other (s), as when the Abbasids, for example, favoured the Nestorians over the Jacobites and Melkites. They acted in line with their political and power interests, directing their support in the way they believed would serve the primary goal of maintaining the stability of the caliphate and preventing the Christians from playing any negative role in Islamic society.

Moreover, the Muslims soon realized that, though they might favour the Nestorians in certain geographical areas of the caliphate (such as Iraq and Persia), in other parts of their domain, such as Syria and Palestine, they needed to tailor their alliances and gain the allegiance of the Jacobites and the Melkites. This strategy eventually meant that the Muslims became keen to understand more deeply the religious teachings that divided these three Christian groups so implacably in order to work out how the state could pre-empt the impact of such theological divisions on Muslim society. This background explains why we find in 8th- and 9th-century manuscripts that it was first of all the caliphs who debated with Christian prelates from the Melkite, Nestorian and Jacobite communities in order to understand the roots and the ramifications of the theological disagreements that kept the Christians in seemingly endless division.

In the intellectual and interreligious context of 8th–9th-century Syria-Palestine, Theodore Abū Qurrah took upon himself the burden of defending orthodox, Chalcedonian Christology and representing it in a rationally plausible, dialogically lucid and religiously acceptable manner. He found himself haunted by this task on the *ad intra* level of Chalcedonian–non-Chalcedonian controversy, as well as on the *ad extra* level of Christian-Muslim interaction and *kalām*.

Abū Qurrah lived in a world where the newly dominant Islamic power ruled over Syria-Palestine's Christian environment. Rather than remaining in the wings, Abū Qurrah deliberately immersed himself in the battle for orthodox Chalcedonian Christology, deciding to defend it not only against the accustomed attacks of the Nestorians, Monophysites, Monoenergists and Monothelites, but, more essentially this time, against the Islamic-Qur'ānic Christological discourse of the new rulers.[734] In Abū Qurrah, the Muslims encountered a Melkite-Chalcedonian of formidable intellect, who was not only aware of the new cultural, religious, social, political and linguistic changes that the Muslims wre bringing to his homeland, but also determined to employ the implications of these changes in his own theological scholarship.

In studying Abū Qurrah's christological legacy, it is important to realize that, though a prelate in a church whose historical allegiance to Hellenism and Byzantine theology was considered by Nestorians, Jacobites and the Muslims alike to be definitive of its Christian identity, the bishop of Ḥarrān did not set himself up in his conversations with the Muslims (or even with other Christians) as a theologian speaking on behalf of Byzantine Christendom or the Constantinopolitan theological school of thought. One may be like to think that this conjecture may perrenially be thought of Theodore's mentor, John of Damascus, whose ecclesial community was still seen as affiliated to the Greek theological tradition up to the middle of the 8th century. But, this was not the case when Abū Qurrah started his theological career in the second half of the 8th and then the 9th century (or even up to the 11th), in the midst of a dominantly Arab-Islamic context, when the Melkite Church of Syria-Palestine had to start using Arabic, even in theological and ecclesial matters.[735] During the 8th and 9th centuries, the patriarchates of the oriental churches lost any serious communication with their sister churches in Constantinople and the other parts of Byzantium,[736] and these oriental patriarchates, especially the Melkites, were now striving to survive in *dār al-Islām* (the Abode of Islam) by demonstrating their integration into the new social and cultural context of their Muslim compatriots. They now had to gain legal recognition and acceptance from the Muslim caliph, as well as to build intellectual and religious bridges with their Muslim surroundings.[737]

---

734 S. Griffith, "Muslims and Church Councils. On this setting, see also the essays in *After Chalcedon: Studies in Theology and Church History*, ed. C. Laga; J. A. Munitiz and L. Van Rompay (Leuven: Peeters, 1985). On the development of the Monophysite-Dyaphesite controversies and divisions in 7th-century Byzantium, see Haldon, *Byzantium in the Seventh Century*, pp. 297–323.

735 See Sidney Griffith's subtle analysis in "The First Christian *Summa Theologiae* in Arabic," pp. 24–25 ff.

736 Griffith, "Muslims and Church Councils," pp. 284, 294. See also Hugh Kennedy, "The Melkite Church from the Islamic Conquest to the Crusades: Continuity and Adoption in the Byzantine Legacy," in *The 17th International Byzantine Congress, Major Papers*, Group of eds., (New Rochelle, NY: Aristide D Caratzas, 1986), 325–343.

737 One of the costly and inappropriate prices the Christians had sometimes to pay for gaining this acceptance was adapting their Christian belief and compromising its content to please the

Among the oriental patriarchates, it was the Melkites of Palestine, despite their staunchly Chalcedonian theological allegiance, who eventually started to demonstrate in the positions they took in public a clear indifference to whether their Christological views concurred with the imperial Christology of Constantinople. They did so, first, because they stopped being informed about theological developments and changes in ecclesial circles in the Byzantine capital, but also, second, because they really had begun to part company with imperial theological position, which remained Monothelite until 680 CE[738] This segregation from Byzantium can be detected in the Syrian-Palestinian Melkites' acknowledgement of only six ecumenical councils and lack of interest in, or even knowledge about, any Christological or theological views beyond the third Council of Constantinople (the sixth ecumenical council) in 680 – 681 CE[739]

In the light of this disconnection with the Byzantine world, and far from being caught up in Byzantium's preoccupation with iconoclasm and icons theology during the 8th–9th centuries, Abū Qurrah and his fellow Melkites of Syria-Palestine found themselves fully engaged with defending Chalcedonian Christology to the followers of Monothelitism and Monoenergism[740] (both rejected at Constantinople in 680 – 681 CE) within the territories of the Islamic caliphate. This is why Abū Qurrah, as Sidney Griffith notes, writes "to rebut any objection to the rejection of the teaching of the sixth council," showing thereby that, because of their rejection of that council's teaching, the Arabic-speaking Monophysites were not following Christian orthodox Christology.[741] It is also the reason

Muslims. The author of a 9th-century Melkite text known as the *Summa Theologiae Arabica* (British Library Or. Ms. 4950), attacks these Christians, calling them 'waverers' (*mudhabdhabīn*). See Griffith, "The First Christian *Summa Theologiae* in Arabic," pp. 16 – 24.

738 Griffith, "Muslims and Church Councils," p. 284.

739 On this council, see Davis, *The First Seven Ecumenical Councils*, pp. 258 – 287. In his presentation of that segregation between the oriental patriarchates, especially the Melkite patriarch of Jerusalem, and Constantinople, Sidney Griffith shows that one of the indicators of the separation is that Abū Qurrah, though he lived after the seventh ecumenical council (Nicaea II), in 787 CE, never shows any real knowledge of this council in his writings. His poor knowledge of Byzantine theological trends at the time also appears, Griffith argues, in his *Maymar fī Ikrām al-Aiqūnāt* (Maymar on the veneration of icons). Though the veneration of icons was the main theme of Nicaea II, Abū Qurrah's ideas and views are actually derived from John of Damascus' writings, and attempt to meet the iconoclastic challenges of the Muslims, not of the iconoclasts of Constantinople: Griffith, "Muslims and Church Councils," pp. 282 – 285, 293 – 296.

740 Griffith, "Muslims and Church Councils," p. 295.

741 Ibid., p. 293. On the historical and theological development of the Monophysite discourse, see also W. H.C. Frend, *The Rise of the Monophysite Movement: Chapters in the History of the Church in the Fifth and Sixth Centuries* (Cambridge: Cambridge University Press, 1972); and

why Abū Qurrah wrote his Christological texts in Arabic, rather than in Syriac (which he used to write thirty complete maymars against the Jacobites and Nestorians)[742] or even in Greek.[743] Abū Qurrah develops his Christological defences with a profound awareness of, and deliberate affiliation to, the Islamic-Arabic intellectual and social milieu, into which he and the Monophysites and Nestorians of the Islamic Caliphate were fully integrated. He writes as an Arab-Chalcedonian *mutakallim*, not as a Byzantine imperial-patriarchal representative, and as one facing and debating in Arabic not only with Muslim interlocutors, but also with other 'local' Christian (Jacobite and Nestorian) *mutakallims* as well (as we gather from his controversy with the Jacobite Abū Rāʾiṭa, with whom Abū Qurrah communicated in Arabic on the subject of Christology).[744] His discourse does not, therefore, stand for Byzantine against Jacobite and Nestorian Christology, if 'Byzantine' is taken to carry political, cultural, linguistic, or even ecclesial connotations. Far from being typically 'Byzantine' or 'Greek,' Abū Qurrah's Christological discourse, as Griffith convincingly conjectures, should be read "as anti-'Jacobite' and anti-'monothelete' in theology, Hellenophone and Arabophone in language," and written by a Christian existing in "the cultural world of the commonwealth of Islam" and identifying with its cultural and intellectual context.[745] He wrote an Arabic Christology that was primar-

Iain R. Torrance, *Christology after Chalcedon: Severus of Antioch and Sergius the Monophysite* (Eugene, OR: Wipf and Stock Publishers, 1998).

742 Abū Qurrah, *Maymar fī Mawt al-Masīḥ* (Maymar on the death of Christ), pp. 60 – 61; Griffith, "From Aramaic to Arabic," p. 20; Griffith, "'Melkites', 'Jacobites' and the Christological Controversies" p. 48.

743 Sidney Griffith even claims that Greek was the most dominant language in Christological controversies at the beginning of the 6th century: "In the first two decades of the sixth century in Syria/Palestine the christological controversies, as they engaged Sabas and the monks of Judean desert and elsewhere, were largely conducted in Greek on all sides": Griffith, "From Aramaic to Arabic," p. 13.

744 Mark Beaumont notes this, commenting: "Indeed Arabic was a necessity not just for communication with Muslims but also between Melkites and Jacobites, since it was in Arabic that Abū Rāʾiṭa argued with Abū Qurrah in his *Replay to the Melkites on the Union* (*of Divine and Human in Christ*)": M. Beaumont, *Christology in Dialogue with Muslims*, p. 45.

745 Griffith, "'Melkites', 'Jacobites' and the Christological Controversies" p. 12. Griffith argues that one should not understand the nomenclature 'Melkites' as simply meaning the followers of Chalcedonian theology, who "remained in communion with the imperial see of Constantinople as 'Emperors' men'": ibid., p. 11, referring to that understanding in *The Oxford Dictionary of the Christian Church*, ed. F. L. Cross and E. A. Livingstone 3rd ed. (Oxford: Oxford University Press, 2005), p. 1067. Griffith considers this understanding of 'Melkite' a modern 'byzantinizing' attempt that is "at once anachronistic, incomplete and, sociologically speaking, inaccurate": Griffith, "'Melkites', 'Jacobites' and the Christological Controversies" pp. 11–18, esp. p. 11. On rela-

ily formulated to respond to the Christology of the followers of the Qur'an, who had prviously been grappling with the non-Chalcedonian Christologies of the Nestorians and the Jacobites.[746]

In the ensuing sections of this chapter, I shall restrict my study of Abū Qurrah's Christology to his discourse on Jesus Christ in response to, and debate with, Muslim charges against Christian (particularly Melkite) orthodox teaching. That is, I leave aside his statements and arguments related to intra-Christian controversies with the Nestorians and the Jacobites. One can deal with these Christological elements in his works from different perspectives and by the help of various methodologies. It is far beyond the scope of this study to cover all Abū Qurrah's Christological proposals, or to do so using more than one analytical method. So, I shall be tackling his answers to Muslims as follows: I shall, first, analyze his interpretations of Jesus as 'Word and Spirit,' Jesus as '*walad*' or '*ibn*,' Jesus as a divine being and Jesus as the incarnate *Logos*. Second, I shall trace the elements that prove Abū Qurrah's allegiance to doctrinal orthodoxy and those, if there be any, that might indicate a compromise of that orthodoxy and a deviation from that tradition with the aim of making the Christian faith more able to be clearly understood in Arabic and rationally defensible before Islam.

II. On Jesus as Kalimat Allāh' and Rūḥ Minhu

A. On Using the Terms 'God's Word' and 'Spirit' in Christian and Muslim *Kalām*

يا أهل الكتاب لا تغلوا في دينكم ولا تقولوا على الله إلا الحق إنما المسيح عيسى ابن مريم رسول الله وكلمته ألقاها إلى مريم وروح منه فآمنوا بالله ورسله ولا تقولوا ثلاثة انتهوا خيرا لكم إنما الله إله واحد سبحانه أن يكون له ولد له ما في السماوات وما في الارض وكفى بالله وكيلا

---

tions between Jerusalem and Constantinople during the 8th and 9th centuries, see also S. Griffith, "What Has Constantinople to Do with Jerusalem? Palestine in the Ninth Century: Byzantine Orthodoxy in the World of Islam," in *Byzantium in the Ninth Century: Dead or Alive?* Ed. Leslie Brubaker (Aldershot: Variorum, 1998), 181–194.

746 Griffith, "Muslims and Church Councils," p. 295: "In Abū Qurrah's instance, this effect is particularly noticeable in that, while he argued against Nestorians and Jacobites, as well as the Muslims, the Jacobites were the special target of his polemics, because, in Abū Qurrah's view, their doctrinal formulae played directly into the hands of the Muslim polemicists." See also Griffith, "'Melkites', 'Jacobites' and the Christological Controversies;" Keating, "Ḥabīb ibn Khidma Abū Rā'iṭa; D. Thomas, "Early Muslim Responses to Christianity;" Griffith, "The Church of Jerusalem and the 'Melkites,'" pp. 173–202.

> O People of the Book, do not exaggerate in your religion nor say about God except the truth. The Messiah, Jesus son of Mary, is a messenger of God, and his Word which he delivered to Mary, and a Spirit from him. So believe in God and his messengers, and say not "Three." Cease, better for you. God is only one god. Glorious is he to have a child, his is all that is in the heavens and in the earth. And God is sufficient as defender.[747]

To both the Muslim and the Christian *mutkallims* of the 8th – 9th centuries CE, if not to those of the later centuries too, this Qur'anic attestation of Jesus as both 'God's Word' and 'a Spirit from him' was foundational. It is prominantly used in both Christian discourses on the biblical and theological view of Jesus Christ and Muslim counter-discourses on the Qur'anic understanding of the prophet called ʿĪsā ibn Maryam. However, when speaking of Jesus as the Word and Spirit of God, the two sides clearly did not mean the same thing. The Christian *mutakallims* would use the phrase to argue from within the Islamic scripture for the divinity and pre-existence of Jesus, while the Muslim *mutkallims* would use the same Qur'anic manner to refute that same divinity.

Within Islamic *kalām*, references to Jesus as 'a Spirit of/from God' (*rūḥ Allāh/ rūḥ minhu*) are prominent in relation to Jesus' birth from Maryam the daughter of ʿImrān. In Q 19:17–22, we read that God sent his Spirit, who took the form of a perfect human, to Maryam in order to bestow upon her a Son, who was going to be sinless, full of abundant goodness and righteousness and pure by nature (*ghulām zakī*). In addition, in other verses, such as Q 21:91 and 66:12, God declares that he blew his Spirit into Maryam, thus making her and her son a sign (*'āya*) to the worlds. It is noticeable that, in these verses, the term 'Spirit' is not used to name Jesus in person, but to designate a godly messenger to Jesus' mother and to represent a godly instrument in her impregnation.[748] By arguing thus, the term 'Spirit' is used to deny Jesus' divine sonship, rather than to declare it, as is the case in the Gospel narrative. Associating Jesus with God's Spirit in the Qur'an, as Harry Wolfson persuasively conjectures, is rather intended to show that "the birth of Jesus, like the creation of Adam, was effected by

747 Q 4:171.

748 Wolfson, *The Philosophy of the Kalām*, pp. 306–307. Wolfson points here to a noticeable similarity with the Lukan narrative in the New Testament (Luke 1:26–28, 31), where the angel Gabriel is the messenger of God, who carries His Spirit. Wolfson believes that this biblical image of an angelic messenger inspired the Qur'ānic association of both God's روح (*rūḥ*/spirit) and God's رسول (*rasūl*/messenger) with an angel sent from God, as one sees in Q 11:72,79,83; 7:11; 6:9; 15:29; 38:72; 32:8. On the similarity between the Gospel and the Qur'anic text on this point, see also Theodore Nöldeke, *Sketches from Eastern History*, trans. John S. Black (London: Adam & Charles Black, 1892; repr. Kessinger, 2007), p. 31.

God's breathing into the womb of Mary a life-giving soul, and thereby creating Jesus as a human being."[749]

On the other hand, the Qur'an first associates Jesus with God's Word when angels proclaim to Zacharias the birth of his son, John (Yaḥya), who will verify the coming of a 'Word' sent from God (Q 3:39).[750] Despite the unmissible similarity with what John's Gospel says about John the Baptist's bearing witness to God's Word (Jesus), in the Qur'an, Wolfson notes, "the 'Word' is taken to mean the word 'Be' (*kun*), by which God caused Jesus to be conceived and born without a human father."[751] It does not, that is, indicate that Jesus had any divine, pre-temporal existence.

So the term 'Word' in the Qur'an is not taken by Muslim exegetes and *mutakallims* to imply any sense of a pre-existent, divine Christ, as it does in the biblical witness. The early Christian *mutkallims* – as we see, for example, in Timothy I's debate with al-Mahdī and the fictional debate with a Saracen, claimed to be written by John of Damascus or Theodore Abū Qurrah – faced this stark difference between the Christian and the Muslim association of Jesus with the 'Word,' and had to offer a persuasive and plausible justification of the Christian construal of the use of 'Word' as indicating Jesus' pre-existence and divinity.

One of the interesting responses given by early Christian *mutkallims* to the Muslims on the Christian understanding of Jesus as God's eternal, divine Word is found in Timothy I's explanation to the Caliph al-Mahdī, that when they speak of two natures in Jesus, the divine and the human, Christians mean one divine which belongs to the Word, and the other one human, which is from Mary.[752] With this answer, Timothy tried to demonstrate that Christians concur with the Qur'anic association of the 'Word' with God himself, in that they consider 'the divinity of Jesus' as expressing this godly Word, which the Qur'an says ʿĪsā is. Recognizing this, some Muslim *mutakallims* did find in the Christians' association of God's pre-existent, eternal Word with the Messiah a plausible way of explaining the relation of God to his Word in Islam. As an example, Wolfson points to the views of two Muʿtazilite scholars on God and his Word: Ibn Ḥāʾiṭ and al-Ḥadathī, who were the disciples of Abū Isḥaq ibn Sayyār ibn

749 Wolfson, *The Philosophy of the Kalām*, p. 308.

750 Ibid., p. 308. Wolfson traces in this Qur'anic story biblical elements found in the Gospels of Luke (1:26–31) and John (1:7).

751 Ibid., p. 309.

752 Mingana, "Woodbrooke Studies: Patriarch Timothy I and the Caliph Mahdi," in *The Early Christian-Muslim Dialogue*, pp. 176–177; M. Heimgartner, *Timotheos I., Ostsyrischer Patriarch: Disputation Mit dem Kalifen al-Mahdī*, pp. 6–7; and H. Wolfson, *The Philosphy of the Kalām*, p. 312.

Māniʿ al-Naẓẓām. These two Muʿtazilites, Wolfson demonstrates, believed that the world had two creators, God and 'the Word of God,' and that the latter is none other than the Messiah Jesus, Son of Mary. So, for these Muslim *mutkallims*, though Jesus is originated (*ḥādith*/*muḥdath*) by the eternal (*qadīm*) God, he still enjoys a co-eternal status like God.[753] Moreover, Wolfson further notes that Ibn Ḥā'iṭ and al-Ḥadathī also believed that "the [pre-existent] Christ clad himself with bodily flesh and He is the eternal Word who was made flesh, as the Christians say."[754]

It must be pointed out here that this incorporation of some Christian theological elements into the Islamic interpretation of the expression 'Word of God' has never been formally recognized in orthodox Islam, whether Sunni or Shiʿi. From the beginning, official Islamic teaching has strictly rejected the Christian version of the association of Jesus with the Word of God, and any assertion that it constitutes evidence of the divine, pre-existence of the Son of Mary. That said, official Islamic doctrine still holds fast to the Qur'anic reference to ʿĪsā ibn Maryam as the 'Word of God and a Spirit from him.' Many Muslim authors during the first five or six centuries of Islam followed the Qurʾan in calling Jesus either 'Word of God' or 'Spirit from him,' but all argued vehemently that being called 'God's Word' does not make Jesus divine or pre-existent. It rather aims at revealing that Jesus was righteous, sinless (ذكي/*zakī*)[755] and close to and appreciated by God. The Muslim *mutakallims* admit that this undoubtedly makes Jesus a special creature in the eyes of God, but it also maintains Jesus' humanness and affirms that, like Adam, Jesus was created by God from soil (*turāb*) (Q 3:59). In his description of the Islamic and Qur'anic discourse on Jesus Christ as the Word and Spirit of God, the contemporary Islamic scholar Mahmoud Ayoub summarizes the Islamic view thus: "The Qur'ān presents a Christology of the human Christ,

753 Wolfson, *The Philosphy of the Kalām*, p. 316.

754 Ibid., p. 317.

755 With regard to Jesus' sinlessness, Mahmoud Ayoub points to an early Ḥadith, in which the prophet Muḥammad states: "Every child born of the children of Adam Satan touched with his finger, except Mary and her Son, peace be upon them both": M. Ayoub, *A Muslim View of Christianity: Essays on Dialogue*, ed. Irfan A. Omar (Maryknoll, NY: Orbis Books, 2007), p. 58; citing this Ḥadith from Aḥmad Ibn Ḥanbal, *Musnad*, ed. Aḥmad M. Shākir (Cairo: Dār al-Maʿārif, 1955), Vol. 15, ḥad. 7902ff, and from Muslim b. al-Ḥajjāj al-Qushayrī, *Ṣaḥīḥ Muslim*, ed. Muḥammad F. ʿAbd al-Bāqī (Cairo: Dār Iḥyāʾ al-Kutub al-ʿArabiyya, 1955), Vol. 4, ḥad. 141–149. In Arabic, the text of this ḥadīth comes as follows:

قال النبي: كل بني آدم يطعن الشيطان في جنبيه بإصبعه حين يولد غير عيسى ابن مريم ذهب يطعن فطعن الحجاب

the Prophet said" every son of Adam Satan pierces with his [Satan's] finger in his [the son] two sides when he [the son] is born except ʿĪsā b. Maryam, [Satan] went to pierce and he [Satan] pierced the vailing curtain instead.

empowered by God and 'fortified with the Spirit' (Q 2:87; 253). It is a fully Islamic Christology based not on borrowed distortions of early Christian heresies, but on the Islamic view of man and God ... Islam differed from Christianity [in that] it denied the divinity of Christ, but without denying his special humanity."[756] That is, Muslims differ from Christians not only in their reading of Christ's identity but also in their reading of the Qur'anic association of Jesus with God's Word and Spirit.

The Lebanese Islamicist, Tarif Khalidi, presents the Islamic understanding of Jesus as recorded in a variety of extra-Qur'anic literature from the 7th to the 16th centuries. He surmises that, though Jesus is depicted after a "general typological framework of prophecy," the prophet of the Christians is equally singled out from the rest of the acknowledged prophets and is granted particular esteem in Islam. Khalidi locates this particular esteem in two specific epithets given to him by the Qur'an: a 'Word' and a 'Spirit' from God.[757] Fully persuaded that they denote Jesus' special place of honour on the prophetic stage, rather than being merely rhetorical expressions, Khalidi cites Ḥadīth and other intellectual, theological and philosophical texts where Jesus is called consistently either 'God's Word' or 'Spirit from God,' ultimately suggesting that these expressions are extra-Qur'anic evidence of Jesus in Islam (or, as he puts it, in the 'Islamic Gospel').

In the 303 passages quoted in Khalidi's collection,[758] Jesus is called the 'Spirit of God' 20 times, 'Word of God' or 'Word from God' only twice,[759] and 'Word

756 Ayoub, *A Muslim View of Christianity*, pp. 158 – 159.

757 Tarif Khalidi (ed. & trans.), *The Muslim Jesus: Sayings and Stories in Islamic Literature* (Cambridge, MA: Harvard University Press, 2003), p. 11. See also T. Khalidi, "The Role of Jesus in Intra-Muslim Polemics of the First Two Islamic Centuries," in *Christian Arabic Apologetics during the Abbasid Period (750 – 1258)*, ed. Samir Khalil Samir and Jørgen S. Nielsen (Leiden: Brill, 1994), 146 – 156.

758 They are found in ʿAbdullah ibn al-Mubārak al-Marwazī, *Kitāb az-Zuhd war-Raqāʾiq* (The book of asceticism and the flakes), ed. Ḥabīb al-Raḥmān al-Aʿẓamī (Beirut: Dār al-Kutub al-'Ilmiyyah, 1962), pp. 77, 121, 225; Aḥmad Ibn Ḥanbal, *Kitāb az-Zuhd* (The book of asceticism), ed. Muḥammad Zaghlūl (Beirut: Dār al-Kitāb al-ʿArabī, 1988), p. 95; Abū ʿUthmān aj-Jāḥiẓ, *al-Bayān wat-Tabyyīn* (The declaration and the indication), ed. ʿAbd al-Salām Hārūn (Cairo: Maṭbaʿat Lajnat at-Taʾlīf wat-Tarjamah wan-Nashr, 1949), Vol. 3, p. 140; Abū Bakr ibn Abī ad-Dunyā, *Kitāb Dhamm ad-Dunyā* (The book of rebuking the world), in *Mawsūʿat Rasāʾil Ibn Abī ad-Dunyā* (The Encyclopedia of Ibn Abī ad-Dunyā's Epistles), ed. Muṣṭafā ʿAṭā (Beirut: Muʾassasat al-Kutub ath-Thaqāfiyyah, 1993), Vol. 2, pp. 128 – 129; Ibn Abī al-Dunyā, *Kitāb aṣ-Ṣamṭ wa-Ādāb al-Lisān* (The book of silence and the conversation's protocols) in *Mawsūʿat Rasāʾil Ibn Abī ad-Dunyā*, p. 392; Abū Ḥayyān at-Tawḥīdī, *al-Baṣāʾir wadh-Dhakhāʾir* (The sagacities and the supplications), ed. Ibrāhīm al-Kaylānī (Damascus: Maktabat Aṭlas, 1965 – 1977), Vol. 1, p. 21; at-Tawḥīdī, *Risālah fī aṣ-Ṣadāqah waṣ-Ṣadīq* (Istanbul: Maṭbaʿat al-Jawāʾib, 1301 AH), p. 64; Abū

and Spirit of/from God' only four times.[760] It is interesting, in the 303 texts quoted, Jesus is called 'the Spirit of God' (*rūḥ Allāh)* far more often than 'God's Word' (*kalimat Allāh*), and also more often than 'God's Word and Spirit.' This indicates the popularity of associating Jesus with the role of these heavenly agents who are sent by God to convey the divine message, which God conveys by means of his Word. This role is usually linked in Islamic thinking to God's angels and Spirit, so, rather than indicating any supernatural or divine status to Jesus, calling him 'the Spirit of God' points to his unique identity, but only as one who conveys the message of God to his creation. This messenger status is not only recognized by God or Jesus' followers. It is also Jesus' universal designation, as this prophet of God, the Son of Mary, is called God's Word or Spirit by all God's creatures, heavenly and earthly alike: angels (such as Gabriel and the fallen angel, Satan);[761] his mother, Mary;[762] his disciples;[763] Isaac (*Isḥaq*);[764] various other people;[765] animals, such as cows and snakes;[766] and even inanimate objects, such as city ruins or skulls.[767]

Khalidi's 303 texts demonstrate the significance of the phrase 'Word of God and Spirit from him' in the Islamic understanding of Jesus. The Muslim *mutakal-*

Nuʿaym al-Iṣbahānī, *Ḥiliyat al-Uliyā' wa Ṭabaqāt al-Aṣfiyā'* (The ornament of the patriarchs and the layers of the chosen) (Cairo: Maṭbaʿat al-Saʿādah, 1932–1938), Vol. 6, pp. 10–12; Abū Ḥāmid al-Ghazālī, *Īḥiyā' 'Ulūm ad-Dīn* (Reviving religious knowledge) (Cairo: Muṣṭafā al-Bābī al-Ḥalabī, 1939), Vol. 4, pp. 339, 411, 448; Ibn Abī Randaqa al-Ṭurṭushī, *Sirāj al-Mulūk* (The monarchs' lantern) ed. J. al-Bayātī (London: Riyāḍ al-Rayyis, 1990), pp. 76, 82; Abū al-Ḥusayn Warrām ibn Abī Firās, *Majmūʿat Warrām: Tanbīh al-Khawāṭir wa Nuzhat an-Nawāẓir* (Warrām's collection: The passion's cautioning and the sighting's cruise) ed. Muḥammad Akhund (Tehran: Dār al-Kutub al-Sulṭāniyyah), Vol. 1, p. 83; Muḥyī al-Dīn ibn ʿArabī, *al-Futūḥāt al-Makkiyyah* (The Meccan conquests) (Cairo: 1305 AH), Vol. 1, pp. 368–369; Kamāl ad-Dīn ad-Damīrī, *Ḥayāt al-Ḥayawān al-Kubrā* (The Grand Animal's Life) (Cairo: al-Maṭbaʿah al-Maymaniyyah, 1305 AH), Vol. 1, pp. 202–203, 252.

759 In ʿAbdullāh ibn Qutayba, *Kitāb 'Uyūn al-Akhbār* (The book of the fountains of chronicles) (Cairo: Dār al-Kitub al-Miṣriyyah, 1925–1930), Vol. 4, p. 123; Abū al-Ḥajjāj al-Balawī, *Kitā 'Alif Bā'* (The book of A and B), (Cairo: Jamʿiyyat al-Maʿārif, 1287 AH), Vol. 1, p. 406.

760 In Ibn al-Mubārak, *az-Zuhd*, p. 520; 'Abd al-Malik ibn Hishām, *Kitāb at-Tījān fī Mulūk Ḥimiyar* (The book of crowns on the kings of Ḥimyar), ed. F. Krenkow (Hyderabad: Dā'irat al-Maʿārif, 1928), p. 27, al-Aṣbahānī, *Ḥiliyat al-Uliyyā' wa Ṭabaqāt al-'Aṣfiyyā'*, Vol. 6, p. 314; al-Damīrī, *Ḥayāt al-Ḥayawān al-Kubrā* , Vol. 1, pp. 202–203.

761 Khalidi, *The Muslim Jesus*, pp. 53, 203.

762 Ibid., p. 197.

763 Ibid., pp. 57, 66, 115, 144, 147, 180, 199.

764 Ibid., pp. 206–208.

765 Ibid., pp. 61, 71, 96, 114–115, 123.

766 Ibid., pp. 108, 209–210.

767 Ibid., pp. 59, 154–157, 189–190.

lims of the 9th century continued to use this description and to employ it as an interpretation of who Jesus was against the Christian Christologies. In their defence of the divinity and pre-existence of Jesus as God's *logos*, the Christian *mutakallims* reveal their awareness of the significance of calling Jesus God's Word and Spirit in the Islamic discourse, in that, in their attempt to present the scriptural evidence for his divinity, they pointed out to their Muslim interlocutors that the Old Testament speaks about Jesus' divinity when it declares that God created the heaven by his Word and all the heavenly powers by his Spirit, or when it addresses God's Word as a praised and glorified true God. Ḥabīb b. Khidmah Abū Rā'iṭah, for example, said:

153. وإنَّ داوود قال في كتابه، بكلمة الله خُلقَت السماوات وبروحِ فِيه كل قواتها...
154. ثم أنه وصف في موضع آخر في كتابه تحقيقاً بأنَّ كلمة الله إلهٌ حق، حيث قال لكلمة الله: "أسبّح". أفكان داوود ممن يسبح لغير الله؟

153. And David said in his book, the heavens were created by the Word of God and all their powers by the Spirit of His mouth [*fīh*] ...
154. Then he described elsewhere in his book a verification that the Word of God is true God, as he addressed the Word of God with "I praise." Was David one of those who praised any else than God?[768]

Before Abū Rā'iṭah, the author of the Melkite text known as *On the Triunity of the One God* also uses the epithets Word and Spirit to point to the divinity of Jesus and his membership in the Trinity by showing that 1) the angels praise and glorify not only God, but also his Word and Spirit as one God and Lord, 2) that God created the heavens and the earth and whatever is in them by his Word, and gave life to the host of angels by the Holy Spirit.[769] This author also argues, moreover, that believing in the divine nature of God's Word is not only biblical, but also Qur'anic, since the Qur'an commands people to believe in God and his Word and Spirit,[770] and to view them as one God and one Lord.[771] Later in the text

768 Dakkāsh, III.3.S101.153–154 (p. 95).
769 Gibson, *An Arabic Version*, f.102b.20 (pp. 74–75).
"وأنت أللهم بكلمتك خلقت السماوات والأرض وما فيهما. وبروح القدس أحييت جنود الملايكة، فنحن نحمدك اللهم ونسبحك ونمجدك بكلمتك الخالقة وبروحك المقدس المحيي."
"And you, O God, by your Word created the heavens and the earth and whatever is therein. And by the Holy Spirit [you] gave life to the host of angels, so we praise you, O God, and glorify you by your creating Word and life-giving Holy Spirit."
770 Ibid., f. 104b.15–20 (p. 77).
"وتجدونه في القرآن...وقال آمنوا بالله وكلمته وأيضاً في روح القدس..."
"And you find it in the Qur'ān...and it said believe in God and His Word and also in a Holy Spirit ..."

of *fī Tathlī Allah al-Wāḥid*, the author hints, like Abū Rā'iṭah, at David to prove the divinity of the Word. He says:

> ولا تقول أنا نؤمن بإلاهين أو نقول ربين: معاذ الله...ولكن الله أوحى إلى عبده ونبيه داوود وبيّن له أنَّ المسيح كلمة الله ونوره إذ طلع للناس برحمته: فإنه إله من الله، وإن كان لبس جسد. فمن أطاعه فقد أطاع الله، ومن عصاه فالله جاعله تحت قدميه ليعلم الناس أنَّ الله ومسيحه في عرش وكرامة واحدة، وليس شيء من الله بعضه دون بعض
>
> And do not say that we believe in two Gods or we speak of two Lords: God forbid ... But, God inspired his servant and prophet David and made it clear to him that the Christ is God's Word and light, who appeared to people by his [God's] mercy. He [Christ] is a divine [*ilāh*] from God [*Allāh*], even if he [Christ] wore flesh. And whoever obeyed him obeyed God, and whoever disobeys him God will place him under his [Christ's] feet, so that people will know that God and his Christ are on one throne and [share] one dignity: nothing in God belongs to one and not the other.[772]

The author of *fī Tathlī Allah al-Wāḥid* and Abū Rā'iṭah are just two examples of how Christian *mutakallims* used the Qur'anic reference to Jesus as God's Word and a Spirit from him to show their Muslim interlocutors that these Qur'anic epithets justify the Christian belief in Jesus' divinity, divine sonship and pre-existence. It is this use of the Qur'anic text, which Muslims considered a deliberate twisting of Qur'anic teaching, that the early Muslim *mutakallims* of the 9th century onwards totally rejected, as we see, for instance, in the writings of the Mu'tazilite, aj-Jāḥiẓ.

In his refutation of Christianity, Abū 'Uthmān ibn Baḥr aj-Jāḥiẓ first rejects the Christian belief in the divine sonship of Jesus and then argues that it cannot be defended (as some of his Christian contemporaries did) by referring to the Qur'an's calling Jesus 'Spirit of God.' This name, aj-Jāḥiẓ affirms, is not an ontological description of Jesus' being but rather an expression of the characteristic and condition of his function, which distinguishes his prophetic role, not his nature as a being, from the roles of other prophetic messengers.

> فإن قال قائل: فكيف لم يقدموه على جميع الأنبياء إذا كان الله قدّمه بهذا الاسم ["روح الله] الذي ليس لأحد مثله؟...
> قلنا: إنَّ هذا الاسم اشتُقَّ له من عمله وحاله وصفته...
>
> So, if someone said: how did not they place him ahead of all the prophets if God, by means of this name [i.e., 'Spirit of God'], which no one else holds, gave him precedence ... .

771 Ibid., f. 104b.20 (pp. 77–78).
"وأنتم تجدونه في القرآن أنَّ الله وكلمته وروحه إله واحد ورب واحد. وقد أُمِرتُم أن تؤمنوا بالله وكلمته وروح القدس..."
"and you find it in the Qur'ān, that God and His Word and Spirit are one God and one Lord. And you are commanded to believe in God and His Word and a Holy Spirit ..."
772 Ibid., f. 115b.5–10 (p. 88).

> We said: This name was derived for him from his work, condition, and attribute ... .[773]

In order to pre-empt any Christian exploitation of calling Jesus 'Spirit of God' to prove his divinity or divine sonship, aj-Jāḥiẓ immediately stipulates that Jesus is called 'Spirit of God' in the Qur'an strictly because of his unusual, un-natural *birth*, and not because of his unnatural nature: God created in the womb of Mary, his mother, soul (*rūḥ*) and flesh (*jasad*) without human intercourse.[774] The core argument aj-Jāḥiẓ presents here is that the Qur'anic witness to Jesus as God's Word and Spirit is an authentic, reliable definition of Jesus' prophetic identity because it is an attestation from the one and only true religious text. At the same time, aj-Jāḥiẓ emphasizes, the Qur'anic naming of Jesus 'God's Word and Spirit' must not be used by Christians as evidence from within Islam of Jesus' divine sonship. In the Islamic discourse, aj-Jāḥiẓ reminds his interlocutors, the angel Gabriel is also called by God 'his Spirit' and 'a Holy Spirit.' So, if this name means divine sonship, we should consider not only Jesus but also Gabriel to be God's son, which is not Islamic at all. Aj-Jāḥiẓ concludes:

> ولو كنا إذا قلنا: "عيسى روح الله وكلمته"...وجب علينا في لغتنا أن يجعله الله ولداً ونجعله – مع الله تعالى – إلهاً...
> فكنا إذا قلنا: إنَّ الله سمى جبريل روح الله وروح القدس، وجب علينا أن نقول فيه ما يقولون في عيسى، وقد علمتم أنَّ ذلك ليس من ديننا ولا يجوز ذلك، بوجه من الوجوه، عندنا فكيف نظهر للناس قولاً لا نقوله وديناً لا نرتضيه؟
>
> And if we said: "'Īsā, God's Spirit and His Word" ... we must in our language assume that God makes him son and we – along with the supreme God – make him a god ...
> So, if we said that God called Gabriel "God's Spirit" and '"Holy Spirit," we must then say of him [i.e., Gabriel] what they [i.e., the Christians] say of 'Īsā, and you already know that this is not of our religion, and it is by no means permissible to us, for how would we disclose to people a saying we do not say and a religion we do not accept ...[775]

B. Abū Qurrah's Use of 'God's Word' and 'Spirit' in *al-Mujādalah* and Other Maymars

How does Abū Qurrah treat the Qur'anic expression, 'God's Word and Spirit,' in his Christological discussions with Muslims? What are the characteristics of the

---

773 Aj-Jāḥiẓ, *al-Mukhtār fī ar-Radd 'alā an-Naṣārā* (The Selected in responding to the Nazarenes), p. 81.
774 Ibid., p. 82.
"وخلق من رحم مريم روحاً وجسداً على غير مجرى العادة وما عليه المناكحة، فلهذه الخاصة قيل له "روح الله"."
"And He [i.e. God] created in Maryam's womb soul and flesh not through the usual process and the act of intercourse; for this specific reason, he [Jesus/'Īsā] is called 'God's Spirit'."
775 Ibid., p. 87.

approach he takes in his attempt to present Jesus the Messiah as the Word and Spirit of God, and does he step into a new hermeneutic circle and develop a different rationale in his understanding of Jesus as the Word and Spirit of God, or does he merely take what other Christian *mutakallims* have presented as an interpretation of these epithets to its natural conclusion?

When we read through the maymars of Abū Qurrah that have survived, it is easy to see that he does not often refer to the Messiah as 'God's Word' or as 'the Word,' and he hardly uses this epithet in any substantial Christological apology in his encounter with Muslims. Rather, what he generally does is to mention this epithet occasionally as merely one of Jesus' titles. He does this in his *Maymar fī Ikrām al-Aiqūnāt* (Maymar on the veneration of icons),[776] and his *Maymar Yuḥaqqiq 'anna li-Allah 'Ibnan hūa 'Adluh fī aj-Jawhar wa-lam Yazal Ma'ah* (Maymar affirming that God has a Son who is equal to him in essence and is still with him [God]).[777] Opposite to this occasional rarity, in his text *Risālah fī Ījābat Mas'ālah Katabaha Abū Qurrah al-Qiddīs ilā Ṣadīq lah kana Ya'qūbiyyan fa-Ṣāra Urthūdhuksiyyan 'inda Raddih 'alayh aj-Jawāb* (An epistle in response to a matter, written by the holy Abū Qurrah to a friend of his, who was Jacobite and became Orthodox, as he responds to him with the answer), Abū Qurrah calls the Messiah 'the Word' and 'the Godly Word' almost throughout the text and in a clear Christological sense,[778] But here Abū Qurrah is not in dialogue with a Muslim interlocutor. He is rather explaining the orthodox understanding of Jesus the Christ to a Christian friend. In other words, 'God's Word' is here used in Christological hermeneutics in a Christian-Christian interaction, so the significations and connotations of the term 'Word' here are all doctrinal and patristic, and not Qur'anic.

776 Abū Qurrah, *Maymar fī Ikrām al-Aiqūnāt* (Maymar on the veneration of icons), III.15.11, 15, 22, where Abū Qurrah speaks of the Messiah as *kalimat Allāh al-azaliyyah* (the eternal Word of God) and as *kalimat Allāh al-mutajassid* (the incarnate Word of God).

777 Abū Qurrah, *Maymar Yuḥaqqiq anna li-Allāh Ibnan hūa 'Adluh fī aj-Jawhar wa-lam Yazal Ma'ahu* (Maymar affirming that God has a Son who is equal to Him in essence and is still with Him [God]), p. 103, where Abū Qurrah refers once to the Messiah as being called in 'the Word' (in Jn 1), and that this Word, by means of whom God created everything, is called by the Apostle Paul 'Son' and also 'God's means for making the ages.'

778 *Risālah fī Ījābat Mas'ālah Katabaha Abū Qurrah al-Qiddīs ilā Ṣadīq lah kana Ya'qūbiyyan fa-Ṣāra Urthūdhuksiyyan 'inda Raddih 'alayh aj-Jawāb* (An epistle in response to a matter, written by the holy Abū Qurrah to a friend of his, who was Jacobite and became Orthodox, as he responds to him with the answer), in *Mayāmir Thā'ūdūrus Abī Qurrah* (The maymars of Theodore Abū Qurrah), ed. Constantine Bacha, pp. 104–141.

One noteworthy use of 'God's Word' in Theodore's maymars is in his *Maymar on the Trinity*, where he points to John's calling the Messiah 'God's Word' and endeavors to elaborate on this title in a Trinitarian context:

> ولذلك سمى مار بولس الابن ضوء مجد الآب...وسمّاه أيضاً حكمة الله وقوته...ويوحنا المبشّر قد سماه كلمة...وإنما سماه قوّالا الإلهيات هذان بهذه الأسماء لا لأنه ليس بأقنوم وإله تام، ولكن ليعلما الناس أنه كما لا يقال كل واحد من هذه الأشياء المضافة التي ذكرنا أنه والمضاف إليه يعملان شيئاً، وإن كان كل واحد منهما يقال أنه يعمل على حدته، كذلك لا يقال الآب والابن أنهما خلقا، وإن كان كل واحدٍ منهما على حدته يقال أنه خلق
>
> Therefore, St Paul named the Son the light of the glory of the Father ... and named him also God's wisdom and power ... and John the evangelist named him Word ... [T]hese two theologians name him with these names not because he is neither *uqnūm* nor perfect god, but to inform people that, just as it is not said that each of the added things and the entity they are added to do something [as if they were two], although we say that each of them acts on its own, also it is not said that the Father and the Son created, although each one of them is said to have created alone.[779]

In this paragraph, Abū Qurrah clearly uses the notion of 'God's Word' to emphasize that God remains strictly one despite, if not by virtue of, his triunity. Speaking about the second *uqnūm* exclusively as 'Word' serves in Abū Qurrah's mind the purpose of emphasizing this oneness. By 'the added thing and the entity they are added to it,' Abū Qurrah is referring actually to the human flesh,[780] its relation to its organs and what the flesh creates through these organs' abilities, which are those of the flesh. This allegorical reference to the human flesh to defend the oneness of God despite his triunity is Abū Qurrah's way of showing his Muslim audience that, just as the mind and its words are one and the same in essence, since the words are expressive of the mind that originated them, so is Christ (the second *uqnūm*) to the Father (the first *uqnūm*) who begot him, since Christ is the Word of the divine intellect.

'Word' here, although serves the primary purpose of defending God's oneness-in-triunity, also points to the organic equality and unity between God

---

779 Abū Qurrah, *Maymar fī ath-Thālūth* (Maymar on the Trinity), p. 39.

780 Ibid., pp. 27–28
وتقول لصاحبك عينك أبصرتني وأنت محقّ. وتقول له أنت أبصرتني وأنت محق. ولا يستقيم أن تقول لصاحبك أنك وعينك أبصرتماني لأنَّ صاحبك إنما يبصرك بعينه. وتقول للنجار يدك صنعت هذا الباب وأنت محق. وتقول له أنت صنعت هذا الباب وأنت صادق. ولا يستقيم أن تقول للنجار أنت ويدك صنعتما الباب لأنَّ النجار إنما يصنع الباب بيده
And you say to your companion 'your eye has seen me', and you are correct. And you say to him 'you have seen me' and you are correct. And it is not right to say to your companion 'you and your eye have seen me', for your companion sees you with his eye. And you say to the carpenter 'your hand has made this door' and you are correct. And you say to him 'you have made this door' and you are speaking the truth. And it is not right to say to the carpenter 'you and your hand have made this door', for the carpenter makes the door with his hand.

and the Messiah, in that this equally creator-divine Word is not another God *beside* God, but the Word of this same one and only true God. This is why, Abū Qurrah concludes, John the Evangelist not only calls the Messiah 'Word,' but also calls him 'God,' for only when the Messiah is both 'God's Word' and 'as divine as God,' can the Creator of creation remain one, and not become either two separate deities, or a deity and an additional creaturely entity.

> فليعلم أنَّ هذا القول الذي ذكرنا أنه في الكتب المقدسة وما شاكله لم يوضَع في الكتب إلا من حرص قوالي الإلهيات أن يعلّموا الناس أنَّ الابن إله تام والروح إله تام لكيلا يظنوا أنَّ الابن والروح في الله بمثل هذه الأشياء المضافة فيما يضاف إليه فيضلون من غلظ قلوبهم.
>
> So, let it be known that this saying, which we have noted that it is in the holy scriptures, and its like was only placed in the scriptures except because of the theologians' concern to teach the people that the Son is perfect God and the Spirit is perfect God, so that they [people] would not assume that the Son and the Spirit are in God in the same way as these additional things are in what they are added to, and be deluded because of the coarseness of their hearts.[781]

So, just as the human and 'his word and spirit' are one entity, God, his Word and Spirit are one and the same deity.[782] Abū Qurrah's use of 'God's Word and Spirit' has inescapable implications for the identity of Jesus the Messiah and his divine nature. These implications notwithstanding, the focus in this maymar is deliberately dominantly Trinitarian, rather than Christological, so one should not construe what this maymar says about the Messiah as 'Word' as an example of how Abū Qurrah argued with Muslims on Christology. He is not here explaining the Christological rationale for calling the Messiah 'God's Word,' but is showing what the title means within a Trinitarian and monotheistic discourse.

We now come to the text of Abū Qurrah's debate in al-Maʾmūn's court, where we find a totally different situation and a different apologetic strategy. Here, Abū Qurrah consistently uses the Qur'anic expression 'God's Word and Spirit' without reservation when he defends Christian Christology. In what follows, I shall make a careful analysis of the way he uses this expression and no other to show the

781 Ibid., p. 41.

782 Ibid., pp. 44–45.
ثم نقول لك إنَّ الله وكلمته وروحه إله واحد، كما أنَّ الإنسان وكلمته وروحه إنسان واحد...فليس يقال الله وكلمته وروحه إلا إلهاً واحداً، كما لا يقال الإنسان وكلمته وروحه إلا إنساناً واحداً.
then, we tell you that God, His Word and Spirit are one God, as the human, his word and spirit are one human being...so, it should not be said that God, His Word and Spirit are [anything] except one God, as it is not said that the human, his word and spirit are [anything] except one human being.

Muslims that their scripture supports the Christian belief in the divinity and pre-existence of Jesus Christ.

The text of the *Mujādalah* tells us that he does this first in responding to the questions of the Muslim interlocutor called Muḥammad ibn ʿAbdallāh al-Hāshimī. The text narrates that al-Hāshimī was intrigued when Abū Qurrah ended his initial conversation with the caliph as follows:

48. ولم نشك [أي النصارى] في أنه [أي السيد المسيح] إله إبراهيم وإسحاق ويعقوب
49. وأنه إله ابن إله، كلمة الله وروحه بغير افتراق بينهم.

48. And we [i.e., the Christians] do not doubt that he [i.e., the Lord Christ] is the God of Abraham, Isaac, and Jacob.
49. And that he is God, Son of God, God's Word and his Spirit, without separation between them.[783]

In other words, Abū Qurrah here is following other *mutakallims*, especially the Melkite author of *On the Triunity of the One God*, in using Qur'anic expressions to argue the case for the validity of Christian christological hermeneutics from within Islamic beliefs. The subtle and creative way in which Abū Qurrah points here to the divinity of God's Word and Spirit is interesting. In particular, he shows that belief in this divinity is supported not only by the Qur'anic reference to the prophet of the Nazarenes as God's Word and Spirit, but also, and more essentially, by the fact that the one who is called 'God's Word and Spirit' is the clear fulfillment of the Old Testament prophecies of the Messiah. Abū Qurrah here deliberately refers to the Messiah, rather than to Jesus (ʿĪsā), because he wants to say that the Christians based their belief in the divinity and divine sonship of Jesus on the Jewish Scripture's attestation to the 'Messiah' as the disclosure of the God of Abraham, Isaac and Jacob himself.

Despite this subtlety, Abū Qurrah inescapably invited a counter-attack from his Muslim audience when, at the end of his response to al-Maʾmūn, he juxtaposed the Old Testament reference to the Messiah with the Qur'anic 'God's Word and Spirit.' By doing this, Abū Qurrah seemed to the Muslims to be imposing inappropriate connotations on the Qur'anic text and twisting its words to prove what it does not actually say. This lay at the core of al-Hāshimī's aggressive reaction, when he rebuked Abū Qurrah:

51. ...ويحك يا أبا قرة، إنّ المسيح كلمة الله وروحه بعثها إلى مريم
52. ومثله عند الله كمثل آدم خلقه من ترابٍ ونفخ فيه من روحه.

783 Abū Qurrah, *Abū Qurrah wal-Ma'mūn: al-Mujādalah* (Abū Qurrah and al-Maʾmūn: The Debate), II.A.3.48–49 (p. 109).

51. Woe to you, Abū Qurrah, Christ is the Word and Spirit of God sent by him to Maryam,
52. and for God he is like Adam: He created him from soil and breathed into him his Spirit.[784]

Al-Hāshimī's reaction was harsh and offensive because he perceived Abū Qurrah's method and decided to oppose it directly by presenting the Qur'anic interpretation and rejecting Abū Qurrah's association of 'God's Word and Spirit' with Maryam, the mother of ʿĪsā. Why? Because al-Hāshimī wanted to tell Abū Qurrah that if he wanted to use the Qur'anic phrase to describe Jesus he would have to read it strictly within the framework of ʿĪsā's birth from a human virgin, that is, as a purely human child, and not reading it as scriptural evidence for Jesus' supra-human ontology. I have shown above that the same criticism was raised by aj-Jāḥiẓ in his refutation of Christian theology. Both aj-Jāḥiẓ and al-Hāshimī reflect a serious weariness with what they consider the exploitative misuse of the Qur'anic text by Christians.

No wonder Abū Qurrah reacted to al-Hāshimī's attack with a remarkably long pause, retreating into silence and pensive contemplation.[785] Abū Qurrah immediately realized that his theologically subtle, yet also rhetorical, presentation of the Jewish and Islamic religious texts was doomed to failure, and needed some minutes to think of an alternative explanation for the Christian belief in Jesus Christ, and his diplomatic skills and wit led him, predictably, to put on before the caliph the garment of an obedient, submissive prelate waiting for permission to speak from his political superior.[786]

In fact, Abū Qurrah was here gaining time to come up with another debating strategy to compensate the failure of his scriptural argument, realizing that he

784 Ibid., II. B.51–52 (p. 110).
785 Ibid., II. B.1.53 (p. 110).

53. فسكت أبو قرة طويلاً ولم يرد جواباً وأطرق إلى الأرض ملياً.

53. So Abū Qurrah remained for a long time silent and gave no answer and stared reflectively at the floor.

786 Ibid., II. B.1.54–55 (pp. 110–111).

54. فقال له المأمون: "لما لا تجيبه يا أبا قرة؟"
55. قال له: "حتى بأمرني أمير المؤمنين"

54. And al-Maʾmūn said to him: 'Why do not you respond to him, Abū Qurrah?'
55. He said to him: 'Till the prince of believers orders me [to do so].'
Notice here Abū Qurrah's diplomatic and rhetorical cunning in addressing the caliph as the 'prince of believers', which acknowledges the latter's leadership over everyone who believed in God in the caliphate, not only the Muslims, and in his use of the Word 'order', giving the caliph a clear impression of Abū Qurrah's personal submission and his reliance on the caliph's mercy. Predictably, the caliph was touched by this gesture, and responded to it courteously: ibid., II. B.1.56–61 (pp. 111–112).

needed to resort to reason and logic, rather than texts alone, and that he had to press on, rather than withdraw, in his argument from within the boundaries of the Qur'anic and Islamic rationale. This strategy of relying on reason and philosophy is expressive, as I demonstrated in chapter two of this study, of Abū Qurrah's hermeneutic methodology: reason is the first and ultimate judge of truth, and when textual arguments fail to convey the truth and substantiate it, rational and philosophical arguments should intervene to fulfil this task. This is exactly what Abū Qurrah's ensuing engagement with al-Hāshimī's rebuke reveals. Abū Qurrah knew that what the Qur'an said about Jesus' generation from Maryam, despite being 'God's Word and Spirit,' was the primary Muslim argument against any idea that ʿĪsā was any more than a mere human being like his mother. In other words, the fact of Jesus' birth from a human mother is the evidence that the prophet who is called 'God's Word and Spirit' is a human, finite being like any other messenger and prophet from God.

Abū Qurrah knew this Islamic conviction and perceived its echo in al-Hāshimī's counter-attack. He therefore decided to defend his use of the phrase 'God's Word and Spirit' to prove the divinity of the Messiah exclusively from the angle of the notion of createdness or human origination, and he said to al-Hāshimī

67. ...'أخبرني عن المسيح، من شيءٍ هو مخلوق أم لا؟' قال [الهاشمي]:'نعم، من كلمة الله وروحه'
68. قال أبو قرة: 'كلمة الله وروحه تُحَدّ وتُكيَّف وتوصَف؟' قال: 'لا، لا تُدرَك'
69. قال أبو قرة: 'أخبرني عن كلمة الله، خالقة هي أم مخلوقة؟'
70. فأطرق محمد بن عبدالله رأسه ساعةً صامتاً، ولم يتهيأ له أن يقول مخلوقة.
71. وكان مفكراً: إن قال خالقة فُيغلَب، وما يتهيأ له أن يقول مخلوقة.
72. فتطلع أبو قرة إلى المأمون وقال: 'شتان بين من تراه ومن لا تراه، يا أمير المؤمنين، ولا يُحَدّ ولا تدرك عظمته ولا يوصَف.
73. فابتهج المأمون لذلك وأعجبه

67. Abū Qurrah said: "Tell me about the Messiah: Is he created from something or not?" He [al-Hāshimī] said: "Yes, [He is created] from the Word of God and his Spirit."
68. Abū Qurrah said: "Can God's Word and Spirit be delimited, adjusted, or described?" He said: "No, it is beyond perception."
69. Abū Qurrah said: "Tell me about the Word of God: Is it creator or creature?"
70. Muḥammad ibn ʿAbdullāh bowed his head in silence for an hour, and he did not think of saying 'created.'
71. And he was thinking if he said [God's Word is] creator, he would be defeated, but he did not imagine himself saying 'created.'
72. Then, Abū Qurrah looked at al-Maʾmūn and said: "There is a great difference between one whom you see and one whom you do not, O prince of believers, and he is unlimited and indescribable and his greatness is incomprehensible."
73. And al-Maʾmūn was pleased with this and admired it.[787]

787 Ibid., II. B.3.67–73 (pp. 113–115). Note here the contrast in the text between Abū Qurrah's contemplative silence 'for a long time' in II. B.1.53, and al-Hāshimī's silence and confusion for a

Abū Qurrah's counter-argument is simple and concise, yet logically and dialogically, let alone Qur'anically, formidable. He takes al-Hāshimī up to the level of the relation of God's Word and Spirit to their owner, the divine, infinite, indescribable and unconditioned God himself. Abū Qurrah makes al-Hāshimī realizes that, if God is infinite, incomprehensible, indescribable and inudjustible, God's Word and Spirit must also be as divine, infinite, incomprehensible and inudjustible as their owner. Al-Hāshimī saw that he could not reject this argument, for attempting to reject it would trap him in the heretical polytheistic idea of division, leveling and splitting in the one, single being of God, which Islamic monotheism decisively rejects.[788] On the other hand, al-Hāshimī could anticipate the intellectual blow that would follow from Abū Qurrah if he said that God's Word and Spirit was a creator and not a creature (which would mean that God's Word and Spirit was as divine, infinite, indescribable and incomprehensible as God). He anticipated Abū Qurrah's response would be: if what belongs to God (that is, his Word and Spirit) must be divine as God per se, then what is originated from God's Word and Spirit must also carry its divine nature in its being. What the Qur'an says about the Messiah as God's Word and Spirit is therefore ground for the Christian belief that Jesus Christ, the son of Mary, is none other than God and Son of God. Jesus is so *because of*, not despite, his birth from Mary as God's Word and Spirit. To deny this is to reject none other than the witness of the Qur'an itself. Abū Qurrah goes even further by bluntly stating that if Muslims do not believe in God's Word and Spirit and that that title designates the divinity and creator status of Christ, they are not real Muslims and have not truly entered into faith.

'whole hour' in II. B.3.70. This is how the narrator of *al-Mujādalah* redeems Abū Qurrah and shows that, though al-Hāshimī was able to corner Abū Qurrah momentarily, the latter ultimately prevailed, leaving the former helpless and speechless. This framework of contrast and competition leads the scribe to interrupt the flow of the theological debate with an entire pericope (II.C.1.74–91 (pp. 116–120)), in which Abū Qurrah explains to his interlocutor and audience why Christians evade engagement with Muslims in debates on religious matters. Christians, Abū Qurrah argues, are not weak or incapable. They just cannot stand the Muslims' lack of commitment to the ethics of conversation with the non-Muslims, which the Qur'an commands them to follow.

788 In his reflection on this conversation in *al-Mujādalah*, Mark Beaumont tries to justify al-Hāshimī's confusion by suggesting that "it is highly unlikely that a Muslim would have made this admission in an actual debate, but the writing shows a level of confidence on the Christian side that is striking.": M. I. Beaumont, "Early Christian Interpretation of the Qur'ān," *Transformation*, 22 (4) (2005), 195–203, p. 199. However, Beaumont does not explain how he arrived at this conclusion or why is it unlikely that a Muslim would have answered as al-Hāshimī did.

.114 فلا تفتخر أيها المسلم بأنك لم تؤمن بكلمة الله وروحه الخالقة لكل شيء
.115 (ولعمري) إنه كذلك أنَّ كل من لا يؤمن بكلمة الله وروحه لم يدخل الإيمان

114. Do not, then, boast, O Muslim, that you did not believe in God's Word and Spirit that created everything.
115. (And I swear) that indeed it is the case, that whoever does not disbelieve in God's Word and Spirit has not entered into faith.[789]

If the Muslims want to truly abide with the Qur'an's teaching and their prophet's belief and commandments, Abū Qurrah declares, they must not oppose the Christians and treat them as enemies just because they believe that God's Word and Spirit is 'creator,' and neither 'created creature' nor 'owned slave,' as the Muslims do.[790] Accusing the Christians of *shirk* because they believe in, and follow, this 'Word and Spirit' sets the Muslims against their own prophet and Qur'an.[791]

A similar argument also forms the strategy in Abū Qurrah's debate with another Muslim interlocutor in the caliph's court, Ṣaʿṣaʿah ibn Khālid, which basically circles around the two natures of Jesus and how his divinity can be accommodated in the incarnation. At one point of their conversation, however, Abū Qurrah also reminds Ṣaʿṣaʿah that taking exception to Christians because of their belief that the Messiah is as divine as God's creating Word and Spirit is contrary to the Qurʿan and the prophet.

.244 قال أبو قرة: 'فتنكر أنَّ المسيح روح الله وكلمته؟' قال صعصعة: 'لا ما أنكر ذلك'.
.245 قال أبو قرة: 'فالله يتوعد بروحه وكلمته ويغضب على من اتبعه'.
.246 وكتابك يقول: إنَّ الله يحقق الحق بكلمته وروحه
.247 ويسمينا في موضع آخر المهتدين بالحق
.248 وأنت بعجبك تخالف ذلك وتسمينا مشركين

244. Abū Qurrah said: "Do you deny that the Messiah is God's Word and Spirit?" Ṣaʿṣaʿah said: "No, I do not deny it."

---

789 Abū Qurrah, *Abū Qurrah wal-Maʾmūn: al-Mujādala* (Abū Qurrah and al-Maʾmūn: The Debate), III. A.3.114–115 (p. 125).
790 Ibid., III. B.3.138–139 (p. 130).

.138 وتعادوننا لأنا لم نقل على كلمة الله وروحه الخالقتين
.139 إنهما خلق مخلوق وعبد مملوك كما تقولون أنتم

138. And you feud us because we did not call God's Word and Spirit the creators
139. and that they are created creature and owned slave, as you say.
791 Ibid., III. B.4.142–161 (pp. 131–161). Abū Qurrah refers here to verses from Q 3 and Q 7. On the general strategic use of Qur'anic verses and citations in Abū Qurrah's debate in the caliph's court, and also by other Christian *mutakallims* in their debates with Muslims, see S. Griffith, "The Qur'ān in Arab Christian Texts"; see also more general appraisals in M. Swanson, "Beyond Prooftexting"; and B. Roggema, "A Christian Reading of the Qur'ān."

245. Abū Qurrah said: "Would God promise His Word and Spirit and then become furious with those who follow Him [the Word and Spirit]?
246. And your book says that God fulfills the truth by his Word and Spirit,
247. and it calls us elsewhere 'those guided with truth,'
248. and you in your boasting contravene this and call us replacers [*mushrikīn*]."[792]

For Abū Qurrah, Christians and Muslims alike believe in 'God's Word and Spirit.' This is not sole property of the Muslims, which the Christians plagiarized from the Muslim Scripture and used in the service of their replacive faith. Christians and those Muslims who adhere to the true Qurʿanic teaching, Abū Qurrah argues, share a belief in God's Word and Spirit that is one in content and meaning, not only in form and words. With this, Abū Qurrah takes his audience full-circle, bringing them back to the Old Testamental witness from where he started at the beginning of his presentation before al-Maʾmūn. Believing in God's Word and Spirit, Abū Qurrah surmises, places on the shoulders of Christians and Muslims alike the obligation to accept the teaching of the prophecies of the Messiah that are found in the Torah and the Gospels.[793] Here, we see Abū Qurrah clearly following the explication style of the earlier Melkite, the author of *On the Triunity of the One God*, in a manner also similar to that of Abū Rāʾiṭah, in referring to David's words in the Old Testament, and speaking of God's Word as the creator of the heavens and earth and God's Spirit as the originator of all their powers.[794] The unique feature in Abū Qurrah's style, however, is his juxtaposition of quotations from Psalms and the Old Testament with similar texts in both the Gospel and the Qur'an

274. وقد قال داوود النبي: إنَّ بكلمة الله خلقت السماوات والأرض وبروح فيه جميع قواتها
275. والإنجيل المقدس يقول: في البدء كان الكلمة والكلمة كان عند الله والله هو الكلمة
276. وكتابك يقول: إن الله يريد تحقيق الحق بكلمته وروحه
277. وكلمة الله هي التي خلقت جميع الخلائق وروحه أحيت الملائكة والناس

274. And David the prophet said: "By God's Word the heavens and the earth were created and by the Spirit of his mouth all its powers."
275. And the Holy Gospel says: "In the beginning was the Word and the Word was with God *and God is the Word.*"
276. And your book says: "God wants to fulfill truth by his Word and Spirit,
277. and the Word of God is the creator of all creatures and his Spirit gave life to the angels and humankind."[795]

792 Abū Qurrah, *Abū Qurrah wal-Maʾmūn: al-Mujādalah* (Abū Qurrah and al-Maʾmūn: The Debate),VI. A.4.244–248 (p. 147).
793 Ibid., IV. A.6.267–285 (pp. 150–153).
794 Ibid., IV. A.6.274 (p. 151); and IV. B.2.298 (p. 156).
795 Ibid., IV. A.6.274–277 (pp. 151–152); and IV. B.2.293–303 (pp. 155–156).

Abū Qurrah's choice of John 1:1 to parallel the quotations from the Qur'an is carefully and effectively made, as is his translation of the verse into Arabic (see particularly the italicized phrase in the translation above)[796] – an admirably precise rendition of the Greek original. In the Arabic translation of the Bible known as the Van Dyke translation, which is still used today by the Arab Protestants in the Middle East, John 1:1 reads:

في البدء كان الكلمة والكلمة كان عند الله وكان الكلمة الله

In the beginning was the Word, and the Word was with God and the Word was God.[797]

In contrast, the Nestle-Aland text of the Greek New Testament has:

Ἐν ἄρχῇ ἦν ὁ λόγος, καὶ ὁ λόγος ἦν πρός τόν θεόν, καὶ θεός ἦν ὁ λόγος

In the beginning was the Word, and the Word was with God, and God was the Word.[798]

This has a different theological connotation from that which may be gleaned from Van Dyke's Arabic translation.

I am not going here to delve into a textual analysis of the Greek Johannine text or discuss which is the most accurate version, but I would like to take this nuance in translation into the discussion of Abū Qurrah's use of John1:1 in *al-Mujādalah*, and note that Abū Qurrah's translation of John1:1 differs from that found in a modern Arabic translation, such as Van Dyke's. Abū Qurrah sticks to the Greek syntax, keeping God as the subject and translating καί θεός ἦν ὁ λόγος directly into Arabic as *Wa-Allah hūa al-Kalimah* (and God is the Word).

---

796 Samir Khalil Samir believes that the Qur'anic reference to Jesus as 'God's Word' is derived from John 1:1, concluding that speaking of one of God's messengers as God's Word "is an astonishing affirmation, ... for it does not correspond to that which is normally said [in the Qur'an] of the messengers of God, who are all created *by* the word of God": S.K. Samir, "The Theological Christian Influence on the Qur'ān: A Reflection," in *The Qur'ān in Its Historical Context*, ed. Gabriel Said Reynolds (London: Routledge, 2008), 141–162, p. 156.

797 *Al-Kitāb al-Muqaddas, aiy Kutub al-ʿAhd al-Qadīm wal-ʿAhd aj-Jadīd wa qadd Turjima ʿann al-Lughāt al-Aṣliyyah* (The Holy Bible, or the books of the Old Testament and the New Testament translated from the original languages) (Beirut: Bible Society in the Near East, 1994)

798 Cited from Alfred Marshall, *The New International Version: Interlinear Greek-English New Testament* (Grand Rapids, MI: Zondervan, 1958), p. 356; on Van Dyke's Arabic translation and its importance for the Eastern Christian churches and Christian-Muslim relations, see David D. Grafton, "The Word Made *Book:* The 1865 Van Dyck Arabic Translation of the Bible and Arab Christian Views of *Wahy*," in *Jesus and the Incarnation: Reflections of Christians from Islamic Contexts*, ed. David Emmanuel Singh (Eugene, OR: Wipf & Stock, 2011), 79–95; and E. Smith and C.V. A Van Dyck, *Brief Documentary History of the Translation of the Scriptures into the Arabic Language* (Beirut: American Presbyterian Mission Press, 1990).

Intriguing in this translation is Abū Qurrah's slight, but immeasurably significant, conjugational editing of this Johannine phrase. The phrase καί θεός ήν ό λόγος may be translated as 'God *was, and is still* the Word.' In his translation of Greek verses from the New Testament, Abū Qurrah reveals his awareness of the continuous tense in Greek and he demonstrates his knowledge here. This is not the first time Abū Qurrah has cited John1:1 in his theological debates (nor was he the first Christian *mutakallim* to use the Gospel of John in dialogue with Muslims[799]). Abū Qurrah also uses John 1:1 in his *Maymar on the Trinity*, and he conspicuously translates the verse into Arabic so as to reflect the Greek continuous tense:

وقال في الإنجيل أنه في البدء لم تزل الكلمة والكلمة لم تزل عند الله وإلهاً لم تزل الكلمة

> And he said in the Gospel that in the beginning was still the Word, and the Word was still with God, and a God [*ilāhan*] the Word still is.[800]

Here, Abū Qurrah follows the Greek text's continuous tense by speaking of the Word as 'still is,' rather than as 'was,' and he offers a particular translation of καί θεός ήν ό λόγος as '*wa īlāhan lam tazal al-Kalimah*' (and a God the Word still is). Here, the subject is the Word, not God, and the translation indicates that the Word is divine, but is not alone or exhaustively God. This translation and its philological connotations in Arabic serve the main purpose of Abū Qurrah's argument in this maymar, namely to defend the triune nature of God by showing that the three *hypostases* are *together* the Godhead of God, rather than three separate Gods, each by himself alone. This is why Abū Qurrah, using John 1:1, would speak of the Word as 'a God' (*ilāh*), rather than 'God.'

---

799 The Gospel of John was probably one of the most used scriptural texts in Christian-Muslim dialogues, and by *mutakallims* from all the existing Christian denominations, despite the fact that the content of this Gospel would be the most rejected by Muslims and the most challengingly opposite to the Qur'anic teaching on ʿĪsā ibn Maryam. See, for instance, David D. Bundy, "The Commentary of Nonnus of Nisibis on the Prologue of John," in *Actes du Premier Congrès International d'Études Arabes Chrétiennes*, pp. 123–133; Julian Faultless, "The Two Recensions of the Prologue to John in Ibn at-Ṭayyib's *Commentary on the Gospels*", in *Christians at the Heart of Islamic Rule*, ed. David Thomas (Leiden: Brill, 2003), 177–198;" M. Accad, "The Ultimate Proof-Text"; and Hikmat Kashouh, "The Arabic Versions of the Gospels: A Case Study of John 1.1 and 1.18," in *The Bible in Arab Christianity*, ed. David Thomas (Leiden: Brill, 2007), 9–36.

800 Abū Qurrah, *Maymar fī ath-Thālūth* (Maymar on the Trinity), p. 32. Abū Qurrah uses the same Arabic translation in his discourse on the Trinity in his other maymar, *Maymar Yuḥaqqiq 'anna li-Allāh 'Ibnan hūa ʿAdluh fī aj-Jawhar wa-lam Yazal Maʿahu* (Maymar affirming that God has a son who is equal to Him in essence and is still with Him), pp. 102–103.

Let me return after this short detour to *al-Mujādalah.* There, Abū Qurrah refers to John1:1 one more time, this time offering yet another Arabic translation with an unmissible nuance. Instead of 'and a God the Word still is,' Abū Qurrah's translation this time reads '*wal-lāh hūa al-Kalimah*' (and God *is* the Word).

Abū Qurrah's Arabic translation thus reveals two crucial nuances. First, instead of the continuous 'was, and still is' tense, we have the absolute affirmative and definitive 'is.' Instead, that is, of speaking about the Word's identity and nature in a temporal sense, within the logic of a before-after framework, we have now a reference to the Word's identity in ontological terms, within the logic of a being and 'is-ness' framework.

Second, instead of presenting the Word as the subject of the phrase, i.e., 'and a God the Word still is,' as in his *Maymar on the Trinity*, Abū Qurrah makes God the subject, i.e., 'and God is the Word,' in his Arabic translation of the same verse in *al-Mujādalah.* This time, the ontological question is about the being of God himself, not the Word alone.

What can we make of this nuance in translation? Did Abū Qurrah forget his earlier translation of John 1:1 in *Maymar on the Trinity*, or give it up, and improvise another, on-the-spot Arabic translation in his debate before the caliph, without actually noticing, or intending to make, these nuances? Or could they be a reflection of the theological thinking of Abū Qurrah's students, followers, or scribes, who recorded the debate in the caliph's court, rather than really being representative of the mind of Theodore Abū Qurrah himself?

Attempting to find plausible and reliable answers to either of the above questions would only lead the inquirer to highly speculative and far from verifiable results, so I prefer to surmise that these nuances in Abū Qurrah's Arabic translations of John 1:1 in *al-Mujādalah* and *Maymar fī ath-Thālūth* in fact resonate with the change Abū Qurrah made in his dialogue strategy in pragmatic response to the needs of the situation. I have already argued in the previous chapter that, in his defence of the Christian doctrine of the Trinity, Abū Qurrah evinced a readiness to invoke any theological argument he can call on from the orthodox patristic legacy and to enlist it in the service of his apologetics, if he thought it would help Muslims to understand the triune faith and stop them from nullifying or denying its rational plausibility. There is no valid reason to assume that Abū Qurrah would not adopt the same pragmatism and a similar eclecticism in his apologetics on Christology. In relation to the variations in the Arabic translations of John 1:1, this entailed a deliberate shift from 'and a God the Word still is' to 'and God is the Word' in order to serve a specific Christological, rather than Trinitarian, purpose on that occasion. The Christological concern made Abū Qurrah revise his translation in a way that would make it clear to the Muslim that he was by no means limiting God, or restricting his infinite being, by what he said about the deity in Jesus.[801]

Let me in the rest of this section propose some ideas that this new translation would provide for Abū Qurrah in his presentation of the Qur'anic phrase 'God's Word and Spirit' as the Islamic expression of the divinity of both the Word and the Spirit and its manifestation in the Messiah.

One of the ideas that Abū Qurrah develops on the basis of his claim that 'God is the Word' is articulated in his dialogue with a noble Muslim interlocutor from the Hāshimī clan, who initially argues against the divine sonship of the Messiah. After Abū Qurrah refutes his criticism, the Hāshimīte turns helplessly to the caliph and says:

304. ... يا أمير المؤمنين، تحيَّر عقلي وهانت عليَّ معرفتي
305. ولكن إعلم أنَّ مثل عيسى عند الله كمثل آدم وقد عييت عن الجواب

304. ... O prince of believers, my mind is confused and my knowledge was degraded in my eyes;
305. but, know that ʿĪsā is for God like Adam, and I failed in responding.[802]

To this comparison of Jesus to Adam, Abū Qurrah responds by referring again to the creating or originating ability of God's Word. This is the way he decides to show that the proof of the Gospel's claim that 'God is the Word' appears in the Word's creation of Adam and the other creatures by saying to them '*kun*' (be), and so Adam and the other creatures were.[803] This creating act by means of speaking the word *kun* not only points to the Word's total equality with

---

801 Kenneth Cragg has eloquently explained this inexhaustibility of God's infinite being by the deity we see in Jesus in the following terms: "'and God was the Word' has a full and yet restrictive sense, as one might say: 'and music was the symphony'. These are differentiated, not in *what* they are, but in *how* they are – not in essence or quality, but in how these reach us in experience": Cragg, *Jesus and the Muslim*, p. 252.
802 Abū Qurrah, *Abū Qurrah wal-Ma'mūn: al-Mujādalah* (Abū Qurrah and al-Ma'mūn: The Debate), IV. B.3.304–305 (pp. 156–157).
803 Ibid., IV. B.3.306–307 (p. 157).

306. قال أبو قرة: 'ألا تعلم أنَّ كلمة الله هي التي خلقت آدم وقالت له كن فكان،
307. وأمرت جميع البهائم أن يكونوا فكانوا'

306. Abū Qurrah said: "Do you not know that the Word of God created Adam and said to him 'be' and so he was
307. and ordered all the animals to be and so they were?"

God, but also affirms that the Word, as God himself, is not at all equal to Adam, its creature, just as God is not on the same level of being as Adam.[804]

Now, speaking of the Word's revelation of God himself in its (the Word's) act of creating by ordering creatures to 'be' symptomizes a very subtle use of the Qur'anic text to convey a Christian belief to Muslims. In the Muslim Scripture, it is God alone who brings entities into existence by ordering them 'be' and so they become: '*kun fa-yakūn*' (Q 2:117; 3:47, 59; 6:73; al-Naḥl 16:40; 19:35; 36:82; 40:68). Furthermore, in Q 3:59, God uses the command *kun* to create Jesus, as he did with Adam. Al-Hāshimī was certainly using this Qur'anic verse to prove the human, creaturely nature of ʿĪsā when Abū Qurrah picked this up and reversed its interpretation, making it a declaration of the Messiah's divine, non-creaturely status. Abū Qurrah does this by picking up the '*kun fa-yakūn*' from Q 3:59, and linking it to other occurrences of *kun fa-yakūn* in the Qur'an, arguing that it refers to God, and to Jesus as the Word of God, before he finally combines these two Qur'anic elements under the Christological formula 'God is the Word.' It is as if, by doing this, Abū Qurrah wants to say that if, according to Qur'an, Jesus is the Word of God, he cannot then be like Adam, or from the creaturely realm created by God's command '*kun*.' On the contrary, being the Word of God, ʿĪsā is above the creaturely realm. Being God's Word, he even commands creatures to be on the same principle as '*kun fa-yakūn*.' In addition, when Jesus, God's Word, creates in this way, he does not stand as a separate God over-against God. He is, rather, God himself in being, commanding things to come into being by means of the Word's *kun*. God is the Word, who created Adam and other creatures by the command, *kun*. So, if ʿĪsā is God's Word, as the Qur'an says, he is the one through whom, and as whom, God utters the command *kun* that brings entities into being (*fa-yakūn*).

This rather sophisticated and sharp-witted re-interpretation of the Qur'anic teaching is one of the hermeneutics that Abū Qurrah developed as an extension of his Arabic translation of the last part of John1:1 as 'and God *is* the Word' (*wallah hūa al-Kalimah*). Within the context of Qur'anic and Islamic philosophical and *kalām* thinking, it is more convenient to say that God *is* his Word, '*kalimatuhu hiya hū/huwa kalimatuhu*' (*his Word in him, he is his Word*), than to speak of the Word as God, for the latter would suggest to Muslims that there is separation and plurality in God, and that there is an entity called 'Word' that exists in itself

---

804 On how Theodore differentiates between God and Adam, see his argument in Abū Qurrah, *Maymar fī Wujūd al-Khāliq wad-Dīn al-Qawīm* (Maymar on the existence of the Creator and the right religion), 2.9.8 – 42.

and stands as a God parallel to, or even over-against, God.[805] According to Telman Nagel, the Muslim philosopher, al-Fārābī argues, for example, that, because God is one and only, he alone must have a supreme being, for:

> Only that is perfectly magnificent next to which there is nothing as magnificent. Only that is perfectly graceful besides which there is nothing that has its kind of gracefulness. Likewise, only that has perfect substance of which we can say: nothing can exist beside it that is of the same substance.[806]

In order not to be trapped in this Islamic logic, Abū Qurrah subtly avoided translating the Johannine phrase as 'and God the Word still is,' because it would suggest to the Muslims that he was claiming that there are two supreme beings alongside each other, and this is totally rejected in Islamic thought. Instead, Abū Qurrah argued that 'God *is* the Word,' so that the Muslim interlocutors are prevented from accusing him of implying two equally supreme Gods. On the contrary, by using this translation, Theodore showed his counterparts that he was actually concurring in his rationale with the Muslims' insistence that God's knowledge/Word is God himself: *hiya hūa* ('it is he'). By deliberately speaking of God as the Word, he wants precisely to affirm that the Word is a manifestation of God, and not another deity with him, such that the 'Word of the Universe' and the 'Real Agent' who brings the universe into being are one and the same, and not a composite cause (*sabab murakkab*).[807]

Probably with this distinction in mind, and being profoundly aware of the Qur'anic and Islamic sensitivity regarding God's oneness, exclusive supremacy and simplicity, Abū Qurrah dispensed with his Arabic translation of John 1:1 in *Maymar fī ath-Thālūth:* 'and God the Word still is.' He knew that this translation would not serve his attempt to rest the Christian belief in Jesus' divinity as God's Word on the shoulders of the Qur'anic 'God's Word and Spirit,' and so he improvised a new translation, *wallah hūa alkalimah* (and God is the Word), because it more conveniently served the goal of showing that Jesus as God's Word and Spirit is none other than God's Word which manifests God in his creation of

805 In his study of the history of Muslim *kalām*, Harry Wolfson shows that the threat of referring to divine attributes to God's oneness was one of the main concerns of the early Muslim *mutakallims*, namely the Muʿtazilites. Wolfson points, for instance, to the rejection of the founder of Muʿtazilism, Wāṣil ibn ʿAṭāʾ al-Baṣrī of the reality of the attributes in God upon his conviction that "first…anything eternal must be a God. Second…the unity of God excludes any internal plurality in God, even if these plural parts are inseparably united from eternity": Wolfson, *The Philosophy of the Kalām*, pp. 132ff., esp. p. 133.

806 Nagel, *The History of Islamic Theology*, p. 191.

807 On this, see Sweetman, *Islam and Christian Theology*, Pt1, Vol. 1, pp. 106–109.

everything by means of the command, *kun*. ʿĪsā does this not as a distinct deity beside God, but rather as a manifestation of the same, and only, God of the command, *kun*. Why? Because, according to Abū Qurrah, God *is* the Word (John 1:1); God is the Word who created Adam and other creatures by ordering them '*kun*' and so they came into being. It is not surprising, after this elaborate theological response, to hear Abū Qurrah give the caliph al-Maʾmūn the following summary:

348. فقال أبو قرة: 'أليس يا أمير المؤمنين الإسلام مُقرّاً أنّ المسيح الذي أتبعه أنا وحفظت وصاياه
349. هو كلمة الله وروحه وأنه من ذاته وجوهريته، خالقٌ غير مخلوق؟' قال: نعم
350. قال أبو قرة: 'فأي شيءٍ للعبد أفخر من أن يصدق ويطيع كلمة مولاه؟'

348. So Abū Qurrah said: "Does not Islam, O prince of believers, affirm that the Christ whom I follow and whose commandments I have kept
349. is God's Word and Spirit and he is from his [God's] self and essence, a non-created creator?" He [the caliph] said: "Yes."
350. Abū Qurrah said: "So what is more honourable to the slave than believing and obeying the word of his master?"[808]

Another use of the Johannine 'and God is the Word' in *al-Mujādalah* appears in Abū Qurrah's debate with a Muslim from the Quraysh clan and another man called Īsmāʿīl al-Kūfī. The conversation with the Qurayshī suggests that the latter was aware of the core purpose of Abū Qurrah's reliance on the Johannine phrase 'and God is the Word,' so he led Abū Qurrah into an inquiry that is directly related to the essential implications of Theodore's hermeneutics:

434. فقال له رجل من وجوه قريش: أليس المسيح كلمة الله وروحه؟
435. فقال أبو قرة: كذلك في قرآنك وكتابك، إن كنت تحفظ القرآن.
436. قال: فأخبرني، عندما كان المسيح في بطن مريم، من كان يدبّر السموات والأرض؟
437. وحيث بعث روحه وكلمته إلى مريم، أليس أنه بقي بلا كلمة ولا روح؟
438. ولو كانت مريم ماتت وهي حبلى بالمسيح، من كان يكون ديّاناً يوم الدين أو من كان يحاسب الخلائق في يوم الحشر.

434. So, a man from the nobles of Quraysh said to him: "Is not the Messiah God's Word and Spirit?"
435. And Abū Qurrah said: "So [he is] in your Qur'an and book, if you memorize the Qur'an."
436. So he [the Qurayshī] said: "Then tell me, when the Messiah was in Maryam's womb, who was managing the heavens and the earth?
437. And since he sent his Word and Spirit to Maryam, did not he remain Wordless and Spiritless?

808 Abū Qurrah, *Abū Qurrah wal-Maʾmūn: al-Mujādalah* (Abū Qurrah and al-Maʾmūn: The Debate), IV.D.2.348–350 (p. 164).

438. And if Maryam had died while she was pregnant with the Messiah, who would be the judge at the day of judgment, and who would hold the creatures accountable on doomsday?"[809]

If God *is* the Word, the Qurayshī asked, then God had to limit himself to time and space when he became the Messiah-child in Mary's womb. He could no longer play his divine role as the Creator and Lord of the heavens and the earth. That is, if the Word of God *is* the Messiah and God is his Word, then God is no longer infinite, omnipresent, or omnipotent, but rather subjected to the spatio-temporal and contingent limitations of the human species. Consequently, one must either say that God is not the Word, or that the Word of God is not the Messiah who was born from Maryam's womb.

How did Abū Qurrah tackle this subtle challenge? First, Theodore cleared the ground about his view of God himself. He did so by appealing to the Qur'anic witness, reminding his interlocutor that his book affirms that:

440. ... الله في كل مكان ولا يخلو منه مكان
441. ولا يدنسه شيء ولا يختلط به شيء ولا يحيط به شيء ولا يحويه شيء ولا تدركه الحواس ولا العقول
442. وكتابك يشهد أنه خالق السموات والأرض وكل شيءٍ وأنه خالق غير مخلوق

440. ... God is everywhere and no place is void of him,
441. and nothing desecrates him, mixes with him, surrounds him, or contains him and neither senses nor minds comprehend him;
442. and your book testifies that he is the creator of the heavens and the earth and everything, and he is an uncreated creator.[810]

From this affirmation of his total concurrence with the Qur'anic understanding of the nature of God, Abū Qurrah brought this Qur'anic theology into the circle of his basic claim that 'God is the Word.' First, he argued that, if God is infinite, omnipresent, omnipotent and incomprehensible, his Word and Spirit must also be infinite, omnipresent, omnipotent and incomprehensible. Otherwise, the Word and Spirit is not the creator of every creaturely thing and is not God's

445. فإذا كانت الكلمة والروح الخالقة لذلك بأسره، كيف يجوز أن يحوط بها شيء أو يحويها مكان؟

445. If the Word and Spirit was the creator of all of this, how could it be surrounded by anything or contained in any place?[811]

---

809 Ibid., V. A.434–438 (p. 180).
810 Ibid., V. A.1.440–442 (p. 181).
811 Ibid., V. A.2.445 (p. 182). Abū Qurrah, nevertheless, does not go as far as calling the Word and Spirit '*rabb al-ʿālamīn*' (Lord of the worlds), as the Qur'an calls God Himself (e.g., Q 1:2), which the author of the *Summa Theologiae Arabica* does bluntly: Griffith, "The Qur'ān in Arab Christian Texts," p. 220.

Second, Abū Qurrah defended his 'God is the Word' by emphasizing God's omnipotence: If God is omnipotent, and if God's Word is him in essence, then why cannot the Word appear in one of its creations, and why should not this option be within the bounds of the Word's infinite capabilities?

446. أو كيف لا يجوز أن تحلَّ في خلقةٍ من خلقها، ظاهرةً على صورتها ومثالها وتتخذها لها حجاباً؟

446. Or how is it not possible [for the Word] to appear in one of its creatures, manifested in its image and likeness and making it its veil?[812]

If God and his Word are omnipotent, they can do anything, even exposing and subduing themselves to the limitations of their creation, if they will to do so. On the other hand, Abū Qurrah continued, the Word of God knows that human senses and minds cannot comprehend God, nor can they grasp in their contingent state God's graciousness toward his creation or follow his orders and obey them.

447. أو عساك ترى أنَّ الله يخلق بيمينه شيئاً طمثاً ويأنف منه ممن اصطفاه له؟
448. وظهوره به لخليقته، لتعرف الناس كرامته على خلقه ويتّبعوا أمره ويعملوا بطاعته

447. Or maybe you think that God creates with his right hand something menstrual [or unclean] and repugnant and chose it for himself?
448. And his appearance in it to his creation was in order for the people to know his generosity toward his creatures and for them to follow his command and act in obedience to him.[813]

---

812 Abū Qurrah, *Abū Qurrah wal-Ma'mūn: al-Mujādalah* (Abū Qurrah and al-Ma'mūn: The Debate), V. A.2.446 (p. 182). The same argument from omnipotence not only in terms of God's ability to do what is beyond our realm of power, but also in terms of his doing what is part and parcel of our limited capabilities, is also used in Abū Qurrah's *Maymar fī Sabīl Maʿrifat Allāh wa-Taḥqīq al-Ibn al-Azalī* (Maymar on the way of knowing God and verifying the eternal Son), p. 80:
فأخبرني أيها الجاحد للابن. أتقول أنَّ الله يقدر أن يلد مثله أم لا يقدر. فإن زعمت أنَّ الله لا يقدر أن يلد مثله فقد أدخلت عليه أعظم المنقصة حيث تجعلنا نحن يقدر أحدنا أن يلد مثله وتجعل الله لا يقدر على ما نقدر نحن عليه من الفواضل
So, tell me, you apostate against the Son, do you say that God can beget another like Himself or that He cannot? If you claim that God cannot beget another like Him, you insert into Him the greatest imperfection, as you make one among us capable of begetting another like himself and God incapable of the excellences we are capable of.
Here, Abū Qurrah seems to be borrowing from early Muʿtazalite *kalām* the idea of inferring the 'unseen' from the 'visible' and using in his argument their conviction that God's being can be known via its manifestation before the creatures in His acts of creating, speaking and knowing. On this early Muʿtazilite view and its refutation by later Muslim Sunni rationalists, such as al-Ashʿarī and al-Fārābī, see Nagel, *The History of Islamic Theology*, pp. 148–194.
813 Abū Qurrah, *Abū Qurrah wal-Ma'mūn: al-Mujādalah* (Abū Qurrah and al-Ma'mūn: The Debate), V. A.2.447–448 (p. 183). Abū Qurrah also elaborates further on the same idea in VI. A-B.1.664–669 (pp. 219–220) and VI. B.7.696–701 (p. 225). An echo of the same idea of God's will-

It is because of the infinite power of God and his Word, and not in spite of it, that the Word can veil his infinity and overcome his transcendence by manifesting himself in the human form of the Messiah without losing his divinity or omnipresence.

This conclusion takes us straightaway to Abū Qurrah's response to Ismāʿīl al-Kūfī. This Muslim interlocutor picked up what Abū Qurrah said about the Word taking the form of a creaturely being and making it his veil, and pushed Abū Qurrah to elaborate further on the idea of veiling. In response to this challenge, Abū Qurrah replied:

.460 ... ألا تعلم أنَّ النفس والروح والكلمة في الجسد لا يظهرون للعيان
.461 ولا يطيق النظر وصف العقل والنفس والروح
.462 ولا يرى شيء منهم ماداموا في الجسد
.463 والجسد بها حياً

460. ... Do not you know that the soul, spirit, and word in the flesh are invisible,
461. and sight cannot describe the mind, soul, and spirit,
462. and does not see anything of them as long as they abide in the flesh,
463. even though the flesh lives by means of them?[814]

---

ingness to humble Himself by means of appearing in creaturely flesh for our sake is found in Abū Qurrah, *Maymar fī Ikrām al-Aiqūnāt* (Maymar on the veneration of icons), 1.5.2.22:

.22 ونُخلص في عقولنا لله الصفة الطاهرة، ونعرف انحطاطه برحمته إلى غير ما يشاكل تجرُّد جوهره، مما فيه خلاصنا، ونحمده على ذلك

22. And we adhere in our minds to God's attribute of holiness, and we acknowledge His merciful lowering of himself into what differs from the transcendence of His essence, wherein lies our salvation, and we praise Him for it.

Elsewhere, Abū Qurrah elaborates on the objection that God would abhor indwelling creaturely flesh, denying that God could by any means be repelled from incarnating Himself in what He Himself had made: Abū Qurrah, *Maymar fī ar-Radd ʿalā Man Yunkir li-Allāh al-Tajassud wal-Ḥulūl fī-mā Aḥabba an Yaḥill fīhi [min khalqihi] wa-annahu fī Ḥulūlihi fī al-Jasad al-Maʾkhūdh min Maryam [al-muṭahharah] bi-Manzalat Julūsihi ʿalā al-ʿArsh fī al-Samāʾ* (Maymar in response to those who deny God [the possibility of] being incarnate and indwelling whatever [of His creatures] He wished to indwell, and that His indwelling in the flesh taken from [the pure] Mary is equal to His sitting on the throne in heaven), in *Mayāmir Thāʾūdūrus Abī Qurrah ʾUsquf Ḥarrān, ʾAqdam Taʾlīf ʿArabī Naṣrānī,* (*Mayāmir* of Theodore Abū Qurrah, Bishop of Ḥarrān, the oldest Arabic, Christian work), 180–186, p. 183.

ولم يكن الله يتقزز من الحلول في أكرم خلقه عليه. بل هذا الخلق الإنسي أولى به أن يحل به الله من كل الخلق لما تقدم، مع أن النجس الذي يتقزز الله منه إنما هو الخطيئة فقط

And God would not abhor indwelling the creature most honourable to Him. Rather, this human creature is more worthy than the rest of creation that God should indwell him because of what has been stated earlier, bearing in mind that the uncleanness that God abhors is only sin.

814 Abū Qurrah, *Abū Qurrah wal-Maʾmūn: al-Mujādalah* (Abū Qurrah and al-Maʾmūn: The Debate), V. A.3.460–463 (p. 185).

The invisibility of the Word abiding in the Messiah is no proof of limitation or a threat to the divine nature of the Word. The Word of God willingly veiled himself in the Messiah's created flesh , just as the human mind, soul and spirit veil themselves in the human flesh and express their presence in that flesh by implicitly providing it with life. Appearing in the human flesh of the Messiah, according to Abū Qurrah's logic, becomes a humanly perceptible means of disclosing before creation that God is the Word, by means of whom everything was commanded to be (*kun*) and so was (*fa-yakūn*). The Word and Spirit is not only God's property and possession. He is God's very self, as what belongs to the human self is that self and is never denied by it.[815] Also, the Word and Spirit, in turn, is God and cannot be called other than God, because he emanates from God and returns to him.[816]

This, in conclusion, is another argument that Abū Qurrah derives from his Arabic translation of the phrase in John 1:1, 'and God is the Word.' The essence of Abū Qurrah's defence of the Christian Christological reading of God's *kalima* and *rūḥ* lies in his persistent and able intellectual endeavour to show his Muslim interlocutors that the Christian understanding of the Messiah as the Word of God is not actually alien to the core teaching of the Qur'an on God's Word and Spirit. If Muslims miss this strong affinity between the Gospel's and the Qur'an's view of God's Word and Spirit in relation to Jesus, it is due to their failure to adhere to the teaching of their holy scriptures and their prophet, and their stubborn refusal to obey it. There is no better expression of this conviction than Abū Qurrah's own words:

509. وقد صغرتم أيها المسلمون كلمة الله وروحه
510. وزعمتم أنها خلق مخلوق وعبد مملوك وكفرتم به
511[817]. وكذبتم قول الله (تعالى) في كتابكم، على لسان نبيكم، إذ يقول أنه خلق الخلق بكلمته وروحه
512. وخالفتم وصيته وتجعلوننا مع الكافرين وتنسبوننا مع المشركين.

---

815 Ibid., V. B.1.478 (p. 188).

478. وكلمته وروحه هي ذاته، كما أنَّ ما كان منك لا تنكره

478. And His Word and Spirit is His self, as what is of you is not denied by you.

816 Ibid., V. B.1.477 (p. 188).

477. يا هذا العجب فما الذي يمكن أن تسمي كلمة الله وروحه إلا إلهاً إذ هما منه وإليه

477. How amazing, for what can you call God's Word and Spirit except God, since they are from Him and to Him

817 It is not very clear which Qur'anic verse Theodore is citing here. No verse in the Qur'an states that God created creation by means of His Word and Spirit (*kalimatihi wa-rūḥih*). Is Abū Qurrah here quoting from memory and making a mistake? This is possible. Strange though, that the Muslim *mutakallims* in the court did not stop him and tell him that there is no such statement in their scripture. Theodore Abū Qurrah's knowledge of the Qur'an, and discovering which text of it was available to read in his time, is an important subject worthy of examination,

509. And you, O Muslims, demeaned God's Word and Spirit
510. and claimed that it is a created creature and an owned slave and blasphemed against it
511. and belied the saying of God (may he be glorified) in your book, on the tongue of your prophet, when he says that he [God] created the creation with his Word and Spirit,
512. and you disobeyed his commandment and you place us with the blasphemers and ally us with the replacers [*mushrikīn*].[818]

Finally, one may validly conclude from this study of Abū Qurrah's arguments that the Qur'anic notion of 'God's Word and Spirit' occupies a central place in Theodore's apologetic Christological discourse in the text of the *Mujādalah* in al-Maʾmūn's *majlis*. Abū Qurrah's use of this Qur'anic witness, and his consistent invitation to his Muslim interlocutors to remember this Qur'anic expression before all else answers the allegation that the Melkite *mutakallim* "did not resort to calling Christ by the more Qur'ānic title 'Word.'"[819] My study of the moments of the debate in the caliph's *majlis* that is presented above suggests that, though Abū Qurrah might not have shown much interest in using the 'God's Word and Spirit' in his other maymars, in *al-Mujādalah* he rather relies on this Qur'anic phrase and employs it explicitly and persistently in his Christological apologies.

and one that has not yet been sufficiently studied. Did Abū Qurrah know the Qur'an we call today ʿUthmān's *Muṣḥaf*, or did he know older, different versions of some *sūras*? This is still an open question. On the different versions and readings of the Qur'an in general, read for example, Alba Fedeli, "Early Evidences of Variant Readings in Qur'ānic Manuscripts," in *The Hidden Origins of Islam*, ed. Karl-Heinz Ohlig and Gerd-R. Puin (Amherst, NY: Prometheus Books), 311–334; and Mondher Sfar, *In Search of the Original Koran: The True History of the Revealed Text* (Amherst, NY: Prometheus Books, 2007).

818 Abū Qurrah, *Abū Qurrah wal-Ma'mūn: al-Mujādalah* (Abū Qurrah and al-Maʾmūn: The Debate), V. B.5.509–512 (p. 194). An echo of the same condemnation of Muslims of disobeying their prophet and holy book is found in al-Kindī's criticism of Muslims: "You see how your master imposes on you the faith of God as one with the Word and Spirit; and declares that Christ, the Word of God, took flesh and became man": al-Kindī, *The Apology of al-Kindī*, in *The Early Christian-Muslim Dialogue: A Collection of Documents from the First Three Islamic Centuries (632–900 A.D.); Translation with Commentary*, ed. N. A. Newman (Hatfield, PA: Interdisciplinary Biblical Research Institute, 1993), 381–516, p. 425.

819 Beaumont, *Christology in Dialogue with Muslims*, p. 94.

III. Jesus' Divine Sonship and the Muslim God, Who *'Lam Yalid Wa-Lam Yūlad'*

A. God's Taking a Child unto Himself in the Qur'an and *Kalām*

Besides the Trinity, and before any other Christological claim, belief in the Messiah's divine sonship to God is, as is well known, the Christian conviction that is the first and most prominently and antagonistically rejected in Islamic apologetic literature. The primary and most important foundation of this rejection by all the Muslim polemicists and *mutakallims* is usually the Qur'anic attestation. Having said that, when we look at the Qur'an, we do not find a single monolithic stance on the idea of divine sonship, but rather various verses with various points of view and intentions. A careful reading of the Islamic scriptures regarding the claim that God has a child or a son reveals that not every verse on the subject contributes to the development of a total rejection of the idea of 'God having a divine Son or begetting one if he willed to do so,' because each passage in the text discusses the issue from a different perspective and suggests a critique of it for a particular purpose. Far from a Qur'anic discourse on 'God's taking unto himself a child,' we have various Qur'anic *discourses* on the subject, as I shall briefly show.

In Q 4:171, for instance, God commands the People of the Book as follows:

> يا أهل الكتاب لا تغلوا في دينكم ولا تقولوا على الله إلا الحق...إنما الله إله واحد سبحانه أن يكون له ولد، له ما في السماوات وما في الأرض وكفى بالله وكيلا
>
> O People of the Book, do not exaggerate in your religion and say only the truth about God … . God is one God, he is far glorified beyond having a child [*walad*]; his is what is in the heavens and what is on earth, and God is enough as an advocate.[820]

A careful reading of this verse shows that the Qur'an here rejects the idea of God having a child in order to defend God's oneness in specific. It particularly says that suggesting that God has a *walad* is a claim against monotheism. It is not, that is, against God's infinity and divinity as an uncreated Creator, who is transcendent and supreme in nature. This verse is not primarily concerned about this divine infiniteness, but rather about the threat that the idea of having a child with an equal divine nature may present to God's oneness and singleness as the definition of authentic monotheism.

820 Unless otherwise stated, all English translations of the Qur'an in this chapter are my own.

The concern of Q 4:171 disappears in other Qur'anic verses' reference to the same idea of 'having a child' and of Jesus' divine sonship. In the well known verse from Q 5:116, we read:

> وإذ قال الله يا عيسى ابن مريم أنت قلت للناس أتخذوني وأمي إلهين من دون الله قال سبحانك ما يكون لي أن أقول ما ليس لي بحق إن كنت قلته فقد علمته تعلم ما في نفسي ولا أعلم ما في نفسك إنك أنت علّام الغيوب
>
> And when God said: "O ʿĪsā son of Maryam, did you say to people, 'Take me and my mother as two gods instead of [*min dūn*] God?'", he [Jesus] said: "Be glorified; it is not mine to say what is not my right [to say]. Had I said it, you would have known it; you know what is within me and I do not know what is within you. You are the knower of the hidden things."

According to the text, the divinity of Jesus, the son of Mary, is rejected in the context of an accusation that he enticed people to deify him and his mother and to worship them as alternative gods. The divinity of Jesus does not represent here a threat to God's oneness, but has the potential to set aside God's divinity altogether by replacing him with other gods, Jesus and his mother. The frequent translation of the Arabic '*īlahayn min dūn Allah*' into English as 'two gods beside God' does not fully capture the meaning of the verse. It suggests that the text is warning against polytheism and associationism – worshiping other gods alongside, or together with, God – whereas the Arabic syntax calls for the translation 'two Gods *instead of* God,'[821] showing that the concern here is with the danger that God may be rejected altogether and be replaced with other deities. Thus, rather than defending monotheism against polytheism in terms of association, this verse uses the idea of Jesus' divinity to argue against any tendency to displace, or replace, orientation to God with orientation to other deities.[822]

---

821 The same idea of taking other gods *instead* of God or in God's place also appears in Q 25:3:
واتخذوا من دونه آلهةً لا يخلقون شيئا وهم يخلقون ولا يملكون لأنفسهم ضرّا ولا نفعا ولا يملكون موتاً ولا حيوة ولا نشورا
And they took gods *instead* of Him, who create nothing, and they are created and can neither hurt nor benefit themselves, and cannot control death or life or resurrection.
The same Arabic expression *min dūn* (instead of/in the place of) is used in the same sense in this verse. The same meaning, 'instead of God', is also found, for example, in Q 2:107; 3:64, 79; 4:119, 123, 173; 5:76; 6:56, 70–71, 107; 7:30, 37, 194, 9:16, 31, 116; 10:18, 37–38, 66, 104; 11:13, 20, 101, 113; 12:40; 13:14, 16; 16:20, 35, 73, 86; 17: 97; 18:14–15, 26, 50; 19:48–49, 81; 21:24, 29, 66–67, 98; 22:12, 62, 71, 73, etc. It is my belief that, in the light of this Qur'anic attestation, we might need to consider speaking about *shirk* in the Qur'an in terms of 'association' and start talking about it in terms of 'replacement'displacement', i.e. replacing/displacing God with other deities. This is how I personally translate and speak about *shirck* in this monograph, using 'replacement' as an English translation to the Arabic term شِرك /*shirk*, and 'replacers' as an English one to the Arabic *mushrikūn*.

822 It is because of this meaning in Arabic that I do not agree with Sidney Griffith's latest suggestion that this verse "recalls the then current theological controversy dividing the largely Sy-

When it comes to the idea of 'having a *walad*,' rather than the divine nature of such a son, the Qur'an is evidently consistent in stating that God is far from having a *walad* (child), but its explanation of this denial varies considerably from one *sūra*, and even from one verse, to another. In Q 2:116, for example, we have:

وقالوا اتخذ الله ولداً سبحانه بل له ما في السموات والأرض كل له قانتون

> And they said: "God has taken a child unto himself." Glorified be he, however, his is all that is in the heavens and the earth; all are obedient to him.

This verse does not reveal exactly who has claimed that God took a child unto himself. It just negates this claim and rejects it as a belief related to God. On the other hand, the verse does not clearly deny the possibility that God is able to have a child. Instead, it repeats an idea similar to the one that is found in Q 4:171, and then tries to present a logical and practical reason for its claim that God does not need such a child: God does not need to have a child of his own, not necessarily because this possibility is forbidden to, or militates in any way whatsoever against, God's deity. The verse does not state this at all. It rather suggests that God does not need to have a child because he has already taken unto himself every entity on earth and in the heavens, and he does not need to take to himself any more. In other words, this verse is not particularly rejecting the idea of 'God's taking a child unto himself' but aims, in fact, at emphasizing God's infinite *sufficiency*, since he already has every created reality as his own and has no need that 'taking a child unto oneself' may satisfy. The same emphatic defence of God's sufficiency is echoed also in Q 10:68, where the idea of sufficiency is even more clearly stated: *subḥānahu wa-hūa al-ghanī lahu mā fī as-samawāt wa-mā fī al-'arḍ* (May he, who is sufficient (*ghanī*), be glorified, his is what is in the heavens and the earth).

---

riac/Aramaic-speaking, Jacobite and Nestorian Christians in the Qur'ān's own milieu over the propriety and veracity of the Marian title *theotokos*, 'Mother of God'": Sidney H. Griffith, *The Bible in Arabic: The Scripture of the 'People of the Book' in the Language of Islam* (Princeton, NJ: Princeton University Press, 2013), p. 35. In principle, I fully side with Griffith in his attempt to read the Qur'anic passages within the context of the contemporaneous Christian-Christian theological debates. I do fully concur that the infiltration of Christians, with their beliefs and theological schools, into Arabia in the first third of the 7th century is historically attested (ibid., p. 36). However, I do not think that a careful reading of the Arabic text of Q 5:116 would actually support associating the content of this verse with the debate on the *theotokos*. The Arabic wording of this verse, at least, does not prove a link between the Qur'an and the Christian traditions on the motherhood of Mary.

In Q 17:111, what the Qur'an says about 'God's taking a child unto himself' takes yet another interesting turn. There, the rejection of God's having a child is used in the service of defending God's status as the only King:

وقل الحمد لله الذي لم يتخذ ولداً ولم يكن له شريك في الملك ولم يكن له ولي من الذل وكبره تكبيرا

And say: "Praise be to God, who did not take unto himself [*yattakhidh*] a child and who has no partner in kingship and has never had a protector from humiliation, and magnify him magnificently."[823]

The rejection of any idea of God having a child is here meant to stress that God is all-sufficiently sovereign and king by himself. He needs no partner to inherit the throne from him (for God is eternal and immortal) or to protect his kingship from any degradation (for God is omnipotent). Again, the rejection of *'ittakhadha waladan'* does not represent a goal in itself. It is an instrument used in another more significant cause, namely affirming God's absolute sufficiency as king.

Elsewhere, as in Q 18:4, the Qur'an explicitly states that God *yundhir allazyn qālū ittakhadha Allah waladan* ([He] warns those who said God has taken a child unto himself). However, the verse does not name those who said such a thing, or explain why such a saying is to be warned against. On the other hand, in Q 19:35 we have traces of an initial attempt at offering some sort of explanation for the rejection of the concept of 'God's taking a child unto himself,' which fits into the broader framework of this *sūra:*

ما كان لله أن يتخذ من ولد سبحانه إذا قضى أمراً فإنما يقول له كن فيكون

It was not for God to take a child unto himself. Glorified is he, if he decreed something, he says to it 'be' [*kun*] and so it is [*fa-yakūn*].

The explanation this verse offers for why God does not take a child unto himself lies in the nature of the natural process of procreation. Begetting children requires a specific procedure, involving a male impregnator, an impregnated female, intercourse between them, and then a period of time during which the seed grows and becomes an offspring. Far from needing to go through all this process, or to subject himself to its requirements and preconditions, God, this verse affirms, usually creates things merely by the command, *kun* (be), and they immediately come into being (*fa-yakūn*). So, as an originator, God is self-sufficient: he does not need another to bring anything into existence. Thus, *making* a child, the verse suggests, rather than *taking one unto oneself ('ittikhādh)*, goes against God's self-sufficient, creating '*kun fa-yakūn*' power. The issue here, then,

823 Almost exactly the same idea and wording are repeated in Q 25:2.

is not the possibility of God 'taking a child unto himself' *per se*, but *how* this possibility could be fulfilled. If God needs to subject himself to the natural, creaturely process of procreation (*'īlād*), it is not believable that God should have a child at all. This is exactly what the Qur'an also wants to emphasize in Q 39:4:

لو أراد الله أن يتخذ ولداً لاصطفى مما يخلق ما يشاء سبحانه هو الله الواحد القهار

> Had God willed to take a child unto himself, he would have selected from what he creates whatever he, be glorified, wants [to make his own]; he is God the one and compelling.

God can undoubtedly will to have a child if he wants to, the verse suggests. His divine, infinite omnipotence and compelling abilities enable him to make this choice. However, this should not mean, the verse implies in the light of Q 19:35, that God compels himself to pursue the natural process of procreation that is required for creatures to have children. God can simply select someone or something from what he has already created to become this 'child' for him.

The same logic also underpins the Qur'anic endeavour to reject God's taking a child unto himself and any related suggestion that God has a female partner or concubine (Q 72:3; 6:101). For, if God needed a consort to be his impregnated partner, he would then be subject to the requirements of procreation, like his creatures. But, God transcends this limitation absolutely. His self-sufficiency negates any need of a partner to help him take a child unto himself. Nevertheless, *mā yanbaghī ll-raḥman an yattakhidh waladan* (The Merciful must not take a child unto himself) (Q 19:92). What God can take unto himself is *'ibād mukarramūn* (honoured worshipers) (Q 21:26). The honoured worshipers fulfill the potential for God to 'take a child unto himself' without jeopardizing his infinite self-sufficiency and omnipotence by the imposition of any limitation or condition related to the natural, creaturely process of procreation. What actually seems to be more central to the Qur'anic rationale is the linkage of the possibility of 'God's taking a child unto himself' to the narrow boundaries of God's self-sufficiency and omnipotence. As long as 'God's taking a child unto himself' is achieved by means of '*kun fa-yakūn*' principle, and as long as it is not suggestive of any lack, need, or limitation in God, the possibility of 'taking a child unto himself' is not in itself contradictory to the divinity of God. However, since entertaining this possibility without proper qualification and explanation would confuse faith and lead believers astray, the Qur'an ultimately states that God '*lam yalid walam yūlad*' (has not begotten, and he is not begotten) (Q 112:3).

This analysis of the Qur'anic texts, and what they say in relation to the idea of 'God taking a child unto himself,' shows that the Qur'an is flexible and multifaceted and does not present a monolithic and absolute prohibition of any such idea or notion in principle. Each Qur'anic *sūra* or verse has its own logic and context that underly its rejection of, or reservations on, the idea of 'God's taking a child unto himself.' One cannot, and should not, read this variety as simply a number of ways of expressing a single position. One needs to be more sensitive to, and perceptive of, the rather significant qualitative nuances, and even relative discrepancies, between the connotations and concerns found in these verses.

Did the Muslim *mutakallims* of the early Abbasid centuries have such an awareness and evince such a sensitivity in their use of the Qur'an in their polemics against Christian Christology? It is not my goal here to develop a comprehensive examination of this significant matter, which would require a separate study. So, I shall restrict myself in the following paragraphs to giving some examples from the Islamic *kalām* tradition that illustrate the early application of the Qur'anic stance on 'God's taking a child unto himself' in debates with Christians over Christology.

A relevant example is found in *ar-Radd ʿalā an-Naṣārā* (The Response to the Christians) by al-Qāsim ibn Ibrāhīm ar-Rassī. In this polemic letter, ar-Rassī uses various Qur'anic verses in his rationalist argument against claiming that God has a child, or alleging that God has begotten (*yalid/walada*) a child.

From the very first lines of his text, ar-Rassī reveals that his point of departure is a philosophical conviction that the transcendent and infinitely eternal God cannot logically be the 'primary origin' for anything whatsoever. Thus, God cannot originate anything from his own being:

الحمد لله الذي لم يزل ولا يزال...المتعالي عن أن يكون لشيءٍ أصلاً متأصلاً...ولو
أنَّ ذلك كان فيه كذلك، لعاد غيره له ندّاً ومثلاً،إذ كان له, سبحانه، محتداً وأصلاً،
ولكان حينئذٍ لكل ما كان منه، ووجِدَ من فروعه وعنه،ما كان من القول له، إذ كان المتولد منه مثله.

> Praise be to God who was, still, and still is ... who is transcendent above being a primary origin for something ... and if this was otherwise in him, his other would become his equal and match, since he [God], the glorified, is his origin and principle, and he would then be to everything that was from him, and to each of the things that emanated from him, whatever is said about him, since what is generated from him would be similar to him.[824]

For ar-Rassī, then, God cannot be a supreme cause, an uncaused cause, or an *arche* because this would mean that what originates from God is totally like him, not only functionally, but essentially and ontologically as well. Attributing any originating ability to God nullifies monotheism and justifies polytheism; that is, it turns the one God against his oneness, against his own self. If God is to remain the one and only supreme, transcendent and eternally infinite deity, God

824 Ar-Rassī, *ar-Radd ʿalā an-Naṣārā* (Response to the Christians), p. 17.

cannot be an *arche*, an originating principle, or uncaused cause of any other thing.

Does this mean that, for ar-Rassī, God is not then 'Creator' and creation was created by another agent? Not at all. Later in this work, ar-Rassī states:

هو الله الخالق الأول القديم، الذي ليس لغيره عليه أولية ولا تقديم

He, God, is the primal, eternal Creator [*al-khāliq al-awwal al-qadīm*]; over him no other has priority or precedence.[825]

What kind of creation did this Creator make? Is it similar to him and equal in nature? Not at all, ar-Rassī states:

ولكن كل ما سواه فخلقٌ ابتدعه، فابتداه، فوجِدَ بالله خلقاً برياً بعد عدمه برياً من مشاركة الله في قدرته وقدمه، بيّنة آثار الصنع والتدبير فيه، شاهدة أقطاره بالحدث والصنع عليه، مختلف مؤلف ضعيف مصرّف مجسمٌ محدود، متوهم معدود قد ناهاه قطره وحدّه وأحصاه مقداره وعدّه، فهو كثير أشتات له نعوت وصفات كثيرة متفاوتات

But everything other than him is a creation, which he innovated and started. So, by virtue of God, a creation existed [and] was created [*bāriyan*] after its nothingness, absolved [*bar-iyyan*] from sharing with God in his power and eternity, exhibiting traces of being made and directed; its parts [that is] testifying to its contingency and fabrication, [and it is] differentiated, composed, weak, diversified, embodied, limited, imaginable, and countable. It is restricted by its location, boundary, computation, magnitude, and number, for it is numerous and sundry, [and] has many, distinct attributes and characteristics.[826]

From this, one concludes that ar-Rassī differentiates between 'Creator' (*khāliq*), on the one hand, and 'originator' (*'aṣl*), on the other.[827] More interestingly still, 'Creator' for him is connotatively and notionally different from 'primary origin,' 'uncaused cause' and '*arche*.' The absolute Being can be the Creator of other entities, but he cannot be any other's originator, or generating cause. For ar-Rassī, the act of creating is definitely distinct from the act of causing by means of origination. This distinction is not only central to the philosophical backbone of his argument, but also controls his reading of the Qur'anic verses and his understanding of their meaning and claims.

825 Ibid., p. 25.

826 Ibid., p. 25.

827 One wonders here if ar-Rassī is invoking a distinction that is similar in conception to the philosophical distinction in Greek between *arche* and *aitia*. It would be worth studying whether this distinction in Greek, which is used in Christian patristic doctrinal hermeneutics of God and the Trinity, is borrowed here by this Muslim *mutakallim* to argue against the Christians from within their own theological, philosophical and linguistic pool of knowledge. This question merits a study of its own and cannot be pursued here.

This 'from-intellect-to-text' method appears clearly in ar-Rassī's application of the 'Creator-primary originator' differentiation to what the Qur'anic says about God. First, he argues that God, being absolute and infinite, cannot be the 'primary origin' (*'aṣl muta'aṣṣil*) of any other; God cannot be the father of any child or of a son if he is understood as being his originator.

> لا يكون واحداً من كان له ولدٌ أبداً، ولا يكون أزلياً من كان والداً أو أباً، لأنّ الابن ليس لأبيه برب، وكذلك الرب فليس لمربوبٍ بأبٍ. إذ كان الابن في الذات هو مثله، فكلاهما من الربوبية قاصٍ مبتعد، إذ ليس منهما من هو بها متفرد متوحد، لأن الربوبية لا تمكّن أبداً إلا لواحدٍ ليس بأصل لشيء، ولا ولدٍ ولا والدٍ.
>
> The one who has a child will never be eternal, and the one who is an originator or father can never be eternal, for the son is not to his father a lord, nor is the lord to his servant a father. Since the son in terms of self is like him, so both are far and remote from lordship, for neither of them is individually and singularly lord, and because lordship can never be mastered except by one who is not the origin for something, or a child, or an originator.[828]

On the other hand, ar-Rassī suggests, we can only surmise that God created other creaturely beings, and that he is these beings' 'maker' (*ṣāni'*) or initiator (*mubdi'*), but not their 'begetter' or 'originator' (*wālid*). For,

> كيف يولد من لم يزل واحداً أولاً، أو يلد من جلّ أن يكون عنصراً متحللاً، لا كيف، والحمد لله أبداً، يكون الله والداً أو ولداً؟
>
> How can he, who is still one and primal, be begotten, or [how can] he beget; [he, that is] who is far above being a decomposed element? There is no way, and thanks be to God forever, that God is a begetter or begotten.[829]

God is a Creator and maker, not a begetter and originator, because he 'innovates his action and fabrication' "neither with tiredness and treatment, or by any instrument or suffering, but He completes His universe and its fabrication, for He wanted and willed it."[830] Ar-Rassī here backs up his argument with quotations from Q 5:116; 2:116; 10:68; 19:88; 43:81; and others, but apparently without first examining whether they all take the same position and sing the same song with regard to the idea of 'God's taking a child unto himself.' His clear priority, as far as one can see, is not to carefull set out the precise content of these verses, but rather to back up the philosophical assumptions behind his apologetic discourse with Qur'anic authority. His assumption is: if God is a Father and Jesus is his origination, then the former's fatherhood and the latter's sonship must mirror all the characteristics and constituents of natural fatherhood and

---

828 Ar-Rassī, *ar-Radd 'alā an-Naṣārā* (Response to the Christians), p. 18.
829 Ibid., p. 26.
830 Ibid., p. 28.
"فإنما قضاؤه له بأن يبتدع صنعه وفعله، لا بنصبٍ وعلاج ولا أداة ولا معناه، ولكنه يتم كونه وصنعه إذ هو أراده وشاءه."

sonship that we see in the creaturely realm of human existence. But if this is the case, we shall ultimately force upon God a status that is against everything definitive of divine eternity and transcendence –for natural fatherhood and sonship are by nature limited, contingent and imaginable. So, we either continue treating God as originating Father and begotten Son, thus compromising God's divinity and 'god-ness' altogether, or we maintain God's divinity and protect his infinite essence from any creaturely contingency, and stop calling him 'primary originator,' 'Father/begetter,' or 'child/begotten.'

> وهل للابن إلا كالأبناء وكذلك الأب فكالآباء؟ فإن لم يكن كهم، زال أن يكون ابناً أو أباً، ولم يكن ذلك أبداً في الأوهام ممكناً، لأنه إن لم يكن أبٌ وابنٌ، كأبٍ وابنٍ في الأبوة والبنوة، زالت الأبوة والبنوة واسمها كلها عنه
>
> Has the Son anything other than what pertains to sons and likewise the Father what pertains to fathers? For if he is not like them, he can no longer be a son or a father, and this is not possible to imagine, because if he was not Father and Son as a father and son in fatherhood and sonship, then fatherhood and sonship and the names of both are removed from him.[831]

For ar-Rassī, then, God can be a Creator but never a primary origin because the Creator only makes things by bringing them into existence out of nothing, whereas the originator brings forth (begets) another by emanation from his own being.[832] Consequently, Christians commit a grave blasphemy against God

---

831 Ibid., p. 30.

832 In the history of Islamic philosophy, the tradition that speaks of God bringing things into being by means of emanation is associated with the names of al-Fārābī and Avicenna. It seems that ar-Rassī opts out of this tradition and prefers to follow the view that sees creation in terms of the '*kun fa-yakūn*' notion, which we also see in the following centuries in the philosophical thinking of people such as Ibn Ṭufayl. On al-Fārābī and Avicenna, see, for example, David C. Reisman, "Al-Fārābī and the Philosophical Curriculum," and Robert Wisnovsky, "Avicenna and the Avicennian Tradition," both in *The Cambridge Companion to Arabic Philosophy*, ed. Peter Adamson and Richard C. Taylor (Cambridge: Cambridge University Press, 2005), 52–71 and 92–136 respectively. See also T. A. Druart, "Al-Fārābī and Emanationism," in *Studies in Medieval Philosophy*, ed. John F. Wippel (Washington, DC: Catholic University of America Press, 1987), 23–43; T. Druart, "Al-Fārābī, Emanation and Metaphysics," in *Neoplatonism and Islamic Thought*, ed. Parviz Morewedge (Albany: State University of New York, 1992), 127–148; Dimitri Gutas, *Avicenna and the Aristotelian Tradition: Introduction to Reading Avicenna's Philosophical Works* (Leiden: Brill, 1988); and J. Janssens, "Creation and Emanation in Avicenna," *Documenti e studi sulla Tradizione filosofica medievale*, 8 (1997), 455–477. On Ibn Ṭufayl and his philosophical views in his work *Ḥayy ibn Yaqẓān*, see, for example, Josep Puig Montada, "Philosophy in Andalusia: Ibn Bājja and Ibn Ṭufayl," in *The Cambridge Companion to Arabic Philosophy*, ed. Peter Adamson and Richard C. Taylor (Cambridge: Cambridge University Press, 2005), 155–179; G. Hourani, "The Principal Subject of Ibn Ṭufayl's *Ḥayy ibn Yaqẓān*," *Journal of Near Eastern Stud-*

when they speak of Jesus Christ as God's begotten (i. e., of God's essence) rather than merely as God's creation or innovation (i. e., like God's other human worshiping servants). This abomination tears God's divine eternal oneness from him.

Again, what catches the attention in ar-Rassī's discourse is that he cites numerous Qur'anic verses to support his philosophical preconception without assessing whether these verses serve this purpose. What the Qur'an refutes in the verses that refer to 'God's taking a child unto himself,' as shown above, is not the plausibility of God's taking a child unto himself, but the functional dimension of actualization of that possibility (i. e., whether having a child would require God to follow a child-generating process that threatened his self-sufficiency and omnipotence). Ar-Rassī, however, seems to be refuting the actual plausibility and possibility of 'God's taking a child unto himself,' or even originating anything in principle, and then twisting meanings of the Qur'anic verses to suit his preconceived project. A careful reading of the text shows that ar-Rassī uses these verses primarily to support his rational-philosophical refutation, instead of trying first to interpret the Qur'anic statements and then gleaning from the interpretation arguments on the validity or invalidity of claiming that God may take a child unto himself. In other words, he uses the Qur'anic verses eisegetically to prove his own philosophical assumptions, instead of examining exegetically whether they serve, support, oppose, or are irrelevant to them.

One also finds in other Muslim *kalām* texts the same tendency to rely on purely philosophical arguments and use Qur'anic texts to give authority to these arguments without offering any serious exegesis of the scriptural verses or any adequate elaboration on how they resonate hermeneutically with the philosophical assumptions. ʿAlī ibn Rabbān aṭ-Ṭabarī, for example, also refutes the Christian belief in the possibility of God's having a child by simply citing as proof-texts Q 112:1–4: *qul hūa Allah 'aḥad, Allah aṣ-ṣamad, lam yalid walam yūlad walam yakun lahū kufū'an aḥad* (say: "He is God One, God the eternal (refuge); he neither begets nor is begotten and none is equivalent to Him"), and Q 3: 64.[833] In his turn, Abū ʿUthmān aj-Jāḥiẓ similarly resorts to absolutist, affirmatively logical polemics against the possibility of God's taking a child unto himself, also quoting Qur'anic verses that he thinks support his own presuppositions, rather than analysing them to unpack their core meanings. He simply

ies, 15 (1956), 40–46; and L. E. Goodman (ed. and trans), *Ibn Ṭufayl's Ḥayy ibn Yaqẓān: A Philosophical Tale* (Chicago: University of Chicago Press, 2009).

833 ʿAlī aṭ-Ṭabarī, *ad-Dīn wad-Dauwlah: fī 'Ithbāt Nubūwat an-Nabī Muḥammad* (Religion and the state: On the verification of the prophethood of the Prophet Muḥammad), ed. ʿĀdil Nuwayhiḍ (Beirut: Dār al-Āfāq aj-Jadīdah, 1982), pp. 34, 55.

states his own position on 'God's taking a child unto himself' (*ittakhadha waladan*), as when he says, for instance:

> وأما نحن – رحمك الله – فإنّا لا نجيز أن يكون لله ولد ولا من جهة الولادة ولا من جهة التبني، ونرى أن تجويز ذلك جهل عظيم وإثم كبير، لأنه لو جاز أن يكون أباً ليعقوب لجاز أن يكون جداً ليوسف، ولو جاز أن يكون جداً وأباً وكان ذلك لا يوجب نسباً ولا يوهم مشاكلة في بعض الوجوه ولا ينقص من عظم ولا يحط من بهاء، لجاز أيضاً أن يكون عماً وخالاً... وهذا ما لا يجوزه إلا من لا يعرف عظمة الله وصغر قدر الإنسان...فالله تعالى أعظم من أن يكون له أبوة من صفاته والإنسان أحقر من أن تكون بنوة الله تعالى من أنسابه
>
> But we – God have mercy upon you – do not allow that God has a child [*walad*], neither in terms of begetting nor in terms of adoption, and we see that allowing this is grave ignorance and a great sin. For, had it been allowed that he could be father to Jacob, it would then be allowed that he would be grandfather to Joseph, and if it were allowed that he is a grandfather and a father, without a genealogical link and without suggesting differentiation in some aspects or belittling the greatness or degrading the glory, then it would also be allowed [for him] to be a paternal and maternal uncle ... and this is not allowed except by those who do not know God's glory and the inferiority of humankind ... for God, glorified he is, is too great to have fatherhood as one of his attributes, and humankind is too base to be related in sonship to the glorified God.[834]

Ar-Rassī, aṭ-Ṭabarī and aj-Jāḥiẓ are just three examples of how Muslim *mutakkalims* developed polemics against the idea that God might take a child by relying on the Qur'anic references to it. It is not my purpose here to offer a study of Muslim *mutakkalims*' hermeneutical approaches and methods of reading the Qur'an and whether their strategies display exegetical or eisegetical approaches to the scripture, which merits a separate and comprehensive study. I intend here simply to propose that the Muslim *mutakkalims*' rejection of divine sonship as expressed in Christian Christology may not actually echo the Qur'anic discourse on God's taking a child, and that it does not demonstrate sufficiently awareness of the serious nuances between the meanings and contexts of the Qur'anic verses. A careful investigation of the variations between these verses suggests that the Qur'anic stance may not in fact be unreservedly and absolutely against the possibility of 'God's taking a child unto himself,' but rather warns specifically against the consequences of thinking that God might make this happen by assimilating God's action to the process of procreating children in the human, creaturely realm.

A contemporary Muslim scholar, who pays explicit and perceptive attention to nuances and variations in the verses of the Qur'an and focuses on their exegeses before using them against the Christian belief in Jesus divine sonship, is

---

834 aj-Jāḥiẓ, *al-Mukhtār fī ar-Radd 'Alā an-Naṣārā* (The selected in response to the Christians), pp. 73–75.

the Lebanese Islamicist, Mahmoud Ayoub. In an essay on the divine sonship of Jesus, Ayoub refers extensively to the use of the terms *walad* (child) and *ibn* (son) in the Qur'anic tradition. Ayoub admits that, despite the exemplary, highly revered status that Jesus enjoys in the Islamic faith, regarding him as the only begotten Son of God "has been the barrier separating the two communities and long obscuring the meaning and significance of Jesus, the 'Word of God,' to Muslim faith and theology."[835] Nevertheless, Ayoub goes on to assert that this barrier "is not an impenetrable wall dividing [the] two communities." It can actually "be transformed into a beacon of light guiding us all to God and the good."[836]

How can we convert Jesus' divine sonship and his begottenness from God from a barrier into this beacon of light? Ayoub surmises that this requires re-interpreting and re-conceptualizing the Qur'anic statements, particularly in relation to the terms *ibn* and *walad*. Ayoub opines that the proper methodological criterion for pursuing this goal should be shaped after the following two-fold principal:

> It is, first, to stress the need to take our scriptures seriously in what they say and not to use one as a criterion to judge the truth and authenticity of the other ... the second ... is to reflect on the situation to which the Qur'ān seems to have addressed its critique of the Christian doctrine of the divine sonship of Christ.[837]

I follow the first element of Ayoub's criterion in the critique presented above of early Muslim *mutakkalims*, such as ar-Rassī and others, in their resort to eisegesis rather than exegesis in their interpretation of Qur'anic texts and then their tendency to use the texts to support their polemic. In contrast, Ayoub invites us to visit with him the Islamic Scripture and Tradition and to read their claims in their terminological, conceptual and historical contexts. Such a reading, Ayoub persuasively conjectures, makes us realize that, while the Qur'an argues strictly against using the term *walad* if it implies that God has an offspring, it, nevertheless, "nowhere accuses Christians of calling Jesus the *walad* offspring of God." Furthermore, maintaining sensitivity to the content variations in both, the Gospel and the Qur'an, Ayoub proceeds, requires an awareness of the symbolic and al-

835 Mahmoud Ayoub, "Jesus the Son of God: A Study of the Terms *Ibn* and *Walad* in the Qur'ān and *Tafsī* Tradition," in *A Muslim View of Christianity: Essays on Dialogue by Maḥmoud Ayoub*, ed. 'Irfān A. 'Omar (Maryknoll, NY: Orbis Books, 2007), 117–133, p. 117 (first published in *Christian-Muslim Encounters*, ed. Yvonne Y. Ḥaddād and Wadī' Z. Ḥaddād, [Gainesville: University Press of Florida, 1995], pp. 65–81. Pagination in the quotations that follow is that of the 2007 edition.

836 Ayoub, "Jesus the Son of God," p. 118.

837 Ibid.

legorical nature of the language of these two scriptures.[838] Neither means to suggest, when speaking allegorically of Jesus' birth and God's involvement in it, that "God had a female consort in Mary, or a physically engendered son in Christ."[839] This is clear, Ayoub argues, in the Qur'an's particular use of *walad* and the rather peculiar phrase, 'God's taking a child unto himself,' drawing attention specifically to the Qur'anic expression '*ittakhadha waladan*.' The word '*ittakhadha*,' Ayoub explains, is philosophically different from '*walada*' (begot), which connotes an actual act of generation, and he concludes that, in using *ittakhadha* rather than *walada*, the Qur'an is referring to God's 'relationship of adoption' rather than his 'actual generation' of Jesus.[840] More importantly still, the Qur'an does not explicitly name those who say that God took a child unto himself as 'Christians,' nor does the Christian Gospel itself make any such claim.

One can glean from Ayoub's subtle reading of the scriptural texts that, in their commentaries on the Qur'anic position on the idea of 'God's taking a child unto himself,' the Muslim *mutakkalims* did not always read the Qur'anic verses sufficiently carefully, nor was their exegesis consistently free of preconceptions. There are occasions when their reference to the Qur'an was motivated entirely and strongly by their zeal to refute the Christian faith in Jesus Christ. While it is true that the Qur'an has a deep concern to afffirm God's self-sufficiency and omnipotence, the *mutakallims* I referred to make it state that, even as a potential act of freewill, God cannot take anyone unto himself other than as a servant worshiper. Any relationship to him other than that of worshipful servanthood would threaten God's infinite oneness and absolute transcendence. Ar-Rassī, as shown above, even goes as far as stressing that God can never be the 'primary, unoriginated originator' of anything whatsoever. This approach is the object of Ayoub's caution against using the scriptures as a means to judge the truth and authenticity of the beliefs of others, let alone pursuing that aim at the high price of missing, or misinterpreting, the exact meaning of the scripture.

This presentation of the Qur'anic positions on 'God's taking a child unto himself,' and the Muslim *mutakallims*' use of the Qur'an in their polemics against the Christian belief in God's fatherhood of Jesus and Christ's divine sonship was necessary because of the clear implication that Muslims could not find any point of reconciliation with Christians on these Christological doctrines. More significantly still, the *mutakallims*' eisegetical readings of the Qur'an

838 Ibid.
839 Ibid., p. 120.
840 Ibid., p. 125.

were not theirs alone but seem also to have been adopted by other lay (non-intellectual or non-scholarly) Muslims. In his dialogue with Timothy I, for example, the caliph al-Mahdī also expresses his rejection of the idea that God needed a partner in order to take a child unto himself, as he asks Timothy at the outset of their discussion how Christians could believe that "God married a woman from whom He begot a Son."[841] The patriarch responds by affirming that Christians consider this to be a blasphemy and do not believe that God needs any instrument to help him fulfill his actions, like other creatures.[842] Earlier than the conversation between al-Mahdī and Timothy I, there are also other 7th-century texts, in which Christian *mutakallims* deal with objections to Jesus' sonship and of 'God's taking a child unto himself' that were raised by Muslim commoners. Sidney Griffith refers to a text from the end of the 7th century, called *Hodēgos* (The guide), written by Anastasios of Sinai to tackle the mistakes of the Monophysites, but also the "false notions of the Arabs." One of the objections to Jesus' sonship these Arab commoners seemingly made is derived from their reading of God's interrogation of Jesus in Q 5:116: "O Jesus, Son of Mary, did you tell people 'take me and my mother as two gods instead of God'?" Against this charge, Griffith maintains, "Anastasios reminds his reader: this is a false notion about Christians that one must condemn before engaging in controversy with Arabs."[843]

The challenge that Anastasios notes, and Griffith refers to, is undoubtedly paramount in the Christian-Muslim inter-*kalām* during the early Abbasid centuries. The refutation of Jesus' divine sonship and reliance on Qur'anic verses in the polemic was a common practice among Muslims, be they *mutakkalims*, rulers, or commoners. Christian *mutakallims* found themselves pushed by Muslims to ask themselves, as Kenneth Cragg once opined, "does not this Christian faith [i.e., in Jesus' divine sonship] somehow unwarrantably and improperly [as the Muslims claim] compromise God? Is not our paramount duty, in the subtleties of idolatry, to refuse resolutely all that might even unintentionally violate divine transcendence above all that they (i.e., the idolaters) associate?"[844] In addition to showing Muslims that Christianity refuses any belief that compromises God's

841 Sweetman, *Islam and Christian Theology*, I.1, p. 72. See also the dialogue in Mingana, "The Apology of Timothy the Patriarch before the Caliph Mahdī," p. 78.

842 Sidney Griffith suggests that the rejection of God's having a consort who helped Him have a child goes back even to the time of Muḥammad, as the prophet himself expressed His dismissal of Jesus' divine sonship by denying that God needed a woman or a child in Q 2:116 and 4:171: Griffith, *The Church in the Shadow of the Mosque*, p. 30. Griffith does not show here any willingness to delve more deeply into the intrinsic substance of these verses to see whether or not they actually reject sonship as such or reject something else by means of it.

843 Ibid., pp. 28–32, esp. p. 30.

844 Cragg, *Jesus and the Muslim*, p. 198.

oneness and divine nature, Christian *mutkallims* were further faced with the challenge of making their interlocutors and antagonists believe that "'God in Christ' [even in terms of sonship and divinity] is continuous with aspects of faith, which Muslims, and Christians, together hold."[845] One of the most outstanding Christian *mutakallim*, and one who set his sights on the task of meeting this challenge at all costs in the 8th-9th centuries was Theodore Abū Qurrah.

B. Abū Qurrah's Defense of Jesus' Divine Sonship before the Muslims

Abū Qurrah's defence of Jesus' divinity (as such and in relation to his humanity), and his apologies for the Messiah's divine sonship, are scattered throughout his Arabic texts, and launched either against Muslim polemic against Christian Christology or against the Jacobites' and Nestorians' refutations of the pro-Chalcedon Melkite teaching. In this section, I shall restrict my attention to Theodore's apologetics in conversation with Muslim interlocutors and readers. I shall trace Abū Qurrah's defence of Jesus' divine sonship and nature before the Muslims, first in his debate in al-Maʾmūn's court that is narrated in the text of *al-Mujādalah*, and then in his Arabic maymars.

The text of *al-Mujādalah* narrates that Abū Qurrah approaches Jesus' divine sonship from various angles, and he addresses it with diverse terms and strategies that are appropriate to the raised Islamic questions and to the intellectual and logical assumptions that underpin his Muslim interlocutors' refutations. I shall consider the answers he gives by proceeding systematically through the chapters in the texts of the debate and reflecting on Theodore's argumentation strategies one by one.

The first time Abū Qurrah tackles the issue of Jesus' divine shonship before al-Maʾmūn occurs when, in the debate's text, a Muslim called Ṣaʿṣaʿa ibn Khālid asks Theodore about Jesus' humanity. Ṣaʿṣaʿa reveals his familiarity with the Gospels when he cites John 20:17, where Jesus says to his disciples, "I ascend unto my Father and your Father and to my God and your God."[846] He then concludes from Jesus' words 'my God and your God' that he was just God's worshipping servant, like his disciples: Jesus, that is, is just *'ʾīnsān min banī ʾAdam'* (a human from the sons of Adam). Abū Qurrah's answer to this inquiry merits quotation at length:

845 Ibid.
846 Abū Qurrah, *Abū Qurrah wal-Maʾmūn: al-Mujādalah* (Abū Qurrah and al-Maʾmūn: The Debate), IV. A.202–203.

204. قال أبو قرة: لو كان إنساناً من بني آدم لم يعمل الآيات والعجائب التي عمل
205. من إحياء الموتى وغير ذلك، مما يطول شرحه
206. بلا معين ولا معضد، بل بأمر نافذٍ وقول جازم
207. ولكنه جاء إنساناً كاملاً وإلهاً كاملاً
208. فقال لتلاميذه "أبي وأبيكم" بألوهيته و"إلهي وإلهكم" بالناسوتية
....
212. وأما قوله "أبي وأبيكم" فالله يُقال أبوه بالتحقيق وأبو التلاميذ بالإنعام والتفضُّل
213. وأما قوله "إلهي وإلهكم" فهو إلهه على مجاز الكلام والإكرام
214. كمثل ابن ملكٍ قال لغلمانه: "قال لكم مولاي ومولاكم"
215. فهو مولاهم بالتحقيق ومولاه بالإكرام. والله (عزَّ وجلَّ) إله التلاميذ [بالتحقيق] وإلهه بالتفضُّل
216. فإن قلت بل هو إله بالتحقيق، قلنا لك فاجعل التلاميذ بني الله بالتحقيق
217. كما أنَّ التلاميذ ليسوا بني الله بالتحقيق، هكذا ليس الله (عزَّ وجلَّ) إله سيدنا المسيح ربنا بالتحقيق.

204. Abū Qurrah said: "If he was a human from the sons of Adam, he would have not performed the miracles and wonders he did,
205. such as bringing the dead to life and other things, which would take a long time to be explained,
206. without a helper or reinforcer, but by means of an effective command and a firm word.
207. No, he came fully human and fully divine
208. and said to his disciples: 'My father and your father' by virtue of his divinity and 'my God and your God' by virtue of the humanity.
...
212. Concerning his saying 'my father and your father,' God is called his father by virtue of fact and the father of the disciples by virtue of benevolence and favour.
213. As for 'my God and your God,' he is his God figuratively speaking, and to honour him,
214. as when a king's son said to his slaves: "My lord and your lord said to you."
215. He is their lord in fact, and his lord as a term of honour. And God (almighty) is the God of the disciples [factually] and his [i.e., Jesus'] God as an expression of preference
216. If you say: "No, he is his God in fact," we say to you: "Make, then, the disciples the sons of God in fact."
217. Just as the disciples are not the sons of God in fact, likewise God (the almighty) is not in fact the God of our master Christ, our lord."[847]

It is interesting here to note what Abū Qurrah says about Jesus' sonship in relation to his two natures, the divine and the human. Theodore states a prominent orthodox, doctrinal belief that Jesus "came to us fully human and fully divine," But his commendable sensitivity to the mindset and intellectual background of his Muslim interlocutors leads him to circumvent the crudely doctrinal terminological expressions and elaborations on it in orthodox Christian Christology. He does not go into a detailed interpretation of doctrinal questions, such as: How do these two natures unite in one person? Are the two natures expressive of one or two hypostatic existences? Does every nature have will, reason, and separate at-

---

847 Ibid., IV.A.1.204–208, 212–217.

tributes, or not? He opts, instead, to simply state the basic orthodox belief in Jesus' two natures, and then moves directly on to differentiating between 'two manners of speech on,' rather than 'two modes of being in,' Christ, on the one hand, and pointing to two distinct connotations in the way the disciples and Jesus address God, on the other.

Basically, Abū Qurrah stipulates that addressing God in the same words does not mean that the addressers have the same ontological or relational rank as each other vis-à-vis the addressee. Using the same words and expressions as the disciples to address God is actually Jesus' way to reveal his true humanity and its perfection. In this, Theodore concedes, Ṣaʿṣaʿa got it right: Jesus is a real human being, like the disciples. For Abū Qurrah, this is consistent with the orthodox belief that "He came fully human and fully divine."[848] That said, confirming his perfect humanity does not logically, or syllogistically, negate his perfect divinity. The fact that Jesus calls God 'my God,' like the disciples, demonstrates his human nature as it does theirs, but that does not mean that it denies the divine nature, since 1) Jesus also calls God 'my father,' and 2) although the disciples are invited to also call God 'our father' (as in the Lord's prayer), it does not mean the same as when Jesus says it. If this were the case, not only Jesus but also the disciples would be God's sons, which is not accepted in either Christianity or Islam. On the other hand, even though both the disciples and Jesus call God 'Father' and 'God,' they address him as such from different angles and according to distinct ranks: the former call him 'Father' by virtue of grace and 'God' as a matter of fact, while the latter calls him 'Father' as a matter of fact and 'God' to do him honour. That being the case, either Ṣaʿṣaʿa should admit this difference in the manner of speaking, thus conceding a substantial distinction between Jesus and the disciples in the matter of their humanity, or he should reject that distinction, ultimately making the disciples sons of God alongside Jesus, regardless of their humanity. What proves the human identity does not disprove the divine nature. Otherwise, what is said of the one human who also has a divine nature must be said of his disciples too (i.e., that they too are God's sons, since they also call God 'our father'), placing the same insistence upon their humanity. Since this is not feasible, Jesus' humanity, and, thus, his human-like verbal communication with God, must not be used to refute, or even to defend, his divinity. This is the core logic of Theodore's answer to Ṣaʿṣaʿa.

Now, Theodore knows that Q 5:116 is used as one of the prominent Islamic offensive arguments against Jesus' divinity. This is the verse that quotes God's

---

848 Ibid., IV. A.1.207.

question to Jesus: "Did you say to people, 'Take me and my mother as two gods instead of God'?" He therefore pre-empts Ṣaʿṣaʿa's quoting this verse by taking the initiative in discussing this text with his interlocutor:

228. ولكن أخبرني عن قول كتابك إنَّ الله قال لعيسى
229. "يا عيسى ابن مريم أنت قلت للناس اتخذوني أنا وأمي إلهين من دون الله؟"
230. فقال: (سبحانك) إن كنت قد قلته فقد علمته لأنك تعلم ما في نفسي ولا أعلم ما في نفسك
231. فأنت تعلم أنَّ سيدنا المسيح لم يقل للناس اتخذوني وأمي إلهين.
232. بل إنه قال: اتخذوني إلهاً. فهو صحيح.
233. أخبرني، يا مسلم، هل علم الله أنَّ عيسى يجيبه بهذا الكلام والجواب المسموع
234. أم لم يعلم حتى يسأله فأعلمه؟
235. فإن قلت إنه لم يعلم صيرته جاهلاً (تعالى) عز وجل اسمه عن ذلك
236. وإن كان قد علم، فما معنى سؤاله عما قد عرف حقيقته؟

228. But tell me about the saying in your book that God said to ʿĪsā:
229. "O ʿĪsā, son of Maryam, did you say to people, 'Take me and my mother as two gods instead of God'?"
230. And [Jesus] said: "(Be glorified), had I said this you would know it, for you know what is in me and I do not know what is in you."
231. So you know that our lord Christ did not say to people "Take me and my mother as two gods,"
232. but he said "Take me a God." For this is true.
233. Tell me, O Muslim, did God know that ʿĪsā would answer him with these audiable words and response,
234. or did he not know until he asked him and [ʿĪsā] made it known to him?
235. If you said He did not know, you make [God] (the almighty) ignorant; His name be praised and glorified above such thing.
236. And if He already knew, then what is the meaning of His asking about what He [already] knew?[849]

In pre-empting the Qur'anic quotation, Abū Qurrah pursued a sharp-witted exegetical strategy to defy the Muslim *mutakallims*' use of the Qur'ān in their apologetics (see the previous section). Earlier in this chapter, I explored the Muslim *mutakallims*' reliance on scriptural texts in their polemics against Christian Christology, giving ar-Rassī, aṭ-Ṭabarī and aj-Jāḥiẓ as examples. I suggested that, instead of offering a genuinely objective exegesis of the Qur'anic verses, these *mutakallims* opted for an eisegetical application of the scripture to support their preconceived ideas, ultimately snatching these verses away from their textual and theological context. In his interaction with Ṣaʿṣaʿa ibn Khālid, Abū Qurrah challenges this hermeneutical exploitation of the text and implicitly invites his Muslim counterpart to attend more carefully to the text's real implications. He pursues this by conjecturing that the main point of this text – which Muslims,

849 Ibid., IV. A.3.228 – 236.

as Abū Qurrah knows, usually use as evidence against Jesus' divine sonship – does not explicitly centre on Jesus, or his divine sonship, but is, rather, concerned with God's omniscience. *En passant*, Abū Qurrah also reminds Ṣaʿṣaʿa that Jesus never asked people to regard his mother as a god, and that he only spoke about divinity in relation to himself.

After commenting rather rapidly on this, Abū Qurrah takes Ṣaʿṣaʿa to the heart of the Qur'anic text itself, stating that what these verses point to is an explicit declaration from God's Word and Spirit, from God's Messiah, that God is all-knowing and that God alone, and no other, not even his Messiah, is as omniscient as he. So, Theodore then concludes, the text tells us that, if God is the absolute all-knowing, he does not need to ask Jesus (or any other) about anything. Otherwise, God would be accused of ignorance, and that would be blasphemous in both Christianity and Islam. So why did God question Jesus? Abū Qurrah's view is that the question is a rhetorical and figurative Qur'anic device that provides the occasion for Jesus' declaration that God is the absolute all-knowing being. Abū Qurrah is here inviting Ṣaʿṣaʿa to realize that, just as figurative language is present in the Islamic scripture, so it is present in the Christian Gospels. And, just as one should read what the Qur'an says about the omniscient God asking a question without accusing God of ignorance, one has equally to read what the Gospels say about Jesus' calling his divine Father 'my God' as a figurative rhetorical expression that does not negate his divine nature. In other words, an accurate and meticulous exegetical approach to religious scriptures requires great sensitivity to the textual language and framework, which in return paves the way for rationally and logically reliable arguments.

The next defence of Jesus' divine sonship that Abū Qurrah presents in *al-Mujāalah*'s text emerges during his interlocution with a Muslim from the Hashimite clan. This Hashimite takes Abū Qurrah from Ṣaʿṣaʿa's broad issue of denying Jesus' divinity to the narrower, more controversial, issue of rejecting the possibility that God can take a child unto himself

286. فانتبه لأبي قرة رجلٌ من بني هاشم وقال: ويحك يا أبا قرة،
287. اسمع، ما نسبناكم إلى الشرك إلا لقولكم إنَّ الله له ولد
288. فقال أبو قرة: اسمع، يا ابن عم الرسول، قول نبيك وابن عمك في سورة الزمر
289. "لو أراد الله أن يتخذ له ولداً لاصطفاه ممن خلق فيمن يشاء"
290. فأنكرت أنت على ربك أن يصطفي كلمته وروحه ويكرمها ويمجدها ويسميها له ولداً
291. وأنت تسمي نبيك رسولاً وإبراهيم يسمىَ خليلاً وموسى كليماً؟ قال "نعم"
292. قال أبو قرة: فمن الذي يمنع الله أن يسمي كلمته وروحه ولداً إذ هما منه؟ كما الذي هو منك لا تنكره.
293. وأنت تعلم أنه قال في سورة البقرة: "قال اتخذ الرحمن ولداً بل لله ما في السموات والأرض"
294. وفي موضع آخر: "إن الرحمن اتخذ ولداً فنحن أول العابدين"
295. وكتابك ونبيك يقولان إنَّ الله قد اصطفى كلمته وروحه وأسماها ولداً
296. وأنت ونحن وجميع الخلائق نقرُّ أنَّ للرحمن كلمة وروحاً
297. وهي التي نادت الملائكة بأسمائها

298. وداوود النبي يسميها رباً وولداً
299. وأنت تنكر ذلك من الزبور والقرآن والإنجيل
300. وتجحد كلمة الله لقسوة قلبك وتغالط نفسك بتوهمك أنك على يقين
301. وتجهل على الله حيث تقيس روحه المحيية الحالة في جسم آدمي
302. الذي اتخذ من مريم ابنة آدم، وآدم بكلمة الله خُلِق وبروحه نشأ
303. وتجعل لروحه ولكلمته نظيراً وشكلاً

286. And a man from the Hashimite clan took note of Abū Qurrah and said: "Shame on you, Abū Qurrah.
287. Listen, we have not related you to *shirk* except for your saying that God has a child."
288. So Abū Qurrah said: "Listen, O cousin of the prophet, to the saying of your prophet and cousin in *surat al-Zumar:*
289. 'Had God wanted to take a child unto himself [*yattakhidh*], he would have selected him out of what he created and from what he wills.'
290. So, you have denied your Lord the right to choose his Word and Spirit and glorify and honour it by calling it a child for him.
291. Do not you call your prophet a messenger, and Abraham is called a friend, and Moses a converser?" He [the Hashimite] said: "Yes."
292. So Abū Qurrah said: "Who, then, prevents God from calling his Word and Spirit a child if they are of him? As you do not deny what is of you.
293. And you know that he said in *sūrat* al-Baqara: 'He said the merciful has taken a child unto himself. But to God belongs all that is in the heavens and on earth.'
294. And elsewhere: 'If the merciful took a child unto himself, we are, then, the first worshipers.'
295. And your book and prophet say that God has chosen his Word and Spirit and called it a child.
296. And you, we, and all creatures admit that the merciful has a Word and Spirit,
297. which is the one who called the angels by their names [or, whose names were said by the angels].
298. And David the prophet calls it lord and child,
299. and you deny this from the Psalms [*Zabūr*], the Qur'an, and the Gospel.
300. And you reject God's word because of your heart's hardness and delude yourself by imagining that you are certain.
301. And you act ignorantly against God as you measure his life-giving Spirit, which indwells a human body [*jism*],
302. which [God] took from Maryam the daughter of Adam, and Adam was created by God's Word and grew up by his Spirit.
303. And you make for his Spirit and Word an equal and a form.[850]

The Hashimite's challenge to Abū Qurrah's defence of Christ's divinity goes to the heart of the Muslim rejection: Christians are 'replacers' (*mushrikūn*) because they allege that God has a child. One wonders why the idea of 'God's taking a child unto himself' is linked here with *shirk*. In making this link, the Hashimite

850 Ibid., IV. B.1–2.286–303.

indirectly concedes that, if God has a child, that child must be as divine and infinite as God, and his birth would, consequently, occur by means of God's order '*kun fa-yakūn*' (be, and so it will). The Hashimite might be thinking that, if this is the case, Christians make God bring forth another deity from his own divine essence, making him breach monotheism and moving into polytheism.

Abū Qurrah's response to the Hashimite suggests that he saw the implications in the latter's statement, which, in turn, hints at Abū Qurrah's motivation in choosing to respond in precisely the way he did. He begins his reply by affirming God's ultimately infinite freedom to will whatever he wishes and to act as he pleases. He cites a verse, which he claims is from *sūrat al-Zumar*, to show his interlocutor that the Qur'an itself affirms God's omnipotence, even in the matter of fulfilling his wish to take anything as a child unto himself. It is plausible that Abū Qurrah refers here to this verse and no other to speak of God's omnipotence because the exegesis of the verse makes it relevant to his purpose. Rather than rejecting the possibility of 'God's taking a child unto himself,' this verse argues that, since God is omnipotent, taking a child unto himself is something God can easily perform and there is nothing to prevent him from doing so. In other words, 'taking a child unto himself' does not threaten monotheism or make God responsible for causing polytheism by his own actions. On the contrary, it points to God's infinite ability and absolute omnipotence. We have here a Christian *mutakallim* using scriptural statements to support his logical argument. In this, Abū Qurrah is no different from the Muslim *mutakallims* in their application of the same methodology, but he shows in his use of scripture a more subtle and perceptive exegetical appreciation of the core meaning and context of each verse. He wants to counter the accusation of 'association' by emphasizing God's omnipotence, so he quotes a Qur'anic verse that speaks of God's omnipotence, rather than referring to any other verse and then imposing his own presuppositions on its meaning.

This is at least what Theodore pursues in his treatment of the Qur'ānic text. In the ensuing lines of his answer to the Hashimite, Abū Qurrah cites other Qur'anic verses (Q 2:116 and 43:81[851]), but without displaying any exegetical subtlety in his quotations, since neither of the two verses actually refers either to God's omnipotence or to the Qur'anic concession that God may be said to

851 Ibid., IV.B.2.293–294. Note here that Abū Qurrah quotes Q 19:88; 21:62 as saying "*He said* the merciful Has taken a child unto Himself," while the verse in the Qur'an in general use today reads: "*They* said the merciful Has taken a child unto Himself." One wonders here whether this variation suggests that a different version of the text was in use, or whether it merely indicates that Abū Qurrah was quoting from memory and made a mistake.

have taken a child unto himself. One may say that these two verses do not link up exegetically with his first response to the Hashimite.

That notwithstanding, reading Abū Qurrah's quotation of Q 43:81 in the context of his *succeeding*, rather than the preceding, argument may help us find a possible explanation of his use of this verse rather than any other. Q 43:81 says: "If the merciful took a child unto Himself, we are the first worshippers." That is, it acknowledges first that the option of taking a child unto Himself *is* possible and tenable for God. The 'if' here must have caught Abū Qurrah's attention as a Qur'ānic admission that *if* God willed to have a child, his infinite and absolute power means that this is an option open to his divine free will. On the other hand, the verse continues, if this was God's choice, we (his servants) would not only see God's omnipotence in it, but we would also bow down in awe before him and assent to his will. If '81a' serves Abū Qurrah's initial emphasis on the infinity of God's free will and the absoluteness of his omnipotence, '81b' serves his subsequent attack on the Hashimite by emphasizing obedience and compliance. The Qur'an, Theodore argues, commands believers to obey God and bow submissively to his free choice, even if he willed to take a child unto himself. Not only the Qur'an, Abū Qurrah adds, but also the prophet Muḥammad, all the creatures of God, all the prophets (such as David) and the religious books (Psalms and the Gospels) equally declare that God willed by his omnipotent freedom to take his Word and Spirit as a child unto himself.[852] If all these references affirm this possibility, Abū Qurrah concludes, who is the Hashimite or any other creature to disobey God's Word and imagine himself correct in his disobedience?[853]

Following this possible rationale, Abū Qurrah's citation of Q 43:81 seems to be serving the purpose of stressing the Qur'an's understanding of God's omnipotence and its commandment to believers to comply with the consequences of belief in that omnipotence. If God willed to take a child unto himself, all we can do is submit to his will and bow down to it in praise and worship. The same idea of compliance with what God's books and prophets declare about God is used later in *al-Mujādalah:*

348. فقال أبو قرة: أليس يا أمير المؤمنين الإسلام مقراً أنَّ المسيح الذي أتبعه أنا وحفظت وصاياه
349. هو كلمة الله وروحه وأنه من ذاته وجوهريته، خالق غير مخلوق؟ قال "نعم"
350. قال أبو قرة: فأي شيءٍ للعبد أفخر من أن يصدق ويطيع كلمة مولاه؟

348. So Abū Qurrah said: "Does not Islam, O prince of the believers, acknowledge that the Messiah, whom I follow and whose commandments I have kept,

852 Ibid., IV. B.2.295–300.
853 Ibid., IV. B.2.300–301.

349. is the Word of God and his Spirit, and he is from [God's] self and essentiality, uncreated Creator?" He said: "Yes."
350. Abū Qurrah said: "So what makes a slave more proud than to believe and obey the word of his master?"[854]

Upon pointing to God's omnipotence and the obligation of obedience and compliance, Abū Qurrah develops his defence of the tenability of the Christian belief in Jesus Christ's divine sonship. This belief, Abū Qurrah argues, is not only Christian but is also validated in the Islamic scripture. The Qur'an itself speaks of the same idea of divine sonship in terms of 'God's taking a child unto himself.' In addition, the Qur'an does not absolutely and without qualification reject the possibility of God's taking a child unto himself. What the Qur'an does, Abū Qurrah suggests, is confessing God's omnipotence and absolute freedom to will whatever he chooses. In addition, it also commands believers to obey God's will and bow down to its consequences, even if one consequence was that God willed to take a child unto himself. The servant, Abū Qurrah stresses, has only to pride himself on his obedience to, and belief in, the will of his master and the teaching and commandments that convey that will in God's scriptures and his messenger's words.

Up to this stage in his debate before al-Ma'mūn, Abū Qurrah has concentrated on defending Jesus' divine sonship by demonstrating its logical and theological tenability and its harmony with the core meaning of the Qur'anic expression 'God's taking a child unto himself.' In some later parts of the *Mujādalah*, Theodore elaborates on Jesus' divine nature, most conspicuously when the caliph personally enters into the discussion:

539. فقال المأمون له: يا أبا قرة، إن كان المسيح إلهكم، كما تزعمون
540. فكيف أكل الطعام وشرب الشراب ودار في الأسواق كما تقولون وتزعمون؟
541. قال أبو قرة: يا أمير المؤمنين...
542. قد وقفت على الصواب بما تقدم من الخطاب وسبق منى الجواب
...
544. قال المأمون: دع، يا أبا قرة، ما مضى وأسرع بجواب وقول صحيح يقبله عقلي ولا ينكره فكري

539. So al-Ma'mūn said to him: "O Abū Qurrah, if Christ is your God, as you claim,
540. how did he eat food and drink beverges and wander around the markets, as you say and claim?"
541. Abū Qurrah said: "O prince of the believers, ...
542. I have held a true position in my previous discourse and earlier response."
...

854 Ibid., IV.C.2.348–350.

544. Al-Ma'mūn said: "Leave, Abū Qurrah, what has passed and hurry up with a response and an accurate statement that my mind can accept and my thought does not reject."[855]

This inquiry is a direct challenge to the Christian belief that Christ was human and divine simultaneously. The challenge runs as follows: if Christ is God's Word and Spirit (which God is free to take as a child unto himself), Jesus must be divine, since God's Word is God per se (*hiya hūa*). If this is the case, how can this Christ also be said to act and live like a human, carrying in his being their limitations, needs and characteristics? Either, the challenge proceeds, Christ is like other human beings, and so is not God's divine Word, or Christ is God's Word, and then he is only divine and not human, since these two (humanity and divinity) cannot be definitive of one and the same being.

A careful reading of this challenging question indicates the noticeable presence of some Christian doctrinal elements in its logic, namely a Nestorian Christological line of thought: a Christological ontological rationale, which one finds in the conventional patristic Nestorian-like separation of the divine from the human, and a Nestorian philosophical assumption that every nature (*kyana/physis*) has its own, self-existing concrete personification (*parsop/prosopon*). According to this, the divine and human natures cannot be one and the same being, for their activities and ways of living are different (e.g., the divine nature does not hunger or thirst, while the human does). Al-Ma'mūn's question indicates that he is an inquirer who is familiar with the Nestorian division between human nature and its existential personification, on the one hand, and the divine nature and its eternal existence, on the other. This is not surprising, given the good relations that the Nestorian prelates in Iraq and Mesopotamia had historically enjoyed with the Abbasid caliphs from the time of al-Ma'mūn's grandfather, and al-Mahdī's good relationship with the Nestorian patriarch, Timothy I.[856] Like the Nestorians, and in contrast to the other Muslim interlocu-

855 Ibid., V.C.539–544.

856 We know that Timothy I conducted theological controversies with other Christian theologians in the court of al-Mahdī, and did not only attend dialogues with Muslim interlocutors. This means that the Abbasid caliphs were familiar with listening to the complicated doctrinal differences of opinion between the Christians denominations and their stark disagreement on serious matters, such as Christology. For some recent studies of Timothy I's Christian-Christian controversies, see, for example, Alexander Treiger, "Could Christ's Humanity See His Divinity? An Eighth-Century Controversy between John of Dalyatha and Timothy I, Catholicos of the Church of the East," *Journal of the Canadian Society for Syriac Studies*, 9 (2009), 3–21. On the culture of the Abbasid court and the Christians' presence in it, see Kennedy, *When Baghdad Ruled the Muslim World*, pp. 243–260. On Christology in the Nestorian Church, see Brock, "The Christology of the Church of the East."

tors in his court, al-Ma'mūn does not actually deny the existence of divinity in Christ, but rather inquires as to how Abū Qurrah interprets that divinity's existence alongside Jesus' undenied humanity. We have here, then, Abū Qurrah's response to an Islamic version of Nestorian Christology.[857]

How did Abū Qurrah answer this Nestorian-like Christological challenge, which al-Ma'mūn invoked to inquire about the divinity and humanity of Christ? Let us first cite the relevant passages from Abū Qurrah's own words as they appear in the text of *al-Mujādalah:*

547. قال أبو قرة: أما بعد يا أمير المؤمنين، أعلم أن القول لك
548. أعرفك أنَّ المسيح الله
549. الآب والابن والروح القدس إله واحد
550. المعروف بوحدانية جوهريته، المعبود بثالوث خواصه

…

563. له أقرّ وإياه أعترف بالربوبية واللاهوتية والعظمة والجلال والقدرة

…

566. وأؤمن أن يجمع جوهر الآب الأزلية والربوبية واللاهوتية والعظمة والجلال والقدرة
567. والابن والروح القدس مثل ذلك الذي للآب

547. Abū Qurrah said: "Furthermore, O prince of the believers, I know that yours is the final word.
548. I make it known to you that Christ is God.
549. The Father, Son, and Holy Spirit is one God,
550. who is known in the singularity of his essentiality, worshiped in the Trinity of his characteristics [*khawāṣṣih*].

…

563. To him I assent and confess his lordship, divinity, majesty, dignity, and power.

…

857 It is not unlikely that early Muslims were familiar with Nestorian theological doctrine, far more than with the theological thought of the Jacobites and Melkites, due to the consistent first-hand contacts with Nestorians since the time of the prophet Muḥammad and the Rightly-Guided Caliphs in the Arabian Peninsula. On the regular interaction between Muslims and Nestorians, see, for instance, Baumer, *The Church of the East*, pp. 137–168; Jeremy Johns, "Christianity and Islam," in *The Oxford History of Christianity*, ed. John McManners (Oxford: Oxford University Press, 2002), 167–204; Chase F. Robinson, *Empire and Elites after the Muslim Conquest: The Transformation of Northern Mesopotamia* (Cambridge: Cambridge University Press, 2000). On the theological encounters between Muslims and Nestorian Christianity, see, for example, Sidney Griffith, "Disputes with Muslims in Syriac Christian Texts: From Patriarch John (d. 648) to Mar Hebraeus (d. 1286)," in *The Beginnings of Christian Theology in Arabic*, ed. S.E. Griffith (Aldershot: Ashgate, 2001), V: 251–273; Griffith 'Muhammad and the Monk Bahira"; and Samir, "The Prophet Muhammad as Seen by Timothy I".

566. And I believe that the essence of the Father combines [the attributes of] infinity, lordship, divinity, majesty, dignity, and power,
567. and [to] the Son and Holy Spirit similarly [belongs] that which is the Father's.[858]

The above does not set out Abū Qurrah's response in full, but only specific sentences relevant to the main focus here. In the lines that are not cited above, Theodore expresses his understanding of God's attributes and 'beautiful names' (*al-'asmā' al-ḥusnā*),[859] and repeats his own understanding of God's oneness-as-trinity, already explained in his responses to other interlocutors. My concentration in this chapter, however, is strictly on the logic of Abū Qurrah's Christological arguments, not on his Trinitarian or theistic discussions, which have been dealt with in the previous chapter. Hence, the selection here is of the Christological points that are made in his response to the caliph.

It is interesting that Abū Qurrah's begins with the Trinity in order to make a Christological point. In his response to the caliph, set out above, Theodore says: '*'u'arrifuka 'annal-Massīḥ Allah*' (I make it known to you that Christ is God). The reader expects this to be followed by a further elaboration on this Christological statement. But intriguingly, this is not the case. Instead of explaining how Christ is God, Abū Qurrah seems to move abruptly from a statement about Christ to rather lengthy declarations on the triune God and his divine attributes: '*al-Āb wal-'Ībn war-Rūḥ al-Qudus Īlah Wāḥid al-Ma'rūf bi-Waḥdāniyyat Jawharih, al-Ma'būd bi-Thālūth Khawāṣṣih*' (The Father, Son and Holy Spirit is one God known in the singularity of his essentiality, worshiped in the Trinity of his characteristics). In Wafīq Naṣrī's edition of *al-Mujādalah*, which is the one consistently followed in this study, sentence 548 says 'Christ is God'; while the ensuing sentences 549 – 583 (pp. 199 – 203 of Na.srī's edition) are all a detailed interpretation of the triune nature and unity of God. Only after this long detour into Trinitarian theology does the text return to the caliph's question on the two natures of Christ (sentences 584 – 597; pp. 203 – 206).

Why do we find in these lines an abrupt shift from answering a question on Christology with a Christological discourse to approaching the question with a lengthy discourse on the Trinity? Why would Abū Qurrah start with a statement on the divine nature of Christ, and then suddenly go into a detailed confession of God's triune nature before bringing his reply back onto the track of the original question about Christ?

858 Abū Qurrah, *Abū Qurrah wal-Ma'mūn: al-Mujādalah* (Abū Qurrah and al-Ma'mūn: The debate), V.C.1.547 – 567.
859 Ibid., V.C.1.561, where he literally says: *lahu al-asmā' al-ḥusnā* (His are the beautiful names).

The scholars of ancient manuscripts and textual criticism may consider the possibility of an editorial or scribal amendment to the oldest version of the text of *al-Mujādalah*. A later scribe or editor may have inserted into the original text fragments of Abū Qurrah's teaching on the Trinity, thinking them to be relevant to the original content that is transmitted by the earlier scribes who recorded Theodore's debate in the caliph's court. If this could be proved, sentences 549 – 583 in Naṣrī's edition would be an additional pericope inserted by a later scribe, while, in the original version of the text, sentence 548 would have been directly followed by sentences 583 – 597, to which it would have been a prelude.

I do not intend to explore the plausibility of this hypothesis and do not believe that such a redactionist reconstruction of the text is the only possible explanation for the abrupt shift from Christology to the Trinity in the response of a rational, systematic and strictly logical thinker like Abū Qurrah. It is my belief that referring to the Trinity to reply to a question on the two natures in Christ in fact demonstrates a genuine 'Abū Qurran' strategy and subtlety, as well as his profound awareness of the roots and assumptions behind the caliph's question. Sentences 549 – 583 in Naṣrī's edition are not, I believe, an editorial addition or later insertion but rather are part and parcel of Abū Qurrah's presenting an explanation of the two natures in Christ in a way that was specifically appropriate to the caliph's Nestorian-like enquiry.

As stated earlier, al-Ma'mūn's inquiry – as to how the divine Word of God cold eat and drink and move around like a normal human being – is loaded with the implications of a Nestorian rejection of Chalcedonian orthodoxy on the basis of the Nestorian belief that the divine and the human could not be one and the same reality, and that, if they stood together for any reason, each nature must have its own, separate personal existence. In the light of this originally Nestorian logic, al-Ma'mūn inquires about how the same person, called Jesus, can have both a human and a divine nature without this means that we are dealing here with two separate persons – the human, who eats, drinks and wanders around, and the divine, God's Word and Spirit, who should not be said to act like human beings. Abū Qurrah seems to have detected traces of this Nestorian influence on al-Ma'mūn's question and decided to answer by relying on an orthodox theological rationale that had, in fact, also been followed by Nestorius of Constantinople himself.

Chapter three of this study has set out a brief analysis of the Christological debate between Nestorius of Constantinople and Cyril of Alexandria in the 5th century.[860] There, I argued that Nestorius believed not only that his understand-

860 See chapter three, section IV.

ing of the unity of the two natures in Christ was the most appropriate theological and philosophical explanation of the ontological aspects of the incarnation, but also, and just as emphatically, that his understanding was the inevitable Christological outcome of the orthodox ontology that was developed in the Trinitarian discourses at the Councils of Nicea in 325 and Constantinople in 381. Among the basic elements in Niceno-Constantinopolitan Trinitarian doctrine are the notions of 'particularity' and 'distinction,' which were expressed, as even Nestorius acknowledged, by using the technical terms *hypostasis* and *ousia* in Greek, or *kyana* and *qnuma* in Syriac. Nestorius believed, as shown in chapter three, that adhering to the Niceno-Constantinopolitan orthodox Trinitarian ontology required that these same notions and their hermeneutical implications be applied in Christology too. Nestorius followed this rule by importing the notions of 'particularity' and 'distinction' from the discussion of the unity-in-threeness of the three divine *hypostases*, into the discussion of the two natures of Christ. He suggested that, as the three persons' oneness lay in the central and foundational factor of their hypostatic distinction, the oneness of Christ could not be maintained, let alone plausibly explained, without similarly emphasizing the clear distinction and total particular hypostatic existence of each nature. Thus, Christ is not truly *fully* divine and *fully* human – as the scripture, Nestorius maintains, attests – unless one maintains a total distinction between his two natures and distinguishes uncompromisingly between the particularities of the divine and the human in him.

I argued in chapter three that Nestorius never actually spoke of separation or division, but always about the concrete particularity of and distinction between the two natures, which appears in their personal representation in Jesus' life and ministry. Cyril and his allies missed this notional specificity in Nestorius' Christology and did not realize that he was developing it within the framework of his adherence to the orthodox, Niceno-Constantinopolitan, Trinitarian ontology. Nestorius' choice of words, I have proposed, is also to be held accountable for Cyril's mis-appraisal of his theology, as he, perhaps unwisely, used the Syriac term *parsop* instead of *qnuma* to convey the Greek notion of *hypostasis*. He did not clarify that, in his understanding of *hypostasis*, he followed the Cappadocian (and Ephraimite) distinction between *hypostasis* and *ousia*, rather than the total equation of these two terms like the one found in Athanasius.

There is no need here for further repetition of the analysis in chapter three, which is recalled in order to develop a proposal on why Abū Qurrah's response to al-Ma'mūn's Christological question began with a discourse on the Trinity. Abū Qurrah hears a Nestorian tone in the caliph's words, so he reverts to an equally Nestorian principle in his response, namely Nestorius' attention to the notions of 'particularity' and 'distinction' in the doctrine of the Trinity and his reliance on them in his understanding of the unity of the two natures in Christ. Thus, in his elaboration on the Trinity in sentences 549–583, Abū Qurrah shows al-Ma'mūn that, even though God's nature is triune, God remains one deity because the Father, Son and Holy Spirit are not three separate and divided essences, but three particular and distinct *khawāṣṣ* (characteristics) of the one and the same God. None of them is separated from the other (just as the sun and the moon are not separate from their light).[861] The Father, Son and Holy Spirit are one God, though the first alone is particularly called 'God the originator,'[862] while the second and third are distinguished by being called 'the creating Word' (Son) and 'the perfecting Spirit' (Holy Spirit).[863]

From the doctrine of the Trinity as Abū Qurrah explains it to the caliph, we learn that 'particularity' and 'distinction,' rather than 'division' and separation,' are intrinsic to the meaning of God's oneness. What Abū Qurrah does not say explicitly, but conveys implicitly, is something like the following: "understanding oneness in terms of 'distinction' and 'particularity' is inherent in the Christian Trinitarian framework of Christian thought, not only of the thought of Melkites like me, but also of those who follow the thinking of Nestorius, which seems to lie behind your question to me."

But, why would Abū Qurrah try to answer the caliph by implicitly alluding to a Trinitarian emphasis on 'distinction' and 'particularity' that is derived from Nestorius? I believe the answer can be found in an earlier section in the text of *al-Mujādalah*. One of the interlocutors in the caliph's court, called Abū al-Ḥusayn al-Dimashquī, expresses his failure before Abū Qurrah's arguments by saying to the caliph

---

861 Abū Qurrah, *Abū Qurrah wal-Ma'mūn: al-Mujādalah* (Abū Qurrah and al-Ma'mūn: The Debate), V.C.3.572–575

572. فقد تعلم أن الشمس والقمر والنار مخلوقات وقوة ضوئها يتولد منها بلا انفصال وحرارتها ظاهرة منها في غير انقطاع

573. فلا الجوهر أقدم من ضوئها وحرارتها ولا الضوء والحرارة أحدث من ذلك الجوهر

574. ولا الجوهر يُعرَف إلا بالضوء والحرارة ولا الضوء والحرارة تُعرَف إلا بالجوهر

575. كذلك الله (عز وجل ثناؤه) هو وكلمته وروحه من غير افتراق بينهم.

572. And you know that the sun, moon and fire are creatures and the power of their light originates from them inseparably and their heat emanates from them unstoppably.

573. So, neither the essence is older than its light and heat, nor the light and the heat are newer than this essence,

574. and the essence is not known except by light and heat, nor are the light and heat known except by essence.

575. Likewise, God (both glorified and dignified is He) and His Word and Spirit are inseparable from each other.

862 Ibid., V.C.1.564, where Abū Qurrah calls fatherhood the origin: *al-ubūwa hiya al-aṣliyyah*

863 Ibid., V.C.3.579–581.

363. ... أبا قرة يرميني بسهام من جعبتي
364. فسلاحي فانٍ وسلاحه باقٍ

363. Abū Qurrah shoots at me with arrows from my own quiver.
364. My weapon is transient, his weapon is immortal.[864]

This strategy of 'shooting at the other with arrows from their own quiver' is also followed when Abū Qurrah tackles the caliph's question on the two natures in Christ. Abū Qurrah perceived that the logic of the caliph's question derives from ideas he may have heard from Nestorians at his court. So, Theodore decided to quench the caliph's thirst by offering him water from the same Nestorian fountain. He was, in other words, shooting at the caliph with arrows from the latter's own quiver.

If this connection with Nestorian thinking in both the question and the answer is plausible, it can be surmised that Abū Qurrah's abrupt shift from Christology (sentence 548) into long comments on the Trinity (sentences 549–583) is neither an editorial or scribal amendment, nor an unintended weakness in the logical progression of Abū Qurrah's argument. Rather, it may be a very deliberate apologetic strategy, in which Theodore perceives his interlocutor's underlying assumptions and counters his presumptions with answers derived from, or shaped after, the same line of reasoning.

Abū Qurrah's Christological statements that follow (sentences 584–597 in Naṣrī's edition) are all developed within the framework of understanding the 'unity-despite-difference' of the two natures in Christ on the basis of the 'unity-in-particularity/distinction' of the three divine persons in the orthodox doctrine of the Trinity. For example:

584. فإن كان المسيح، يا أمير المؤمنين، أكل الطعام مثل إنسان
585. فقد أشبع بلاهوته من خمس خبزات سبعة آلاف نفسٍ
...
587. وإن كان قد شرب الماء بناسوته فقد حول الماء خمراً في عرس قانا الجليل بعظم لاهوته
588. وإن كان مشى في الأسواق فقد شفى الأمراض

584. So, if Christ, O prince of the believers, ate food as a human,
585. he fed seven thousand souls with five loaves through his divinity.
...
586. And if he drank water in his humanity, he transformed water into wine at the wedding of Cana in Galilee by the greatness of his divinity.
587. And if he walked in the markets, he also cured diseases.[865]

864 Ibid., IV. D.4.363–364.
865 Ibid., V. C.4.584–585, 587–588.

The key to unlocking the puzzle of Christ's two natures, Abū Qurrah concludes, lies in viewing Jesus' seemingly contradictory, natural and supernatural, actions and modes of existence from the angle of the Trinitarian notions of 'distinction' and 'particularity.' Eating food and drinking water like any other human does not negate Christ's divine nature any more than feeding the multitudes miraculously does not disproving his humanity. Eating, drinking and moving around ultimately point to the authentic reality of Jesus' humanity as particularities that belong to human nature (e.g., drinking and eating and walking). Similarly, Jesus' supernatural abilities and miraculous acts of healing reveal the authenticity of Christ's divinity as actions that are particular to divinity (e.g., healing and miraculous activities). Such particularity does not stand against the unity of the two natures or imply their division. It rather protects their unity by founding it on the distinctness of the two natures. This applies successfully in Christology just as it does in relation to the unity of the three in the Trinity (as was conceded even by Nestorius, who struggled with the concept of the two natures in Christ).

It is certainly intriguing to see a prominent father of the Melkite Church and staunchly orthodox-Chalcedonian theologian like Abū Qurrah riding the wave of a 'non-orthodox,' or even (for the Melkites) 'heretical,' theologian like Nestorius to explain a central element in Christian Christology. The fact that he chose this rather courageous and far from conformist approach shows, first, Abū Qurrah's thorough knowledge of the theological teachings of past and contemporary patristic, orthodox and heterodox traditions. He even seems to be familiar with the writings of the non-Melkite fathers themselves, not only with commentaries on them, and to be ready to draw on their theological and conceptual resources quite ably and reliably. Second, Abū Qurrah's readiness to use Nestorius' rationale in a Melkite discourse demonstrates his apologetic strategy: responding to his opponents' challenges *from within* the same intellectual and conceptual framework as that from which they derived their polemic. Al-Maʾmūn's reliance on Nestorian logic in his question invited Abū Qurrah to develop an answer with the help of a parallel Nestorian logic, in an attempt to show that the Nestorian spring that brought forth the question could also produce an answer to it, showing his interlocutors that the arrows in their quiver can be shot back at them.

The pages above have presented an analysis of Abū Qurrah's response to Muslim objections to Christ's divine nature and sonship that was raised in the debate at al-Maʾmūn's court. In the rest of this section, I shall look at what Abū Qurrah had to say elsewhere in his maymars about the divine nature and sonship of Christ.

In his, *fī Ikrām al-Aiqūnāt* (On the veneration of icons), Abū Qurrah presents the Christian doctrines regarding the divine nature and sonship of Christ on two occasions. The first is when he blames Christians for being obsessed with pleasing Muslims (*al-barrāniyyūn*, to use Abū Qurrah's term) and compromising basic Christian practices and rituals (in this case the veneration of icons) in order to gain the Muslims approval. Abū Qurrah strictly rebukes these approval-seeking Christians and warns them that compromising on ritual practices would become the thin end of the wedge and would take them along the costly and unforgivable track of sacrificing fundamental elements of faith. If the Muslims abhor prostration to icons, they reject even more harshly Christian christological and theological doctrines, so what would save those who avoid a liturgical practice in order to satisfy Muslims from the pitfall of abandoning basic confessions of faith if the Muslims went as far as expecting it. Abū Qurrah argues:

7. فمن من أولئك يسمع النصارى يقولون أن لله ابناً هو عدله من جوهره إلا قال أنَّ هؤلاء مجانين
8. وإذا سمعهم يقولون إنَّ هذا الابن المولود من الله ليس الله بأقدم منه، أليس يظنهم أشد الناس مكابرة؟

7. For who of those who hear the Christians say that God has a Son, who is equal to him and from his essence, would not say that they are mad?
8. And if he heard them say that God is not older than this Son, who is born from God, would not he assume that they are the most arrogant people?[866]

The second place, where Abū Qurrah states Christ's sonship and divinity, is when he tries to explain why God revealed his Trinitarian nature to the Christians and not to the Jews before them. Theodore says that God did this because the Jews were not ready to receive a coherent understanding of this truth and to act according to it in a correct religious manner. They would have mistaken the triune nature of God for polytheism and associated the real God with false deities. The minds of the Christians, however, are ready to welcome this Trinitarian truth and to apprehend it accurately by virtue of the Holy Spirit and the grace of the cross

22. وأيضاً بنو إسرائيل...
23. ... كتمهم الله ابناً ورِوحاً كل واحدٍ منهما إله تام مثله ومن جوهره يستحقان السجود مثله
24. لكي لا يكون ذلك علّة لهم ليتخذوا آلهة مع الله لكَلبِهِم على عبادة آلهة شتى والسجود لها
25. ودفن معرفة ذلك في كتبه كلها لتظهر في زمانه
26. فأما النصارى فإنه أفصح لهم بأعلى الصوت أن لله ابناً وروحاً كل واحدٍ منهما إله مثل الله ومن جوهره
27. فهم يعبدون الابن والروح مع الله ولا يعبدون آلهة شتى بل يقولون إنَّ الله وابنه وروحه إله واحد
28. لأنَّ لعقولهم لطاقة تفهم ذلك إذ قد فاض عليها روح القدس بصليب المسيح الذي هو تسبحته كما قلنا

22. And also the children of Israel ...
23. ... God has hidden from them a Son and a Spirit, each of whom is a perfect God like him and from his essence, who merit prostration like him,
24. so that this would not be [the Israelites'] excuse to take gods with God unto themselves, since they rush into worshipping various deities and prostrating to them.

866 Abū Qurrah, *fī Ikrām al-Aiqūnāt* (On the veneration of icons), I.2.7–8 (pp. 91–92).

> 25. And he buried the knowledge of this in all his scriptures in order to appear in his [Jesus'] time.
> 26. As for the Christians, he disclosed to them with the loudest voice that God has a Son and a Spirit, each of whom is a God like God and is from his essence.
> 27. So they worship the Son and the Spirit with God, and they do not worship many gods, but say that God and his Son and Spirit is one God,
> 28. for their minds have the subtlety to apprehend this, since the Holy Spirit has been poured out upon them by the Cross of Christ, who is [God's] praise, as we stated.[867]

It is clear that Abū Qurrah does not develop on either occasion an apologetic explication or a detailed justification for the Christian belief that God has a divine, eternal and ontologically equal Son. He only invokes this belief in support of his primary elaboration on the Christian understanding of the veneration of icons. He acknowledges the Muslims' rejection of this belief and the Jews' ignorance of it, but rather than setting it aside to please the followers of the other two monotheistic, Abrahamic religions, Abū Qurrah states that Christians alone are enabled rationally to comprehend this belief because they are enlightened by the Holy Spirit. The alleged foolishness of the belief that God Has a divine Son proves, in Abū Qurrah's view, the poor rational abilities of those who make this allegation, as well as it demonstrates the reliable cognitive perception of those who would otherwise be accused of madness, because they believe in this divine sonship. Traces of the same strategy of 'shooting at others with arrows from their own quiver,' which we witnessed in *al-Mujādalah*, can also be detected in this maymar.

After looking at Abū Qurrah's defence of Christ's divine sonship in *al-Mujādalah* and *fī Ikrām al-Aiqūnāt*, let us now finish this part with some analysis of Abū Qurrah's attempt to defend the divinity and eternal sonship of Christ in his other Arabic maymars. One of the most relevant in this regard is his *Maymar fī Sabīl Maʿrifat Allah wa-Taḥqīq al-Ibn al-Azalī* (Maymar on the way of knowing God and verifying the eternal Son). In this work, Theodore presents a defense of the logical plausibility of believing that God 'took a child unto himself.' He starts his apology with an explanation of the possibility of knowing God through logic and reason. He suggests three epistemological means for obtaining such knowledge: 1) an Aristotelian causal argument;[868] 2) an analogical argument that proposes assimilation (opposite to the Muʿtazilites' rejection of analogy in relation to God) as a reliable means of knowing God;[869] and 3) an appophetic ar-

867 Ibid., III.18.22–28 (pp. 184–185).
868 Abū Qurrah, *Maymar fī Sabīl Maʿrifat Allāh wa-Taḥqīq al-Ibn al-Azalī* (Maymar on the way of knowing God and verifying the eternal Son), pp. 75–91, esp. pp. 76–78.
869 Ibid., pp.78–79.

gument that deduces knowledge of God via an ontological differentiation between God and the human beings.[870] For Abū Qurrah, these three epistemological means not only give us rational access to God's existence and being. They can also become reliable instruments for testing the logical plausibility of the belief in God's taking a Son (*ibn*) unto himself and in that Son's eternal divinity that is totally equal to his originator's eternal and divine nature. Theodore thinks that the analogical and the appophetic arguments in particular fulfill this purpose. Thus, in the rest of the maymar, he uses these two arguments to defend the divinity and eternal being of God's Son.

Abū Qurrah introduces his reader to this shift from the possibility of acquiring knowledge of God analogically and appophetically to using these means to test the Son's divinity and infinity in the following words:

> فإذ تقرر عندنا أنَّ معرفة الله إنما أفضينا إليها على أحد هذه الثلاثة أوجه فهلم حتى نعلم إن كان العقل يودينا إلى أنَّ لله ابناً من جوهره هو عدله كما يشهد الإنجيل والناموس والأنبياء وقد اتفقنا أنه لا يصلح أن نصف الله بشيءٍ من المناقص التي عندنا
>
> Since it was decided by us that we acquire knowledge of God by one of these three ways [i.e., causal, analogical, and apophatic], let us find out whether the mind would claim that God has a Son from his essence, who is his equal, as the Gospel, the law [*nāmūs*], and the prophets testify. And we have agreed together that it is inappropriate to attribute to God any of the deficiencies which we [i.e., humans] have.[871]

Abū Qurrah's emphasis on the Muslim and Christian consensus on God's ontological difference from us is his subtle reminder that the Christian do emphasize God's transcendence and total otherness, despite their claim that he took a Son unto himself. In other words, God's origination of a Son is not an anthropomorphic proof that God and his creatures are one and the same. Christians are not, that is, idolators or crude anthropomorphists, but rather analogical and apophatic in their logic. This insistence on God's total transcendence and otherness suggests that Abū Qurrah's Muslim opponents in this maymar are primarily the Muʿtazilites, who refused to ascribe any attributes to God. They emphatically stood against speaking of God's reality in any relational, metaphorical, or anthropomorphic manner because they believed that this would threaten God's oneness and eternity (*qidam).* The Muʿtazalites developed this conviction and propagated it from the time they were established as an intellectual movement

---

870 Ibid., pp.79–80.
871 Ibid., p.80.

in Islam in the first half of the 8th century CE by the Baṣran thinker Wāṣil ibn ʿAṭāʾ.[872]

In this maymar, Abū Qurrah is probably responding to a Muʿtazilite refutation. He therefore starts by stating three ways of knowing God by reason, one of which the Muʿtazilites in particular were known to follow, namely the causal argument.[873] This is Abū Qurrah's way of assuring his Muʿtazilite interlocutors that the Christians also follow the causal rational argument in their reasoning about God. Furthermore, by stating that there is between Christians and Muslims an agreement (*qad ittafaqnā*) that no human deficiency must be ascribed to God, Abū Qurrah also assures them that Christians side primarilly with the Muʿtazilites in their insistence that God's unity is absolute, provided that absoluteness designates God's total otherness from humans.[874]

Having confirmed these common elements to his Muʿtazilite readers, Abū Qurrah, also states the elements of disagreement between Christian and Muʿtazilite thought. He shows in the ensuing lines that, contrary to the Muʿtazilites, Christians do not depend on the causal argument alone for acquiring knowledge of God, but equally rely on analogical and apophatic reasoning. Christians even believe that these two epistemic arguments are sound enough to defend the rational plausibility of God's taking a child unto himself. In the next pages of his maymar, Theodore endeavours to show how analogy and apophaticism support the tenability of such a belief.

---

872 Wolfson, *The Philosophy of the Kalām*, pp. 132–143. On the Muʿtazilites and their debates with the Ashʿarites on God's absoluteness and the divine attributes, see, for instance, Richard M Frank, *Early Islamic Theology: The Muʿtazilites and al-Ashʿarī: Texts and Studies on the Development and History of Kalām*, ed. Dimitri Gutas (Burlington, VA: Ashgate, 2007). On the development of Arab-Islamic philosophy in Muʿtazilite *kalām* and the development of the Ashʿarite opposition to it in general, see also Majid Fakhry, *History of Islamic Philosophy*, 3rd ed. (New York: Columbia University Press, 2004), pp. 43–66; 170–186; 209–222; and Tilman Nagel, *The History of Islamic Theology*, pp. 125–170.

873 Tilman Nagel even believes that the causal argument was consistently the sole focus of Muʿtazilite rational thinking about God: "The Muʿtazilites had focused their attention strictly on causality in nature in order to understand better the nature of the Creator-God and to explain why human beings, who were obliged to act in this world, were rewarded and punished in the next world": Nagel, *The History of Islamic Thought*, p. 157.

874 Harry Wolfson perceives this concern, and suggests that the entire Islamic discussion on the attributes is actually derived from Christian thinking: "The views of the orthodox Muslims and the Muʿtazilites on the problem of attributes, as well as the arguments employed by them, correspond exactly to the views of orthodox Christians and the heretical Sabellians on the question of the persons of the Word and the Holy Spirit in the Trinity": Wolfson, *The Philosophy of the Kalām*, p. 139.

This is how Abū Qurrah articulates in his defence from analogy the tenability of claiming that God took a child unto himself. Theodore's words are cited in full here as they appear in Constantine Bacha's edition:

فأخبرني أيها الجاحد للابن، أتقول أنَّ الله يقدر أن يلد مثله أم لا يقدر. فإن زعمت أنَّ الله لا يقدر أن يلد مثله، فقد أدخلت عليه أعظم المنقصة حيث تجعلنا نحن يقدر أحدنا أن يلد مثله وتجعل الله لا يقدر على ما نقدر نحن عليه من الفواضل. لأنَّ الولد قد علم كل الناس أنه من مكارم ما عندنا وفواضله. فلا بد لك من أن تقول أنَّ الله يقدر أن يلد مثله. فنقول لك إذ قد أقررت بهذا فإنَّ الله لا يمتنع أن يلد مثله (إذ كان قادراً أن يلد) إلا لأحد ثلاثة أسباب. إما لكلفة تنوبه في الولادة يكسل عنها ويعجز. وإما لأنه لا يحب أن يرى مثله حسداً وإما أن يكون فيه قوة على ذلك لا يعرفها وإنما يمتنع عن أن يستعملها جهلاً بها. فكل هذا اسمج من أن يقال على الله وهو نفي منه. فلعمري ما يعتريه كسل ولا يدخل عليه حسد ولا يدنو منه جهل. إذاً تبارك وتعالى قد ولد ولداً هو عدله لا محالة وليس لأحد أن ينكر أنَّ لله ابناً وإلا فقد أدخل على الله النقص والعيب والسماجة العظيمة.

So tell me, you who disbelieve in the Son, do you say that God can or cannot beget one like himself? If you allege that God cannot beget one like himself, you have introduced into him the greatest deficiency, since you count one of us capable of begetting his like and count God incapable of the virtues of which we are capable. For, everyone knows that a child is [made up] of the dignities and virtues which we have [ourselves]. So [in like manner], you are bound to say that God can beget his like. And, we say to you, if you admit this, that God would only refrain from begetting his like (since he is capable of begetting) for one of three reasons: either because some inconvenience befalls him that delays or incapacitates him, or because, out of envy, he does not want to see another like him, or because he has in him the power to do this but is unaware of it and refrains from using it because of his ignorance of it. All this is too disgusting to be said of God and must be repudiated. I swear that he is not afflicted by any laziness, and no envy enters unto him, and no ignorance draws near to him. So, may he be blessed and glorified, he has begotten a Son who is undoubtedly his equal, and no one can deny that God has a Son, for he would then introduce into God a deficiency and imperfection and gross unseemliness.[875]

The core logic of Abū Qurrah's use of analogy circles around hermeneutical variations on God's omnipotence. His discussion runs as follows: Begetting children is one of the known abilities of God's creatures, the human beings, and one aspect of this ability is the begetting of others who are similar to those who beget them. Now, if a human person is capable of begetting another like him, and is God's creature, God must be able at least to have in himself what he has already causally bestowed upon his creation. Either God can perform what his creatures perform as one of the abilities that God bestowed on them, or God is impotent, limited and far from absolutely divine. Either, that is, God is omnipotent, or he is deficient, envious and repugnant, and not God at all. That being the case, saying that God, by analogy with his creatures, can take a child (who is from his essence

---

875 Abū Qurrah, *Maymar fī Sabīl Maʿrifat Allāh wa-Taḥqīq al-Ibn al-Azalī* (Maymar on the way of knowing God and verifying the eternal Son), pp. 80 – 81.

and equal to him) unto himself is rationally consistent with belief in God's omnipotence and the Creator-creature causal relation with humankind.

In the next lines of the maymar, Abū Qurrah also develops a parallel apophasis-centred argument for God's taking a child unto himself. The first question that comes to mind here is: Why did Abū Qurrah opt for such an argument? He probably perceptively anticipated his Muʿtazilite interlocutors' reaction to the analogical explanation given above. He must have known that the Muʿtazilites, who gave God's transcendence and infinite otherness absolute priority, would weary of this comparison of the Creator to his creation and conclude that the consequence of Theodore's argument would be: if God can have a child just because his creatures can beget children equal to them, then God must also follow in his generation of a child the same process that humans follow. Thus, if a human begets another through a 'before-and-after' temporal process, God, if we are to use the argument of analogy, must also beget a Son in the same way. If this is the case, God and his child cannot be the same, since the former is eternal, while the latter (since he is begotten) is not. In other words, the starting point contradicts the outcome, while the conclusion defies logically the conceptual point of departure.

Anticipating this counter-argument to his analogical hermeneutics, Abū Qurrah resorts to another well known rational argument in the Christian orthodox theological circles, namely the appophetic argument: acquiring knowledge of God by discerning what God is not and on the basis of how God differs ontologically from his creatures.[876]

لكن تقول أيها الجاحد للابن إن كان الله ولد ولداً فإن الله أقدم من ابنه. فينبغي لك أن تذكر أنّا اتفقنا بالاضطرار أن نصف الله بمكارم ما عندنا وننفي عنه مناقصنا لمخالفتها جوهره الكريم وحده. وقِدَم الآب على الابن إنما يكون من نقص طبيعة الوالد عندنا. وذلك أنَّ أحدنا يولد غير تام ولا بالغ حد مقدرة الولادة: فذلك الزمان الذي بين مولده وبين بلوغه طاقة الولادة لابد أن يكون فيه أقدم من ابنه. وإذا بلغ الإنسان منا طاقة الولادة لا بد أن يكون فيه أقدم من ابنه. وإذا بلغ الإنسان منا طاقة الولادة فهو ولو كان أحرص الناس على الولد لا يقدر أن يلد إلا بالزواج وتمضي عليه أزمان قبل أن يصل إلى زمان الزواج يكون فيها أقدم من ابنه...فأما الله تعالى فإنه لم يكن قط غير قادر أن يلد مثله. ولم يكن قط لا يعلم أنه يقدر أن يلد مثله ولم يكن قط لا يشاء أن يلد مثله لئلا يدخل عليه العيوب التي ذكرناها من فوق ولا يحتاج إلى غير هذا ليلد. وليس بين مشيئته وبين أن يكون ما يريد طرفة عين. وإلا فذلك ضعف به وعجز في جوهره. فقد ولد الله لا محالة وليس الله بأقدم من المولود منه.

But, you who disbelieve in the Son, say that if God begot a child, God would be older than his Son. You should recall that we agreed that we must impute to God the virtues that we

876 For some of the classical literature on the apophatic or mystical tradition in Christian theology, see, for example, Vladimir Lossky, *The Mystical Theology of the Eastern Church* (New York: St Vladimir's Seminary Press, 1997); Vladimir Kharlamov, *The Beauty of the Unity and the Harmony of the Whole: The Concept of Theosis in the Theology of Pseudo-Dionysius the Areopagite* (Eugene, OR: Wipf and Stock, 2009); and Andrew Louth, *The Origins of the Christian Mystical Tradition: From Plato to Denys* (Oxford: Oxford University Press, 2007).

> have, but negate from him our deficiencies because they are incompatible with his uniquely dignified essence. The precedence of the father over the son is due to a deficiency in the nature of the begetter in our case, for when one of us is begotten he is incomplete and not yet capable of begetting. So, this time between his birth and his attaining the ability to beget inevitably means that he is older than his son. And if one of us humans reached the [stage of the] ability to beget, he must then be older than his son. And, if one of us, humans, reached the [stage of the] ability to beget, no matter how concerned he was to beget a child, he could only beget by mating, and a period of time must pass before he reaches the time to mate, and this will make him older than his son … . But, God, may he be glorified, has never been unable to beget another like him. And, he has never been ignorant of his ability to beget another like him, and he has never been unwilling to beget another like him, lest he introduces into himself the imperfections we referred to above, and he does not need anything else in order to beget. And, there is not [even] blinking of an eye between his willing and the coming to be of what he willed. Otherwise, it would be a weakness in him and a disability in his essence. Therefore, God has undeniably begotten, and God is not older than the one begotten from him.[877]

The creature, Abū Qurrah states, is an image of the Creator and provides epistemic access to the Creator's reality, but he then immediately confirms that this image is analogical and never ontological in nature. It not only reveals what God is in the sense that his abilities are imaged in the human person, but also demonstrates what God *is not* by virtue of his ontological difference from his creatures. The analogical argument, Theodore suggests, is incomplete and deficient if used alone and so is not sufficient to lead to a reliable knowledge of God. It must, rather, be complemented by an apophatic argument (based on what God is not) in order to provide us with a plausible explanation of God's begetting ability in relation to his omnipotence. In other words, Abū Qurrah seems to be suggesting that, in relation to knowing God, apophasis without analogy leads to complete silence and ignorance, while analogy without apophasis leads us to a complete mythologization of the divine.

Interesting here, systematically speaking, is Abū Qurrah's inclusion of analogy, apophasis and causality in a triadic network. He seems to be inviting the Muʿtazilites to take their trust in the causal argument to its natural, logically inevitable conclusion, which lies in developing both analogical (positive) and apophatic (negative) understandings of the organic relation that logically links the caused (creation) to its primal cause (Creator). The theological rationale behind this invitation is: if God is the causer of creation, understanding the causal relation between the cause and its caused entities requires the discerning of common, similar attributes that usually originate from a causer-caused relation,

---

877 Abū Qurrah, *Maymar fī Sabīl Maʿrifat Allāh wa-Taḥqīq al-Ibn al-Azalī* (Maymar on the Way of God's Knowing and the Verification of the Eternal Son), pp. 81–82.

thus pursuing an analogical interpretation. However, if this analogical similitude between the causer and its caused creatures is not to mar the ontological distinction between them, understanding this causal relation equally requires giving attention to what is not definitive of the causing Creator by also pursuing an apophatic interpretation. Causality is logically incoherent apart from analogy and apophasis. Ultimately, staying rationally with the triad of 'causality-analogy-apophasis' will lead to a tenable and authentic confirmation of belief in God's begetting of an equally eternal and divine Son.

This rationally subtle argument is not the only one Abū Qurrah pursues in his Arabic maymars. We find another defence of the Son's divine sonship in his, *Maymar Yuḥaqqiq anna li-Allah Ibn hūa ʿAdluh fī aj-Jawhar wa-Lam Yazal Maʿah (*Maymar affirming that God has a Son who is equal to him in essence and is still with him). There, in question-answer dialogue fashion, Abū Qurrah offers a rational justification of the belief that God Has a co-eternal and *homoousius* Son, but instead of verifying the notion of sonship per se, let alone reflecting on the knowability of God, Theodore this time begins with an elaboration on God's supreme lordship. He argues that God's lordship is not restricted to his superiority as Creator over his creation. Nor is it preconditioned by that creation's existence, or in need of such an existence. God is Lord eternally; in his own self-existence. He is Lord before the existence of his creation, and he will remain so after his creation's disappearance. God's lordship, that is, expresses his ontological infinite omnipotence, which is far from being derivable from creation or bestowed upon God by that creation in fulfillment of some divine need. This is how Theodore articulates this argument:

فأن قلت أنه لم تكن له رياسة قبل الخلق فقد جعلته يتخذ الشرف من الخلق لأنَّ الرياسة شرف لمن هي له لا محالة. وإن كان الخلق هم الذين شرفوه وحاشا له ذلك فإنه لا منّة له عليهم بخلقه إياهم لأنَّ حاجته إلى أن يشرَّف بالرياسة عليهم هي التي دعته إلى خلقه إياهم وهذا استئصال لجوده وإبطال لطيبه وكفر بنعمته.

So, if you say that he had no lordship before creation, you have made him derive honour from creation, for lordship is definitely an honour to the one who has it. And, if it is creatures who bestow honour on him – far be it from him – his creation of them would be no favour to them on his part, since it would be his need to be honoured by lordship over them that which made him create them, and this would be the eradication of his generosity, the revocation of his kindness, and disbelief in his grace.[878]

---

878 Abū Qurrah, *Maymar Yuḥaqqiq 'anna li-Allāh Ibnan hūa ʿAdluh fī aj-Jawhar wa-lam Yazal Maʿahu* (Maymar affirming that God has a Son who is equal to Him in essence and is still with Him), p. 92.

If God is Lord over all creation, it is because he is eternally and infinitely omnipotent, regardless of the created reality. And, since God is different from the human (in the apophatic sense), God's lordship must not be understood in comparison to, but in contrast with human lordship.[879]

After stressing God's absolute omnipotence and ontological lordship, Abū Qurrah moves on to specify the object of God's lordship: either God is Lord over another less than him, another better than him, or another who is his equal. If God's lordship is ontologically inherent to his eternal being, he must not be seen as merely Lord over lesser creatures, because that would place a condition on God. On the other hand, God's lordship cannot be exerted over others who are better than him: '*wa-'ammā afḍal min Allah falays shay', jalla wa-tabarak*' (and better than God there is no else, blessed and glorified is he).[880] Therefore, Abū Qurrah concludes, God must be Lord over another who is his equal.

What kind of lordship would God have over his equal? Abū Qurrah here suggests three forms of known lordship: by coercion (*qahr*), by agreement, or by nature (*ṭibāʿiyyah*). Lordship by coercion is inapplicable to God, since God's lordship is not over lesser things but over his equal. On the other hand, lordship by agreement is also inapplicable to God, since 'agreement' suggests temporary and circumstantial compliance from the one under his lordshop that may change and make God's honour contingent.[881] God's lordship over his equal must therefore be by virtue of his nature and nothing else, and this '*riyāsa ṭibāiyya*' can only be seen in the father-son relationship:

وأما الرياسة الطباعية فهي التي تكون للآب على الابن التي لا زوال لها ولا نيلت بالقهر ولا فيها كلفة ولا وهم وهي ممتلئة سروراً وحباً. فلعمري أنَّ الآب مسرور بالابن يحبه كما شهد عليه إذ اصطبغ متجسداً في الأردن فقال هذا ابني الحبيب الذي به سررت (متى 3: 17) فجمع له المحبة والمسرة. والابن مسرور بالآب يحبه كما قال في الإنجيل في مواضع كثيرة (يو 15: 9)

And concerning lordship in terms of nature, this is what the Father has over the Son, and it is immortal, not obtained by means of coercion, without affectation or delusional, and is full of happiness and love. I swear that the Father is pleased with the Son, loving him as he testified to him, when he [the Son] was baptized incarnate in the Jordan [river], say-

---

879 Ibid.

فأما الله تبارك وتعالى فإنه لا شيء من الخلق بتة يعدله في شيءٍ جلّ عن ذلك. فإنَّ أرفع خليقته في الخلق لأبعد عن طبيعة الله من الصورة عن الإنسان المصوَّر ومن الظل عن الجسد ومن الشخص البادي في المرآة عن الوجه الذي يطلع فيها ومما هو أبعد من هذا عن صاحبه بما لا يتوهم

Concerning God, may He be praised and glorified, He has no equal whatsoever in creation – far be that from Him – for the noblest creature in creation is unimaginably further from God than a picture is from the person in the picture, and than the shadow is from the flesh, and than the person who appears in a mirror is from the face that appears in it, and than anything further from its [the face's] owner

880 Ibid., p. 93.

881 Ibid., pp. 93–94.

> ing: "This is my beloved Son in whom I was pleased" (Matthew 3: 17), bringing together love for and happiness in him. And, the Son is pleased with the Father, and loves him as he said in many places in the Gospel (John 15: 9).[882]

God's lordship over the one baptized in the Jordan is not the lordship of a Creator over his creatures, or of a master over his servant. It is, rather, the lordship of a Father over his equal Son: a lordship of mutual love and pleasure. Any other form of lordship between the Son and the Father is not against the Son's sonship, but more dangerously against God's very own omnipotence and being.

It is not made explicit why Abū Qurrah would begin in his justification of God's having a Son with a rational elaboration on God's lordship. Why did he opt for this instead of starting immediately with the question of God's begetting a Son, as he does later in his maymar? Is there here, again, the suggestion of a later editorial or scribal decision to combine into one work two different texts on Christology known to have come from Abū Qurrah, each of which presents an apology for Christian Christology in response to a distinct set of questions from distinct Muslim interlocutors? In principle, there is nothing that would stand against such a hypothesis, since the versions of the texts in our hands are not Abū Qurrah's originals. On the other hand, there is no historical or scriptural evidence to prove that this maymar is the product of an editorial, redactionist emendation by later scribes. Nevertheless, since this study attempts systematically to analyse the theological content of Theodore Abū Qurrah's Arabic apologetic works, rather than to trace their historical and textual roots and origins, I simply raise these questions and move on to consider the content of the rest of this maymar.

If the first pericopes of *Maymar Yuḥaqqiq anna li-Allah Ibn hūa ʿAdluh fī aj-Jawhar wa-Lam Yazal Maʿah* (Maymar affirming that God aas a Son who is equal to him in essence and is still with him) represent a response to an inquiry on the logical tenability of claiming that God can *in principle* 'take a child unto himself,' the ensuing parts of this maymar seem to be focusing on developing a rational explanation for the possibility of 'begetting' a child, or the tenability of saying that God takes a child unto himself *specifically by means of begetting*, and how Christians can present an apology for this in the face of the Islamic belief that God *'lam yalid wa-lam yūlad'* (Has not begotten, and is not begotten) (Q 112:3). This transition from an inquiry on 'taking a child unto himself' *per se* to an inquiry as to how is it possible to say that God does so specifically by means of 'begetting' emerges as follows:

---

882 Ibid., p. 94.

ولكن تقول كيف يلد الله وقد نرى الوالد تنوبه النوائب التي لا يخلو منها أحد من الجماع والحبل وتوابع ذلك مما لا يحسن أن نقوله على الله؟

But you say how can God beget when we can see that the begetter would follow the processes that none is exempt from, including intercourse and pregnancy and their consequences, which we cannot appropriately say concerning God.[883]

To Abū Qurrah's ear, this question is not ontological (that is, it is not related to God's nature or identity as Lord), but rather functional in character. It asks *how* God can perform a specific action in a certain way, rather than how can God *be* the deity he is and have another deity beside him. Because Theodore reads the question from this functional perspective, he emphasizes in his reply the incomprehensibility of God's actions, implicitly relying on the biblical, Old Testamental assertion that God's ways are far different from humans' (Is. 55:1–2). Abū Qurrah starts his response by almost saying to his interlocutor: "Who are you to know God's ways, and to be able to comprehend their intrinsic operational nature?" God's actions transcend in their nature and possibilities even the minds of the angels and the heavenly hosts. If God's actions and identity are restricted to what our human minds can apprehend and our rational intelligence can conceive, Abū Qurrah proceeds, then everything we say about God to express his glory and nature in human terms is false and unreliable. As we tend to deny God the ability to beget because it does not concur with our rational ideas about deity, we must, equally, reject every other claim that our minds accept about God's being and characteristics, for we either accept what our human cognitive expressions and descriptions apply to God, including the ability to beget, or we reject every expression our minds produce about God's actions and identity, including not only the ability to beget, but also every other claim, such as 'God is a living being,' 'God can hear and see,' 'God is wise,' or 'God is a maker.'[884] Abū Qurrah then asks his opponent: "How can you accept the use of these statements, which your mind has created, about God, the infinite and perfect deity, even though you know that each of these abilities or attributes has its own deficiencies and limitations, according to human reason?" "What you do," Abū Qurrah argues, "is that you free these abilities and attributes from their deficiencies first and then apply them to God. Now, if doing this is allowable in speaking about God in terms of 'living, hearing, speaking, thinking wisely, and making,' why is it not tenably allowable in speaking about God in terms of 'begetting'?"

883 Ibid.
884 Ibid., pp. 94–96.

وإلا فما بالك تحقق على الله هذه الأسماء التي ذكرناها من السمع والحكمة والصنعة وغير ذلك وأنت تراها لا تبلغ إلى فهمك فواضلها إلا مع مناقصها وقد رضيت بنفيها من مناقصها وإخلاص فواضلها لله ولا تحقق على الله الولادة وإن كان اسمها لا يبلغ إلى فهمك فضله إلا مع نواقصه فتجعل لاسم الولادة أسوة بغيره من تلك الأسماء وتوقعه على الله كما توقع تلك، هذا منك ليس بعدل.

Or, what is the matter with you applying to God these terms that we have mentioned, of hearing, wisdom, workmanship, and others, whose virtues, you realize, cannot be perceived apart from their deficiencies, and so you are happy to deny their deficiencies and apply their virtues to God, while you do not apply begetting to God, perceiving its virtues only along with its deficiencies, so you treat this term of begetting in the same way as the other terms and apply it to God as you apply the others. This is unjust of you.[885]

Theodore concludes from this logic of 'either equally confirm all the terms, or equally reject all of them' that any denial of God's ability to take a child unto himself specifically by means of 'begetting' is an act of obstinacy before, if not also against, God and his omnipotence and an attempt to deny God an ability that is far superior to merely 'creating things out of nothing' (*yakhluq al-'ashiyā' min lā shaiy'*). Denying God the ability to 'beget' would in fact mean making him less in power, let alone in being, than his creatures, for whom the begetting of others is one of their virtues. "How can God create out of nothing creatures, who can beget others and lack that ability Himself?" Abū Qurrah seems to be asking. God would either then be less than his creatures in terms of ability, which makes him less than God, or God would be limited in his abilities (he can 'create out of nothing,' but he cannot beget), which makes God far from omnipotent. In either case, denying God the ability to beget, while stressing his ability to create out of nothing, Abū Qurrah concludes, would lead:

إلى تعطيل رياسته التي ساقك إليها العقل الصدوق باضطرار. وقد رضيت أن تقصر بالله تقصيراً تزيل به من قبلك شرف ملكه وعلو قدرته نفاراً من اسم الوالد الذي الهمت نفسك بغضه لجاجةً ووافقك تكذيب عقل أحق من العيان قد ألجأك باستقامة إلى أن تقرّ بالابن الأزلي جماحاً في الفرار مما لا حياة لك إلا به وحسبك مخلصاً من الهلكة والعار يوم الدين....

to crippling his lordship, which is what sincere reason has necessarily led you to. And you have agreed to limit God with a limitation by means of which you remove the honour of his kingship and the greatness of his might, abhorring the name of 'father,' which you insisted on deluding yourself into avoiding and contenting yourself with counting false a reason, [which is] more truthful than sight, that invited you with integrity to accept the eternal Son, fleeing from the one [i.e., the Son] apart from whom you have no life, who is sufficient to save you from perishing and disgrace on the day of judgment.[886]

885 Ibid., p. 97.
886 Ibid.

From this argument, Theodore bluntly calls on everyone, Muslim, Christian, Jew, or otherwise, to believe in the eternal Son, who is begotten from the Father before all ages, who saved us by means of his incarnation from the Virgin Mary, and who saves us from our sins if we accept his redemption and believe in his divinity and avoid the hypocrisy that leads us away from the path of reason.[887]

Abū Qurrah's elaboration in the rest of this maymar demonstrates his consistent implementation of his 'first reasoning, then searching scripture' apologetic method, analysed above in chapter two, and he now takes his interlocutors straight into the scriptural attestations to the eternal generation of the Son. This is how he bridges his discussion of his logical-rational defence and his biblical-textual argument:

> واعلم أن هذا الابن قد تحقق أيضاً من وجوهٍ كثيرة غير الوجه الذي حققناه وإن كان هذا حسبك إن كنت ذا لبٍّ أو لك رغبة في الحياة الدائمة. ومع هذا كله وأفضل من هذا قد تنبأت عليه الأنبياء الذين كتبهم بايدي النصارى واليهود جميعاً وأخبروا بمولده الأزلي من الآب ومولده الثاني من مريم العذراء وبأوجاعه وصلبه ودفنه وكل تدبيره غير الذي يصرح به الإنجيل المقدس من ذلك. وكتب الحديثة كلها ومصاحف العتيقة والحديثة مبذولة لكل من أراد معرفة ذلك وعليه أن يطلب ذلك فيها ولا يكلفنا تتبعه مما قد تكلفنا له من سبيل العقل على ما نحن عليه من الضعف في عقولنا ونياتنا التي بصحتها نجتلب نور المعرفة من روح القدس الذي أفاضه علينا المسيح بصلبه مع أننا لئلا نعطل أمر الابن الأزلي من شهادات الكتب المنزلة سنأتي بأقرب ما يحضرنا عليه من ذلك
>
> And know that this Son has been also affirmed in many ways other than the one in which we affirmed him, even though that would be sufficient for you if you have a mind and you want immortal life. Despite all this, even better than all of this, the prophets, whose books are in the hands of both the Christians and the Jews, have prophesied about him and told about his eternal begetting from the Father and his second begetting from the Virgin Mary and about his pains and crucifixion and burial and all his providence, apart from what the Holy Gospel states, and all the books of the New [Testament] and the old and new books [*maṣāḥif*] are all offered to anyone who wants to know this. It is up to him to seek [this knowledge] therein, the following of which does not cost us what it cost us when we followed [in our defence] the path of reason, given the weakness we have in our minds and intention, and its truth brings us the light of knowledge from the Holy Spirit, whom Christ poured out on us by his cross, although we, lest we hinder the decree of the eternal Son found in the testimony of the revealed books, will cite from them here as closely as we can.[888]

Searching the Old and New Testaments to producee biblical attestations to the Son's eternal generation takes Abū Qurrah back to the Book of Psalms (Ps. 10:3; 44:7; 83:8) and the Wisdom Literature (Prov. 8), where he equates Jesus with 'wisdom' and speaks of the Messiah as being with the Lord God from eternity and as being God's pleasure and instrument in creating the entire

---

887 Ibid., p. 98.
888 Ibid.

creation.[889] Then, he moves to the prophetic literature, quoting Isaiah (9:6; 44) on the divine one, who established heaven and earth and was commissioned by the Father and the Holy Spirit to be one of us:

> فمن هو هذا الأول وإلى الأبد الذي أسس الأرض وصلب السماء ودعا بابل ووضع طريقها والآن الرب أرسله وروحه إلا الابن الأزلي الذي صار رسولاً للآب والروح القدس حيث تجسد وولد من مريم العذراء...فلعمري قد صار الابن الإله معنا في تجسده وعدّ فينا.
>
> So who is this first, and forever, who established the earth and the firmament of heaven, and called Babel and set its path, and who has now been sent by the Lord and his Spirit, except the eternal Son, who became a message of the Father and the Holy Spirit when he was incarnate and was born from the Virgin Mary ... I swear that the divine Son has become with us in his incarnation and was counted among us.[890]

The next lines of the maymar show Abū Qurrah reciting, clearly from memory, various other scriptural claims and statements, from Galatians 4:4; Jeremiah 1; John 1:1, 6:38; Genesis 1:26; Micah 5:1–2; Matthew 20:28; Hosiah 1:6, etc. He even refers sometimes to apocryphal, extra-canonical texts, such as Baroch 3:36,[891] when they serve his argument. One cannot but notice that all these biblical texts are presented without a proper exegetical explanation of their content and context. On the contrary, Abū Qurrah seems here to be quoting the Bible in a way that seems to be as remote from an accurate exegesis as the use by some of the Muslim interlocutors we met in *al-Mujādalah* of Qur'anic verses to argue against the possibility of 'God's taking a child unto himself by means of begetting.' The apologetic concern to support rational argument with prooftexts from scripture clearly takes here priority and precedence over approaching the biblical text exegetically rather than eisegetically. Scriptures here are used to serve the rational justification of the Son's eternal divine origin.[892]

---

889 Ibid., pp. 98–99.
890 Ibid., p. 100.
891 Ibid., pp. 101–104.
892 Ibid., p. 103.
ألا ترى أنه [يوحنا] يسميه [المسيح] "كلمة" ويقول أنه إله. وهذه الكلمة التي بها خلق كل شيء مار بولس يسميها ابناً ويقول أنّ الله بها صنع الدهور. ويسمي هذا الابن ضوء مجد الله (عب 1: 2) ليعلم الناس أنه لم يزل مع الله كما أنَّ ضوء الشمس لم يزل في الشمس
Do not you see that [John] calls Him [Christ] 'Word' [*kalima*] and he says that He is God. And, this Word, by means of which [God] created everything, St Paul calls 'Son' and he says that God made the ages by it. And, he calls this Son the light of God's glory (Heb 1:2), so that people might know that He [the Son] is still with God, as the sun's light remains in the sun.

IV. The Incarnation in Abū Qurrah's Christology

Scholars of Christian-Muslim polemics tend to study the arguments and counter-arguments over both Jesus' divine sonship and his divine-human nature as part and parcel of the study of the Christian-Muslim differences over the notion of 'incarnation.' Here, however, I deliberately distinguish the subjects of 'divine sonship' and 'divine-human identity,' on the one hand, from the subject of the incarnation, on the other, because, in Theodore Abū Qurrah's Arabic apologetic texts, his defences of each of these three topics are distinct, treated as various separate, yet not totally unrelated, components of the Christian discourse on Jesus Christ, Christology. He answers the question of how God could take a child unto himself (divine sonship) almost separately from the question of how an ordinary human being can also be divine in nature and equal in that divinity to God himself (divine-human identity), as the discussions in the previous parts of this chapter have shown.

In what follows, I shall show that Abū Qurrah offers still more logical explanations and apologies in defence of the possibility of God's *logos* becoming human and dwelling amongst us as a real Man-God, i.e., the incarnation. In my view, missing this theologically and methodologically very subtle distinction between understanding the tenability of the incarnation, on the one hand, and the divine sonship and divine-human identity, on the other, would hinder a fair hermeneutic treatment and a proper apprehension of Theodore Abū Qurrah's theological thought. Abū Qurrah's defence of the rational tenability of the incarnation will be the last subject to be analysed in this chapter on Abū Qurrah's Christology in his debates with Muslims. This chapter will then end with an investigation of whether, in his attempt to defend the possibility of 'God taking a child unto himself,' Jesus' having two natures, divine and human, and the Word of God becoming flesh and dwelling amongst us, Abū Qurrah remained firmly within the boundaries of Melkite Christian doctrinal orthodoxy or he failed to do so.

A. The Incarnation between *Tajassud/Ta'nnus* and *Ḥulūl*

Christians and Muslims alike usually concede that belief in the incarnation is one of the divisive subjects between the two monotheistic faiths. In his appraisal of Christian-Muslim dialogues throughout history, Badru Kateregga expresses the Islamic rejection of the Christian theology of the incarnation when he claims that the incarnation in particular is "the point where Muslims and Christians painfully part company." He then proceeds to state that this doctrine "seems to compromise God's transcendence and sovereignty while at the same time exalting a mere man to God-like status."[893] The late Kenneth Cragg in turn also realizes that the incarnation is one of the most friction-creating elements between Islam and Christianity. Cragg, first, points out that the core meaning of the idea of the 'incarnation' in Christianity is simply "the human expressibility of God."[894] He, then, suggests that 'incarnation' is the Christian synonym of the Arabic-Islamic notion of *tanzīl* (descent), as both terms "denote in concept and conceal in mystery the divine/human, the eternal/temporal, relationship."[895] This notwithstanding, Cragg admits that God in Islam is exempted from engagement with creation in general and humankind in particular. Such an involvement, Cragg states, is disavowed as "unfitting to divine sovereignty." And, if it is ever conceded, God's involvement is then strictly seen as exerted via "law, guidance, exhortation and judgment, yet never via anything related to incarnation."[896] In stark contrast to this Islamic view, Cragg goes on, Christians believe that in the humility of the incarnation in the redeeming grace of the cross, and nowhere else, lies a way towards comprehending divine transcendence in a manner broader than the limits of 'prophecy.'[897]

Despite the above, the question to be reckoned with here is whether Islam rejects the notion of 'incarnation' altogether, or whether it stands against a specific theological understanding of this notion in Christian thought. It may be that Islamic *mutakallimūn* and thinkers stand specifically against the Christian interpretation of the idea of incarnation as an expression of *union* between the infinite, transcendent divine reality of God and the finite, mortal and contingent reality of the human.

It is well known among scholars that this understanding of the incarnation as divine-human union is not alien to Christian theology. In his comparative study of Christian and Muslim theologies, Windrow Sweetman points out that Church fathers such as Theodore of Mopsuestia, Paul of Samosata and John of Damascus, to mention just few, do interpret the incarnation as basically a divine-human union. That said, Sweetman draws our attention to the fact that

893 Badru D. Kateregga and David W. Shenk, *Islam and Christianity: A Muslim and a Christian in Dialogue*, (Nairobi: Uzima Press, 1980), p. 132; also cited in Rollin G. Grams, "Revealing Divine Identity: The Incarnation of the Word in John's Gospel," in *Jesus and the Incarnation: Reflections of Christians from Islamic Contexts*, ed. David Emmanuel Singh (Eugene, OR: Wipf & Stock, 2011), 47–59, p. 47.

894 Kenneth Cragg, *Muhammad and the Christian: A Question of Response* (London: Darton, Longman & Todd, 1984), p. 110.

895 Ibid., p.83.

896 Ibid., p.137.

897 Ibid., p. 139.

they also conjecture that such a union is fundamentally voluntary and never substantial: it is performed out of the divine *Logos*' free goodwill (*εὐδοκία*). These fathers maintain that this voluntariness protects the two united natures from any possible conflation and "shows that the person (*Πρόσωπον*) made up of both is one and indivisible."[898] What is thought-provoking in Sweetman's exposition of this patristic view is his realization that, in relation to the Muslim stance on the incarnation, "it is worth noting that [the stress on God's free will] is precisely the argument against substantial union which is used against incarnation in Muslim theology."[899]

If Sweetman's view is correct, one may say that Muslims' concern for God's freedom and transcendence is what energizes their rejection of what Christians say about the incarnation. Their main objection stems not essentially from their refusal to confess God's ability to do voluntarily whatever he pleases – including interaction with the human on a very intimate level – if he decides to do so. It rather stems from their refusal, first, to bestow upon Jesus any divine status that would make him God's Son or equal, as well as, second, from their conviction that any surmised union between divinity and humanity in any act of (substantial) incarnation is logically implausible, let alone impossible.[900]

In both their ancient and contemporary Arabic theological texts, Eastern, Arabic-speaking Christians speak of the incarnation using one of the following three Arabic words: '*tajassud*' (embodiment, or maybe 'enfleshment'), '*ta'annus*' (literally 'en-humanization'), and '*ḥulūl*' (indwelling). It is interesting and intriguing that, when the Qur'an touches upon the idea of incarnation in relation to Christian Christology, it overwhelmingly uses yet another Arabic term, the noun *wilāda* (birth) or the verb *'īlād* (birthing), thus associating the incarnation with Jesus' birth from, or by, either the Spirit, or the angel Gabriel, who conveys the Spirit.[901] in the Qur'anic witness, it is worth considering the silence about how Mary conceived the child, on one hand, and the association of the messen-

898 Sweetman, *Islam and Christian Theology*, 1/II, p. 104.
899 Ibid., 1/II.p. 104. Sweetman is right in detecting, in this Islamic view, traces of the Nestorian denial of any union in terms of substance between the divine and the human that can lead to a conflation between them (ibid.). Yet, the concern about forbidding any mixing or conflation between the human and the divine is not just a Nestorian concern. It is a principal orthodox, Chalcedonian patristic concern as well. The difference between Nestorian and Chacedonian Christologies lies in the solution each opted for to avoid this threat of conflation: the former emphasized division and separation, the latter emphasized togetherness and alongside-ness.
900 See on this Mark I. Beaumont, "Defending the Incarnation in the Early Christian Dialogue with Muslims," in *Jesus and the Incarnation: Reflections of Christians from Islamic Contexts*, ed. David Emmanuel Singh (Eugene, OR: Wipf & Stock, 2011), 155–168.
901 See Q 19:17–22; 21:91; 66:12.

ger of the miraculous birth (the Spirit) (rather than the conceived child) with the act of taking a human form (as if the Spirit is experiencing a form of an 'en-humanization' or *ta'annus*).This is particularly the case in Q 19:17–22, where the Spirit is represented as an angelic messenger with human features (mouth and voice, at least) conveying to Mary the news of the birth (in a clear evocation of the nativity story in Luke 1:26–28, as Harry Wolfson correctly notes[902]).

On the other hand, understanding the incarnation in terms of 'birth' is also associated in the Qur'an with the notion of the 'Word' (*al-Kalimah*), as we read in Q 3:45. Here, we have the angels, rather than the Spirit, conveying to Mary the message of God's Word, who is named ʿĪsā b. Maryam, and who is going to have honour in this world and the hereafter and be very close to God.[903] One can see here an indirect claim that Jesus is none other than the divine Word of God, who is going to become *someone* honourable and dignified (en-humanized!) through his birth from Maryam.

Nevertheless, in both the Spirit-centred and the Word-centred references to the incarnation in terms of virginal birth-giving, one cannot but realize, as Harry Wolfson persuasively suggests, that there is in the Qur'an a clear denial of the divinity of Jesus – which I believe reflects a refusal to interpret the incarnation as divine-human union, or as divinization – while still affirming the miraculous birth from a virgin[904] – which invites, in my view, consideration of possible room for accepting the incarnation in terms of the miraculous birth of God's Word as an honourable human who will be intimately favoured by God. One cannot but wonder here whether this dissociation of the miraculous birth from divinity is the Qur'anic method of finding an acceptable form of the idea of incarnation by interpreting it in terms of a 'birthing' (*'īlād*) that is expressive of God's power. This interpretation may just be the Qur'anic way of countering the interpretation of the incarnation in Christian Christology as an expression of the divine nature of the child that was born vis-à-vis this birthing and was called Emmanuel. In other words, one wonders whether this hermeneutical editing is the Qur'an's way of preserving the concept of 'incarnation,' rather than an indication of the Islamic scripture's complete rejection and denial of its usefulness.

A similar possible tendency to re-interpret, rather than discard, the notion of 'incarnation' in a manner that opposes its Christian theological connotations can

902 Wolfson, *The Philosophy of the Kalām*, pp. 306–307.
903 "إذ قالت الملائكة: يا مريم إنَّ الله يبشركِ بكلمة منه اسمه المسيح عيسى ابن مريم وجيهاً في الدنيا والآخرة ومن المقربين" Behold the angels said: "O Mary God giveth thee glad tidings of a Word from Him; his name is the Messiah, ʿĪsā the son of Mary honourable in this world and the hereafter and one of those who are close [to God]."
904 Wolfson, *The Philosophy of the Kalām*, p. 310.

also be extracted from some Muslim *mutakallimūn*'s and interlocutors' critiques of, and reflections on, Christian Christology. One of the common stances of these Muslim apologists is their unanimous rejection of interpreting the incarnation, or using the miraculous virginal birth, as evidence of Jesus' divine sonship or God's union with the human. One can find traces of such rejection, for example, in the conversation between Patriarch John I (Sedra) and ʿUmar ibn al-ʿĀṣ (according to F. Nau[905]), or ʿUmayr ibn Saʿd al-Anṣārī (according to K. Pinggéra and B. Roggema[906]) – British Museum manuscript ADD.17193 – which is assumed to have occurred in 639 CE The text states that ʿUmar/ʿUmayr asks the Patriarch "when Christ was in the womb of Mary, He of whom you say He is God, who carried and ruled heaven and earth?", before the Muslim prince later demands that Jesus' divine sonship must be proved to him through reason and Old Testament texts, or John must recant.[907]

The rejection of viewing the incarnation as evidence of divine sonship, or of God's involvement with humans, is also reflected in the Caliph al-Mahdī's engaging of Patriarch Timothy I in a dialogue over Christianity. We have here the caliph saying to the prelate: "O Catholicos, a man like you, who possesses all this knowledge and utters such sublime words concerning God, is not justified in saying about God that He married a woman from whom He begat a son."[908] To this accusation, Timothy responds: "And who, O God-loving king, has ever uttered such a blasphemy concerning God?"[909] This exchange, eventually, takes the two men into a detailed discussion of the nature and identity of both Jesus and Muḥammad from a Christian point of view.

We also find a similar rejection of the Christian view of the incarnation in the polemics of Abū ʿĪsā al-Warrāq. In his treatise, *Against the Incarnation*, al-Warrāq not only rejects the notion of 'incarnation' in terms of birth, but also argues that

---

905 This what F. Nau believes to be the identity of the Muslim interlocutor: F. Nau, "Dialogue between the Patriarch John I and the Amir of the Hagarenes," in *The Early Christian-Muslim Dialogue: A Collection of Documents from the First Three Islamic Centuries (632–900 AD), Translations with Commentary*, ed. N. A. Newman (Hatfield, PA: Interdisciplinary Biblical Research Institute, 1993), pp. 11–46.

906 Karl Pinggéra, "Johannes I. (III.) von Antiochien ('Johannes Sedra')," in *Giographisch-Bibliographisches Kirchenlexicon*, 23(2004), pp. 734–737; and Barbara Roggema, "The Disputation of John and the Emir," in *Christian-Muslim Relations, A Biographical History (600–900)*, Vol. I, pp. 782–785.

907 F. Nau, "Dialogue between the Patriarch John I and the Amir of the Hagarenes, pp. 24–26, pts. E, G.

908 Mingana, "Woodbrooke Studies: Patriarch Timothy I and the Caliph Mahdi," p. 175; and Heimgartner, *Timotheos I., Ostsyrischer Patriarch*pp. 3–4.

909 Mingana, p. 175; and Heimgartner, p. 4.

'incarnation' per se is inappropriate logically and conceptually in its Christian theological version.[910] Rather than just dismissing the notion of 'incarnation' altogether, al-Warrāq makes a sweeping attack on the Christian theology of the incarnation, accusing it of suggesting, against any rational, logical, or textual plausibility, that God took to himself a wife to give birth to a son, or of believing in the possibility of divine-human union. In his refutation, al-Warrāq presents two presumed meanings of the incarnation in Christian writings: "an *appearance* of the divine Word in a bodily form," and "a *control* of the divine Word of Christ."[911]

The Christian-Muslim debates on Christology conspicuously reveal that the Christian *mutakallimūn* strictly and bluntly rejected the accusation of al-Warrāq and other Muslims. For example, in the dialogue between Timothy I and al-Mahdī, the patriarch assures the caliph that Christians concur with Muslims about the absurdity of thinking that God took to himself a wife to give birth to a child. Timothy states explicitly that Christians have never uttered such a blasphemy in their discourse on the incarnation.[912] In addition, against al-Warrāq's elaboration on the twofold meaning given to the incarnation by Christians, the 10th-century Jacobite *mutakallim*, Yaḥyā ibn ʿAdī affirms that neither of the two meanings that al-Warrāq extrapolates actually reflects the actual Christian understanding of the icarnation. Mark Beaumont perceptively captures Ibn ʿAdī's core logic when he realizes that his reply to al-Warrāq's misinterpretation is conducted by referring back to Christ's original statements in the Scriptures. This is Ibn ʿAdī's way of showing al-Warrāq that the developed theology of the incarnation is a true re-iteration of the original teaching of the master, Jesus

910 Thus David Thomas, "Christian Theologians and New Questions," p. 273. One of the indications of this stance, according to Thomas, is al-Warrāq's willingness to engage with the incarnation, rather than just dismiss the notion altogether without any further ado.

911 Beaumont, "Defending the Incarnation in the Early Christian Dialogue with Muslims," p. 162.

912 Mingana, "Woodbrooke Studies: Patriarch Timothy I and the Caliph Mahdi," p. 175; and Heimgartner, *Timotheos I., Ostsyrischer Patriarch*, pp. 3–4. In a similar fashion, ʿAbd al-Masīḥ al-Kindī also refutes the claim that God took to himself a wife to give birth to a child, insisting in his response to ʿAbdullāh al-Hāshimī that the Christians have never said at any time that God took to Himself a lover. Such vices (*radhāʾil*) and vilenesses (*khasāʿis*), al-Kindī affirms, are not said by the Christians,but rather by the Jews, who invented these allegations against the Christians to the Muslims: ʿAbd al-Masīḥ al-Kindī, *Risālat ʿAbdalmasīḥ al-Kindī* (The Epistle of ʿAbd al-Masīḥ al-Kindī), in *Risālatān fī al-Ḥiwār wal-Jadal bayn al-Masīḥiyyah wal-Islām fī ʿAhd al-Khalifa al-Maʾmūn (m 813–834 t)* (Two epistles on dialogue and debate between Christianity and Islam in the era of the Caliph al-Maʾmūn [c. 813–834 AD]), ed. Georges Tartar (Paris: Asmar, 2011), 119–379, pp. 138–139.

Christ.[913] Unltimately, Ibn ʿAdī's refutation shows that the Muslim *mutakallimūn*'s rejection of the two implications of the incarnation that al-Warrāq assumes is grounded in their *mutakallimūn*'s theological presuppositions and preconceived ideas, not in what Christianity itself declares. Mark Beaumont takes this seriously and proposes convincingly that the ground of these Muslim *mutakallimūn*'s rejection is their assumption that God's otherness would be seriously damaged by any conjectured union between the divine and the human. This is what Beaumont also deduces from the argument of the Muslim *mutakallim*, al-Qāsim ibn Ibrāhīm, who argues, Beaumont says, "that associating the created with the Creator weakens His power, and believing that God should take a body is to limit Him."[914] Beaumont's convincing threefold conclusion is that, with regard to the incarnation

> Christian apologists first of all had to defend the nature of the incarnation from Muslim misunderstanding of the kind of relationship Jesus had with his Father ... secondly, they needed to develop appropriate justification for Jesus' divinity in the light of Muslim refusal to countenance any union of divine and human ... [and], thirdly, they took pains to so portray the union of divinity with humanity in Christ that there would be no adverse effects on the divinity from uniting with the humanity.[915]

The question that is still worth raising here is: Does this rejection of divine sonship and divine-human union mean that the Muslim *mutakallimūn* refused altogether the notion of 'incarnation' itself? This may not necessarily be the case and there are elements in their writings that invite the proposal that, rather than discarding the idea altogether, what they specifically rejected is what they *presumed* to be the Christian theological doctrine concerning the implementation of the 'incarnation.' Quite a few Muslim authors would use the notion of incarnation in their contemplation of the divine reality and presence of God. The difference between them and the Christians in this regard lay in their avoidance of the Arabic terms *tajassud* (embodiment/en-fleshment) and '*ta'annus*' (en-humanization), and in their consistent use, instead, of the term '*ḥulūl*' (indwelling) to express exactly the same connotations as those contained in the Christian theology

913 Beaumont, "Defending the Incarnation in the Early Christian Dialogue with Muslims," p. 162. Beaumont uses here Yaḥyā ibn ʿAdī's text *Jawāb Yaḥya Ibn ʿAdī ʿan Radd Abī ʿIsā al-Warrāq ʿalā an-Naṣārā fī al-Itiḥād* (A reply to the response of Abū ʿĪsā al-Warrāq on the union to the Christians), in *Abū ʿIsā al-Warrāq, Yaḥyā ibn ʿAdī De l'Incarnation*, CSCOV, 490–491 (Louvain: Peeters, 1987), p. 88.
914 Beaumont, "Defending the Incarnation in the Early Christian Dialogue with Muslims," p. 163.
915 Ibid., p. 166.

of the incarnation.[916] And, far from using this term only to articulate their own point of view, *ḥulūl* is used to re-iterate what Christians said in their theology on the divine that became human.

The Arabic term *'ḥulūl'* corresponds to the Greek term for indwelling, *ἐνοίκησις*. According to Windrow Sweetman, as indicated earlier, this word was used by the Church fathers, as we see, for example, in the pre-Islamic Christian works of Nestorius and Theodore of Mopsuestia.[917] One can also find in Paul of Samosata's works some references to the incarnation that speak of the *Logos* living in Jesus as in a temple.[918] With the idea of 'indwelling,' Nestorius and Theodore wanted to defend the distinction between the substance of the divine and the human and to affirm that God's substance did not suffer substantial limitation because of the union with the human. Rather than uniting ontologically with the human and becoming circumscribed in space and time, the divine *Logos* indwelt the human freely and by grace.[919]

It is quite plausible that almost the same understanding of 'indwelling' can be found in what Muslim *mutakallimūn* said about *ḥulūl*. This understanding of incarnation as *ḥulūl* is valued positively and used systematically by some Muslim mystics, such as Abū Manṣūr al-Ḥallāj. This famous Muslim Sufi is even accused in Islam of supporting *ḥulūliyyah*, because in one of his ecstatic experiences he called himself 'Creative Truth'[920] or 'I am the Real.'[921] In al-Ḥallāj's Sufism, Muslim scholars recognize the advocacy of a particular type of incarnationism (*ḥulūliyyah*) according to which two spirits are infused within one flesh. They believe

---

916 Mark Beaumont suggests that the Arabic term *'tajassud'* was used for the first time in relation to the incarnation in the dialogue between al-Mahdī and Timothy I: "whether *tajassud* was first used in this dialogue is not certain, but it is the first surviving record of its use in Christian writing in Arabic": Beaumont, *Christology in Dialogue with Muslims*, p. 24.

917 Sweetman, *Islam and Christian Theology*, Vol. 1 p. 105. See also on the use of the Greek term in patristic literature, especially Theodore of Mopsuestia, Kelly, *Early Christian Doctrines*, pp. 304–309.

918 Öhlig, "Syrian and Arabian Christianity and the Qur'ān," p. 375. Paul of Samosata, as Öhlig states, would even go as far as arguing that "Mary did *not* give birth to the *Logos*, on the contrary, she gave birth to a human being, one who was like us," which resonates with the later Islamic Christologiccal view of ʿĪsā b. Maryam. This is yet another invitation to trace the influence of Syrian-Aramaean Christianity on the theological content of the Islamic scripture.

919 Sweetman, *Islam and Christian Theology*, Vol. 1 p. 105.

920 Ibid., p. 112.

921 Alexander Treiger, "Al-Ghazālī's 'Mirror Christology' and Its Possible East-Syriac Sources," *The Muslim World*, 101 (2011), 698–713, p. 699. On ecstatic experiences in other Islamic Sufi texts, see Carl W. Ernst, *Words of Ecstasy in Sufism* (Albany: State University of New York Press, 1985); and Muhammad Abūl-Qasem, "Al-Ghazālī's Evaluation of Abū Yazīd al-Bisṭāmī and His Disapproval of the Mystical Concepts of Union and Fusion," *Asian Philosophy*, 3(2) (1993), 143–165.

that in advocating this, al-Ḥallāj adopts none other than the Christian understanding of God's presence in Jesus Christ to refer to his own ecstatic experience.[922]

One who detected a borrowing of Christological elements from Christian theology in al-Ḥallāj's thought, according to Alexander Treiger, is the renowned 12th-century Muslim scholar Abū Ḥāmid al-Ghazālī. In his critical reading of the al-Ḥallāj's spiritual-ecstatic view of God-human relationship, al-Ghazālī accuses him of misinterpreting the notion of incarnation by reducing 'indwelling' (*ḥulūl*) to 'union' (*ittiḥād*). For al-Ghazālī, this notional misnomer is the evidence that al-Ḥallāj and other Sufis had fallen into the grave Christological errors of the Christians.[923] Al-Ghazālī argues that the indwelling (*ḥulūl*) of the divinity in Jesus should not be understood as a 'union,' but merely as a way of expressing the 'reflection' or 'mirroring' of the divinity in Jesus' human heart.[924] It is not my goal here to analyse al-Ghazālī's so-called 'mirror christology.' I simply wish to draw the attention to the fact that a careful reading of Alexander Treiger's presentation and analysis of al-Ghazālī's critique of al-Ḥallāj indicates that al-Ghazālī is not dismissive of the notion of *ḥulūl* (indwelling) in itself. He only disagrees with its *interpretation* as a state that leads to a union between the divine and the human. For al-Ghazālī, it seems, *ḥulūl* is a valid way of understanding the relation between the human and the divine, insofar as it means that the divinity reflects, or mirrors itself in the hearts and spiritual lives of human subjects, without ever uniting with them.[925]

---

922 Lloyd Ridgeon, "Christianity as Portrayed by Jalāl ad-Dīn ar-Rūmī," in *Islamic Interpretations of Christianity*,ed. Lloyd Ridgeon (Richmond, UK: Curzon, 2001), 99–126, pp. 113–114. It was al-Rūmī more than others who emphasized in al-Ḥallāj's Sufism this attempt at imitating Jesus, especially in al-Ḥallāj's personal fate: like Jesus, he was condemned as a powerless victim and sentenced to death on a cross for the sake of purifying his community (ibid., p. 114). For ar-Rūmī and his writings, see Jelāluldīn ar-Rūmī, *The Rūmī Collection*, ed. Kabīr Helminski (Boston, MA: Shambala, 1998); and Reynold A. Nicholson (trans.), *Rūmī: Poet and Mystic* (London: Oneworld, 1995).

923 Treiger, "Al-Ghazālī's 'Mirror Christology' and Its Possible East-Syriac Sources," pp. 699–701.

924 Ibid., p. 703. For al-Ghazālī, this confusion of *ḥulūl* and *ittiḥād* "leads, in the Christian case, to erroneous beliefs regarding Jesus, and in the ṣūfī case, to heretical ecstatic pronouncements (*shaṭaḥāt*)" (ibid.).

925 Treiger interestingly suggests that, in his notion of 'mirroring' or 'reflecting', al-Ghazālī is not opposing the Christian theology of the divine-human union in the incarnation by borrowing from Christianity another Christological concept, i.e. the notion of mirror Christology that is prominent in Eastern-Syrian traditions. Treiger, nonetheless, concedes that al-Ghazālī does not take the 'mirror christology' concept directly from primary Christian resources, but rather

In the writings of Muslim Sufis, then, the notion of *ḥulūl* is not rejected out of hand, but is rather re-interpreted and re-examined, lest it convey ideas about God that express the Christians' misuse of the concept in their Christology. It is in essence a matter of interpretation, not of usage. W. Sweetman also points to another notable example of the acceptance of the idea of *ḥulūl* by some 9th-century Shiʿite authors, such as Aḥmad ibn Ḥāʾiṭ, or groups such as the 'Janāḥites' and 'Shuraiʿites,' who believed in God's embodying in five corporal beings, namely Muḥammad, ʿAlī, Fāṭima, Ḥassan and Ḥusayn.[926] *Ḥulūliyyah*, therefore, did find a foothold in early Islamic thought, and the idea of the in-dwelling of the divine in humanity (without there being union between them) was attractive to a few of Muslim *mutakallimūn*. Even among Muslims who rejected the notion of *ḥulūl*, there may be seen a willingness to acknowledge some extent of divine indwelling in the human.[927] 'Indwelling' was acceptable to Muslims because, to them, it did not connote union of substance between the divine and the human, or that the divine had become human. It rather meant the manifestation of the divine in the human without any kind of change of the divine essence into a human one. It meant becoming seen, sensed and experienced in the human; as water or liquid becomes visible when it fills a jar or cup. In fact, this is how some Christian *mutakallimūn* also tried to present a logically tenable interpretation of the incarnation to Muslims in the 10th and 11th centuries.[928]

---

from the Muslim polemical tradition, and specifically that of Abū ʿĪsā al-Warrāq and the judge ʿAbd aj-Jabbār al-Hamadhānī (ibid., pp. 704 – 707).

926 Sweetman, *Islam and Christian Theology*, 1/II, pp. 110 – 111; and Wolfson, *The Philosophy of the Kalām*, p. 315. In his book on early Islamic theology, Josef van Ess narrates the story of the Shi'ite, Abū Mansūr al-ʿIjlī, who, due to a specific spiritual experience of ascension to heaven and a supernatural meeting with God (in a *miʿrāj*-like manner) came back to earth and considered himself the son of God, and his followers "called him *Logos* (*al-kalima*) and took oaths using that word," and Abū Mansūr started to also call himself 'the Messiah' (*al-Masīḥ*): Josef van Ess, *The Flowering of Muslim Theology*, trans. Jane Marie Todd (Cambridge, MA: Harvard University Press, 2006), p. 74.

927 Sweetman, *Islam and Christian Theology*, 1/II, p. 113, where Sweetman cites some exponents of the doctrine of *tawḥīd* (monotheism) "speaking of the perfect man as the temple of God and of the tabernacling of God with man. He looked to find the world His image, and so set up His tent in Adam's field."

928 Ibid., 2/I, pp. 296 ff. Sweetman gives as an example here the explanation of the Nestorian Ibn aṭ-Ṭayyib in his *Commentary on the Four Gospels*, where he interprets John's prologue, 'the Word became flesh', in a manner that shows that the Son of God's indwelling (*ḥulūl*) in the flesh (*laḥm*) does not pertain to that which changes essence. Ibn aṭ-Ṭayyib continues: "'Zayd became a grammarian', meaning that he acquired the art of grammar, but his essence remained unchanged" (ibid., p. 296).

Thus, although the Qur'an and early Islamic *kalām* may not accept the actuality of the incarnation, some branches of Islamic thought do demonstrate a readiness to consider certain interpretations of the incarnation and do not stand against, but rather allow, the possibility of it. The logic behind this margin of acceptability might not be far from Kenneth Cragg's suggestion: "One should not deny to the divine what might be perceptibly within divineness ... veto on the possibility of 'incarnation' ... would be denying divine sovereignty by limiting its prerogatives and doubting its freedom."[929] These sovereignty and freedom are two divine prerogatives that the Qur'an seems unwilling to deny or ever underestimate. Finally, there is in Islam an attempt to recognize a form of incarnation that is related to the existence of the Qur'an itself. As the objective equivalent of the Word that became flesh in Christianity, many interfaith dialogue scholars recall the Islamic claim that the eternal Qur'an also became, or appeared in the form of, a physical book, as 'the word made book.'[930]

B. On the Incarnation as *Ḥulūl* in Abū Qurrah's Apologies

These Christian and Muslim elaborations on the incarnation as either *ḥulūl* or *tajassud* may also validly be taken to be the intellectual framework and apologetic context of Abū Qurrah's discourse on the plausibility of the 'incarnation' idea. In this section, I shall visit Theodor's Arabic mayamers to see how he speaks of the incarnation to Muslims, focusing first on some of his claims in *al-Mujādalah*, and then on the manuscript of his *fī ar-Radd ʿalā man Yunkir li-Allah at-Tajassud wa al-Ḥulūl fīmā Aḥabba an Yaḥulla fīh 'min Khalqih' wa-annahu fī Ḥulūlih fi aj-Jasad al-Mā'khūdh min Maryam al-Muṭahharah bi-Manzilat julūsih ʿalā al-ʿArsh fī as-Samā'* (In response to those who deny to God the [possibility of] incarnation and indwelling (*ḥulūl*) in whatever of 'his creatures' he wished to indwell, and that his indwelling in the flesh taken from the pure Maryam is equal to his sitting on the throne in heaven). This is probably Abū Qurrah's most complete extant apologetic discourse on the incarnation.

Let us first look at the text of *al-Mujādalah*, in which we have already seen how Abū Qurrah defends the theological and logical tenability of the Christian

---

929 Kenneth Cragg, "Ismāʿīl al-Fārūqī in the Field of Dialogue," in *Christian-Muslim Encounters* (ed. Yvonne Yazbeck Ḥaddād and Wadīʿ Zaidān Ḥaddād, Gainesville: University Press of Florida, 1995), 399–410, p. 106.

930 David E. Singh, "'The Word Made Flesh': Community, Dialogue and Witness," in *Jesus and the Incarnation: Reflections of Christians from Islamic Contexts*, ed. David Emmanuel Singh (Eugene, OR: Wipf & Stock, 2011),. 3–18, p. 4.

belief that 'God took a child unto himself' and that Jesus was not a merely human, but also and equally divine. In parallel to his defence of these two Christological elements, Abū Qurrah also argues in support of the plausibility in principle of the belief that God willed the appearance of his Word and Spirit (*kalimatuh wa-rūḥuh*) in a physical, corporal form. The text of *al-Mujādalah* sets out a debate between Theodore and Ṣaʿṣaʿa ibn Khālid on this specific idea. Abū Qurrah draws Ṣaʿṣaʿa's attention to the Qur'anic assertion that "if God (may He be praised and glorified) wanted to carry out the miracles Christ performed on earth while He [Christ] was [still] in heaven, He [God] would have been able to do so."[931] Abū Qurrah's reminder is his way of affirming that Christians agree with Muslims in believing that God's omnipotence and free will are transcendentally infinite. Earlier, Abū Qurrah also begins his argument for the plausibility of 'God taking a child unto himself' by emphasizing God's omnipotence and freedom. Here, Theodore starts from the same premise, deriving it, as he himself says, from the Islamic intellectual tradition, to argue for the plausibility of God's indwelling in human flesh. As God had a clear purpose from 'taking a child unto himself,' though he could have decided freely not to do so, God also has a clear goal in his divine logic behind asking Christ to perform his miracles on earth, though God could have made Christ perform them while he (Christ) was still in heaven. God's purpose in this, Abū Qurrah surmises, is to test humankind and make himself known to them. God decided to achieve this by revealing some of his unimaginable, all-surpassing power, by sending his 'Word and Spirit' into Mary and making 'his light' appear incarnated (*mutajassid*) to people

219. وإنما الله (سبحانه) أراد أن يمتحن الخلق ويعرفهم ما هو عليه
220. إذ أظهر لهم بعض قدرته فأرسل كلمته وروحه إلى مريم العذراء الطاهرة
221. فحملت نور الله الذي هو من الله وظهر للناس متجسداً [في مخطوط باريس: في جسدٍ أخذه منها]

> 219. For God (may he be praised) wanted to test the creatures and make what he is known to them.
> 220. So he disclosed to them part of his power by sending his Word and Spirit to the pure Virgin Mary,
> 221. who bore the light of God, who is from God, and he [the light] appeared to people incarnated [in the Paris MS: in flesh he took from her].[932]

---

931 Abū Qurrah, *Abū Qurrah wal-Ma'mūn: al-Mujādalah* (Abū Qurrah and al-Maʾmūn: The debate), IV. A.2.218.
218. ولكن أخبرني عن قولكم إنَّ الله (عز وجل) لو أراد أن يعمل ما عمله المسيح من العجائب على الأرض وهو في السماء لقدر على ذلك.

932 Ibid., IV. A.2.219 – 221.

Abū Qurrah's words here are very subtle. They convey the Christian theology of the incarnation in terms, expressions and notions that cannot be rejected by Muslims, for they are borrowed from their own religious vocabulary. It is common in Islamic thought to speak of God testing humans and his desire to make his omnipotence and divinity clearly known to them.[933] Aware of this, Abū Qurrah argues that appearing to people in flesh is part and parcel of God's way of making it known that he tests creatures (*yamtaḥin*) and he is omnipotent and all powerful, able to perform anything (*ʿalā kulli shayʾyin qadīr*). With the intention of partially disclosing his supreme power (*baʿḍ qudratih*), God decided to make his Word and Spirit known. It is important here that Abū Qurrah is careful to say that what is made tangible or visible, is not God himself, but God's Word and Spirit and God's light. It is this light in particular that appeared to people in flesh taken from Mary. Thus the incarnation is referred to here not as 'indwelling' (*ḥulūl*), nor 'en-humanization' (*ta'nnus*), but rather as 'apperance' (*zuhūr*), which is close in connotation to the Qur'anic '*tajallī*' or '*zuhūr*.'[934] Neither is it referred to as a moment when God becomes human. Rather, it is a moment when God's power shines forth visibly before creatures by appearing in human flesh.

The question that might now logically follow is: Why would God decide to disclose, to show (*yuẓhir*), his light, Word and Spirit and power in a bodily form in the first place? Abū Qurrah anticipates the question, so he takes his interlocutor from the theme of what Islam says about God's omnipotence to the theme of another, no less orthodox, Islamic emphasis on God's free goodwill and benevolent mercy.[935] This is what Abū Qurrah says about the appearance of God's Word and Spirit in a bodily form, seen from the perspective of God's free goodwill and mercy:

222. إذ لم تطق العيون البشرية النظر إلى قدرة الله ومجده
223. ولولا احتجابه بذلك الجسد، لم يهبط من سمائه إلى الأرض ولم يخالط الناس
224. فصارت كلمة الله شبه إنسان بلا خطيئة
225. وهو إله يقدر أن يعمل العجائب التي عمل
226. كما أنَّ كتابك يشهد بذلك إذ يقول: "وبعثنا إلى مريم من روحنا فتمثل لها بشراً سوياً"
227. أعني بذلك أنه صار شبه إنسان بالجسد

933 See Q 49:3; 2:20, 106, 148, 259, 284; 3:29, 165, 189; 4:133; 5:17, 19, 40, 120; 6:17; 8:41; 9:39; 11:4; 16:77; 22:6; 24:45; 29:20; 30:50; 33:27; 35:1; 41:39; 42:9, 29; 46:33; 48:21; 57:2; 59:6; 64:1; 65:12; 66:8; 67:1.

934 See, for example, the use of *tajallī* and *ẓuhūr* in Q 7:143; 92:2; 91:3; 98:33, 48.

935 On *raḥma* in the Qur'an, see Q 2:157, 178; 3:8, 107, 159; 4:96, 175; 6:12, 54, 133, 147, 157; 7: 203' 9:21; 10:21, 27; 11:9, 28, 63; 15:56; 17:87, 100; 18:10, 58, 65, 82, 98; 19:2; 28:46; 30:36, 33:17; 35:2.

> 222. For human eyes could not bear to look upon God's power and his glory,
> 223. and without his being veiled in this flesh, he would not have descended from his heaven to earth and would not have mingled with people.
> 224. So the Word of God became like a human being, without sin.
> 225. And he [God] is a God, who can perform the miracles he did,
> 226. as your book testifies, when it says: "And we sent to Maryam from our Spirit, and it appeared to her in the image of a normal human."
> 227. By this, I mean that he [the Word and Spirit] became like human in flesh.[936]

God disclosed his might in a human form because he mercifully and benevolently sympathizes with the human inability to encounter God's glory and power face-to-face. Moreover, God did not jeopardize his transcendence when he decided to show mercy and disclose his power visibly to humankind. God's transcendence and omnipotence remained paradoxically uncompromised in God's appearance, for in this bodily appearance God himself remained hidden. Had God's transcendence and substance not remained incomprehensible and infinitely beyond grasp, God would not have allowed his Word and Spirit (Christ) to descend from heaven and perform his miracles on earth, although God could have made his Christ conduct them from heaven. The intention here is to show that Christians also believe in God's infinite transcendence and incomprehensibility, and that God's equally essential mercy and free goodwill, which made him disclose his power to us, do not compromise his infiniteness and divine aloofness.

Abū Qurrah's choice of words here is intriguing. He insists that the one who appeared in a physical form is not God, but his Word. He also proposes the incarnation of the Word as a miraculous action that is conducted directly by God through his Word. Sentence 225 of *al-Mujādalah* says *wahūa 'īlah yaqdir an ya'mal al-'ajā'ib allatī 'amil* (and he is a God who can perform the miracles he did). It is my conviction that the Arabic word *'ilāh* in this verse should not be translated as if it refers to the 'Word of God,' or as if it means to speak of the Word as 'God from God.' Rather, I believe that Abū Qurrah is not here referring to God's Word (Christ) when he says *wahūa 'īlah* (and he is a God), but is making a statement about the almighty and transcendent God Hemself. What leads me to this conclusion are Abū Qurrah's words in the lines that follow in *al-Mujādalah*, 226–227. Here, Abū Qurrah does not cite texts from the New Testament, which may invite the interpretation 'and he is a God,' echoing the Christian Christolog-

936 Abū Qurrah, *Abū Qurrah wal-Ma'mūn: al-Mujādalah* (Abū Qurrah and al-Ma'mūn: The debate), IV. A.2.222–227.

ical notion of 'God from God' (*homoousius*). Instead, Theodore sticks to the interfaith setting of his debate and cites a Qur'anic verse (Q 19:17) that serves his theological, rather than Christological concern in this debate. Theodore recalls here (seemingly from memory): *fa-'arsalnā īlayha min rūḥina fatamath-thal lahā basharan sawyyah* (and, we sent to her our Spirit, who appeared to her as a normal human). Abū Qurrah seems to be here offering (from the Qur'an) relevant evidence of God's miraculous power; evidence, that is, that demonstrates God's power precisely in relation to his Word's appearance in a bodily form derived from Mary. Of great significance here is Abū Qurrah's attempt to tell his Muslim interlocutors that the Qur'an itself says that God himself performed an appearance in a physical form (incarnation) when his Spirit (which is God *per se: hiya hūa*) appeared to Mary as a normal human.

This is a thought-provoking and innovatively challenging theological reading of the Qur'an to the ears of any Muslim interlocutor. We can see ourselves in the place of Ṣaʿṣaʿa, the caliph al-Maʾmūn and the rest of the audience and imagine them hearing Abū Qurrah saying: "If we all concede that God is almighty and mercifully performs surprising miracles without compromising his transcendence. And, if we all acknowledge as truthful the Qur'anic teaching about the divine Word's appearance in a bodily form through Mary, then we should all submit to the Qur'anic attestation that the miracle worker, almighty God, and not only his Word, has also experienced a form of incarnational appearance in the disclosure of his Spirit before Mary in a human-like form. We either follow the Qur'an's teaching and surrender to God's miraculous power (conceding that the appearance in a human-like form was a sign of God's mercy and goodwill), or we disobey the Qur'an, deny God's miraculous power and, ultimately, reject God's mercy and benevolent goodwill,"[937] For Abū Qurrah, the first option is valid not only in Christianity but also in Islam. God Spirit's appearance in a physical form, he argues, does not militate against God's incomprehensibility and transcendence, for, even in its disclosure in the human form of Mary's child, the Spirit and the Word of God are still mysteriously hidden and paradoxically veiled. Abū Qurrah seems to stay with this argument, as he repeats the same logic in his ensuing discussions in *al-Mujādalah*

---

937 Later in *al-Mujādalah*, Abū Qurrah would continue speaking about the incarnation as both the appearance and the indwelling of God's Spirit in human flesh and via Mary: Ibid., IV.B.2.300–303; D.1.326–341. He seems now, however, to be building another level on the edifice he has constructed in the preceding lines.

446. أو كيف لا يجوز [للكلمة والروح] أن تحلّ في خلقةٍ من خلقها ظاهرةً على صورتها ومثالها وتتخذها لها حجاباً

446. Or, how is it not possible [for the Word and the Spirit] to indwell a creature from its creation, appearing in [this creation's] image and likeness, and to make [this creature] a veil for it [i.e., for the Word and the Spirit]?[938]

Ultimately, the divine will to appear in a human physical form is, first and foremost, God's declaration of his mercy and love, in a way that humans can perceive, and an affirmation of his miraculous power: God put on flesh to speak to the flesh by means of another flesh.[939]

I will move now to Abū Qurrah's maymar *fī ar-Radd ʿalā man Yunkir li-Allah at-Tajassud wa al-Ḥulūl* (In response to those who deny God's incarnation and indwelling). This maymar is wholly dedicated to the question of the incarnation, and it focuses on defending the incarnation specifically in relation to God's omnipresence. A good way to start analysing this maymar is by pausing briefly to consider Theodore's vocabulary. It is striking that Abū Qurrah uses the Arabic word *ḥulūl* (indwelling) to speak of the incarnation. In contrast to other Christian traditional Arabic theological texts, Abū Qurrah's maymar does not contain the word en-humanization (*taʾannus*), and it contains only once, at the end of the text, the word embodiment (*tajassud*).[940] Apart from this exception, Abū Qurrah consistently uses the Arabic term *ḥulūl* (indwelling). He even describes this indwelling as a state of containment (*iḥtiwāʾ*) of the divine Word, or God's Son, in human flesh, as if the flesh was a vessel or a garment, which God freely indwelt, or wore, to fulfill a specific divine purpose. The use of the word *ḥulūl* to refer to the incarnation, rather than other terms that are more common in Christian Arabic, strongly suggests that Abū Qurrah was addressing a Muslim. As discussed in the previous section, *ḥulūl* was the main term used by Muslims, wheth-

938 Ibid., V.2.446.

939 Ibid., VI. A.665–666.

665. فنزل من علو سمائه إلى أرضه ولبس جسداً ليخاطب الجسد بالجسد

666. إذ كانت العيون الجسدانية لا تطيق النظر إلى جوهر اللاهوت

665. So He descended from the height of His heaven down to His earth and put on flesh to converse with the flesh by means of the flesh ,

666. for fleshly eyes could not bear to look upon the essence of the divinity.

940 Abū Qurrah, *Maymar fī ar-Radd ʿalā Man Yunkir li-llāh at-Tajassud wal-Ḥulūl* (In response to those who deny to God [the possibility of] incarnation and indwelling ...), p. 186.

"فللابن الذي ولي خلاصنا بتجسده من مريم العذراء المطهرة الحمد والمجد والبركات مع الآب وروح القدس إلى دهر الداهرين"

"So to the Son, who undertook our salvation by His embodiment/en-fleshment/incarnation from the pure virgin Mary, praise and glory and blessings with the Father and Holy Spirit to the ages of ages."

er to present their own understanding of God's presence in the human realm, or to set out their reading of the Christian belief in the incarnation.

Even more significant than the term itself is the content of Abū Qurrah's defence of God's indwelling human flesh. Theodore decides to defend the indwelling from the specific angle of God's presence on the heavenly throne. Why does he opt for this? Because in Muslim *kalām* on the incarnation, we repeatedly find the question: When God indwelt the womb of Mary as a Child, who was ruling the universe from the heavenly throne of divine lordship? Abū Qurrah himself, as the text of *al-Mujādalah* informs us, heard this question from a Qurayshī noble in the court of al-Maʾmūn,[941] and we also find the same inquiry raised before the Patriarch John I by the Muslim leader.[942] In *On the Triunity of the One God*, we also see the Christian author responding indirectly to the same question by stating that, even when the Messiah descended from heaven to save his worshipers, he never abandoned the throne, but remained upon it with the Father and the Spirit.[943] So, in this maymar on the incarnation, Abū Qurrah argues for the possibility of God's sending his Word to indwell human flesh in relation to the idea of God's throne.

How does Abū Qurrah develop his argument? He first addresses the audience's question about the reason behind the decision of God's Son, who is 'God and equal to God' (*'īlāh wa-ʿadl 'ilāh*), to be contained in flesh (*'an yaḥwyhi jasad*) and for God to allow his Son to experience physical suffering, which otherwise would not touch him.[944] Abū Qurrah's answer is similar to the one he gives in the de-

---

941 Abū Qurrah, *Abū Qurrah wal-Maʾmūn: al-Mujādalah* (Abū Qurrah and al-Maʾmūn: The debate), V. A.434–436

434. فقال له رجلٌ من وجوه قريش: أليس المسيح كلمة الله وروحه؟
435. فقال أبو قرة: كذلك في قرآنك وكتابك، إن كنت تحفظ القرآن
436. قال: فأخبرني عندما كان المسيح في بطن مريم من كان يدبِّر السماوات والأرض؟

434. And a nobleman of Quraysh said to him: "Is not Christ God's Word and Spirit?"
435. And Abū Qurrah said: "Thus [He is] in your Qur'an and your book, if you follow the Qur'an."
436. He said: "Then tell me when Christ was in Mary's womb, who was governing the heavens and the earth?"

942 Nau, "Dialogue between the Patriarch John I and the Amir of the Hagarenes," pp. 24–25, pt. E: "The famous Amir asked him yet this: 'When Christ was in the womb of Mary, He, of whom you say He is God, who carried and ruled heaven and earth?"

943 Gibson, *Fī Tathlīth Allah al-Wāḥid* (On the Triunity of the One God), p. 82. 10–15 (p. 84. 10)
"وهو الذي هبط من السماء خلاصاُ لعباده: ولم يفارق العرش. فإنّ الله وكلمته وروحه على العرش وفي كل مكان لا ينتقص"
"He is the one who descended from heaven for the sake of His worshipers' salvation. He did not desert the throne, for God and His Word and Spirit are upon the throne and they are everywhere whole, never detract."

944 Abū Qurrah, *fī ar-Radd ʿalā Man Yunkir li-llāh at-Tajassud wal-Ḥulūl* (In response to those who deny God [the possibility of] incarnation and indwelling…), p. 180.

bate at al-Ma'mūn's court: God's Son indwelt flesh and bore physical suffering because he wanted to reveal his work and words to humankind in a humanly accessible and perceptible way.[945] Had the Son not done so, people's minds would have been distracted, and they would have not had any opportunity to know him or find peace and comfort in perceiving his truth. For Abū Qurrah, this is not only the purpose of the indwelling in human flesh (*ḥulūl*), but also the ultimate intention behind God's establishment of a heavenly throne in the first place. As God does not need to indwell flesh unless he finds it necessary for us to do so, so also he does not need to have a throne in heaven unless he finds it useful for us to do so.

This association of indwelling with the establishment of a throne, and the linking of both to God's benevolent will and mercy is a subtle argument, as far as the Islamic belief in God's throne is concerned. In the Qur'an, the idea of 'God sitting on a throne' is quite prominent in various *sūras*,[946] and, as Abū Qurrah demonstrates, the heavenly throne of God is also a prominent theme in the Christian, Old Testament scriptures.[947] By showing that God's throne is attested to in the Qur'an and the Bible, and by comparing the 'indwelling in the flesh' with the 'establishment of a throne,' Theodore wants to validate the former by virtue, and on the basis, of the scriptural support of the latter: God does not personally need a throne to sit on, but he established a throne in heaven in order to help us perceive him and know the location of his will and decrees (*maḥallat qarārih*). In the same way, God sent his Son or Word to indwell flesh in order to enable us to visibly encounter his words and actions and to benefit us by making us able to apprehend his salvation. God did this, even though neither God nor his Word, or eternal Son, needed to indwell anything whatsoever. So, if we concede the first decision to sit upon a throne in heaven, why would not we accept God's decision to allow his Son, or even himself, to indwell (*yaḥill*) in human flesh, if that happened to be God's will. In principle, God does not need to be located in any specific place in heaven since he is omnipresent. The same also applies, Abū Qurrah goes on saying, to the eternal Son, who is also omnipresent like his Fa-

---

945 Ibid., pp. 180 – 181.

لكنه شاء تبارك أن يظهر لخلقه من حيث أنه أحب أن يظهر لهم أفعاله وكلامه من الموضع الذي يصلح لهم

But He, may He be blessed, willed to appear to His creatures, for He wished to reveal to them His actions and words, from an angle that suits them.

946 Q 7:54; 9:129; 10:3; 11:7; 13:2; 20:5; 21:22; 23:88; 116; 25:59; 27:38; 32:4; 39:75; 40:7,15; 43:82; 57:4; 69:17; 81:20; 85:15.

947 Abū Qurrah cites 2 Kings 22:16 – 32; Isaiah 1 – 3; Daniel 7:9; Daniel 3:54; Psalms 102:19: Abū Qurrah, *fī ar-Radd ʿalā Man Yunkir li-llāh at-Tajassud wal-Ḥulūl* (In response to those who deny God [the possibility of] incarnation and indwelling...), pp. 181 – 182.

ther. However, just as locating his presence on a throne is God's expression of mercy and goodwill to the angels, so is the indwelling of the divine in a specific human flesh an expression of the Word's/Messiah's mercy and redemptive grace that is shown to humankind. This is how Abū Qurrah puts it:

> ولا أحد منهم يقدر أن يقول أنَّ الله لجلوسه على الكرسي لا يكون في كل موضع من السماء بل نعلم كلنا أنَّ الله في كل المواضع ونعلم أنه مالئ السماء كلها غير أنه لا يبدو لملائكته في السماء إلا من العرش وإلى ما هنالك يرفعون التمجيد لله لحلول الله فيه وهم لا يجهلون. كذلك نحن نعرف أنَّ الابن الأزلي هو في كل موضع ولا نهاية له ولا يحويه شيء ولا يحتاج إلى الحلول في موضع من المواضع غير أنه تبارك برحمته لحاجتنا نحن البشر إلى مخلص حل في الجسد الذي أخذه من مريم العذراء المطهرة وعرضه إلى الآلام والأوجاع التي كانت إذا حلَّت به فدانا بذلك من لعنة الناموس ولأجل ذلك حلَّ فيه برحمته وصار لنا هذا الجسد بمنزلة العرش في السماء لأنَّ الجسد بفعل اللاهوت الذي كان متحداً به أخلص وارفع اتحاداً تعرض للمصائب حتى حلّت به فداءاً عن الناس.
>
> And none of them can say that God, because of his sitting on the throne, is not everywhere in heaven. On the contrary, we all [Christians and Muslims] know that God is everywhere and we know that he fills the whole heaven, yet he only appears to his angels in heaven from the throne, and it is toward that location they give glory to God, for God indwells it, and they are not unaware of that. Likewise, we know that the eternal Son is everywhere and is infinite and nothing contains him and he does not need to indwell anything. However, he, may he be blessed for his mercy, and because of our need, we humans, of a saviour, [the Son] indwelt the flesh that he acquired from the pure virgin Mary, and exposed it [the flesh] to pains and sufferings, through which when they came upon him [*ḥallat bih*], he redeemed us from the curse of the law. This is why he [the eternal Son] indwelt it in his mercy, and this flesh became for us equal to the throne in heaven, for the flesh, by virtue of the divinity that was united most sublimely and truthfully to it, was exposed to misfortunes till they [the misfortunes] indwelt it in redemption of the people.[948]

Abū Qurrah concludes through this syllogistic logic that those who reject the 'indwelling in flesh' yet adhere to the 'indwelling in a throne' are self-contradictory and self-defeating. They can either support both or deny them altogether. There is no third option.

> فما بال المخالفين لنا ينكرون لله الحلول في الجسد المأخوذ من مريم العذراء المطهرة وهم يقولون أنَّ الله يجلس على العرش في السماء وقد كان يحق عليهم إما أن لا يعيبوا مثل الذي يقولون أو أن لا يقولون مثل الذي يعيبون
>
> So what is the matter with our adversaries denying God the indwelling in the flesh that is derived from the pure virgin Mary while they say that God sat on the throne in heaven? They should either not scorn what is similar to what they affirm, or not affirm what is similar to what they scorn.[949]

---

948 Ibid., pp. 182–183.
949 Ibid., p. 183.

Abū Qurrah anticipates in the following sections of the maymar that the Muslim interlocutor may then argue that one should not equate the indwelling of the throne and the indwelling in human flesh. For, while the heavenly throne is spacious and does not limit God's omnipresence, the human flesh is spatio-temporally limited and narrow, and prevents God's omnipresence.

ولكن لعلك تقول أنَّ العرش واسع والجسد المأخوذ من مريم ضيق فلذلك لا ينكر الله أن يحل في العرش وقد ينكر له أن يحل في الجسد

But you might say that the throne is spacious and the flesh taken from Maryam is narrow. So one does not deny that God may indwell the throne, but may deny that God could indwell the flesh.[950]

To this, Abū Qurrah responds by affirming that not only the flesh, but also heaven and earth and every created thing is narrow for God and cannot contain his glory and presence. So, in principle, no created thing can match God's omnipresence, including the heavenly throne, which is also created. Yet, since we accept a divine indwelling in a *created* heavenly throne, despite its inability by nature to contain God's presence, then God's indwelling, whether in a throne or elsewhere, must be founded on criteria other than space. From God's perspective, Theodore states, '*laysa mā ḍāqa 'aū ittasʿa 'illā wāḥidan ʿindah*' (what narrows down or widens up are but one to him).[951]

On the other hand, Abū Qurrah also imagines another interlocutor who may argue that the indwelling of a throne is acceptable while the indwelling of flesh is not, because the former is pure, while the latter is defiled. Against this, Theodore reminds his readers that both Christianity and Islam believe that the human being is God's most honourable creature. And, since the human, and not heaven, is so dignified in God's eyes, God would never abhor indwelling his most honourable creatures.

وإن قلت أنَّ العرش طاهر والجسد الأنسي لا يعدله في هذا الحد، قلنا لك أنَّ العرش في الخلقة ليس بأطهر من الناسوت، بل تقول أنت ونقول نحن أنَّ الله لم يخلق خلقاً أكرم عليه من الإنسان. ولم يكن الله يتقزز من الحلول في أكرم خلقه عليه. بل هذا الخلق الأنسي أولى به أن يحل به الله من كل الخلق لما تقدم مع أنَّ النجس الذي يتقزز الله منه إنما هو الخطيئة فقط.

And if you said that the throne is pure and the human flesh is unlike it in this regard, we said to you that the throne in nature is not purer than humanity. [On the contrary,] you and we say that God created no creation more honourable to him than humankind. And, God does not abhor indwelling his most honourable creatures. Rather, this human creature, ac-

950 Ibid.
951 Ibid.

> cording to what has been already stated, merits God's indwelling more than other creatures, for the only impurity that God abhors is sin.[952]

Abū Qurrah here concedes that the human flesh is defiled by sinfulness, but he also says that sinfulness does not prevent God's indwelling in Jesus' flesh. For, unlike every other human being, the flesh of Emmanuel, which is taken from Mary, is fully human in everything except sin. Sinfulness is not characteristic of the flesh of Mary's child, which is far from any sinfulness, though it bears all the forms of suffering and degradation that the sinfulness of others imposed upon it:

> هذا الجسد لم يؤخَّذ من مريم العذراء حتى طهرها روح القدس من أوساخ الخطيئة كلها وأخذه منها الابن الأزلي نقياً طاهراً مهذباً متهيئاً لحلول اللاهوت فيه. وبعد حلول اللاهوت فيه صار عيناً تفيض منه كل مفاخر اللاهوت من البر والحكمة والقوة غير أنَّ الابن الأزلي حصر حلول لاهوته فلم يظهره في جسده إذ كان يتقلب بين الناس وترك الأفعال الأنسية تظهر فيه من الأكل والشرب والنوم وغير ذلك لكيلا ينكره الشيطان ويجتري عليه حتى تحل به على يد أهل طاعته تلك الأوجاع التي كان حلولها به خلاصاً من خطيئتنا وإبطالاً لحجة الشيطان التي كانت على آدم بدخوله في طاعته غير مكره.

> This flesh was not taken from Maryam the virgin until the Holy Spirit had purified her from all the defilements of sin and the eternal Son took it from her pure, immaculate, refined, and prepared for the indwelling of divinity in it. And, after the indwelling of the divinity, [the flesh] became a fountain from which overflows all the divinity's acts of righteousness, wisdom, and power. Yet, the eternal Son limited the glory of his divinity and did not disclose it in his flesh. For he was mingling with people and he allowed the human actions of eating, drinking, and sleeping to appear in him, so that Satan would not ignore him, but would rather be bold so that, by the hands of his [Satan's] followers, sufferings would come upon him, which were salvation from our sin and an annulment of Satan's plea that Adam had freely decided to obey him.[953]

This paragraph summarizes just as clearly and sharply Abū Qurrah's understanding and appreciation of the meaning and plausibility of the indwelling of the divine Son in human flesh. The final lines of the maymar only confirm what Theodore has already argued for and defended. His core theme is again that one cannot use double-standard, allowing, on the one hand, a divine indwelling in a throne, or a burning bush (as when God spoke with Moses), or a pillar of cloud (like the one God appeared in to the children of Israel), but, on the other, rejecting such an indwelling in the human flesh (God's most honourable creature).[954] One either denies the possibility of indwelling altogether or one accepts the possibility of indwelling as a divine action and then affirms the eter-

---

952 Ibid.
953 Ibid., pp. 184–185.
954 Ibid., p. 185.

nal Son's indwelling in human flesh. Either indwelling is a logical and plausible theological notion, or it is not.

V. Abū Qurrah and Melkite/Chalcedonian Christological Orthodoxy

In the last part of this chapter, I will bring my analysis of Abū Qurrah's Christological apologetics back to the basic question that is addressed by the whole of the present study: In his defence of Christian theology in dialogue with Muslims, does Abū Qurrah merely echo an orthodox, doctrinal voice without any change or revision, or does he sometimes choose theological expressions and approaches that take him away from the orthodox doctrine of his church's Melkite theological heritage? As in the previous chapter, on Theodore Abū Qurrah's Trinitarian discourse, I shall pursue an answer to this question by comparing and contrasting Abū Qurrah's Christological expressions and rationale with some of those of his two Melkite, orthodox theological mentors, John of Damascus and Maximus the Confessor. I deliberately say 'some' of their Christological views, because it is not my intention, either in this chapter or in this study overall, to present a comprehensive analysis of the Christologies of these two Church fathers. As in the previous chapter, I shall be also consulting other Arabic *kalām* works, both Melkite and non-Melkite, whenever necessary, to shed light on Abū Qurrah's Christological language and ideas.

A. Some Christological Views from John of Damascus

My visit to John of Damascus' Christological discourse will be restricted, first, to John's rational explanation of the belief that God has a divine Word, who relates to him as a Son to his Father, and, second, to the Damascene's rationalization of the incarnation. John's interpretation of these two Christological themes occupies Chapter 6 of Book I and Chapter 2 (46, in the Greek text) of Book III in *De Fide Orthodoxa*, respectively. I choose these two chapters in particular because they touch upon two central Christological themes that Theodore Abū Qurrah passionately defends in his debates with Muslim *mutakallims*.

In Chapter 2 in Book I of *De Fide Orthodoxa*, John speaks of the Word as God's Son. First, it is significant that in Book I, the Damascene elaborates on the Son of God strictly after, and never before or without, developing a chapter on the strict oneness of God (not venturing here to speak of God's triune nature, for instance). It is even more thought-provoking to realize that John is not beginning with monotheism for apologetic or interreligious dialogical purposes. As has been said above, John does not need to reckon with dialogical strategies, because his text is not primarily an apologetic text (like his discussion of Islam in Chapter 101 of *On Heresies*) to counter Islamic polemics against the Christian faith. It is rather a catechetical *didache* composed to survey hermeneutically the doctrinal elements of faith for Christian, monastic and ecclesial, novices. John's defence of the oneness of God in Chapter 5 of Book I – that is, immediately before he explains the divine sonship of God's Word – is the Damascene's attempt to teach his Christian fellows that the emphasis on God's oneness is not a diplomatic 'word-game' that Christians need to play when they engage with staunch monotheists, but is a confessional conviction that is at the heart of the Christian catechism.

That said, John of Damascus does not develop his *didache* on orthodox faith without a context. He is an experienced, clear-headed Christian theologian with a deep knowledge of the religious and socio-cultural context in which the Christians of Syria and Palestine lived during the 7th and 8th centuries: the world of Islam. One can hardly, therefore, discount that, despite his primary concern to educate Christians in the orthodox faith of the Melkite Church, the Damascene must have been aware of his Christian contemporaries' need for theological interpretations that would enable them to deal confidently and successfully with any inquiry about Christian faith. Sidney Griffith is quite articulate and thought-provoking in opining that:

> It seems likely that the Islamic conquest, which claimed Palestine definitively in the year 638, was a major factor among the circumstances which prompted John to produce a compendium of the faith in the first place, ... the need for a convincing apologetic in the face of a strong non-Christian intellectual challenge had not been so strong since the days of the early Greek apologists.[955]

One wonders whether this contextual need for convincing apologetics can be indirectly sensed in what John says about the oneness of God in Chapter 5, Book I, of *De Fide Orthodoxa* and his emphasis there that God's oneness is a foundational prolegomenon in the Church's holy scripture: "That God is one and not many is no matter of doubte to those who believe in the holy scriptures."[956] In the same chapter, the Damascene's teaching that God's oneness is a constitutive biblical

---

955 Sidney E. Griffith, "Theodore Ab Qurrah's Arabic Tract on the Christian Practice of Venerating Images," *Journal of the American Oriental Society*, 105 (1985), 53–73, pp. 53–54. See also on John of Damascus' Islamic intellectual age S. Griffith, "John of Damascus and the Church in Syria," pp. 23–31.

956 John of Damascus, *Exposition of the Orthodox Faith*, Bk I, Ch. 5.

belief is also notable. One cannot miss realizing here that John is attempting to provide a rational explanation and justification of this oneness that can be applied to defend it before those who do not believe in the reliability of the Christian scriptures. It is worth wondering whether by "those who do not believe in the holy Scripture" John means the Muslims, who, as John unsurprisingly knows, rely exclusively on Qur'anic texts alone when it comes to saying anything about God, and who also expect Christians to prove their faith by application to reason and logic alone. One can probably assume that, because John knows this from his long career in Islamic ruling, administrative and intellectual circles,[957] he says in his exposition that he "will *reason*" on the oneness.[958]

John goes on, in the same chapter, to give his rational explanantion of the necessity of saying that God is 'one and only.' In contrast to the Muslim, Muʿtazilite-like reduction of God's attributes to one, single predicate and then deeming this nominalism evidence of divine oneness, John starts by acknowledging various divine attributes: God is perfect, all good, wise, powerful, eternal, infinite, and uncircumscribed. All of these are attributes of God's perfection, but they do not indicate a state of plurality that entails ontological differentiation within the divine being (as the Muʿtazilites would say in their argument against the plurality of the divine attributes). Rather, these attrinbutes express one, divine perfection that belongs to the one and only God. This is how John states this claim:

> Should we say, then, that there are many Gods, we must recognize difference among the many [attributes]. For, if there is no difference among them, they are one rather than many. But if there is difference among them, what becomes short of perfection, whether it be in goodness, or power, or wisdom, or time, or place, could not be God. But it is this very identity in all respects that shews that the Deity is one and not may.[959]

This is a clear, rational, far from merely scriptural, argument for the oneness of God, which John of Damascus wants his Christian audience to adopt and use in their propagation, or even defence, of Christian faith before those who do not believe in the Christian scriptures. To come back now to his Christology, it is es-

---

957 Some scholars even believe that John of Damascus was also an active interreligious debator in the Christian-Muslim controversies that took place in the caliphs' court: see, for example, ʿAzīz ʿAṭiyya, "St John Damascene. Survey of the Unpublished Arabic Versions of His Work in Sinai," in *Arabic Islamic Studies in Honour of Hamilton A.R. Gibb*, ed. George Makdisi (Cambridge, MA: Harvard University Press, 1965); and Portillo, "The Arabic Life of St John of Damascus."

958 John of Damascous, *Exposition of the Orthodox Faith*, I.5 (my italics): "but with those that do not believe in the holy scriptures, we will reason thus."

959 Ibid., I.5.

sential for any reader of John's text to realize that his reasoned proof of the Word's divine sonship to God is structured upon no other foundation than the strict oneness of God. It is a Christological elaboration that aims first and foremost at plausibly explicating that oneness and emphasizing, not challenging or refuting, it. Missing this methodological link between God's oneness and the divine sonship of God's Word in the discourse of the Christian theologians through the ages is one of the central mistakes in which Muslim iterlocutors and polemicists have trapped their refutations of Christian Christology.

To stay with *De Fide Orthodoxa*, from Chapter 5 on God's oneness, the Damascene moves on to develop another rational explanation of how and why this one and only God has a divine Word that is no less than a divine Son to him. John begins with an elaboration on the logic of believing that God has a Word because "God is not wordless," or without reason (*ἄλογον*),[960] arguing that God cannot be wordless, and then stressing that God and his Word are substantially one and co-eternal,[961] One cannot but realize an intriguing similarity between this and the Islamic belief that God's Word (*kalimatuh*) is none other than God himself: *kalimatahu hiya hūa*.[962] If God's Word is God, John concludes, then this Word "is not proceeding out of Himself [as human words do], but ever existing within Himself."[963] In this sense and no other, John states, Christians understand and speak of God's Word as God's Son. Christians do not mean, in other words, that God decided at some point to take unto himself a child after having none before, or that God needed to take a child unto himself for a certain specific time and then let that child perish. By calling God's Word 'Son,' John implies, Christians want only to show the unique nature of the divine Word as different in substance from the human word: God's Word is as close in causality to God as a son is close in substantial causality to a father. Here, John indirectly compares the causal link of the human and her words, on the one hand, with the causal link of father-son, on the other. He then argues that the latter is more expressive of God's relation to his Word than the former: the 'father-son' causality is more congenially expressive of this relation because 1) it connotes total eqauality be-

960 Ibid., I.6.

961 Ibid. "For there never was a time when God was not Word." Note here that John says 'God *was* not Word' rather than 'God *has* no Word.'

962 This remains an interesting similarity even if one cannot affirmatively prove that John has it in mind here and even if it remains a hypothetical comparison and contrast. It may actually invite a study of the possible impact of John of Damascus' theological reasoning on Muslim *kalām* with regard to aspects and dimensions that have not yet been touched upon seriously by modern scholars.

963 John of Damascous, *Exposition of the Orthodox Faith*, I. 6.

tween the causer (father) and the caused (son), and 2) it shows that what the causer causes is not without subsistence and is not making the causer reliant on another for his existence.

By applying this 'father-son' causal metaphor to God's relation to his Word, one can describe the divine Word as 'Son' to the divine causer, who can, in turn, be seen as a 'Father' of what he substantially caused. Why is this valid? Because, John surmises, as in the case of 'father-son' causality, and since the divine causer is everlasting and perfect, so everything he causes would be him *a se* in essence, and not a separate other.[964] When, therefore, it comes to the nature of the Word of God, which is who God is as such, the divine Word reflects in itself all God's attributes, thus it is of the same nature as God (just as the caused son is of the same nature as the causing father: the human begets another human, not a non-human being): "just as absolute perfection is contemplated in the Father, so also is it contemplated in the Word that is begotten of Him."[965]

In conclusion, what John presents in *De Fide Orthodoxa*, Book I, Chapter 6 is not just a theological interpretation of the divine sonship of God's Word, but also a rational justification of the logic of calling God's Word subsistent with God, as a son is subsistent with a father, ready for Christians to use as a hermeneutic tool in their interaction with those 'who do not believe in the Scripture.' Why is it plausible to say that 'God took a child unto himself' who is none other than his Word itself? Because, 1) it is rationally plausible to say that God is not word-less, 2) it is, thus, as plausible to believe that God's relation to his Word is not at all temporal or non-substantial, as is the human's relation to her words, and 3) it is more appropriate to express the fact that God's Word is him himself by means of a 'father-son,' rather than a 'human speaker-words,' metaphorical causality.

Time now to turn to John of Damascus' elaboration on the divine incarnation in *De Fide Orthodoxa*, Book III, Chapter 2 (46). I intend in what follows to unpack the content of this chapter by drawing attention to three very significant conceptual choices that John makes in his attempt to explain the incarnation.

The first choice is to be seen in John's explication of the incarnation from the perspective of the synoptic Gospels' virginal birth stories, and not from the Johannine prologue on the divine, eternal *Logos* who became flesh. Rather than starting with the eternal Son who was with God and who was God, the Damascene decides to speak of the Word as the saving agent of God, whose human

---

964 Ibid. "But since God is everlasting and perfect, He will have His Word subsistent in Him, and everlasting and living, and possessed of all the attributes of the begetter."
965 Ibid.

birth was announced to the Virgin Mary.[966] This beginning with the Synoptic Gospels instead of the Gospel of John is not coincidental. It is intended to show that Christians do not improvise a metaphysical and purely philosophical idea about the Word who became flesh, and then search for verification of their speculation in their scriptures. Far from it; Christians base their belief in the rational possibility of such an incarnation on the scriptural witness to the angel of God's declaration to Mary of the birth of the divine Word by the Spirit of God to be the Saviour of humankind.

If John of Damascus' first conceptual choice is to start with the virginal birth, his second lies in what he says about the incarnation as 'indwelling,' rather than as any form of enfleshment (*tajassud*) or en-humanization (*ta'annus*). John says that the divine Word:

> taking up His abode in the womb of the Holy Virgin, He unreservedly in His own subsistence took upon Himself through the pure blood of the eternal virgin a body of flesh animated with the spirit of reason and thought, thus assuming to Himself the first-fruits of man's compound nature, Himself, the Word, having become a subsistence in the flesh.[967]

John here speaks of the incarnation as the divine Word's act of being animated in the creaturely realm in visible human flesh, which never conflates with the divine nature. Nor is it ever implied, the Damascene emphasizes, that what we have in this act of indwelling is a human being becoming God.[968] Rather, the divine Word inhabits the Virgin's womb and takes upon himself a human body that is "animated with the spirit of reason and thought."[969] In other words, Christians do not make any claim about a human child being ontologically transformed supernaturally into a deity, but rather perceive the incarnation to be an instance of God's omnipotent ability to indwell anything he wills, in this case a human womb, and to take upon himself a created dwelling place, in this case a human body.

This takes us immediately straight on to John's third conceptual choice. The distinction between speaking of deification ontologically (i.e., as a man becoming God in his being) and speaking existentially of God indwelling a human body as his animated abode gives the only meaningful explanation of why John of

---

966 On John of Damascus' understanding of the incarnation in the context of the history of salvation, see the analysis in Louth, *St John Damascene*, pp. 144–146.
967 John of Damascous, *Exposition of the Orthodox Faith*, III.2 (46). Let us realize here that John speaks about 'body' more often, in contrast to Abū Qurrah, who tends to dominantly use the Arabic term 'جسد /*jasad*', which means rather 'flesh.'
968 Ibid.
969 Ibid.

Damascus speaks of the incarnation of the Word in terms of 'subsistence' (*enhypostasis*[970]) rather than 'substance.' The Greek term the Damascene uses for 'subsistence' is a variation on *hypostasis*, which means a personal concrete existence of a specific nature or substance. In patristic, especially Cappadocian, theological ontology, as I have shown in chapter three above and elsewhere, the term *hypostasis* (subsistence) is notionally distinguished from *physis* (nature) and *ousia* (essence).[971] John of Damascus' decision to us *enhypostasis* in this chapter is not coincidental or unconsidered. He consistently maintains his theological position in line with the Cappadocian distinction between nature and essence (*physis/ousia*) and subsistence (*hypostasis*),[972] and he uses this distinction to speak of the incarnation as a state of concrete existence, or, one may say, a 'particular manner of presence or appearance,' in a bodily abode. This is how John uses 'subsistence' in this very specific sense to explain the incarnation:

> the Son of God … formed flesh animated with the spirit of reason and thought … not by procreation but by creation through the Holy Spirit; not developing the fashion of the body by gradual additions, but perfecting it at once, He himself, the very Word of God, standing to the flesh in the relation of subsistence.[973]

This insistence on denying that the Word's human indwelling place was procreated or developed like other human bodies is meant to show that what is happening in the dwelling of the Word in the womb of Mary is not primarily about the being or nature of the divine Word, or even of the born child. Rather, it points to the form of *existence* that the divine Word has in a bodily abode, which is related to this divine Word merely in terms of subsistence and not in terms of substance. John seems to conjecture that the incarnation in Christian

---

970 'Enhypostasis' literally means "having one's subsistence in the subsistence of another." The term is used post-Chalcedon, especially by John of Damascus, to safeguard the union of the two natures by affirming the oneness of the person of the incarnate being: Richard A. Muller, *Dictionary of Latin and Greek Theological Terms* (Grand Rapids, MI: Baker Books, 1985), 'enhypostasis', p. 103.

971 On the distinction between *hypostasis* (subsistence) and *ousia* (substance), see my discussion in chapter three of this study and see also N. Awad, *God Without a Face?*, pp. 184–191; and C. Stead, *Divine Substance*, pp. 131–139 ff.

972 It is not clear whether John of Damscus is simply following the Cyrillian, almost total equation and identification of *hypostasis* and *physis*, although he can rightly be seen, as Andrew Louth notes, to be in line with Cyrillian Chalcedonianism: Louth, *St John Damascene*, pp. 150–151, 157. I agree with Louth's claim that John, who clearly echoes the Cappadocians' theological views in almost all his ideas on the Trinity, also maintains his Cappadocian orientation in his Christology (ibid., p. 174).

973 John of Damascus, *Exposition of the Orthodox Faith*, III.2 (46).

thought has existential rather than ontological connotations. The 'incarnation' idea is not meant to suggest that the divine Word himself became flesh, but rather that the divine Word willed to "become a *subsistence in* the flesh" and "found *existence*" in it.[974] In other words, by taking a body upon himself, the *Logos* hypostatized the animated flesh and gave it a concrete personalized existence. One may say here that, for John, it seems that the flesh was embraced by the *Logos* (was hypostatized), rather than that the *Logos* indwelt the flesh.

Missing this very intelligent nuance that John makes between 'becoming body' and 'subsisting/existing in animated flesh' would prevent the reader from seeing the core logic behind John's statement: "We speak not of man as having become God, but of God as having become man," as well as his insistence that the Word "did not change the nature of his divinity into the essence of flesh, nor the essence of flesh into the nature of his divinity, and did not make one compound nature out of his divine nature and the human nature He had assumed."[975] This deliberate language invites us to think that John is not only here teaching his readers about the constituents of orthodox faith, but also indirectly equipping them with a specific way of speaking that can enable them to express this faith in a subtle theological manner. This concern is unique to this text and is not common in John's other doctrinal apologetic works.

In contrast with his manner of speaking in *De Fide Orthodoxa*, John of Damascus elaborates on the incarnation in slightly different language in his treatise, *On the Divine Images*. Rather than referring simply to the divine Word, John here explicitly and unreservedly calls the Word 'the eternal Son and Lord,' the 'visible God,' and the eternal person from the divine Godhead. In addition, instead of speaking of the Word embracing human flesh and hypostatizing it in a concrete form of existence, the Damascene now speaks of the incarnation of the eternal invisible God (or Son of God) as an ontological *union* (not in terms of embrace or 'taking upon himself') between the divine Word and the flesh, which led to the transformation of both:

> The flesh assumed by Him is made divine and endures after its assumption. Fleshly nature was not lost when it became part of the Godhead, but just as the Word made flesh remained the Word, so also flesh became the Word, yet remained flesh, being united to the person of the Word.[976]

---

974 Ibid.

975 Ibid.

976 John of Damascus, *On the Divine Images: Three Apologies against Those Who Attack the Divine Images*, trans. David Anderson (Crestwood, NY: St Vladimir's Seminary Press, 1980), Bk I, pt 4. One may therefore say here that Sweetman's belief that John of Damascus understood the incarnation as 'divine-human union' might actually be derived from a reading of John's text on the

Here, the Damascene depicts the incarnation of the Word not only as subsistence in human animated flesh, as he does in *De Fide Orthodoxa*, but also as an act of self-emptying, whereby the invisible God took in *substance* the form of a servant.[977] Within the framework of this ontological tone, the Damascene finds it normal to speak of the substantial union of the Son of God with the flesh as a union of the flesh with the second divine person that enabled the flesh to "participate in the divine nature and by this communion become unchangeably God. Not only by the operation of divine Grace, as was the case with the prophets, but by the coming of Grace Himself."[978] One may go as far as saying that, while in *De Fide Orthodoxa* John declares that he is not talking about 'a man becoming God,' in his apology for the divine icons, the Damascene allows himself to speak of the incarnation as a moment of deification of both human flesh and of the human saints alike.

The question I want to tackle in relation to this view is: Why would the Damascene allow himself to speak of the incarnation in the language of high ontological Christology in *On the Divine Images* but not do so in *De Fide Orthodoxa?* The answer lies in the context of the composition of each text, the imagined audience, as John of Damascus saw it, and the counter-arguments that might be raised. John wrote his apology on the veneration of icons within the context of the iconoclastic controversy, which began in the 8th century by the Byzantine Emperor Leo III (717–741) and continued into the reign of Constantine V (741–775). This apology is thus written for the Byzantine world, and specifically for Christian iconoclast readers, not for the Arab-Islamic world and its Jewish and Muslim iconoclasts (who became the addressees of Theodore Abū Qurrah and the reason for his defence of the veneration of icons in later decades). John's presumed addressees are fellow Christian believers and church prelates and hierarchs, whom John personally calls in the apology 'brothers'[979] and 'my masters.'[980] His targets, in other words, are within the Christian circle, and are well acquainted with the ontological expressions and metaphysical rationale of the doctrinal discourse of high Christology. The case is surmisibly different in *De Fide Orthodoxa*. John there is not writing an apology, but primarily a catechistic *didache* on the components of orthodox faith for monastic novices and

---

icons, but it does not take into consideration the different language John uses in *De Fide Orthodoxa*, particularly in the chapters studied in this section: Sweetman, *Islam and Christian Theology*, 1/II, p. 104.

977 John of Damascus, *Exposition of the Orthodox Faith*, I.8.

978 Ibid., I.19.

979 Ibid., I.5.

980 Ibid., II.1.

clerical apprentices, although John still keeps in mind that they should, in their future ministry, be able to share their education in a coherent, accurate and authentically orthodox manner.

B. Some Christological Views from Maximus the Confessor

There is a considerable amount of truth in Andrew Louth's conviction that the title 'confessor' was bestowed upon Maximus ultimately by virtue of his theological defence of the orthodox doctrine of the person of Christ.[981] Maximus is deservedly one of the most prominent heroes of Chalcedonian Christology, who struggled against Monoenergism and Monothelitism in the history of orthodox doctrine. The extant texts of Maximus' works clearly show that interpreting the identity and work of the incarnate Son/*Logos*, Jesus Christ, is the cornerstone, the governing purpose and the inclusive basis of all his theological reasoning. Louth is again right in his perception that "Christology is so central to his theological reflection that it is rarely far from his thought."[982]

This section will not analyse Maximus the Confessor's multifaceted, highly sophisticated Christological rationale. This has already been thoroughly pursued by numerous scholars around the world, and it would also go beyond boundaries of this study of Theodore Abū Qurrah. Moreover, I do not believe that a detailed study of Maximus' apologetic Christology in response to Monothelitism and Monoenergism offers a first-hand, direct, or relevant contribution to the context of interreligious debate about Christ between the Arab-speaking Christians and the Muslim *mutakallim*s in the early Abbaside era. The bulk of Maximus' Christological elaborations were composed in direct dialogue with Byzantine Christianity and Christological trends in Constantinopolitan Christendom, not with Islam.

This means that the number of texts in Maximus' works that are relevant to the dialogue with Islam is minimal, and so the task of finding any influence of Maximus' Christology on Theodore Abū Qurrah's discussions with Muslims about Christ produces rather scant results. Nevertheless, one can still trace

---

981 Louth, *Maximus the Confessor*, p. 48.

982 Ibid. The same idea is also expressed by Ian McFarland: "If Maximus the Confessor is mentioned at all in most introductory courses in church history or systematic theology, it is invariably for his defence of Christ's having a distinct human will over against the movement, known as monothelitism, which denied it": Ian A. McFarland, "Fleshing Out Christ: Maximus the Confessor's Christology in Anthropological Perspective," *St Vladimir's Theological Quarterly*, 49 (4) (2005), 417–436, p. 417.

some forms of expression and modes of speech about Christ in Theodore Abū Qurrah back to his study of, and learning from, John of Damascus' and Maximus the Confessor's discourses on Christology. That being so, I shall visit very few texts in Maximus' works and to point out specific notions that he uses in relation to the incarnation and shall indicate some theological views and implications that could have caught Abū Qurrah's attention and influenced his method of dialogue with Islam in a way or another. This limited approach may not quench the intellectual thirst of the Maximian scholars, but I hope that it will serve the purpose of shedding a brighter light on the roots of Abū Qurrah's Christological orthodoxy and the soil in which it grew.

Relevant to my concern with the incarnation in Maximus the Confessor's works is what he says about the threefold 'birth' of the *Logos* in *Ambiguum* 42. There, he refers back to some texts from Gregory Nazianzus, where the latter speaks of the incarnation, baptism and resurrection of the *Logos* as "three births for us: bodily birth, birth through baptism and birth through resurrection."[983] Maximus notes in the Nazianzen's discourse an attempt to express the incarnation, or even the three forms of birth, in terms of "original and vital *inbreathing*."[984] 'Inbreathing' is a term worth pondering. It describes how the *Logos* honoured the act of birthing in his incarnation. In *Ambiguum* 42, Maximus uses two Greek words in reference to the act of 'inbreathing':[985] *emphysema* (ἐμφυσεμα) and *empneusis* (ἐμπνευσις). Both can be validly translated as 'breathing in.' Maximus uses this term to speak not of the conception of Christ as a child (γέννεσις), but rather of the origination of the human flesh (γένησις) into which the *Logos* was breathed. He is trying to differentiate between the creation of Adam from earthly matter as a living, creaturely body and soul, and the breathing into the Virgin Mary to originate for the *Logos* a human, fleshly abode in her womb.

What is most intriguing in this use of *emphysema* (inbreathing) in relation to the present study, however, is what I see as a striking similarity between it and the Qur'an's use of the verb 'to breathe' (*nafakha*) in, for example, Q 15:29: "So, when I have made him and have breathed into him of My Spirit, do ye fall down, prostrating yourselves unto him;"[986] Q 21: 91: "And she who was chaste, therefore

---

983 Maximus Confessor, *Ambiguum* 42, in *On the Cosmic Mystery of Jesus Christ; Selected Writings from St Maximus the Confessor*, pp. 79–95 (PG. 91:1316 A-1349 A), 1316 A (p. 79).
984 Ibid., 1316C (p. 79).
985 For my observations on the implications of the Greek terms Maximus uses in this text, I am grateful to Prof. Dr Assaad Elias Kattan and his expertise on Byzantine theology, in general, and Maximus the Confessor's thinking, in particular.
986 Q 15:29
"فإذا سوّيتهُ ونفخت فيه من روحي فاقعوا له ساجدين"

We breathed into her (something) of our Spirit and made her and her son a token for (all) peoples;"[987] Q 38:72: "And when I have fashioned him and breathed into him of my Spirit, then fall down before him in prostration,"[988] and Q 66:12: "And Maryam, daughter of ʿImrān, whose body was chaste, therefore We breathed therein something of our Spirit. And she put faith in the words of her Lord and His scriptures, and was of the obedients."[989] One must not fail to note that the Qur'an speaks of both the conception of the son of Mary and the creation of the first man, Adam, in terms of 'breathing God's spirit into them,' whereas inbreathing in Maximus the Confessor is only spoken of in relation to the conception of the incarnate *Logos*. Despite this distinction, the similarity between the Qur'anic use of the idea of 'breathing' (*nafkh fī*) and Maximus the Confessor's use of 'inbreathing' (*emphysema*/*empneusis*) cannot be denied. It may be that it stems from the influence on both Maximus and the Qur'an of the Old Testament text (as, for instance, in the story of the creation of Adam in the Septuagint version of Genesis 2:7[990]). The Qur'an is here more reminiscent of the Old Testament text in that it uses the expression 'breathing into' to refer to the creation of Adam as well as to the conception of the son of Mary, while Maximus uses it only in what he says about the conception of Christ.

Be that as it may, one wonders whether this linguistic similarity indicates that Maximus was speaking of the incarnation with Islamic/Qur'anic thinking somehow in his mind. I think this is quite unlikely. None of the Confessor's known works addresses Muslims or touches on any element in the Islamic faith. Having said that, the similarity in the vocabulary must have been striking enough to catch the attention of Christian Arab *mutakallimūn* after the 7th century, as much as it does that of present-day readers, like me.

What makes the notion of 'breathing' more theologically significant in *Ambiguum* 42 is Maximus' use of it to demonstrate the substantial difference between the birth of the *Logos* in a bodily form and the creation of the first Adam. Adam was created by supreme Creator different from himself, and his human nature suffered from the transgression, sin and limitations of its creaturely origin, while the *Logos* was not created, or re-originated in a bodily form by

987 Q 21:91

"والتي أحصنت فرجها فنفخنا فيها من روحنا وجعلناها وابنها آيةً للعالمين"

988 Q 38:72

"فإذا سويته ونفخت فيه من روحي فقعوا له ساجدين"

989 Q 66:12

"ومريم ابنت عمران التي أحصنت فرجها فنفخنا فيه من روحنا وصدقت بكلمات ربها وكتبه وكانت من القانتين"

990 Again, I am indebted here to Prof. Kattan who drew my attention to this possible textual derivation from the Septuagint.

Creator other than himself, and his bodily form was subjected to all the human body's limitations except sinfulness, without his becoming another created Adam. The *Logos* was breathed into the human body in a voluntary action of self-emptying, and "through His incarnated birth, … [the *Logos*] voluntarily assumed the likeness of corruptible humanity (cf. Phil 2:7), He willingly allowed Himself to be made subject virtually to the same natural passion as us, yet without Sin (cf. Heb 4:15)."[991]

In *Ad Thalassium* 21, Maximus goes even more deeply in his elaboration on the creation of Adam and the incarnation of the *Logos*, building the core distinction between the incarnation of the *Logos* and the creation of Adam on a subtle notional differentiation between 'origination/formation' (γένεσις) and 'sexual procreation' (γέννησις). Adam, the first human, Maximus argues, "received his existence from God and came into being at the very origins of his existence."[992] Adam was given birth as a human being (γέννεσις) by virtue of God's power, and he was created perfect and sinless, but Adam broke God's commandment and corrupted his human nature and origin. So, "he was condemnd to birth based on sexual passion and sin." Accordingly, Maximus concludes, "there is no human being who is sinless, since everyone is naturally subject to the law of sexual procreation that was introduced after man's true creaturely origin in consequence of his sin."[993] In other words, Adam's birth is now defined not only be means of its origination from God, but also in terms of his sinful humanity, which imposes on his descendents the burden of origination through 'sexual procreation.'[994]

Regardless of his rather problematic and unfruitful association of sexuality and procreation with sinfulness and transgression (probably inspired by Genesis 3:16), Maximus' differentiation between Adam and the *Logos* is meant to show that 1) the *Logos* is really human and has experienced real human birth, yet without his flesh being contaminated with sinfulness and human corruption, which could nullify his divinity, and 2) the incarnate *Logos* is not subjected, either in his birth or in his humanity, by the limitations of sexual procreation. What the

991 Maximus, *Ambiguum* 42, 1316D (p. 80).

992 Maximus, *Ad Thalassium* 21, in Blowers and Wilkens, *The Cosmic Mystery of Jesus Christ* (CCSG 7:127–133), pp. 109–113, Q.127 (p. 109).

993 Ibid., Q.127 (p. 110).

994 Ibid. "The more human nature sought to preserve itself through sexual procreation," Maximus opines, "the more tightly it bound itself to the law of sin, reactivating the transgression connected with the liability to passion."

incarnate *Logos* assumed in his original birth in a human body is "the liability to passion" alone, and not the sinful consequences of the procreation process.[995]

It is within this notional framework of the distinction between 'γέννησις' and 'γένεσις' that Maximus the Confessor calls the incarnate *Logos* 'the new Adam' in *Ambiguum* 42.[996] The incarnate One is called 'Adam' not because he and Adam are identical in origin and human identity. As well as being liable to passion, the incarnate One shares with Adam his original humanity before his (Adam's) fall and damnation, but with regard to dependence on the process of sexual procreation, the *Logos* is not like Adam, and only Adam's humanity is tormented by this punishment. The incarnate *Logos*, Maximus affirms, "did not assume this passion and corruption [which lies in γέννησις']."[997]

It is not my intention, again, to suggest here that Maximus is consciously and deliberately launching an apologetic interpretation of the incarnation that aims at dealing with Muslim polemics. This would, in my view, be a highly speculative and hypothetical assumption. Nevertheless, it is acceptable to consider whether there are in Maximus' understanding of the incarnation some dialogical aspects that could convey the Christian idea of the incarnation in a tone that is accessible, and positively audible, to the Muslim ear. I suggest that an elaboration on the incarnation with the Muslim imagination in view can be gleaned from what Maximus says on the incarnation: 1) from the use of the term 'inbreathing', of breathing the *Logos* into the womb of Mary; 2) from the emphasis that the *Logos'* inbreathing was absolutely voluntary and came from the divine free will and omnipotence; and, finally, 3) from his demonstration that, though the *Logos* was given human birth(γέννεσις), he was still different in his human dwelling place from Adam in that, unlike Adam, the incarnate *Logos* was not cursed in his human origin by the 'transgression' of sexual procreation. There is a striking resonance between these three elements and the following aspects of Islam: 1) what the Qur'an says about the *kalimah*'s conception by Maryam through an act of breathing God's Spirit into her womb; 2) the Qur'anic and Islamic belief that ʿĪsā and Adam are both God's made and both originate (γένεσις)

---

995 Ibid., Q.127 (p. 111).

996 Maximus, *Ambiguum* 42, 1317 A (p. 80). On the *Logos* as the 'new Adam' in relation to sin in Maximus' thought, see also Daniel Haynes, "The Transgression of Adam and Christ the New Adam: St Augustine and St Maximus the Confessor on the Doctrine of Original Sin," *St Vladimir's Theological Quarterly*, 55 (3) (2011), 293–317.

997 Maximus, *Ambiguum* 42, 1317B (p. 81).

from a supreme Originator;[998] and 3) the emphasis in Islamic *kalām* on God's omnipotence and absolute free will, even in the act of the indwelling of God's *kalimah* in Maryam's womb. One can ostensibly, then, propose that we have in Maximus' elaboration one of the earliest examples of some useful and subtle interpretations of Christology, from which later Christian *mutakallims*, particularly the Melkites, could have taken inspiration in their interreligious apologies.

I shall now show that this conclusion also applies to another significant choice of words by Maximus the Confessor. I refer to his use of the Greek word *enhypostaton* (ἐνυπόστατον). Maximian scholars generally agree that this word occupies as significant a place in the Confessor's understanding of the incarnation as terms like*hypostasis*, *ousia* and *perichoresis*.[999] The belief among scholars is that it was a prominent term in the Christology of the 6th-century father, Leontius of Byzantium.[1000] While some scholars believe that Maximus uses *enhypostaton* exactly as Leontius does,[1001] others express their conviction that this is far from evident.[1002]

One of the latter group, who believe that Maximus' use of *enhypostaton* was unique, is Melchisadec Törönen. In his book, *Union and Distinction in the Thought of St Maximus the Confessor*, Törönen suggests that *enhypostaton* has a twofold meaning in Maximus' works. The first is something "which by no means subsists by itself, but is considered in others, as a species in the individ-

998 In one of my discussions with Assaad Elias Kattan, he suggested that there may be here a Pauline influence on both Maximus and Islam with regard to this idea. This is, again, a very intriguing suggestion that merits a detailed study, but it cannot be pursued here.

999 On *enhypostaton*'s role and connotations in Maximus the Confessor's Christology, see Törönen, *Union and Distinction in the Thought of St Maximus the Confessor*, pp. 101–104ff; and Eric Perl, *Methexis: Creation, Incarnation and Deification in Saint Maximus Confessor* (PhD. thesis, Yale University, 1991), pp. 188–220.

1000 On the use and the meaning of *enhypostaton* in the theology of Leontius of Byzantium, known among scholars and often referred to is Brian Daley's unpublished 1979 essay, "The Christology of Leaontius of Byzantium: Personalism or Dialectics?"; see also Matthias Gockel, "A Dubious Christological Formula? Leontius of Byzantium and the *Anhypostasis-enhypostasis* Theory," *Jouranl of Theological Studies*, 51 (2000), 515–532.

1001 Thus Perl, *Methexis*, p. 188.

1002 Andrew Louth believes that the notion of '*enhypostaton*' is not at all the key to Maximus' own Christology, no matter what recent Maximian scholars suggest. Louth calls this mistaken proposal "the exorcism of the ghost of the doctrine of '*enhypostasia*'": A. Louth, "Recent Research on St Maximus the Confessor. A Survey," Review Essay in *St Vladimir's Theological Quarterly*, 42 (1) (1998), 67–84, p. 73. I shall not take sides in the matter, which is beyond both my own expertise and the scope of this study. I shall simply rely on the fact that the term is used by Maximus in his writings on the incarnation and Christology, regardless of whether or not he deemed it a key notion.

uals subordinated to it," and the second is "something which is put together with another, different by essence, to bring about a whole."[1003] When it comes to his understanding of the incarnation, Törönen suggests, Maximus opts to use *enhypostaton* in this second meaning to speak of the *Logos*' becoming human. This particular meaning, in Törönen's view, is consistent with Maximus' understanding of "composite *hypostasis*, as a particular entity made up of two essentially different realities, 'that which is put together with another different by essence, to bring about a whole.'"[1004] From this angle, Törönen adds, Maximus did not view the flesh of the incarnate *Logos* as a concrete personal hypostatic entity that exists by itself in separation from the concrete personal existence of the *Logos* (had he done so, the Confessor would have become a Nestorian). Rather, he views the flesh as an expression of a state of *enhypostaton*, that is an expression of a state of *subsistence* of generic humanity in the *Logos*, which itself gained existence when the *Logos* assumed (or, one may say, 'dwelt in') this fleshly form of subsistence.[1005]

It is within the 'subsisting' framework that Maximus the Confessor treated the incarnation, approaching it as 'composite' with the help of a 'body-soul' analogy: as the soul indwells the flesh and subsists in it without compromising its own nature, so the *Logos* indwelt human flesh and subsisted therein without jeopardizing its divine nature by any possible mixing or conflation. And, in order not to fall into the trap of Monophysitism, Maximus speaks of a 'composite *hypostasis*' rather than a 'composite nature.'[1006] While the Monophysites insisted upon considering 'mixture' the mode of union in the incarnation and spoke of an '*ousia* of union,'[1007] Maximus avoids this emphasis on substance and focuses, instead, on 'subsistence,' using the term '*enhypostaton*' in a sense that is probably reminiscent of the stoic notion of *krasis* (κράσις), which means a mutual and

1003 Törönen, *Union and Distinction in the Thought of St Maximus the Confessor*, p. 103. According to Törönen, Maximus gives this description in *Epistual* 15 (PG 91), 557D-560 A; and *Opusculum* 14 (PG 91), 152D-153 A (Ibid.nt.93).

1004 Törönen, *Union and Distinction in the Thought of St. Maximus the Confessor*, p. 103.

1005 Ibid., n. 93.

1006 The notion of 'compsite nature', scholars believe, originated from the Monophysites' mistaken reading of Cyril of Alexndria's use of the body-soul analogy when he spoke of 'the one *hypostasis* of the union in/as Jesus Christ.' One can glean such a reading, for instance, from the works of Severus of Antioch in the 6th century and the 10th-century Jacobite bishop, Severus Ibn al-Muqaffaʿ: Törönen, *Union and Distinction in the Thought of St Maximus Confessor*, pp. 95–101; and Aloys Grillmeier, *Christ in Christian Traditon*, Vol. 2, Pt 2, pp. 34, 127.

1007 For this the valuable analysis, see Torrance, *Christology after Chalcedon*, pp. 59–71.

total interpenetration, wherein those that interpenetrate maintain unaltered their particular properties and their distinction.[1008]

It is not surprising that Maximus the Confessor was heavily reliant on the Trinitarian notion of reciprocity[1009] in his understanding of the union and relationship between the two actions and wills of the incarnate One, for this notion expresses exactly the idea of 'mutual interpenetration without mixture,' as well as resonating with the idea of *enhypostaton*. Nor is it surprising that Maximus also spoke of the flesh as a 'garment' and of the relationship between the soul and the flesh in terms of 'ensouled flesh.' This suggests that the *Logos* clothed his divine glory as in a garment manner and sometimes hid, or veiled, it within it, lest we dare unworthily to claim control of what lies beyond our comprehension. This seems to be Maximus' view of the incarnate Word's relation to his bodily and visible appearance to human eyes in *Ambiguum* 10, where the Confessor says that the Word wears white clothing (symbolizing his divine awesomeness), as a garment that shines with his blessed radiance, as the words of scripture indirectly represent the divine law.[1010] Here, the Confessor seems to be resisting any implication that the incarnate Word's divine substance was transformed ontologically into any bodily, created nature when it indwelt a physical form. After all, Maximus stresses, God is simply and indefinably beyond all beings, both what circumscribes and what is circumscribed.[1011] The incarnation is an act of dwelling in, subsistence in, or wearing of the flesh as a garment in order to make God's glory and salvation encounterable and conceivable by the finite and sinful human mind. Maximus sees Christ's body, as Thomas Cattoi notes in his comparative study of *Ambiguum* 10, "[as] the *dwelling* place of divine wisdom [*Logos*], the *'tent'* which God has planted in the midst of humanity."[1012] And the reason for, and implications of, the *Logos*' making of the body his dwelling place, his tent, or his garment, is definitely epistemological and existential, not ontological, in nature or extent. It is a sign of God's mercy toward us, in that he

1008 Ibid., p. 61. See also Richard A. Norris, *God and the World in Early Christian Theology* (New York: Seabury Press, 1965), pp. 69–70.

1009 On *perichoersis* in Maximus the Confessor's Christology, see Lars Thunberg, *Microcosm and Mediator: The Theological Anthropology of Maximus the Confessor*, 2nd ed., (Peru, IL: Open Court, 1995), pp. 23–36; Assaad E. Kattan, "The Christological Dimension of Maximus Confessor's Biblical Hermeneutics," *Studia Patristica*, 42 (2006), 169–174; and A. E. Kattan, *Verleiblichung und Synergie: Grundsüge de Biblehermeneutik bei Maximus Confessor* (Leiden: Brill, 1995).

1010 Maximus the Confessor, *Ambiguum* 10, in A. Louth, *Maximus the Confessor*, 94–154, 17.D, 1128 A (p. 109).

1011 Ibid., 26.B, 1153 A (p. 124).

1012 Thomas Cattoi, "The Incarnate *Logos* and the *Rūpakāya:* Towards a Comparative Theology of Embodiment," *Religion East & West*, 8 (2008), 109–129, p. 117.

made himself and his salvation known and perceived by us because we are completely unable in our broken, limited and sinful condition to know by ourselves his will, glory and grace. According to Maximus in *Chapters on Knowledge*, the dwelling of the *Logos* in human flesh occurred because human beings "cannot with their naked mind reached naked spiritual realities." They need such an indwelling in fleshly garment to be able to realize that the *Logos* "converses in a way familiar to them in a variety of stories, enigmas, parables and dark sayings."[1013]

Again, it is not my intention here to delve into a theologico-philological study of Maximus the Confessor's Christological terminology. My only intention in this presentation of Maximus' use of *enhypostaton* is to show that John of Damascus concurs with Maximus' reading of the incarnation and, most importantly, with his way of speaking about it: both John and Maximus refer to the *Logos'* becoming human in terms of 'subsistence,' not 'substance'; in terms, that is, of 'indwelling' and existential concrete presence in fleshly embodiment. They both seem to be speaking of the incarnation not as an ontological transformation into either fleshly human nature (enfleshment) or an essential human being (enhumanization[1014]), and both, finally, seem to take care to give balanced attention to the dimensions of veiling and disclosure in their understanding of how the divine truth made itself able to be encountered by the finite human mind in the incarnate *Logos*. This equal attention to veiling and disclosure may not be maintained by Theodore Abū Qurrah, who seems rather to emphasize the veiling dimension in order to assure Muslims that, in their belief in the incaranation, Christians do not want to deny God's transcendence or subordinate it to the human mind. Theodore maintains that, even in his incarnation, God's Word and Spirit (as shown in the previous section) remains infinite and transcendent, and his glory and divine nature remain hidden behind the human flesh in which he dwelt.

Pointing to this linguistic similarity between John of Damascus and Maximus the Confessor, on the one hand, and Maximus and later Arab Christian apol-

1013 Maximus the Confessor, *Chapters on Knowledge*, in Berthold, *Maximus Confessor, Selected Writings*, pp. 127–180, II.60 (p. 159).

1014 They were not apllying the understanding of incarnation in terms of *enanthropesis*, which Origen developed in his *Logos* Christology. See on Origen's Christology, for example, J. N.D. Kelly, *Early Christian Doctrines*, (London: A&C Black, 1993), pp. 154–158; Basil Studer, *Trinity and Incarnation: The Faith of the Early Church*, Matthias Westerhodd (trans.), Andrew Louth (ed.), (Edinburgh: T&T Clark, 1993), pp. 77–89; David L. Paulsen, "Early Christian Belief in a Corporeal Deity: Origen and Augustine as Reluctant Witnesses," in *Harvard Theological Review*, 83:2 (1990), pp. 105–116; and Christopher A. Beeley, *The Unity of Christ; Continuity and Conflict in Patristic Tradition*, (New Haven: Yale University Press, 2012), pp. 3–47.

ogists, on the other, is not intended to undermine the generally accepted fact that Maximus the Confessor is by no means a Christian apologist to Islam. Comparing with John of Damascus, who wrote on Islamic scripture and beliefs and left polemic works on them, Maximus is no Christian interlocutor in any significant Christian-Muslim dialogue. Even when he occasionally mentions Islam, as in *Epestula* 14, Maximus, as Gregory Benevich accurately notes, "speaks only in terms that contrast a barbarian invasion with a civilization; he does not at all discuss the faith of the [Muslim] invaders."[1015] Far from being a defender of faith before Islam, Maximus is known in history as the guardian of Chalcedonian orthodoxy over against Monophysitism and Monothelitism. As Benevich realizes, Maximus' defence of the incarnation was at a time "when in Byzantium the teaching about God's incarnation was corrupted to the extent that church officials began to profess the absence of a human will in Christ."[1016] Maximus does not seem to have much knowledge of the Islamic faith, at least not as extensive as his knowledge of Judaism.

C. Abū Qurrah's Christology and the Melkite Tradition: Concurrence or Divergence?

The apologetic path that Maximus the Confessor and John of Damascus (especially the former) trod in their defence of Chalcedonian Christology against Jewish and Christian heresies (Monophysitism, Nestorianism, Monoenergism, Monothelitism) in the Byzantine Empire was also trodden by Theodore Abū Qurrah in his attempt to interpret Christology in Arabic to the Muslim population of the Abbasid Caliphate. This is the conclusion that can be drawn from the above presentation of some theological Christological hermeneutics in the works of the Confessor and the Damascene.

In addition, when it comes to the detailed apologetic context of each of these Church fathers, one must realize that the questions on Christology that Maximus and John, on the one hand, and Theodore, on the other, had to deal with differed substantially due to the backgrounds of their interlocutors. Maximus and John were primarily attending to specific non-Orthodox Christological trends raised

---

1015 Grigory I. Benevich, "Christological Polemics of Maximus the Confessor and the Emergence of Islam onto the World Stage," *Theological Studies*, 72 (2011), 335–344, p. 338. Some scholars even believe that Maximus did not really have any reliable knowledge of the religious content of Islam. See, for example, Karl Heinz Öhleg, *Der frühe Islam: Eine historisch-kritische Rekonstruktion anhand Zeitgenösischer Quellen* (Berlin: Hans Schiler, 2007).
1016 Benevich, "Christological Polemics of Maximus the Confessor," p. 343.

by Nestorians, Jacobites and other non-Chalcedonian groups, so their christological treatises consist basically of elaborate theological answers to questions such as: What is the relation of the divine and human natures in the incarnate Son of God or *Logos*, Jesus Christ? How do the human and the divine *hypostases* stand together, and how do they relate to each other in the union of the two natures? Did Jesus Christ have two sets of activities, divine and human, or did he carry out one form of actions in both his natures? Can we speak of two wills or minds, one divine and one human, in the *hypostasis* of union, and can we then assume a *perichoresis*, or a division, between the characteristics (*communicatio idiomatum*) between the humanity and the divinity of the incarnate *Logos?*

Such questions indicate that both those who raise them and those who attempt to find plausible answers to them, start their deliberations from a normative belief that 1) God has a Son, who is equal to him in divinity, infinity and essence, 2) that this Son has freely willed to become human like us and to be incarnate in and as Jesus Christ, and 3) that Jesus Christ, as this incarnate Son of God, is both human and divine in nature and one in personal concrete subsistence (*hypostasis*). *That* God has a Son, and *that* this Son has been incarnated in/as Jesus of Nazareth were major, taken for granted convictions by Christians. The debates between the Christian factions were about determining *how* the divine and the human came together in one person without clash, contradiction, or conflation, and *how* can we reconcile the *Logos*' identity with his human life.

When we come to Theodore Abū Qurrah, this Arab Melkite father's thought and rationale cannot be accurately understood without an awareness of the major differences between his apologetic context and that of his predecessors, Maximus and John. Theodore's interlocutors are predominantly Muslims of the Abbasid Caliphate, who speak a new language, not Greek or Syriac, and who do not share any common religious or theological ground with Abū Qurrah. Even when Abū Qurrah found himself debating with Jews or Jacobite and Nestorian Christians, he often pursued these debates either within the Arab-Islamic intellectual context, or physically in the presence of the Muslim Caliph and Muslim *mutakallims*. As his works show, this must have forced him to present Christian doctrines using a form of speech free of Christian jargon and technical terms (such as *ousia* and *hypostasis*) and in a logical style that was lucid, accessible and easily understood by his audiences. Abū Qurrah elaborated on, and interpreted, Christology from the perspective of questions that are totally different from those that faced Maximus and John.[1017] While Maximus' and John's audien-

1017 I principally concur fully here with Mark Beaumont's perceptive note that, in Theodore

ces (mainly Christians) took for granted that God is an eternal Father and a divine, equally eternal Son, Theodore's audiences (mainly Muslims) rejected totally that God could take a child unto himself (*itakhadha lahu waladan*) and one of their main challenges to the Christian faith had to do with how Christians could really justify and defend their belief that God has a Son. On the other hand, the nature of Maximus' and John's audiences meant that their point of departure was the undisputed belief among Christians that the Son of God became human and dwelt amongst us. They then debated with non-Chalcedonian Christians about how the meeting of the divine and the human in Jesus should be interpreted. Theodore Abū Qurrah's audiences, on the other hand, were Muslims, whose holy book and theological teaching told them that God is absolutely transcendent and cannot in any way become one of his creatures.

In other words, what the audience of Maximus and John took for granted, Theodor's audience considered highly problematic and blasphemous. This is why we see in Theodore's maymars lengthy attempts to defend the logical and theological tenability of saying that 'God took a child unto himself.' This is also why Theodore had a serious concern to present an explanation of how the divine and the human could meet together in one person without God's transcendence and omnipotence being threatened. Developing arguments on these points was not a priority for Maximus and John, and they were considered secondary to other more urgent questions for the divided Christian factions. In contrast, Theodore Abū Qurrah found himself pushed into making it his primary and most urgent task to argue for the plausibility of these basic Christian premises. For his Muslim audience, the question as to whether Jesus had two wills and energies or one, or how the human and the divine *ousiai* made one single *hypostasis* was only secondary.

In the previous lines above, my aim was to point out the importance of discerning central differences between Theodore Abū Qurrah's Arabic-speaking dialogical context and the Greek-Byzantine environment of his Melkite-Chalcedonian predecessors. Now I shall go on to give attention to the fact that, despite these differences, both Maximus and John, on the one hand, and Theodore, on the other, pay noteable attention to the idea of the 'incarnation' and are careful to explain it to their interlocutors in as plausible, meaningful and lucid manner as possible. And. it is specifically in relation to the notion of 'incarnation' that

Abū Qurrah's Christological apologies before Muslims, "there is no discussion of varieties of Christological positions held by Christians. Muslims were not asking questions about differences between Christian views, so what was essential debate in his Confession of the Orthodox Faith, is irrelevant to his apologies for Muslim. He was trying to find openings in Muslim thought for the presentation of Christ as he saw Him": Beaumont, *Christology in Dialogue with Muslims*, p. 43.

one can clearly discern Abū Qurrah's reliance on the teaching of his two Melkite theological mentors, Maximus and John.

In his *Mujādalah* at al-Maʾmūn's court, Abū Qurrah speaks of the incarnation using various forms of the Arabic word for indwelling: *ḥulūl, ḥalla, yaḥillu, taḥillu*. For example:

445. فإذا كانت الكلمة والروحِ الخالقة لذلك بأسره...
446. ...كيف لا يجوز أن تَحِلّ في خلقةٍ من خلقها ظاهرةً على صورتها ومثالها وتتخذها لها حجاباً

445. If the Word and Spirit was the Creator of all this entirely ...
446. ... how should it not be that it would indwell [*taḥill*] one of its creatures, appearing in its image and likeness, and making it a veil [*ḥijāb*] for itself?[1018]

Earlier in the same text, Abū Qurrah repeats from memory the angel's proclamation to Mary, replacing the words in the Gospel: *wa-quwwat al-ʿaliyy tuẓalliluki* (and the power of the almighty overshadows you) with *rūḥ al-ʿaliyy taskunuki* (the Spirit of the almighty inhabits/indwells you).

329. يا مريم إنّ الرب يحل فيكِ وروح العلي تسكنكِ

329. O Maryam, the Lord indwells you and the Spirit of the almighty inhabits you.[1019]

It is striking here that Abū Qurrah's changes the original text and translates it in a way that fits his own theological and rational hermeneutics of the incarnation. This is another example of his using of the religious text to serve rational argument and logic, rather than subjecting his rational argument to the literal wording of the religious text. Here, Abū Qurrah, like other Muslim and Christian *mutakallims* of his time, is sometimes eisegetical rather than exegetical in his approach.

1018 Abū Qurrah, *Abū Qurrah wal-Maʾmūn: al-Mujāalah* (Abū Qurrah and al-Maʾmūn: The debate), V. A.2.445–446. Abū Qurrah uses the same vocabulary, as shown in earlier sections of this chapter, in Abū Qurrah, *fī ar-Radd ʿalā Man Yunkir li-llāh at-Tajassud wal-Ḥulūl* (In response to those who deny to God [the possibility of] incarnation and indwelling ...), pp. 180–186.

1019 Abū Qurrah, *Abū Qurrah wal-Maʾmūn: al-Mujādalah* (Abū Qurrah and al-Maʾmūn: The Debate), IV. D.1.329. In the older Melkite text, M. D. Gibson, *Fi Tathlīth Allah al-Wāḥid* (On the trinuity of the one God), f.110b.15 (p. 83), we find yet another Arabic form of this verse:قال جبريل روح الله عليكِ تنزل وقوة العليّ فيكِ تحلّ (Gabriel said: the Spirit of God upon you descends and the power of the almighty within you dwells). These descrepancies may simply be due to lack of a single, official Arabic translation of the whole Bible in the 8th-9th centuries. Translating biblical verses into Arabic from Greek, Aramaiac and Hebrew was left to the Arab Christian *mutakallims*' linguistic skills and discretion. But one may add here that it also depended on each *mutakallim*'s theological needs and dialogical circumstances.

In addition, Abū Qurrah's avoidance of terms such as *tāʾannus* and *tajassud* to speak of the incarnation is also striking. He opts rather for 'indwelling' and 'inhabiting' or *ḥulūl* and *sakan*. This is not just a haphazard linguistic choice. If one wants to connect Abū Qurrah with John and Maximus and propose that Theodore derives his theological thinking from these two fathers, it could be suggested that Abū Qurrah's use of *ḥulūl* and *sakan* is a possible reflection of his mistranslation into Arabic, or even misunderstanding, of the reference in John of Damascus and Maximus to 'subsistence' or *enhypostaton* in relation to the incarnation (as shown in the previous two sections). What Maximus and John explained by using '*enhypostaton*' Abū Qurrah endeavoured to convey to Muslims by using the Arabic term *ḥulūl*, whose use and presence in Islamic literature he must also have been aware of. However, the connotations of Abū Qurrah's translation show that his understanding of *enhypostaton* is different from the way Maximus and John understood and used it; for Maximus and John, *enhypostaton* signifies the hypostatization of the body by its being embraced by the *Logos* in the womb of the virgin Mary. To the contrary for Abū Qurrah, *ḥulūl* tends to connote the body embracing the *Logos* and concealing it behind a human veil. This may be a creative and ingenious way of speaking to Muslims about the incarnation using the Arabic terms they used and they were familiar with. But, from the perspective of Theodore's alignment with the theological orthodoxy of his Melkite predecessors and intellectual mentors, John and Maximus, this rather inaccurate translation of *enhypostaton* as *ḥulūl* may lead us to conclude that Abū Qurrah here diverges from the precise conceptual connotations of Chalcedonian Christological doctrine.

It is also worth noting that Abū Qurrah adopts Maximus the Confessor's reference to the 'veil' or 'garment' of the glory of the divine *Logos*, and speaks of the Word and Spirit indwelling the creaturely body in terms of the creature being a veil (*ḥijāb*) for the divine.[1020] Abū Qurrah must have found this idea of 'clothing the divine glory' an appropriate expression of his thinking about the indwelling of the Word in a human body that would not make the incarnation sound to Muslim ears like an ontological transformation of God's Word from its eternal identity with God (*hiya hūa*) into a mere creaturely being. Abū Qurrah wanted to enable Muslims to realize that Christians do not say that the divine *Logos* was transformed into a human creature in stustance, but that the *Logos* decided to dwell in a human body and to subsist in it as if standing behind a veil. The question here is whether the notions of 'veil' (*ḥijab*) and 'indwelling' (*ḥulūl*) are prob-

1020 Abū Qurrah, *Abū Qurrah wal-Maʾmūn: al-Mujāalah* (Abū Qurrah and al-Maʾmūn: The debate), V. A.2.446.

ably and accurately derived from Maximus the Confessor's understanding and use of the notion of *enhypostaton*, or even from John of Damascus' explanation of the incarnation as an expression of an existential hypostatization of the flesh by the divine *Logos*. The contradiction between Abū Qurrah's understanding of the notion of *enhypostaton* and that of his two mentors hardly proves Abū Qurrah's full allegiance to the exact theological views of the Damascene and the Confessor. This notwithstanding, we must also be fair to Abū Qurrah here and admit that in his choice of Arabic terms, he reveals an admirably subtle attentiveness to the intellectual background of his Muslim audience and his evident ability to speak to them using words from their conceptional and terminological resources. Is this a sacrifice of orthodoxy? Not necessarily. It can be seen as an attempt to re-explain orthodoxy in a way that makes it as plausible and accessible as possible to non-Christians.

In his letter to a Jacobite friend who converted to orthodoxy, Abū Qurrah does not worry much about his Arabic vocabulary and is more relaxed in his choice of words when he speaks about the incarnation. Instead of *ḥulūl*, Abū Qurrah uses without embarrassment the Arabic term *tajassud* and even states that in using that term he wants to say that the *Logos* (*kalima*) not only clothed himself with the flesh (took it as a garment), but that he also truly *united* with and connected to it

ونقول أنَّ هذه الكلمة الإله تجسَّد من العذراء المصطفاة مريم فولد منها إنساناً...فأما قولنا أنَّ الكلمة تجسَّد فإنّا إنما نعني به أنه حديثاً هبط إلى حال تدبير التواضع من أجل فكنا وخلاصنا. ونحن نريك أيضاً أنه صار إنساناً هذا الكلمة حتى نوضِّح بذلك أنَّ تجسّده ليس نعني به التحاف الجسد الالتزاق به ولكن الاتصال الحق والاتحاد الذي هو أرفع من كل اتصال واتحاد.

And we say that this divine Word was en-fleshed [*tajassad*] from the chosen Virgin Maryam and was born a human from her … . concerning our saying that the Word [*kalmia*] was en-fleshed [*tajassad*], we mean by it that he in recent times descended to a state of deliberate humility in order to release and save us. And we also show you that this Word become human [*insān*] in order to clarify that we do not mean by his 'en-fleshment' [*tajassudih*] [simply] clothing with [*iltiḥāf*] the body and clinging to it [*iltizāq*], but a real connectedness [*ittiṣāl*] and union [*ittiḥād*] that is more sublime than any [other] connectedness and union.[1021]

Later in this epistle, Theodore reflects extensively on the union and relationship of the two natures using the analogy of the relation between the body and the soul (thus drawing on the neo-Chalcedonian theology of 6th-century authors

1021 Abū Qurrah, *Risālah fī Ījābat Mas'alah Katabahā Abū Qurrah al-Qiddīs ilā Ṣadīq lahu kāna Ya'qūbiyyan fa-Ṣār Urthūdhuksiyyan 'Inda Raddihi 'alayhi aj-Jawāb* (An epistle in response to a matter, written by the holy Abū Qurrah to a friend of his, who was Jacobite and became orthodox, as he responds to him with the answer), p. 118.

such as Leontius of Byzantium and Leontius of Jerusalem). He does this in a manner clearly reminescent of Maximus the Confessor's Christology, almost simply reiterating Maximus' assertions on the union of the two natures, but in Arabic. Thus the difference between Theodore's elaborations on the incarnation in *al-Mujādalah* and the maymar on the Incarnation, on the one hand, and in his responses to non-Chalcedonian Christians, such as his epistle to a Jacobite friend, on the other, is clear: in the former, the Word 'indwells' (*ḥulūl*) the body, while in the latter, the Word truly unites with the body (*tajassud*). In the former, the body is just a veil (*ḥijāb*) to conceal the *Logos*' transcendent, infinite and glorious divinity, while in the latter the body is a sign of a real human nature (*'insāniyyah*) and evidence of real unity between the divine and the human.

Is this discrepancy a sign of Theodore Abū Qurrah's intellectual inconsistency and evidence of an unreliable fluctuation and ambivalence in his Christology? I think not. This apparent discrepancy is, rather, an indication of his admirable sensitivity and profound perception of his audiences' and readers' intellectual, religious and philological mind-set and context; for Muslims, the language of *ḥulūl* and *iḥtijāb* makes sense, while for Christians, the language of *tajassud* and *'ittiḥād* is normal and part and parcel of familiar doctrines and beliefs about Jesus Christ.

Is this decision to use different logical arguments and vocabularies to speak of the incarnation a proof of Theodore Abū Qurrah's readiness to compromise Chalcedonian-Melkite orthodoxy and take a divergent path, upon the belief that this would enable him to gain Muslim approval? I believe that this is far from a real compromising or abandonment of orthodoxy. After all, both Abū Qurrah's ways of explaining the incarnation – as 'dwelling in a veil/garment' (*ḥulūl/ḥijāb*) and as 'uniting-with and becoming a human person' (*tajassud/tā'annus*) – are found in the Christological discourses of the Church, and are not Theodore's own, unprecedented invention. Both, therefore, could be derived by Abū Qurrah from the Tradition and used by him, each in its suitable context and before the appropriate audience, in the belief that both were within the boundaries of orthodoxy and does not contradict it. It is true that that orthodoxy may not be Melkite in substance and may be different in conception from the orthodox understanding of the incarnation that is found in the works of Maximus the Confessor and John of Damascus, but a relative and temporary departure from the Melkite path is not the same as completely drifting away from orthodoxy, which was not, after all, exclusively Melkite or Greek but was also Syrian.

In his essay "Syrian and Arabian Christianity and the Qur'ān," Karl-Heinz Öhlig relates the development of Syrian theology and the thinking behind it from pre-Nicene time up to the Islamic era, when that theology was Arabicized. Öhlig pays specific attention to Christology, shedding important lights on the development of the Syrian theology of the incarnation. One of the interesting hermeneutics of the incarnation in Syrian theology, according to Öhlig, is the tradition that interprets the incarnation as meaning that the *Logos* lived in Jesus 'as in a temple' and that the Virgin Mary "did not give birth to the *Logos*. On the contrary, she gave birth to a human being, one who is like us."[1022] An example of this is found, for example, in Paul of Samosata, a representative of Syrian theology from the Euphrates before Nicea, when he speaks on the incarnation. The same idea of abiding in a temple continues in later Syrian theology, after Nicea, as we see, for example in the 4th-century Syrian theologian, Diodore of Tarsus' reference to the *Logos* as 'dwelling in' the Son of Man.[1023] This tradition, Öhligh surmises, continues through later Syrian theological discourse, too, so that one may say that, in the Syrian theological tradition, "the incarnation is thought of in terms of 'enrobing' or 'enclothing.'"[1024]

Now, if Öhlig's construction is correct, it seems that there was in this Syrian theological tradition, and, more intriguingly, in Theodore Abū Qurrah's theological discourse on the incarnation, a valid and plausible space for serious comparison between understanding the incarnation in terms of 'indwelling,' 'enclothing,' 'abiding in' and the idea of *ḥulūl* in Muslim *kalām*. We do know that Theodore Abū Qurrah was born into a Syrian context (or family) and knew Syriac, and he even wrote maymars in that language in the course of his theological career. It is not far from likely that Theodore could also have versed himself in Syriac theological traditions, as much as he educated himself after the Greek one.

In the perivous chapter, I argued that, in his attempt to present a rationally plausible interpretation of Christian theology of the Trinity to Muslims, Abū Qurrah was ready to borrow from marginal trends in Christian orthodoxy some terms and notions (e.g., the idea of *wajh*, which he developed along the lines of the notions of *prosopon* and *parsop*), which he believed to be more useful in conveying what Christian orthodox theology of the Trinity wants to say when it speaks of three *hypostases* in the Godhead. I think that Theodore follows the same strategy in what he says to Muslims on the incarnation. He uses the Arabic term *ḥulūl* – though he knows that its connotations differ from the understanding of *enhypostaton* in the texts of John of Damascus and Maximus the Confessor – beause he seems to be thinking that this term resonates with other, this time Syrian,

1022 Karl-Heinz Öhlig, "Syrian and Arabian Christianity and the Qur'ān," p. 375.
1023 Ibid., p. 378.
1024 Ibid., p. 381.

trends in orthodoxy that speak of the incarnation in terms of 'indwelling a temple' or 'enclothing a human body.'

This proposal explains the source of Theodore's Arabic vocabulary by rooting it in his knowledge of Syrian theological traditions. The question here is: But does he then remain still within the bounds of theological orthodoxy? The answer would be 'yes' if this Syrian tradition, from which we propose that Theodore was borrowing, is considered part and parcel of theological orthodoxy. Öhlig shows that, from the 4th century, the Syrian fathers were willing to incorporate into their theological thinking some Hellenistic theological trends (specifically the Antiochene). In his view, from the 5th century onwards, one can safely call Syrian theology 'Antiochene,' as it adopted "a monarchian doctrine of God and a dyophysite Christology."[1025] One can say, Öhlig concludes, that "from here on, Syrian theology was marked at its foundation by 'Byzantine' trinitarian and Christological ideas, even if these were interpreted through an 'un-Cyrillian' and 'Antiochene' lens."[1026] If Öhlig's argument is correct, we have here a Syrian theological orthodoxy that developed in parallel to the Greek-Byzantine one and was just as widespread and prevalent as the latter in the territories of Syria-Palestine. More importantly, a theologian like Theodore Abū Qurrah, who was born in and grew up and served as a bishop in the Syriac-speaking context of Edessa and the famous city of Ḥarrān, must have been knowledgeable about this Syrian orthodox tradition. It is then not at all surprising to see him borrowing some terms and notions from this line of theological reasoning in his debates with Muslims.

The above leads us not only to see how innovative and intelligent Abū Qurrah is in his use of every available orthodox tradition, both Greek and Syrian, in the service of his apologetics, but also to wonder whether the same Syrian theological tradition was not equally familiar to the ears of his Muslim interlocutors, which ultimately raises the question of whether the Islamic idea of *ḥulūl* was itself derived from the same Syrian theological thought that Theodore drew upon for his ideas on the incarnation. This question merits an entire study of its own and cannot be pursued here. The brief presentation above is made to show that Abū Qurrah, in his reliance on two parallel traditions to speak of the incarnation (one Greek-Byzantine and the other Syrian) in his various writings, was shaping his discourse on christology in ways and forms of expressions that were accessible to his audiences' backgrounds, thought forms and cognitive capacities.

1025 Ibid., p. 383.
1026 Ibid., p. 385.

If this is what Abū Qurrah was doing, he would not have been the first Arabic-speaking apologist to take this route. He may have been inspired by a similar attempt to speak of the incarnation as both a real union with the human, on the one hand, and as a clothing of the divine glory with a 'garment,' on the other, in a Maximian (or even an older Nyssan) tradition of writing that had been adopted by other Melkite authors before him. For example, we find in the Melkite Arabic text known as *fī Tathlīth Allah al-Wāḥid* (On the Trunity of the One God) that the author insists on the real humanity of the incarnate 'Word and Spirit,'[1027] while at the same time, speaking of the incarnation as an act of veiling (*iḥtijāb*) in Maryam and an act of clothing in a body (*labisa jasad*).[1028] Speaking of the incarnation in terms of veiling, as Mark Swanson reminds us, is also reminiscent of Gregory of Nyssa's reference in his Catechetical Orations to "God's divinity [as] hidden by the veil (*prokalymma*) of our nature."[1029] One can also find the understanding of the incarnation as 'veiled behind a human body' in various Greek and Syriac patristic works.[1030]

Abū Qurrah reveals a more subtle and intelligent use of this twofold Maximian-Nyssan, orthodox expression of the incarnation, as he avoids speaking of the incarnation as 'ontological union' and 'existential veiled indwelling' in the same way without differentiating between audiences, as the author of *On the Trunity of the One God* seems to be doing. With Muslims, Theodore speaks of the incarnation using only the idea of 'indwelling and subsisting behind a veil,' as in the text of *Mujādalah* and the maymar on the incarnation, but,

---

1027 Gibson, *Fi Tathlīth Allah al-Wāḥid* (On the trunity of the one God), f.110b.20, p. 83:"إنسان كامل بالنفس والجسد من غير خطية" (A perfect human in soul and flesh, without sin).

1028 Ibid., f.109b.5, p. 83, and f.115b.10, p. 88, respectively:ولبس هذا الإنسان الضعيف المقهور من مريم الطيبة... فاحتجب بها وأهلك به الشر... (and He clothed Himself in with this weak, oppressed human human from the good Maryam...so, He veiled Himself in Her and demolished by it evil...); and فإنه إله من الله وإن كان لبس الجسد (for He is divine from God, though He clothed Himself in the flesh).

1029 Mark Swanson, "Beyond Prooftexting," pp. 297–298. Swanson believes that the author of *Fi Tathlīth Allah al-Wāḥid* (On the triunity of the one God) does not derive these terms and notions from the tradition of Christian theological vocabulary, but rather directly from the Qur'an, suggesting a direct quotation from Q 3:42. On this derivation, Swanson, then, comments "the Christian author needs no clumsy citation formula or footnote to let the reader know that he is citing the Qur'ān; many with ears to hear will hear. For them, four or five carefully chosen words in *Tathlīth* are sufficient to bring the biblical and the Qur'ānic stories of the annunciation into sympathetic resonance" (ibid., p. 298).

1030 On this the analysis, see in Barbara Roggema, "*Ḥikāyāt Amthāl Wa Asmār*...King Parables in Melkite Apologetic Literature," in *Studies on the Christian Arabic Heritage, in Honour of Father Prof. Dr Samir Khalil Samir S.I. at the Occasion of His Sixty-Fifth Birthday*, ed. Rifaat Ebied and Herman Teule (Leuven: Peeters, 2004), 113–131, pp. 124–131.

when addressing other Christians, Abū Qurrah was more relaxed in his christological language and spoke of the incarnation as a 'real substantial union,' as we see in the epistle to the Jacobite convert.

VI. Conclusion

In his attempt to enter into dialogue on Christology with Muslims, Theodore Abū Qurrah focuses on defending the Christian belief in the divinity of Jesus Christ, his sonship to God and his incarnation by emphasizing 1) God's absolute omnipotence, 2) God's gracious and merciful free will, 3) the logic of claiming that God's Word dwelt in human flesh in order to make it possible for us to perceive his will, and 4) the argument that not only the religious texts of the Christian Church, but the holy texts of the Qur'an itself, can reasonably be understood to support such a belief.

But it is particularly in Abū Qurrah's interpretation of the incarnation that we find an interesting and creatively original re-articulation of the Christian belief in terms accessible to the Muslim mind. It has been noted in the study of Abū Qurrah's Trinitarian apologies in the previous chapter that he innovatively chooses the Arabic word *wajh* to refer to the three *hypstases* (Greek) or *qnome* (Syriac) when addressing his Muslim interlocutors. This was Theodore's ingenious way of conveying to Mulims in Arabic what Christians are trying to say when they recognize three *hypostases*, Father, Son and Holy Spirit, in the one divine Godhead. In what he says about the incarnation, which has been one of the subjects of this chapter, Abū Qurrah makes another innovative vocabulary choice: he uses the Arabic word *ḥulūl* to convey the mode of the incarnation of God's Word and Spirit in human flesh. My study of the way Maximus the Confessor and John of Damascus spoke of the incarnation has shown that Abū Qurrah seems to have thought of taking up their use of the Greek technical term *enhypostaton*.Yet, in so doing he seems to have added to the definitions of the Greek term new connotations and meanings borrowed from a parallel, Syrian orthodox tradition that speaks of the incarnation in terms of 'indwelling' 'robing' and 'clothing.' This attempt at mixing two distinct, though equally orthodox, manners of theological expression eventually produced his admittedly rather peculiar interpretation of *enhypostaton* as equivalent to the Arabic *ḥulūl*, and his, then, bestowal on the latter a meaning that is not quite found in the former. The consequence is that Theodore's translation of orthodoxy into Arabic may lead some to see in this mixing of ideas evidence that his theology on the incarnation wandered off the main path of doctrinal orthodoxy.

The above acknowledged, one should not deny that Abū Qurrah's attempt to speak of the incarnation in Arabic was innovative and worthwhile from a dialogical and interreligious point of view. Though the word *ḥulūl* appears in other Arabic Christian *kalām* texts, it is used in Theodore's texts on Christian orthodoxy to Muslims in a systematic and sophisticated hermeneutic way that seems based on a conviction that the Syrian and Greek lines of orthodox Christian thought were in harmony and consistent with each other. By specifically using *ḥulūl*, Abū Qurrah seems to be suggesting to his fellow Christians that, with Muslims, one should not stick to just one tradition of orthodox teaching, but use every useful item in recognized orthodox theology, whether Greek or Syrian. That is, one should not speak of the incarnation using the terms *tajassud* or *tāʾannus*, but only using *ḥulūl* (indwelling). The reason for this lies, first, in the fact that the idea of 'indwelling' or 'clothing' exists in the Syrian orthodox tradition of Christianity that is native to the Islamic territories and is therefore familiar to the Muslim *mutakallims*' ears. *Tajassud* and *tāʾannus*, on the other hand, are neither used nor accepted in Islam. The second reason for this terminological option is that terms other than *ḥulūl*, such as *tajassud* and *tāʾannus*, have highly metaphysical and irrational connotations to the Muslim mind; they imply that God, the divine and infinite in nature, has experienced a change of substance and become a creaturely human being. It is better to use *ḥulūl*, Abū Qurrah decides, because it implies that an existential subsistence took place when the Word of God made his dwelling in flesh and made it his veil for the sole purpose of making God's will able to be perceived by our limited and sinful minds. It did not, that is, force on the Word of God any transformation or conversion, but enabled the Word to come and save us by dwelling within fleshly veil.

The interpretation of the term *ḥulūl* in the discourse on the incarnation may be more intriguing and slightly more problematic in Arabic Christian orthodox *kalām* than Theodore's incorporation of the term *wajh* in his hermeneutics of the Trinity. However, and from the specific perspective of interreligious dialogue, the way in which Theodore uses the term *ḥulūl* to speak of the incarnation is no less innovative in content and subtle in conception than his use of *wajh* in what he says about the Trinity. *Wajh* and *ḥulūl* are the words Abū Qurrah chose to convey theological orthodoxy (in its two versions, the Syrian and the Greek) and to re-articulate its core content afresh, and not to compromise it or dispense with the orthodox discourse altogether. Mark Beaumont is, therefore, quite correct in his conclusion that

> Abū Qurrah's Christology in dialogue with Muslims is largely a defence of the Nicene-Chalcedonian tradition … . The language of the detailed description of the incarnation … reflects

the Creed of Constantinople … . He translates the orthodox creeds into Arabic, finding terminology to suit the purpose.[1031]

1031 M. Beaumont, *Christology in Dialogue with Muslims*, pp. 41–42. Beaumont also acknowledges the importance of the word *ḥulūl* in Abū Qurrah's works and his preference of this term over *tāʾannus* and *tajassud*.

Concluding Postscript. Theodore Abū Qurrah: A Melkite Orthodox *Mutakallim* in *Dār al-Islām*

In this study, I have ventured through the Arabic apologetic literature of one of the most prominent Arabic-speaking Melkite theologians of the 8th – 9th centuries, whose textual legacy it is our good fortune and privilege to have extant today. Theodore Abū Qurrah ought not to be approached just as a late-Byzantine, staunch orthodox-Chalcedonian theologian from the Melkite Church of Syria-Palestine. The Bishop of Ḥarrān is also one of the most, if not even *the* most, influential, seminal and able Christian theologians of the early Abbasid era, who not only defended the orthodox Christian faith against the attacks of other Christians, but also attempted brilliantly to argue with Muslims, in their own mother-tongue, for the logical and rational tenability of Christian orthodoxy.

I did not aspire in this study to present a comprehensive exposition of all Theodore's theological works, nor did I promise a philosophical and doctrinal analysis of every theme Abū Qurrah touched upon in his extant writings (which I hope I shall have the opportunity of pursuing one day). I have limited my attention, first, to Theodore's apologies to Muslims, leaving aside his apologies to the non-Chalcedonian branches of Christianity in his time. I have focused, second, on Abū Qurrah's theological dialogues and controversies with Muslim interlocutors specifically on the doctrine of the Trinity and some selected themes from Christology. The Trinity and Christology, as every scholar of Christian-Muslim relations knows, are not simply two subjects of controversy between the followers of these two religious traditions in present-day interreligious interactions alone. They have also clearly been the most divisive issues between Muslims and the Christians, and those that have caused the most antagonism, ever since the invaders from the Arabian Peninsula entered the lands of Syria-Palestine in the early 7th century and encountered the local Aramaic- and Greek-speaking people of those territories. I have given comprehensive analytical attention to these two doctrinal issues to show that they were similarly central to, and primary in, almost all of Theodore Abū Qurrah's conversations with Muslims. By centralizing these two subjects in his discourse with them, Abū Qurrah definitely became the man of his time, and his texts are not only evidence of his own bright, highly sophisticated mind, but also mirror the intellectual and cultural complexity and intensity of the 8th – 9th-century context at the geographic heart of the Islamic caliphate.

In my study of Abū Qurrah's discourses to Muslims on the Trinity and Christ's divinity, sonship and incarnation, I took my analytical-critical examination beyond the narrow boundaries of the impact and implications his theological logic would have had for the Muslim ear, and I also went beyond these boundaries to examine the impact and implications of Abū Qurrah's interpretation of Trinitarian and Christological orthodoxy to the ears of his fellow Melkite and orthodox-Chalcedonian Christians of Syria-Palestine (who were alive during Theodore's life-time and either witnessed personally, heard about or read some of his Arabic hermeneutics and apologetic reasoning with Muslims on orthodoxy). I explored whether or not, in his attempt to convey Christian orthodox thought to Muslims in their own language and via their own conceptual, logical and textual Islamic webs of meaning, Abū Qurrah would have seemed to his fellow Melkites to be compromising the core content of orthodoxy and twisting and bending its notions and claims in such a pragmatic, un-orthodox manner that he ultimately emptied it of its original, ecclesially and creedally authorized meaning. In other words, I explored whether or not, in his attempt to communicate with Islam, and regardless of whether he succeeded or failed to do so, Abū Qurrah's method shows a theologian who avoids innovation in confessing his faith, or, rather, one who is keen to innovate because he believes it will help him conveying that faith.

In his reflection on the understanding of the Church fathers' authority and its relation to originality and independence in theological thinking, Jaroslav Pelikan considers Maximus the Confessor to be an example of the meaning of authority in relation to theology. Pelikan's indirect question that is implicit in this view seems to be something like: What makes a Church father's theological contribution authentic and ultimately authoritative in the Church? Is it that theology's originality and the results it achieves, or is it its adherence to the traditional confession of the Church? According to Pelikan, Maximus the Confessor gives us an answer that leans towards the latter answer, for Maximus, Pelikan explains, is considered by Church historians to be "the most universal spirit of the 7th century," and the "real father of Byzantine theology."[1032] Maximus ultimately earned these epithets of praise, as Pelikan notes, not because of the innovative, original and productive theological contributions (with which his the-

1032 Pelikan, *The Christian Tradition*, Vol. 2, p. 8. Pelikan cites here Hans-Georg Beck, *Kirche und theologische Literature im Byzantinischen Reich* (Munich: Beck Verlag, 1959), p. 432; Werner Elert, *Der Ausgang der altkirchlichen Christologie: Eine Untersuchung über Theodore von Pharan und seine Zeit als Einführung in die alte Dogmangeschichte*, ed. Wilhelm Maurer and Elisabeth Bergsträsser (Berlin: Lutherisches Verl-Haus, 1957), p. 259; and John Meyendorff, *Christ in Eastern Christian Thought* (Washington, DC: St Vladimir's Seminary Press, 1975), p. 99.

ology is seminally pregnant), but rather because of his strict confession of the faith of the church.

> the very title confessor implied any thing but being independent, original or productive ... as a confessor and theologian, Maximus was obliged to preserve, protect and defend the doctrine that had been handed down by the fathers, for to 'confess with soul and mouth' meant to affirm 'what the fathers have taught us'[1033]

The authority of the theologian's teaching stems from the excellence of his 'confessing with soul and mouth' the official teaching that the church had inherited unchanged and strictly preserved from generation to generation. This glorification of 'preservation, protection and defensiveness' over 'innovation, originality and creative re-articulation,' Pelikan continues, is a general characteristic of Byzantine Christendom, if not of all other branches of Christian theology, orthodox and heterodox alike: "all parties of Christians in all controversies ... had in common a wish to conform themselves to that authority."[1034] They all believed that theological authority should be founded on the theologian's degree of conformity to the traditional patristic testimony and his unquestioning loyalty to it. Authoritative and authentic confessions of the orthodox faith, then, are those that express the theologian's commitment to the orthodox belief that "the word of truth is ... uniform and unsharable by its very nature, and it cannot be subjected to differences in viewpoints or to temporal changes."[1035] Confessionality and conformism, rather than originality, in sum, seems to be construed the defining characteristic of the Byzantine approach to Christian doctrine. The Byzantine theologian, as Kallistos Ware once stated, "saw himself as heir to a rich Christian inheritance from the past, which it was his duty and privilege to transmit unimpaired to future generations."[1036]

According to this understanding of theological authority, Theodore Abū Qurrah would not be truly 'Byzantine' in his rational and theological approaches. The study presented in this book on his Trinitarian and Christological discourses conspicuously demonstrates that he was not a 'confessor' like his intellectual mentor, Maximus the Confessor, nor was he a steady, conservative, unfaltering

---

1033 Pelikan, *The Christian Tradition*, Vol. 2, p. 8.

1034 Ibid., p. 9. Pelikan also refers here to Joan Mervyn Hussey, *Church and Learning in the Byzantine Empire 867–1185* (London: Russell & Russell, 1963), p. 29.

1035 Pelikan, *The Christian Tradition*, Vol. 2, pp.13–14. In contrast to falsehood, which is considered to be "splintered into many parts and theories...it never remains fixed in the same place, for it is subject to changes and to the exigencies of mutation."

1036 Kallistos Ware, "Christian Theology in the East 600–1453," in *A History of Christian Doctrine*, ed. Hubert Cunliff-Jones (Edinburgh: T&T Clark, 1997), 183–226, p. 184.

transmitter of the fathers' teaching, like his other mentor, John of Damascus. In this sense, Abū Qurrah's writings do not present before us a 'Byzantine mind' such as Pelikan and Ware describe.

Nevertheless, this is not evidence that Abū Qurrah compromised his Byzantine identity or formally rejected such 'Byzantine' orthodoxy(ies).[1037] The reason for the inappropriateness of such an accusation is rather simple: in none of his extant works does Abū Qurrah state that he considers himself either a 'Byzantine' theologian or a spokesman for the 'Byzantine' doctrinal cause. He neither speaks in support of, nor declares that he is breaking with, Byzantine Christendom. In fact, Theodore never considered himself part of this form of Christendom in the first place, and did consider patristic orthodoxy as existing strictly and exclusively in the Byzantine tradition. In other words, one cannot accuse Theodore of abandoning what he did not attribute to himself or identify himself with in the first place.

Abū Qurrah's commitment to innovation and originality in his theological discourse shows his dissociation from the Byzantine centralization of conformism and rejection of innovation, but this does not automatically mean that he parted company in his methods with orthodoxy and its understanding of Tradition. It is one of the fundamental factors of the 8th–9th centuries context, as shown on chapter two of this study, that theological orthodoxy was patronised and defended by two Christian Chalcedonian church bodies: the Greek-speaking church that had until then flourished within the territories of the Byzantine Empire, and the Arabic-speaking church that flourished from that time onwards within the territories of the Islamic Caliphate. During the time of Abū Qurrah, this second church body, to which he belonged and which he served, that Chalcedonian church called 'Melkite,' had a publically declared 'Arab' identity and no longer considered itself 'Byzantine.' Even so, the Melkite Church never stopped being 'orthodox' in its theology and in its understanding of patristic Tradition. So, 'Byzantine' and 'orthodox' ceased being synonymous for this Chalcedonian Syro-Palestinian community, not only ecclesiologically, but theologically as well.

1037 On the multiple forms and aspects of Byzantine orthodoxies, read for example Andrew Louth and Augustine Casiday (eds), *Byzantine Orthodoxies: Papers from the Thirty-Sixth Spring Symposium of Byzantine Studies, University of Durham, 23–25 March 2002* (Aldershot, UK: Ashgate, 2006); Hannah Hunt, "Byzantine Christianity," in *the Blackwell Companion to Eastern Christianity*, ed. Ken Parry (Oxford: Blackwell, 2010), pp. 73–93; and Derek Kruger, "The Practice of Christianity in Byzantium," in *Byzantine Christianity*, ed. D. Kruger (Minneapolis, MN: Augsburg Fortress, 2010), 1–18.

This distinction between 'orthodox' and 'Byzantine' means that making innovations and developing original hermeneutics of Tradition makes Theodore non-orthodox in the Byzantine sense, or a 'non-Byzantine.' However, it does not *per se* make him non-orthodox in the absolute, or in any non-Byzantine sense. What decides whether Theodore is orthodox despite his innovation, rather than non-orthodox because of it, is whether or not, in his innovation and originality, Abū Qurrah remained on the authentic orthodox path, or he left it and forged for himself an entirely different, far from orthodox one. To find out which represents Theodore's position, the nature of 'orthodoxy' itself must be clear: What is orthodoxy? Is it primarily 'Tradition' or essentially a 'straight path'?

Scholars concede in principle that there is some ambiguity in the meaning of the word 'orthodoxy,' as it may mean 'right belief' as well as 'right worship,' or 'right thinking about God and faith in him,' which leaves scholars divided between regarding 'orthodoxy' as an expression either of ideas or of actions.[1038] The history of the Christian Church, nevertheless, indicates that the term 'orthodoxy' is trans-denominational, as it is used within Orthodox, Catholic and Protestant church circles alike to describe the boundaries that delineate and justify each church's separate existence.[1039] In addition, scholars identify the core meaning of 'orthodoxy' from its historical usage to signify "belief in, or assent to, the fundamental truths of the faith."[1040] During the patristic era, 'orthodoxy' did not just name these fundamental truths of faith, but also meant that the criterion of their correctness was the consensus of the Church fathers on "that which has been believed everywhere (*quod ubique*) always (*quod simper*) and by all (*quod ab omnibus*)."[1041] This understanding of 'orthodoxy' was the by-product of the Church's preoccupation with the challenge of variety and difference in theological reasoning. This challenge was ultimately dealt with by tidy-

1038 Art. "Orthodoxy", in Alan Richardson and John Bowden (eds), *A New Dictionary of Christian Theology* (London: SCM Press, 1989), 421–422, p. 422; and Timothy (Kallistos) Ware, *The Orthodox Church*, (Baltimore, MD: Penguin Books, 1969). According to Ware, "the Orthodox , therefore, make what may seem at first a surprising claim: they regard their church as the church which guards and teaches the true belief about God and which glorifies Him with right worship, that is, *as nothing less than the church of Christ on earth*" (ibid., p. 16). Ware then adds "it has been truly said of the Byzantines: 'dogma with them is not only an intellectual system apprehended by the clergy and expounded to the laity, but a field of vision wherein all things on earth are seen in their relation to things in heaven, first and foremost through liturgical celebration" (ibid., p. 271).

1039 Richardson and Bowden, *A New Dictionary of Christian Theology*, p. 421.

1040 Ibid.

1041 Ibid.

ing up divisions and differences and developing what was called the 'right/straight path of faith,'[1042] or the "right thinking" about God and faith in him.[1043] Seeing 'orthodoxy' as an expression of 'straight/right path of faith' makes it a "hermeneutical principle and method."[1044] This means that 'orthodoxy' is not just about the transmission of inherited doctrinal Tradition that is consisting of "a fixed core or complex of binding propositions." it is, rather, a manner of perception, a hermeneutic path, whose straightness and accuracy lies in the nature of its "insight into the meaning and impact of the revelatory events, of the revelation of the God who acts."[1045]

This understanding of 'orthodoxy' is not, however, the only meaning this term has had in the history of Christian theology. The history of Eastern theology also reveals a trend in interpreting 'orthodoxy' that approaches it from the perspective of the Church's role of preserving fixed what it deems as 'true faith' and passing it on intact. Here, 'orthodoxy' becomes the name of that general faith that was "contained in the church's continuous tradition of teaching."[1046] Here, 'orthodoxy' and 'Tradition' are totally identified, and mean the teaching on faith that is handed down and transmitted from one generation of ecclesial *magisterium* to another, in a manner that represents an authoritative delivery of the doctrinal faith, which initially committed to the Church by Christ and his apostles.[1047] Within this conceptual framework, it was believed that "not the will of the majority, nor the use of the emperor, nor the subtlety of the learned could determine what was orthodox,"[1048] but rather the authoritative episcopacy of the Church fathers, whose authority lay in their confessing *verbatim* the word of truth and passing it on to the next generations without change.[1049] Understanding 'orthodoxy' as 'Tradition' is, therefore, different in conception and practice from the understanding of 'orthodoxy' that the Eastern

---

1042 Karen King, "Which Early Christianity?" in *The Oxford Handbook of Early Christian Studies*, ed. Susan A. Harvey and David G. Hunter (Oxford: Oxford University Press, 2009), 66–86, p. 67.

1043 Marcus Ward, *The Byzantine Church: An Introduction to the Study of Eastern Christianity* (Madras: Christian Literature Society, 1953), pp. xi, xvi.

1044 George Florovsky, "The Function of Tradition in the Ancient Church," in *Eastern Orthodox Theology: A Contemporary Reader*, ed. Daniel B. Clendenin (Chicago, IL: Revell, 1995), 97–114, p. 103.

1045 Ibid.

1046 Kelly, *Early Christian Doctrines*, pp. 29–31.

1047 Ibid., p. 30.

1048 Pelikan, *The Christian Tradition*, Vol. 2, pp. 144–145.

1049 On Tradition as transmission first and foremost, see, for instance, Vladimir Lossky, *In The Image and Likeness of God* (Crestwood, NY: S. Vladimir's Seminary Press, 1985), pp. 141–168.

Church started to develop in the 17th century, which views 'orthodoxy' as "a combination of ... the repetition of ancient truths in ancient words, and the response to contemporary challenges in words appropriate to them."[1050]

To take this brief presentation back to the 8th–9th centuries, my reading of the theological works of John of Damascus and Maximus the Confessor indicates that the Hellenic, Greek-speaking Christendom of the Byzantine sphere of influence reflects in its orthodoxy an identification of orthodoxy with Tradition. To be orthodox here, means to confess the doctrinal teaching of the fathers as literally as possible, and then to pass that teaching on to the next generation in a fixed and unchanged form. In the Byzantine Empire, this form of orthodoxy became part and parcel of the Empire's Hellenistic, national identity,[1051] so that one's orthodoxy was measured not only by one's sincere confession of the teaching of the Byzantine Church, but also by one's loyalty and adherence to the Byzantine imperial cause. The question here is whether Abū Qurrah was orthodox in the sense of blind loyalty to Tradition, or whether his theological thinking indicates otherwise.

One treatise in particular from among Theodore Abū Qurrah's maymars, his *Maymar on the Veneration of Icons*, may suggest a possible answer to this question. In the seventh chapter of the second part of this maymar, Abū Qurrah argues with those who claim that the veneration of icons should be abolished because it has no textual support in either the Old or New Testament.[1052] Abū Qurrah replies that, if textual evidence was the Church's sole criterion for correctness, Christians would stop practising almost all their sacramental rituals, since they do not have any textual foundation in the Bible, either. What the Church relies on besides the proof-texting, Theodore suggests, is the inheritance that has been transmitted to the Church community from past generations of believers.

4. فنحن نقول له: إنَّ كثيراً من عظيم ما في أيدينا إنما أصبناه ووصل إلينا توارثاً
من غير أن نجد له ثبتاً في مصحف من مصاحف العتقية والحديثة التي أسلم إلينا التلاميذ

1050 Pelikan, *The Christian Tradition*, Vol. 2, p. 287.

1051 Ward, *The Byzantine Church*, p. 41: "orthodoxy and nationality were so related that to be a good Byzantine meant being an orthodox churchman."

1052 Abū Qurrah, *Maymar fī Ikrām al-Aiqūnāt* (Maymar on the veneration of icons), II.7.3 (pp. 111–112).

ولعلَّ قائلاً يقول من أولئك: كيف لنا أن نعلم أنَّ السجود للصور نشأ في
الكنيسة على عهد السلحيين ونحن لا نجد كتاباً ينطق به؟

And one of them may say: and how can we know that prostration before icons originated in the Church in the time of the apostles when we do not find a book that speaks about it?"

> 4. So we say to him: many of the greatest things in our hands we have received, and they have reached us, by inheritance, without our finding for them any evidence in one of the old and new books that the apostles passed on to us.[1053]

It is noteworthy that Abū Qurrah speaks of two 'inheritances' that were transmitted to the Church from the apostles: the inheritance that the Church follows in its veneration of icons and other rituals, and the other inheritance, which is the written books, old and new. One wonders here, since Abū Qurrah refers to what the Church inherited, why he does not speak of one single inheritance, rather than two, since the source is one and the same? Does he want to differentiate here between two sources, one inherited (*tawāruth*) and one not? It does not seem so, for Theodore uses two Arabic words that have the same meaning *tawāruth* ([passing on inheritance) and *taslīm* (handing in). So, for Theodore, both the written texts and the seemingly oral or non-textual ones are both inherited from the apostles; both are, so to speak, a 'Tradition' that is transmitted from generation to another.

If we accept this logic, does Abū Qurrah mean here to differentiate between the oral Tradition of the Church fathers' doctrinal teachings and the written texts of the scripture? Making such a distinction would in fact be imposing on Theodore's text an anachronistic interpretation based on the distinction that theologians today tend to make between 'Tradition' and 'scripture.' It is not certain in the text of the maymar whether Abū Qurrah's reference to *maṣāḥif al-ḥadīthah wal-ʿatīqah* (the old and new books) means the Old and the New Testaments. What if, instead, he is referring here to the old and new writings of the Church fathers, or the patristic teaching in the early centuries and in his own time? And, what if, for Abū Qurrah, the written and the oral patristic teachings alike are part and parcel of what has the Church inherited?

If this proposal is plausible, we have in this maymar an indication of what sort of 'orthodox' Abū Qurrah is, and how he understands 'orthodoxy': as a 'confessional transmission of fixed traditional teaching,' or as an 'attempt to follow the right/straight path of thinking about the faith in the light of the patristic mind.' If this reading (i.e., the attempt to follow the right/straight path of thinking about the faith in the light of the patristic mind) of Abū Qurrah's words in his maymar is plausible, he is presenting a revised and, rather, broadened interpretation of 'Tradition': the inherited Tradition of the Church is not only the fixed dogmatic rules that we find in the writings of the apostles and the Church fathers. It is also that inherited oral, practised apostolic and patristic teaching and spirituality that are sculpted, engraved and preserved in the historical life

1053 Ibid., II.7.4 (p. 112).

and worship of the Christian churches throughout the generations. Abū Qurrah points to this ecclesial and life-centred inheritance when he speaks of the practice of venerating icons not as a fixed dogmatic or conciliar rule, but as a general and public custom (*taʿmīm ʿādāt/publically disseminated habits*) observed throughout the churches, which, in his view, makes it an authentic practice.[1054] By expanding the definition of what is inherited in the Church, Theodore is not undermining the fixed dogmatic, written teaching of the Church fathers or degrading the orthodox authority of the old and new patristic heritage. He is, rather, affirming that these teachers have a very high status in the church, as they follow directly after the apostles and the prophets in rank and authority.[1055] Abū Qurrah, is, however, expanding the boundaries of the patristic 'Tradition' beyond the understanding that assesses one's orthodox adherence to Tradition by his confessional, almost literal transmission of the fathers' dogmatic teaching as found in their written works that have been passed down. The point I want to propose from this discussion is that Abū Qurrah's orthodoxy goes beyond the fixed, official perception of 'Tradition' and 'orthodoxy' in Byzantine Christendom. This takes him out of the circle of the Hellenistic-Byzantine Christian identity, but, it does not expel him from the sphere of 'orthodoxy,' because in his expansion of the patristic Tradition into the non-textual practice of the church, Theodore, follows the second understanding of orthodoxy as right thinking or straight hermeneutics of faith in the footsteps of the Church fathers.

Theodore Abū Qurrah's relation to the teaching of the Church fathers, and his highly creative and intelligent implementation of the impact of their thinking on the lived and experienced history of the Church, both show that he was not a Byzantine orthodox, but a creative and particular *Arabophone* orthodox, who was ready to give up mere confession and literal transmission and to opt for innovation and originality whenever it was needed. It is, therefore, valid and fair to

1054 Ibid., II.7.8–9 (p. 113)

8. وليعلم أنه لا شيء من تلك الأنواع بأعمَّ في الكنيسة من الصور فما من بلادٍ لعمري إلا وفي كنائسها صور القديسين

9. وإن كان عمومها لا يحققها أنها جرت من الأصل فأوشك أن يبطل وغيرها مما قد عمَّ عمومها ويزعم أنه دخيل

8. And let him know that none of these kinds is more general and public in the Church than icons. For, I swear, there is no country whose churches do not contain icons of the saints.

9. And if its general dissemination does not prove its authenticity, this would almost abolish it and other general public things, and would consider them all spurious.

1055 Ibid., II.8.32 (32–34) (p. 122).

ومن بعد هذين المعلمين الذين لا يفوقهما أحدٌ، إعلم أنَّ للمعلمين مرتبة عالية درجتهم في الكنيسة فوق مراتبها كلها بعد مرتبة السليحيين والأنبياء .32

32. And after these two teachers [Eusebius and Gregory Nazianzus], above whom there is no one, know that the teachers have a very high status and their rank in the Church is above any other, with nothing higher in rank after the rank of the apostles and the prophets.

attribute this innovative form of orthodoxy not to the Byzantine legacy, but rather to a unique Melkite Arabic-speaking Christianity, which, by the 8th–9th centuries, had become willingly integrated into Islamic, Arab culture and identity in preference to the Greek-Hellenistic culture of Byzantium. And the most prominent theologian of the Melkite Church, Theodore Abū Qurrah, was ready to practice orthodoxy as ultimately a 'right/straight path of thinking,' rather than simply as a confession of Tradition in its ancient form of words.

Sidney Griffith is, thus, right to recognize in the Melkite context of the 8th century "an attitude toward the world of Islam that finds in it not only a major challenge to Christian faith, but also a cultural transformation that furnishes both a new idiom in which that faith must be articulated if it is to continue to carry conviction and a new opportunity for the proclamation of the Gospel."[1056] Within this milieu, it is quite tenable, let alone necessary, to see Theodore Abū Qurrah following the right path of orthodoxy in a way no other theologian affiliated to orthodoxy in its Byzantine version would do. Even when Abū Qurrah elaborates on orthodoxy, he does so, as Griffith eloquently notes, with the help of "the kerygmatic posture of Islam," ultimately providing "an Arabophone Christian's apology for his beliefs, in the face of what one Muslim controversialist of the 9th century called the 'silencing questions' to be put to Christians."[1057] What is actually more significant and worth noting in Abū Qurrah's extant legacy is the contextual implication of his attempt to go beyond the mere confessional transmission of orthodoxy to undertake an innovative, productive approach. In his commitment to, rather than abomination of, innovation, Abū Qurrah presents to us an early Arab Christian contextual theologian in dialogue with Islam.

In one of his studies on the relation between religiosity and contextuality, Olivier Roy asks: "Does the expansion of a religion go along with the spreading of a new culture ... or does it expand, on the contrary, precisely because this religion has nothing to do with any specific culture?"[1058] Roy focuses on those religions that expanded in history through either conquest or conversion, and thereby were "grafted into different cultures and experienced territorialization."[1059] Roy believes that religions assert themselves when they explicitly dissociate themselves from culture, positing the latter as 'otherness.'[1060]

1056 Griffith, *The Church in the Shadow of the Mosque*, p. 57.
1057 S. Griffith, "Muslims and Church Councils," p. 277.
1058 Olivier Roy, *Holy Ignorance: When Religion and Culture Part Ways*, trans. Ros Schwartz, (London: Hurst, 2010), p. 24.
1059 Ibid.
1060 Ibid., p. 28.

Of the various relational modes between religion and culture, Olivier Roy highlights four in particular: 1) religion attempting to eradicate a certain culture (*de*culturation), 2) religion trying to adapt to an already existing dominant culture (*ac*culturation), 3) religion trying to control a specific cultural context and make itself its sole center (*in*culturation), and 4) religion rejecting a certain cultural context and alienating itself from it, after first identifying itself with it, because of particular changes, deemed destructive, that the culture faces (*ex*culturation).[1061] Usually, what determines a religion's choice of one of these four stances, Roy suggests, is whether it calls people to belong to it and follow its faith (conversion) by alienating them from their original culture, or by converting them within own culture. For Roy, Christianity is a religiosity that practices an acculturating approach by converting people within their culture and by adapting itself to the new culture, refusing to deculturate or exculturate them. In the Roman Empire, Roy says, Christianity "did not introduce a new culture of foreign origin," nor did it try to make itself "superior to or as a competitor with Hellenism from the cultural point of view."[1062] Later, he continues, Christianity did not seem to have changed this relation to cultural contextuality, as it "did not seek to rule over another people," or "regard the native as a potential 'subject of the king' …"[1063]

I do not intend here to make a comprehensive analysis of Olivier Roy's rather perceptive and thought-provoking socio-religious thesis. Rather, and lest I fall into anachronism, I shall just use his fourfold understanding of the relationship between religion and culture (deculturation, acculturation, inculturation and exculturation) in my consideration of Theodore Abū Qurrah as an early Arab Christian theologian, who makes a unique attempt to contextualize his theology in the land of Islam. The question one may ask from the angle of contextuality is: What was Abū Qurrah doing in his theological career in the land of Islam; was he deculturating, acculturating, inculturating, or exculturating Christianity?

If deculturation means that religion stands over against culture and eradicates it, Abū Qurrah is not a deculturator. He can be seen as one who certainly takes Christian religion beyond the boundaries of the Byzantine-Hellenistic and native Syrian-Palestinian Aramaean cultures by determinedly arabizing his theological discourse and endeavouring to draw the theological mind into the sphere of Muslim intellectual rationale. Yet, this does not make him a deculturator, because there is no evidence that Theodore tried to eradicate the Christian, pre-Is-

1061 Ibid., pp. 33 ff.
1062 Ibid., p. 37.
1063 Ibid., p. 50.

lamic, Hellenistic and Syrian, cultural heritage from his own scholarship and ministry. We certainly know that Abū Qurrah never stopped composing works in Syriac (and Greek!), or communicating in these two languages, though he clearly presented himself as an Arabic-speaking theologian in the land of Islam. Finally, this non-aggressive, non-hostile stance on Byzantine culture not only reveals that Theodore is not a deculturator, but also shows that he is not an exculturator either.

Second, if 'acculturation' means, as Roy says, adapting the mainstream culture, and 'inculturation' means controlling culture and claiming its centre-stage location, Abū Qurrah is, as I have argued in this study, an acculturator, not an inculturator. He does not seem to be aiming to put Christianity at the centre of the Arab-Islamic culture of his time. He certainly intends to demonstrate to Muslims that the Christian faith is *the* straight, most rationally and logically authentic and right religion. Yet, he does not seem to be using this conviction to persuade Muslims to accept the cultural values of the Christian religion as the criteria on which to base the state and the society, or to concede that the followers of this religion-culture called Christianity are more qualified to run, or even rule, the affairs of the caliphate. Though Abū Qurrah is a staunch defender of Christian faith, he does not seem to be leading a converting-inculturating campaign to Christianize, the Arab-Islamic culture of the Abbasid caliphate. Far from it; Abū Qurrah's contextuality actually lies in an innovative, perceptive and quite consistent endeavour to acculturate Christian faith itself by working doggedly to make the Christian theological mind adapt to the cultural context of the Arab-Muslim sphere in Syria-Palestine.

In some contemporary Greek Orthodox studies on Muslim-Christian relations, one finds a Roy-like realization of the organic link between cultural encounters and religious dialogues. The Greek Orthodox theologian, Mario Begzos, for example, certainly expresses the influence of this awareness on modern Greek Orthodox theology when he says: "It is impossible to establish communication between two cultural traditions without the active intervention of their religious expression. Whoever ignores these elements makes a great error."[1064] However, when it comes to specifying the two sides of the cultural encounter that he sees in the history of Christian-Muslim relations in the early Islamic era, Begzos sees it to be an encounter between the 'Byzantine' and the 'Muslim,'

1064 Marios P. Begzes, "Inter-Religious Dialogue in Byzantine Thought: the Philosophical and Theological Contribution of John of Damascus," in *Two Traditions, One Space: Orthodox Christians and Muslims in Dialogue*, ed. George C. Papademetriou (Boston, MA: Somerset Hall Press, 2011), 37–76, p. 37,

the 'Greek' and the 'Arab.'[1065] Another Greek Orthodox author goes even further in construing the Byzantines as none other than "the forerunners of the Christian-Muslim dialogue."[1066]

Contrary to this, and in the light of Olivier Roy's interpretation of acculturation, I believe that giving the Byzantine-Greeks the credit for being in the forefront of religious dialogue between Christianity and Islam does not apply to the context of Syria-Palestine in the 8th and 9th centuries. Theodore Abū Qurrah's interreligious encounter with Muslims in that time and place reveals that the Melkites wanted to liberate themselves from Greek-Byzantine culture, rather than representing it or speaking on its behalf. Abū Qurrah's acculturating contextuality proves that the tendency of the Melkite Church within the territories of the Islamic caliphate was to integrate fully into their Arab-Islamic context, and to live there as citizens, not foreigners. An accurate description of the cultural encounter that took place in the early Abbasid era in contextual terms, at least in the texts of Theodore Abū Qurrah, suggests that it was an encounter between Arab Christians, on one side, and Arab Muslims, on the other.

Pointing out the acculturating nature of Abū Qurrah's theological legacy brings us back to the main question of this study, regarding Abū Qurrah's adherence to, or deviation from, Christian orthodoxy in his attempt to interpret Christian doctrines in Arabic and following an Islamic rationale. Is it right to conclude from his acculturation that Abū Qurrah drifts so far in his intellectual innovation that he should be considered not just as an innovative contextualizer, but a waverer in his Christian faith for the sake of satisfying the Muslims?

In one of his numerous studies of the situation of Christians under Islamic rule, especially during the 8th and 9th centuries, Sidney Griffith points to the serious challenge with which the newly emergent Arab-Islamic context faced Christians. The Christians of Syria-Palestine, Griffith explains, "were now faced with the task of defending their criticized doctrines ... in a vigorously new *lingua sacra*, whose religious lexicon was inevitable to be determined by the burgeoning Islamic sciences, and not by the apologetic or polemical requirements of the older Christian, Jewish, or other theological establishment."[1067] Pondering carefully the contextual implications of this challenge, Griffith visits the Arabic *kalām* text known as the *Summa Theologiae Arabica*, and finds there its author's description of how the Christian inhabitants of that Arab-Islamic milieu dealt

1065 Ibid., p. 38.

1066 Anastasios Yannoulatos, "Byzantine and Contemporary Greek Orthodox Approaches to Islam," in *Two Traditions, One Space*, ed. George C. Papademetriou (Boston, MA: Somerset Hall Press, 2011), 147–178, p. 153.

1067 Griffith, "The First Christian *Summa Theologiae* in Arabic," p. 15.

with the new cultural and social situation. The author of the *Summa* does not hide his blatant resentment of his Christian contemporaries, who "were accustomed to conceal the specifics of their faith behind Islamic phrases, which in the Islamic community could only be interpreted to state the opposite of the traditional Christian doctrines … ."[1068] Griffith detects in this attitude a clear assimilation to Islamic society by a group of second-generation Arabophone Christians.[1069] Rather than following the *Summa* author's bluntly offensive rebuke of these Christians and accusing them of being 'waverers,' Griffith follows a neutral descriptive reading of this 'wavering' approach as part of the Melkite Christians' endeavour "to meet the Muslim challenge with a full statement of Christianity's religious claims in the Arabic of the Qur'ān."[1070]

Neutral as Griffith's assessment may be, the author of the Arabic Melkite text, *Summa Theologiae Arabica*, does not hesitate in harshly and crudely accusing these Christians with wavering in their faith for the sake of gaining security and acceptance by the Muslims. If this wavering is condemned in Christian commoners, how much more disgraceful and abominable would it be if it were committed by the church's prelates and theologians. Had Abū Qurrah's innovative acculturation been perceived as an act of 'wavering,' his legacy and reputation would never have been praised, preserved, and transmitted to later Melkite generations. The fact that he enjoyed a praised and revered position in the memory and historical records of the Arab Melkite Church indicates that Theodore's innovation was not deemed by the church to be an attempt to conceal the Christian faith before Muslims and to say what suited Muslim audiences and made them happy. Had Abū Qurrah's acculturation been a strategy of wavering, his writings would not explicitly have spoken of God as triune in nature, of Christ as affirmatively the divine Son of God, who was incarnate in a human body, died on a cross and was raised from the dead, or even of Christianity itself as the only straight and truly rational religion. Abū Qurrah's innovative acculturation was actually pursued in such a subtle, balanced and profound manner that it makes him a very valuable example of an interreligious dialogician, not only in his own time, but also in ours.

1068 Ibid., p. 21. Griffith cites from the text the following expressive lines: "a group (*qawm*) in the midst of the people of this community who rule over them, a group born among them, grown up with them, and educated in their culture (*ta'ddabu bi-adābihim*). They conceal their faith, and disclose to them what suits them…this [practice] comes from their forebears, and their children have followed their example in an obliging evasion."

1069 Ibid. They even, Griffith continues, go to those who refuse to follow the same strategy and rebuke them: "What preoccupies you to be so distracted from your situation?"

1070 Ibid., p. 25.

In his study of Christian-Muslim dialogues on Christology, Mark Beaumont notes that contemporary Christianity in the West is experiencing challenges of co-existing with Islam in the Western homelands, as well as of dialoguing with the Muslims over faith and religious conviction, that are similar to those faced by Christians of the 8th–9th centuries in their life within *Dār al-Islām*.[1071] Following their newly developed conviction that "theological formulations are always both fallible and culture-relative,"[1072] some Western theologians have started calling for building relations of complementarity rather than superiority, between Christianity and Islam. They propose achieving this complementarity by emancipating Christian faith from all the theological and doctrinal statements that divide Christians and Muslims, considering such statements as merely contingent, linguistic, dispensable improvisations that are no longer valid and useful in today's interreligious context. The beginning of real religious coexistence and complementarity between Christianity and Islam, according to these compromising theologians, lies, as Beaumont notes, in showing willingness to expose Christian doctrine to "severe reductionism," especially in relation to controversial doctrines, such as Christology, the Trinity and the atonement.[1073] These reductionist theologians justify their approach by claiming, Beaumont continues, that "the Christological [and theological] formulations of Nicaea and Chalcedon are no longer useful ... since they emphasize being rather than doing, static nature rather than active commitment."[1074]

Beaumont's exposition of the modern compromising strategies of some Christian theologians in today's Christian-Muslim relations is reminiscent of a similar accommodationist attitude that the author of *Summa Theologiai Arabica* invites his 8th-century Christian readers to see in the attitude of some Arab Christians toward their Muslim environment. In his reading of this text, Sidney Griffith unpacks this Melkite author's criticism of these wavering and accommodationist Arabophone Christians, who, haunted by fears for their survival and se-

---

1071 Beaumont, *Christology in Dialogue with Muslims*, pp. 154–173. Beaumont notes that this challenge has made important Christian theological figures "turn their attention to a global context for theology," which demonstrates, in his opinion, "a shift in the self-understanding of some Western Christian leaders away from simply doing theology in the traditionally Christian world of Europe and North America, to thinking about the Christian faith in non-Christian contexts" (ibid., p. 154).

1072 Ibid., p. 155; citing from John Hick, "A Recent Development Within Christian Monotheism," in *Christians, Muslims and Jews*, ed. David Kerr and D. Cohn-Sherbok, (Canterbury: University of Canterbury Press, 1983), 1–19, p. 2.

1073 Beaumont, *Christology in Dialogue with Muslims*, pp. 160–162.

1074 Ibid., p. 171.

curity, speak of Jesus Christ and God as the Muslims do, evincing a readiness to dispense with the Christian orthodox faith:

> If you ask them about Christ our Lord, they maintain that He is a messenger (*rasūl*) like one of the messengers ... in public they avow the opposite of the Trinity of the oneness of God and His incarnation ... they say, "What compels us to say 'Father', 'Son' and 'Spirit', and to maintain that the Messiah is God?[1075]

This one-sided emphasis on the commonalities at the expense of the differences is not at all an antique, archaic, or closed chapter in the history of Christian-Muslim relations. Opting for accommodationism and reductionism, and a willingness to compromise orthodoxy, for the sake of achieving co-existence and complementarity is similarly characteristic in modern times of the stance on Islam of some well-known European theologians (e.g., John Hick, Hans Küng, Kenneth Cragg) and North America (e.g., Miroslav Volf). One may even go as far as to argue that the same tendency to seek approval and tolerance from Islam toward Christianity also haunts contemporary Arabophone Christians in the Arab Middle East.[1076] The Christians of the Arab World, due to various challenging circumstances and tensions, sometimes have a tendency to waver due toconcerns and worries about coexistence that are similar to those of both Arabophone Christians in the early Abbasid period and some Western Christian theologians today. Christians of the present Middle East sometimes find themselves developing "an interaction with their Muslim context in such a manner that would eventually, as they hope, grant them safe life and secure co-existence for the survival of their families," which makes them "ready to compromise substantial components of their religious and cultural worldview for the sake of gaining the satisfaction and approval of the dialogue's Muslim counterparts."[1077]

The present study of Theodore Abū Qurrah's apologetic orthodoxy invites us to realize that, in the theological voice of this 8th–9th-century Melkite Church father, we find a Christian who ably dialogues with Muslims with a solid integrity that does not compromise orthodoxy's content, waive its claims, or sacrifice its accuracy out of a personal concern for his survival and security in his non-Christian environment. I fully concur with Sidney Griffith's perceptive reading of The-

1075 Griffith, "The First Christian *Summa Theologiae* in Arabic," p. 23.

1076 For more on these aspects and tendencies in present-day Christian-Muslim relations in the Arab world, see Najib George Awad, *And Freedom Became a Public-Square: Political, Sociological and Religious Overviews on the Arab Christians and the Arabic Spring* (Berlin: LIT Verlag, 2012), pp. 156–171.

1077 Ibid., p. 166.

odore Abū Qurrah's dialogical stance alongside the critical and condemnatory stance of the author of *Summa Theologiai Arabica*. Griffith persuasively explains that the latter rebukes his fellow Christians who "hide their faith and divulge [to the Muslims] what suits them," deeming them eventually "hypocrites (*munāfiqūn*) among [the Christians], marked with [the Christians'] mark, standing in [their] congregations, contradicting [their] faith, forfeiters of themselves (*al-khāsirūn*), who are Christians in name only."[1078] Griffith, then, compares this attitude with Theodore Abū Qurrah's, concluding that the latter stands in full agreement with the author of the *Summa*'s rejection of this obsession with 'life-dialogue' and co-existence. Abū Qurrah, Griffith accurately notes, refuses in his apologies to give up the core teaching of Christian orthodoxy, despite of his determination to convey that orthodoxy, and nothing but that orthodoxy, in a linguistically accessible and contextually perceptive and sensitive manner, notwithstanding his awareness of the threat of dangerous consequences for his life and to his safety that may arise from his decision.

Abū Qurrah sets a very thought-provoking and challenging dialogical example that is truly relevant to present-day Christian-Muslim relations. In his theological-dialogical character, as Sidney Griffith says, we encounter an Arabophone interlocutor, who

> wants the standard Christian doctrines [i.e., orthodoxy] to be clearly stated in Arabic, in spite of the fact that Muslims … would claim that the radical absurdity of the doctrines appeared clearly in their Arabic expression. It was precisely the task of the Christian *mutakallims*, Abū Qurrah would argue, to state the faith clearly even in the face of the charge of absurdity from the wise men of this world …[1079]

In his brief presentation of minorities in the Middle East, the Israeli Islamic and Middle Eastern Studies scholar, Moshe Ma'oz says:

> Like the Copts in Egypt, many Christians in Palestine … were already living in the area before the seventh century Arab Islamic conquest. They underwent a thorough process of Arabization and many of them … also shared common customs with their Muslim neighbours.[1080]

The prelates and theologians among these Syrian-Palestinian Christians soon knew that this Arabization process was not going to be merely linguistic, socio-

1078 Griffith, "The First Christian *Summa Theologiae* in Arabic," pp. 19–20.

1079 Ibid., p. 26.

1080 Moshe Ma'oz, *Middle Eastern Minorities, between Integration and Conflict*, (Washington, DC: Washington Institute for Near Eastern Policy, 1999), p. 27.

logical and cultural in nature, but, more demandingly, intellectual and rational too. During the early Islamic period, the theologians and *mutakallims* among the Muslim occupiers of Syria-Palestine knew clearly that they needed to prove the authentic truth of their religious faith to the indigenous inhabitants of the land, who were non-Muslims, and who had not yet taken Islam or the Muslims themselves seriously in any religious or intellectual sense. The early Muslim *mutakallims*, as Josef Van Ess correctly conjectures, perceived that relying on their holy book, the Qur'an, alone to prove the truth of their religion was far from sufficient. The Muslims were no longer living in the purely Islamic environment of the Arabian Peninsula, as these Muslim *mutakallims* realized. In this new land, the Muslims now lived in a "pluralist society, [where] non-Muslims could not be persuaded by quotations drawn from Qur'ānic revelation."[1081] Theology, thus, had to take on "an apologetic task, among others, and that task [could] be performed only through reason."[1082]

The contextual and cultural changes generated by the Muslims' arrival in Syria-Palestine, which Ma'oz and van Ess point to, were also faced, in fact and in consequences, by the indigenous Christian inhabitants of Syria-Palestine. Like their Muslim counterparts, the Christian *mutakallims* were also aware of the newly emerging pluralist society of which they were newly becoming members. They also realized that Christian theology needed to be as apologetic and imbedded in reason as that of the Muslims.

It is within this very particular historical context of seminal cultural, societal, intellectual and religious evolution in 8th- and 9th-century Syria-Palestine that one should read, interpret, and even edit and translate, Abū Qurrah's theological orthodoxy and apologetic maymars. Only by probing this specific context will researchers successfully unearth the substance of the particularity of Abū Qurrah's hermeneutics of the orthodox doctrine of the Trinity and Christology. Only then will they piece together accurately the components of his subtle and plausible linguistic choices and philological and conceptual strategies. Only within the theological and notional context, analysed in this study, can one perceive the distinctiveness of Theodore Abū Qurrah's interpretations of orthodoxy, which prove him to be an undoubtedly innovative, not merely traditionalist, orthodox voice, and a particularly creative witness to the patristic doctrinal legacy, not just a passive adhering guardian and transmitter of it.

This is what makes Theodore Abū Qurrah an exemplary pedagogical and profoundly inspiring voice for Arabophone Christians in my homeland, if not

1081 Van Ess, *The Flowering of Muslim Thought*, p. 158.
1082 Ibid.

for all Christians around the world, today. As I write these final lines, the historic, monumental and crucial uprisings in the Arab world (the so called 'Arabic Spring'), which exploded in 2011, are still running their course in some parts of the Arab world and about to emerge in others. I and almost all modern-day Arabophone Christians realize day by day, and ever since the tsunami of these uprisings brought turmoil to the Arab world, that "no matter how long the birth-operation of the new Arab world takes, sooner or later all that we know of the political, societal and even cultural context of the Arab world will be no more."[1083] As Christian Arabs deeply rooted in the Middle East, whose destiny is tied to the wagon of post-revolutionary Arab countries, we concede, more than we were willing to do before, that the experience our ancestors underwent during the 7th – 10th centuries is paying us another visit today, and that we shall soon face the exponential fact that we can no longer relax as we mistakenly did under the old dictatorships, indifferent to the state of our relationships with our broader Islamic environment and giving little time to assessing whether these relationships are still tangible, reliable and vital. Today, we have no guaranteed support to protect our existence and ensure a peaceful life and constructive role for us in our homeland, unless we maintain, revive, or re-build true relationships with our Muslim societies.[1084] Dialogue, especially interreligious dialogue, is now not only a need, but a destiny that cannot be avoided or postponed. And in confronting this destiny, Middle Eastern Christians need not primarily to seek lessons and guidance on dialogue with Islam from any foreign, external source. They need first of all simply to study carefully and painstakingly the indigenous interreligious dialogue experiences of the past, into which their ancestors put their hearts and minds during the early Islamic era. Arab Christians of the Near East seem today to be in grave need of reading, studying and learning from the experience of *mutakallims* like Abū Qurrah of living among Muslims and dialoguing with Islam about faith. This study has endeavoured to show that the unique voice of this Melkite father, Theodore Abū Qurrah, is one of the most important sources from which, in the midst of our attempt to maintain our existence in the new Middle East, we can draw many lessons on how to live and how to convey our religious convictions without losing integrity or falling into cultural seclusion or religious hostility. The Bishop of Ḥarrān is an inspiring asset in our dream of witnessing the dawn of a better, more interreligiously tolerant, constructive and promising future.

1083 Awad, *And Freedom Became a Public-Square*, p. 219.
1084 Ibid., p. 220.

Bibliography

Abel, A. *Le livre de la réfutation des trois sectes chrétiennes de Abū 'Īsā Muḥammad ibn Harūn al-Warrāq. Sa date, son importance, sa place dans la littérature polémique arabe*, Bruxelles: Perseus, 1949)

Abūl-Quasim, Muhammad. "Al-Ghazālī's Evaluation of Abū Yazid al-Bistāmī and His Disapproval of the Mystical Concepts of Union and Fusion," *Asian Philosophy*, 3(2) (1993), 143–165.

Abū Qurrah, Theodore.*Mayāmir Thā'ūdūrus Abī Qurrah Usquf Ḥarrān, Aqdam Ta'līf 'Arabī Naṣrānī*, ed. Constantine Basha, Beirut: Maṭba'at al-Fawā'id, 1904.

= *Maymar fī al-Ḥuriyyah* (Maymar on Freedom), ed. Samir Khalil Samir, S.J., *Al*-Mashriq, 79(2) (2005), 437–468, and 80(1) (2006),. 191–222.

= *Maymar fī Ikrām al-Aiqūnāt* (Maymar on the veneration of icons), ed. Ignace Dick, Jounieh: Librairie St Paul/Dhūq Mikhāyil: Christian Arabic Heritage/Rome: the Papal Oriental Institute, 1986.

= *Maymar fī Mawt al-Masīḥ* (Maymar on the death of Messiah), ed. Ignace Dick, (Jounieh: Librairie S. Paul/Rome: Papal Oriental Institute, 1982.

= *Maymar fī ar-Radd 'alā Man Yunkir li-Allāh al-Tajassud wal-Ḥulūl fī-mā Aḥabba an Yaḥill fīhi [min khalqihi] wa-annahu fī Ḥulūlihi fī al-Jasad al-Ma'khūdh min Maryam [al-muṭahharah] bi-Manzalat Julūsihi 'alā al-'Arsh fī al-Samā'* (Maymar in response to those who deny God [the possibility of] being incarnate and indwelling whatever He wishes to indwell [of His creatures] and that His indwelling in the body taken from Mary [the purified] is equal to His sitting on the throne in heaven), in *Mayāmir Thā'ūdūrūs Abī Qurrah usquf Ḥarrān, aqdam ta'līf Nuṣrānī 'Arabī* (*Mayāmir* of Theodore Abū Qurrah, Bishop of Ḥarrān, the oldest Arabic, Christian work), ed. Constantine Bacha (Beirut: Al-Fawā'id Press, 1904), 180–186,

= *Maymar fī Sabīl Ma'rifat Allāh wa-Taḥqīq al-Ibn al-Azalī* (Maymar on the way of knowing God and verifying the eternal Son), in *Mayāmir Thā'ūdūrus Abī Qurrah, usquf Ḥarrān, aqdam ta'līf 'Arabī Naṣrānī* (*Mayāmir* of Theodore Abū Qurrah, Bishop of Harran, the oldest Arabic Christian text), ed. Constantine Bacha, Beirut: Maṭba'at al-Fawā'id, 1904, 75–91.

= *Maymar fī Taḥqīq Nāmūs Mūsā wal-Anbiyā' alladhīna Tanabba'ū 'alā al-Masīḥ wal-Injīl at-Ṭāhir alladhī Naqalahu ilā al-Umam Talamīdh al-Masīḥ al-Mawlūd min Maryam al-'Adhrā' wa-Taḥqīq al-Urthūdhuksiyya allatī Yansibuhā al-Nās ilā al-Khalkīdūniyya wa-Ībṭāl Kull Milla Tantaḥill al-Naṣrāniyya Siwā hādhihi al-Milla Waḍa'ahu al-Mu'allim al-'Āmil wal-Faylasūf al-Kāmil wal-Ab al-Fāḍil Kīr Thā'ūdūrus 'Usquf Ḥarrān* (Maymar in confirmation of the law of Moses and of the prophets who foretold Christ and the pure Gospel, which was conveyed to the nations by the disciples of Christ who was born of the Virgin Mary, and a confirmation of the orthodoxy that people attribute to Chalcedonianism and refuting every group that claims to be Christian other than this group, written by the active teacher, and the perfect philosopher and the righteous father Kir Theodore, Bishop of Ḥarrān), in *Mayāmir Thā'ūdūrus Abī Qurrah, usquf Ḥarrān, aqdam ta'līf 'Arabī Naṣrānī* (*Mayāmir* Theodore Abū Qurrah, Bishop of Harran, the oldest Arabic Christian text), ed. Constantine Bacha, Beirut: Maṭba'at al-Fawā'id, 1904, 140–179.

= *Maymar fī Wujūd al-Khāliq wad-Dīn al-Qawīm* (Maymar on the existence of the Creator

and the right religion), ed. Ignace Dick, Jounieh: Librairie St. Paul/Rome: The Papal Oriental Institute, 1982.
= *Maymar Yuḥaqqiq annahu lā Yalzam an-Naṣārā an Yaqūlu Thalāthat Āliha īdh Yaqūlūn al-Āb Īlāh wal-Ibn ilāh war-Rūḥ al-Qudus. Wa-anna al-Āb wal-Ībn war-Rūḥ al-Qudus Īlāh wa-law Kāna kull Wāḥid Minhum Tāmm ʿalā Ḥidatih* (Maymar affirming that the Christians do not necessarily speak of three gods when they say the Father is God, the Son is God and the Holy Spirit. And that the Father, Son and Holy Spirit are God even if each of them is perfect in Himself), in *Mayāmir Thā'ūdūrus Abī Qurrah, usquf Ḥarrān, aqdam ta'līf ʿArabī Naṣrānī* (*Mayāmir* of Theodore Abū Qurrah, Bishop of Harran, the oldest Arabic Christian text), ed. Constantine Bacha, Beirut: Maṭbaʿat al-Fawā'id, 1904, 23–47.
= *Maymar Yuḥaqqiq anna li-llāh Ibnan hūa ʿAdluh fī aj-Jawhar wa-lam Yazal Maʿahu* (Maymar affirming that God has a Son who is equal to Him in essence and is still with Him), in *Mayāmir Thā'ūdūrus Abī Qurrah, usquf Ḥarrān, aqdam ta'līf ʿArabī Naṣrānī* (*Mayāmir* of Theodore Abū Qurrah, Bishop of Harran, the oldest Arabic Christian text), ed. Constantine Bacha, Beirut: Maṭbaʿat al-Fawā'id, 1904), 91–104.
= *Risālah fī Ījābat Mas'alah Katabahā Abū Qurrah al-Qiddīs ilā Ṣadīq lahu kāna Yaʿqūbiyyan fa-Ṣār Urthūdhuksiyyan 'Inda Raddihi ʿalayhi aj-Jawāb* (An epistle in response to a matter, written by the holy Abū Qurrah to a friend of his, who was Jacobite and became orthodox, as he responds to him with the answer), ed. Ignace Dick, (Jounieh: Librairie S. Paul/Rome: Papal Oriental Institute, 1982
= *A Treatise on the Veneration of the Holy Icons Written in Arabic by Theodore Abū Qurra, Bishop of Harrān (c. 755–c. 830 A. D)*, trans. Sidney Griffith, Louvain: Peeters, 1997.
Accad, Martin. "The Ultimate Proof-Text: The Interpretation of John 20.17 in Muslim-Christian Dialogue (Second/Eighth-Eighth/Fourteenth Centuries)," in *Christians at the Heart of Islamic Rule*, ed. David Thomas, Leiden: Brill, 2003, 199–214
Adamson, Peter and Richard C. Taylor (eds). *The Cambridge Companion to Arabic Philosophy*, Cambridge: Cambridge University Press, 2005.
Ahrweiler, Hélène. "The Geography of Iconoclasm," in *Iconoclasm*, ed. Anthony Bryer and Judith Herrin (Birmingham: University of Birmingham/Centre of Byzantine Studies, 1977), 21–27.
Alexander, Paul J. *The Patriarch Nicephorus of Constantinople: Ecclesiastical Policy and Image Worship in the Byzantine Empire*, rev. ed., Oxford: Oxford University Press, 2001.
Alfeyev, Bishop Hilarion, "Theological *Popevki* of the Fathers, Liturgy and Music," in *Shaping a Global Theological Mind*, ed. Darren C. Marks, Aldershot: Ashgate, 2008, 15–26.
Allen, Pauline and Bronwen Neil (trans, and ed.). *Maximus the Confessor and his Companions: Documents from Exile*, Oxford: Oxford University Press, 2004.
and C.T. Hayward, *Severus of Antioch*, New York: Routledge, 2005.
Altaner, Berthold. "Augustinus in der griechischen Kirche bis auf Photius," in *Kleine patristische Schriften*, Berlin: Akademie-Verlag, 1967.
"Augustinus und die grieschiche Patristik," *Revue Bénédictine*, 62 (1952), 201–213.
Anastos, Milton V. "Nestorius was Orthodox," in *Studies in Byzantine Intellectual History*, ed. M.V. Anastos, London: Variorum Reprints, 1979, VI 119–140.
Anatolios, Khaled. *Athanasius, the Coherence of His Thought*, London: Routledge, 1998.
= *Retrieving Nicaea: The Development and Meaning of Trinitarian Doctrine*, Grand Rapids, MI: Baker Academic, 2011.

Anawati, G.C. "Factors and Effects of Arabization and Islamazation in Medieval Egypt and Syria," in *Islam and Cultural Change in the Middle Ages*, ed. Speros Vryonis, Wiesbaden: Harrasswovitz, 1975, 17–41.
Anselm of Canterbury, *Monologion*, trans. and ed. J. Hopkins and H. Richardson, London: SCM Press, 1974.
Aquinas, Thomas. *The Summa Theologia*, 2nd ed. ed. M.D. Jordon, London: Burns, Oates & Washbourne Ltd, 1920.
Armstrong, A.H (ed.). *The Cambridge History of Later Greek and Early Medieval Philosophy*, Cambridge: Cambridge University Press, 1967.
"The Way and the Ways: Religious Tolerance and Intolerance in the Fourth Century," in *Vigiliae Christianae*, 38 (1984), 1–17.
Ashe, Geoffrey. *The Virgin*, London: Routledge & Kegan Paul, 1976.
Athanasius, *Defense of the Nicene Definition*, in *Nicene and Post-Nicene Fathers*, eds. Philip Schaff and Henry Wace, Grand Rapids, Mich: W.B. Eerdmans Publishing Company, 1987, Vol. 4.
= *Deposition of* Arius, in *Nicene and Post-Nicene Fathers*, eds. Philip Schaff and Henry Wace, Grand Rapids, Mich: W.B. Eerdmans Publishing Company, 1987, Vol. 4.
= *On the Incarnation of the Word*, in *Nicene and Post-Nicene Fathers*, ed. P. Schaff and H. Wace, Peabody, MA: Hendrickson, 1995, Vol. 4.
'Aṭiyya, 'Azīz Suryal. *A History of Eastern Christianity*, London: Methven, 1968.
= "St. John Damascene: Survey of the Unpublished Arabic Versions of His Work in Sinai," in *Arabic Islamic Studies in Honour of Hamilton A.R. Gibb*, ed. George Makdisi, Cambridge, MA: Harvard University Press, 1965.
Augustine, St. *De Trinitate*, trans. Edmund Hill, in *The Works of St Augustine*, ed. John E. Rotelle, Brooklyn, NY: New City Press, 1996.
Awad, Najib G. *And Freedom Became a Public-Square: Political, Sociological and Religious Overviews on the Arab Christians and the Arabic Spring*, Berlin: LIT Verlag, 2012.
= "Between Subordination and Koinonia: Toward a New Reading of the Cappadocian Theology," *Modern Theology*, 23 (2) (2007), 181–204.
= *God without a Face? On the Personal Individuation of the Holy Spirit*, Tübingen: Mohr Siebeck, 2011.
= "'Another puzzle is . . . the Holy Spirit': *De Trinitate* as Augustine's Pneumatology," in *Scottish Journal of Theology*, 65(1), 2011, pp. 1–16.
= "Is Christianity from Arabia? Examining Two Contemporary Arabic Proposals on Christianity in the Pre-Islamic Period," in *Orientalische Christen und Europa: Kulturbegegnung zwischen Interferenz, Partizipation und Antizipation*, ed. Martin Tamcke, Wiesbaden: Harrassowitz, 2011, 33–58.
= "Personhood as Particularity: John Zizioulas, Colin Gunton and the Trinitarian Theology of Personhood," *Journal of Reformed Theology*, 4 (1) (2010), 1–22.
Ayoub, Mahmoud. "Jesus the Son of God: A Study of the Terms *Ibn* and *Walad* in the Qur'ān and *Tafsīr* Tradition," in *A Muslim View of Christianity: Essays on Dialogue by Maḥmoud Ayoub*, ed. Irfan A. Omar, Maryknoll, NY: Orbis Books, 2007, 117–133.
= *A Muslim View of Christianity: Essays on Dialogue*, ed. Irfan A. Omar, Maryknoll, NY: Orbis Books, 2007.
Ayres, Lewis. *Nicea and Its Legacy: An Approach to Fourth-Century Trinitarian Theology*, Oxford: Oxford University Press, 2006.
= *Augustine and the Trinity*, Cambridge: Cambruidge University Press, 2010.

= "On Not Three People: The Fundamental Themes of Gregory of Nyssa's Trinitarian Theology as Seen in *To Ablabius: On Not Three Gods*," *Modern Theology*, 18 (4) (2002), 445–474.
Bacha, Constantine [Qustanṭīn Bāshā] (ed.). *Mayāmir Theodore Abū Qurrah, Usqūf Ḥarrān, Aqdam Taʾlīf ʿArabī Naṣrāni* (*Mayāmir* of Theodore Abū Qurrah, Bishop of Harran, the oldest Arabic Christian work), Beirut: Al-Fawāʾid Press, 1904.
al-Baghdādī, Abū Manṣūr b. Ṭāhir. *Al-Farq bayn al-Firaq* (The difference between the sects), Cairo: 1910.
al-Bakhīt, Muḥammad and Iḥsān ʿAbbās (eds.), *Proceedings of the Second Symposiumon the History of Bīlad ash-Shām during the Early Islamic Period up to 40 A. H/640 A. D.; The Fourth International Conference on the History of Bīlad ash-Shām.* (Arabic papers), Amman: University of Jordan, 1987, Vol. II.
al-Balādūrī, Aḥmad b. Yaḥyā. *Kitāb Futūh al-Buldān*, trans. Philip Hitti, New York: Columbia University Press, 1916, Vol. 1.
Barnard, L. W. "The Origins and Emergence of the Church at Edessa during the First Two Centuries A. D.," *Vigiliae Christianae*, 22 (1968), 161–175.
Barnes, Michel René. "Eunomius of Cyzicus and Gregory of Nyssa: Two Traditions of Transcendent Causality," *Vigiliae Christianae*, 52 (1998,) 59–87.
= "Divine Unity and the Divided Self: Gregory of Nyssa's Trinitarian Theology in Its Psychological Context," *Modern Theology*, 18 (4) (2002), 475–496.
= "Rereading Augustine's Theology of the Trinity," in *The Trinity: An Interdisciplinary Symposium on the Trinity*, ed. Stephen T. Davis, Daniel Kendall, and Gerald O'Collins, Oxford: Oxford University Press, 2001, 145–176
Basil of Caesarea, *Letters*, in *Nicene and Post-Nicene Fathers*, Vol. 8, ed. P. Schaff and H. Wace, Peabody. MA: Hendrickson, 1995.
= *On the Holy Spirit*, trans. Stephen M. Hildebrand, Crestwood, NY: St Vladimir's Seminary Press, 2001.
Baum, Wilhelm and Dietmar W. Winkler, *The Church of the East: A Concise History*, London: Routledge Curzon, 2010.
Baumer, Christoph. *The Church of the East: An Illustrated History of Assyrian Christianity*, London: I. B. Tauris, 2006.
Beaumont, Mark Ivor. "ʿAmmār al-Basrī's Apology for the Doctrine of the Trinity," *Orientalia Christiana Analecta*, 218 (1982), 169–191.
= *Christology in Dialogue with Muslims: A Critical Analysis of Christian Presentations of Christ for Muslims from the Ninth and Twentieth Centuries*, Eugene, OR: Wipf & Stock, 2005.
= "Defending the Incarnation in the Early Christian Dialogue with Muslims," in *Jesus and the Incarnation: Reflections of Christians from Islamic Contexts*, ed. David Emmanuel Singh, Eugene, OR: Wipf & Stock, 2011, 155–168.
= "Early Christian Interpretation of the Qur'ān," *Transformation*, 22 (4) (2005), 195–203.
Beck, Hans-Georg. *Kirche und theologische Literature im Byzantinischen Reich*, Munich: Beck Verlag, 1959.
Beeley, Christopher A. "Cyril of Alexandria and Gregory Nazianzen: Tradition and Complexity in Patristic Christology," *Journal of Early Christian Studies*, 17 (3) (2009), 381–419.
= "Divine Causality and the Monarchy of God the Father in Gregory of Nazianzus," *Harvard Theological Review*, 100 (2007), 199–214.
Gregory of Nazianzus on the Trinity and the Knowledge of God: In Your Light We Shall

See Light, Oxford: Oxford University Press, 2008.
= (ed.). *Re-Reading Gregory of Nazianzus: Essays on History, Theology and Culture*, Washington, DC: Catholic University of America Press, 2012.
= *The Unity of Christ; Continuity and Conflict in Patristic Tradition*, New Haven: Yale University Press, 2012.

Begzes, Marios P., "Inter-Religious Dialogue in Byzantine Thought: The Philosophical and Theological Contribution of John of Damascus," in *Two Traditions, One Space: Orthodox Christians and Muslims in Dialogue*, ed. George C. Papademetriou, Boston, MA: Somerset Hall Press, 2011, 37–76.

Behr, John. *The Nicene Faith: Formation of Christian Theology 2*, Crestwood, NY: St Vladimir's Seminary Press, 2004.

Benevich, Grigory I. "Christological Polemics of Maximus the Confessor and the Emergence of Islam onto the World Stage," *Theological Studies*, 72 (2011), 335–344.

Berkey, Jonathan P. *The Formation of Islam: Religion and Society in the Near East, 600–1800*, Cambridge: Cambridge University Press, 2003.

Bertaina, David, "The Debate of Theodore Abū Qurrah," in *Christian-Muslim Relations, A Bibliographical History*, Vol. 1: *(600–900)*, ed. David Thomas and Barbara Roggema, Leiden: Brill, 2009, 556–564.

Berthold, George C. "Did Maximus the Confessor Know Augustine?" *Studia Patristica*, 17 (1982), 14–17.
(ed. and trans). *Maximus the Confessor: Selected Writings*, Mahwah, NJ: Paulist Press, 1985.

Betts, Robert B. *Christians in the Arab East: a Political Study*, Athens: Lycabettus Press, 1975.

Bijlefeld, Willem A. "Christian-Muslim Relations: A Burdensome Past, a Challenging Future," *Word & World*, 16 (1996), 117–128.
="Eschatology: Some Muslim and Christian Data," *Islam and Christian-Muslim Relations*, 15(1) (2004), 35–54.

Blau, Joshua. *A Grammar of Christian Arabic*, CSCO 267, 276, 279, Louvain: Peeters, 1966–1967.

Block, C. Jonn. "Philoponian Monophysitism in South Arabia at the Advent of Islam with Implications for the English Translation of '*Thalātha*' in Qur'ān 4.171 and 5.73," *Journal of Islamic Studies*, 23 (1) (2012), 50–75.

Blois, Francois, "*Naṣrānī* (ναζωραιος) and *Ḥanīf* (εθνικος): Studies on the Religious Vocabulary of Christianity and Islam," *Bulletin of the School of Oriental and African Studies*, 65 (2002), 1–30.

Blowers, Paul and Robert Wilkens (trans.), *On the Cosmic Mystery of Jesus Christ: Selected Writings from St Maximus the Confessor*, Crestwood, NY: St Vladimir's Seminary Press, 2003.

Bowersock, Glen. W. *Roman Arabia*, Cambridge: Cambridge University Press, 1983. "A Report on *Arabia Provincia*," *Journal of Religious Studies*, 61 (1971), 219–242.

Brock, Sebastian P. (trans.), 1 *The Apocalypse of Pseudo-Methodius*, in *The Seventh Century in the West-Syrian Chronicles*, ed. Andrew Palmer, Sebastian Brock and Robert Hoyland (Liverpool: Liverpool University Press, 1993), 233–234
= "The Christology of the Church of the East," in *Fire from Heaven: Studies in Syriac Theology and Liturgy* (Aldershot: Ashgate, 2006), III, 159–177.
= "The Christology of the Church of the East in the Synods of the Fifth to Early Seventh Centuries: Preliminary Considerations and Materials," in *Studies in Syriac Christianity:*

History, Literature and Theology, Hampshire: Variorum, 1992, 125–142.
= "An Early Syriac Life of Maximus the Confessor," *Analecta Bollandiana*, 1 (1973), 302–319.
= ed., *Fire from Heaven: Studies in Syriac Theology and Liturgy*, Aldershot,: Ashgate, 2006.
= "From Antagonism to Assimilation: Syriac Attitudes to Greek Learning," in *East of Byzantium: Syria and Armenia in the Formative Period*, ed. N. Garsoian, T. Matthews and R. Thompson (Washington, DC: Dumbarton Oaks, 1980), 17–34.
= "Greek into Syriac and Syriac into Greek", in *Syriac Perspectives on Late Antiquity*, ed. S. Brock, London: Variorum, 1984.
= "Iconoclasm and the Monophysites," in *Iconoclasm*, ed. Anthony Bryer and Judith Herrin (Birmingham: University of Birmingham/Centre of Byzantine Studies, 1977), 53–57.
= "North Mesopotamia in the Late Seventh Century. Book XV of John Bar Penkāyē's *Rīš Mellē*," *Jerusalem Studies in Arabic and Islam*, 9 (1987), 51–75.
= "The Orthodox-Oriental Orthodox Conversations of 532", in *Syriac Perspectives on Late Antiquity*, ed. S. Brock, London: Variorum Reprints, 1984.
= "Some Aspects of Greek Words in Syriac", in *Syriac Perspectives on Late Antiquity*, ed. S. Brock, London: Variorum Reprints, 1984.
Syriac Perspectives in Late Antiquity, London: Variorum, 1984.
= "Towards a History of Syriac Translation Technique", *Orientalia Christiana Analecta*, 221 (1980), 1–14.
= "Two Letters of the Patriarch Timothy from the Late Eighth Century on Translations from Greek," *Arabic Sciences and Philosophy*, 9 (1999), 233–246.
= with Aaron M. Butts; George A. Kiraz and Lucas Van Rompay (eds.). *Gorgias Encyclopedic Dictionary of the Syriac Heritage*, Piscataway, NJ: Gorgias Press/Beth Mardutho: Syriac Institute, 2011.

Brubaker, Leslie (ed.), *Byzantium in the Ninth Century: Dead or Alive?* Aldershot: Ashgate, 1998.
= and John Haldon. *Byzantium in the Iconoclast Era, c. 680–850: A History*, Cambridge: Cambridge University Press, 2011.

Bryer, Anthony and Judith Herrin (eds.). *Iconoclasm*, Birmingham: University of Birmingham/Centre of Byzantine Studies, 1977.

Bulliet, Richard W. *The Camel and the Wheel*, Cambridge, MA: Harvard University Press, 1977.
= *Conversion to Islam in the Medieval Period: An Essay in Quantitative History*, Cambridge, MA: Harvard University Press, 1979.
= "Conversion Stories in Early Islam," in *Conversion and Continuity: Indigenous Christian Communities in Islamic Lands, Eighth to Eighteenth Centuries*, ed. Michael Gervers and Ramzī Jibrān Bikh'āzī, Toronto: Pontifical Institute of Medieval Studies, 1990, 123–134.

Burgess, Stanley M. *The Holy Spirit: Eastern Christian Traditions*, Peabody, MA: Hendrickson, 1997.

Busse, Heribert. "'Omar b. al-Khattāb in Jerusalem," in *Jerusalem Studies in Arabic and Islam*, 5 (1984), 73–119.
= "'Omar's Image as the Conqueror of Jerusalem," *Jerusalem Studies in Arabic and Islam*, 8 (1986), 149–168.

Butts, Aaron M, "Theodoros Abū Qurra," in *Gorgias Encyclopedic Dictionary of the Syriac Heritage*, ed. Sebastian P. Brock, Aaron M. Butts, George A. Kiraz and Lucas Van Rompay, Piscataway, NJ: Gorgias Press/Beth Mardutho: the Syriac Institute, 2011, 403–405.

Cameron, A, "The Eastern Provinces in the 7th Century A.D: Hellenism and the Emergence of Islam," in *ΕΛΛΗΝΙΣΜΟΣ: Quelques jalons un histoire de L'identitè grecque Actes du Colloque de Strasbourg*, ed. S. Said, Leiden: Brill, 1991, 287–313.

=and Lawrence I. Conrad (eds). *The Byzantine and Early Islamic Near East*, Vol. 1: *Problems in the Literary Source Material*, Studies in Late Antiquity and Early Islam 1, Princeton, NJ, University of Princeton Press, 1992.

Catholic University of America (ed.). *New Catholic Encyclopaedia*, New York: McGraw-Hill, 1967, Vol. 11.

Cattoi, Thomas. "The Incarnate *Logos* and the *Rūpakāya:* Towards a Comparative Theology of Embodiment," *Religion East & West*, 8 (2008), 109–129.

Chabot, Jean-Baptiste. *Anonymi Auctoris Chronicon ad A.C. 1234 pertinens*, coll. *CSCO* 81, 82, 109, 354, Louvain: 1916, 1920, 1937 & 1974.

Chadwick, Henry. *East and West: The Making of a Rift in the Church. From Apostolic Times until the Council of Florence*, Oxford: Oxford University Press, 2005.

"John Moschus and His Friend Sophronius the Sophist," *Journal of Theological Studies*, 25 (1974), 41–74.

Chesnut, Roberta C. *Three Monophysite Christologies: Severus of Antioch, Philoxenus of Mabbug and Jacob of Sarug*, Oxford: Oxford University Press, 1976.

Coakley, Sarah. "Re-thinking Gregory of Nyssa: Introduction-Gender, Trinitarian Analogies, and the Pedagogy of *the* Song," in *Modern Theology*, 18 (4) (2002), 432–443.

Cook, David. "Syria and the Arabs," in *A Companion to Late Antiquity*, ed. P. Rosseau and J. Raithel, Chichester: Blackwell, 2009, 467–478.

Cook, M. "The Origins of Kalām," *Bulletin of the School of Oriental and African Studies*, 43 (1980), 32–43.

Cotton, Hanna M., Robert G. Hoyland, Jonathan J. Price and David J. Wasserstein (eds.). *From Hellenism to Islam: Cultural and Linguistic Change in the Roman Near East*, Cambridge: Cambridge University Press, 2009.

Courbage, Youssef and Philippe Fargues. *Christians and Jews under Islam*, trans. Judy Mabro, London: I.B. Tauris, 1997.

Courcelle, Pierre. *Late Latin Writers and Their Greek Sources*, Cambridge, MA: Harvard University Press, 1969.

Cragg, Kenneth. *The Arab Christians: a History in the Middle East*, London: Mowbray, 1992.

= "Ismāʿīl al-Fārūqī in the Field of Dialogue," in *Christian-Muslim Encounters*, ed. Yvonne Yazbeck Ḥaddād and Wadīʿ Zaidān Ḥaddād, Gainesville: University Press of Florida, 1995, 399–410.

= *Jesus and the Muslim: An Exploration*, Oxford: Oneworld, 2003

= *Muhammad and the Christian: A Question of Response*, London: Darton, Longman & Todd, 1984.

Crone, Patricia. "Islam, Judeo-Christianity and Byzantine Iconoclasm," *Jerusalem Studies in Arabic and Islam*, 2 (1980), 59–95.

= and Martin Hinds. *God's Caliph: Religious Authority in the First Centuries of Islam*, Cambridge: Cambridge University Press, 2003.

Cross, F. L and E. A. Livingstone (eds). *The Oxford Dictionary of the Christian Church*, 3rd ed. Oxford: Oxford University Press, 2005.

Cross, Richard. "Two Models of the Trinity?" *Heythrop Journal*, 43 (2002), 275–294.

Cunliff-Jones, Hubert (ed.). *A History of Christian Doctrine*, Edinburgh: T&T Clark, 1997.

Cyril of Scythopolis. *The Lives of the Palestinian Monks*, trans. R. M. Price, annotated by John Binns, Kalamazoo, MI: Cistercian Publications, 1991.

D'Ancona, Cristina. "Greek into Arabic: Neoplatonism in Translation," in *The Cambridge Companion to Arabic Philosophy*, ed. Peter Adamson and Richard Taylor, Cambridge: Cambridge University Press, 2010, 10–31.

Dakkāsh, Salīm, *Abū Rā'iṭa al-Takrītī wa-Risālatuh fī al-Thālūth al-Muqaddas: Dirāsah wa-naṣṣ* (Abū Rā'iṭah al-Takrītī and his epistle on the holy Trinity: Study and text), Beirut: Dār al-Mashriq, 1996.

Daley, Brian. "The Christology of Leontius of Byzantium: Personalism or Dialectics?", unpublished essay, 1979.

Davis, Leo Donald. *The First Seven Ecumenical Councils (325–787), Their History and Theology*, Collegeville, MN: Liturgical Press, 1990.

Davis, Stephen T; Daniel Kendall, SJ and Gerald O'Collins, SJ (eds.). *The Trinity: An Interdisciplinary Symposium on the Trinity*, Oxford: Oxford University Press, 2001.

Debié, Muriel. "Muslim-Christian Controversy in an Unedited Syriac Text: *Revelations and Testimonies about our Lord's Dispensations*," in *The Encounter of Eastern Christianity with Early Islam*, ed. E. Grypeou, M. Swanson and D. Thomas, Leiden: Brill, 2006, 225–236

Declerk, José (ed.). *Quaestiones et Dubia*, Turnhout: Brepols, 1982.

Demacopoulos, George E and Aristotle Papanikolaou, "Augustine and the Orthodox: 'The West' in the East," in *Orthodox Readings of Augustine*, ed. George E. Demacopoulos and Aristotle Papanikolaou, Crestwood, NY: St Vladimir's Seminary Press, 2008, 11–40.

Donner, Fred. *The Early Islamic Conquests*, Princeton, NJ: Princeton University Press, 1981.

Downey, Glanville. *A History of Antioch in Syria: From Seleucus to the Arab Conquest*, Princeton, NJ: Princeton University Press, 1961.

Drijvers, Han J. W. "Early Forms of Antiochene Christology," in *After Chalcedon: Studies in Theology and Church History*, ed. C. Laga; J. A. Munitiz and L. Van Rompay, Leuven: Peeters, 1985, 99–114.

"Early Syriac Christianity; Some Recent Publications," *Vigiliae Christianae*, 50 (1996), 159–177.

"East Antioch: Forces and Structures in the Development of Early Syriac Theology," in *East of Antioch: Studies in Early Syriac Christianity*, ed. Han J. W. Drivers, London: Variorum Reprints, 1984, 1–27.

Druart, T. A. "Al-Fārābī and Emanationism," in *Studies in Medieval Philosophy*, ed. John F. Wippel, Washington, DC: Catholic University of America Press, 1987), 23–43. = "Al-Fārābī, Emanation and Metaphysics," in *Neoplatonism and Islamic Thought*, ed. Parviz Morewedge, Albany: State University of New York, 1992), 127–148.

Dvornik, F. *Early Christian and Byzantine Political Philosophy: Origins and Backgrounds*, 2 vols. Washington, DC: Dumbarton Oaks Studies, 1966.

ʿEbayd, Rifʿat and Herman Teule (eds.). *Studies on the Christian Arabic Heritage: in Honour of Father Prof. Dr. Samir Khalil Samir, S. I. at the Occasion of his Sixty-Fifth Birthday*, Leuven: Peeters, 2004.

Egan, John P. "Aitios/'Author', Aitia/'Cause' and Arche/'Origin': Synonyms in Selected Texts of Gregory Nazianzen," *Studia Patristica*, 32 (1995), 102–107.

= "Primal Cause and Trinitarian Perichoresis in Gregory Nazianzen's Oration 31.14," *Studia Patristica*, 27 (1993), 21–28.

Elert, Werner. *Der Ausgang der altkirchlichen Christologie: Eine Untersuchung über Theodore von Pharan und seine Zeit als Einführung in die alte Dogmangeschichte*, ed. Wilhelm Maurer and Elisabeth Bergsträsser, Berlin: Lutherisches Verl-Haus, 1957.

El-Khoury, N. "The Use of Language by Ephraim the Syrian," *Studia Patristica*, 16(2) (1985), 93–99.

Emery, Gilles, O.P. and Matthew Levering (eds.). *The Oxford Handbook of the Trinity*, Oxford: Oxford University press, 2011.

Epha'l, I. *The Ancient Arabs*, Leiden: Brill, 1982.

Ephraim the Syrian. *The Homily on Our Lord*, in *The Fathers of the Church*, ed. K. McVey, trans. Roy J. Deferrari, Vol. 91, Washington, DC: Catholic University of America Press, 1977.

= *Hymns on the Nativity*, in *Nicene and Post-Nicene Fathers*, ed. Philip Schaff and Henry Wace, Vol. 13, Peabody, MA: Hendrickson, 1995.

Ernst, Carl W. *Words of Ecstasy in Sufism*, Albany: State University of New York Press, 1985.

Eutychius of Alexandria (Saʿīd b. Batrīq). *Annals*, Corpus Scriptorum Christanorum Orientalium 51, ed. Louis Cheikho, B. Carra de Voux and H. Zayyat, Louvain: Imprimerie Orientaliste, 1954.

= *The Book of the Demonstration (Kitāb al-Burhān)*, ed. Pierre Cachia, 2 vols, Louvain: Secrétariat du CorpusSCO, 1961.

Fakhry, Mājid. *History of Islamic Philosophy*, 3rd ed. New York: Columbia University Press, 2004.

Fedeli, Alba, "Early Evidences of Variant Readings in Qur'ānic Manuscripts," in *The Hidden Origins of Islam*, ed. Karl-Heinz Ohlig and Gerd-R. Puin, Amherst, NY: Prometheus Books, 2010, 311–334

Fisher, Elizabeth. "Planoudes' *De Trinitate*, the Art of Translation, and the Beholder's Share," in *Orthodox Readings of Augustine*, ed. George E. Demacopoulos and Aristotle Papanikolaou, Crestwood, NY: St Vladimir's Seminary Press, 2008, 41–61.

Florovsky, Georges. *The Byzantine Fathers of the Sixth to Eighth Century*, trans. Raymond Miller et al., Vaduz: Büchervertriebsanstalt, 1987.

= "The Function of Tradition in the Ancient Church," in *Eastern Orthodox Theology: A Contemporary Reader*, ed. Daniel B. Clendenin, Chicago, IL: Revell, 1995, 97–114.

Frank, Richard M. *Beings and Their Attributes: The Teachings of the Basrian School of the Mu'tazila in the Classical Period*, Albany, NY: State University of New York Press, 1978.

= *Early Islamic Theology: The Muʿtazilites and al-Ashʿarī: Texts and Studies on the Development and History of Kalām*, ed. Dimitri Gutas, Burlington, VA: Ashgate, 2007.

= "Al-Ma'nā: Some Reflections on the Technical Meanings of the Term in the Kalām," *Journal of the American Oriental Society*, 87 (1967), 248–259.

Frend, W.H.C. *The Rise of the Monophysite Movement: Chapters in the History of the Church in the Fifth and Sixth Centuries*, Cambridge: Cambridge University Press, 1972.

Friedrich, Gerhard (ed.). *Theological Dictionary of the New Testament*, trans. Geoffrey Bromiley, Grand Rapids, MI: W.B. Eerdmans, 1918.

Fulford, Ben. "'One Commixture of Light': Rethinking Some Modern Uses and Critiques of Gregory of Nazianzus on the Unity and Equality of the Divine Persons," *International Journal of Systematic Theology*, 11 (2) (2009), 172–189.

Fürst, Alfons. "Augustinus im Orient," *Zeitschrift für Kirchengeschichte*, 110 (1999), 294–303.

aj-Jāḥiẓ, Abū ʿUthmān ʿAmr ibn Baḥr. *Kitāb al-akhbār,* in F. Rosenthal, *The Classical Heritage of Islam*, London: Routledge & Kegan Paul, 1975.

= *al-Mukhtār fī ar-Radd ʿalā an-Naṣārā* (The selected in response to the Christians), ed. Muḥammad ʿAbdullāh al-Sharqāwī, Beirut: Dār aj-Jīl, 1991.

Radd ʿalā an-Naṣārā (A response to the Christians), in *Rasāʾil aj-Jāḥiẓ* (Aj-Jāḥiẓ's Letters), Vol. 3, ed. A. M. Hārūn, Cairo: al-Khānjī, 1979.

Garsoïan, Nina, Thomas Mathews and Robert Thompson (eds.). *East of Byzantium: Syria and the Armenian in the Formative Period,* Washington, 1982.

Geddes, C. L. "The Messiah in South Arabia," *The Muslim World*, 57 (1967), 311–320.

Gemeinhardt, Peter, *Die Filioque-Kontroverse zwischen Ost- und Westkirche in Frühmittelalter*, Berlin & New York: Walter De Gruyter, 2002.

Gervers, Michael & Ramzī Jibrān Bikhʿāzī (eds.). *Conversion and Continuity: Indigenous Christian Communities in Islamic Lands, Eighth to Eighteenth Centuries*, Toronto: Pontifical Institute of Mediaeval Studies, 1990.

Gibson, Margaret Dunlop (ed. and trans.). *An Arabic Version of the Acts of the Apostles and the Seven Catholic Epistles, with a treatise on the Triune Nature of God*, Studia Sinaitica 7, London: C. J. Clay and Sons, 1899.

Gilliot, Claude, "Christians and Christianity in Islamic Exegesis," in *Christian-Muslim Relations: A Bibliographical History*, Vol. 1: *600–900*, ed. David Thomas and Barbara Roggema, Leiden: Brill, 2009, 31–56.

Giulea, Dragoş, "The Divine Essence, That Inaccessible *Kabod* Enthroned in Heaven: Nazianzen's *Oratio* 28,3 and the Tradition of Apophatic Theology from Symbols to Philosophical Concepts," *Numen*, 57 (2010), 1–29.

Glei, Reinhold and Adel Theodor Khoury (eds.). *Johannes Damaskenos und Theodor Abū Qurra Schriften zum Islam*, Altenberge: Oros Vorlag, 1995.

Gockel, Matthias, "A Dubious Christological Formula? Leontius of Byzantium and the *Anhypostasis-enhypostasis* Theory," *Journal of Theological Studies*, 51 (2000), 515–532.

Goodman, L. E. (ed. and trans), *Ibn Ṭufayl's Ḥayy ibn Yaqẓān: A Philosophical Tale*, Chicago, IL: University of Chicago Press, 2009.

Grabar, Oleg. "Islam and Iconoclasm," in *Iconoclasm*, ed. Anthony Bryer and Judith Herrin (Birmingham: University of Birmingham/Centre of Byzantine Studies, 1977), 45–52.

The Shape of the Holy: Early Islamic Jerusalem, Princeton, NJ: Princeton University Press, 1996.

Graf, George. "Die arabischen Schriften des Abū Qurra," in *Forschungen zur Christlichen Literature – und Dogmengeshichte*, ed. G. Graf, Vol. 10, (Paderborn: Ferdinand Schöningh, 1910), 67–78.

= *Die arabischen Schriften des Theodor Abū Qurra, Bischofs von Harrān (ca. 740–820)*, Paderborn: Ferdinand Schöningh, 1910.

= *Geschichte der christlichen arabischen Literature*, Vol. 2, Studi e Testi 133, Vatican City: Biblioteca Apostolica Vaticana, 1947.

= *Des Theodor Abū Kurra Traktat über den Schöpfer und die wahre Religion,* Münster: W. Schendorf, 1913.

Grafton, David D. "The Word Made *Book:* The 1865 Van Dyck Arabic Translation of the Bible and Arab Christian Views of *Wahy*," in *Jesus and the Incarnation: Reflections of Christians from Islamic Contexts*, ed. David Emmanuel Singh, Eugene, OR: Wipf & Stock, 2011, 79–95.

"The Politics of Pre-Islamic Arab Christianity in Contemporary Western Scholarship," in *Theological Review*, 34(2013), 3–21.

Grams, Rollin G. "Revealing Divine Identity: The Incarnation of the Word in John's Gospel," in *Jesus and the Incarnation: Reflections of Christians from Islamic Contexts*, ed. David Emmanuel Singh, Eugene, OR: Wipf & Stock, 2011, 47–59

Gregory of Nyssa, *Against Eunomius*, In *Nicene and Post-Nicene Fathers*, Vol. 5, ed. Philip Schaff and H. Wace, Peabody, MA: Hendrickson Publishers, 1995.

= *On 'Not Three Gods' to Ablabius*, In *Nicene and Post-Nicene Fathers*, Vol. 5, ed. Philip Schaff and H. Wace, Peabody, MA: Hendrickson Publishers, 1995.

Gregory Nazianzen. *Gregory of Nazianzus: Select Orations*, trans. Martha Vinson, Fathers of the Church 107, Washington, DC: Catholic University of America Press, 2003.

Orations, in *Nicene and Post-Nicene Fathers*, Vol. 7, ed. Philip Schaff and H. Wace, Peabody, MA: Hendrickson Publishers, 1995.

Gregory of Nyssa. *Against Eunomius*, In *Nicene and Post-Nicene Fathers*, Vol. 5, ed. Philip Schaff and H. Wace, Peabody, MA: Hendrickson Publishers, 1995.

Commentary, Hatfield, PA: Interdisciplinary Biblical Research Institute, 1993.

Griffith, Sidney H. "ʿAmmār al-Baṣri's *Kitāb al-Burhān:* Christian *Kalām* in the First Abbasid Century," in *The Beginnings of Christian Theology in Arabic: Muslim-Christian Encounters in the Early Islamic Period*, Aldershot, UK: Ashgate Variorum, 2002, 145–181.

= "Answers for the Shaykh: A 'Melkite' Arabic Text from Sinai and the Doctrines of the Trinity and the Incarnation in 'Arab Orthodox ' Apologetics'," in *The Encounter of Eastern Christianity with Early Islam*, ed. Emmanouela Grypeou, Mark Swanson and David Thomas (Leiden: Brill, 2006), 277–309,

= "Apologetics and Historiography in the Annals of Eutychios of Alexandria: Christian Self-Definition in the World of Islam," in *Studies on the Christian Arabic Heritage: in Honour of Father Prof. Dr. Samir Khalil Samir, S. I. at the Occasion of his Sixty-Fifth Birthday*, ed. Rifaat Ebied and Herman Teule, Leuven: Peeters, 2004, 65–90.

= "The Arabic Account of ʿAbd al-Masīḥ an-Nağrānī al-Ghassānī," *Le Muséon*, 98 (1985), 331–374.

= *Arabic Christianity in the Monasteries of Ninth-Century Palestine*, Aldershot, UK/Brookfield, USA: Ashgate/Variorum, 1992.

= "Arguing from Scripture: The Bible in the Christian/Muslim Encounter in the Middle Ages," in *Scripture and Pluralism: Reading the Bible in the Religiously Plural Worlds of the Middle Ages and Renaissance*, ed. Thomas Hefferman and Thomas Burman, Leiden: Brill, 2006, 29–58.

= *The Beginnings of Christian Theology in Arabic: Muslim-Christian Encounters in the Early Islamic Period*, Aldershot: Ashgate, 2002.

= *The Bible in Arabic: The Scripture of the 'People of the Book' in the Language of Islam*, Princeton, NJ: Princeton University Press, 2013.

= "Byzantium and the Christians in the World of Islam: Constantinople and the Church in the Holy Land in the Ninth Century," *Medieval Encounters*, 3 (1997), 231–265

= "Christians, Muslims and Neo-Martyrs: Saints' Lives and Holy Land History," in *Sharing the Sacred: Religious Contacts and Conflicts in the Holy Land, First-Fifteenth*

Centuries CE, ed. Guy G. Stroumsa and Arieh Kofsky, Jerusalem: Yad Izhak Zvi, 1998, 163–208.
= "The Church of Jerusalem and the 'Melkites': The Making of an 'Arab Orthodox' Christian Identity in the World of Islam, 750–1050 *CE*, in *Christians and Christianity in the Holy Land: from the Origin to the Latin Kingdom*, ed. Ora Limor and Guy G. Stroumsa, Turnhout: Brepols, 2006. 173–202
= *The Church in the Shadow of the Mosque: Christians and Muslims in the World of Islam*, Princeton, NJ: Princeton University Press, 2008.
= "Comparative Religion in the Apologetics of the First Christian Arabic Theologians," in *The Beginnings of Christian Theology in Arabic: Muslim-Christian Encounters in the Early Islamic Period* (Aldershot, UK: Ashgate Variorum, 2002), I, 63–87.
= "The Concept of *al-Uqnūm* in ʿAmmār al-Baṣrī's Apology for the Doctrine of the Trinity," in *Actes du premier congrès international d'études arabes chrétiennes (Goslar, septembre 1980)*, ed. Samir Khalil Samir, Orientalia Christiana Analecta 218, Rome: Pontificium Institutum Studiorum Orientalium 1982, 169–191.
= *The Controversial Theology of Theodore Abū Qurrah (c. A. D. 750–c. 820); A Methodological, Comparative Study in Christian Arabic Literature*, PhD Diss., Washington: the Catholic University of America/Ann Arbor, Mich: University Microfilms, 1978.
= "Crosses, Icons and the Image of Christ in Edessa: The Place of Iconophobia in the Christian-Muslim Controversies of Early Islamic Times," in *Transformation of Late Antiquity, Essays for Peter Brown*, ed. Philip Rousseau, Farnham, UK: Ashgate, 2009, 63–84.
= "Disputes with Muslims in Syriac Christian Texts: From Patriarch John (d. 648) to Mar Hebraeus (d. 1286)," in *The Beginnings of Christian Theology in Arabic*, ed. S. E. Griffith, Aldershot: Ashgate, 2002, V: 251–273
= "Faith and Reason in Christian *Kalām:* Theodore Abū Qurrah on Discerning the True Religion," in *Christian Arabic Apologetics during the Abbasid Period (750–1258)*, ed. Samir Khalil Samir and Jørgen S. Nielsen, Leiden: Brill, 1994, 1–43
= "Faith Seeking Understanding in the Thought of St Ephraem the Syrian," in *Faith Seeking Understanding: Learning and the Catholic Tradition*, ed. G. Berthold (Manchester, NH: St Anselm College Press, 1991), 35–55.
= "The First Christian *Summa Theologiae* in Arabic: Christian *Kalām* in Ninth-Century Palestine," in *Conversion and Continuity: Indigenous Christian Communities in Islamic Lands Eighth to Eighteenth Centuries*, ed. Michael Gervers and Ramzī Jibrān Bikhʿāzī (Toronto: Pontifical Institute of Medieval Studies, 1990), 15–31.
= "Free Will in Christian Kalām: the Doctrine of Theodore Abū Qurrah," *Parole de l'Orient*, 14 (1987), 79–107.
= "From Aramaic to Arabic: The Languages of the Monasteries of Palestine in the Byzantine and Early Islamic Periods," in *The Beginnings of Christian Theology in Arabic: Muslim-Christian Encounters in the Early Islamic Period* (Aldershot: Ashgate, 2002), X, 11–31
= "Greek into Arabic: Life and Letters in the Monasteries of Palestine in the 9th Century; the Example of the *Summa Theologiae Arabica*," *Orientalia Christiana Analecta*, 226 (1986), 123–141.
= "Ḥabīb Ibn Ḫidmah Abū Rā'iṭah: A Christian *Mutakallim* of the First Abbasid Century," in *The Beginnings of Christian Theology in Arabic: Muslim-Christian Encounters in the*

Early Islamic Period Aldershot: Ashgate, 2002), 161–201
= "Islam and the Summa Theologiae Arabica, *Rabīʿ* I, 264 A.H.," *Jerusalem Studies in Arabic and Islam*, 13 (1990), 225–264.
= "John of Damascus and the Church in Syria in the Umayyad Era: The Intellectual and Cultural Milieu of Orthodox Christians in the World of Islam," *Hugoye: Journal of Syriac Studies*, 11(2) (2008), 1–34.
= "A 'Melkite' Arabic Text from Sinai and the Doctrines of the Trinity and the Incarnation in 'Arab Orthodox Apologetics'," in *The Encounter of Eastern Christianity with Early Islam*, ed. Emmanouela Grypeou, Mark Swanson and David Thomas, Leiden: Brill, 2006, 277–310
= "'Melkites', 'Jacobites', and the Christological Controversies in Arabic in Third/Ninth-century Syria," in *Syrian Christians under Islam, the First Thousand Years*, ed. David Thomas, Leiden: Brill, 2001, 9–55.
= "Michael the Martyr and Monk of Mar Sabas Monastery at the Court of the Caliph ʿAbd al-Malik: Christian Apologetics and Martyrology in the Early Islamic Period," *Aram*, 6 (1994), 115–148.
= "The Monks of Palestine and the Growth of Christian Literature in Arabic," *The Muslim World*, 78 (1988), 1–28.
= "Muhammad and the Monk Bahira: Reflections on a Syriac and Arabic Text from Early Abbasid Times," *Oriens Christianus*, 79 (1995), 146–174.
= "Muslims and Church Councils: The Apology of Theodore Abū Qurrah," *Studia Patristica*, 25 (1993), 270–299.
= "A Ninth Century *Summa Theologiae Arabica*," in *Actes du Deuxième Congrè International d'Etudes Arabes Chrètiennes (Oosterhesselen, Septembre 1984)*, ed. Samir Khalil Samir, *Orientalia Christiana Analecta*, 226 (1986), 93–121, 123–141.
= "The Prophet Muhammad, His Scripture and His Message According to the Christian Apologies in Arabic and Syriac from the Abbasid Century," in *Vie du prophète Mahomet*, ed. T. Fahd, Starbourg: Colloque de Strasbourg, 1980 1983, 118–121.
= "The Qurʾān in Arab Christian Texts: The Development of an Apologetical Argument: Abū Qurrah in the *Majlis* of al-Maʾmūn," *Parole de l'Orient*, 24 (1999), 203–233.
= "Reflections on the Biography of Theodore Abū Qurrah," *Parole de l'Orient*, 18 (1993), 143–170.
= "Some Unpublished Arabic Sayings Attributed to Theodore Abū Qurrah," *Le Musèon*, 92 (1979), 29–35.
= *Theodore Abū Qurrah. The Intellectual Profile of an Arab Christian Writer of the first Abbasid Century*, Tel. Aviv: Tel Aviv University, 1992.
= "Theodore Abū Qurrah's Arabic Tract on the Christian Practice of Venerating Images," *Journal of the American Oriental Society*, 105 (1985), 53–73; also in *Arabic Christianity in the Monasteries of Ninth-Century Palestine*, ed. S.H. Griffith, Aldershot: Ashgate , 1992, 53–73.
= "Theology and the Arab Christian: The Case of the 'Melkite' Creed," in *A Faithful Presence: Essays for Kenneth Cragg*, .de David Thomas, London: Melisende, 2003, 184–200.
= "The View of Islam from the Monasteries of Palestine in the Early 'Abbāsid Period: Theodore Abū Qurrah and the *Summa Theologiae Arabica*," *Islam and Chistian-Muslim Relations*, 7(1) (1996), 9–28.
= "What Has Constantinople to Do with Jerusalem? Palestine in the Ninth Century:

Byzantine Orthodoxy in the World of Islam," in *Byzantium in the Ninth Century: Dead or Alive?* ed. Leslie Brubaker, Aldershot: Variorum, 1998, 181–194.
Grillmeier, Aloys, SJ, *Christ in Christian Tradition*, Vol. 1: *From the Apostolic Age to Chalcedon (451)*, trans. John Bowden, Atlanta, GA: John Knox Press, 1975.
= *Christ in Christian Traditon*, Vol. 2: *From the Council of Chalcedon /451/to Gregory the Great /590–604/*, trans. J. Cawte and P. Allen (trans.), London: Mowbray, 1995.
Gruendler, B. *The Development of the Arabic Scripts from the Nabataean Era to the First Islamic Century*, Atlanta, GA: Scholars Press, 1993.
Grypeou, E, M. Swanson and D. Thomas (eds). *The Encounter of Eastern Christianity with Early Islam*, Leiden: Brill, 2006.
Guillaume, Alfred. "A Debate between Christian and Muslim Doctors," *Journal of The Royal Asiatic Society of Great Britain and Ireland*, centenary supplement (1924), 233–244.
"Theodore Abū Qurra as Apologist," *The Moslem World*, 15 (1925), 42–51.
Gunther, John J. "Syrian Christian Dualism," *Vigiliae Christianae*, 25 (1971), 81–93.
Gunton, Colin E. *The Promise of Trinitarian Theology*, 2nd ed., Edinburgh: T&T Clark, 1999.
Gutas, Dimitri. *Avicenna and the Aristotelian Tradition: Introduction to Reading Avicenna's Philosophical Works*, Leiden: Brill, 1988.
= *Greek Thought, Arabic Culture: The Graeco-Arabic Translation Movement in Baghdad and Early 'Abbāsid Society (2nd-4th/8th–10th Centuries)*, New York: Routledge, 1999.
Ḥaddād, Yvonne Y. and Wadīʿ Z. Ḥaddād (eds). *Christian-Muslim Encounters*, Gainesville: University Press of Florida, 1995.
Haldon, John F. *Byzantium in the Seventh Century: The Transformation of a Culture*, rev. ed., Cambridge: Cambridge University Press, 1997.
al-Hamadhānī, ʿĀbd aj-Jabbār ibn Aḥmad. *Tathbīt Dalāʾil an-Nubuwwa* (Confirming the evidences of prophecy), in *ʿĀbd aj-Jabbār: Critique of Christian Origins*, ed. and trans. Gabriel Said Reynolds and Samir Khalil Samir, Provo, UT: Brigham Young University Press, 2010.
Ḥamza, Firās; Sajjad Rizvi and Farḥana Mayer (eds). *An Anthology of Qur'anic Commentaries*, Vol. 1: *On the Nature of the Divine*, Oxford: Oxford University Press, 2008.
Hanson, Craig L. "Manuel I Comnenus and the 'God of Muhammad': A Study in Byzantine Ecclesiastical Politics," in *Medieval Christian Perceptions of Islam*, ed. John V. Tolan, New York: Routledge, 2000, 55–82.
Hanson, R.P. "The Doctrine of the Trinity Achieved in 381," *Scottish Journal of Theology*, 36 (1) (1983), 41–57.
= *The Search for the Christian Doctrine of God: The Arian Controversy 318–381*, Edinburgh: T&T Clark, 1988.
Hatch, Edwin. *The Influence of Greek Ideas and Usages upon the Christian Church*, ed. A.M. Fairbairn, 5th ed., Peabody, MA: Hendrickson, 1995.
Haynes, Daniel, "The Transgression of Adam and Christ the New Adam: St Augustine and St Maximus the Confessor on the Doctrine of Original Sin," *St Vladimir's Theological Quarterly*, 55 (3) (2011), 293–317.
Hefferman, Thomas and Thomas Burman (eds). *Scripture and Pluralism: Reading the Bible in the Religiously Plural Worlds of the Middle Ages and Renaissance*, Leiden: Brill, 2006.
Heimgartner, Martin. *Timotheos I., Ostsyrischer Patriarch: Disputation Mit dem Kalifen al-Mahdī*, in *Corpus Scripturum Christianorum Orientalium*, (Leuven: Peeters, 2011.
= *Die Brief 42–58 Des Ostsyrischen Patriarchen Timotheos*, in *Corpus Scriptorum Christianorum Orientalium*, (Leuven: Peeters, 2012.

Heron, Alasdair I.C. *The Holy Spirit: The Holy Spirit in the Bible, in Historical Thought and in Recent Theology*, London: Marshall, Morgan & Scott, 1983.

Hick, John, "A Recent Development within Christian Monotheism," in *Christians, Muslims and Jews*, ed. David Kerr and D. Cohn-Sherbok, Canterbury: University of Canterbury, 1983, 1–19.

Hildebrand, Stephen M. "A Reconsideration of the Development of Basil's Trinitarian Theology: The Dating of Ep. 9 and *Contra Eunomium*," *Vigiliae Christianae*, 58 (2004), 393–406.

= *The Trinitarian Theology of Basil of Caesarea: A Synthesis of Greek Thought and Biblical Truth*, Washington, DC: Catholic University of America Press, 2007.

Holmberg, Bo. "'Person' in the Trinitarian Doctrine of Christian Arabic Apologetics and Its Background in the Syriac Church Fathers," *Studia Patristica*, 25 (1993), 300–307.

Hourani, G. "The Principal Subject of Ibn Ṭufayl's *Ḥayy ibn Yaqẓān*," *Journal of Near Eastern Studies*, 15 (1956), 40–46.

Howard-Johnston, James. *Witnesses to a World Crisis: Historians and Histories of the Middle East in the Seventh Century*, Oxford: Oxford University Press, 2011.

Hoyland, Robert G. "Arabic, Syriac and Greek Historiography in the First Abbasid Century: An Inquiry into Inter-Cultural Traffic," *Aram*, 3 (1999), 217–239.

= "Arab Kings, Arab Tribes and the Beginning of Arab Historical Memory in Late Roman Epigraphy," in *From Hellenism to Islam: Cultural and Linguistic Change in the Roman Near East*, ed. Hannah M. Cotton, R.G. Hoyland, J.J. Price and D.J. Wasserstein, Cambridge: Cambridge University Press, 2009, 374–400.

= "Language and Identity: The Twin Histories of Arabic an Aramaic," *Scripta Classica Israelica*, 23 (2004), 183–199.

= *Seeing Islam As Others Saw It: A Survey and Evaluation of Christian, Jewish and Zoroastrian Writings on Early Islam*, Princeton, NJ: The Darwin Press, 2007.

Hunt, Hannah, "Byzantine Christianity," in *the Blackwell Companion to Eastern Christianity*, ed. Ken Parry, Oxford: Blackwell, 2010, 73–93.

Hurst, T.R. "The Syriac Letters of Timothy I (727–823): A Study in Christian-Muslim Controversy," PhD Diss., Catholic University of America, 1986.

Hussey, Joan Mervyn. *The Orthodox Church in the Byzantine Empire*, Oxford: Oxford University Press, 2010

= *Church and Learning in the Byzantine Empire 867–1185*, London: Russell & Russell, 1963.

Ibn Ḥanbal, Aḥmad. *Musnad*, ed. Aḥmad M. Shākir, Cairo: Dār al-Maʿārif, 1955.

Ibn Khuzayma, Muhammad. I.I. *Kitāb al-tawḥīd wa-ithbāt ṣifāt al-Rabb* (The book of monotheism and the verification of the Lord's attributes), ed. M.K. Harras, Beirut: Dār al-Jīl, 1983.

Ibn al-Munqidh, Usāma. *Kitāb al-iʿtibār* (The book of construal), trans. Philip Hitti, Beirut, 1964.

Ibn an-Nadīm, Muḥammad Ibn Isḥaq. *Al-Fihrist*, Cairo: Al-Maktaba al-Tijariyya al-Kubrā, 1929.

Ibn ar-Rawandī, "Origins of Islam: A Critical Look at the Sources," in *The Quest of the Historical Muhammad*, ed. and trans. Ibn Warraq, Amherst, NY: Prometheus Books, 2000, 89–124.

Ibn Warrāq (trans. and ed.). *The Quest of the Historical Muhammad*, Amherst, NY: Prometheus Books, 2000.

Ibrahim, Gregorios Yuhanna. *Al-Suryān wa-ḥarb al-iqūnāt* (The Syrian Christians and the war over icons), Aleppo: The Syriac Orthodox Patriachate, 1980.
Ibrahim, Mahmood, "Religious Inquisition as a Social Policy: the Persecution of the Zanadiqa in the Early Abbasid Caliphate," in *Arab Studies Quarterly*, 2(16), 1994, pp. 20–53.
Irwin, Robert. *For Lust of Knowing: The Orientalists and their Enemies*, London: Penguin, 2007.
Jacobs, Nathan. "On 'Not Three Gods' – Again: Can a Primary-Secondary Substance Reading of *Ousia* and *Hypostasis*, Avoid Tritheism?" *Modern Theology*, 24(3) (2008), 332–358.
Jansma, T. "The Establishment of the Four Quarters of the Universe in the Symbol of the Cross: A Trace of an Ephraemic Conception in the Nestorian Inscription of Hsi-an fu?" *Studia Patristica*, 13(2) (1971), 204–209.
Janssens, J. "Creation and Emanation in Avicenna," *Documenti e studi sulla Tradizione filosofica medievale*, 8 (1997), 455–477.
Jeffery, Arthur, "Ghevond's Text of the Correspondence between ʿUmar II and Leo III," in *The Early Christian-Muslim Dialogue: A Collection of Documents from the First Three Islamic Centuries (632–900 A.D.): Translations with Commentary*, ed. N.A. Newman, Hatfield, PA: Interdiscplinary Biblical Research Institute, 1993.
Jenkins, Philip. *The Lost History of Christianity: The Thousand-Year Golden Age of the Church in the Middle East, Africa and Asia – and How it Died*, New York: Harper One, 2008.
Jenson, Robert. *The Triune Identity: God according to the Gospel*, Philadelphia, PA: Fortress Press, 1982.
John of Damascus. *Exposition of the Orthodox Faith*, trans. S.D.F. Salmond, in *Nicene and Post-Nicene Fathers*, Vol. 9, ed. Philip Schaff and Henry Wace, New York: Cosimo, 2007.
= *On the Divine Images: Three Apologies against Those Who Attack the Divine Images*, trans. David Anderson Crestwood, NY: St Vladimir's Seminary Press, 1980.
John of Nikiu, *Chronicle*, trans. R.H. Charles, London: Oxford University Press, 1916.
Johns, Jeremy. "Christianity and Islam," in *The Oxford History of Christianity*, ed. John McManners, Oxford: Oxford University Press, 2002, 167–204
Kägi [Kaegi], Walter Emil. *Byzantinum and the Early Islamic Conquest*, Cambridge: Cambridge University Press, 1992.
= "The Early Raids into Anatolia and Byzantine Reactions under Emperor Constans II," in *The Encounter of Eastern Christians with Early Islam*, ed. Emmanouela Grypeou; Mark Swanson and David Thomas, Leiden: Brill, 2006, 73–93
= "Initial Byzantine Reactions to the Arab Conquest," *Church History*, 38 (1969), 139–149.
Kany, Roland, *Augustine Trinitätsdenken: Bilanz, Kritik und weiterführung der modernen Forschung zu 'De Trinitate'*, Tübingen: Mohr Siebeck, 2007.
Kashouh, Hikmat. "The Arabic Versions of the Gospels: A Case Study of John 1.1 and 1.18," in *The Bible in Arab Christianity*, ed. David Thomas, Leiden: Brill, 2007, 9–36
Kateregga, Badru D. and David W. Shenk, *Islam and Christianity: A Muslim and a Christian in Dialogue*, Nairobi: Uzima Press, 1980.
Kattan, Assaad E. "The Christological Dimension of Maximus Confessor's Biblical Hermeneutics," *Studia Patristica*, 42 (2006), 169–174.
Verleiblichung und Synergie: Grundsüge de Biblehermeneutik bei Maximus Confessor, Leiden: Brill, 1995.

Keating, Sandra Toenies. "Ḥabīb ibn Khidma Abū Rā'iṭa al-Takrītī's 'The Refutation of the Melkites Concerning the Union [of the Divinity and Humanity in Christ] III," in *Christians at the Heart of Islamic Rule*, ed. David Thomas, Leiden: Brill, 2003, 39–54.

Kelly, J. N. D. *Early Christian Doctrines*, 5th ed., London: A & C Black, 1993.

= "The Nicene Creed: A Turning Point," *Scottish Journal of Theology*, 1(36) (1983), 29–39.

Kennedy, Hugh. "The Melkite Church from the Islamic Conquest to the Crusades: Continuity and Adoption in the Byzantine Legacy," in *The 17th International Byzantine Congress, Major Papers*, Group of eds. New Rochelle, NY: Aristide D Caratzas, 1986, 325–343.

= *The Prophet and the Age of the Caliphates: the Islamic Near East from the Sixth to the Eleventh Century*, London: Routledge, 1986.

= *When Baghdad Ruled the Muslim World: The Rise and Fall of Islam's Greatest Dynasty*, Cambridge, MA: Da Capo Press, 2005.

Kennedy, Philip. "Abū Nuwās, Samuel and Levi," *Studies in Muslim-Jewish Relations*, 2 (1995), 109–125.

Al-Khālidī, Ṭarīf (ed. and trans.), *The Muslim Jesus: Sayings and Stories in Islamic Literature*, Cambridge, MA: Harvard University Press, 2003.

= "The Role of Jesus in Intra-Muslim Polemics of the First Two Islamic Centuries," in *Christian Arabic Apologetics During the Abbasid Period (750–1258)*, ed. Samīr Khalīl Samīr and Jørgen S. Nielsen, Leiden: Brill, 1994, 146–156.

Khalīfe-Hāshim, Elias. "Does the Council of Ephesus Unite or Divide?", in *Syriac Dialogue: Second Non-Official Consultation on Dialogue within the Syriac Tradition*, ed. A. Stirnemann and G. Wilflinger, Arabic trans. M. Taraqjii, Vienna: Pro Oriente, 1996, 164–178.

Kharlamov, Vladimir. *The Beauty of the Unity and the Harmony of the Whole: The Concept of Theosis in the Theology of Pseudo-Dionysius the Areopagite*, Eugene, OR: Wipf and Stock, 2009.

al-Kindī, Abū Yūsuf Ya'qūb ibn 'Isḥāq aṣ-Ṣabbāḥ, *The Apology of al-Kindī*, in *The Early Christian-Muslim Dialogue: A Collection of Documents from the First Three Islamic Centuries (632–900 A. D.); Translation with Commentary*, ed. N.A. Newman, Hatfield, PA: Interdisciplinary Biblical Research Institute, 1993, 381–516

= *Risālat 'Abd al-Masīḥ al-Kindī* (The Epistle of 'Abd al-Masīḥ al-Kindī), in *Risālatān fī al-Ḥiwār waj-Jadal bayn al-Masīḥiyyah wal-Islām fī 'Ahd al-Khalīfah al-Ma'mūn (t. 813–834 m)* (Two epistles on dialogue and debate between Christianity and Islam in the era of the Caliph al-Ma'mūn [c. 813–834 AD]), ed. Georges Tartar, Paris: Asmar, 2011, 119–379.

King, Karen. "Which Early Christianity?" in *The Oxford Handbook of Early Christian Studies*, ed. Susan A. Harvey and David G. Hunter, Oxford: Oxford University Press, 2009, 66–88.

Klinge, Gerhard. "Die Bedeutung der syrischen Theologen als Vermittler der grieschischen Philosophie an den Islam," *Zeitschrift für Kirchengeschichte*, 58 (1939), 375–383.

Kofsky, Arieh and Guy Stroumsa (eds). *Sharing the Sacred: Religious Contacts and Conflicts in the Holy Land, First-Fifteenth Centuries CE*, Jerusalem: Yad Izhak Ben Zvi, 1998.

Koonammakkal, Thomas. "Divine Names and Theological Language in Ephrem", *Studia Patristica*, 25 (1993), 318–324.

Kruger, Derek. "The Practice of Christianity in Byzantium," in *Byzantine Christianity*, ed. D. Kruger, Minneapolis, MN: Augsburg Fortress, 2010, 1–18.

Laga, Carl, J. A. Munitiz and L. Van Rompay (eds). *After Chalcedon: Studies in Theology and Church History*, Leuven: Peeters, 1985.

Laga, Carl and Carlos Steel (eds). *Maximi Confessionis Quaestiones ad Thalassium*, CCG 22, Turnhout: Brepols, 1990.

Laird, Martin, "Apophasis and Logophasis in Gregory of Nyssa's *Commentarius in Canticum Canticorum*," *Studia Patristica*, 37 (1999), 126–132.

Lampe, G.W.H. *Patristic Greek Lexicon*, Oxford: Clarendon Press, 1961.

Lamoreaux, John C. "The Biography of Theodore Abū Qurrah Revisited," *Dumbarton Oaks Papers*, 56 (2002), 25–40.

= "Early Eastern Christian Responses to Islam," in *Medieval Christian Perceptions of Islam*, ed. John V. Tolan, New York: Routledge, 2000, 3–21.

= "Theodore Abū Qurra," in *Christian-Muslim Relations, a Bibliographical History*, Vol. 1: *600–900*, ed. David Thomas and Barbara Roggema, Leiden: Brill, 2009, 439–491.

= (trans.). *Theodore Abū Qurrah*, Provo, UT: Brigham Young University Press, 2005.

= "Theodore Abū Qurrah and John the Deacon," *Greek, Roman and Byzantine Studies*, 42 (2001), 361–386.

Larchet, Jean-Claude. *Maxime le Confessor, médiateur entre l'Orient et l'Occident*, Paris: Les Editions du Cerf, 1998.

Leirvik, Oddbjørn. *Images of Jesus Christ in Islam*, London: Continuum, 2010.

Levine, Lee I. *The Ancient Synagogue: The First Thousand Years*, New Haven, CT: Yale University Press, 1999.

Levtzion, Nehemiah. "Conversion to Islam in Syria and Palestine and the Survival of Christian Communities," in *Conversion and Continuity: Indigenous Christian Communities in Islamic Lands Eighth to Eighteenth Centuries*, ed. Michael Gervers and Ramzī Jibrān Bikh'āzī, Toronto: Pontifical Institute of Medieval Studies, 1990, 289–311.

Lienhard, J.T. "The 'Arian' Controversy: Some Categories Reconsidered," *Theological Studies*, 48 (1987), 415–436.

= *Contra Marcellum: Marcellus of Ancyra and Fourth Century Theology*, Washington, DC: Catholic University of America Press, 1999.

= "*Ousia* and *Hypostasis:* The Cappadocian Statement and the Theology of 'One *Hypostasis*' in *The Trinity*, ed. S.T. David Kandall and G. O'Collins, SJ, Oxford: Oxford University Press, 1999, 99–121.

Limor, Ora and Guy G. Stroumsa (eds). *Christians and Christianity in the Holy Land: from the Origin to the Latin Kingdom*, Turnhout: Brepols, 2006.

Lindemann, Andreas, and Henning Paulsen (eds). *Die apostolischen Väter* [Greek-German parallel edition], Tübingen: Mohr Siebeck, 1992.

Lisān al-'Arab in www.alwaraq.net/lisanSearchutf8.htm.

Little, Donald P. "Conversion to Islam in Syria and Palestine and the Survival of Christian Communities," in *Conversion and Continuity: Indigenous Christian Communities in Islamic Lands, Eighth to Eighteenth Centuries*, ed. Michael Gervers and Ramzī Jibrān Bikh'āzī, Toronto: Pontifical Institute of Medieval Studies, 1990, 263–288.

Lossky, Vladimir. *In the Image and Likeness of God*, Crestwood, NY: St Vladimir's Seminary Press, 1985.

= *The Mystical Theology of the Eastern Church*, New York: St Vladimir's Seminary Press, 1997.

Lössl, Josef. "Augustine in Byzantium," *Journal of Ecclesiastical History*, 51(2) (2000), 267–273.

Louth, Andrew. "Late Patristic Development on the Trinity in the East," in *The Oxford Handbook of the Trinity*, ed. Gilles Emery, OP, and Matthew Levering (Oxford: Oxford University press, 2011), 138 – 151.
= *Maximus the Confessor*, Abingdon: Routledge, 1996.
The Origins of the Christian Mystical Tradition: From Plato to Denys, Oxford: Oxford University Press, 2007.
= "Recent Research on St Maximus the Confessor: A Survey," Review Essay in *St Vladimir's Theological Quarterly*, 42(1) (1998),. 67 – 84.
= *St John Damascene: Tradition and Originality in Byzantine Theology*, Oxford: Oxford University Press, 2002.
= and Augustine Casiday (eds). *Byzantine Orthodoxies: Papers from the Thirty-Sixth Spring Symposium of Byzantine Studies, University of Durham, 23 – 25 March 2002*, Aldershot: Ashgate, 2006.
Luxenburg, C. *Die syro-aramäsche Lesart des Koran*, 2nd ed., Berlin: Schiller, 2002; translated into English as: *The Syro-Aramaic Reading of the Koran: A Contribution to the Decoding of the Koran*, Berlin: Schiller, 2007.
Lynch, John J. "*Prosopon* in Gregory of Nyssa: A Theological Word in Transition," *Theological Studies*, 40(4) (1979), 728 – 738.
Mahdi, Muhsen, "Language and Logic in Classical Islam," in *Logic and Classical Islamic Culture*, ed. G. E. Van Grunebaum, Wiesbaden: Harrassowitz, 1970, 51 – 83.
Maqdisī, George (ed.). *Arabic Islamic Studies in Honour of Hamilton A. R. Gibb*, Cambridge, MA: Harvard University Press, 1965.
Maʿlūf, Louise, "Aqdam makhṭūṭ ʿArabī Masīḥī" (The Oldest Arabic Christian Manuscript), *Al-Mashriq*, 6 (1903), 1011 – 1023.
Mango, Cyril. *The Art of the Byzantyine Empire, 312 – 1453: Sources and Documents*, New York: Prentice-Hall, 1972.
Ma'oz, Moshe. *Middle Eastern Minorities: Between Integration and Conflict*, Washington, DC: Washington Institute for Near Eastern Policy, 1999.
Marshall, Alfred. *The New International Version: Interlinear Greek-English New Testament*, Grand Rapids, MI: Zondervan, 1958.
Martin, Richard C.; Mark R. Woodward and Dwi S. Atmaja, *Defenders of Reason in Islam: Muʿtazalism from Medieval School to Modern Symbol*, Oxford: Oneworld Publishing, 2003.
McFarland, Ian A. "Fleshing Out Christ: Maximus the Confessor's Christology in Anthropological Perspective," *St Vladimir's Theological Quarterly*, 49(4) (2005), 417 – 436.
McGuckin, John A. "'Perceiving Light From Light in Light" (Oration 31.3): The Trinitarian Theology of St Gregory the Theologian', *Greek Theological Review* 39 (1994), 24 – 45.
= *St Cyril of Alexandria: The Christological Controversy: Its History, Theology and Texts*, Leiden: Brill, 1994.
= "The Trinity in the Greek Fathers," in *The Cambridge Companion to the Trinity*, ed. Peter C. Phan, Cambridge: Cambridge University Press, 2011, 49 – 69.
McLeod, Frederick G. SJ. *The Image of God in the Antiochene Tradition*, Washington, DC: Catholic University of America Press, 1999.
McVey, Kathleen. "Ephrem the Syrian's Theology of Divine Indwelling and Aleia Pulcharia Augusta", *Studia Patristica*, 35 (2001), 458 – 465.

= *The Fathers of the Church*, Vol. 91: *St Ephrem the Syrian*, Washington, DC: Catholic University of America Press, 1994.

Meijering, E. P. "The Doctrine of the Will and the Trinity in the Orations of Gregory of Nazianzen," in *God Being History: Studies in Patristic Philosophy*, ed. E. P. Meijering, Amsterdam: North Holland Publishing Company, 1975, 224–234.

= "God Cosmos History: Christian and Neo-platonic Views on Divine Revelation," *Vigiliae Christianae*, 28 (1974), 248–276.

Menze, Volker L. *Justinian and the Making of the Syrian Orthodox Church*, Oxford: Oxford University Press, 2008.

Meredith, Anthony, SJ. "Gregory of Nyssa and Plotinus," *Studia Patristica*, 17(3) (1982), 1120–1126.

Metallidis, George. "Theology and Gnoseology and the Formation of Doctrine in St John Damascene," *Studia Patristica*, 42 (2006), 341–346.

Meyendorff, John. "Byzantine Views of Islam," *Dumbarton Oaks Papers*, 18 (1964), 115–132.

= *Christ in Eastern Christian Thought*, Washington, DC: St Vladimir's Seminary Press, 1975.

= *Imperial Unity and Christian Divisions: the Church 450–680 AD*, Crestwood, NY: St Vladimir's Seminary Press, 1989.

Mingana, Alphonse. "The Apology of Timothy the Patriarch before the Caliph Mahdi," *Bulletin of the John Rylands Library*. 12 (1928), 137–292.

Sources Syriaques, Leipzig: Harrassowitz, 1908.

Woodbrooke Studies: Christian Documents in Syriac, Arabic and Garshūni, Edited and Translated with a Critical Apparatus, Vol. 2, Cambridge: Heffer, 1928.

= "The Dialogue of Patriarch Timothy I and the Caliph al-Mahdi," in *The Early Christian-Muslim Dialogue: A Collection of Documents from the First Three Islamic Centuries (632–900 A. D.): Translations with Commentary*, ed. N. A. Newman, Hatfield, PA: Interdisciplinary Biblical Research Institute, 1993, 169–267.

Montada, Josep Puig. "Philosophy in Andalusia: Ibn Bājja and Ibn Ṭufayl," in *The Cambridge Companion to Arabic Philosophy*, ed. Peter Adamson and Richard C. Taylor, Cambridge: Cambridge University Press, 2005, 155–179.

Moorhead, John. "The Monophysite Response to the Arab Invasions," *Byzantion*, 51 (1981), 579–591.

Morewedge, Parviz (ed.). *Neoplatonism and Islamic Thought*, Albany: State University of New York, 1992.

Morony, Michael G. "The Age of Conversions: A Reassessment," in *Conversion and Continuity: Indigenous Christian Communities in Islamic Lands, Eighth to Eighteenth Centuries*, ed. Michael Gervers and Ramzī J. Bikh'āzī, Toronto: Pontifical Institute of Medieval Studies, 1990, 135–150

Muir, William. *The Apology of Al Kindy, Written at the Court of Al-Mamun, in Defence of Christianity*, London: Smith, Elder & Co., 1887.

Muller, Richard A. *Dictionary of Latin and Greek Theological Terms*, Grand Rapids, MI: Baker Books, 1985.

Murray, Robert. "The Characteristics of the Earliest Syriac Christianity," in *East of Byzantium: Syria and Armenian in the Formative Period*, ed. N. Garsoïan; T. Mathews and R. Thompson (Washington, DC: Dumbarton Oaks, 1982), 3–16.

Symbols of Church and Kingdom: A Study in Early Syriac Tradition, Cambridge: Cambridge University Press, 1977.

"The Theory of Symbolism in St Ephrem's Theology," *Parole de l'Orient*, 6 – 7 (1975 – 1976), 1 – 20.
Muslim b. al-Ḥajjāj al-Qushayrī, *Ṣaḥīḥ Muslim*, ed. Muḥammad F. ʿAbd al-Bāqī, Cairo: Dār Iḥyāʾ al-Kutub al-ʿArabiyya, 1955
Nagel, Tilman. *Geschichte der Islamischen Theologie*, Munich: Verlag C.H. Beck, 1994; in English translation, *The History of Islamic Theology: From Muhammad to the Present*, trans. Thomas Thornton, Princeton, NJ: Markus Wiener, 2010.
Naṣrī, Wafīq, SJ *Abū Qurrah wa-al-Maʾmūn: Al-Mujādalah*, Beirut: CEDRAC/Jounieh: Librairie St Paul, 2010.
= "Abū Qurrah, Al-Ma'mūn and Yaḥyā Ibn Akṯam," *Parole de l'Orient*, 32 (2007), 285 – 290.
Nassif, Bassam A. "Religious Dialogue in the Eighth Century: Example from Theodore Abū Qurrah Treatise," *Parole de l'Orient*, 30 (2005), 333 – 340.
Nau, F. "Dialogue between the Patriarch John I and the Amir of the Hagarenes," in *The Early Christian-Muslim Dialogue: A Collection of Documents from the First Three Islamic Centuries (632 – 900 AD), Translations with Commentary*, ed. N.A. Newman, Hatfield, PA: Interdisciplinary Biblical Research Institute, 1993, 11 – 46.
Neusner, Jacob. *From Tradition to Imitation: The Plan and Program of Pesiqta Rabbatic and Pesiqta de Rab Kahana*, Brown Judaic Series 80, Atlanta: Scholars Press, 1987.
Nevo Yehuda D. and Judith Koren. *Crossroads to Islam: The Origins of the Arab Religion and the Arab State*, Amherst, NY: Prometheus Books, 2003.
Newman, N.A. (ed.). *The Early Christian-Muslim Dialogue: A Collection of Documents from the First Three Islamic Centuries (632 – 900 A.D.): Translations with Commentary*, Hatfield, PA: Interdisciplinary Biblical Research Institute, 1993.
Nicholson, Reynold A. (trans.). *Rūmī: Poet and Mystic*, London: Oneworld, 1995.
Nöldeke, Theodore. *Sketches from Eastern History*, trans. John S. Black, London: Adam & Charles Black, 1892; repr. Kessinger, 2007.
Norris, Frederick. *Faith Gives Fullness to Reasoning: Five Theological Orations of Gregory Nazianzen*, Leiden: Brill, 1990.
Norris, Richard A. *God and the World in Early Christian Theology*, New York: Seabury Press, 1965.
Öhlig, Karl Heinz. *Der frühe Islam: Eine historisch-kritische Rekonstruktion anhand Zeitgenösischer Quellen*, Berlin: Hans Schiler, 2007.
= "Syrian and Arabian Christianity and the Qur'ān," in *The Hidden Origins of Islam: New Research into Its Early History*, ed. Karl-Heinz Ohlig and Gerd-R. Puin, Amherst, NY: Prometheus Books, 2010, 361 – 401.
= and Gerd-R. Puin. *The Hidden Origins of Islam: New Research into Its Early History*, Amherst, NY: Prometheus Books, 2010.
O'Leary, D.E. *How Greek Science Passed to the Arabs*, London: Goodword Books, 1949.
Olster, David. "Ideological Transformation and the Evolution of Imperial Presentation in the Wake of Islam's Victory," in *The Encounter of Eastern Christianity with Early Islam*, ed. Emmanouela Grypeou; Mark Swanson and David Thomas, Leiden: Brill, 2006, 45 – 72.
= "Justinian, Rhetoric and the Church," *Bzyantinoslavica*, 50 (1989), 65 – 76.
'Omar, Fāroq, "Some Observation on the Reign of the Abbasid Caliph al-Madhi 185/775 – 196/785," in *Arabica*, 2(21), 1974, pp. 139 – 150
Osborn, Kenan B. "The Trinity in Bonaventure," in *The Cambridge Companion to the Trinity*, ed. Peter C. Phan, Cambridge: Cambridge University Press, 2011, 108 – 127.

ʿOṣmān, Ghāda, "Pre-Islamic Arab Converts to Christianity in Mecca and Medina: An Investigation into the Arabic Sources," *The Muslim World*, 95 (2005), 67–80.

Ouspensky, Leonid. *Theology of the Icon*, trans. Anthony Gythiel and Elizabeth Meyendorff, 2 vols, Crestwood, NY: St Vladimir's Seminary Press, 1992.

Oxford Dictionary of the Christian Church, ed. E.A. Livingston, Oxford: Oxford University Press, 1997.

Palmer, Andrew, Sebastian Brock and Robert Hoyland (eds and trans.). *The Seventh Century in the West-Syrian Chronicles*, Liverpool: Liverpool University Press, 1993.

Pannenberg, Wolfhart. *Systematic Theology*, Vol. 1, trans. Geoffrey W. Bromiley, Grand Rapids, MI: W.B. Eerdmans, 2001.

Papademetriou, George C. (ed.) *Two Traditions, One Space: Orthodox Christians and Muslims in Dialogue*, Boston, MA: Somerset Hall Press, 2011.

Papanikolaou, Aristotle, "Is John Zizioulas an Existentialist in Discourse? Response to Lucian Turcesco," *Modern Theology*, 20(4) (2004), 601–607.

Parrinder, Geoffrey. *Jesus in the Qur'an*, Oxford: Oneworld, 1995.

Parry, Ken (ed.). *The Blackwell Companion to Eastern Christianity*, Oxford and Malden: Blackwell, 2010.

Patronos, George. "Jesus as a Prophet of Islam," trans. George C. Papademetriou, in *Two Traditions, One Space: Orthodox Christians and Muslims in Dialogue*, ed. George C. Papademetriou, Boston, MA: Somerset Hall Press, 2011, 15–36.

Paulsen, David L. "Early Christian Belief in a Corporeal Deity: Origen and Augustine as Reluctant Witnesses," in *Harvard Theological Review*, 83:2(1990), pp. 105–116.

Pelikan, Jaroslav. *The Christian Tradition: A History of the Development of Doctrine*, Vol. 2: *The Spirit of Eastern Christendom (600–1700)*, Chicago, IL: University of Chicago Press, 1974.

Percival, Henry R. *The Seven Ecumenical Councils of the Undivided Church, their Canons and Dogmatic Decrees,* in *Nicene and Post-Nicene Fathers*, ed. P. Schaff and H. Wace. 2nd ser. Oxford: Benediction Classics, 2011.

Perl, Eric. *Methexis: Creation, Incarnation and Deification in Saint Maximus Confessor*, PhD Diss., Yale University, 1991.

Perrone, L. "Four Gospels, Four Councils – One Lord Jesus Christ: The Patristic Development of Christology within the Church of Palestine," *Liber Annuus Studium Biblicum Franciscanum*, 49 (1999), 357–396.

Peters, Johannes R.T.M. *God's Created Speech: A Study in the Speculative Theology of the Mu'tazilî Qâḍî l-Quḍât Abû l-Ḥasan ʿAbd al-Jabbâr bn Aḥmad al-Hamaḏânî*, Leiden: Brill, 1976.

Petersen, William L. "The Christology of Aphrahat, the Persian Sage: An Excursus on the 17th *Demonstration*," *Vigiliae Christianae*, 46 (1992), 241–256.

Phan, Peter C (ed.). *The Cambridge Companion to the Trinity*, Cambridge: Cambridge University Press, 2011.

Phillips, Dewi Z. *Faith after Foundationalims: Plantinga – Rorty – Lindbeck – Berger: Critiques and Alternatives*, Boulder, CO: Westview Press, 1995.

Phillips, F.E. *Scholia on Passages of the Old Testament by Mar Jacob, Bishop of Edessa*, London: Williams and Norgate, 1864.

Pines, Shlomo, "Some Traits of Christian Theological Writing in Relation to Moslem *Kalām* and to Jewish Thought," *Proceedings of the Israel Academy of Science and the Humanities*, 5 (1976).

Pinggéra, Karl, "Johannes I. (III.) von Antiochien ('Johannes Sedra')," in *Giographisch-Bibliographisches Kirchenlexicon*, 23(2004), pp. 734–737.
Popov, Radko, "Speaking His Mind in a Multi-Cultural and Multi-Religious Society: John of Damascus and His Knowledge of Islam in Chapter 101 ("The Heresy of the Ishmaelites") of His Work Concerning Heresy," in *Two Traditions One Space: Orthodox Christians and Muslims in Dialogue*, ed. George C. Papademetriou, Boston, MA: Somerset Hall Press, 2011, 109–143.
Portillo, Rocio Daga. "The Arabic Life of St John of Damascus," *Parole de l'Orient*, 21 (1996), 157–188.
Possekel, Uti. *Evidences of Greek Philosophical Concepts in the Writings of Ephrem the Syrian*, Leuven: Peeters, 1999.
Potts, D. T. "Camel Hybridization and the Role of *Camelus Bactrianus* in the Ancient Near East," *Journal of the Economic & Social History of the Orient*, 47(2) (2004), 143–165.
Prestige, G. L. *God in Patristic Thought*, London: SPCK, 1981.
Qāchā, Suhayl. *Ṣafaḥāt min Tārīkh al-Masīhiyyīn al-ʿArab Qabl al-Islām* (Pages from the history of the Christian Arabs before Islam), Jounieh: Paulist Press, 2005.
ar-Rassī, al-Qāsim ibn Ibrāhīm ibn Ismāʿil. *Ar-Radd ʿalā an-Naṣārā* (Response to the Christians), ed. Imām Ḥanafī ʿAbdullāh, Cairo: Dār al-Āfāq al-ʿArabiyyah, 2000.
Reed, William L. and Fredric V. Winnett (eds.). *Ancient Records from North Arabia*, Toronto: University of Toronto Press, 1970.
Reinink, Garrit J. "The Beginning of Syriac Apologetic Literature in Response to Islam," *Oriens Christianus*, 7 (1993), 165–187.
Reisman, David C. "Al-Fārābī and the Philosophical Curriculum," in *The Cambridge Companion to Arabic Philosophy*, ed. Peter Adamson and Richard C. Taylor, Cambridge: Cambridge University Press, 2005), 52–71.
Reller, Jobst. "Christian Views of Muslims in Syria before 1300 AD, Some Remarks on Christian-Muslim-Relations," *Ostkirchliche Studien*, 59(1) (2010), 55–69.
Retsö, J. "The Earliest Arabs," *Orientalic Suecova*, 38/39 (1989–1990), 131–139.
Reynolds, Gabriel Said (ed.). *The Qur'ān in Its Historical Context*, London: Routledge, 2008.
Riedinger, Rudolf. "Die Lateransynode von 649 und Maximos de Bekenner," in *Maximus Confessor: Actes du Symposium sur Maxime le Confesseur, Fribourg 2–5 September 1980*, ed. Felix Heinzer and Christoph Schönborn, Fribourg: Editions Universitaires, 1982, 111–121.
Richardson, Alan and John Bowden (eds). *A New Dictionary of Christian Theology*, London: SCM Press, 1989.
Ridgeon, Lloyd. "Christianity as Portrayed by Jalāl al-Dīn Rūmī," in *Islamic Interpretations of Christianity*, ed. Lloyd Ridgeon, Richmond, UK: Curzon, 2001, 99–126
Robertson, David G. "Stoic and Aristotelian Notions of Substance in Basil of Caesarea," *Vigiliae Christianae*, 52 (1998), 393–417.
Robertson, Jon M. *Christ as Mediator: A Study of the Theologies of Eusebius of Caesarea, Marcellus of Ancyra and Athanasius of Alexandria*, Oxford: Oxford University Press, 2007.
Robinson, Chase F. *Empire and Elites after the Muslim Conquest: The Transformation of Northern Mesopotamia*, Cambridge: Cambridge University Press, 2000.
Roggema, Barbara. "A Christian Reading of the Qurʾān: The Legend of Sergius-Baḥīrā and Its Use in Qurʾān and Sīra," in *Syrian Christians under Islam, the First Thousand Years*, ed. David Thomas, Leiden: Brill, 2001, 57–74.

= "*Ḥikāyāt Amthāl Wa Asmār* ... King Parables in Melkite Apologetic Literature," in *Studies on the Christian Arabic Heritage, in Honour of Father Prof. Dr Samir Khalil Samir S.I. at the Occasion of His Sixty-Fifth Birthday*, =ed Rifaat Ebied and Herman Teule, Leuven: Peeters, 2004, 113–131.

"Muslims and Crypto-Idolaters: A Theme in the Christian Portrayal of Islam in the Near East," in *Christians at the Heart of Islamic Rule, Church Life and Scholarship in 'Abbasid Iraq*, ed. D. Thomas, Leiden: Brill, 2003, 1–18.

= Barbara Roggema, "The Disputation of John and the Emir," in *Christian-Muslim Relations, A Biographical History (600–900)*, Vol. I, pp. 782–785.

Rosenthal, Franz. *The Classical Heritage of Islam*, trans. Emile and Jenny Marmorstein, London: Routledge, 1994.

Rousseau, Philip and Jutta Raithal (eds). *A Companion to Late Antiquity*, Chichester: Blackwell, 2009.

= *Transformations of Late Antiquity: Essays for Peter Brown*, Farnham, UK: Ashgate, 2009.

Rouwhorst, G. "Jewish Liturgical Traditions in Early Syriac Christianity," in *Vigiliae Christianae*, 51 (1997), 72–93.

Roy, Olivier. *Holy Ignorance: When Religion and Culture Part Ways*, trans. Ros Schwartz, London: Hurst, 2010.

Rubin, Milka. "Arabization Versus Islamazation in the Palestinian Melkite Community during the Early Muslim Period," in *Sharing the Sacred: Religious Contacts and Conflicts in the Holy Land, First-Fifteenth Centuries CE*, ed. Guy G. Stroumsa and Arieh Kofsky, Jerusalem. Yad Izhak Ben Zvi, 1998, pp. 149–162.

Ar-Rūmī, Jelāluldīn. *The Rūmī Collection*, ed. Kabīr Helminski, Boston, MA: Shambala, 1998.

Russel, Paul S. *St. Ephraem the Syrian and St Gregory the Theologian Confront the Arians*, Kerala: St Ephraem Ecumenical Research Institute, 1994.

Saadī, Abdul-Massīḥ, "Nascent Islam in the Seventh Century Syriac Sources," in *The Qur'ān in its Historical Context*; ed. Gabriel Said Reynolds, London: Routledge, 2008, 217–222.

Sahas, Daniel J. "The Arab Character of the Christian Disputation with Islam: The Case of John of Damascus (ca. 655-ca. 749)," in *Religionsgespräche im Mittelalter*, ed. Bernard Lewis and Friedrich Niewöhner, Wiesbaden: Otto Harrassowitz, 1992, 185–205.

= "The Art and Non-Art of Byzantine Polemics: Patterns of Refutation in Byzantine Anti-Islamic Literature," in *Conversion and Continuity: Indigenous Christian Communities in Islamic Land*, ed. Michael Gervers and Ramzī J. Bikh'āzī, Ontario: Pontifical Institute of Medieval Studies, 1990, 55–73.

= "The Face to Face Encounter between Patriarch Sophronius of Jerusalem and the Caliph 'Umar Ibn Al-Khattāb: Friends of Foes?" in *The Encounter of Eastern Christianity with Early Islam*, ed. Emmanouela Grypeou, Mark Swanson and David Thomas, Leiden: Brill, 2006, 33–44,

= "'Holosphyros'? A Byzantine Perception of 'The God of Muhammad'," in *Christian-Muslim Encounters*, ed. Yvonne Yazbeck Ḥaddād and Wadī' Zaidān Ḥaddād, Gainesville: University Press of Florida, 1995, 109–125.

Icon and Logos: Sources in Eighth-Century Iconoclasm, Toronto: University of Toronto Press, 1986.

= *John of Damascus on Islam: The 'Heresy of the Ishmaelites'*, Leiden: Brill, 1972.

= "Why Did Heraclius Not Defend Jerusalem, and Fight the Arabs?" *Parole de l'Orient*, 24 (1999), 79–97.

Sako, Louis. "Does the Council of Ephesus Unite or Divide?", in *Syriac Dialogue: Second Non-Official Consultation on Dialogue within the Syriac Tradition*, ed. A. Shternman and G. Wolflinger, Vienna: Pro Orente, 1996, 158–163.

Samir, Samir Khalil. *Abū Qurrah: Al-mu'allafāt* (Abū Qurrah: Works), Beirut: Dar al-Mashriq, 2000.

= *Abū Qurrah: Al-sīrah wa-al-marāji*ʿ (Abū Qurrah: Life and sources), Beirut: Dār al-Mashriq, 2000.

= (ed.). *Actes du Premier Congrés International d'Études Arabes Chrétiennes*, Pizza: Pontificium Institutum Studiorum Orientalium, 1982.

= "The Earliest Arab Apology for Christianity (c. 750)," in *Christian Arabic Apologetics during the Abbasid Period (750–1258)*, ed. S.K. Samir and J.S. Nielsen, Leiden: Brill, 1994, 57–114.

= "Kitāb jāmiʿ wujūh al-īmān wa-mujādalat Abī Qurrah ʿan ṣalb al-Masīḥ," *Al-Maçarrat*, 70 (1984),. 411–427.

= "Lāhūt al-Sharq al-Adnā al-Ḥadīth fī al-Ṣila bayn al-Ḥawiyya wal-Ghayriyyah" (The theology of the Near East on the link between identity and otherness)," *Al-Mashriq*, 75 (1) (2001), 25–55.

= "The Prophet Muḥammad as Seen by Timothy I and Other Arab Christian Authors," in *Syrian Chrisians under Islam, the First Thousand Years*, ed. David Thomas, Leiden,: Brill, 2001, 75–106.

= "Religion et culture en Proche-Orient: arabe-islam et christianisme comme facteurs d'intégration et d'éclament," *Proche-Orient Chrétien*, 39 (1989), 251–309.

= *The Significance of Early Arab-Christian Thought for Muslim-Christian Understanding*, Washington, DC: Center for Muslim-Christian Understanding, History and International Affairs, 1997

= "La somme des aspects de la foi, œuvre de Abū Qurrah?" in *Actes du quatrième congrès international d'ètudes arabes chrètiennes, II*, ed. Samir Khalil, *Parole de l'Orient*, 1986, 93–121,

= "The Theological Christian Influence on the Qur'ān: A Reflection," in *The Qur'ān in its Historical Context*, ed. Gabriel Said Reynolds, London: Routledge, 2008, 141–162.

= and Jørgen S. Nielsen (eds). *Christian Arabic Apologetics during the Abbasid Period (750–1258)*, Leiden: Brill, 1994.

Schadler, Peter, "The Dialogue between a Saracen and a Christian," in *Christian-Muslim Relations, A Bibliographical History (600–900)*, David Thomas and Barbara Roggema, et. al., (Leiden: Brill, 2009), Vol. 1, pp. 367–370.

Schick, Robert. *The Christian Communities of Palestine from Byzantine to Islamic Rule: A Historical and Archaeological Study*, Princeton, NJ: Princeton University Press, 1995.

Schwöbel, Christoph and Colin Gunton (eds). *Persons, Divine and Human*, Edinburgh: T&T Clark, 1991.

Seale, Morris S. *Muslim Theology: A Study of Origins with Reference to the Church Fathers*, London: Luzac, 1964.

Sfar, Mondher. *In Search of the Original Koran: The True History of the Revealed Text*, Amherst, NY: Prometheus Books, 2007.

Shahīd, 'Irfān, "Byzantium in South Arabic," *Dumbarton Oaks Papers*, 33 (1979), 25–94.

= *Byzantium and the Arabs in the Fifth Century*, Washington, DC: Dumbarton Oaks Library and Collection, 1989.

= *Byzantium and the Arabs in the Sixth Century*, 2 vols, Washington, DC: Dumbarton

Oaks, 1995.
= "Islam and *Oriens Christianus:* Makka 610–622 AD." in *The Encounter of Eastern Christianity with Early Islam*, ed. Emmanouela Grypeou, Mark Swanson and David Thomas, Leiden: Brill, 2006, 9–32
= *The Martyrs of Najrān: New Documents*, Subsidia Hagiographica, 49, Brussels: Soc. des Bollandistes, Bd. Saint-Michel, 1971.
= "The Martyrs of Najrān: Miscellaneous Reflexions," *Le Muséon*, 93 (1980), 149–161.
ash-Shahristānī, *Kitāb al-Milall wan-Niḥal* (The book of religious sects and groups), ed. W. Cureton, London: Society for the Publication of Oriental Texts, 1846.
Sharf, Andrew. *Byzantine Jewry, from Justinian to the Fourth Crusade*, New York: Oxford University Press, 1984.
Shboul, Aḥmad M. H. "Arab Islamic Perceptions of Byzantine Religion and Culture," in *Muslim Perceptions of Other Religions: A Historical Survey*, ed. Jacques Waardenburg, New York: Oxford University Press, 1999, 122–135.
Shepardson, Christine. "Syria, Syriac, Syrian: Negotiating East and West," in *A Companion to Late Antiquity*, ed. Philip Rousseau and Jutta Raithel, Chichester: Blackwell, 2009, 455–466.
Siecienski, A. Edward. "The Authenticity of Maximus the Confessor's *Letter to Marinus:* The Argument from Theological Consistency," *Vigiliae Christianae*, 61 (2007), 189–227.
= *The Filioque: History of a Doctrinal Controversy*, Oxford: Oxford University Press, 2010.
Singh, David Emmanuel (ed.). *Reflections of Christians from Islamic Contexts*, Eugene, OR: Wipf & Stock, 2011.
= "'The Word Made Flesh': Community, Dialogue and Witness," in *Jesus and the Incarnation: Reflections of Christians from Islamic Contexts*, ed. David Emmanuel Singh, Eugene, OR: Wipf & Stock, 2011, 3–18
Smith, E. and C.V.A Van Dyck. *Brief Documentary History of the Translation of the Scriptures into the Arabic Language*, Beirut: American Presbyterian Mission Press, 1990.
Sophronius. *Christmas Sermon*, ed. H. Usener, *Weihnachtspredigt des Sophronios*, *Rheinisches Museum Fuer Philologie*, 41 (1886), 500–516.
= *Epistola Synodica*, in *Patrologiae Graecae Cursus Completus*, ed. J.P. Migne, Vol. 87, Paris,1866,
Soro, Mar Bawai. "Does the Council of Ephesus Unite or Divide: Re-evaluation of the Council of Ephesus – The Point of View of the Assyrian Oriental Church", in *Syriac Dialogue: Second Non-Official Consultation on Dialogue within the Syriac Tradition*, ed. A. Stirnemann and G. Wilflinger, Vienna: Pro Oriente, 1996, 179–204.
Stein, D. *Der Beginn des byzantinischen Bilderstreites und seine Entwicklung bis in die 40er Jahre des 8. Jahrhunderts*, Miscellanea Byzantina Monacensia 25, Munich: Institut für Byzantinistik und Neugriechische Philologie der Universität München, 1980.
Stead, Christopher G. "The Concept of Divine Substance," *Vigiliae Christianae*, 29 (1975), 1–14.
= *Divine Substance*, Oxford: Clarendon Press, 1977.
= "Why Not Three Gods? The Logic of Gregory of Nyssa's Trinitarian Doctrine," in *Studien zu Gregor von Nyssa und der christlichen Spätanke*, ed. Hubertus Drobner and Christoph Kock, Leiden: Brill, 1990, 149–162.
Stramara, Daniel F., Jr. "Gregory of Nyssa's Terminology for Trinitarian Perichoresis," *Vigiliae Christianae*, 52 (1998), 257–263.
Straub, Johannes (ed.). *Acta Conciliorum Oecumenicorum*, Berlin: Walter de Gruyter, 1971.

Studer, Basil. *Die theologische Arbeitsweise des Johannes von Damaskus*, Ettal, Germany: Buch-Kunstverlag, 1956.
= *Augustine De Trinitate, Eine Einführung*, Paderborn: Ferdinand Schöningh, 2005.
= *Trinity and Incarnation: The Faith of the Early Church*, Matthias Westerhodd (trans.), Andrew Louth (ed.), Edinburgh: T&T Clark, 1993.

Swanson, Mark N. "Are Hypostases Attributes? An Investigation into the Modern Egyptian Christian Appropriation of the Medieval Arabic Apologetic Heritage," *Parole de l'Orient*, 16 (1990–1991), 239–250.
= "Beyond Prooftexting: Approaches to the Qur'ān in Some Early Arabic Christian Apologies," *The Muslim World*, 88(3–4) (1998), 297–319.
= "Ibn Taymiyyah and the *Kitāb al-Burhān:* A Muslim Controversalist Responds to a Ninth-Century Arabic Christian Apology," in *Christian-Muslim Encounters*, ed. Yvonne Yazbeck Ḥaddād and Wadīʿ Zaidān Ḥaddād, Gainesville: University Press of Florida, 1995, 95–107.
= "The Martyrdom of ʿAbd al-Masīḥ, Superior of Mount Sinai (Qays al-Ghassani)," in *Syrian Christians under Islam: The First Thousand Years*, ed. David Thomas, Leiden: Brill, 2001, 107–130.
= "Some Considerations for the Dating of *Fī Tathlīth Allāh al-Wāḥid* (Sinai Ar. 154) and *Aj-Jāmiʿ wujūh al-Īmān* (London British Library Or. 4950)," in *Actes du quatrième congrès international d'ètudes arabes chrètiennes*, ed. Samir Khalil Samir, *Parole de l'Orient*, 18 (1993), 117–141.
= "The Trinity in Christian-Muslim Conversation," *Dialog: A Journal of Theology*, 44(3) (2005), 256–263.

Sweetman, James W. *Islam and Christian Theology: A Study of the Interpretation of Theological Ideas in the Two Religions*, 4 vols, Cambridge: James Clark, 2002.

aṭ-Ṭabarānī, Sulaymān b. Aḥmad. *Musnad al-Shamiyyīn*, ed. Ḥamdī ʿAbd al-Majīd al-Silafī, 4 vols, Beirut: Muʾassasat al-Risāla, 1996.

aṭ-Ṭabarī, ʿAlī b. Rabbān. *Al-dīn wad-Dawla: Fī Īthbāt Nubuwwāt al-Nabī Muḥammad* (Religion and the state: On the verification of the prophethood of the Prophet Muḥammad), ed. ʿĀdil Nuwayhiḍ, Beirut: Dār al-Āfāq aj-Jadīdah, 1982.

Taft, Robert F. *Liturgy in Byzantium and Beyond*, Aldershot: Ashgate , 1995.

Tanner, R. G. "Stoic Influence on the Logic of St. Gregory of Nyssa," *Studia Patristica*, 18 (3) (1989), 557–584

Tartar, George (ed.). *Risālatān fī al-Ḥiwār waj-Jadal bayn al-Masiḥiyya wal-Islām fī ʿahd al-Maʾmūn (C. 813–834 AD)* (Two Epistles on Dialogue and Debate between Christianity and Islam in the Era of the Caliph al-Maʾmūn [c. 813–834 AD]), Paris: Asmar, 2011.

Theological Dictionary of the New Testament, ed. Gerhard Friedrich, trans. Geoffrey Bromiley, Grand Rapids, MI: Eerdmans , 1968.

Theophanes, *Anni Mundi 6095–6305 (A. D. 602–813)*, ed. and trans. Harry Turtledove, Philadelphia: University of Pennsylvania Press, 1982.

Theophylact Simocatta, *History*, trans. Michael and Mary Whitby, Oxford: Oxford University Press, 1986

Tertullian, *Against Praxias*, in *The Ante-Nicene Fathers*, Vol. 3, ed. Robert Alexander and James Donaldson, Grand Rapids, MI: Eerdmans, 1968.

Thomas, David. *Anti-Christian Polemic in Early Islam: Abū ʿĪsā al-Warrāq's "Against the Trinity"*, Cambridge: Cambridge University Press, 1992.

(ed.), *The Bible in Arab Christianity*, Leiden: Brill, 2007.
= "Changing Attitudes of Arab Christians towards Islam," *Transformation*, 22(1) (2005), 10–19.
= *Christian Doctrines in Islamic Theology*, Leiden: Brill, 2008.
= "Christian Theologians and New Questions," in *The Encounter of Eastern Christianity with Early Islam*, ed. Emmanouela Grypeou, Mark Swanson and David Thomas, Leiden: Brill, 2006, 257–276.
= "The Doctrine of the Trinity in the Early Abbasid Era," in *Islamic Interpretations of Christianity*, ed. Lloyd Ridgeon, Richmond, UK: Curzon, 2001, 78–98.
= *Early Muslim Polemic against Christianity: Abū ʿĪsā al-Warrāq's "Against the Incarnation"*, Cambridge: Cambridge University Press, 2002.
= "Early Muslim Responses to Christianity," in *Christians at the Heart of Islamic Rule*, ed. David Thomas, Leiden: Brill, 2003, 231–254,
= (ed.). *Syrian Christians under Islam, the First Thousand Years*, Leiden: Brill, 2001.
= and Clare Amos (eds). *A Faithful Presence: Essays for Kenneth Cragg*, London: Melisende, 2003.
= and Barbara Roggema (eds.). *Christian-Muslim Relations, a Bibliographical History*, Vol. 1: *600–900*, Leiden: Brill, 2009.

Thunberg, Lars. *Man and the Cosmos in the Vision of St Maximus the Confessor*, Crestwood, NY: St Vladimir's Seminary Press, 1985.
Microcosm and Mediator: The Theological Anthropology of Maximus the Confessor, 2nd ed., Peru, IL: Open Court, 1995.

Tolan, John V (ed.). *Medieval Christian Perceptions of Islam*, New York: Routledge, 2000.
= *Saracens: Islam in the Medieval European Imagination*, New York: Columbia University Press, 2002.

Tollefsen, Torstein Theodor. *The Christocentric Cosmology of St Maximus the Confessor*, Oxford: Oxford University Press, 2008.

Törönen, Melchisedec. *Union and Distinction in the Thought of St Maximus the Confessor*, Oxford: Oxford University Press, 2007.

Torrance, Iain R. *Christology after Chalcedon: Severus of Antioch and Sergius the Monophysite*, Eugene, OR: Wipf and Stock Publishers, 1998.

Treiger, Alexander, "Could Christ's Humanity See His Divinity? An Eighth-Century Controversy between John of Dalyatha and Timothy I, Catholicos of the Church of the East," *Journal of the Canadian Society for Syriac Studies*, 9 (2009), 3–21.
= "Al-Ghazālī's 'Mirror Christology' and Its Possible East-Syriac Sources," *The Muslim World*, 101 (2011), 698–713.

Trimingham, J. Spencer. *Christianity among the Arabs in Pre-Islamic Times*, London: Longman, 1979.

Turcescu, Lucian. *Gregory of Nyssa and the Concept of Divine Persons*, Oxford: Oxford University Press, 2005.
= "'Person' Versus 'Individual', and Other Modern Misreadings of Gregory of Nyssa," *Modern Theology*, 4(18) (2002), 527–539.
= "*Prosopon* and *Hypostasis* in Basil of Caesarea's *Against Eunomius* and the Epistles," *Vigiliae Christianae*, 51 (1997), 374–395.

van Ess, Josef. *The Flowering of Muslim Theology*, trans. Jane Marie Todd, Cambridge, MA: Harvard University Press, 2006.

= *Theologie und Gesellschaft im 2 und 3. Jahrhundert Hidschra: Eine Geschichte des religiösen Denkens im frühen Islam*, Berlin & New York: Walter De Gruyter, 1991, Vol. II.
van Ginkel, Jan J., "The Reception and Presentation of the Arab Conquest in Syriac Historiography: How Did the Changing Social Position of the Syrian Orthodox Community Influence the Account of their Historiographers," in *The Encounter of Eastern Christianity with Early Islam*, ed. Emmanouela Grypeou; Mark Swanson and David Thomas, Leiden: Brill, 2006, 171 – 184.
Vaporis, N. M. (ed.). *Orthodox Christians and Muslims*, Brookline, MA: Holy Cross Press, 1986.
Varsanyi, Orsolya. "The Role of the Intellect in Theodore Abū Qurrah's *On the True Religion* in Comparison with His Contemporaries' Use of the Term," *Parole de l'Orient*, 34 (2009), 51 – 60.
Vasiliev, A. A. "The Iconoclastic Edict of the Caliph Yazid II, A. D. 721," *Dumbarton Oaks Papers*, 9 – 10 (1955 – 1956), 25 – 47.
Vine, Aubrey R. *An Approach to Christology*, London: Independent Press, 1948.
von Grunebaum, G. "Byzantine Iconoclasm and the Influence of the Islamic Environment," *History of Religions*, 2 (1962), 1 – 10.
Vööbus, A. *History of the School of Nisibis*, CSCO 266, Louvain: Peeters, 1965.
"New Sources for the Symbol in Early Syrian Christianity," in *Vigiliae Christianae*, 26 (1972), 291 – 296.
Vryonis, Speros. *The Decline of Medieval Hellenism in Asia Minor and the Process of Islamization from the Eleventh through the Fifteenth Century*, Aldershot: Ashgate Variorum, 2001.
Waardenburg, Jacques. *Muslims and Others: Relations in Context*, Berlin: Walter de Gruyter, 2003.
= (ed.) *Muslim Perceptions of Other Religions: A Historical Survey*, New York: Oxford University Press, 1999.
Wallace-Hadrill, D. S. *Christian Antioch: A Study of Early Christian Thought in the East*, Cambridge: Cambridge University Press, 1982.
Waltzer, R. *Greek into Arabic: Essays ion Islamic Philosophy*, Oxford: Oxford University Press, 1962.
Ward, Marcus. *The Byzantine Church: An Introduction to the Study of Eastern Christianity*, Madras: Christian Literature Society, 1953
Ware, Kallistos, "Christian Theology in the East 600 – 1453," in *A History of Christian Doctrine*, ed. Hubert Cunliff-Jones, Edinburgh: T&T Clark, 1997, 183 – 226.
The Orthodox Church, Baltimore, MD: Penguin, 1969.
Watt, W. Montgomery. "The Christianity Criticized in the Qur'an," *The Muslim World*, 57 (1967), 197 – 201.
= *The Formative Period of Islamic Thought*, Edinburgh: Edinburgh University Press, 1973.
Webb, C. *God and Personality*, New York: Macmillan, 1918.
Wendebourg, Dorothea. "From the Cappadocian Fathers to Gregory Palamas: The Defeat of Trinitarian Theology," *Studia Patristica*, 17 (1982), 194 – 197.
Wessels, Antonie. *Arab and Christian? Christians in the Middle East*, Kampen: Kok Pharos, 1995.
Whitby, Michael and Mary (trans.). *The History of Theophylact Simocatta: An English Translation with Introduction and Notes*, Oxford: Clarendon Press, 1986.

Whitby, Mary. *The Propaganda of Power: the Role of Panegyric in Late Antiquity*, Leiden: Brill, 1998.
Wickham, L.R. "Severus of Antioch on the Trinity," *Studia Patristica*, 24 (1993), 360–372.
Wilken, Robert L. *The Land Called Holy: Palestine in Christian History and Thought*, New Haven, CT: Yale University Press, 1992.
Wisnovsky, Robert. "Avicenna and the Avicennian Tradition," in *The Cambridge Companion to Arabic Philosophy*, ed. Peter Adamson and Richard C. Taylor, Cambridge: Cambridge University Press, 2005, 92–136.
Witakowski, Witold. "The Syriac Chronicle of Pseudo-Dionysius of Tel-Maḥrē: A Study in the History of Historiography," Motala: Diss., Uppsala University, 1987.
Wolfson, Harry Austryn. "The Muslim Attributes and the Christian Trinity," *Harvard Theological Review*, 49 (1956), 1–18.
= *The Philosophy of the Kalām*, Cambridge, MA: Harvard University Press, 1976.
= "An Unknown Splinter Group of Nestorians," *Revue des Études Augustiniennes*, 6 (1960), 249–253.
Wood, Philip. *'We Have no King but Christ', Christian Political Thought in Greater Syria on the Even of the Arab Conquest (c. 400–585)*, Oxford: Oxford University Press, 2010.
Woodberry, J. Dudley, "The Muslim Understanding of Jesus," *Word & World*, 14(2) (1996), 173–178.
Yannoulatos, Anastasios, "Byzantine and Contemporary Greek Orthodox Approaches to Islam," in *Two Traditions, One Space: Orthodox Christians and Muslims in Dialogue*, ed. George C. Papademetriou, Boston, MA: Somerset Hall Press, 2011, 147–178.
Young, Frances M. *From Nicaea to Chalcedon: A Guide to the Literature and its Background*, London: SCM Press, 1983.
Zadok, R, "Arabians in Mesopotamia during the Late-Assyrian, Chaldean, Achaemenian and Hellenistic Periods," *ZDMG*, 131 (1981), 42–84.
"On Early Arabians in the Fertile Crescent," *Tel Aviv*, 171990), 223–231.
Zaman, Muhammad Qasim. *Religion & Politics under the Early 'Abbāsids, the Emergence of the Proto-Sunnī Elite*, Leiden: Brill, 1997.
Zizioulas, John. *Being as Communion: Studies in Personhood and the Church*,
Crestwood, NY: St Vladimir's Seminary Press, 1993.
= "On Being a Person: Towards an Ontology of Personhood," in *Persons, Divine and Human*, ed. Christoph Schwöbel and Colin Gunton, Edinburgh: T&T Clark, 1991, 33–46.
= "The Teaching of the Second Ecumenical Council on the Holy Spirit in Historical and Ecumenical Perspective," in *Credo in Spiritum Sanctum*, ed. J.S. Martins, Teologia et filosofia 6, Rome: Libraria Editrice Vaticano, 1983, 29–54.

Name Index

ʿAbbās, al-, 48
ʿAbdul-ʿAzīz, ʿUmar b., 209 n.543
Ablabius, 127
Abū Ḥāritha, 229 n.593
Abū Hāshim, 223
Abū Rāʾiṭah, Ḥabīb b. Khidmah, 11, 68, 107, 113, 173, 283, 290, 291, 301
Accad, Martin 71 n.171
Aetius of Antioch, 131 n.334
Afrahat, 140 n.358, 142, 143, 217
Ahrweiler, Hélène, 97, 98
Alfeyev, Hilarion, 140 – 141 n.359
Anastasius of Antioch, 253 n.674
Anastasius the Sinaite, 253 n.674, 327
Anatolios, Khaled, 105 n.271
Al-Anṣārī, ʿUmayr ibn Saʿd, 363
Anselm, 146
Aristotle, 48, 73 n.177, 74
Arius, 121 n.297, 134 – 135 n.343
Arsas, George, 278 n.729
Al-Aṣfahānī, Abū al-Faraj, 275 n.721
Ashʿarī, al-, 216 n.561, 310 n.812
Ashe, Geoffrey, 143 n.368
Athanasius, 118 n.281, 120 – 123, 124, 135 – 136 n. 347, 136 – 137, 138, 139, 155, 157, 230
Augustine, 104, 146, 164, 172, 173 – 178, 179, 181 – 182, 183, 184, 203
Avicenna, 322 n.832, 341
Ayoub, Mahmoud, 287 – 288, 324 – 326
Ayres, Lewis, 230
Āzmaʿ, Rumī bint, 273 n.715

Babai the Great, 275 n.723
Bacha, Constantine, 1 n.3, 5 – 6, 17, 18, 193, 194 – 195, 204, 213, 216 n.562, 218, 349
Baḥīrā, Sargīs, 274
Balādhurī, al-, 27 n.59, 66
Barnes, Michel René, 232, 233 n.605
Basil of Caesarea, 118 – 119, 125 n.313, 126 n.316, 128, 129 – 132, 133 – 134, 135 n.345, 141 n.361, 143, 187, 188 – 189, 190, 191, 232, 233, 239 – 240, 243 – 244, 251, 254, 263
Al-Baṣrī, ʿAmmār, 68, 79 n.191, 113
Al-Baṣrī, al-Ḥasan, 87 n.217
Baum, Wilhelm, 40, 41 n.101, 275 n.721, 279 n.733
Beaumont, Mark, 283 n.744, 299 n.788, 364, 365, 366 n.916, 399 – 400 n.1017, 409 – 410, 425
Beck, E., 140
Beeley, Christopher A., 128 n.325, 133 n.340, 135 – 136 n.347
Begzos, Mario P., 422
Benevich, Gregory I., 398
Berkey, Jonathan P., 66 n.158
Berthold, George C., 181 – 182 n.472, 182
Beser, 95
Block, C. Jonn, 229 n.593
Blowers, Paul M., 246 – 247 n.650, 250
Börjesson, Johannes, 179 – 180
Bonaventure, 236 – 237
Brock, Sebastian, 96, 115 – 116, 117, 138, 140, 141 n.362, 142, 151 n.394, 155 n.406, 158, 160 n.421, 161 n.424, 259 n.695
Burgess, Stanley, 146

Cappadocian fathers, 8, 12, 118 n.281, 123 – 124, 125 n.313, 126 n.316, 128, 136, 138, 139, 143, 149, 157, 164, 187, 188, 203, 217, 231, 232, 243, 248, 251, 253, 261, 263, 264, 341, 386
Cattoi, Thomas, 396
Chadwick, Henry, 177, 178 n.400
Clement of Alexandria, 75, 216 n.563
Constans II, 46, 62
Constantine IV, 64
Constantine V, 83 n.200, 388
Constantine VI, 62
Cook, David, 33 n.81, 59 – 60
Cragg, Kenneth, 277 – 278, 305 n.801, 327, 360, 369, 426
Crone, Patricia, 61
Cross, Richard, 244 n.642
Cyril of Alexandria, 8, 12, 114, 135 – 136 n.347, 136, 138 – 139, 140, 150, 151, 153, 154, 155, 159, 160, 161, 177 n.456, 217,

258 n.692, 270, 272, 275 n.723, 340, 341, 386 n.972, 395 n.1006
Cyril of Scythopolis, 31 – 32, 181
Cyrus of Phasis, 278 n.729

Dakkāsh, Salīm, 107
Daley, Brian, 394 n.1000
Debié, Muriel, 34 – 35
Demacopoulos, George E., 176 – 177
Democritus, 74
Dick, Ignace, 2, 3 n.11, 4 – 6, 17, 18, 92, 93, 99, 218
Dimashqī, Ghaylān ad-, 87 n.217
Al-Dimashquī, Abū al-Ḥusayn, 342 – 343
Diodore of Tarsus, 232 n.604, 405
Dionysius the Areopagite, 131, 237
Dionysius of Tel Maḥrē, 29 – 30, 31, 33 – 34, 36, 49 – 52, 53, 56
Drijvers, Han J. W., 142

Egan, John P., 132 – 133 n.338
Elias of Nesseben, 107
Ephraim the Syrian, 139 – 150, 156 – 157, 158, 217, 341
Epiphanius of Salamis, 177 n.456
Euclid, 74
Eunomius, 124, 126 n.315
Eusebius, 419 n.1055
Eutyches, 161 n.424
Eutychius of Alexandria, 179 n.464
Evagrius, 250 n.662

Fārābī, al-, 307, 310 n.812, 322 n.832
Florovsky, Georges, 245
Fredegarious, 28
Fulford, Ben, 133 n.339

Gabrielius, 181
Galen, 74
Gammala, Athanasius I, 278
Gaon, Saadia, 216 n.561
George of Rish ʿAyna, 29 n.69
Al-Ghassānī, ʿAbd al-Masīḥ al-Najrānī, 44 n.107, 66
Ghazālī, Abū Ḥāmid al-, 367
Graf, Georg, 5, 6
Gregory Nazianzen, 119, 128, 132 – 135, 141 n.361, 144, 147, 149, 177, 181, 187, 188, 190 – 191, 200 – 201, 204, 232 n.603, 234, 240 – 241, 242, 243, 244, 248 – 249, 251 – 254, 257, 263, 390, 419 n.1055
Gregory of Nyssa, 119, 124 – 129, 130, 132, 133 – 134, 135 n.345, 137 – 138 n.350, 140 – 141 n.359, 143, 230, 231 – 233, 239, 246, 258 n.691, 258 n.692, 263, 407
Griffith, Sidney H., 1 n.1, 4, 5, 6, 7, 9, 10 – 11, 18, 39, 45, 53 – 56, 73, 74, 76 n.182, 77, 79, 80 n.193, 82 n.198, 83 n.201, 85 – 86 n.210, 87, 93 n.231, 95 – 96, 99, 106, 107 n.275, 141 n.361, 142 n.364, 178, 180, 218 n.564, 223 n.574, 226 – 227, 235 n.607, 235 n.609, 236 n.610, 267, 272 n.713, 274 n.717, 275 n.723, 276 n.724, 282, 283, 315 – 316 n.822, 327, 381, 420, 423 – 424, 425 – 427
Grillmeier, Aloys, 121 n.297, 123, 124, 135 n.345, 151 – 152, 154 n.405
Guillaume, Alfred, 18
Gutas, Dimitri, 63 – 64 n.155, 71 – 72 n.173, 73

Ḥadithī, al-, 286 – 287
Ḥakīm, ʿNaṣṭūr al-, 222, 223, 225, 226 n.580
Haldon, John F., 63
Al-Ḥallāj, Abū Manṣūr, 366 – 367
Al-Hamadhānī, ʿAbd aj-Jabbār, 2, 196 n.510, 367 – 368 n.925
Hanson, Craig L., 79 – 80
Hanson, R. P., 136 n.348
Al-Ḥārith, an-Nabīl, 273 n.715
Al-Hāshimī, ʿAbdullāh, 296 – 299, 306, 364 n.912
Ḥawwāla,ʿAbdullāh b., 33 n.81
Heimgartner, Martin, 42 n.102
Heraclius, 24, 46, 49, 64, 278 – 279
Heron, Alasdair I. C., 248 – 249 n.658
Hick, John, 426
Hinds, Martin, 61
Hippocrates, 74
Holmberg, Bo, 144 – 145
Hoover, Jon, 214 n.552

Howard-Johnston, James, 26 – 27 n. 59, 32 n.78
Hoyland, Robert G., 33 n.82, 59 n.141, 81
Hussey, John M., 62, 97 n.246

Ibn ʿAbbās, 229 n.593
Ibn ʿAbdullāh, Muḥammad, 298
Ibn ʿAdī, Yaḥya, 107, 173 n.441, 216 n.561, 364 – 365
Ibn al-ʿĀṣ, ʿUmar, 363
Ibn ʿAllāf, Abū al-Ḥuḏayl, 223 – 224
Ibn ʿAṭāʾ, Wāṣil, 87 n.217, 307 n.805, 347 – 348
Ibn Ḥāʾiṭ, 286 – 287, 368
Ibn Ḥazm, 71, 216 n.561, 222 n.570
Ibn Isḥaq, 27 n. 59
Ibn Khālid, Ṣaʿṣaʿa, 167, 300, 328, 330 – 332, 370, 373
Ibn Khuzayma, Abū Bakr Muḥammad ibn Isḥaq, 214 – 215
Ibn Kullāb, ʿAbdullāh, 216 n.561
Ibn Munqidh, Ūsāmah, 277
Ibn an-Nadīm, 2 – 3
Ibn Ṣafwān, Jahm, 87 n.217
Ibn Ṭufayl, 322 n.832
Ibn ʿUbayd, ʿAmr, 87 n.217
Ibn aṭ-Ṭayyib, 368 n.928
Ibrāhīm, Gregorios Yūḥannā, 93, 99
Ignatius of Antioch, 216 n.563, 230
Al-ʿIjlī, Abū Mansūr, 368 n.926
Irenaeus, 157
Irwin, Robert, 163
Ishoʿyahb II, 150, 155 n.407

Al-Jabbār, ʿAbd, 214
Jacob of Edessa, 28
Jāḥiẓ, al-, 11, 74 – 75, 196 n.510, 291 – 292, 297, 323 – 324, 331
Jarīr, Sulaymān b., 223
Jenson, Robert, 122 n.303
John of ar-Rahā, 92 – 93, 99
John of Damascus, 2, 6, 7 – 8, 11, 12, 15, 16 – 17, 52 – 53, 62, 66, 67, 77, 79 – 87, 88, 94, 95 – 96, 98 n.251, 103, 104, 164, 165, 172, 177, 180 n.466, 181, 182 n.475, 193 – 194, 200, 201, 232 n.604, 234, 235 – 245, 246 – 248, 251, 258, 259 – 260, 261 – 262, 263, 264, 265, 266, 281, 282 n.739, 286, 360, 380 – 389, 390, 397 – 401, 402 – 403, 404, 405, 408, 414, 417
John of Nikiu, 28
John of Phenek, 29
Al-Juhānī, Maʿbad, 87 n.217
Justin Martyr, 75
Justinian I, 160

Kaegi, Walter, 23 – 24, 25, 28, 46
Kateregga, Badru D., 359 – 360
Kattan, Assaad Elias, 243 n.636, 245 n.643, 258 n.691, 262 n.700, 390 n.985, 391 n.990, 394 n.998
Kelly, J.N.D., 159, 160
Kennedy, Hugh, 44 – 45
Khalidi, Tarif, 288 – 290
Al-Khaṭṭāb, ʿUmar b., 29 n.67, 32 n.77, 36 n.91, 66
Kindī, al-, 313 n.818, 364 n.912
Koonammakkal, Thomas, 147
Koren, Judith, 25 – 26
Al-Kūfī, Īsmāʿīl, 308, 311
Küng, Hans, 426

Lamoreaux, John C., 3, 4, 5, 6 – 7, 18, 27, 50 n.121, 193, 194 – 195, 196, 202, 204 – 205, 207, 210 n.545, 212 – 213, 259 n.694
Leo I, 271 – 272
Leo III, 95, 209 n.543, 388
Leontius of Byzantium, 394, 404
Leontius of Jerusalem, 404
Lössl, Josef, 176
Louth, Andrew, 67 n.162, 80 n.193, 82 n.198, 86 n.211, 94, 98 n.251, 181, 243 n.636, 245 n.644, 246 n.647, 253 n.675, 262 n.700, 386 n.972, 389, 394 n.1002
Lynch, John J., 125 n.314, 230 – 231

Madāʾinī, al-, 27 n.59
Mahdī, al-, 1, 30, 37, 38 – 39, 40 – 41, 42, 43, 45, 47 – 48, 64 n.155, 65, 183, 286, 327, 337, 363, 364, 366 n.916
Maʾmūn, al-, 1, 2, 5, 17, 61 n.148, 63 – 64 n.155, 71, 74, 88, 100 n.254, 108, 164,

183, 218, 222, 224, 296, 297 n.786, 298, 301, 308, 328, 336–344, 373, 375, 401
Ma'oz, Moshe, 427, 428
Martin I, 46
Marwān, ʿAbd al-Malik b., 60 n.144
Masʿūdī, al-, 222 n.570
Maximus the Confessor, 2, 8, 11, 12, 16–17, 62–63, 164, 165, 178, 179–183, 234, 245–259, 260–261, 262, 263, 264, 265, 266, 279, 380, 389–401, 402–403, 404, 405, 408, 412–413, 417
Maximus the Philosopher, 131
McFarland, Ian A., 389 n.982
McGuckin, John A., 153
McLeod, Frederick G., 119, 152, 153
McVey, Kathleen, 141 n.363, 143 n.368
Michael the Great, 28 n.62, 29–30, 31 n.71, 49–50, 51–52, 53, 55, 56
Michael the Sabaite, 44 n.107, 66
Mingana, Alphonse, 37 n.93, 39
Monte Croce, Ricoldo de, 163, 266
Mundell, Marlia, 96–97
Al-Muqaffaʿ, Severus b., 395 n.1006
Mutawwakil, al-, 44–45

Nagel, Tilman, 61 n.48, 307, 348 n.873
Narsai, 275 n.723
Nasrallah, Joseph, 6, 18
Naṣrī, Wafīq, 17, 18, 218 n.564, 339, 340
Nassif, Bassam A., 180 n.466
Naṣṭūr of Adiabene, 222
Nau, F., 363
Al-Naẓẓām, Abū Isḥaq b. Sayyār b. Māniʿ, 286–287
Nestorius, 3 n.11, 114, 115–116, 123, 124 n.307, 136, 139 n.356, 150, 151–156, 159, 160, 161, 217, 222, 270, 340–341, 342, 344, 366
Neusner, Jacob, 49
Nevo, Yehuda D., 25–26, 31 n.72

Öhlig, Karl-Heinz, 232 n.604, 278 n.728, 366 n.918, 398 n.1015, 404–406
Olster, David, 51–52 n.123,
Origen, 75, 118, 121 n.297, 172, 250 n.662, 397 n.1014

Palaiologos, Michael VIII, 178
Pamphilus, 253 n.674
Papanikolaou, Aristotle, 176–177
Pascal, Blaise, 104
Paul the Blind, 278 n.729
Paul of Samosata, 360, 366, 405
Pelikan, Jaroslav, 105, 145, 151 n.392, 178, 264–265, 412–413, 414
Penkāyē, John Bar, 31
Peter of Capitolas, 44 n.107
Peter of Sebaste, 130 n.328
Phillips, Dewi Z., 103–104
Philoponus, John, 229
Philoxenus of Mabbug, 275 n.723
Photius, 177
Pinggéra, Karl, 363
Planoudes, Maximus, 178
Plato, 74
Possekel, Uti, 119 n.286, 141, 142
Prestige, G. L., 120 n.292, 137
Prophet Muḥammad, 33 n.81, 35, 37, 38–39, 41, 42, 43, 44, 46, 47, 48, 53, 61, 63, 64 n.155, 81, 84, 88 n.218, 167, 169, 229 n.593, 268, 269, 273, 274 n.719, 275 n.721, 275 n.723, 279–280, 327 n.842, 335, 368
Pseudo-Dionysius, 238, 248, 250 n.662, 261

Qāchām, Suhayl, 273 n.715, 275 n.722

Al-Ramlī, Stephen, 67, 79, 178
Al-Rashīd, Hārūn, 2, 92
Ar-Rassī, al-Qāsim b. Ibrāhīm, 70, 197 n.511, 319–323, 324, 325, 326, 331, 365
Renan, Ernst, 141 n.359
Riedinger, Rudolf, 180 n.467
Robertson, Jon M., 136 n.348
Roggema, Barbara, 363
Rosenthal, Franz, 108
Roy, Olivier, 420–423
Russel, Paul S., 141–142, 147, 149

Saadi, Abdul-Massih, 29
Sabellius, 121 n.297, 132, 134–135 n.343
Sahas, Daniel J., 29 n.67, 32 n.77, 58–59, 80 n.193, 82–83 n.199, 84, 95
Saʿida, Quss b., 275 n.721

Said, Edward W., 141 n.359
Samir, Samir Khalil, 5, 6, 17, 18, 36 n.90, 39, 42 n.102, 302 n.796
Sarjūn, Manṣūr b., 66, 80
Schleiermacher, F.D.E., 104
Sebokht, Severus, 33 n.82
Sedra, John I, 363, 375
Sergius of Constantinople, 278 n.729
Severus of Antioch, 160, 264 n.702, 275 n.723, 278 n.729, 395 n.1006
Shahristānī, al-, 222
Shboul, Ahmad M. H., 95 n.239
Shepardson, Christine, 34 n.84
Siecienski, A. E., 181, 182, 256, 258 n.691
Simeon of Thessalonica, 264 n.701
Simocatta, Theophylact, 32
Sophia, Empress Consort of Byzantium, 62
Sophronius of Jerusalem, 29 n.67, 32–33, 65–66, 279
Soro, Bawai, 116, 117, 138, 161
Sozomen, 143
Stead, Christopher, 120
Stramara, Daniel F., Jr., 128 n.324
Sulaymān, Muqātil b., 229 n.593
Swanson, Mark N., 14 n.42, 71 n.172
Sweetman, Windrow, 360–361, 366, 368, 387–388 n.976, 407

Tabarī, al-, 27 n.59, 323, 324, 331
Ṭālib, ʿAlī b. Abī, 275 n.722
Terentius, 130 n.332
Tertullian, 216 n.563, 258 n.692
Theodora, Empress Consort of Byzantium, 62
Theodore of Mopsuestia, 360, 366
Theodore of Pharan, 278 n.729
Theodore of Raithu, 253 n.674
Theodore the Studite, 62
Theodoret of Antioch, 4, 5
Theophanes, 97 n.247
Theophilus of Antioch, 118
Thomas Aquinas, 104, 146, 236
Thomas, David, 38, 39, 49, 52–53, 69–70, 72 n.174, 193, 235–236 n.609, 236, 364 n.910
Thunberg, Lars, 245–246 n.646, 250 n.662, 257 n.689
Timothy I, 30, 37–48, 64 n.155, 65, 107, 183, 286, 327, 337, 363, 364, 366 n.916
Törönen, Melchisedec, 232 n.604, 253 n.674, 394–395
Treiger, Alexander, 367
Turcescu, Lucian, 125 n.313, 131 n.332, 233

Varsányi, Orsolya, 103 n.267
Van Ess, Josef, 368 n.926, 428
Van Ginkel, Jan, 29, 30, 49, 50
Volf, Miroslav, 426

Waardenburg, Jacques, 105 n.270
Al-Walīd, Khālid b., 66
Wāqidī, al-, 27 n.59
Ward, Marcus, 417 n.1051
Ware, Kallistos, 413, 414, 415 n.1038
Al-Warrāq, Abū ʿĪsā, 2, 70, 363–364, 367–368 n.925
Webb, Clement, 124
Wendebourg, Dorothea, 240
Wilken, Robert Louis, 246–247 n.650, 250
Wolfson, Harry Austryn, 215–216, 222–224, 226, 285–287, 307 n.805, 348 n.874, 362
Wood, Philip, 62 n.150

Yazīd II, 95, 97 n.247
Young, Frances M., 122 n.303, 137–138 n.350

Zizioulas, John D., 125 n.313, 189 n.496

Subject Index

Abū Qurrah, Theodore
and apologetics, 8–14, 17, 76, 88–92, 100, 102, 104–107, 163–164, 169, 191–192, 194–197, 226–229, 261–266, 280–284, 292–293, 294–313, 328–337, 341–358, 369–380, 399–400, 402–404, 405–410, 411–412, 420–429
– biography of, 1–8
– on Christology, 165, 168, 204–206, 211–212, 292–313, 399–410
– on the incarnation, 369–380, 400–410
– on Jesus' divine sonship, 328–359, 400
– on John 1:1, 301–313
– on icons, 92, 98–101
– and John of Damascus, 6, 7–8, 16–17, 259–264, 400–401, 40, 406, 413–414
– and Maximus the Confessor, 8, 16–17, 179–182, 260–261, 263–264, 400–401, 402, 406, 413–414
– and modalism, 229–230
– and orthodoxy, 11–14, 108–109, 162, 259–265, 398–410, 412–420
– on the Trinity, 164–187, 191–212, 217–234, 258–266, 294–295, 304, 338–339, 341–344, 405, 408
– on true religion, 89–92, 100–102, 104–106, 107
– writings of, 17–18
Arab conquests, 23–30

Christian–Muslim relations, 31–56, 58–61, 64–68, 70–76, 163–164, 192, 267–268, 272–274, 278–280, 359–360, 363, 364, 425–426, 428–429
– and apologetics (Christian), 64–65, 72–74, 75–76, 77–80, 85, 87–89, 102, 103–104, 226–227, 261, 267–269, 277–278, 286–287, 290, 327–328, 368, 389–390, 393–394, 397–398
– in John of Damascus, 52–53, 80–87, 380–383, 397–398
– in Timothy I, 37–48
– and apologetics (Muslim), 68–74, 286–287, 289–290, 319–328, 359–366
– Christology, 29–30, 51, 52, 57, 70, 78, 84–85, 86, 106, 120–123, 136–137, 138–139, 247, 255, 256–257, 267–410
– in Athanasius, 120–123, 136–137
– in John of Damascus, 380–388, 398–399, 400–401, 403
– in Maximus the Confessor, 389–398, 399, 400–401, 402–403, 404
– and Muslim responses, 272–280, 287–293, 319–328, 359–366, 369
– in Nestorian controversy, 115–117, 123, 136, 138–140, 150–161, 217, 270–271, 337–344
– in Niceno-Constantinopolitan orthodoxy, 270–272
– in the Qur'an, 268–270, 285–286, 287–288, 290–291, 292, 295–302, 306, 309, 314–319, 323–324, 330–331, 334–336, 361–362, 369, 373, 393–394
– two natures, 9, 12–13, 86, 115–117, 139–140, 145, 150–162, 217, 270–272, 286, 300, 329–330, 337–344, 359, 399

icon debates, 94–98, 388

philosophy, 74–76, 108, 119, 140–142

religion–state relations, 60–64

terminology, Arabic
– *ḥulūl* ('indwelling'), 359–376, 401–410
– *ibn* ('son'), 270, 284, 325, 347
– *jawhar* ('essence'), 12, 113, 144, 220, 223, 226
– *kalima* ('word'), 170, 261–262, 269, 284–312, 358, 362, 368, 370, 383, 393, 394, 403
– *rūḥ* ('spirit'), 269, 284–312
– *shakhṣ* ('individual'), 145 n.374, 206 n.536, 227
– *shirk* ('idolatry'), 165–167, 192, 197, 262, 300, 315 n.821, 333
– *ta'annus* ('en-humanization'), 359–369, 374, 385, 402–404, 409–410

– *tajassud* ('embodiment'), 359 – 369, 374, 385, 402 – 404, 409 – 410
– *uqnūm* ('person'), 12, 18, 99, 113, 144 – 145, 206 n.536, 208 – 221, 233, 268, 294
– *wajh* ('face'), 12, 13, 18, 113, 202 – 207, 212 – 228, 233 – 234, 264, 266, 405, 408, 409
– *walad* ('child'), 168 – 169, 198, 270, 284, 314 – 358, 400
terminology, Greek
– *aitia*, 133, 190, 320 n.827
– *archē*, 133, 185, 240 – 243, 261, 319 – 320
– *enhypostasis*, 386, 394 – 397, 402 – 403, 405, 408
– *homoousios*, 121, 122, 131 – 132, 137, 244 n.642, 352, 373
– *hypostasis*, 12 – 13, 18, 113, 116 – 140, 141 n.361, 144 – 145, 148, 149, 151 – 162, 165, 170, 185, 187, 190, 200 – 201, 203 – 204, 208 – 218, 223 – 224, 227, 230 – 233, 240 – 245, 247, 253 – 257, 264, 303, 341, 386, 394 – 395, 399 – 400, 405, 408
– *hypostasis* of union, 12 – 13, 153, 159 – 161, 399
– *monarchia*, 132 – 134, 190, 200 – 201, 234, 242 n.634, 244 n.642, 252 – 255, 263
– *ousia*, 113, 117, 118, 120 – 139, 144, 149, 151, 152, 155, 162, 170, 187, 191, 213, 226 – 227, 230, 231 – 232, 252, 341, 386, 394, 395, 399, 400
– *perichoresis*, 132 – 133, 257, 394, 399
– *persona*, 134
– *physis*, 12, 113, 127 – 128, 135 n.346, 138, 155 n.406, 158, 230, 337, 386
– *prosopon*, 113, 115 – 117, 118 – 119, 121 n.297, 123, 130 – 131, 132, 134 – 135, 144 – 145, 151 – 161, 216 – 217, 220, 228 – 233, 337, 405
terminology, Syriac
– *ituta/itya* ('essence'), 113, 139, 143 – 145, 149 – 150, 162, 170, 213
– *kiana/kyana* ('nature'), 113, 117 n.280, 139, 158, 162, 170, 213, 337, 341
– *parsopa* ('face'), 116 – 117, 144 – 145, 151 – 161, 216, 217, 337, 341, 405
– *qnoma* ('person'), 18, 113, 116 – 117, 138, 139 – 162, 212, 217, 227
Trinity, doctrine of, 9, 18, 42, 47, 52 – 53, 57, 70, 78, 85, 106, 116, 117, 118 – 140, 142 – 150, 151, 153 – 155, 161 – 162, 163 – 266
– in Athanasius, 120 – 123
– in Augustine, 173 – 175
– in Basil of Caesarea, 129 – 132, 188 – 189
– in Ephraim the Syrian, 140 – 150
– in Gregory Nazianzen, 132 – 135, 190 – 191, 200 – 201
– in Gregory of Nyssa, 124 – 129
– in John of Damascus, 201, 235 – 245, 264, 265
– in Maximus the Confessor, 245 – 259, 264, 265

FSC
www.fsc.org
MIX
Papier aus verantwortungsvollen Quellen
Paper from responsible sources
FSC® C141904